Investment Management

THEORY AND APPLICATION

Investment Management
THEORY AND APPLICATION

Sarkis J. Khoury
University of Notre Dame

MACMILLAN PUBLISHING CO., INC.
New York
COLLIER MACMILLAN PUBLISHERS
London

*To the Phoenicians, who
were the first to sail the sea, who
were the first to internationalize
portfolios, and who gave the world the
greatest gift of all: the alphabet.*

Macmillan Publishing Co., Inc.
866 Third Avenue, New York, New York 10022

Collier Macmillan Canada, Inc.

Library of Congress Cataloging in Publication Data

Khoury, Sarkis J.
  Investment management theory and application.

  Includes index.
  1. Investments. I. Title.
HG4521.K453   1983   332.6'78   82–4627
ISBN 0–02–362440–X

Printing 1 2 3 4 5 6 7 8   Year: 3 4 5 6 7 8 9 0

ISBN   0–02–362440–X

Foreword

This book is intended to serve as a basic text for advanced undergraduate and MBA students enrolled in an investments course or as a basic text for courses in portfolio theory and speculative markets. The book is best used for a two-semester course in investments, however. The first eleven chapters should be ample for a background in the basics of investments, covering such topics as the nature and operations of securities markets, risk analysis, portfolio theory, the capital asset pricing model, valuation models for stocks and bonds, investment strategies in fixed-income securities, and the various aspects of investment companies. The remaining seven chapters—along with a casebook in investments—should complete the comprehensive treatment of investment theory, strategy, and instruments usually reserved for the second semester in investments. Chapters 12 through 17 cover the balance of investment vehicles, with substantial treatment of various hedging and speculative vehicles, such as financial and commodities futures, stock options, and gold and gold futures; these chapters also look closely at the major considerations for investing within a global framework and for financial planning over the life of a hypothetical individual.

All chapters in this text include ample examples and limit complex mathematical derivations to the necessary minimum. The prerequisites for the course are a course in finance and at least one course in statistics. Some sections of almost all the chapters can be skipped without loss of continuity. The instructor's discretion in this regard is required.

The questions and problems at the end of each chapter are intended not only to test the knowledge of the student but also to stimulate curiosity and offer a better perspective on investment theory.

The overall structure of the book and the contents of the chapters, the latter ones in particular, are intended to bring Wall Street to the classroom. Several investment texts have not sufficiently recognized that academic courses have tended to fall behind Wall Street in terms of the strategies and instruments covered. This text takes a major turn in the belief that the latest techniques, strategies, and instruments can be mastered by students as easily as they are by practitioners, with time and extent of interest being the reasonable constraints.

This text also enjoys a considerable international flavor, which is becoming more palatable to the taste of portfolio managers, academicians, and students as the economies of the world become increasingly interdependent and as money managers adopt a more geocentric approach to investments.

The contents of this book were successfully used in my investment courses, which helped significantly in the shaping of this final version. I hope that this material will serve the users of this text as well as it has served my students and me.

ACKNOWLEDGMENTS

Works of this magnitude require the cooperation, goodwill, and insight of many persons. I have been very fortunate to receive the assistance and encouragement of competent scholars within and without Notre Dame. Special thanks go to Frank Bonello, Animesh Ghoshal, Ken Milani, Kevin Misiewicz, Michael Morris, James Rakowski, James Wittenbach, Owen Gregory, and Lemma W. Senbet, who pointed out many errors in fact or in judgment and made valuable suggestions that contributed to my own understanding of certain issues and to the quality of this book. Very special thanks go to William Knight for his patience in reading and rereading and for his extensive comments on parts of this work.

I owe a great deal to Michael Grantio of Morgan Guaranty Trust Co. for his many insightful comments, his patience, and his encouragement, and to my tennis partners at Windingbrook Park for improving my endurance.

Many thanks are due to Professor Richard Rendelman, to Paul Wilkinson, to many anonymous referees, and to my speculative markets class of the spring of 1982.

There should be no doubt that this work could not have been completed without the exceptional assistance of Frank Oelerich (he is just brilliant), Todd Hooper, Frank Connor and his group, Michael Hartmann, Brian Robbins, Jane Herbstritt, and Ed McAree. The typing of this manuscript was a product of patience, love, and tolerance. I acknowledge with deep gratitude the work of Bee Recker, and particularly, that of Joyce Khoury. Joyce has been an inspiration and a source of strength throughout the preparation of this work.

Special thanks go to Chip Price, Eileen Schlesinger, William Winchief, and all the other dedicated people at Macmillan Publishing Co. Their commitment to this project was exemplary indeed.

The kindness and support these people have shown and given me does not allow me, unfortunately, to shift the blame for any remaining errors onto their shoulders. I, therefore, accept all responsibility for whatever errors remain and ask the reader who might encounter such defects to point them out.

Sarkis J. Khoury

Contents

PART
TWO   **Portfolio Theory**

CHAPTER
5

6

PART
THREE   **Equity Securities**

CHAPTER
7

PART
FIVE   **Stock Options**

CHAPTER
12

PART SEVEN International Investments Considerations

CHAPTER 16 The Foreign Exchange Markets 521

PART
EIGHT   **Looking Toward the Future**

CHAPTER
18

An Overview of Investments and of Financial Markets

1 | Investments: An Overview

1.1 INVESTMENT DEFINED

There are two distinct definitions of *investment,* one given by economists and the other offered by financial analysts and theorists.

The Economist's Definition

Investment is the replacement of and net addition to fixed capital stock (used for both business and residential purposes) by business and nonprofit institutions.

Fixed investment consists of nonresidential fixed investment (new and replacement buildings, stores, warehouses, and producers' durable equipment, including machinery, office equipment, and motor vehicles) and of residential structures (new single-family houses, apartments, hotels, dormitories, and nursing homes).

The Financial Analyst's Definition

Investment is the commitment of funds with the expectation of a positive return commensurate with the level of risk assumed. Such funds may be committed to government or corporate securities; commodities, currency, and financial futures; real estate; options; and other vehicles (gems and antiques, for example) with a potential for preserving and adding to the investor's wealth.

This book will deal with investment as seen by the financial analyst; it will discuss in detail the instruments available to investors, the techniques used to measure and deal with risk, and systematic methods for constructing portfolios of seemingly unrelated securities.

1.2 THE INVESTMENT ENVIRONMENT—A PERSPECTIVE

Developments in the U.S. economy and that of the world have proceeded at breakneck speed and continue at the same pace. The 1970s brought about some fundamental changes in the character of the private enterprise system in the United States; in the attitudes of people toward government, business, and each other; in the role the United States plays in the world community; in the very nature of the political process; and in the operations of the financial markets. The distribution of the gross national product (GNP) between the goods sector and the service sector also shifted. By 1975 the service sector accounted for over 50 percent of GNP—$697.6 billion (service) vs. $686.6 billion (goods).

The 1970s were characterized by increased uncertainty about the course of the U.S. economy. Americans added a new word to their vocabulary—*stagflation*—meaning accelerated inflation coupled with economic slowdown. Americans stood in line, hostages to the Arab oil embargo, and watched helplessly as events unfolded in Iran. Energy issues surfaced in a dramatic way. As a consequence, the very nature of the role the United States was expected to play in world affairs was subjected to intense discussion. Questions about the military power of the United States and its reliability in protecting the nation's markets and vital interests were loudly raised. Changes in America's corporate boardrooms also took place. When Douglas Frasier was elected to the board of the ailing Chrysler Corporation, many felt that U.S. business was being swept by the European tide.

The 1970s also brought about some dramatic changes in technology. Major advances were realized in medicine, human beings walked on the moon, genes were manipulated, a whole new set of industries emerged (e.g., silicon chips, robots), and a whole new set of problems—resulting in part from technology—were identified, including pollution, job stress, waste disposal, and so on.

The changes in the securities markets were no less dramatic. Daily volume on the New York Stock Exchange, which topped 100 million shares only recently, is now almost consistently in the 50- to 60-million-share range, while only in the mid 1970s a 35-million-share day was considered a bonanza. The explosion in trading volume is evidenced in Table 1.1. From a daily average of 6.2 million shares in the mid-1960s, daily trading volume increased to 44.9 million shares in 1980. Also recording a dramatic increase were large-block (10,000 shares or more) transactions. This was an increase both in absolute terms and relative to total reported volume (Table 1.2).

Also registering a significant increase was the number of individuals owning stocks. Between 1975 and 1980, the number of people owning stocks increased by 18 percent, to 30 million. The median age of the stockholder dropped between 1975 and 1980 from 50 to 45.5 years. The new young entrants into the stock market and portfolio diversification dropped the average size of the stock portfolio from $10,000 to $4,000 during the same five years. During the same period, the median family income of shareholders families rose from $19,000 to $27,700. The number of owners of shares listed on the New York Stock Exchange, the American Stock Exchange, and traded in the over-the-counter market increased by 31, 43, and 66 percent respectively.

The activities of institutions also proceeded at a fast pace. Table 1.3 clearly illustrates their level of activity both on the buy and on the sell side. Leading the way in dollar terms were the noninsured private pension funds.

The 1970s also witnessed, on May 1, 1975, the emergence of a negotiated (competitive) commission structure. This translated into lower commission fees for both individuals and institutions. Other developments with wide-ranging impact on market efficiency involved a stream of mergers among brokerage firms and the acquisition of many brokerage firms by institutions outside the brokerage industry, such as the acquisition of Dean Witter Reynolds Organization, Inc., by Sears Roebuck and Co.

Investments on an international scale also increased dramatically in the 1970s. Foreign

TABLE 1.1
Daily Reported Share Volume: Average, High, and Low Record Days (thousands)

Year	Daily Average[a]	High Day		Low Days[b]	
		Shares	Date	Shares	Date
1900	505	1,627	11/12	89	8/22
1910	601	1,656	2/3	111	12/23
1920	828	2,008	4/21	227	6/29
1930	2,959	8,279	5/5	1,090	8/1
1940	751	3,940	5/21	130	8/19
1945	1,422	2,936	6/28	492	8/6
1950	1,980	4,859	6/27	1,061	3/13
1955	2,578	7,717	9/26	1,230	8/15
1960	3,042	5,303	12/30	1,894	10/12
1965	6,176	11,434	12/6	3,028	7/7
1966	7,538	13,121	5/6	4,268	6/6
1967	10,080	14,954	12/29	5,998	1/3
1968	12,971	21,351	6/13	6,707	3/25
1969	11,403	19,950	10/14	6,683	8/11
1970	11,564	21,345	9/24	6,660	5/11
1971	15,381	31,731	8/16	7,349	10/25
1972	16,487	27,555	12/29	7,945	10/9
1973	16,084	25,962	9/20	8,970	8/20
1974	13,904	26,365	10/10	7,402	7/5
1975	18,551	35,158	2/13	8,670	9/15
1976	21,186	44,513	2/20	10,301	1/2
1977	20,928	35,261	11/11	10,582	10/10
1978	28,591	66,370	8/3	7,580	1/20
1979	32,237	81,619	10/10	18,346	1/2
1980	44,871	84,297	11/5	16,132	12/26

[a]A trading session of 3 hours or less is counted as one half day.
[b]Full days only, four or more trading hours.

Series Record (thousands)

Daily average, low year	1914	270	Low Day	12/30/14	50
Daily average, high year	1980	44,871	High Day	11/5/80	84,297

Source: New York Stock Exchange Fact Book, 1981, p. 64.

TABLE 1.2
NYSE Large Block Transactions

Year	Transactions		Shares (thousands)	% of Reported Volume
	Total	Daily Average		
1965	2,171	9	48,262	3.1%
1966	3,642	14	85,298	4.5
1967	6,685	27	169,365	6.7
1968	11,254	50	292,681	10.0
1969	15,132	61	402,064	14.1
1970	17,217	68	450,908	15.4
1971	26,941	106	692,536	17.8
1972	31,207	124	766,406	18.5
1973	29,233	116	721,356	17.8
1974	23,200	92	549,387	15.6
1975	34,420	136	778,540	16.6
1976	47,632	188	1,001,254	18.7
1977	54,275	215	1,183,924	22.4
1978	75,036	298	1,646,905	22.9
1979	97,509	385	2,164,726	26.5
1980	133,597	528	3,311,132	29.2

Source: New York Stock Exchange Fact Book, 1981, p. 64.

investors of all nationalities invested larger and larger sums in U.S. securities, U.S. property, and U.S. land. Foreigners hold about 13 percent of the national debt of the United States. The tiny country of Kuwait is reported to hold $7 billion in U.S. securities, including ownership interests in leading U.S. companies like Dow Chemical, J. C. Penney, K-Mart, McDonald's, General Electric, and—most recently—Santa Fe International, Inc. The citizens of Lichtenstein own American land three times the size of their own country. The flow of investment funds across national borders has been distinctly a two-way street, however. American investments overseas continued unabated throughout the 1970s (see Chapter 17).

The decade of the 1970s also brought about a sharp increase in the volatility of prices of metals (both precious and other) as well as diamonds and credit. These changes increased the need for hedging and thus necessitated the creation of new financial instruments.

New Financial Instruments

The 1970s and 1980–81 witnessed an explosion of new financial instruments. Instruments that were not even contemplated in the early 1970s now play important roles in many investment strategies and portfolios.

The International Monetary Market (IMM), a division of the Chicago Mercantile Exchange, began trading futures contracts[1] in seven foreign currencies on May 16, 1972.

---

[1] A financial futures contract is an obligation to buy or sell a specified amount of a financial instrument at some future date at a price negotiated today.

TABLE 1.3
Institutional Activity on the NYSE

Institutional Purchases and Sales of Common Stock (millions)

Period	Noninsured Private Pension Funds	Open-end Investment Companies	Life Insurance Companies	Property & Liability Companies	Total Purchases and Sales
I 1980	$27,587	$11,170	$ 6,364	$3,393	$ 48,514
II	21,381	7,914	4,804	3,020	37,119
III	31,284	10.578	6,116	3,647	51,625
IV	N/A	11,953	6,520	N/A	N/A
Year	N/A	$41,615	$23,804	N/A	N/A
1979	$59,109	$29,012	17,296	$9,432	$114,849
1978	43,120	27,287	12,785	7,154	90,346
1977	35,772	20,914	10,176	4,560	71,422
1976	33,418	23,912	10,082	6,282	73,694
1975	29,405	23,095	8,545	5,390	66,435
1974	21,105	18,455	6,365	5,625	51,550
1973	35,115	33,065	10,670	7,375	86,225
1972	38,870	43,495	11,340	7,870	101,575
1971	34,485	42,730	9,005	6,115	92,340
1970	23,325	33,030	5,745	6,335	68,435

Annual Purchase and Sales Rates of Common Stock

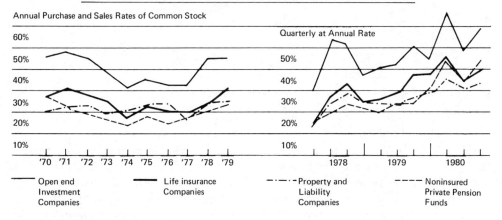

Source: *New York Stock Exchange Fact Book 1981*, p. 22.

The Chicago Board Options Exchange began operations on April 26, 1973, trading 16 classes of options.[2] By the end of 1980, calls and puts on every major stock were traded on this and other exchanges. Prior to 1973, stock options were available but were not traded on any exchange. Various brokerage houses matched the supply of options with the demand.

On Dec. 31, 1974, trading in gold bullion futures contracts began after the U.S. government lifted restrictions against private ownership of gold.

The trading in treasury bill futures contracts on the IMM began on Jan. 6, 1976. Between that date and Dec. 31, 1976, a total of 110,223 contracts changed hands. In 1978, between January and August alone, 339,415 contracts (each $1 million in size) traded.

---

[2] An option is a contract that gives the buyer the right to purchase (sell) a stock during the contract life at a specified price.

FIGURE 1.1   Graphic summary of trading in futures contracts.

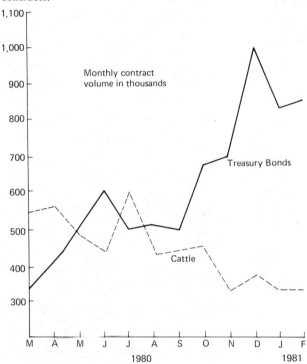

Sources: Chicago Board of Trade and Chicago Mercantile Exchange.

On Oct. 20, 1975, the Chicago Board of Trade (CBT) began trading Government National Mortgage Association (GNMA) futures contracts. On Aug. 22, 1977, CBT introduced another instrument: the T-bond futures contract. And in August 1981, yet another futures contract in 90-day certificates of deposit was introduced by CBT.

These futures contracts proved very popular. Trading in T-bond futures contracts far outdistances that of futures contracts in livestock and meat, for example, as shown in Figure 1.1.

On Feb. 24, 1981, the Securities and Exchange Commission (SEC) "voted to let the Chicago Board Options Exchange trade options on Government National Mortgage Association securities, the first time exchange trading has been approved for nonstock options."[3]

The usefulness and popularity of financial futures contracts has yet to cease improving. On July 5, 1981, in an unprecedented move, the Federal Home Loan Bank Board decided to loosen trading restrictions for Savings and Loan associations:

> *Under the new rules, the nation's nearly 4,000 federally insured S&L's will be allowed to take positions hedging all their assets. The old rules didn't allow contracts to total more than an S&L's net worth, typically only 5% of assets.*

---

[3] *The Wall Street Journal,* Feb. 25, 1981.

TABLE 1.4
What the Exchanges Want to Offer Next

Exchange	Futures	Options	Regulator
American Stock Exchange	–	Treasury issues	SEC
Chicago Board of Trade	Treasury issues, 11 stock portfolios, U.S. and Eurobank certificates of deposit	Government National Mortgage Assn. futures, Treasury bond futures	CFTC[a]
Chicago Board Options Exchange	–	Treasury issues	SEC
Chicago Mercantile Exchange	U.S. and Eurobank CDs, stock index, 180-day T-bills, Italian lira	T-bill futures, foreign currency futures	CFTC
Commodity Exchange (Comex)	Stock index, one-year T-bill	GNMA futures, two-year T-note futures, 90-day T-bill futures	CFTC
Kansas City Board of Trade	Stock index	–	CFTC
Mid America Commodity Exchange	Treasury bonds, notes	–	CFTC
New York Futures Exchange	GNMA certificates, U.S. and Eurobank CDs, stock index	–	CFTC
New York Stock Exchange	–	Stock index, GNMA certificates, T-bills, T-bonds, foreign currencies	SEC
Philadelphia Stock Exchange	–	Foreign currencies	SEC

[a] CFTC = Commodity Futures Trading Commission.

> *. . . the new rules also allow trading in any contracts based on securities in which the S&L's can legally invest. This will permit trading in Treasury securities futures and bank certificate of deposit futures. Currently, only Government National Mortgage Association futures can be traded.* [4]

Buoyed by the success of their current contracts or those of other exchanges, several exchanges have adopted ambitious plans for the future. These plans are summarized in Table 1.4.

The Dec. 22, 1981 issue of *The Wall Street Journal* reported that the Chicago Mercantile Exchange plans to form a new division on which stock index futures contracts and options on futures contracts will be traded. The new market was referred to as the Index and Options Market (IOM). Trading in an S&P-based index futures contract on the IOM began on April 21, 1982 after the successful introduction of a Value Line stock index futures contract by the Kansas City Board of Trade on Feb. 24, 1982. Also reported were plans by the Chicago Board of Trade to link up with the futures arm of the New York Stock Exchange and with the Chicago Board Options Exchange.

The Dec. 24, 1981 issue of *The Wall Street Journal* reported approval by the Securities and Exchange Commission for options trading on U.S. treasury bonds, notes, and bills on the New York, American, and the Chicago Board Options Exchanges.

All the exchanges are gearing up for this revolutionary trend in the financial markets. Other financial instruments that have recently emerged are:

1. The deep-discount (zero coupon) bonds to finance business. This instrument was introduced by the Martin Marietta Corp. in March 1981. By May 1981, "2.5 billion

---

[4] *The Wall Street Journal*, July, 16, 1981.

in such bond issues have been completed—usually as quick sellouts in an otherwise dreary market."[5]

2. The all-savers certificate, inaugurated on Oct. 1, 1981, is a creature of the Economic Recovery Tax Act of 1981. This certificate is issued by thrift institutions and banks, has a one-year life, and could only be issued between Oct. 1, 1981, and Dec. 31, 1982. Up to $1,000 ($2,000 on joint tax returns) of interest on these securities is exempt from federal income taxes.

3. Shares in money market funds. Money market funds proved to be an excellent alternative to savings deposits and certificates in an inflationary period. From a very humble beginning at the end of 1972, money market funds grew to 126 in number and their assets reached $185.96 billion by Dec. 16, 1981. Money market funds proved to be a bonanza for nondepository institutions, as did cash management accounts and other instruments.

Other Important Developments

While their first attempt has failed, the proponents of the Corporate Democracy Act of 1980 are still waiting for the right moment. The expressed purpose of the legislation is to turn board directors from representatives of shareholders to representatives of constituencies and special-interest groups. This type of philosophy, if it prevails, could have serious repercussions on the securities industry as it is known today.

Several securities scandals broke open in the 1970s and the early 1980s. One of them involved officers at Morgan Stanley and Co. trading on insiders' information. The ability of the SEC to monitor insider's trades was brought into question.

The Federal Reserve Board, in an attempt to lure offshore banking business back into the United States, "authorized banks to establish international facilities in this country beginning December 3, 1981."[6] This development could affect the operations and the profitability of international banks. The impact on profitability, whatever its nature, will ultimately be reflected in the securities markets.

Another recent (August 1981) and dramatic development involves the passage and signing into law of the most extensive tax reform bill since 1933. The Economic Recovery Tax Act of 1981 will have dramatic effects on the securities markets, since it provides considerable incentives for people to save and invest.

Two proposals currently under consideration should be carefully watched, for they could have considerable impact on the financial markets. One is a bill to decontrol the banking industry and the other involves a user fee on futures transactions. The bank decontrol bill is given a good chance of passage, although its exact contents are still not well defined.

One other memorable event in 1981 occurred on Jan. 7, 1981. An investment advisor named Joseph E. Granville succeeded, almost single-handedly, in bringing panic to Wall Street. By the end of that trading day, the Dow-Jones Industrial Average had dropped 23.8 points on a record volume of 92.89 million shares. Those promoters of and believers in smoothly functioning and efficient markets had much to think about on that day and since.

---

[5] *The Wall Street Journal,* May 28, 1981.

[6] *The Wall Street Journal,* June 10, 1981.

In brief, investors today are operating in a much more complex world, but its complexities offer both challenges as well as opportunities.

The objective of this book is to present the readers with a comprehensive review of the literature on investment and of investment vehicles in the hope of helping them identify and capitalize on investment opportunities.

A summary and definitions of key financial terms is offered at the end of this chapter so the reader may start on the right footing.

1.3 PREVIEW OF UPCOMING CHAPTERS

The chapters to follow use the simplest possible mathematics and are intended to be as consistent as possible.

Chapter 2 deals with the securities markets—their organization, their regulation, the role of the investment banker, and the operations of the investment banking industry.

Chapter 3 discusses the types of orders and positions available to the investor, the various ways of measuring market performance, and other important factors one ought to keep in mind when investing in stocks.

Chapter 4 discusses the concept of market efficiency, the various forms of efficiencies, and the various levels of efficiency. It concludes with a statement that the market appears to be efficient in a semistrong sense. In this chapter we also discuss the various techniques used by technicians to improve their performance in the market.

Chapter 5 discusses risk and utility and the various ways of measuring them. Portfolio theory is then introduced and the efficiency frontier is derived. Decision making under conditions of certainty and uncertainty is then discussed and a way for identifying the most suitable point along the efficiency frontier is presented.

Chapter 6 discusses the Capital Asset Pricing Model (CAPM) in great detail and surveys the empirical evidence on CAPM. After exposing the limitations of CAPM, an alternative model—the Arbitrage Pricing Theory (APT), developed by Stephen Ross— is introduced. The little empirical evidence on APT is also presented.

Chapter 7 discusses the various common stock valuation models, reviews all the important theories on dividends and stock prices, and presents the empirical evidence.

Chapter 8 covers the whole process of financial analysis, from the level of the economy to that of the firm. The effects of the economic cycle on the industry and the effect of both economy and industry factors on the performance of the firm are also discussed. We then examine the effects of various types of earnings and earning-generating processes on the predictability of share prices.

Chapter 9 deals with investment companies—their nature, goals, size, regulation, and the reasons for their prosperity. It also deals with the various methods of evaluating their performance and the empirical evidence thereon.

In Chapter 10 we move to debt securities. The various types of debt instruments and their valuation models are discussed. Also discussed are some trading strategies.

Chapter 11 continues with the discussion of debt-related issues. The component parts of interest rates, the various theories on interest rates, and the various methods utilized in predicting interest rates are also presented. There is also an extensive discussion of bond immunization.

Chapters 12 and 13 deal with all types of options and options strategies from both the buyer's and seller's perspective. Major option strategies are discussed, as is the Black-Scholes option-valuation model. The advantages and disadvantages of options trading compared with appropriate (short or long) positions in the underlying stock are also presented. Chapter 12 concludes with a discussion on other forms of options: stock warrants and stock rights. Chapter 13 concludes with a note of caution on the prerequisites for involvement in the options markets.

Financial futures contracts are discussed in detail in Chapter 14. The operations of the exchanges on which these contracts are traded, the various types of contracts, and the models for their valuation are presented in great detail. The uses of T-bill contracts as hedging, investment, or speculative vehicles are extensively discussed.

Chapter 15 deals with the various aspects of commodities futures, the valuation of futures contracts, the manner in which they are utilized by different economic agents, and the operations and requirements of the futures markets. The chapter also deals with the spot market for gold and discusses a few strategies for using gold futures contracts.

The international dimensions of investments are discussed in Chapters 16 and 17. The nature and operations of the foreign exchange markets are closely examined in Chapter 16. Forward and futures exchange contracts are analyzed and compared, and the various methods for forecasting exchange rates are presented. Chapter 17 reviews the considerations in international investments and sketches a profile of those countries of greatest interest to U.S. investors. In addition, the Eurobond market is discussed, as are American Depository Receipts and internationally diversified mutual funds.

In Chapter 18, we review the tax laws to include the provisions of the Economic Recovery Tax Act of 1981. A hypothetical doctor with two children and a certain set of objectives is picked and a financial plan is developed for him or her starting from an assumed level of assets and income.

The problems and questions at the end of each chapter should increase the readers' interest and help them further their understanding of the subject matter.

QUESTIONS

1. Do the recent developments in the capital markets represent a threat to the small investor? A threat to institutional investors?

2. Do the new instruments increase the need for professional money managers?

3. The Economic Recovery Tax Act of 1981 reduces the capital gains tax as well as the personal income tax. How might these changes in the tax law affect the investment decision-making process?

4. Should an investor be concerned with the increasing volume of trades by institutions, both in absolute and in relative terms? Why?

5. Can an investor ignore the developments in the financial markets and still realize the maximum rate of return given the risk inherent in his or her portfolio?

6. Do you see the emergence of "financial supermarkets" as a benefit to the small investor? How?

7. How important are taxes (both federal and state) in establishing trading strategies and in financial planning?

8. Does inflation and the general increase in the level of uncertainty about economic performance increase the need for information? Why?

9. "The emergence of stock options and financial futures is directly attributable to the volatility of the stock and bond markets." Do you agree?

10. Investors should be quite vigilant in tracking new technologies and significant changes in management. Why? What are the specific payoffs?

11. The 1970s were characterized by increased uncertainty about the economic environment, increased inflation, and unstable monetary policy. How do you suppose this affects the decision to commit funds to the stock market as opposed to fixed income securities?

12. "If banks are allowed to enter the securities industry, they will practically put all securities firms out of business because of their size and market position." Comment.

13. How important to the securities industry is the consumer's decision to save?

14. You have $10,000 in savings, no retirement plan, and no insurance policy. How would you rank the following investment opportunities in light of your financial condition?
    Buy stocks
    Buy a life insurance policy
    Buy corporate bonds
    Put money in a savings account
    Buy government bonds.

A Glossary of Financial Terms

annuity: a guaranteed series of payments at regular intervals bought for a lump sum. With a **deferred annuity,** payment begins at a specific future date; no income tax is paid on the interest earned during the accumulation period, only when repayment begins.

appreciation: the increase in value of any property over time.

assets: everything that is owned—cash, bank deposits, cars, stocks, bonds, investments, land, buildings, machinery, furniture; property that can be used to repay debts.

averaging, or dollar-cost averaging: buying a fixed dollar amount of a certain stock at regular intervals. Although prices may fluctuate, the price an investor pays, over the long run, is an average.

bear: one who believes the price of investments will decline. A **bear market** is a declining market.

big board: the New York Stock Exchange.

blue chip: stock in a company with a reputation for steady growth and profit; the term often refers to one of the 30 Dow Jones industrial stocks.

board of directors: a group of individuals elected by the shareholders to manage a company according to established policies.

bond: a long-term IOU from a government, bank, company, or other institution promising to repay a loan, with a specified interest, after a specified time.

broker: an agent, working on commission, who handles orders between buyers and sellers in a market.

bull: one who believes the price of investments will rise; a speculator who buys in the belief that prices will rise and he can sell at a profit. Thus, a **bull market** is an advancing market.

capital: wealth in the form of money or property; sometimes the basic sum in an investment enterprise.

CEO: chief executive officer of a company.

certificate of deposit: a bank savings plan that pays a higher interest than a passbook savings account. A considerable amount of interest is forfeited for early withdrawal.

certificate (stock): physical evidence of stock ownership, usually on contract or watermarked paper.

collateral: property offered to secure a loan and subject to seizure upon failure to pay.

collectibles: hobby items, such as baseball cards, beer cans, comic books, and stamps, purchased as an investment.

commercial paper: short-term promissory notes (IOU's) issued by major corporations. The cost is very high, but so usually is the return.

commission: a fee charged by an agent who handles purchases for the public; usually a percentage of the purchase.

commodities futures: contracts to buy and receive, or sell and deliver a commodity, such as pork bellies or wheat, at a future date. The contracts, not the commodities themselves, are bought and sold by investors.

convertible bonds: bonds that can be exchanged for stocks or other interests in the company.

credit: money loaned in the present to be repaid in the future.

creditor: a person or agency owed money in a credit agreement.

debenture: a promissory note (IOU), such as a bond, that is backed by the general credit of the company.

debt: money owed to a creditor.

default: failure to meet the terms of a credit agreement.

depreciation: a bookkeeping entry that subtracts a dollar amount from the net worth of any property that decreases in value over time.

dividend: a proportionate payment distributed to shareholders of a company. For common stocks, the payment can vary with the fortunes of the company.

Dow Jones Industrials: 30 stocks that are monitored closely; their collective performance indicates the movement of the market.

equity: the value of an individual or corporation that exceeds its debt.

estate: an individual's total cash and property holdings.

finance charge: interest charged for the use of credit.

full-service bank: a bank that offers checking, savings, lending, and a wide range of programs for borrowers and lenders.

GNP, or gross national product: the combined annual money value of all products and services in any country, not including any deductions.

guaranteed stocks and bonds: issues of a company guaranteed by another company.

hedge: to avoid committing oneself, or counterbalancing investments to limit potential losses in the event of a change in price. See **options.**

holding company: a corporation that owns the securities of and has voting control over another corporation.

index: a statistical measurement for comparing a quantity (prices or industrial activity, for example) with the same quantity over some "baseline" time.

indicators: business-related activities that economists analyze to predict trends.

inflation: the rise of prices generally over time.

interest: payments to a borrower from a lender for the use of money.

investment: any property from which one hopes to realize a profit.

IRA, or individual retirement account: an account established as a form of investment for retirement by an employee not covered by an employer's pension plan. Most banks can advise on this matter. See **Keough plan.**

issue: any security of a company, or its distribution.

Keough plan: a tax-deferred retirement fund that may be established by self-employed persons not covered by a conventional retirement plan.

La Salle Street: Chicago's equivalent of Wall Street.

liabilities: All financial claims against an individual or organization, including wages that must be paid, dividends, taxes, and mortgages.

lien: a charge against property to secure payment of a debt or the performance of an obligation.

liquidation: the process of converting investment holdings into cash.

liquidity: the ease with which holdings can be converted into cash. Liquidity depends on market conditions.

margin buying: buying properties with money, part of which is borrowed from another party, usually a broker.

market: the place or process by which buyers and sellers meet for the exchange of goods or services for money.

maturity: the date on which a loan, bond, or debenture must be repaid.

merger: the consolidation of two or more companies into one.

money markets: financial institutions that deal in short-term investments, such as treasury bills, certificates of deposit, and commercial paper. Money market funds are minimum risk, short-term investment mutual funds. Pooled assets make possible buying short-term investments not available to the average investor.

mortgage: the pledge of an asset to a creditor as security until a loan is repaid; often used in borrowing money from a bank or savings institution to purchase a home.

municipal bond: a bond issued by a local government to finance public works projects. In general, interest on these bonds is exempt from federal income tax.

mutual fund: a company that combines the investment funds of many whose investment goals are similar and invests the money in a wide variety of securities, usually stocks.

NYSE common stock index: a figure representing price movements of all common stocks listed on the New York Stock Exchange.

option: the purchased right to buy or sell at a specified price within a given time, should the holder of the option choose to do so.

over-the-counter: a means of trading securities not listed on a regular stock exchange.

portfolio: the total securities held by any investor.

point: one point equals $1 in common stock quotations.

probate: the legal establishment and enactment of a will. Also, the taxes administered on the estate of the deceased.

profit: the difference between revenues and costs, when revenues are higher than costs.

promissory note: a written promise to pay the bearer a specific sum at some future time.

rally: a rise in stock market prices following a decline.

recession: a long-term downswing in the national economy characterized by rising unemployment as well as industrial cutbacks.

revolving credit: a credit account, usually represented by a plastic card such as Visa or Master Charge, that allows credit up to a certain dollar amount.

savings and loan: an institution specializing in home mortgage loans.

seat on the exchange: a membership in an organized stock exchange.

securities: Shares or interest in a corporation; properties pledged for the payment of an obligation.

security: property pledged to a creditor to repay a loan or obligation. Also called **collateral.**

Standard & Poor's composite index: an index of the price movements of a group of 500 industrial, rail, and utility stocks.

stock: An investment in a company or organization. Owners of **common stock,** the standard form of stock investment, share fully the risks and opportunities of corporate activity. **Preferred stockholders** get first crack at any distribution of profits, called **dividends,** and usually are entitled to priority in payments if the company should fold. The market for **preferred stock** generally is less active than that of **common.**

tax shelters: investments, such as real estate and oil-drilling, designed to direct income into nontaxable areas.

ticker: An electronically operated transmitter that relays nationwide the prices and volumes of transactions from the floor of a stock or commodity exchange.

treasury bonds and bills: investments in the United States government.

trust: a right or interest in property controlled by one person for another. The trustees distribute money to the beneficiaries in accordance with the rules of the trust.

volume of traffic: a measure of how many shares were traded on the market on any given day.

Wall Street: The New York equivalent of La Salle Street; home of the New York Stock Exchange, symbol of the Big Apple's financial district, and center of the American financial community.

wholesale price index: monthly index of wholesale prices, based on selected goods, a measure designed to reflect changes in the cost of living.

yield: the return received from an investment or property; the income from a security as a proportion of its current market price.

CHAPTER 2 | Securitities Markets

2.1 INTRODUCTION

The primary function of securities markets is to facilitate the flow of funds from economic agents with surplus funds to those in need of funds. The greater the transmission efficiency is, the higher the rate of capital formation and consequently the higher the growth rate of the economy.

By their mere presence and their efficient functioning, securities markets increase the liquidity of capital assets and, consequently, minimize transaction costs and improve rates of return. Securities markets characterized by depth (size of issues), and breadth (diversity of issues, domestic and international) afford lower transactions costs and constitute, therefore, an inducement to investments in financial assets.

In this chapter we shall concentrate on the nature and operations of the stock markets and on the laws and regulations governing their operations. While much of the discussion here is relevant to other markets—options markets, bond markets, futures markets— we shall leave the discussion of these markets to other chapters.

2.2 NATURE OF SECURITIES MARKETS

Two types of securities markets may be distinguished:

Money markets. Money markets are markets for short-term (less than one year) debt instruments.
Capital markets. Capital markets are markets for long-term funds.
Securities markets are constituted in two forms: the organized exchanges and the over-the-counter market. Before discussing the operations of these markets, we shall consider the important role played by investment bankers.

2.3 INVESTMENT BANKING

Definitions

Investment banking is essentially a mechanism through which funds flow from savers to investors. It is also a channel for information intended to improve the quality and effectiveness of the investment decision for both firms and individuals.

An investment banker, on the other hand, is a firm that uses its own equity capital

TABLE 2.1
Securities Registrations for Cash Sale 1976–1981 (Under Securites Act of 1933)[a]

| | | | Primary Corporate Offerings | | | | | |
| | | | Stock | | | | | |
	Debt	Preferred	Unseasoned	Seasoned	Warrants and Other Equity Securities	Closed-End Investment Companies	Secondary Offerings	Foreign Governments
			Amounts in Millions of Dollars					
1976	25,367	2,359	185	7,221	897	44	774	3,827
1977	21,938	2,421	197	6,078	1,554	27	394	4,096
1978	18,878	1,758	296	4,969	2,459	15	558	4,100
1979	24,844	1,963	545	5,306	2,831	11	934	4,272
1980	42,210	3,284	1,667	10,997	6,445	19	1,979	2,008
Year to date								
1980 Jan–Apr	10,486	908	164	2,827	2,946	19	708	697
1981 Jan–Apr	12,021	873	1,031	3,686	2,497	0	459	1,343
1980 Apr	3,893	223	56	400	205	19	305	0
May	6,562	191	268	1,350	754	0	33	125
Jun	7,020	338	91	694	173	0	92	497
Jly	5,102	360	191	613	182	0	122	0
Aug	3,755	130	96	863	145	0	214	0
Sep	2,696	402	129	918	652	0	114	0
Oct	2,364	484	206	1,321	511	0	293	399
Nov	1,414	256	193	980	323	0	305	90
Dec	2,811	215	329	1,431	759	0	98	200
1981 Jan	2,663	360	113	966	715	0	51	0
Feb	2,072	136	160	516	382	0	94	249
Mar	3,564	297	287	1,154	512	0	117	100
Apr	3,722	80	471	1,050	888	0	197	994
			Number of Issues					
1976	391	71	43	209	96	4	97	50
1977	374	61	58	177	130	2	61	40
1978	339	51	70	222	173	2	81	26
1979	320	55	110	203	191	2	72	23
1980	556	78	281	394	337	1	153	14
Year to date								
1980 Jan–Apr	106	22	48	87	82	1	29	4
1981 Jan–Apr	119	19	162	144	141	0	88	9
1980 Apr	35	6	18	22	14	1	7	0
May	98	6	17	27	28	0	8	1
Jun	73	8	21	39	20	0	15	3
Jly	51	8	32	27	23	0	17	0
Aug	52	5	24	32	21	0	10	0
Sep	47	7	39	33	43	0	11	0
Oct	49	9	28	50	36	0	25	3
Nov	30	8	32	41	37	0	16	1
Dec	50	5	40	58	47	0	22	2
1981 Jan	33	7	22	39	30	0	15	0
Feb	25	6	36	25	30	0	16	1
Mar	35	3	33	40	16	0	21	1
Apr	46	3	71	40	45	0	36	7

Source: SEC Monthly Statistical Bulletin, U.S. Securities and Exchange Commission, June 1981.

[a] Figures may not add due to rounding.

or borrowed capital to establish positions and to trade in securities. It is primarily involved in new issues—primary distributions (issues sold to the public for the first time; Table 2.1) and frequently in secondary issues (redistribution of shares already issued to the public). The sale of 10,000 shares of IBM to the public by a wealthy owner through an investment banker is an example of a secondary offering or distribution.

Investment bankers are also extensively involved as agents in the distribution of securities and in placing securities directly with institutional investors.

Underwriting as an integral part of the capitalist economic life began to take hold in England in the seventeenth century. Merchants were the original underwriters. They gathered at Lloyd's Coffee House to underwrite part of all the risk associated with certain seafaring ventures. In the United States, the first underwriting was of U.S. government bonds during the second half of the nineteenth century. Jay Cooke, with the help of other professionals, was able to market $2 billion in U.S. government securities in 1871. From this modest beginning, the investment banking industry has continued to evolve; its reach today extends to several aspects of the nation's financial life. Investment bankers continue to add new lines of business activity, further capitalizing on their large wealth of knowledge about money markets, capital markets, corporate financial positions, industry and company trends, and the attitude and behavior of investors; they also capitalize on their strong ties with the business community.

Types of Agreements

The most frequently concluded agreement between an investment banker and an issuing corporation (whether the issue is stocks, bonds, warrants, etc.) involves the purchase (the underwriting) of the whole issue. The issuing firm receives payment for the entire value of the issue.

Other types of agreements are:

1. *The best-effort agreement.* As the name implies, this agreement does not obligate underwriters actually to purchase an issue but rather to do their best to sell it. The underwriter acts as an agent here.
2. *The all-or-none agreement.* Under this arrangement the issue is simply withdrawn if it is not all sold.
3. *The stand-by agreement.* This agreement obligates the underwriter to purchase at a fixed price the remainder of the issue not subscribed to by the holders of stock rights (see Chapter 12).

Selection of the Investment Banker

The selection of an investment banker is done in either of two ways:

1. *The negotiated method.* The terms of the deal are negotiated between the investment banker and the issuing company.
2. *The competitive bidding method.* This method is required for most government and municipal securities. Underwriters submit a sealed bid to be opened by a certain date. The best bid wins the deal.

The Underwriting Process

The underwriting process begins with an information session about the needs and the condition of the company in need of funds. The process continues generally in accordance with the following steps:

1. A thorough investigation is undertaken by the investment banker to assess the condition of the company and the industry, and the appropriate vehicle to be issued in order to meet the financial needs of the company. The financial records of the company are carefully scrutinized with an eye on liquidity, profitability, leverage, and operating efficiency of the company. The quality of the management, actual and prospective, is of great importance as well. In light of the findings and of prevailing conditions in the bond and the equity markets, the investment banker makes a recommendation as to whether, if any, equity or bonds should be issued.

2. The registration statement and the prospectus are prepared and filed with the Securities and Exchange Commission.[1] Both documents must contain all pertinent information regarding the issuing company so as to allow for an enlightened decision by the investor. This step is required under the Securities Act of 1933, which is discussed later in this chapter.

3. The underwriting and selling groups are formed.

The underwriting group is a form for spreading the risk of underwriting. Here a group of underwriters (sometimes referred to as the *underwriting syndicate*) pool their resources (not necessarily with equal commitments) to purchase the entire issue of stocks or bonds. The syndicate is dissolved upon completion of the underwriting transaction.

The selling group, on the other hand, is assembled to help in the marketing of the issue. Members of this group do not have a commitment to buy the securities but simply to sell their share. This group is made up of members who are not necessarily in the underwriting group.

4. The due diligence meeting is held. This meeting takes place between the issuing company and the underwriters, with various experts (lawyers and accountants, ordinarily) taking part. The purpose of this meeting is to discuss the registration statement and prospectus. The meeting takes place toward the end of the required 21-day waiting (cooling) period before the registration statement with the SEC becomes effective and the underwriter can proceed with the sale of the securities.

It must be noted, however, that the approval of the registration statement by the SEC in no way implies that the SEC approves of the investment merits of the issue— that is, that the SEC considers it a "good investment."

5. The issue is qualified under the various state laws where the issue is going to be sold. This is referred to as "blue-skying" the issue.

6. The underwriter is now ready to discuss the terms of the issue. These include the public offering price (the price at which the issue will be sold to the public), the underwriting spread, and the sales commission. The underwriting spread is the difference

---

[1] Rule 415, promulgated by the SEC, was intended to take effect on March 16, 1982. Under this rule major corporations are permitted to file a single "shelf registration" for nine months and offer unlimited securities against the registration statement any time during that period. The investment banking community lobbied hard against Rule 415.

between what the underwriter pays for the securities and the public offering price. The underwriting spread varies from one issue to another and from one underwriter to another. On average the underwriting spread amounts to one-half to three-quarters of 1 percent of the value of the issue. The selling commission is approximately 1 percent of the public offering price and is paid by the issuer. There are no explicit commission costs to the investor on the purchase of new issues.

7. Having agreed on the terms of the underwriting, the underwriter pays the issuing firm for the securities to be sold.

8. The securities of the issuing firm are sold by the selling group. The SEC requires that sales solicitations be accompanied by a prospectus to be made available to the investor free of charge. For a specified time during the sales period, if agreed to by the other members of the underwriting group, the managing underwriter engages in price-stabilizing transactions. The managing underwriter may establish short or long positions in the security in order to maintain a certain price level or range.

Complex as the process discussed above appears to be, it is almost always handled efficiently and expediently.

Methods of Disposal

Underwriters dispose of their securities in either of two ways:

1. *Public offering.* The issue is sold directly to the public at the offering price.
2. *Private placement.* The investment banker approaches a small group of investors—usually insurance companies or pension funds—trying to place (sell) the entire issue with them.

The distribution of sales between public offerings and private placements from 1934 until 1980 is shown in Table 2.2

Other Functions of Investment Banking Houses

Investment banking has taken on many new dimensions. Investment banking houses handle large block trades, recruit and counsel firms in acquisition and merger cases, act as dealers for government and municipal securities, manage portfolios, offer investment advisory and management services, structure real estate and other tax shelters, and deal in a host of other investment related endeavors.

2.4 THE ORGANIZED STOCK EXCHANGES

There exist two national stock exchanges—the New York Stock Exchange (NYSE) and the American Stock Exchange (ASE)—and 11 regional exchanges. The highest dollar volume of transactions take place on the New York Stock Exchange. In fact, the NYSE accounted for 85.27 percent of the dollar value of all stocks traded on registered stock exchanges (Table 2.3) in April 1981 and for 80.62 percent of the value of all stocks, options, warrants, and rights traded on the same exchanges during the same period.

TABLE 2.2
New Corporate Securities Offered for Cash in the United States by Method of Offering and Type of Security (Millions of Dollars)[a]

	Total				Publicly Offered				Privately Placed			
	All Issues	Bonds & Notes	Pfd.	Common	All Issues	Bonds & Notes	Pfd.	Common	All Issues	Bonds & Notes	Pfd.	Common
	All Industries											
1934	397	372	6	19	305	280	6	19	92	92	0	0
1935	2,333	2,225	86	22	1,946	1,840	84	22	387	385	2	0
1936	4,572	4,029	271	272	4,199	3,660	270	269	373	369	1	3
1937	2,309	1,618	406	285	1,979	1,291	403	285	330	327	3	0
1938	2,155	2,044	86	25	1,463	1,353	85	25	692	691	1	0
1939	2,164	1,979	98	87	1,457	1,276	95	86	707	703	3	1
1940	2,677	2,386	183	108	1,912	1,628	181	103	765	758	2	5
1941	2,667	2,389	168	110	1,854	1,578	167	109	813	811	1	1
1942	1,062	917	111	34	642	506	102	34	420	411	9	0
1943	1,170	990	124	56	798	621	124	53	372	369	0	3
1944	3,204	2,670	369	165	2,417	1,892	362	163	787	778	7	2
1945	6,011	4,855	758	398	4,989	3,851	747	391	1,022	1,004	11	7
1946	6,899	4,882	1,126	891	4,982	3,019	1,084	879	1,917	1,863	42	12
1947	6,576	5,036	761	779	4,341	2,889	682	770	2,235	2,147	79	9
1948	7,080	5,973	492	615	3,993	2,965	433	595	3,087	3,008	59	20
1949	6,051	4,890	424	737	3,549	2,437	382	730	2,502	2,453	42	7
1950	6,361	4,920	631	810	3,681	2,360	519	802	2,680	2,560	112	8
1951	7,740	5,690	838	1,212	4,326	2,364	762	1,200	3,414	3,326	76	12
1952	9,535	7,602	564	1,369	5,533	3,645	522	1,366	4,002	3,957	42	3
1953	8,899	7,084	489	1,326	5,581	3,856	406	1,319	3,318	3,228	83	7
1954	9,515	7,487	815	1,213	5,846	4,003	652	1,191	3,669	3,484	163	22
1955	10,241	7,420	635	2,186	6,764	4,119	516	2,129	3,477	3,301	119	57
1956	10,938	8,002	635	2,301	7,052	4,225	573	2,254	3,886	3,777	62	47
1057	12,004	9,957	411	2,516	8,959	6,118	376	2,465	3,925	3,839	35	51
1958	11,557	9,652	571	1,334	8,068	6,332	434	1,302	3,489	3,320	137	32
1959	9,747	7,189	531	2,027	5,993	3,557	444	1,992	3,754	3,632	87	35
1960	10,123	8,081	408	1,634	6,657	4,806	220	1,631	3,466	3,275	188	33
1961	13,165	9,420	450	3,295	8,143	4,700	217	3,226	5,022	4,720	233	69
1962	10,703	8,969	421	1,313	6,063	4,440	336	1,287	4,640	4,529	85	26
1963	12,237	10,872	343	1,022	5,824	4,714	159	951	6,413	6,158	184	71
1964	13,958	10,866	412	2,680	6,454	3,623	180	2,651	7,504	7,243	232	29
1965	14,782	12,585	726	1,471	6,485	4,688	361	1,436	8,297	7,897	365	35
1966	17,385	14,903	581	1,901	9,853	7,640	435	1,878	7,532	7,363	146	23
1967	24,012	21,205	881	1,926	17,040	14,443	784	1,813	6,972	6,762	97	113
1968	21,261	16,740	636	3,885	14,440	10,215	574	3,651	6,821	6,525	62	234
1969	25,995	17,666	690	7,639	20,218	12,338	598	7,282	5,777	5,328	92	357
1970	37,450	29,025	1,390	7,035	32,526	24,366	1,310	6,850	4,924	4,659	80	185
1971	43,227	30,059	3,684	9,484	36,144	23,293	3,556	9,295	7,083	6,766	128	189
1972	39,716	25,639	3,372	10,705	29,664	16,926	2,408	10,330	10,052	8,713	964	375
1973	31,694	20,701	3,346	7,647	22,908	12,898	2,400	7,610	8,786	7,803	946	37
1974	37,733	31,497	2,257	3,978	31,031	25,337	1,745	3,949	6,701	6,160	512	29
1975	53,637	42,763	3,459	7,415	42,858	32,590	3,089	7,179	10,779	10,173	370	236
1976	53,319	42,214	2,804	8,301	36,740	26,095	2,353	8,292	16,579	16,119	451	9
1977	54,233	42,270	3,918	8,045	34,489	24,209	2,423	7,857	19,744	18,061	1,495	188
1978	48,212	37,445	2,832	7,935	29,984	20,472	1,755	7,757	18,228	16,973	1,077	178
1979r	53,090	40,858	3,526	8,706	37,018	26,473	1,966	8,579	16,072r	14,335	1,560	127
1980	78,355	55,723	3,636	18,996	66,024	44,110	3,196	18,718	12,331	11,613	440	278

Source: *SEC Monthly Statistical Bulletin*, U.S. Securities and Exchange Commission, June 1981.

[a]Totals differ from earlier presentations due to changes in rounding procedures.

+ = Greater than $0.0 but less than $500,000.

r = revised.

TABLE 2.3
Market Value and Volume of Equity Sales on U.S. Securities Exchanges (Data in Thousands)

	Total Market Cash Value	Stocks Cash Value	Stocks Shares	Options[a] Cash Value	Options[a] Contracts	Warrants Cash Value	Warrants Units	Rights Cash Value	Rights Units
Registered Stock Exchanges, April 1981									
American	3,464,794	2,439,920	123,894	995,814	2,838	29,061	1,981	0	0
Boston	249,181	249,181	8,275	0	0	0	0	0	0
Chicago Option	1,449,315	0	0	1,449,315	4,376	0	0	0	0
Cincinnati	153,554	153,554	5,001	0	0	0	0	0	0
Midwest	2,581,755	2,581,755	71,697	0	0	0	0	0	0
New York	41,605,784	41,575,392	1,204,433	0	0	30,392	4,481	0	0
Pacific	1,216,332	1,090,565	40,366	125,571	510	196	40	0	0
Philadelphia	884,875	665,173	20,227	219,192	724	510	89	0	0
Intermountain	72	72	92	0	0	0	0	0	0
Spokane	2,034	2,034	1,313	0	0	0	0	0	0
Latest 13 Months									
1980 April	28,068,449	26,247,976	963,193	1,782,420	6,084	38,053	4,247	0	0
1980 May	29,811,523	28,029,110	960,028	1,745,475	5,875	36,599	3,157	338	901
1980 June	35,713,482	33,490,129	1,140,785	2,201,372	6,705	19,340	4,669	2,641	15,380
1980 July	41,700,000	38,610,633	1,258,105	3,052,225	8,400	35,868	4,349	1,274	13,919
1980 August	47,080,619	43,794,553	1,433,202	3,245,766	7,483	39,886	5,725	413	2,307
1980 September	46,284,072	41,216,444	1,335,904	5,024,452	8,896	42,815	4,988	361	560
1980 October	55,681,770	50,640,989	1,501,010	5,000,811	9,700	38,305	4,594	1,666	1,556
1980 November	49,745,339	43,157,058	1,279,508	6,533,206	9,796	54,957	6,566	118	48
1980 December	56,101,474	49,346,976	1,515,313	6,714,420	9,333	39,980	5,041	97	2,070
1981 January	46,178,334	42,443,237	1,286,083	3,709,097	9,131	25,994	4,521	6	591
1981 February	35,442,820	33,153255	1,038,501	2,265,640	7,073	23,925	3,384	+[b]	1
1981 March	52,431,454	49,120,245	1,525,630	3,260,737	9,663	50,472	6,226	0	0
1981 April	51,607,696	48,757,646	1,475,298	2,789,892	8,448	60,159	6,591	0	0
	80.62	85.27							

Source: SEC Monthly Statistical Bulletin, U.S. Securities and Exchange Commission, Washington, D.C., June 1981.
[a]Includes all exchange trades in puts and calls. Value and volume of call trading and exercises are shown in Table M-210. Exercises are not included in these totals.
[b]+ = Less than $500.

A Brief History of the NYSE

The eventful history of the NYSE reflects the dramatic changes that have taken place in the financial markets. The NYSE originated as an auction (a one-sided affair in which only buyers of securities competed against each other) held under a buttonwood tree in Manhattan; it moved indoors to the Tontine Coffee House in 1793. Not only stocks, but also merchandise and bonds were traded. As the economic life of the nation began to move forward, new banks, insurance companies, shipping companies, oil companies, and railroad companies began to emerge, expanding the need for an exchange to provide capital and liquidity. These expansions coincided with an increase in state and federal financing, which increased the number of bonds available to investors.

In 1817, the NYSE board's first constitution, setting certain standards of conduct and membership requirements, was drawn.

By 1842, the NYSE board had moved to the new Merchant's Exchange Building. The auction room was characterized by long tables at which each member occupied a certain seat. Thus the reference today to an exchange membership as a "seat."

In 1863, the exchange adopted its present official name and soon after (1865) acquired the building that remains its headquarters. Around this time too, trading on the exchange became continuous, the participating brokers having leased a room from the exchange so that they could trade among themselves between the auctions ("calls") in the main room. Also, brokers began to gather in certain parts of the room to trade certain securities. Membership in both rooms was unified and became salable in 1868. The calls for stocks were abandoned in 1882 and those for bonds in 1902. It was then that today's type market was effectively born.

In 1920, the Stock Clearing Corporation was formed to clear transactions between members and the system for delivering securities was centralized.

Today the NYSE has 1,366 seats and is governed by a board of directors made up of ten industry members and ten nonindustry members. The operations of the exchange are managed by a paid president and staff. The price of a NYSE seat on Dec. 16, 1981, was $220,000.

Exchange Operations

The primary functions of securities exchanges are to provide a continuous marketplace for listed securities, thus ensuring their liquidity; to allow for "fair" (competitive) price determination; and to transmit accurate information on prices and trading volume.

The liquidity provided by the exchange is essential to investors and to speculators in particular. The larger and more centralized the market is, the more "fair" prices will be, for then a trader moves ever closer to the best possible bid or ask price. As prices move closer to their fair value the allocational efficiency of the market is enhanced, since funds are directed to the most efficient users of capital.

The information value of the exchanges lies in the continuous price and volume information they provide about the auction market and in the requirement that corporations with listed securities disclose vital information about their operations to the public. NYSE-listed firms disclose earnings statements on a quarterly basis.

The system used in determining the prices of securities on the NYSE and the American Stock Exchange is known as the *double-auction system*. On the floor of the exchange, two auctions take place simultaneously. The buyers try to outbid one another (submit the highest bid) and sellers try to outask one another (submit the lowest ask). The best bid and the best offer are known as the *bid-ask quotation.* The trading rules are based on the first-come-first-served principle. The first bid at a particular price has precedence unless it is superseded by a market order on the next sale at that price up to the number of stocks or bonds specified in the bid. If the execution of the bid does not clear all the stocks offered, then the remaining bid (at that particular price) for the largest number of the balance of shares offered will have precedence regardless of the chronological order it occupies.

NYSE Membership

The NYSE is an association of 1,366 members. Membership is achieved through the purchase of a seat that only an individual can own.

Four types of members own seats on the New York Stock Exchange:

1. *The commission or floor broker.* The role of a commission broker is to execute orders for customers and their member firms.
2. *The floor trader.* The floor trader transacts for his own account. He does not deal with the public or for other brokers.
3. *The odd-lot dealer.* The odd-lot dealer deals exclusively with commission brokers acting on behalf of their clients. He buys round lots (100 shares) and odd lots (1 to 99 shares) and sells odd lots. Odd-lot dealers' functions have largely been taken over by brokerage firms.
4. *The specialist.* The specialist occupies one of the trading posts (a horseshoe-shaped post where certain designated listed shares are traded) on the floor of the exchange and specializes in a certain number of listed securities.

Five hundred of the exchange seats are owned by specialists. The specialist's functions are many. First, specialist is charged with maintaining an orderly market—that is, with preventing wide fluctuations in the price of the securities in which they specialize, which may require them to buy or sell for their own accounts. In this capacity, the specialist is acting as a dealer and, in the process, is providing continuity and liquidity to the market by supplying securities when the supply by the public is insufficient and by demanding securities when the demand by the public falls short of the supply. These actions are not intended to reverse the direction of the market but simply to smooth out the rise or the decline in securities prices—that is, to reduce their volatility. The net effect is that the spread (difference between bid and ask prices) is kept to a minimum (one-eighth of a point). Second, the specialist acts as a broker's broker for limit orders (orders to buy or sell at a specific price). The commission broker ordinarily leaves limit orders with the specialist, who executes them when the stock price reaches the specified level or a more advantageous one. Specialists must execute all the public orders they hold at a certain price before buying and selling at that price for their own accounts.

The exclusive access of the specialist to the supply and demand for listed securities at "limit prices" represents a monopoly power over vital stock information. That is why the behavior of the specialist is constantly monitored by the NYSE. The specialist is the sole market maker on the floor of the exchange. The information in the specialist's book can be used as a forecasting tool for stock prices. A specialist with substantial buy limit orders and few sell limit orders may, and should, conclude that the stock price will rise and decide to build inventory in the hope of realizing a profit.

The role of the specialist has become more important as trading by institutions has increased. Block trades (trades of 10,000 shares or more) can be destabilizing to the market at a sensitive time. The specialist on occasion absorbs the whole block offered in order to protect the market price from wide fluctuations. NYSE Rule 127, however, requires the specialist to execute all public limit orders (up to 1,000 shares or 5 percent of the block, whichever is larger) whenever he or she opts to purchase a block of securities. Block purchases by specialists are not made public. Rule 113 prohibits specialists from dealing directly with institutions and thus directly handling block transactions.

The function of specialists and their impact on market efficiency has been subjected to much criticism and is now the subject of much controversy as the market moves closer to a fully computerized national system capable of bypassing the specialist. Specialists have been able to realize consistenlty above-average rates of return, which, as we shall discuss in Chapter 4, decidedly renders the stock market inefficient.

2.5 OVER-THE-COUNTER MARKET

The over-the-counter market is a negotiated market made up of brokers and dealers mostly connected by an elaborate electronic network. When acting as a broker, the investment house negotiates with a third party on behalf of the customer. If, on the other hand, the investment house is acting as a dealer, it buys from or sells to the customer from its own account.

Companies that do not qualify for listing their securities on the exchanges or that choose not to list them trade their securities in the over-the-counter market. Dealers in this market may buy or sell for their own accounts or on behalf of a client. The dealers' bid and asked prices are reported through the National Association of Security Dealers Automated Quotations (NASDAQ). Participating dealers make a market in the securities they trade, which requires them to maintain firm bid and offer prices in the security. NASDAQ involves multiple market-makers. The average stock has seven market-makers.

The over-the-counter market is supervised by the National Association of Securities Dealers (NASD), a voluntary, self-regulating organization of security dealers.

Third Markets

Third markets emerged as a consequence of high transactions costs over the exchanges. The third market consists of listed securities traded over the counter.

In a move to foster competition among the exchanges, the SEC permitted (June 1980) recently listed stocks on exchanges to

> be traded by exchange members away from the exchange floor; that is, over-the-counter. Exchange rules generally bar such trading by members for their own account, leaving floor specialists with a monopoly on trading their designated securities. Currently, about 150 newly listed stocks can be traded both on and away from exchange floors, but fewer than 40 are, the SEC staff says, partly because current equipment automatically sends most trades in exchange-listed stocks to an exchange floor.[2]

---

[2] *The Wall Street Journal*, Feb. 6, 1981.

Fourth Markets

The fourth market goes one step further than the third market: it bypasses the dealer/broker. Here securities owners trade securities among themselves through a computerized system called *Instinet.*

A Centralized Market?

The emergence of the third and fourth markets contributed to the decentralization of the market. The floor of the exchange, even that of the NYSE, was no longer the focus of all trades. Investors were shopping around for better prices and lower transactions costs. This meant that the full mission of the exchange was not being fulfilled. Steps toward centralization and the emergence of a truly centralized market had to be taken. The momentum was provided by the Securities Act Amendments of 1975, which we discuss later in this chapter.

A truly centralized market system requires a multidimensional effort: a centralized system for reporting transactions and quotations and for dealing with limit orders. The objectives of such a system should be to increase the flow, speed, and concentration of information and thus optimize the competitiveness of the securities markets.

In mid-1975, the NYSE began reporting on one tape all transactions (no matter on which exchange they were traded or even if they were traded in the OTC market) in NYSE-listed securities. This consolidated tape is used simply to report transactions and does not report quotations.

The first real sign of a centralized market where all securities are traded appeared in August 1978, when the Composite Quotation System (CQS) began reporting prices and volume of shares traded on the organized exchanges, the over-the-counter market, and the third market. CQS is simply a system from which a trader gets price quotations.

Three other giant steps have been taken since. The first is the Central Limit Order Book (CLOB), which assures nationwide market protection for limit and stop orders; the second is the Intermarket Trading System (ITS), which connects the six major stock exchanges—Pacific, Philadelphia, Midwest, Boston, New York, and American; and the third is the National Securities Trading System (NSTS). Stocks listed on more than one exchange should sell at the same price at any given time. If for some reason the prices are different, the investor can shop around and lower his or her cost. ITS and NSTS allow for precisely this possibility.

The CLOB represents a threat to specialists on the NYSE, who opposed its creation and its scope. The more the CLOB prospers, the more diluted the monopoly power of specialists on limit orders becomes. It appears that the trend indicates more problems for specialists unless they show a more positive attitude toward sharing market power and toward the mandated national market system which may not be dominated by the NYSE or by its specialists.

ITS is a centralized computer facility connecting the member exchanges. For every participating stock (currently—April 1982—950 shares, 850 of which are NYSE listed stocks), the current quotes (bid/ask) can be called up on a screen, indicating to the broker that market on which it would be most advantageous to execute the customer's order. The mere entry on the order does not guarantee execution, however. A New York broker—observing, for example, that the bid on XYZ stock is 10⅜ on the NYSE and 10½ on the Pacific—would want to sell his stock on the Pacific Exchange. Using the facilities of ITS, he would place an order (limit or market) to sell (this is referred to as "commitment to trade") on the Pacific Exchange.

A limit order to sell, say, 500 shares at 10½ would be executed in its entirety if the bid is 10½ when the order reaches the exchange and if the bid covers 500 shares or more. On the other hand, a market order to sell 500 shares at market would be executed at the bid price if the bid covers at least 500 shares. Otherwise, at least 100 shares, or the displayed size of the bid are executed at the current bid and the remaining shares at the higher price.

ITS gets its price quotations from CQS. It is a system through which a trader can trade.

The National Securities Trading System (NSTS) is different from ITS in that it allows any qualified market maker to enter a bid or an ask or a limit order for any of the qualified stocks. Once the order is accepted, it is executed automatically within the system. Limit orders are stored on time and price bases. The maximum-size order is 1,000 shares, with the execution guaranteed provided the size of the bid or ask equals or exceeds the number of shares being sold or bought.

NSTS is the brainchild of the Cincinnati Stock Exchange and is still in its infancy. By April 1982, there were 71 shares traded on NSTS, the majority being NYSE stocks. Of these, only two were fully listed on the Cincinnati Exchange, the remainder being traded under the unlisted trading privileges.

March 1, 1981, was the deadline set by the SEC for the installation of a link between ITS and the Computer Assisted Execution System (CAES) of the NASD. This link would permit CAES market makers to transmit their orders through ITS. The securities industry missed the March deadline primarily for technical reasons. The problems were later worked out, however (May 17, 1982).

CAES was created by the NASD to complement their quotation system (NASDAQ). In contrast to NASDAQ, CAES is both a quotation and an order execution system for Rule 19C3 securities (90 securities as of April 1982). These securities are NYSE securities listed after April 1979. NASDAQ is simply a quotation system for OTC stocks, listed stocks, and stocks traded in the third market.

The actions cited above appear to be the extent to which the SEC is willing to go for now. Yet the drive toward a truly national market continues. Advocates of a centralized market system continue to apply pressure on the grounds that a truly national market would increase convenience, lower transactions costs, and allow for an even fairer price determination.

2.6 REGULATIONS OF SECURITIES MARKETS

The issuance and trading of financial instruments, the underlying contractual agreements between issuer and holder, and the operations of the markets in which these securities are traded are governed by federal and state laws and regulations. Indeed, every phase of the securities industry is regulated in one form or another.

The intent of the various laws and regulations is to prevent fraud and manipulation of security prices and to maximize the flow of accurate and relevant information to the marketplace. Equal access to information, it is theorized, should give every participant in the securities market the same probability of realizing a fair rate of return on his or her investment. The underlying assumption (a weak if not an erroneous one) is that all recipients of information possess an equal ability to process and act on information and that the transactions costs for entering and leaving the securities markets are equal for all participants.

The acts and regulations we shall concentrate on are:

1. The Securities Act of 1933
2. The Securities Exchange Act of 1934
3. The Maloney Act of 1938
4. The Trust Indenture Act of 1939
5. The Investment Company Act of 1940
6. The Employment Retirement Income Act of 1974 (ERISA)
7. The Securities Acts Amendments of 1975
8. Rule 390

The Securities Act of 1933 (May 27, 1933, Chapter 38, Title I)

The Securities Act of 1933 is sometimes referred to as the *Truth-in-Securities Act.*

Its basic purpose is to ensure full disclosure of information in the registration statement and prospectus for *new* securities. In the language of the Act, "to provide full and fair disclosure of the character of securities sold in interstate and foreign commerce and through the mails, and to prevent frauds in the sale thereof, and for other purposes."

The SEC is the government agency in charge of ensuring full disclosure of all significant material facts concerning a security offered to the public. In so doing, the SEC does not pass any judgment on the investment value (merits) of the security.

Not *all* new issues are subject to the 1933 act. Those exempted are:

1. Intrastate issues, which are sold only to persons residing in one state where the issuer is a resident doing business within that state.
2. Securities of any political subdivision of the United States, including those of the federal and state governments and of religious and not-for-profit organizations.
3. An issue offered to the public when the total amount is less than $1.5 million. For these issues the SEC has adopted Regulation A, which requires notification of the intention to offer such stock to the public. The company must provide certain information to prospective purchasers, however. The usual registration requirements do not apply. The SEC is currently (1981) in the process of reviewing proposed rules intended to further ease the guidelines for smaller companies raising money, particularly from accredited investors. An accredited investor is generally defined as a buyer of $100,000 of stock or as one with gross income of $100,000 or a net worth of $750,000. It is theorized that accredited investors do not need the watchful eyes of the SEC as much as small investors do.
4. Securities issued by common carriers subject to the Interstate Commerce Act, since these issues are supervised by the Interstate Commerce Commission.
5. Annuity contracts issued by insurance companies.

The Securities Exchange Act of 1934

The Securities Exchange Act of 1934 extended the reach of the 1933 act to all phases of trading in existing securities. To enforce its provisions, the act set up the SEC and authorized the Federal Reserve System (the "Fed") to regulate the use of credit for the purchase or carrying of securities. The Fed has exercised this authority through Regulations T and U.

The SEC consists of five members appointed by the President with the advice and consent of the Senate. No more than three of the five members can be from one political party.

The Securities Exchange Act of 1934 requires many different groups and organizations to register with the SEC. Among them are:

1. Corporations with listed securities.
2. Brokers and dealers involved in interstate commerce and in transactions not con-summated on the exchanges.
3. Securities exchanges (for example, NYSE, ASE). Strict requirements must be met before approval of registration.
4. Securities traded on the exchanges.
5. National securities associations.

Directors and officers of the issuing corporation and owners of more than 5 percent of the shares outstanding must file a statement with the SEC. Any changes in ownership position must also be reported within ten days from their occurrence. Such individuals are barred from establishing short positions in the securities and are required to turn to the stockholders any short-term profits realized on inside information. Section 16(b) of the Securities Act of 1934 requires insiders to return all profits from purchase and subsequent sale (or a sale and subsequent purchase) occurring within six months from each other.

The 1934 act outlaws the use of any "manipulative, deceptive, or other fraudulent devices or contrivances" such as churning (unauthorized or imprudent transactions in an investor's account with the primary intent of generating commissions), matching orders (simultaneous buy and sell orders on the same security by the same person to give the impression of active trading), wash sales (buying and selling the same day in order to establish a tax loss or selling to one's spouse at a lower price in order to purchase the same security later at that lower price), and pooling (setting up a group for the purpose of trading securities within the group with the intent of manipulating the price upward or downward). Manipulative and deceptive devices and contrivances are dealt with in Sections 10(b) (1–17) of the act. A review of these sections is recom-mended.

The act also outlaws, according to SEC statements, the practice of predicting specific results from positions in securities or of recommending securities without adequate in-quiry.

In addition, the act sets limits on borrowing by member brokers and dealers. The prescribed rule is referred to as the *20-to-1 rule;* that is, a broker dealer's aggregate indebtedness to all other persons cannot exceed 2,000 percent of net capital. The act also sets the requirements for proxies (transference by the stockholder of his or her rights and privileges to another party) and their solicitation and the conditions for short sales.

When and if the SEC suspects wrongdoing, it holds an investigation. Everyone who is subpoenaed must testify. If the fifth amendment is invoked, testimony is still required. However, the testimony and the documents presented cannot be used for prosecution.

The SEC, through its *SEC Statement of Policy,* provides guidelines intended to elimi-nate misleading statements in literature distributed in the sale of securities.

Regulation T

Regulation T is concerned with the extension and maintenance of credit in the purchase or sale of securities. Cash transactions are expected to be settled within seven days. Margin requirements are also set by Regulation T. They specify the maximum percentage of the value of the investment which the investor may borrow from the broker/dealer. Regulation T also identifies those securities that are marginable—purchasable on credit—and those that are exempt. U.S. government securities, municipal bonds, and bonds of the International Bank for Reconstruction and Development are exempt from Regulation T.

Maloney Act of 1938

The Maloney Act amends the Securities Exchange Act of 1934 by adding section 15A. This section provides for "The establishment of regulation among over-the-counter brokers and dealers operating in interstate and foreign commerce or through the mails to prevent acts and practices inconsistent with just and equitable principle of trade and for other purposes."

National securities associations or affiliated securities associations are required to register with the SEC. Copies of their constitutions, charters, articles of incorporation, and bylaws must be filed with the SEC. Disciplinary actions taken against a member of the association can be appealed to the SEC. The commission's decision is then final. The commission can, under this act, suspend (12-month limit) or revoke the registration, suspend or expel an individual member, or remove an officer or director of an association who has not enforced the rules.

Trust Indenture Act of 1939

The Trust Indenture Act of 1939 was intended to protect the holders of debt securities by requiring issuing corporations to live up to the provisions of the indenture agreement (the contract between the bondholder and the bond issuer). The bond issuer, under this act, is required to file periodic financial statements with the trustee. In the words of the act, the intent is "To provide for the regulation of the sale of certain securities in interstate and foreign commerce and through the mails, and the regulation of the trust indentures under which the same are issued and for other purposes."

Some securities are exempted from the act. These include all securities exempted under the Securities Act of 1933 and any security other than a note, bond, debenture, and certain other certificates of interest.

The act requires a bond issuer to have one or more trustees clear of conflict-of-interest considerations. The duties of the trustee are specified in the act. A trustee is required to submit a report at least once a year to the indenture security holders, stating among other things the issuer's eligibility and qualifications, any unpaid advances in excess of one-half of 1 percent of indenture securities, and the inventory of the property and funds in its possession at the time of such report. The trustee must within 90 days of default give notice to bondholders unless the board of directors or another authorized body instructs him or her, based on the best interest of the bondholder, not to. The trustee is expected to follow the "prudent man" rule, that is, to do only what a reasonable, prudent man would do in the discharge of his duties.

The issuing company is required to furnish the indenture's trustee with opinion of counsel as to proper recording of lien and two annual opinions of counsel as to maintenance of lien.

Investment Company Act of 1940

Part A of the Investment Company Act of 1940 provides for the registration of investment companies with the SEC; Part B, also called the Investment Advisors Act, provides for the regulation of investment companies and investment advisors. The intent of the act is to ensure maximum disclosure of information and fair treatment of those who hold securities handled by investment companies (generally referred to as mutual funds). A discussion of the provisions of the act appears in Chapter 9.

ERISA

The Employment Retirement Income Security Act (ERISA), also referred to as the Pension Reform Act, was signed into law by President Gerald Ford on Labor Day, 1974.[3]

ERISA replaced all the provisions of the Welfare and Pension Plans Disclosure Act of 1958 and amended sections of the Internal Revenue Code; it supersedes all state laws related to employee benefit plans. ERISA also created the Individual Retirement Account (IRA), under which wage earners not covered by a retirement plan may set aside up to 15 percent of their income or $1,500, whichever is less. The contributions to an IRA plan and income thereon are not taxable. The sum withdrawn upon retirement is fully taxable, however. The Economic Recovery Tax Act of 1981 changed the requirements of ERISA with regard to IRA plans. The maximum contribution is now $2,000, and an IRA can still be set up even though the wage earner is covered by another retirement plan. More details are given in Chapter 18.

ERISA covers all pension plans except government plans, church plans (unless an election for coverage is made), unfunded excess-benefit plans; plans set up and maintained outside the United States and benefiting primarily nonresident aliens; and plans set up for compliance with workers' compensation, unemployment compensation, or disability insurance laws.

Before discussing the provisions of the act—those with a direct effect on the securities industry in particular—we shall examine the role of pension funds in the capital markets.

The activity of pension funds in the stock market is illustrated in Table 2.4. Their activity rate (the ratio of gross annualized purchases and sales of stocks to the average market value of holdings) for the fourth quarter of 1980 was 42.6, which compares rather favorably with that of other financial institutions and suggests that pension funds are important participants in the stock market.

The size of the assets controlled by private noninsured pension funds is second only to that of life insurance companies. At the end of 1979, private, noninsured pension funds controlled $225.1 billion in assets, with $122.7 billion or 54.5 percent of total assets invested in common stock. This size holding of common stock far exceeds that of any major institutional group (Table 2.5). In fact, it represents four times the holdings of common stock by the life insurance industry.

---

[3] U.S. Congress, Public Law 93–406, HR-2, Sept. 2, 1974.

TABLE 2.4

Quarterly Common-Stock Transactions and Activity Rates of Selected Financial Institutions (Millions of Dollars)[a]

	1979				1980			
	1Q	2Q	3Q	4Q	1Q	2Q	3Q	4Q
Private noninsured pension funds[b]								
Purchases	5,743	7,057	8.834	10.952	14,100	12,045	17,355	19,189
Sales	5,615	6,199	6,610	8,099	13,487	9,336	13,929	16,296
Net purchases (sales)	128	858	2,224	2,853	613	2,709	3,426	2,893
Activity rate	20.8	23.5	26.2	31.2	45.4r[e]	33.1r	42.1r	42.6
Open-end investment companies[c]								
Purchases	2,738	2,962	3,739	3,650	5,161	3,607	5,021	6,105
Sales	3,571	3,875	4,592	3,885	6,009	4,307	5,557	5,848
Net purchases (sales)	(833)	(913)	(853)	(235)	(848)	(700)	(536)	257
Activity rate	40.3	42.9	50.6	44.2	69.1	49.4	58.8	60.0
Life insurance companies — total								
Purchases	1,546	1,603	2,503	2,730	3,394	2,095	3,274	3,597
Sales	1,853	2,209	2,242	2,610	2,970	2,709	2,842	2,923
Net purchases (sales)	(307)	(606)	261	120	424	(614)	432	674
Activity rate	26.9	29.8	35.7	38.4	46.4	34.7	40.4	38.9
Life insurance companies — general accts.								
Purchases	531	690	1,448	1,371	1,401	768	1,249	1,367
Sales	560	986	1,136	1,311	1,396	1,171	1,038	1,084
Net purchases (sales)	(29)	(296)	312	60	15	(403)	211	283
Activity rate	15.9	24.1	35.8	35.5	37.5	26.2	29.1	29.0
Life insurance companies — separate accts.								
Purchases	1,015	913	1,055	1,359	1,993	1,327	2,025	2,230
Sales	1,293	1,223	1,106	1,299	1,584	1,538	1,804	1,839
Net purchases (sales)	(278)	(310)	(51)	60	409	(211)	221	391
Activity rate	39.9	36.6	35.5	41.8	56.8	44.5	52.6	49.1
Property-liability insurance companies								
Purchases	1,331	1,302	1,347	1,702	1,885	1,734	2,027	2,093
Sales	660	735	1,237	1,118	1,508	1,286	1,620	1,498
Net purchases (sales)	671	567	110	584	377	448	407	595
Activity rate	24.3	23.4	28.1	29.8	36.7	31.2	33.3	29.7
Total selected institutions								
Purchases	11,358	12,924	16,423	19,034	24,540	19,481	27,677	30,984
Sales	11,699	13,018	14,681	15,712	23,974	17,638	23,948	26,565
Net purchases (sales)	(341)	(94)	1,742	3,322	566	1,843	3,729	4,419
Activity rate	25.3	27.6	31.8	34.2	48.6r	35.6r	43.6r	43.6r
Foreign investors[d]								
Purchases	4,693	5,054	6,226	6,667	10,394r	6,501r	10,184r	13,240
Sales	4,008	4,703	6,021	6,284	8,229r	6,094r	9,430r	11,291
Net purchases (sales)	685	351	205	383	2,165r	407r	754r	1,949

Source: SEC Monthly Statistical Review, U.S. Securities and Exchange Commission, Washington, D.C., May 1981.

[a] *Activity rate* is defined as the average of gross purchases and sales (annualized) divided by the average market value of holdings.

[b] Includes deferred profit sharing and pension funds of corporations, unions, multiemployer groups and nonprofit organizations.

[c] Mutual funds reporting to the Investment Company Institute, a group whose assets constitute about 90 percent of the assets of all open-end investment companies.

[d] Transactions of foreign individuals and institutions in domestic common and preferred stocks. Activity rates for foreign investors are not calculable.

[e] r = revised.

The distribution of the assets of pension funds measured in terms of book value is shown in Table 2.6. That distribution—measured both in terms of book value and market value—is shown in Table 2.7. The total market value of listed stocks at the end of 1980 was $1,215 billion. The common stockholdings by private noninsured pension funds, therefore, account for (approximately) 14 percent of the value of all equity shares outstanding at the end of 1980. The percentage becomes even more significant (almost double) if the stockholdings of state and local retirement funds are included in the calculation.

The other important components in the asset structure of noninsured pension funds are corporate debt securities and U.S. government securities.

The role played by pension funds in the capital and money markets cannot be underestimated. The activities of pension fund managers, while significant in a securities market context, are of critical importance to the actual and potential beneficiaries of the pension plans. This is where ERISA plays an important role.

TABLE 2.5
Market Value of Total Assets and Common Stockholdings of Major Institutional Groups (Billions of Dollars, End of Year)

	1972	1973	1974	1975	1976	1977	1978	1979
Private noninsured pension funds								
Assets	154.4	132.2	111.7	145.6	173.9	181.6	201.5	225.1
Common stock	113.4	89.5	62.6	87.7	108.5	100.9	106.7	122.7
Percent stocks of assets	73.4	67.7	56.0	60.2	62.4	55.5	53.0	54.5
Investment Companies[a]								
Assets	79.8	66.2	52.9	67.6	78.3	73.9	80.4	115.1
Common stock	64.0	48.9	34.1	43.1	47.9	38.6	36.3	34.3
Life insurance companies[b, c]								
Assets	239.7	252.4	263.3	289.3	320.6	350.5	393.4	436.3
Common stock	21.8	19.6	14.9	20.3	25.8	23.5	24.5	28.5
Property-liability insurance companies[c, d]								
Assets	78.9	83.9	82.1	94.0	111.9	133.1	155.9	185.4
Common stock	18.9	16.3	10.0	11.2	13.6	13.3	15.2	18.9
Personal trust funds								
Assets	168.7	157.3	131.5	151.9	167.4	174.5	179.3	192.6
Common stock	114.1	98.0	70.2	84.3	97.5	92.3	92.7	104.0
Mutual savings banks[e]								
Assets	100.6	106.7	109.5	121.1	134.8	147.2	158.1	163.4
Common stock	2.5	2.8	2.9	2.9	2.8	3.0	3.0	2.9
State and local retirement funds[e]								
Assets	80.6r[f]	80.7r	88.0r	104.8r	120.6r	132.6r	153.0r	178.9
Corporate equity	22.2	20.2	16.4	24.3	30.1	30.0	33.3	37.1
Foundations								
Assets	39.5	36.0	29.9	34.2	38.6	37.6	38.5	51.9
Common stock	28.0	24.1	18.0	22.3	28.6	25.7	26.5	39.6
Educational endowments								
Assets	16.2	14.3	11.4	13.8	16.1	16.1	16.3	16.9
Common stock	10.6	9.5	6.7	8.7	10.4	9.7	10.1	10.1

Source: Statistical Bulletin, Securities and Exchange Commission, Washington, D.C., July 1980.
[a]Includes open-end, closed-end, face amount, and unit trust companies.
[b]Includes separate accounts.
[c]Statement value.
[d]Excludes holdings of insurance company stock.
[e]Stock value.
[f]r = revised.

Among the major provisions of ERISA with implications on the securities markets are the following:

1. *Eligibility and vesting.* ERISA liberalized the vesting and eligibility requirements. Vesting gives the wage earner a nonforfeitable right to the contributions made to the pension fund. All contributions made by the employee are fully and immediately vested. Contributions made by the employer are vested in accordance with the following requirements:

a. *Graded vesting.* At least 25 percent vesting after five years of service followed by 5 percent for each of the succeeding five years and by 10 percent each year thereafter. One hundred percent vesting is achieved after 15 years.

b. *One hundred percent vesting after ten years.* No vesting is realized at anytime before the ten years.

c. *Rule of 45.* The rule of 45 deals with the sum of the age of the wage earner and his or her years of service. Under this rule an employee with five years of service

TABLE 2.6
Assets of Private, Noninsured Pension Funds—Quarterly, Book Value (Millions of Dollars)[a]

	1978 1Q	2Q	3Q	4Q	1979 1Q	2Q	3Q	4Q	1980 1Q	2Q	3Q	4Q
Cash and deps	4,369	5,483	7,400	8,110	7,840	7,767	8,741	8,609	8,199	7,475	7,854	9,290
U.S.gov't sec.	21,272	21,533	19,862	19,695	21,011	21,876	21,357	22,459	24,720	25,612	27,287	28,312
Corp. & other debt	49,009	50,858	51,511	53,824	55,589	57,021	58,091	59,537	60,926	62,665	63,422	63,910
Preferred stock	1,152	1,136	1,119	1,274	1,072	1,328	1,324	1,350	1,251	1,190	1,521	1,322
Common stock	95,238	95,113	97,728	100,424	102,238	104,375	108,161	110,943	114,395	117,235	123,038	128,473
Mortgages	2,520	2,584	2,705	2,789	2,791	2,801	2,991	3,091	2,934	3,161	3,669	4,085
Other assets	12,850	13,431	15,668	16,121	16,841	17,196	17,342	17,476	17,897	18,750	21,643	21,506
Total assets	186,410	190,138	195,993	202,237	207,382	212,364	218,007	223,465	230,322	236,088	248,434	256,898

As a Percent of Total Assets

	1978 1Q	2Q	3Q	4Q	1979 1Q	2Q	3Q	4Q	1980 1Q	2Q	3Q	4Q
Cash and deps	2.3	2.9	3.8	4.0	3.8	3.7	4.0	3.9	3.6	3.2	3.2	3.6
U.S.gov't sec.	11.4	11.3	10.1	9.7	10.1	10.3	9.8	10.1	10.7	10.8	11.0	11.0
Corp. & other debt	26.3	26.7	26.3	26.6	26.8	26.9	26.6	26.6	26.5	26.5	25.5	24.9
Preferred stock	0.6	0.6	0.6	0.6	0.5	0.6	0.6	0.6	0.5	0.5	0.6	0.5
Common stock	51.1	50.0	49.9	49.7	49.3	49.1	49.6	49.6	49.7	49.7	49.5	50.0
Mortgages	1.4	1.4	1.4	1.4	1.3	1.3	1.4	1.4	1.3	1.3	1.5	1.6
Other assets	6.9	7.1	8.0	8.0	8.1	8.1	8.0	7.8	7.8	7.9	8.7	8.4
Total assets	100.0	100.0	100.0	100.0	100.0	100.0	100.0	100.0	100.0	100.0	100.0	100.0

Source: *SEC Monthly Statistical Review*, U.S. Securities and Exchange Commission, Washington, D.C., May 1981.
[a]Includes deferred profit sharing and pension funds of corporations, unions, multiemployer groups, and nonprofit organizations.

TABLE 2.7
Assets of Private, Noninsured Pension Funds (Millions of Dollars)[a]

	1973	1974	1975	1976	1977	1978	1979	1980
Book Value, End of Year								
Cash and deposits	2,336	4,286	2,962	2,199	3,721	8,110	8,609	9,290
U.S. government securities	4,404	5,533	10,764	14,713	20,138	19,695	22,459	28,312
Corporate and other bonds	30,334	35,029	37,809	39,070	45,580	53,824	59,537	63,910
Preferred stock	1,258	1,129	1,188	1,250	1,168	1,274	1,350	1,322
Common stock	80,593	79,319	83,654	93,359	96,984	100,424	110,943	128,473
Own company	4,098	4,588	5,075	N.A.	N.A.	N.A.	N.A.	N.A.
Other companies	76,495	74,731	78,579	N.A.	N.A.	N.A.	N.A.	N.A.
Morgages	2,377	2,372	2,383	2,369	2,497	2,789	3,091	4,085
Other assets	5,229	6,063	6,406	7,454	11,421	16,121	17,476	21,506
Total assets	126,531	133,731	145,166	160,414	181,509	202,237	223,465	256,898
Market Value, End of Year								
Cash and deposits	2,336	4,286	2,962	2,199	3,721	8,110	8,609	9,290
U.S. government securities	4,474	5,582	11,097	14,918	20,017	18,767	21,516	26,334
Corporate and other bonds	27,664	30,825	34,519	37,858	42,754	48,633	51,261	59,987
Preferred stock	985	703	892	1,212	1,009	1,162	1,099	1,367
Common stock	89,538	62,582	87,669	108,483	100,863	106,732	122,703	174,437
Own company	6,947	5,230	6,958	N.A.	N.A.	N.A.	N.A.	N.A.
Other companies	82,591	57,352	80,711	N.A.	N.A.	N.A.	N.A.	N.A.
Mortgages	2,108	2,063	2,139	2,160	2,362	2,554	2,664	3,814
Other assets	5,140	5,681	6,341	7,073	10,838	15,585	17,336	21,980
Total assets	132,247	111,724	145,622	173,906	181,564	201,545	225,188	297,209

Source: SEC Monthly Statistical Review, U.S. Securities and Exchange Commission, Washington, D.C., May 1981.
[a] Includes deferred profit-sharing funds and pension funds of corporations, unions, multiemployer groups, and nonprofit organizations.
N.A. = not available.

and meeting the 45 requirement must be at least 50 percent vested with additional 10 percent vesting each succeeding year. A plan participant with ten years of service must be 50 percent vested, with additional 10 percent vesting each succeeding year.

The Internal Revenue Service has the authority to further liberalize the vesting requirements if it deems appropriate.

The eligibility rule requires that any employee with one year of service who is at least twenty-five years of age must be included in a pension plan. A tradeoff is permitted, however. Participation may be postponed until the age of twenty-five and three years of service provided 100 percent vesting accrues thereafter.

The liberalization of eligibility and vesting requirements increased corporate pension contributions and thus decreased net profits. It has been estimated that corporate pension contributions account for about 15 percent of before-tax profits.

2. *Funding.* ERISA requires that certain plans be subject to minimum funding standards and that these plans maintain an account called the "funding standard account" (FSA). This account is used to determine compliance with minimum funding standards.

The minimum funding requirement is equal to the plan's normal cost for the period, the amortization of the unfunded past service liability, annual interest on unfunded amounts, the increase or decrease in past service liability due to plan amendements, gains or losses, and actuarial gains or losses from changes in actuarial assumptions.

3. *Disclosure and reporting.* The disclosure and reporting requirements under ERISA compel the pension plan administrator to:

a. File a disclosure report with the Department of Labor.
b. Report on plan description and submit a summary annual statement to plan participants and beneficiaries. The summary must include a statement of plan assets and liabilities, a statement of plan receipts and disbursements and other pertinent information.
c. Provide each vested terminated employee with a complete statement of deferred vested benefit rights, that is, state when he or she qualifies to receive the first payment and how much he or she should expect to receive.

Under certain circumstances additional special reports must be submitted by the employer to the Pension Benefit Guaranty Corporation.

4. *Employer liability.* The employer liability clause was at the origin of the legislation. The seeds for ERISA were planted in 1964, when the Studebaker Co. declared bankruptcy and left its employees without jobs and without a pension. An employer has a contingent liability limited to the unfunded liability for insured benefits but no more than 30 percent of the firm's net worth. The balance is made up by the Pension Benefit Guaranty Corporation (PBGC), which was created by the act. The insurance premium is paid by the employer. The maximum guarantee by PBGC is equal to the lesser of 100 percent of the average monthly wages paid the plan participant during the five highest earning years in the plan or $750 per month initially with upward adjustments tied to social security wage-base increases.

Employers are also required under ERISA to reassess their actuarial assumptions in light of actual experience every three years. Employers must also adjust their contributions in accordance with the "experience" of gains and losses.

5. *Fiduciary responsibility.* The Pension Reform Act goes a long way in defining the responsibility of those charged with the management of the assets of a pension plan (fiduciaries).

Fiduciaries are expected (among other things) to follow the "prudent man rule" and diversify the portfolio in order to minimize risk. Tables 2.6 and 2.7 show that diversification has in fact taken place. Stocks as a percent of total fund assets have slipped from 73.4 percent in 1972 to 54.5 percent in 1979 (Table 2.5). Several funds are currently invested in real estate, precious metals, fixed-income securities, and the options market (Chapter 7). This diversification is shown in Tables 2.6 and 2.7.

Prudence, the reader must note, is not to be equated with a conservative investment policy. This point should become clearer later in this book with the discussion of portfolio theory. Prudence, however, may encourage fiduciaries to seek outside managers and/ or to consult frequently with experts in the investment and legal areas.

To quote the act, a fiduciary is expected to discharge his or her duties "with the care, skill, prudence, and diligence under the circumstances then prevailing that a prudent man acting in like capacity and familiar with such matters would use in the conduct of an enterprise of like character and with like aims."

In addition, he or she may not make a loan to or acquire securities in a party of interest (the sponsoring corporation for example).

Finally, a fiduciary must compensate the plan for any losses resulting from a breach of fiduciary responsibility. Profits made on the illegal use of plan assets must be returned to the plan.

All these requirements make the fiduciaries' task quite critical indeed, and necessarily so. Many wage earners' dreams are built on the promise of a secure, stable retirement.

Securities Act Amendments of 1975[4]

The Securities Act Amendments of 1975, the most significant amendment to the Securities Act of 1934, was intended

> to remove barriers to competition, to foster the development of a national securities market system and a national clearance and settlement system, to make uniform the Securities and Exchange Commission's authority over self-regulatory organizations, to provide for the regulation of brokers, dealers and banks trading in municipal securities, to facilitate the collection and public dissemination of information concerning the holdings of transactions in securities by institutional investment managers, and for other purposes.

Briefly, the act is intended to improve the efficiency of the market and to further decrease the chance of fraud and deception.

The act tightens membership requirements in national security exchanges, specifies due process for disciplinary action against a member, and sets conditions for a summary suspension of a member by a national securities exchange.

The act forbids any national securities exchange from imposing "any schedule or fixed rates of commissions, allowances, discounts, or other fees to be charged by its members." Exceptions to this rule were also provided. The basic intent, however, is to increase competition in the securities markets and lower transactions costs.

The act, while expressing a strong sentiment for a national market system for securities, left it to the discretion of the SEC to decide on the appropriate design for a national

---

[4] Public Law 94–29 (S.249); June 4, 1975.

market that would use "New data processing and communications techniques [to] create the opportunity for more efficient and effective market operations" and would recognize that

> *It is in the public interest and appropriate for the protection of investors and the maintenance of fair and orderly markets to assure*
>   *(i) economically efficient execution of securities transactions;*
>   *(ii) fair competition among brokers and dealers, among exchange markets, and between exchange markets and markets other than exchange markets;*
>   *(iii) the availability to brokers, dealers, and investors of information with respect to quotations for and transactions in securities;*
>   *(iv) the practicability of brokers executing investors' orders in the best market; and*
>   *(v) an opportunity consistent with the provisions of clause (i) and (iv) of the subparagraph, for investors' orders to be executed without the participation of a dealer.*

Finally, the SEC was charged with the creation of a national system that would link all markets for qualified securities through a network of communication and data processing facility. The expressed intent is once again the improvement of market efficiency.

The act also amended the registration requirements for securities under the Securities Exchange Act of 1934, further defined manipulation and fraudulent acts, and required certain security measures to reduce the chance of fraud.

Rule 390

There are two 390 rules: the original Rule 390 (initially referred to as Rule 394) and the new Rule 390. The new Rule 390 really refers to the modified Rule 394 of the NYSE. Both rules deal with "off-floor" transactions in listed stocks. Under the old rule (abolished by the SEC in June 1977), the NYSE did not permit member firms to trade NYSE listed securities off the floor of the exchange. The SEC felt that the rule hindered price competition and consequently fair pricing of securities for the investor.

The new Rule 390 permits exchange members to act as agents for their clients and transact NYSE-listed securities in the third market.

Exchange members are not permitted to act as principals in third market transactions—that is, to buy or sell for their own account, nor are they permitted to act as agents for both parties to a transaction.

Rule 19C3 of the Securities and Exchange Commission permits member firms to trade securities listed after April 26, 1979, in any way they please in the third market. Member firms may act as principals or as agents for one party or for both parties to the transaction.

Rule 390, however, is still marked by the SEC for complete extinction.

CONCLUSIONS

The operations and the regulation of the securities markets are complex. In this chapter we were able to introduce the basic considerations and to outline the key provisions of major laws and regulations. The reader should not, however, assume that regulatory matters can be settled without competent legal advice.

QUESTIONS

1. Differentiate between a secondary and a primary market. What are the essential functions preformed by each?

2. What is the essential function of an investment banker? Why could commercial banks not perform the same function?

3. Which member of the NYSE plays the most important role in the efficient functioning of the market?

4. Is the NYSE a primary or a secondary market? Explain.

5. What accounts for the dominance of the NYSE? Is this dominance likely to be diluted by the emergence of a truly national market?

6. What are the major differences between the organized exchanges and the over-the-counter market?

7. Do the third and fourth markets represent a positive or a negative development with regard to the objective of a truly centralized market?

8. How does the emergence of ITS help the small investor? Could a stock listed on more than one exchange sell at different prices? Can this condition last long? Why?

9. Why would specialists be opposed to Rule 390? Would this opposition diminish had they been allowed to deal with institutions (if Rule 113 were eliminated)?

10. Discuss the importance of the underwriting function that investment bankers perform.

11. "The regulation of securities markets is intended to eliminate market risk." Comment. What kind of other risks do securities laws eliminate or limit?

12. Which of the securities acts is most important to the investor?

13. Does the SEC pass a judgment as to the merits of a given investment? Explain.

14. What is the underlying motivation behind securities laws?

15. What are the objectives of ERISA? How does this act affect the functioning of the capital markets?

16. Why do some major companies persist in not listing their securities?

17. The emergence of stock index contracts (futures contracts on stock indexes allowing a speculator to "bet" on the direction of a market index, such as the Dow Jones) raised some jurisdictional questions with regard to who should set the margin requirement on such contracts. Should the Federal Reserve System, which sets the margin requirement on stock purchases, also set the margin requirement on futures contracts based on a group of stocks? (Currently the exchanges set the margin requirements on futures contracts.)

3 | Considerations for Investing in Equity Securities

3.1 INTRODUCTION

The considerations for investing in equity securities range from the very simple to the very complex. An investor having overheard and believed a "tip" on a stock, for example, would only have to call her investment broker and simply indicate her interest in the stock and her intention to buy x number of shares. On the other extreme is that investor who wants to be aware of every possibility for capitalizing on an expected upward or downward move in a security price having closely examined the company's records both in absolute and in relative terms and having also carefully scrutinized the management of the company and its plans for the future.

Investing in equity securities must be approached as an integral part of an overall portfolio strategy. An outline of a financial planning program appears in Chapter 18. The objective of this chapter is to discuss the various types of orders an investor may place with a broker, the various types of equity positions that can be established, the major market indicators, and the critical sources of investment information.

3.2 TYPE OF ACCOUNT

An investor typically opens with his or her broker either a cash account or a margin account. The cash account requires settlement of the full value of the purchase or the delivery of securities in the case of a sale within five business days. The margin account requires initially the deposit of the higher of 50 percent (current margin requirement on stocks) of the value of the securities acquired or the minimum standard commitment set by the broker, whichever is higher. The remaining 50 percent is effectively being borrowed from the broker at a rate tied to the prime rate. The margin requirement is set by the Federal Reserve System. Total margin debt on May 1981 was $14.7 billion; the number of margin accounts for the same date was 1,290,000.

Certain transactions, like short sales, can only be executed in the margin account regardless of whether they are buy or sell transactions.

3.3 TYPES OF ORDERS

Buy or sell orders differ in terms of the time limit, price limit, discretion of the broker handling the order, and nature of the position.

Time limit orders are of two types: time-limited orders and good-'til-canceled orders (GTC). If not executed, a time-limited order expires at the end of the specified time period (usually a day). A GTC order is in effect unless canceled by the investor.

The price limits available to the investor are as follows:

1. *Market order.* The limit here, in a way, is set by the market. The investor buys at the ask and sells at the bid. This is guaranteed for at least one round lot or the displayed size of the bid. If the order is for more than one round lot—say, for 300 shares—the investor could pay more than the ask price. Market orders are the quickest but not necessarily the cheapest way to buy or sell a security.

2. *Limit order.* The investor using a limit order specifies the maximum buy price or the minimum sale price at which the transaction will be consummated.

3. *Stop order.* A stop order is an order to buy or sell a security when a certain price is reached or passed. A stop order can be used on the sell or on the buy side. A stop order to sell is treated as a market order when the stop price is reached or passed if the stock is listed on the NYSE. However, a limit may be specified. If the stock is listed on the ASE, the stop order must specify the stop price and the limit price (they do not have to be different). If the stock does not trade at the limit, the limit price must be respecified by the investor.

No stop order can be placed on unlisted securities.

Stop orders are used in order to preserve a level of profit in a security, to purchase a security as it begins a vigorous upward movement, or to protect the investor from loss.

An investor who purchased a stock at 50 and watched it appreciate to 90 may wish to "lock in" at least 35 points if the stock begins to show weakness. This is done by placing a stop sell order at, say, 85. This order, however, does not guarantee a sale at 85, for the stock can fall substantially below 85 before the position of the investor is closed. Another disadvantage of a stop order emanates from the unpredictable nature of the stock market. The stock may fall below 85, causing the order to be executed, and the stock may then reverse course and rise to 100. The investor in this case would have missed a 10-point appreciation in the price of the stock.

An investor who had just purchased a security that began to show weakness after the purchase date may wish to place a stop-loss (sell) order at below the current market price in order to limit the potential loss in the security. Similarly, an investor with a short position (a position intended to profit from a decline in securities price (see next section)) would place a stop-buy order at above currently prevailing prices to gain protection against an appreciation in the price of the underlying security that causes a loss in a short position.

4. *Discretionary order.* This type order gives the broker a discretion over when, at what price, and how an order is executed. The broker is liable if negligence is proved in the event a "good" opportunity in the market is missed.

3.4 TYPE OF POSITION

Two positions in securities are available to the investor: a long position and a short position.

A long position represents actual ownership of the security regardless of whether personal funds, leverage, or both are used in its purchase. Profits are realized through appreciation in the price of the security.

A short position, on the other hand, involves a sale first, followed by a purchase at, it is hoped, a lower price. The anatomy of a short sale is illustrated in Figure 3.1. The process begins with a sale of a borrowed security. The securities must be borrowed, for settlement of the transaction (the delivery of shares and the payment by the buyer) must be done within five business days. The reader must keep in mind, however, that not every security can be sold short. Listed securities are all eligible, but only some (about 1,500) of the over-the-counter securities are. The security being sold is borrowed from the investment broker, who ordinarily holds a substantial number of shares in street name and/or who has access to the desired security from other investment brokers. The more risk-averse short sellers are, the more likely they are to use some vehicle to limit their loss in case the price of the security rises instead of falls. One way to protect a short position is to use the stop-buy order discussed in the preceding section. Other ways to protect a short position are discussed in Chapters 12 and 13. The stop-buy order is placed at 15 percent above the price at which the short sale was established and is usually reduced ("trail") as the stock price declines. After the stock price has fallen sufficiently, the short position is covered; that is, the stock is bought at the prevailing market price and is returned to the investment broker to settle the loan of shares. The investor could have elected to increase the size of his or her short position as the stock price moved in the right direction.

Three facts must be kept in mind with regard to short positions:

1. The security, if qualified, must be available to be borrowed. This is not usually a problem.
2. Short selling can only be effected on an "uptick"; that is, the price at which the short position is established must be a price that is higher than that on the preceding transaction. An order to sell short at 59½ could not be transacted unless the 59½ is an uptick, that is, the 59½ follows, say, a trade at 59¼.
3. The short seller is liable for the dividends on the stocks borrowed.

As the above scenario makes clear, a short position is ordinarily established if an investor is bearish on the stock. An appreciation in the price of the stock after the short sale would produce a loss because the borrowed shares would have to be replaced at a higher price. A "bad market" is, therefore, not an excuse to stay out of the stock market. Furthermore, short selling is not necessarily riskier than a long position. The probability of a decline in the price of a security could be significantly higher than that of an appreciation in its price.

Short sales can also be used to lock in profits in a long position and to postpone the tax liability from one tax year to another. The latter use is discussed in Chapter 18. The former use is best illustrated with an example.

FIGURE 3.1   The anatomy of a short sale.

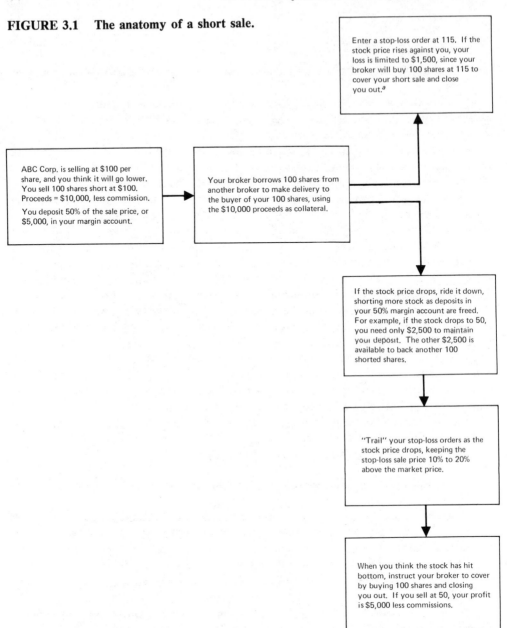

[a] Alternatively, as we shall discuss in Chapter 12, the short seller may choose to buy a call option to protect his short position. The option market can also be used to capitalize on an expected decline in stock prices.

An investor with a long position established at $50 a share would have a book gain of $20 per share if the stock trades at $70. If the volatility in the price of the stock increases from its historical level, the investor may well decide to get some protection. Convinced that the security is still a good investment, but still concerned about its downside risk, the investor can use one of the following methods:

1. Sell the stock and buy it later at a lower price. The danger here is that immediately after the sale the stock may move vigorously upward instead of falling in price.
2. Place a stop-buy order. The advantages and the disadvantages of this type order were discussed in the previous section.
3. Buy a put option or sell a call option (see Chapter 12).
4. Go short against the box, that is, establish a short position for the same number of shares held long.

Method 4 would require a short position at $70. The investor now has perfectly offsetting positions. Every $1 appreciation in the price of the stock yields profits of $1 per share in the long position and a simultaneous $1 loss in the short position. The reverse is true if the price of the stock falls by $1.

In the event of a price decline, the investor's costs of protection are the transactions costs incurred when the short position is established and when it is covered. These costs are likely to be lower than those resulting from a depreciation in the price of the security. In the case of price appreciation, the investor would incur the same costs as above and would forego in addition the appreciation in the price of the security. The sooner the short position is covered, the smaller the foregone profit from a price appreciation will be.

Short selling, if wisely used, should prove to be a valuable tool in portfolio management. Short selling in conjunction with current or expected long positions has proved to be of great value to hedgers, spreaders, and arbitragers in the fixed securities and futures markets. This should become clearer from the chapters to follow.

3.5 DATES TO REMEMBER

Three dates are important in trading securities:

1. *Trade date.* The trade date is the date when the transaction is consummated.
2. *Settlement date.* The settlement date refers to the date when the transaction is settled. For stocks and bonds, it is the fifth business day from the trade date.
3. *Ex-dividend date.* This is the date on which the investor buys a stock without dividend. The recently declared dividend belongs to the seller of the stock. The ex-dividend date is the fourth business day prior to the record date (the date at which the actual ownership of the stock is confirmed by the corporation).

Open buy and sell stop orders and sell stop-limit orders are reduced by the value of the dividend on the ex-dividend date. Both the stop price and the limit price (if any) are reduced by the dividend.

3.6 INVESTMENT PHILOSOPHIES

There are as many investment philosophies as there are investors to formulate them, if not more. Some investors refuse to buy stocks in companies that manufacture arms or defense-related equipment, others refuse to buy stocks in unionized companies, still others insist on only buying stocks of unionized companies, some insist on low-priced securities, others on companies with few shares outstanding, and some investors insist on low P/E shares or low price-to-book-value shares or on shares in new-frontier technology. These are but a few of the philosophies (biases) of investors.

All the different philosophies are intended to maximize the rate of return on investment. Chapter 5 introduces the element of risk which, when incorporated in a portfolio strategy, can radically redefine it. The risk we speak of is the risk inherent in the investment itself as it relates to the risk profile of the investor.

Whatever the philosophy, a method for selecting among competing stocks in a group must be available. Its success depends on how carefully it is thought out, how comprehensive it is, and to what extent it incorporates the financial status and needs of the investor and those of his or her immediate family. Additionally, any philosophy should be sufficiently flexible and adaptable to an ever-changing world and to the changing attitude, environment, and financial position of the investor. In this regard the tax laws, both federal and state, are of great importance, for they have a considerable influence on the vehicle chosen, the portfolio strategy, the timing of purchases and sales, and most certainly on the net realized rate of return.

The analytical tools offered in the chapters to follow present a systematic approach for stock evaluation, selection, and measurement of portfolio performance. In addition, they provide a comprehensive review of the elements of a successful financial plan, taking into consideration the biases of the investors and a detailed analysis of all the major investment vehicles available to investors.

We now look at market indicators that can be used to gauge the direction of the market and the relative performance of a portfolio.

3.7 STOCK MARKET INDICATORS

Various indicators of the level and general direction of the market are used by investors to assess the movement of stock prices, as a standard of comparison to measure the relative performance of the portfolio, and to help identify special opportunities. A security trading at an earning multiple (price–earning ratio) below that of the average of the market may be considered underpriced, or overpriced if the opposite is true. The proper question, therefore, is: What is the market and how do you measure its performance?

The Dow Jones Averages

The Dow Jones averages are the oldest and most publicized of market indicators. Four Dow Jones averages are published by Dow Jones & Co. on a daily basis: the Industrial Average (30 securities), the Transportation Average (20 securities), the Utilities Average (15 securities), and the Composite Average (65 securities). The Dow Jones Industrial Average (DJIA) represents the average value of 30 "blue chip" stocks listed on the NYSE. These stocks are considered as representative of the market. When the DJIA was first published, it consisted of only 12 securities, the increase to 30 securities came in 1928. The securities included in the DJIA are not all the same as those incorporated in 1928. Anaconda and Chrysler, for example, were dropped in favor of stronger, more representative companies. The stocks that make up the DJIA, their history, their earnings per share, their P/E ratio, and their dividends appear in Table 3.1. The replacement of companies included in the DJIA requires adjustment. Also requiring adjustments to the average are stock splits and stock dividends. All adjustments are reflected in the value of the divisor.[1]

---

[1] The divisor is that value by which the sum of the prices of stocks included in the Dow Jones averages is divided to arrive at the reported average.

TABLE 3.1
Spotlight on the Dow

	This Week																
	Vol-ume	Close	Price Change	Market Value	Pc T.												
	00	$	$	$Mil													
Dow Jones Ind.	224,611	886.51	−6.18	226,156.5	10												
Allied Corp	2,392	47.00	.50	1,584.1													
Alum Co Am	3,789	26.00	.75	1,920.0													
Am Brands	1,246	36.25	−2.62	1,976.8													
Am Can	1,468	35.25	1.13	682.6													
Am Tel & Tel	12,522	58.63	−.75	46,921.0	2												
Bethlehem Stl	4,439	22.75	−.37	993.8													
DuPont	8,520	39.25	−1.12	9,223.7	4.08	56.00	36.75	56.00	31.13	6.10	32.61	14	6.4	11.2	8.1	2.75	7.0
Eastman Kodak	8,509	70.00	.75	11,297.9	5.00	85.38	60.63	120.75	41.13	7.89	22.14	17	8.9	17.1	107.	3.50	5.0
Exxon	26,836	31.25	−1.50	27,009.3	11.94	42.88	29.50	44.38	21.34	6.78	4.47	24	4.6	8.3	6.3	3.00	9.6
Gen Electric	10,124	59.63	−.25	13,586.1	6.01	69.88	51.13	69.88	43.63	7.07	8.27	12	8.4	11.2	8.6	3.20	5.4
Gen Foods	3,889	32.00	.50	1,581.8	.70	35.00	27.75	37.00	23.50	4.79	1.70	9	6.7	8.4	6.3	2.20	6.9
Gen Motors	15,451	38.00	.00	11,325.6	5.01	58.00	33.88	78.88	33.88	.88	NE	−58	43.2	6.7	5.1	2.40	6.3
Goodyear Tire	3,757	18.50	−.12	1,328.9	.59	20.25	15.25	28.38	10.75	2.96	24.37	7	6.3	9.4	6.5	1.30	7.0
Inco Ltd	2,783	13.88	−1.12	1,061.2	.47	23.63	12.50	37.00	12.50	.66	−78.00	−11	21.0	19.0	11.2	.72	5.2
Intl Bus Mach	26,720	54.38	−.25	31,960.3	14.13	71.50	48.38	80.50	48.38	5.91	3.32	9	9.2	15.2	11.7	3.44	6.3
Intl Harvester	4,785	7.50	.62	242.4	.11	27.25	7.25	45.50	7.25	−19.67	NE	−40	NE	5.0	3.3	.00	0
Intl Paper	3,660	41.75	.00	2,068.3	.91	51.50	37.13	79.75	30.50	6.80	29.77	5	6.1	11.1	7.5	2.40	5.7
Manville Co	2,152	14.63	−.37	339.3	.15	26.50	13.75	38.25	13.75	1.42	−44.75	−14	10.3	9.5	6.2	1.92	13.1
Merck & Co	5,764	87.63	2.75	6,502.9	2.88	103.00	73.75	103.00	47.38	5.38	.37	12	16.3	18.0	13.3	2.80	3.2
Minn Mng Mfg	6,752	55.00	.63	6,457.3	2.86	65.00	48.00	66.63	43.00	4.92	−13.99	13	11.2	15.0	11.2	3.00	5.5
Owens-Illinois	2,405	29.75	−.25	885.4	.39	33.00	23.75	33.00	17.13	5.05	9.78	13	5.9	7.8	5.7	1.56	5.2
Proct & Gambl	3,139	77.88	−2.50	6,443.5	2.85	80.63	63.00	100.13	62.75	8.39	7.15	10	9.3	13.6	10.8	4.20	5.4
Sears, Roebuck	9,413	16.00	−.87	5,046.2	2.23	20.88	14.38	39.63	14.38	2.14	2.88	−3	7.5	12.0	9.2	1.36	8.5
Std Oil Cal	9,542	44.38	−.37	15,181.1	6.71	54.00	35.13	58.75	14.56	7.37	13.56	29	6.0	7.6	5.1	2.40	5.4
Texaco	12,337	34.63	.13	9,114.3	4.03	52.25	31.50	54.38	22.13	8.65	2.73	30	4.0	7.9	5.9	3.00	8.7
Union Carbide	3,949	52.88	1.13	3,562.0	1.58	62.13	45.25	76.75	33.63	9.73	−1.32	11	5.4	7.7	5.5	3.40	6.4
US Steel Corp	18,660	31.88	2.25	2,843.7	1.26	35.25	22.00	59.38	16.25	9.08	696.49	70	3.5	55.4	36.4	2.00	6.3
Unit Technols	2,960	42.63	−.50	2,202.6	.97	65.75	40.00	65.75	23.19	7.00	11.64	15	6.1	9.8	6.6	2.40	5.6
Westinghouse	4,220	26.38	−.37	2,240.5	.99	34.50	23.00	34.50	13.00	5.15	9.57	15	5.1	7.0	4.6	1.80	6.8
Woolworth FW	2,428	18.63	−.62	563.9	.24	27.63	17.00	32.00	17.00	3.35	−33.40	7	5.6	6.9	4.8	1.80	9.7

Source: The Media General Financial Weekly, Dec. 14, 1981.

The Transportation Average, on the other hand, consists of 20 stocks, and the Utilities Average of 15 stocks. An overall average of the 65 stocks is also calculated and reported regularly in the Dow Jones publications (*The Wall Street Journal* and *Barron's*). See Figure 3.2.

The representativeness of the Dow Jones averages has been frequently assaulted. The companies making up the DJIA are not very representative of American industry, although they account for 25 percent of the corporate wealth of the United States. The average is heavily weighted by stodgy companies not characterized by great innovations and substantial corporate dynamism. The service sector, which accounts for approximately 50 percent of the U.S. economy, is vastly underrepresented in the average.

The other deficiency in the DJIA is mathematical. The average is a price-weighted index. This procedure allows the highest-priced stocks to have a disproportionate impact on the average. A 10 percent change in the price of the stock with the highest market value produces a change in the average much larger than a similar percentage change in the price of a low-price stock. If a high-price stock is split, say 2 for 1, an adjustment is made in the divisor. This reduces the significance of the stock on the average and consequently the impact of its price fluctuation on the level of the average. The average is also very sensitive to factors that have nothing to do with underlying strengths and weaknesses in the marketplace. On Aug. 9, 1976, for example, 9 of the 30 stocks in the DJIA went "ex-dividend," causing the average to drop by 2.31 points.

The DJIA is calculated daily as follows:

$$\text{DJIA} = \sum_{i=1}^{30} \frac{P_{i,t}}{\text{divisor}}$$

where $P_{i,t}$ = closing price of the ith DJIA stock at time t.

An easy way to illustrate how the DJIA is calculated is to assume that it contains two securities X and Y. If the market price of X = \$40 and that of Y = \$60, the average price would then equal to $(40 + 60)/2$ = \$50. If stock Y undergoes a two-for-one split, the price per share would now drop to \$30. The average, unless adjusted (and it must be), would now equal $(40 + 30)/2$ = \$35. This average indicates a considerable drop in the wealth of investors holding both X and Y. This obviously did not materialize. To prevent these illogical situations from occurring, the denominator (the divisor) is adjusted to reflect a stock split. The divisor must be equal to 1.4 for the original average price level to be maintained $(40 + 30)/1.4$ = \$50. This would obviously prevent the Dow Jones averages from giving an incorrect signal to its followers. The divisor for the Dow Jones averages appears in *Barron's* every Sunday and in *The Wall Street Journal* daily.

The narrow focus of the Dow Jones averages and the method of calculating them have frequently been assaulted. If put in perspective, these drawbacks would not be as significant as they appear to be. The broad appeal of the Dow Jones averages and the related psychological impact they have on the market give them considerable market power. Technical analysts consistently use the Dow Jones averages and find them to be a valuable tool in predicting the direction of the market. Furthermore, the averages were intended to be a measure of investment grade and not of the market as a whole; since the Dow Jones stocks account for about 10 percent of the volume on the NYSE, they are meaningful in terms of trading volume despite their weakness in measuring investment trends.

FIGURE 3.2 The Dow Jones averages, March 12–June 11, 1982.

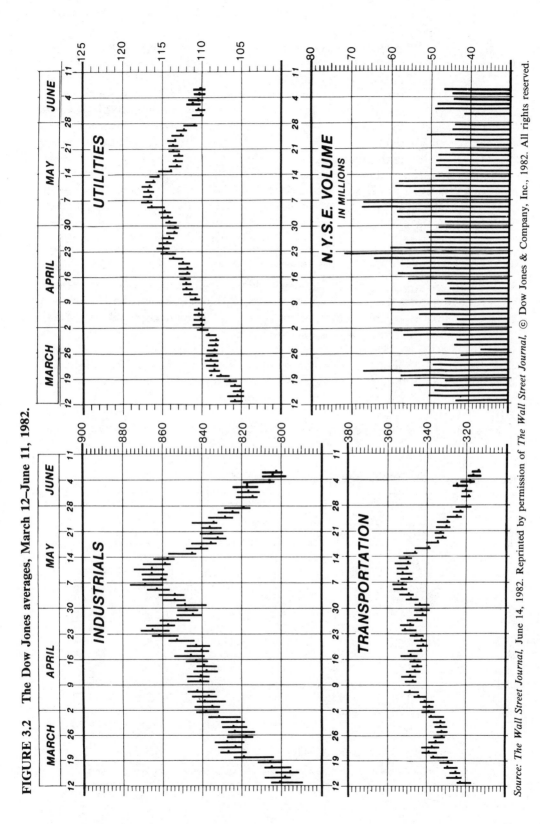

Source: The Wall Street Journal, June 14, 1982. Reprinted by permission of *The Wall Street Journal*, © Dow Jones & Company, Inc., 1982. All rights reserved.

Despite the qualifications offered above, investors find little reason for happiness when the market performance over the past 14 years is measured by the price changes in the DJIA. The record is not even commensurate with that of a certificate of deposit.

When the DJIA is measured in real dollars, its performance can only be characterized as dismal. In real terms, the DJIA was at a 32-year low in December 1981. The data on the "constant-dollar Dow" are provided by the *Media General Financial Weekly* and are arrived at simply by developing an index with 1913 price levels used as a base. The problem, however, is that the feasibility of the methodology is suspect, for the DJIA level is not a dollar amount. Imperfect as the measure is, it still provides a reasonable indication of how well the market has kept pace with inflation. The constant-dollar Dow is shown in Table 3.2. When the market performance is measured by different index averages, the results appear to be brighter, however.

Standard & Poor's Stock Indexes

Standard & Poor's (S&P) Corporation publishes five indexes: Standard & Poor's Industrial Index, made up of 400 stocks; Standard & Poor's Transportation Index, made up of 20 stocks; Standard & Poor's Utility Index, made up of 40 stocks; Standard & Poor's Financial Index, made up of 40 stocks; and Standard & Poor's 500 Composite Index.

Standard & Poor's Composite Index is far more representative of the performance of the market than the DJIA. The market value of the 500 shares making up the S&P in equal to 80 percent of the value of all stocks listed on the NYSE. Standard & Poor's 500 Stock Index shows a superior market performance for the last 14 years over the DJIA.

Standard & Poor's is a value-weighted index where the weight of each stock is equal

TABLE 3.2
Dow Jones Industrials Adjusted for Inflation

	Dow		Consumer Price Index		Constant Dow	
	High	Low	CPI	Deflator	High	Low
Oct. 1980	972.44	971.75	253.9	8.6361	112.60	106.27
Nov	1000.17	932.42	256.2	8.7143	114.77	107.00
Dec	974.40	908.45	258.4	8.7891	110.86	103.36
Jan. 1981	1004.69	938.91	260.5	8.8605	113.39	105.97
Feb.	974.58	931.57	263.2	8.9524	108.86	104.06
Mar.	1015.22	964.62	265.1	9.0170	112.59	106.98
Apr.	1024.05	989.10	266.8	9.0748	112.85	108.99
May	995.59	963.44	269.0	9.1497	108.81	105.30
Jun	1011.99	967.88	271.3	9.2279	109.67	105.68
Jul.	967.66	924.66	274.4	9.3333	103.68	99.07
Aug.	953.58	881.47	276.5	9.4048	101.39	93.73
Sept.	884.23	824.01	279.3	9.5000	93.08	86.74
Oct.	878.14	832.95	279.9	9.5204	92.24	87.49

Source: Media General Financial Weekly, Dec. 14, 1981.

This table shows the performance of the Dow Jones industrial average for the past year on a monthly high and low basis, along with the Consumer Price Index, and the Dow deflator showing the effect of inflation.

to its market value in relation to that of all stocks included in the index. The base value (1941–1943) of the index is 10. Stock splits and stock dividends do not affect Standard & Poor's because the total market value of an S&P index would remain constant (more shares multiplied by a lower market value).

Standard & Poor's 500 Index is computed as follows:

$$\frac{(\text{Market value of 500 stocks})_t}{\text{Market value in 1941–1943}} \times 10$$

The weaknesses of Standard & Poor's Composite Index lie in its insufficient breadth in terms of the number of securities covered, in the disproportionate influence few stocks have on its direction (IBM accounts for 3.9 percent of the S&P 500 Stock Index, while Foster Wheeler accounts for only 0.06 percent) and in the fact that dividend returns are not included when the rates of returns are calculated. The performance of the Standard & Poor's Composite Index over the last 24 years is shown in Figure 3.3.

The NYSE Indexes

In 1966, the NYSE inaugurated the Stock Exchange Common Stock Index (Fig. 3.4), which covered the prices of all the 1,260 or so common stocks then listed on the exchange. Separate transportation, utility, finance, and industrial indexes were also introduced.

The anatomy of the NYSE Index is similar to that of Standard & Poor's. The NYSE is also a value-weighted index. The market value of each listed common stock is multiplied

FIGURE 3.3   Graphic summary of quarterly stock price averages.

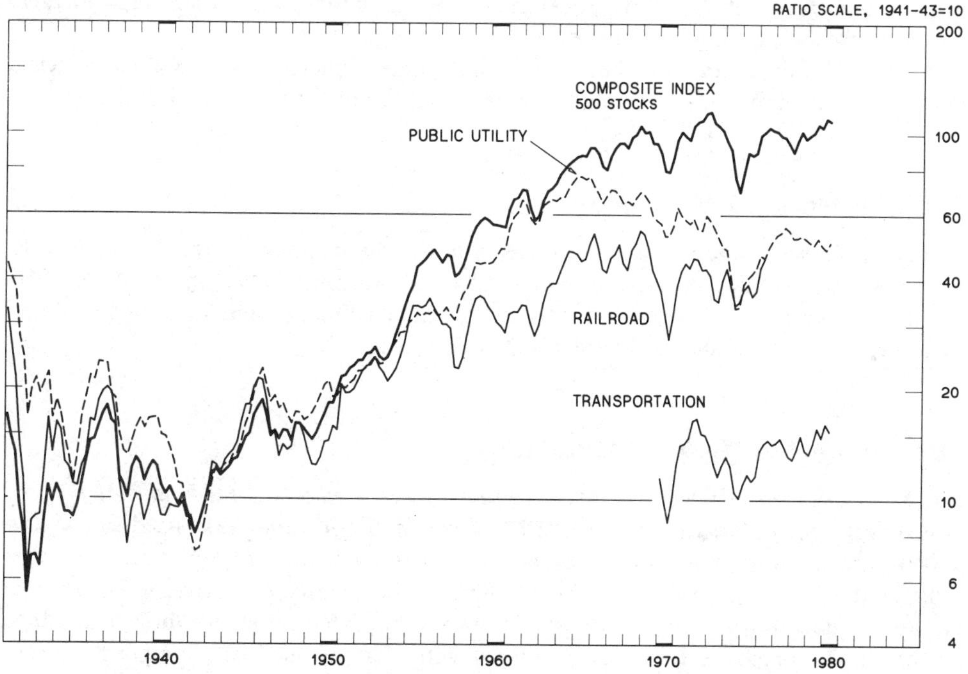

Source: 1980 Historical Chart Book, Board of Governors of the Federal Reserve System, 1981.

FIGURE 3.4   NYSE Composite Average, 1971–1981

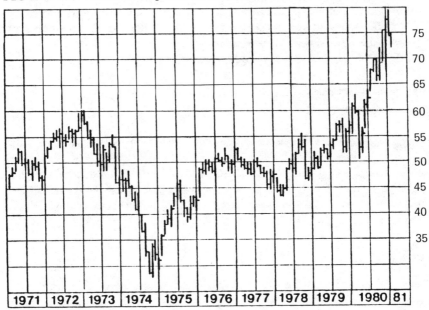

Source: New York Stock Exchange Inc.

by the number of shares outstanding, and the results are added to obtain total market value. This total is then divided by a base value which is adjusted to reflect changes in the capitalization of listed firms, changes in the listing (new listing, delisting), mergers and acquisitions, and other factors.

The NYSE is a broad index but is not, some argue, sufficiently so. Another criticism deals with the dominance of a small number of stocks over its level and direction.

The ASE Market Value Index

The ASE Market Value Index is constructed in a fashion similar to that of the NYSE. It represents the value of all common stocks and warrants listed on the ASE. This index is not as representative as that of the NYSE and its direction and level are dominated by a fewer number of shares than is the NYSE Index.

M/G Composite Market Value Index

The M/G Composite Index is published weekly in the *Media General Financial Weekly*. It is a very broad index which consists of all of the NYSE- and ASE-listed stocks and 840 over-the-counter stocks. The absence of widely available daily quotations on this index and its relative newness (1970) account for its relative obscurity, although it is getting considerably more attention as time wears on. Table 3.3 shows the performance of the M/G Composite Index as compared with that of the S&P Composite during the 1980–1981 period.

TABLE 3.3
Market Value Indexes

End of	Media General				S&P 500
	NYSE	ASE	O-T-C	Composite	
Month					
Feb. 1980	130.60	161.36	134.66	132.97	113.66
Mar.	115.77	126.23	112.22	116.45	102.09
Apr.	121.14	134.31	120.31	122.18	106.29
May	127.23	141.62	129.41	128.56	111.24
June	131.18	152.78	135.49	133.04	114.24
July	139.01	161.28	146.53	141.15	121.67
Aug.	140.95	164.70	153.65	143.52	122.38
Sept.	145.31	167.37	162.33	148.09	125.46
Oct.	148.69	167.03	164.12	151.19	127.47
Nov.	163.16	179.17	174.63	165.29	140.52
Dec.	156.92	168.70	168.62	158.88	135.46
Jan. 1981	149.71	166.63	164.12	152.08	129.55
Feb.	151.06	163.18	165.36	153.17	131.27
Mar.	157.09	171.79	176.82	159.70	136.00
Apr.	154.38	172.07	182.83	157.68	132.81
May	154.60	181.00	187.90	158.60	132.50
June	152.51	171.03	181.88	155.91	131.25
July	152.30	164.10	177.50	155.10	130.92
Aug.	142.95	160.08	165.45	145.79	122.79
Sept.	133.88	134.49	153.04	135.62	116.18
Oct.	141.60	141.90	164.80	143.60	121.89
Nov.	147.11	151.76	171.36	149.44	126.35
Week					
Nov. 6	142.90	147.60	160.10	115.40	122.67
Nov. 13	141.90	144.70	169.50	144.40	121.67
Nov. 20	142.30	145.10	168.10	144.70	121.71
Nov. 27	145.70	150.60	170.70	148.10	125.09
Dec. 4	146.90	150.70	170.90	149.20	126.26
Day					
Nov. 30	147.11	151.76	171.36	149.44	126.35
Dec. 1	146.73	150.72	171.27	149.04	126.10
Dec. 2	145.23	149.81	170.63	147.62	124.69
Dec. 3	145.79	149.79	170.16	148.09	125.12
Dec. 4	146.90	150.70	170.90	149.20	126.26

Source: The Media General Financial Weekly, Dec. 7, 1981.

Value Line Indexes

The Value Line Indexes are a measure of "what has happened to the price of most stocks." The Value Line Composite Index consists of all the stocks (about 1,700) that are under continuous review by the Value Line Investment Survey. Eighty-five percent

FIGURE 3.5   Composite, industrials, rails, and utilities averages representing some 1,700 stocks.

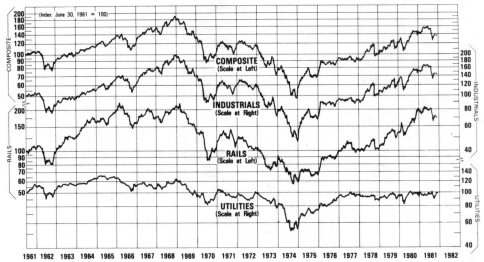

1961 1962 1963 1964 1965 1966 1967 1968 1969 1970 1971 1972 1973 1974 1975 1976 1977 1978 1979 1980 1981 1982

Source: The Value Line Investment Survey, Nov. 27, 1981. Copyright 1981 by Arnold Bernhard & Co., Inc. Reprinted by permission of the publisher.

of these stocks are listed on the NYSE. Four indexes are published: composite, industrials, rails, and utilities (Fig. 3.5). The base period of the indexes is 1961 = 100.

All component stocks are equally weighted. A 10 percent fluctuation in a stock with 1 million shares outstanding will have the same impact on the indexes as a 10 percent fluctuation in a stock with 10 million shares outstanding. Each stock is assigned equivalent percentage weight in the index. Each index is computed as follows:

> *Each market day the closing price of each stock is divided by the preceding day's close, with the preceding day set at an index of 100. The resulting indexes of change are geometrically averaged for all the stocks. The geometric average of change for the day is then multiplied by the value of the average on the preceding day to get the latest value.*[2]

Stock splits and stock dividends are incorporated by adjusting the preceding day's price. The deficiency of this index lies in the method of computation. The geometric averaging would underestimate the gain and overestimate the loss. This distortion is magnified over time, diminishing in the process the usefulness of this indicator.

Unweighted Market Indexes

The distortions caused by various weighting schemes led to the development of various unweighted indexes. An unweighted index gives every stock an equal weight regardless of its price (P) or value (P times the number of shares outstanding). It is constructed under the assumption that an equal dollar amount is committed to each security in

---

[2] *Value Line Stock Market Averages,* vol. 35, no. 1.

FIGURE 3.6   Comparison of leading stock indicators.

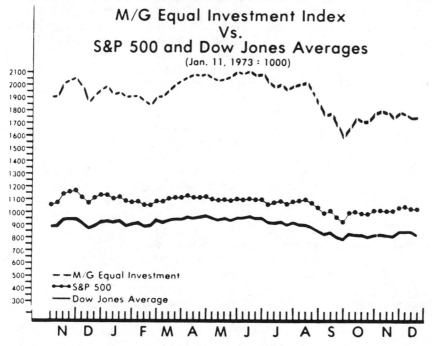

M/G Equal Investment Index
Vs.
S&P 500 and Dow Jones Averages
(Jan. 11, 1973 : 1000)

N D J F M A M J J A S O N D

Source: The Media General Financial Weekly, Dec. 21, 1981.

the index. Among them are the Indicator Digest Average (IDA) and ZUPI, which is constructed by the Zweig Forecast. All these indexes are based on data supplied by Quotron Systems, Inc. Price changes are biased downward in these indicators because a price rise, for example, from 50 to 100 is shown as a 50 percent increase (50/100) instead of 100 percent.

One unweighted market index that is getting considerable attention is the M/G Equal Investment Index. Using Jan. 11, 1973 = 1,000 as a base, the index is developed on the basis of all shares listed on the NYSE and the ASE, assuming an equal investment in each. The results are compared to those of the S&P and the DJIA after converting these two indicators to a base of 1,000 as of Jan. 11, 1973. The results are shown in Figure 3.6.

A summary of the major stock market indexes appears in Table 3.4. Another market index published by *Inc. Magazine* should also be mentioned for those investors interested in new issues. Referred to as the Inc. Index, it covers 55 new growth companies.

3.8 SOURCES OF INVESTMENT INFORMATION

Information on all types of investment vehicles and on issues relating to them, to investment strategy, and to portfolio management abounds. So much information, in fact, is available from so many different sources that the best of us can only sample it, no matter what our station in life or our employment. Our sample consists of the following five categories of sources.

TABLE 3.4

Stock Market Indicator	Sample	Representation	Weighting and Computation
Dow Jones Industrial Average	30 major NYSE industrial companies.	Less than 2% of all NYSE stocks and less than 1% of all actively traded stocks. Accounts for about 25% of market value of NYSE stocks and about 20% of all stock values.	Price weighted arithmetic average with divisor adjusted for stock splits.
S&P 500	400 industrials, 40 utilities, 20 transportation, 40 financial companies (mostly NYSE issues). Separate indexes for each of these groups.	About 75% of NYSE market value and 30% of NYSE issues. Large capitalization companies have heavy influence on index movement.	Value weighted index, as a percentage of the average during 1941–1943.
NYSE Composite Index	Approximately 1,550 NYSE listed stocks. Separate indexes for industrial, utility, transportation, and financial stock groups.	Complete coverage of NYSE stocks. Major movements still dominated by stocks of large companies.	Value-weighted index, with base of 50.
AMEX Market Value Index	About 1,000 American Stock Exchange stocks.	Complete coverage of smaller companies listed on the American Stock Exchange. Accounts for less than 5% of market value of all stocks.	Value-weighted index, with base of 100.
NASDAQ OTC Composite Index	Over 2,000 stocks traded over the counter. Separate indexes for industrial, insurance, and bank stocks.	Covers many small company stocks, but is heavily influenced by about 100 of largest NASDAQ stocks.	Value-weighted index, with base of 100.
Value Line Composite Average	1,681 stocks, which include 1,484 industrials, 19 rails, and 178 utilities. Separate averages for each of these groups.	Broad representation of stocks, mostly from the NYSE. All stocks have equal influence on indicator's movement.	Equal weighting, with average expressed as a percentage of a 100 base value.

Source: Investment Analysis and Portfolio Management, by Sid Mittra with Chris Gassen. Copyright © 1981 by Harcourt Brace Jovanovich, Inc. Reprinted by permission of the publisher.

Macroeconomic Information

The most often used sources of macroeconomic data are as follows:

1. *Federal Reserve Bulletin.* Published monthly by the Board of Governors of the Federal Reserve System. It is an excellent publication containing extensive monetary, banking, output, and international data.
2. *Survey of Current Business.* Published monthly by the United States Department of Commerce. It covers extensively GNP data, national income statistics, labor data, interest rates, and international statistics.
3. *Economic Report of the President.* Published annually in January. It contains an extensive data base on various economic indicators and is an excellent source on budget related matters.
4. *The various economic services.* Commercial banks, investment bankers, research centers, and economic research groups—such as the Wharton Econometric Forecasting Associates (WEFA) and others—publish regular assessments of the conditions of the economy and forecasts of things to come. A regular review of the publications of any of these services, such as WEFA's, should prove quite helpful.

Aggregate Stock Market Data

Some of the valuable sources are the following:

1. *Statistical Bulletin.* Published monthly by the SEC. It contains valuable information on trade activity on the exchanges and the OTC market and on new issues registered with the SEC.
2. *The Wall Street Journal.* Published daily by Dow Jones, it contains a wealth of information and is "must" reading for investors.
3. *Barron's.* Published weekly by Dow Jones, it contains comprehensive data on stocks, stock markets, and financial markets.
4. *Barron's Market Laboratory.* Summarizes the data found in the weekly *Barron's* in an annual publication.
5. *S&P Trade and Security Statistics.* Published by Standard & Poor's, it contains extensive business and financial data and historical data on the S&P indexes.

Industry-Specific Reports

Once again, several important sources should be examined:

1. *Reports of investment banking houses.* Every major investment banking house publishes its own industry studies and forecasts. Investors should ask their brokers for such publications.
2. *Standard & Poor's Industry Survey.* An excellent source on 69 major industries, it is both historical and prospective in nature.
3. The various publications by trade associations and industry groups—such as *The ABA Banking Journal* and *Chemical Week*—should be consulted, depending on the industry involved.

TABLE 3.5
A Sample from *Standard & Poor's Stock Reports*

Sears, Roebuck

NYSE Symbol S   Put & Call Options on CBOE

Price	Range	P-E Ratio	Dividend	Yield	S&P Ranking
Sep. 1'81 16¾	1981 20⅞-14⅞	8	1.36	8.1%	A-

Summary

Sears realigned its operations into five separate business groups in early 1980—Merchandise, All-state, Credit, International, and Seraco, which develops and operates real estate, etc. A corporate restructuring program and streamlining of merchandising operations was completed around the end of 1980. Profitability in retailing, which receded in recent years, appears to be in a recovery trend, and progress in other areas is also expected over the longer term.

Current Outlook

Earnings for calendar 1981 could reach $2.40 a share, versus the prior year's $1.92.

Dividends should continue at $0.34 quarterly.

Strength in domestic merchandising profits should continue over the balance of 1981. Pressure on underwriting results will continue to restrict profits at Allstate. Losses may continue in credit and international operations. The trend of interest rates, currency adjustments, changes in LIFO reserves, and the provision for taxes will continue to impact net earnings.

[6]Total Revenues (Billion $)

Quarter:	1981-2	1980-1	1979-80	1978-9
Apr.	6.10	5.47	3.63	4.07
Jul.	6.78	6.00	4.25	4.49
Oct.		6.46	4.53	4.46
Jan.		7.26	5.10	4.93
		25.19	17.51	17.95

Revenues for the six months ended July 31, 1981 increased 12.3%, year to year, but an advance of 12.7% in costs and expenses lowered operating income 18.4%. Much larger other income and capital gains increased pretax income 24.6%, and large tax benefits lifted net income 36.6%. Earnings rose to $0.83 a share, from $0.61.

Capital Share Earnings ($)

Quarter:	1981-2	1980-1	1979-80	1978-9
Apr.	0.30	0.19	0.47	0.48
Jul.	0.53	0.42	0.60	0.63
Oct.		0.43	0.67	0.73
Jan.		0.88	0.80	1.02
		1.92	2.54	2.86

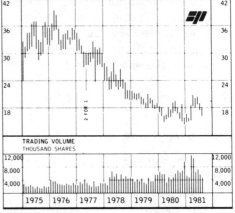

TRADING VOLUME
THOUSAND SHARES

Important Developments

Aug. '81—First half results reflected wide improvement in merchandising income, a slight dip at Allstate, and Seraco profits bolstered by a large capital gain. Interest expense of $710 million was up from $547 a year earlier, the LIFO charge was $9.55 million less, and currency exchange losses were $14.7 million versus $2.5 million a year earlier. Tax benefits totaled $37.4 million, against a $7.6 million credit a year before.

May '81—Financial reporting is to be changed to a calendar year from a January fiscal year, with the switch to occur with the quarter ending September 30. Capital spending for 1981 will be about unchanged, with 31 stores to be opened, five fewer than in 1980; 16 of the planned stores would be in new markets.

Next earnings report due in late November.

Per Share Data ($)

Yr. End Jan. 31 [1]	[7]1980	1979	1978	1977	1976	1975	[2]1974	1973	[2]1972	1971
Book Value	24.38	23.53	21.98	20.27	18.61	16.72	16.60	15.87	14.38	13.05
Earnings[3]	1.92	2.54	2.86	[4]2.62	[4]2.18	1.65	1.63	2.16	1.96	1.78
Dividends	1.36	1.28	1.27	1.08	0.80	0.92½	0.92½	0.87½	0.80½	0.75
Payout Ratio	71%	50%	44%	41%	37%	56%	57%	40%	41%	42%
Prices[5]—High	19⅝	21⅞	28⅛	34⅝	39⅝	37⅛	45⅛	61⅝	59¾	52
Low	14⅜	17¾	19¾	27	30¾	24⅛	20¾	39⅛	48⅝	37⅜
P/E Ratio—	10-7	9-7	10-7	13-10	18-14	22-15	28-13	28-18	30-25	29-21

Data as orig. reptd. Adj. for stk. div(s). of 100% Jul. 1977. **1.** Of fol. cal. yr. **2.** Reflects merger or acquisition. **3.** Bef. spec. item(s) of +0.02 in 1972. **4.** Ful. dil.: 2.61 in 1977, 2.17 in 1976. **5.** Cal. yr. **6.** Net sales prior to 1980-1. **7.** Reflects acctg. change. NA-Not Available.

Standard NYSE Stock Reports
Vol. 48/No. 173/Sec. 15

September 9, 1981
Copyright © 1981 Standard & Poor's Corp. All Rights Reserved

Standard & Poor's Corp.
25 Broadway, NY, NY 10004

Sears, Roebuck and Co.

Income Data (Million $)

Year Ended Jan. 31 [1]	Revs.	Oper. Inc.	% Oper. Inc. of Revs.	Cap. Exp.	Depr.	Int. Exp.	Net Bef. Taxes	Eff. Tax Rate	[4]Net Inc.	% Net Inc. of Revs.
[5]1980	25,195	2,081	8.3%	[6]368	279	[7]1,150	[3] 698	12.2%	606	2.4%
1979	17,514	1,336	7.6%	372	218	634	[3]1,029	21.3%	810	4.6%
1978	17,946	1,423	7.9%	324	209	527	[3]1,264	27.1%	922	5.1%
1977	17,224	1,267	7.4%	262	196	356	[3]1,194	29.8%	838	4.9%
1976	14,950	1,304	8.7%	229	170	264	[3]1,076	35.5%	695	4.6%
1975	13,640	1,234	9.0%	282	166	279	[3] 915	42.9%	[5]523	3.8%
[2]1974	13,101	1,135	8.7%	411	149	381	[3] 816	37.3%	511	3.9%
1973	12,306	1,248	10.1%	401	127	277	[3]1,113	38.9%	680	5.5%
[2]1972	10,991	1,104	10.0%	352	120	148	[3]1,030	40.4%	614	5.6%
1971	10,006	1,038	10.4%	362	106	139	[3] 950	42.0%	551	5.5%

Balance Sheet Data (Million $)

Jan. 31 [1]	Cash	Current Assets	Current Liab.	Ratio	Total Assets	Ret. on Assets	Long Term Debt	Common Equity	Total Cap.	% LT Debt of Cap.	Ret. on Equity
1980	787	NA	NA	NA	28,054	2.7%	[9]3,382	7,689	12,495	27.1%	8.0%
1979	284	10,256	6,261	1.6	16,422	5.2%	2,474	7,467	10,161	24.3%	11.2%
1978	225	9,676	5,926	1.6	15,262	6.1%	2,040	7,092	9,336	21.9%	13.5%
1977	237	9,642	6,059	1.6	14,746	6.1%	1,990	6,524	8,687	22.9%	13.4%
1976	223	8,201	5,039	1.6	12,712	5.7%	1,564	5,937	7,672	20.4%	12.3%
1975	277	7,454	4,807	1.6	11,577	4.6%	1,326	5,302	6,769	19.6%	9.9%
1974	192	7,248	4,896	1.5	11,339	4.7%	1,095	5,241	6,444	17.0%	10.0%
1973	198	6,772	4,393	1.5	10,427	6.9%	981	4,993	6,034	16.2%	14.3%
1972	233	6,207	3,877	1.6	9,326	6.9%	916	4,515	5,449	16.8%	14.3%
1971	198	5,615	3,556	1.6	8,312	6.9%	696	4,061	4,757	14.6%	14.1%

Data as orig. reptd. 1. Of fol. cal. yr. 2. Reflects merger or acquisition. 3. Incl. equity in earns. of nonconsol. subs. 4. Bef. spec. item(s) in 1972. 5. Reflects accounting change. 6. Net of curr. yr. retirement and disposals. 7. Net of interest income.

Business Summary

Sears' retail operations are supplemented by four other major operations which in 1980-1 (new basis) contributed as follows:

Groups	Sales	Income
Merchandise	67%	30%
Allstate	25%	64%
Credit	4%	-5%
International	3%	4%
Seraco (real estate & fin.)	2%	7%

Retailing is conducted through 854 stores with 116.3 million gross sq. ft., about half of which is net selling space. Catalog orders account for about one-fifth of sales, credit sales for about 52%, durables for 65%, and nondurables for 35%.

The Allstate Group is engaged in the property-liability insurance, life insurance, and financial services businesses.

The Credit Group has about 25 million active customer accounts with an outstanding balance of about $1 billion. It sells each month, without recourse, selected account balances.

The International Group services 72 stores and 55 sales offices in Central and South America, Spain, Mexico and Puerto Rico. A 40% equity interest is held in Simpsons-Sears Ltd. (Canada).

The Seraco Group develops, invests in and operates real estate. Financial services include savings and loan, mortgage banking and insurance. Homart Development owns 16 regional shopping centers and is a partner in 11.

Dividend Data

Dividends have been paid since 1935. A dividend reinvestment plan is available.

Amt. of Divd. $	Date Decl.	Ex-divd. Date	Stock of Record	Payment Date
0.34	Nov. 18	Nov. 21	Nov. 28	Jan. 2'81
0.34	Feb. 10	Feb. 19	Feb. 25	Apr. 2'81
0.34	May 18	May 22	May 29	Jul. 2'81
0.34	Aug. 11	Aug. 20	Aug. 26	Oct. 2'81

Next dividend meeting: mid-Nov. '81.

Capitalization

Long Term Debt: $3,015,600,000.

Capital Stock: 315,388,651 shs. ($0.75 par). Institutions hold about 43%. Shareholders: 350,000.

Office—Sears Tower, Chicago, Ill. 60684. Tel—(312) 875-2500. Chrmn & Pres—E. R. Telling. VP-Secy—C. W. Harper. VP-Treas—R. F. Gurnee. Investor Contact—R. Greer. Dirs—W. O. Beers, A. R. Boe, E. A. Brennan, A. V. Casey, E. M. deWindt, L. H. Foster, R. M. Jones, P. Martin, C. A. Meyer, N. Pace, C. B. Rogers, J. Rosenwald II, D. H. Rumsfeld, W. I. Spencer, E. B. Stern, Jr., E. R. Telling, A. M. Wood, C. C. Wurmstedt. Transfer Agent—Co's. Office. Registrar—First National Bank of Chicago. Incorporated in New York in 1906.

Source: Standard & Poor's Stock Reports, New York Stock Exchange, October 1981.

TABLE 3.6
A Sample Page from *The Value Line Investment Survey*

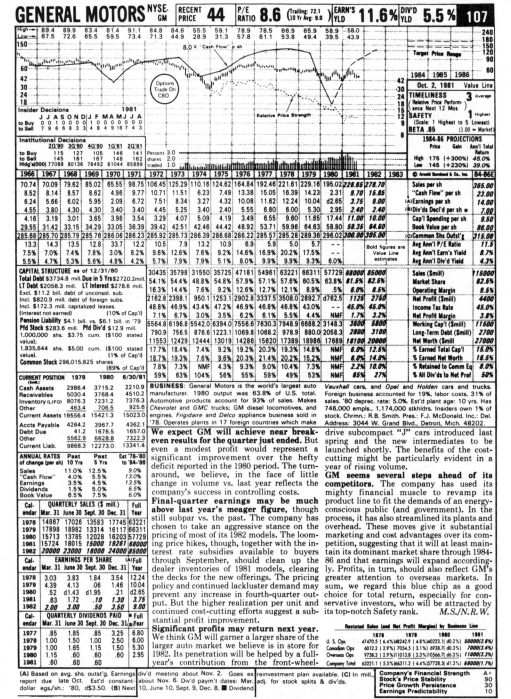

Source: The Value Line Investment Survey, Oct. 2, 1981. Copyright 1981 by Arnold Bernhard & Co.,
    Inc. Reprinted by permission of the publisher.

Company-Specific Reports

The sources here are many and could vary considerably in their level of sophistication and their emphases. The indispensable ones are:

1. *Corporate reports.* These reports consist of the annual reports distributed to the shareholders by publicly owned corporations and of the various reports filed with the SEC, such as the 10-K form.
2. *The Standard & Poor's publications.* The most valuable for a "quick look" at a stock is the *Standard & Poor's Stock Reports.* An example appears in Table 3.5. Another S&P publication that reports on stocks with certain characteristics, in addition to other market related issues, is the *Outlook.*
3. *The Value Line Investment Survey.* This publication is quite thorough and gives past and expected data on the 1,700 stocks followed by Value Line. An example appears in Table 3.6.
4. *Research reports by investment banking firms.* These reports, usually very timely and very well done, are available free of charge from all major firms. The reports vary in length depending on the stock and the investment banking firm's interest in it.

Other Sources

Several regularly published magazines and journals cover all aspects of investment on both the macro and the micro levels. The nonacademic publications that should be consulted are *Business Week* (weekly), *Forbes* (biweekly), *Financial World* (biweekly), and *Institutional Investor* (monthly). The academic journals that lead the field of finance and investments are *The Journal of Finance* (quarterly), *Financial Management* (quarterly), *Journal of Financial and Quantitative Analysis* (quarterly), *Financial Analysts Journal* (bimonthly), and the *Journal of Portfolio Management* (quarterly). All these journals tend to be very technical and are written by academicians for academicians and also for sophisticated portfolio managers.

Conclusions

The securities markets are complex and are becoming increasingly so. To navigate their waters requires skill but—most importantly—also information. To measure their performance requires several techniques and yardsticks, all of which could lead to confusion or to clarity. We hope that the reader reaches the latter after completing the remaining chapters in this book.

Questions

1. Which dates must an investor keep in mind with respect to investments in equity?

2. How can investors and analysts use market indexes? What criteria would you use before choosing a market index? Is one market index, no matter its merits, ever sufficient?

3. "The Dow Jones Industrial Average rose 2.45 to 949.52." Evaluate this information. How useful is it to an investor wishing to learn the performance of the market as a whole?

4. How would you expect inflation to affect stock prices—positively or negatively? Why?

5. Describe how shorting against the box enables an investor to postpone the payment of taxes. Under what conditions would an individual consider such a strategy?

6. Outline the advantages and disadvantages of margin accounts. What is "marking to the market," and how does this affect purchases on margin?

7. "The market is terrible, stay out of it." Comment.

8. The market tends to be more active on Monday than on days in the middle of the week. Provide a possible explanation for this.

9. "A person who does not like to assume much risk will never go short." True or false? Why?

10. "It is unpatriotic to be short on the market." Comment.

11. John Fortunate has a paper profit of $20 per share on a stock purchased at $50. He is nervous about the recent weakness in the stock. Suggest ways to protect his paper profit.

12. Might psychological factors, such as the DJIA breaking 1,000, affect the stock market? How? Do you perceive any fault in a market that reacts to such events?

13. Discuss the advantages and the limitations of a limit order and of a market order.

14. How might a high-grade stock covary with the DJIA? Why?

15. Which of the market indexes are most relevant to the typical investor?

16. Should investors rely on one source of information for data on stock valuation or economic forecasts? Why?

17. Why do exchanges prohibit short sales unless those sales are preceded by an uptick? Provide an argument to counter the reasoning of the exchanges.

18. What are the major weaknesses of value weighted indexes?

19. Who gets the proceeds of a short sale? What opportunities does this offer?

20. Some investors restrict their portfolios to certain industries or types of securities. What are the benefits and drawbacks of such a strategy?

CHAPTER 4 | Market Efficiency

4.1 AN OVERVIEW[1]

The words *efficient* and *optimal* pervade the economic literature. The economist looking at a planet with finite resources is concerned with optimum allocation of resources in order to minimize waste and consequently prices. Efficient resource distribution in a two-input (a,b) two-output (x,y) case requires that

$$\frac{\text{MPP}_{ax}}{\text{MPP}_{bx}} = \frac{\text{MPP}_{ay}}{\text{MPP}_{by}}$$

The ratio of the marginal physical product (MPP) of input a to that of input b in the production of output x should equal that in the production of output y. These conditions obtain in a purely competitive structure in the factors markets. Under such a system the production process is at maximum efficiency.

In the output market, efficiency is assured when the marginal rate of substitution of one product for another for a given consumer is equal to that of another consumer. That is, the maximum amount of an output y a consumer c_1 is willing to give up in order to receive one additional unit of output x must be equal to that of another consumer c_2.

$$\text{MRS}_{xy}^{c_1} = \text{MRS}_{xy}^{c_2}$$

This condition is referred to as *Pareto optimality* and is achieved under a purely competitive market system.

Financial analysts are as much concerned with efficiency as are economists. Their limited inputs are labor, capital, and information and their output is information on

---

[1] This section has greatly benefited in terms of organization and ideas from the excellent work by **James Lorie** and **Louis** and **Mary T. Hamilton,** *The Stock Market: Theories and Evidence.* Richard D. Irwin, Homewood, Ill., 1973, chapters 4, 5, and 6.

the basis of which investment decisions are made and financial resources are shifted from one sector to another, from one industry to another, and from one firm to another.

The concern on the macro level is, therefore, with the allocational efficiency of the market—that is, with how well the financial markets channel resources to the most efficient users. Alternatively stated, the concern is with how well the market allows its participants to correctly gauge the actual and expected performance of a business entity and penalizes it (through higher cost of equity and/or cost of debt) or rewards it (through lower cost of equity and/or cost of debt).

As investors shift their resources from the "bad" firm to the "good" firm, the efficiency of the market is gauged further in how quickly and cheaply this is done. This is called *operational efficiency.*

Our focus, therefore, must be on the market for information. A perfectly competitive information market allows for "equal" access to all investors in the market and, consequently, for equal results (in terms of risk/return tradeoff). This is equivalent to arguing that all the players in a poker game have equal abilities and hence equal probability of winning, assuming they are playing with a "fair" deck of cards. The conditions for efficiency in the financial markets are, therefore, essentially the same as those required by economists in the factors and goods markets.

On the firm's level, the concern is with the disclosure of all relevant information and with whether that information has been discounted in such a way that the expected at time t_0 will in fact materialize.

From the point of view of the investor, the concern with efficiency arises from the process of assessing one's chances in earning a rate of return higher than is generally available in the marketplace. In an efficient market, all investors should realize the same rate of return for a given level of risk. A higher rate of return would imply that the market has incorrectly assessed the potential of a firm and/or its risk profile. Equivalently, a rate of return higher than the market's implies a superior ability of an investor in sourcing or in interpreting information. This is not possible, however, if the market for information is perfectly competitive.

4.2 A FORMAL STATEMENT ON EFFICIENCY

There exist several definitions of efficiency, each with its own strengths and drawbacks. Originally, the definition of efficiency relied on the intrinsic value (the theoretically correct value, the present value of a stream of cash flows) as its foundation. Deviations from intrinsic value were indications of inefficiencies.

Later, a more intuitive (although much harder to test empirically) definition of efficiency emerged. Fama argued that "in an efficient market prices 'fully reflect' the information available."[2]

The problem with Fama's definition lies in the absurd conclusions one can draw from it. For example, how does one know that information is fully reflected in prices? One can simply look at prices and conclude that they reflect all available information, otherwise they would not be at their observed levels.

[2] **E. Fama,** "Efficient Capital Markets: A Review of Theory and Empirical Work." *Journal of Finance,* May 1970, pp. 383–417.

A major step forward in the definition of efficiency was taken by W. Beaver.[3] After exposing the weaknesses of the previous definitions, Beaver advanced his own definition, which seems to circumvent many of the problems from which other definitions have suffered. The full contents of the new definition are rather complex for this level of discussion. We shall settle for his "casual" definition: "A securities market is efficient with respect to an information system if and only if security prices act as if everyone knows that information system."[4]

Some of the advantages Beaver sees in such a definition are that it:

> *(1) permits a definition of market efficiency in a world of individuals who are heterogeneous with respect to beliefs and information . . . (3) permits individuals to perceive the market to be inefficient even if it is not, (4) gives the term "fully reflect" a well defined meaning . . . (6) focuses upon prices as opposed to beliefs or actions . . . and (11) avoids the* use of ill-defined terms, *introduced in previous definitions."*[5]

To delve further into this issue and to pick one definition over another (although some readers may feel that we have done so by the time they finish reading this chapter) could only be confusing to the reader at this level. The various definitions were presented in order to show that even the definition of what is efficient is not as yet fully sorted out.

The sections to follow will deal with the implications of market efficiency, the levels of market efficiency, and the empirical evidence regarding market efficiency. The focus is the efficiency of the stock market.

4.3 IMPLICATIONS OF EFFICIENCY

An efficient market should render obsolete any and all devices intended to outperform the market. No scheme, however carefully devised, should result in consistently higher returns than those realized on a naive buy-and-hold strategy. A review of the strategies employed by various investors should, therefore, be helpful at least in showing what does not work and persuade investors as to the fruitlessness of their attempts. An efficient market should also be reassuring to small investors who compete with large investment companies, banks, and investment banks in the marketplace. The price of a security in an efficient market should not be influenced by the behavior of any participant or any group of participants. In an efficient market, professional money managers could not have access to privileged information that allows them consistently to outperform the market. In such a market, a small investor should not be fearful of playing an active role because of actual or perceived inferior ability in assembling, interpreting, or digesting actual or anticipated information. In summary, an efficient market in its various forms (details below) argues that with or without analysis (thorough or shallow), the rates of return on an investment will not be higher than those obtained from a random

---

[3] **William H. Beaver,** "Market Efficiency." *Accounting Review,* vol. 56, no. 1 (January 1981), pp. 23–37.

[4] Ibid., p. 23.

[5] Ibid., p. 35.

selection of stocks of similar risk. While answering these questions, an efficient market raises new ones, mainly about the economic justification for the employment of 12,000 security analysts[6] by some of the most prestigious money managers in the world. Could it be that the labor market is so inefficient as to pay positive wages to security analysts while their marginal product is zero? Could it be that investors are so foolish as to pay a price for a book based on the premise that markets are inefficient while the weight of empirical evidence indicates otherwise? Could it be that investors can be repeatedly fooled by the same firms or by different firms using variations of the same sales techniques in order to sell advisory services based on the hypothesis that securities markets are inefficient?

The market efficiency hypothesis has produced two schools of thought: one that accepts it and one that rejects it. We discuss the merits of each of the schools in the sections to follow.

4.4 THE FUNDAMENTAL SCHOOL

The fundamental school concentrates on the determination of the "intrinsic" value of the security; that is, the present value of all net cash flows to be derived from the ownership of the security, mathematically:

$$MP_0^s = \sum_{t=1}^{n} \frac{D_t}{(1 + K_e)^t} + \frac{MP_n^s}{(1 + K_e)^n} \tag{4.1}$$

where MP_0^s = current market price of a security

MP_n^s = selling price at time n

D_t = dividend at time t

K_e = investor's required rate of return

The dividends in the stock price equation are a proxy for the earnings of the firm, as we shall discuss in Chapter 7. The concentration by fundamental analysts on future earnings requires sorting of all variables that come to bear on the levels and growth rate of earnings—variables like:

1. Quality and depth of management
2. Standing of the company relative to the industry in terms of the competitive position of its product line
3. Degree of company participation in growth areas
4. Strength of company balance sheet and its accounting policies
5. The nature of the economic, human, and technological environment in which the company will be operating
6. The industry environment and the industry characteristics
7. Investor perception of the company and of its product

---

[6] The superior ability of security analysts to forecast earnings was documented by **Lawrence D. Brown** and **Michael S. Rozeff,** "The Superiority of Analyst Forecasts as Measures of Expectations: Evidence From Earnings." *Journal of Finance,* vol. 33, no. 1 (March 1978), pp. 1–16.

The higher the level of excitement about the company's position and prospects and the larger the company's participation in the "hot" areas (silicon chips, artificial hearts, machines that can see or hear or talk, etc.), the higher the multiple (the price/earnings ratio) the investor must be willing to pay for the company's earnings.

The question in the context of these complex and detailed analyses is the following: Can fundamental analysis be of any value if securities markets are efficient?

The answer is in the affirmative. Fundamental analysis is used in the following ways:

1. To determine whether a given security is underpriced or overpriced in relation to its intrinsic value. This value is not constant and changes as new information becomes available. A security is underpriced only in the opinion of the analyst; it is not underpriced as far as the market is concerned. The analyst's forecast should occasionally (not consistently) produce an above-average rate of return given that it is accurate, unique, and significantly different from the market's. As special opportunities are identified, arbitragers move in to capitalize on them and bring the market to equilibrium.

2. The collection and processing of data may be increasingly useful if economies of scale are present in the information market. Declining marginal cost of information, to the extent it exists, encourages the formation of larger research departments.

3. Security analysis is further justified as a tool in assessing risk of securities (total, systematic, and unsystematic risk—see Chapter 6) and of portfolios, and in evaluating ways to diversify risk. Portfolio theory has come a long way since it was introduced in the early 1950s by Harry Markowitz. Elaborate mathematical and statistical models are currently being employed in order to keep portfolios on the efficient frontier; that is, in order to ensure that the highest rate of return is realized for a given level of risk or that the lowest risk is assumed for a given level of return.

4. Security analysis is very helpful as a tool to minimize transactions costs in all their forms. Taxes are very important considerations for many investors, as are commissions and other fees. The structuring of portfolios in such a way as to minimize tax liability and the cost of trade should substantially improve net returns on invested capital.

5. While there exists a large array of securities from which to choose, knowledge about the various characteristics of securities should be of considerable help in the attempt to match them with the needs and requirements of individual investors. Attitude toward risk, cash-flow requirement, personal biases (buy or do not buy defense issues, for example), tax considerations, and other matters are all very important in the selection of suitable securities.

The risk profile of an individual should prove most important from an asset-selection standpoint. According to the prescriptions of the capital asset pricing model (CAPM), investors wishing to diversify their portfolios will hold the market portfolio that includes every security in the market. The distribution of funds among the securities should be in accordance with the value of each security in relation to the total value of all securities in the market. The only choice left to the investor according to the CAPM is the extent of risk he or she is willing to bear. This will determine the extent to which investors are willing to leverage themselves, or the extent to which they are willing to commit portions of their capital to risk-free government securities. As new information becomes available and as the investor's needs and attitudes shift, portfolios must be adjusted to reflect the changes. In fact, frequent reviews of a portfolio are the norms and the recommended course on Wall Street.

6. While efficiency may characterize the securities market (evidence to follow) in the long run, the market is not in a permanent state of equilibrium. Markets may drop or rise substantially in price for a variety of reasons, such as (*a*) euphoria (panic) over an election of a president (sickness or death), (*b*) threats to the flow of oil supplies, (*c*) the recommendation of an investment advisor with a large following, (*d*) one major holder deciding to "dump" securities as a result of portfolio adjustments, and (*e*) for other reasons, some of which elude the most astute of market observers.

Those deviations from intrinsic value, while temporary, provide many opportunities for investors as the market moves back to equilibrium.

One additional comment worth making deals with the difference between available and observable data. It took some very astute auditors to uncover the scandal at Equity Funding Corporation. The auditors discovered in March 1973 that 66 percent of the insurance policies the company was holding were bogus policies. The stock fell 13 points by March 19, 1973. By March 27 the stock was trading at $14. Trading in the stock was suspended by the SEC on March 28, 1973. The company was later reorganized and started operations in October 1976 under the name Orion Corporation. There simply is no substitute for careful scrutiny of data.

In conclusion, it can be said that an active pursuit of information coupled with active portfolio management are very likely to pay handsome dividends in the long run, whether the market is efficient or not.

4.5 THE TECHNICAL SCHOOL

The technical school is at the opposite pole of the fundamental school. It asserts that market prices are not a random process: expected price changes are not independent of past price changes nor are distributions of rates of returns independent from past distributions. Market prices exhibit identifiable patterns that are bound to be repeated. The "art" lies in devising the proper technique to identify trends, interpret them, and interpret any deviation from them.

The technical school places little if any emphasis on earnings, dividends, market share, size of order backlog, and other fundamental factors. The argument of the school is basically that too many factors come to bear in the evaluation of a stock. To sort these factors out, identify the exact weight each has in the determination of the market value of a security, and gauge the time lag necessary for the impact of each factor to manifest itself are not practical if indeed possible considerations. What is important, the school argues, are supply and demand factors that are internal to the securities market. Investors should spend their valuable time trying to understand the "psychology" of the market; that is, they should grasp the determinants of supply and demand in order to be able to time their purchases and sales properly. Technicians have, therefore, a short-run outlook. In practical terms, the technical school suggests various techniques to beat the naive buy-and-hold strategy (the long-run fundamental view).

The overwhelming empirical evidence we shall detail below supports the efficiency hypothesis. Many curious observations and phenomena are worth noting, however:

1. The substantial drop in the market on Jan. 7, 1981, as a result of a sell recommendation by an investment advisor named Joseph Granville. The DJIA declined by 23.80 points on an unprecedented volume of 92,890,000 shares. Similar events occurred overseas as a result of the prognosis of the same man. The Financial Times Index declined by 20.5 points on Sept. 23, 1981, after Granville predicted doom for the London stock market. The next day (Sept. 24, 1981), the Nikkei Dow Jones average, the Tokyo version of the Dow Jones, fell 128.93 points.

2. The observation made by Martin E. Zweig in a May 16, 1977, issue of *Barron's*. Zweig noted that:

> *Off its own form chart, as it happens, the Dow tends to run not with but counter to the ups and downs of results reported for its 30 component stocks. What the record shows is that the market appreciates at about twice its normal rate when these key fundamentals are trending down. But the bad news is that when one or both are rising, especially at a fast pace, the Dow usually manages to underperform, if not steeply decline.*

Among the many tools used by technicians are the following:

The Dow Theory

The Dow theory was promulgated by Charles Dow, one of the more important figures in the financial world and editor of *The Wall Street Journal* around 1900. The theory is based on the performance of the Dow Jones industrial and rail averages. The market is in a bullish trend, the theory argues, if one of the averages advances beyond an important previous high and this advance is *confirmed* by a similar advance in the other average. On the other hand, if one of these averages dips below a previous important low and the other average confirms this, the market is in a bearish trend. The Dow theory does *not* attempt to forecast the future direction of stock prices but rather seeks evidence for claims that a new bull or a bear trend is under way and not just beginning. The value of the theory stems from the fact that it has many followers. The Dow theory has succeeded in calling major market trends more often that it has failed.

Patterns of Stock Price Movements

Stock price movements are summarized in charts. Bar charts are widely used. A bar chart is constructed by plotting time on the horizontal axis and the daily (weekly or longer period) trading range on the vertical axis, as shown in Figure 4.1.

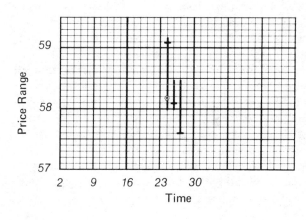

FIGURE 4.1 Typical chart summarizing stock price movements. *Source:* Merrill Lynch Pierce Fenner & Smith, Inc.

The length of the bar indicates the high and the low of the day. The small horizontal line drawn across the bar (the tick mark) indicates the closing price for the chosen time period—in Figure 4.1, the closing price for the day.

Successive bars form a "trend." Technical analysts do not concur with academic findings, that price movement is a series of random events. Trends may be up, down, or sideways, as shown in Figure 4.2.

Figure 4.2b shows an uptrend (suggesting a buy—a long position). The trend line is drawn under the prices. Figure 4.2a shows a downtrend (a sell, or a short position). The trend line is drawn over the prices. The price movement from point B to point C, which fails to exceed the previous high at A, and the subsequent drop below B confirms a downtrend, technicians argue. Figure 4.2c shows a sideways trend, where stock prices are contained between two parallel horizontal lines. Here the trader must be very skillful to realize short-term gains. Picking tops and bottoms is much harder than following a distinct trend.

Trend channels are shown in Figure 4.3. These channels represent major thrusts in one direction characterized by minor price setbacks. The channel represents the development of a trend over a period of time. It is identified by drawing lines connecting high market prices and low market prices. The longer prices move within the channel, the stronger the trend is. A "breakout," a price advance or decline outside the boundaries of the channel, could signal a new direction in the price of the security. The price breakout below the channel in Figure 4.3 could signal a very bearish market (a sell or a short position) unless a countertrend quickly sets in. Traders usually wait until closing time after the breakout before they establish their positions. If the stock price at closing remains outside the channel, a long or a short position is established, depending on whether the closing price is above or below the channel. The stock may well establish a sideways trend for a period of time before a clear upward or downward direction is established once again.

Technicians also believe that the market remembers resistance and support levels. Resistance represents price levels beyond which the market has failed to advance, and support represents price levels at which falling stock prices are arrested. Chartists usually identify several resistance and support levels, as Figure 4.4 indicates. A penetration of either level on a high volume is considered a strong indication of the direction of the market.

Several other formations are helpful, some technicians argue, in predicting the direction of the stock market. One hears descriptions such as "head and shoulders top," "head and shoulders bottom," "right triangle" or "coil top," "double tops," "double bottoms," "triple bottoms and tops," "flag," "symmetrical triangle," "V-bottom," "pennants," "ascending triangle," and so on. (see Fig. 4.5). The art of chart reading is getting even more creative. We shall now discuss a few of the price formations.

The triangles and flags represent consolidations or corrective moves in market trends. A flag is a well-defined price movement contrary to the main trend. Ordinarily, stock prices break out of a flag and rejoin the main trend. A line drawn across the high prices of the corrective phase and another across the low prices form either an ascending or a descending triangle. The tip of the triangle represents the breakout point. Stock prices at this stage are expected to rejoin the main trend.

Double tops form an inverted W (M). They represent a price high followed by a drop and then a rise to the previous high, indicating that price trends may be changing. Double bottoms are exactly the opposite, resembling a regular W with two equal price

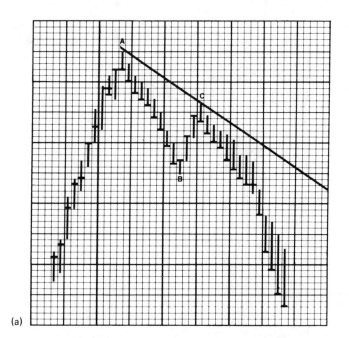

(a)

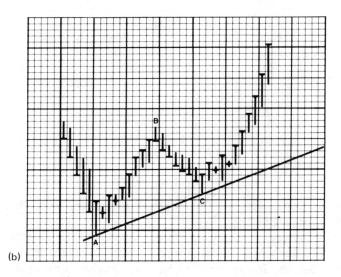

(b)

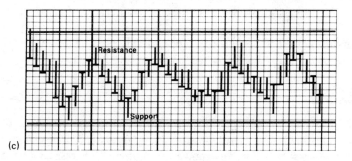

(c)

FIGURE 4.2 Successive bars, showing (a) downtrend; (b) uptrend; and (c) sideways trend. *Source:* Merrill Lynch Pierce Fenner & Smith Inc.

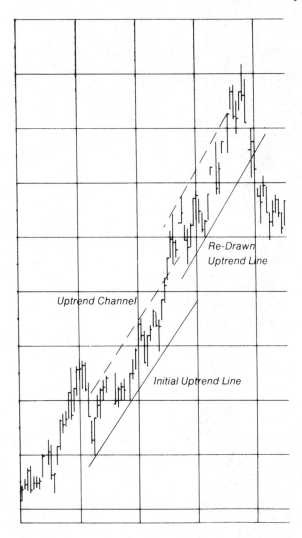

FIGURE   4.3   Trend   channels.
Source: Merrill Lynch Pierce Fenner & Smith Inc.

lows separated by a price rise. Double bottoms, and triple bottoms as well, are bullish indicators. Double and triple tops are bearish indicators.

The head-and-shoulder formations can be either top or bottom. In the "bottom" case, for example, a major market low is flanked on both sides (shoulders) by two higher lows. Cutting across the shoulders is some resistance level called the neckline. The breakdown of a bottom head-and-shoulder formation is a very bullish indication, as shown in Figure 4.6. The breakdown of a top head-and-shoulder formation is a bearish signal.

The analysis of other formations is beyond the scope of this book. The interested reader should consult one of the many books on technical analysis.

Point-and-Figure Charts

The point-and-figure chart is an alternative to the bar chart in the representation of the trends in stock prices. This method of chart construction ignores small price changes and the time dimension and discounts the importance of volume. With respect to the

FIGURE 4.4   Trend channels showing resistance and support levels.

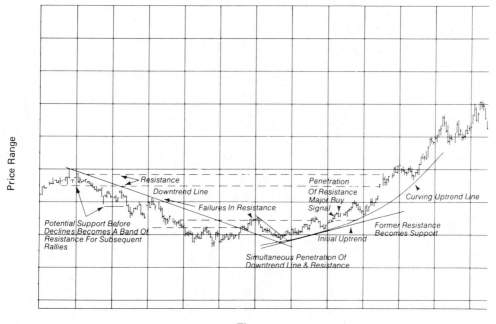

Time

Source: Merrill Lynch Pierce Fenner & Smith Inc.

former, the concern is more with price movement over a broad time period as opposed to movement over subperiods; hence the small concern for calendar time. Point-and-figure charts are constructed merely to show the direction of price changes.

Point-and-figure charts are constructed in a series of columns once the required size of the price change has been decided. An entry is made in a new column when price reversals of the designated magnitude (regardless of the length of the period) occur. Consecutive positive price changes x each equal in size to the minimum required would

$$x$$

be entered in a column like so: x. As soon as a price reversal of the minimum required

$$x$$
$$x$$

level occurs, a new column is introduced. The chart now looks like so: x 0, where 0

$$x$$

marks a price decline, although it is not always used. The various forms that point-and-figure charts can assume are shown in Figure 4.7. A buy signal is usually generated when a new column of x's moves higher than the previous x column; a sell signal is generated when a new 0 column moves lower than the previous 0 column.

Other Market Barometers

There are as many barometers as there are inventive people to make them. Among these are the following:

FIGURE 4.5 Various types of trend channels.

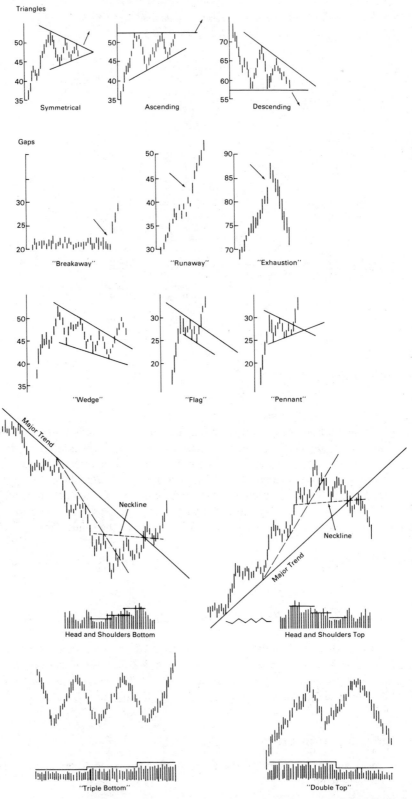

Source: Alan R. Shaw, "Technical Analysis," in Sumner N. Levine, ed., *Financial Analyst's Handbook.* Dow Jones-Irwin, Inc., Homewood, Ill., 1975.

FIGURE 4.6 Head and shoulder formations.

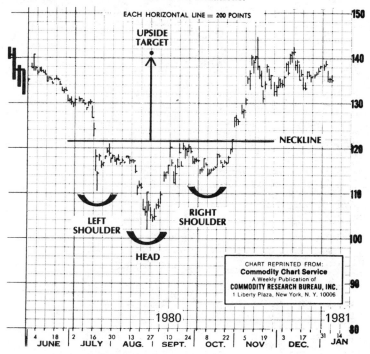

Source: Archer Commodities, Inc., Chicago.

The Dow Jones 20-Bond Average

When this bond average falls and the DJIA rises, a weakening stock market in the future is signaled because the yield on bonds becomes more and more attractive and investors would sell stocks to buy bonds. The opposite circumstances indicate a strengthening stock market. Widening yield spreads between the bond market and the stock market are considered bearish. Investors may shift out of stocks for the higher yields.

Dow Jones Price/Earnings Ratio

The lower the Dow Jones industrials P/E ratio in relation to its trend value, the more undervalued investors consider the stock market to be and the more bullish they are. The common wisdom is that the market "cannot go much lower" and an upward trend is inevitable. A low P/E translates into a high E/P—the (simplified) cost of equity—which reduces if not eliminates the attractiveness of financing corporate growth through equity financing.

NYSE Odd-Lot Trading

Odd-lot trades are trades in less than 100 shares. The common wisdom is that odd-lot traders, particularly those on the short side of the market, do not know what they are doing. The logical thing to do, therefore, is to establish a position opposite those of odd-lot short sales. Other technicians use the ratio of odd-lot sales to odd-lot purchases

FIGURE 4.7   Point and figure chart pattern.

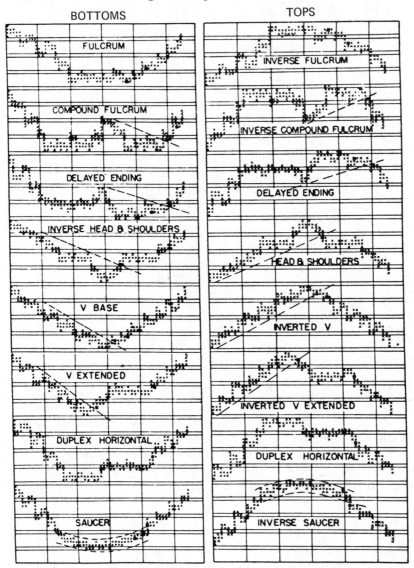

Source: Alan R. Shaw, "Technical Analysis," in Sumner N. Levine, ed., *Financial Analyst's Handbook.* Dow Jones-Irwin, Inc., Homewood, Ill., 1975.

(known as the *Balance Index*) in trying to predict the peaks and troughs of the stock market. If the ratio is significantly higher, then investors should be buying stocks, which is the opposite of what odd-lotters are doing. Tests conducted by Stanley Kaish[7] showed that an odd-lot index gave the correct buy signal but the incorrect sell signals. Thomas

---

[7] **Stanley Kaish,** "Odd-Lot Profit and Loss Performance." *Financial Analyst's Journal,* vol. 25, no. 5 (September–October 1969), pp. 83–90.

Kewley and Richard Stevenson[8] did not find much merit in the odd-lot index as a tool for outperforming the market.

Odd-lot trades are reported weekly in *Barron's* and in *The Media General Financial Weekly* and daily in *The Wall Street Journal.*

Member Trading

Trading by members of the exchanges is carefully watched by market traders. Purchases by members are netted out from sales by members in order to get net sales (+ or −). Excessive high net sale positions indicate a weakening stock market; a stronger stock market is presumed if net sales are negative. Also carefully watched by the public and by the members are net short positions. Short positions established by the public in excess of 30 percent of total short positions are considered signs of excessive pessimism and indicate a bullish market. When covered, short positions lead to higher stock prices. Some have disputed this hypothesis. Joseph Seneca argues that an increase in short interest is a sign of weakness in the stock market.[9]

Barron's Confidence Index

Barron's Confidence Index consists of the ratio of yields on AAa bonds to the yield on Baa bonds. The maximum value the ratio can assume is 1. The closer to 1 the ratio is, the more bullish the market, because investors are willing to accept lower yields on the riskier bonds. The lower the ratio is, the more bearish the indication. Investors are losing confidence in lower-quality issues and are requiring higher-risk premiums in order to hold the bonds. The record of this indicator is mixed.

Volume of Trade

High volume in a market trending upward indicates a strong rally. High volume in a market trending downward is an indication of a bearish market. That is why price movements must always be analyzed in conjunction with volume movements.

Advance/Decline Line

The advance/decline line, sometimes referred to as the overbought/oversold index, is the ratio of the number of shares advancing during a given period to that of shares declining. The higher the ratio, the more "overbought" the market is thought to be; the smaller the ratio, the more "oversold" the market is. The market is considered overbought if the ratio exceeds 1.25 and oversold if the ratio is lower than 0.75. Substantial and spontaneous movements in one direction or another indicate a very bullish (if up) or very bearish (if down) market. Some traders focus on the advance − decline line (instead of advance/decline) for the DJIA and on the DJIA breadth (percentage of

---

[8] **Thomas Kewley** and **Richard A. Stevenson,** "The Odd-Lot Theory as Revealed by Purchase and Sales Statistics for Individual Stocks." *Financial Analyst's Journal,* vol. 23, no. 5 (September–October 1967), pp. 103–109.

[9] **Joseph J. Seneca,** "Short Interest: Bullish or Bearish?" *Journal of Finance,* vol. 22, no. 1 (March 1967), pp. 67–71.

DJIA components appreciating in value during a week) to gauge the direction of the market (Figure 4.8). A rising advance — decline and breadth is a bullish indication.

NYSE Active Stocks

The 20 most active shares (in terms of trading volume) are usually indicative of the "quality" of the rally or the seriousness of the decline. If members of the most active list are traditionally good (blue-chip) securities, then the quality of the rise (in a bull market) is different from that if the list contains securities that are not identified with healthy, well-established companies. The latter case could be considered as excessive speculation auguring a declining market.

Moving Averages

Moving averages are utilized by securities traders as a mechanism for identifying trends and to help develop trading strategies.

FIGURE 4.8   DJIA advance-decline line and DJIA breadth.

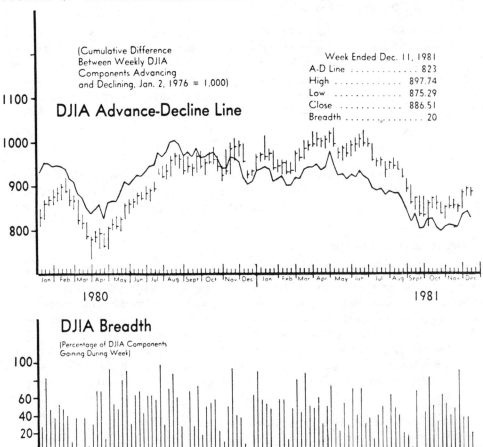

Source: The Media General Financial Weekly, Dec. 14, 1981.

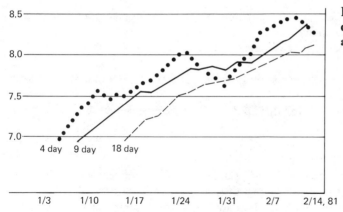

FIGURE 4.9 Four-day, 9-day, and 18-day moving averages.

The development of a moving average is quite simple. First, decide on the length (in days, weeks, or months, etc.) of the time period over which the moving average is to be calculated. Then, calculate the average price and proceed to calculate the next average by dropping the earliest observation and adding a new one. If this continues, a trend should become apparent, as is shown in Figure 4.9. The variation in the number of observations in the moving average allows chartists to reinforce their interpretation of price movements and to devise new trading strategies.

Some chartists use the double moving average, which is the moving average of a moving average, and various levels of exponential smoothing (see Chapter 8) to forecast stock prices.

Chartists use the averages depicted above in various ways. A sustained upward movement in all the averages is clearly bullish. A downward movement in all the averages is bearish. A 4-day moving average cutting across rising 9-day and 18-day moving averages is considered bearish; it is bullish if the 9-day and 18-day averages are trending downward.

Theory of Contrary Opinion

This theory attempts to capitalize on the hypothesis that there is an unwise stampede in the market toward conformity. When a substantial majority of "experts" (financial analysts) agree that the market is likely to improve, the trader should establish a short position, and a long position if the expectations are bearish. This should prove, it is argued, that the trader has not lost the capacity for critical thought.

What the above indicators suffer from as a unit is the conflicting-signal syndrome. What if two of these indicators say buy and the remainder say sell? How does one construct the weighting system that gives consistently correct signals? The answers to these complex questions have not been provided as yet.

4.6 CONDITIONS FOR AN EFFICIENT MARKET

The optimal conditions for an efficient market are:

1. No transactions costs
2. Costless information being available to any investor

3. Homogeneous expectations, all investors holding the same expectations with regard to the future of the company
4. Investors having the same time horizon

If these conditions are obeyed, the market is efficient and stock prices follow a random process.[10]

Fama,[11] on the other hand, showed that the necessary conditions for efficiency require much less restrictive assumptions.

1. "Reasonable" transactions costs
2. Information available to a "sufficient" (large enough to influence price; that is, bring back the market to equilibrium value) number of investors
3. If expectations are heterogeneous, they are not systematically so, with a group of investors showing consistent superiority in assessing information and in capitalizing on it in the form of higher-than-average rates of return

Tests for efficiency require, therefore, the determination of how "reasonable" transactions costs are, the presence of a trading rule(s) that consistently outperforms the market, the existence of elements of monopoly in the sourcing or the processing of information, and the speed of adjustment in securities prices to new information.

Efficiency is not uniform, however. There exist various levels of efficiency: the weak form, the semistrong form, and the strong form.

4.7 THE WEAKLY EFFICIENT MARKET

The weakly efficient market is essentially a refutation of technical analysis. Past price and volume data are already impounded in the market price of a stock and no amount of chart reading is likely to outperform the naive buy-and-hold strategy.

To prove that securities markets are efficient in a weak form, one needs to show that successive price changes are independent.[12] Samuelson[13] and Mandelbrot[14] both showed that such independence is consistent with an efficient market. Some of the earliest

---

[10] See **Paul A. Samuelson,** "Proof that Properly Anticipated Prices Fluctuate Randomly." *Industrial Management Review,* vol. 6 (Spring 1965), pp. 41–48.

[11] **Eugene Fama,** "Efficient Capital Markets: A Review of Theory and Empirical Work." *Journal of Finance,* vol. 25, no. 2 (May 1970), pp. 383–417.

[12] Several of the empirical studies we cite in this chapter utilize statistical techniques and make certain assumptions that have recently been subjected to close scrutiny. The reader should consult the following: **Menachem Brenner,** "The Sensitivity of the Efficient Market Hypothesis to Alternative Specifications of the Market Model." *Journal of Finance,* vol. 34, no. 4 (September 1979), pp. 915–929; and **Robert J. Shiller,** "The Use of Volatility Measures in Assessing Market Efficiency." *Journal of Finance,* vol. 36, no. 2 (May 1981), pp. 291–304.

For an excellent background on the various tests and issues in the area of efficiency, consult Paul H. Cootner, ed., *The Random Character of Stock Market Prices.* MIT Press, Cambridge, Mass., 1964.

While every author believes that his evidence is "conclusive," the remainder of this chapter should be read with some skepticism.

[13] **Samuelson,** 1965.

[14] **Benoit Mandelbrot,** "Forecasts of Future Prices, Unbiased Markets, and Martingale Models." *Journal of Business,* vol. 39, part 2 (January 1966), pp. 242–255.

tests on the randomness of prices were undertaken by Maurice G. Kendall[15] and a physicist named Osborne.[16]

Kendall found that the behavior of securities prices was similar to the outcomes from a roulette wheel. Osborne tested the hypothesis that stock prices follow a Brownian motion similar to that characterizing the movement of very small particles suspended in a chemical solution. The results of Osborne's test confirmed the validity of the hypothesis; that is, stock prices do follow a random process.

Testing the "random-walk" theory requires testing whether successive price changes are independent and identically distributed. The following hypothesis is the one generally tested:

$$H_0 : E_t(P_{t+1}) = P_t$$
$$H_1 : E_t(P_{t+1}) \neq P_t$$

where $E_t(P_{t+1}) =$ period $t + 1$ price expected at time t
$P_t =$ period t price

A stronger test would consist of simultaneously testing the above hypothesis and an autoregressive model:

$$H_0 : E_t(P_{t+1}) = \sum_{k=0}^{m} a_k P_{t-k}$$

$$H_1 : E_t(P_{t+1}) \neq \sum_{k=0}^{m} a_k P_{t-k}$$

where $k =$ length of lag

Rejecting the autoregressive model and accepting the random-walk model should provide the necessary support for the random-walk theory.

Other tests of the random-walk theory consisted of devising trading strategies and measuring the rate of return derived therefrom against those of a naive buy-and-hold strategy. Alexander[17] tested the effectiveness of the "filter rule." From a trough, wait until the stock advances x percent; buy the stock and wait until it falls by x percent from a subsequent peak. At that time, close the long position and establish a short position. By varying the value of x, traders would be able to measure their ability to outperform the market, that is, their ability to capitalize on a price move resulting from the momentum set by an earlier move in the same direction.

Alexander discovered that his filter rule worked, only, however, to have Fama[18]

[15] **Maurice G. Kendall,** "The Analysis of Economic Time Series I." *Journal of the Royal Statistical Society.* Series A, vol. 116 (1953), pp. 11–25.

[16] **M. F. M. Osborne,** "Brownian Motion in the Stock Market," *Operations Research.* vol. 7 (March–April 1959), pp. 145–173.

[17] **Sidney S. Alexander,** "Price Movements in Speculative Markets: Trends or Random Walks." *Industrial Management Review,* vol. 2 (May 1961), pp. 7–26; also **S. Alexander,** "Price Movements in Speculative Markets: Trends or Random Walks, No. 2." *Industrial Management Review,* vol. 5 (Spring 1964), pp. 25–46.

[18] **Eugene F. Fama,** "The Behavior of Stock Market Prices." *Journal of Business,* vol. 38, no. 1 (January 1965), pp. 34–105.

and Fama and Blume[19] point out that he had incorrectly accounted for dividends and failed to include transactions costs in his calculations. Once these factors were taken into consideration and buying and selling prices were made to reflect realistic market opportunities, all profits from the filter rule evaporated.

While the filter rule measures the extent of positive serial correlation in price changes, it fails to detect price reversals. Negative serial correlation could confirm that and would allow for higher rates of return if accurately gauged. Serial correlation measures the relationship between a price change and preceding price changes:

$$\rho(\Delta P_t, \quad \Delta P_{t-k})$$

where k = length of lag

Test conducted by M. Osborne,[20] H. Roberts,[21] and A. Moore[22] confirmed the absence of serial correlation. The stock market follows a random walk.

Could it be that the market is random overall but not over specific spans of time? Runs tests were used to determine whether successive price changes are consistent with random walk. The results indicate that the market is efficient in a weak sense.

Robert Levy[23] set out to test the validity of bar charts as a predictive tool. His test was conducted between July 3, 1964, and July 14, 1969, on 548 stocks listed on the NYSE. None of the 32 stock-price patterns tested outperformed the naive buy-and-hold strategy. Indeed, once transactions costs were accounted for, the patterns were found to give the wrong signals as to the direction of the market.

Some analysts argue that trends in earnings lead to a trend in stock prices if the following equation holds:

$$\mathrm{MP}_0^s = \sum_{t=1}^{n} \frac{D_t}{(1 + K_e)^t}$$

The evidence suggests however, that earnings follow a martingale process which generates independent series of earnings changes behaving as a series of random numbers; that is, there is no trend or pattern to changes in earnings. The evidence overwhelmingly supports the randomness of earnings.[24] A few important exceptions reported by R.

[19] **Eugene F. Fama** and **Marshall E. Blume,** "Filter Rules and Stock Market Trading." *Journal of Business,* vol. 39, no. 1, part 2 (January 1966), pp. 226–241.

[20] **M. F. M. Osborne,** "Brownian Motion in the Stock Market." *Operations Research,* vol. 7 (March–April 1959), pp. 145–173.

[21] **Harry V. Roberts,** "Stock Market 'Patterns' and Financial Analysis Methodological Suggestions." *Journal of Finance,* vol. 14, no. 1 (March 1959), pp. 1–10.

[22] **Arnold B. Moore,** "A Statistical Analysis of Common Stock Prices." Unpublished doctoral dissertation, University of Chicago, 1962.

[23] **Robert Levy,** "The Predictive Significance of Five-Point Chart Patterns." *Journal of Business,* vol. 44, no. 3 (July 1971), pp. 316–334.

[24] See Chapter 6 and the following:
I. M. D. Little, "Higgledy Piggledy Growth." *Bulletin of the Oxford University Institute of Economics and Statistics,* vol. 24, no. 4 (November 1966), pp. 389–412.
J. Lintner and **R. Glauber,** "Higgledy Piggledy Growth in America." Paper presented at the

Brealey[25] and R. Watts[26] are worth noting. Firms with the least fluctuation in earnings were found by Brealey to have significant nonrandomness in earnings. Similar findings were reported by Watts when he analyzed a subsample of 6 firms out of a sample of 32 firms. Generalizations about the randomness of earnings must be avoided.

More studies have been performed recently on the issue of randomness. We discuss their contents in Chapter 6. Suffice it to say that recent work has not resolved the controversy over randomness of earnings and stock prices. Indeed, these studies may have fueled it.

4.8 THE SEMISTRONG EFFICIENT MARKET

The semistrong efficient market requires randomness of stock prices and, in addition, that the market price of a stock reflect all publicly available information.

The efficiency tests should, therefore, consist of measuring the ability of the market to anticipate new information and the speed with which it adjusts to such data.

R. Ball and P. Brown[27] analyzed the effects of annual earnings announcements on stock prices. Their purpose was to see if the market had correctly anticipated earnings changes prior to their public announcement. Using a sample of 261 corporations, they found that, over a 20-year period, earnings were correctly anticipated.

M. Scholes[28] attempted to measure the price effects of secondary offerings on stock prices. He found that stock prices declined between 1 and 2 percent, but he attributed this decline to the information contents of the offering. That is, the market is efficient because it adjusts quickly to new information.

James Millar[29] studied whether stock splits and stock dividends have a differing effect on stock prices. Efficient markets require that they should have the same effects, since they are practically the same thing. His findings were that stock splits and stock dividends caused "no particular difference in stock price behavior," and his conclusion was that "the investing market appears to be efficient."[30]

The effect of stock splits on stock prices were judged neutral to positive until Cope-

---

seminar on the analysis of security prices, Graduate School of Business, University of Chicago, May 11–12, 1967.

R. H. Trent, "Corporate Growth Rates: An Analysis of Their Intertemporal Association." *Southern Journal of Business,* vol. 4 (October 1969), pp. 196–210.

R. A. Brealey, *An Introduction to Risk and Return from Common Stocks.* Cambridge, Mass., MIT Press, 1969.

R. Ball and R. Watts, "Sometime Series Properties of Accounting Income." *Journal of Finance,* vol. 27 (June 1972), pp. 663–681.

[25] Brealey, pp. 98–100.

[26] R. Watts, "The Informational Content of Dividends." Graduate School of Business, University of Chicago, October 1970, appendix A.

[27] Ray Ball and Philip Brown, "An Empirical Evaluation of Accounting Income Numbers." *Journal of Accounting Research,* vol. 6 (Autumn 1968), pp. 159–178.

[28] Myron S. Scholes, "The Market for Securities: Substitution Versus Price Pressure and the Effects of Information on Share Prices." *Journal of Business,* vol. 45, no. 2 (April 1972), pp. 179–211.

[29] James A. Millar, "Split or Dividend: Do the Words Really Matter?" *Accounting Review,* vol. 52, no. 1 (January 1977), pp. 52–55.

[30] Ibid., p. 55.

land[31] reported his findings. Copeland reported that the increase in the number of securities held led to higher transactions costs (commission costs and bid-ask spreads as percent of value increased) and lower net rate of return to holders of securities. This is an indication of market inefficiency.

The fundamental conclusion of Copeland was supported by a recent study by F. Reilly and E. Drzycimski.[32] While providing support for Copeland, the study contradicts earlier studies, which showed that abnormal profits resulted from stock splits indicating market inefficiency.[33] After examining daily price movements and volume changes surrounding the stock split of 130 common NYSE-listed stocks that split two for one during the 1964–1976 period, Reilly and Drzycimski concluded that:

> *In general, the results consistently supported the semi-strong efficient market hypothesis, because they indicate that stock prices either adjusted prior to or very shortly after the public announcement of stock splits. The results indicate that abnormal profits were not available to the general public or to professionals who had to pay normal transaction costs. The results do not support the strong form EMH [efficient market hypothesis], because it appears that abnormal profits are available to investors with inside information about the forthcoming split announcement.*
>
> *A small caveat appears to be in order at this point. Throughout the discussion of profit opportunities, we referred to normal transactions costs of 2%. Clearly the results would be different for investors who were not required to pay the normal commission, such as floor traders on the Exchange. Also, with the requirement of fully negotiated commissions on May 1, 1975 ("May Day"), the normal discount for institutions has been approximately 40% from the fixed commission schedule in effect on May 1, 1975. Also individuals who trade actively in large amounts can likewise derive discounts from proclaimed "discount brokers." Therefore, the standard 2% is probably above the current "normal" transactions cost. While different results are then possible, most of the results we have found would hold, except in the case of those investors with substantially lower costs, because the abnormal returns were typically less than 1.5%.[34]*

A recent study by Stewart Brown set out to improve on the analysis of Ball and Brown. The responsiveness of the market to earnings per share (EPS) announcements was different from expected EPS for periods shorter than one month. The results of the study do not support the efficient market hypothesis. S. Brown found that:

[31] **Thomas E. Copeland,** "Liquidity Changes Following Stock Splits." *Journal of Finance,* March 1979.

[32] **Frank K. Reilly** and **Eugene F. Drzycimski,** "Short-Run Profits from Stock Splits." *Financial Management,* vol. 10, no. 3 (Summer 1981), pp. 64–74.

[33] See **P. Kimball** and **R. Papera,** "Effect of Stock Splits on Short-Term Market Prices." *Financial Analyst's Journal,* May–June 1964, pp. 75–80.

James A. Millar and **Bruce D. Fielitz,** "Stock Split and Stock-Dividend Dimensions." *Financial Management,* Winter 1973, pp. 35–45.

Anna Merjos, "Sell on the News—When Stock Split Take the Money and Run." *Barron's,* May 31, 1976, pp. 11, 16–17.

Guy Charest, "Split Information, Stock Returns and Market Efficiency." *Journal of Financial Economics,* June/September, 1978, pp. 265–296.

[34] **Reilly** and **Drzycimski,** pp. 73–74.

> *Based on the sample of securities chosen, results indicate that the announcement of unusual EPS significantly affects stock prices, that the prices do not adjust instantaneously, and that an abnormal return in excess of transaction costs could be earned by using the forecast models.*[35]

The lengthy (45 days) adjustment process to EPS announcements and the higher rates of returns realized from purchasing "qualifying" securities point to inefficient securities markets.

A study supporting the efficient market hypothesis was undertaken by George Pinches and J. Clay Singleton.[36] Using 207 bond-rating changes (111 upgraded, 96 downgraded), the authors conclude that the evidence supports their hypothesis that abnormally high (low) returns on common stocks do accrue prior to the announcement of a bond-rating change. Also supported is the hypothesis that abnormally high (low) returns are expected prior to the change in rating, to be followed by normal returns after the month of the rating change. The acceptance of these hypotheses indicates that the market had correctly anticipated rating changes and that "reliance on bond rating changes as an early warning of impending financial difficulty appears to be questionable investment management strategy."[37]

In conclusion it can be said, based on the weight of the evidence, that the stock market is efficient in the semistrong sense.

4.9 THE STRONGLY EFFICIENT MARKET

Stock prices in a strongly efficient market should reflect all information, whether available to the public or not. The securities markets must, therefore, be perfect and not merely efficient.

To test the validity of the hypothesis, several academicians concentrated on the performance of professional managers. Do their portfolios earn a higher rate of return on a consistent basis? The evidence is almost uniformly negative. The most significant studies are those of I. Friend, M. Blume, and J. Crockett[38] and P. Williamson.[39] Both studies, covering essentially the same period (1960–1969 and 1961–1971, respectively), showed that the professional managers did not outperform the market. Williamson found that mutual fund managers exhibited superior abilities neither in the selection of securities nor in predicting the direction of the market. Mutual funds did not add to or subtract from market efficiency.

The extensive coverage given by *The Wall Street Journal* (Feb. 13, 1981) to a scheme (devised by two officers at Morgan Stanley and Lehman Brothers Kuhn & Loeb, Inc.) to capitalize on privileged information is but an illustration of the ease of uncovering

---

[35] **Stewart L. Brown**, "Earnings Changes, Stock Prices and Market Efficiency." *Journal of Finance,* vol. 33 (March 1978), pp. 17–18.

[36] **George E. Pinches** and **J. Clay Singleton**, "The Adjustment of Stock Prices to Bond Rating Changes." *Journal of Finance,* vol. 33, no. 1 (March 1978).

[37] Ibid., p. 41.

[38] **Irwin Friend, Marshall Blume,** and **Jean Crockett,** *Mutual Funds and Other Institutional Investors.* McGraw-Hill, New York, 1970.

[39] **Peter J. Williamson,** "Measuring Mutual Fund Performance." *Financial Analysts Journal,* November–December 1972, pp. 78–84.

evidence against the strongly efficient market. The officers would pass information to a market trader on pending merger deals. The trader, in turn, established positions in the securities of the target firm and split the resulting profits with the officers. More evidence of insider trading was provided by *The Wall Street Journal* only ten days later (Feb. 23, 1981).

The *Journal* also reported (Sept. 14, 1981) the activities of a law partner in Wachtell, Lipton, Rosen & Katz. The partner had placed stock orders based on inside information on merger cases in which his firm was involved. More transactions related to insider information were being investigated by the SEC, as again reported by the *Journal* (Oct. 27, 1981). The first of the two cases involved the Grumman Corporation, which allegedly tipped off the Madison Fund about planned purchases of Grumman stock by Grumman's pension fund. The second concerned the trading by a Kuwaiti investor in Sante Fe International, a merger target for Kuwait Petroleum Co.

Results from insiders' transactions should also provide additional evidence on the strongly efficient hypothesis. The SEC requires insiders (officers, directors, and stockholders with more than 5 percent beneficial ownership in the company) to report their transactions. These are reported in the *Official Summary of Insider Trading,* which is published by the SEC. What the summary fails to report on are transactions entered into by friends, relatives, or "partners" of insiders on the basis of tips from insiders. Nor does the *Summary* contain information on transactions entered into by insiders of one company but involving the security of another company, typically a competitor. An example of this is a short position established in the stock of Company X by an officer of its competitor, Company Y, based on the privileged knowledge that Company X has just lost a major contract to Company Y.

Extensive studies have been conducted on insider trading. The data used were those supplied by the SEC, which accounts only for transactions actually undertaken by insiders themselves and not any subsidiary transactions. The studies up to 1972 are summarized by Jeffrey Jaffe.[40] Most of the studies reported support the hypothesis that corporate insiders are able to outperform the market. Specifically Rogoff,[41] Glass,[42] Lorie and Niederhoffer[43] showed that insiders were able to outperform the market. Indeed, they were able to forecast the direction of stock prices six months in advance. Wu[44] and Driscoll[45] found no such evidence.

The study by Jaffe is most comprehensive and elegant, using a sample of 200 largest securities from the *Chicago Research in Security Prices* (CRSP) and observing insiders' transactions in five separate months during the 1962–1968 period. The five months were selected in accordance with a random process. Five random numbers (between

[40] **Jeffrey F. Jaffe,** "Special Information and Insider Trading." *Journal of Business,* July 1974.

[41] **Donald L. Rogoff,** "The Forecasting Properties of Insider Transactions." Unpublished doctoral dissertation, Michigan State University, 1964.

[42] **Gary S. Glass,** "Extensive Insider Accumulation as an Indicator of Near Term Stock Price Performance." Unpublished doctoral dissertation, Ohio State University, 1966.

[43] **James H. Lorie** and **Victor Niederhoffer,** "Predictive and Statistical Properties of Insider Trading." *Journal of Law Economics,* vol. 11 (April 1968), pp. 35–51.

[44] **Hsiu Wu,** "Corporate Insider Trading Profitability and Stock Price Movement." Unpublished doctoral dissertation, University of Pennsylvania, 1963.

[45] **Thomas E. Driscoll,** "Some Aspects of Corporate Insider Stock Holdings and Trading Under Section 16b of Securities and Exchange Act of 1934." Unpublished doctoral dissertation, University of Pennsylvania, 1963.

12 and 18) were picked and the five months were selected with the first month equal to the random number chosen, the second to the sum of the second random number with the first random number, and so on.

Jaffe examined the residuals of rates of returns on insider trading by looking at their magnitude and their randomness. His conclusions were that insiders were in fact able to outperform the market and that intensive trading (by a large number of insiders) yielded profits larger than commission costs.

F. Reilly and J. Nielsen[46] and F. Reilly and E. Drzycimski[47] analyzed the activities of the specialist who has access to privileged information regarding unfilled limit orders. Both studies found that the specialist is able to realize consistently above-average rates of return through block trades and in reacting to unexpected world events. This evidence rejects the strongly efficient market hypothesis.

It can be said, in conclusion, that the evidence presented here, combined with what is generally known about illegal or unethical transactions, offers considerable proof against the validity of the strongly efficient hypothesis.

CONCLUSIONS

The evidence presented in this chapter indicates that markets are efficient in a weak and semistrong sense. Of what value, then, is technical analysis? The vindication of the technical hypothesis lies in its usefulness in *timing* stock purchases or sales. As stock prices fluctuate around their intrinsic value, financial opportunities present themselves. The ability of an investor to capitalize on these opportunities is enhanced by a thorough knowledge of technical analysis. There exists no other trading tool in the very short run, for fundamentals rarely change that dramatically and that swiftly; yet stock prices are almost never stagnant for an extended period. This tempts many traders to make that extra effort in the hope of wrenching extra returns from the market.

QUESTIONS

1. Why should an investor be concerned with the efficiency of the market? Explain.

2. Are there levels of efficiency? What are they? Is the concept of efficiency sufficiently developed and understood?

3. Of what value is an investment course if markets are efficient?

4. What are the fundamental premises of technical analysis? Do any of their tools appeal to you? Why?

5. What are the foundations of fundamental analysis?

---

[46] **Frank K. Reilly** and **James F. Nielsen,** "The Specialist and Large Block Trades on the NYSE." Paper presented at the Southern Finance Association meeting, Atlanta, Georgia, November, 1974.

[47] **Frank K. Reilly** and **Eugene F. Drzycimski,** "The Stock Exchange Specialist and the Market Impact of Major World Events." *Financial Analysts Journal,* vol. 31, no. 4 (July–August, 1975), pp. 27–32.

6. Could fundamental analysis be used for trading stocks (active short-term trading)? Why?

7. What is the most effective way to utilize technical analysis?

8. Investors and speculators continue to use technical analysis despite the overwhelming evidence offered by academicians that markets are efficient. Why?

9. The tests of technical tools cover those tools that are in the public eye. Sophisticated traders who may have devised profitable trading strategies would obviously choose not to talk about them. How might disclosure of the presence of such tools affect our conclusions about the efficiency of the market?

10. What are the conditions for an efficient market?

11. Can the stock market ever be strongly efficient? Is the evidence (for or against) market efficiency hard to find? Can you recall instances indicating market inefficiencies?

12. Outline some drawbacks of relying on the P/E ratio to determine a stock's potential.

13. From the evidence discussed in the chapter, can you conclude that the stock market is efficient in a semistrong sense? What implications does this have for the trading strategies of the investor?

14. Does the conclusion that the market is efficient in the long run merit much attention, or should our focus be on short-run efficiency (inefficiency)?

15. Do you expect capital markets in small European nations to be more or less efficient than the U.S. capital market? Why?

16. How can the technician use volume of trading to determine when to enter/exit the market?

17. John Brilliant has just sold his stock which he held for a year at a substantial profit. His rate of return was 60 percent, while the average rate of return in the market was 15 percent. Could you consider this as evidence of an inefficient market?

18. If the strategy that positions opposite to those of odd lot traders pays off, what are the implications for market efficiency?

19. A chimp tosses ten darts at the stock quotations listed in *The Wall Street Journal.* The securities hit are then purchased. If the portfolio's returns exceed the average returns on similar-risk portfolios, does this support market efficiency? Market inefficiency?

20. The stock market appears to be divided into two segments, (1) stocks purchased by individuals and institutions to be included in portfolios and (2) stocks whose companies are takeover targets. The latter trade at a substantial premium above their price levels prior to revelation of the takeover. Is this fact in and of itself indicative of market inefficiency? Why?

PART
TWO

Portfolio Theory

CHAPTER 5 | Risk and Utility

5.1 INTRODUCTION

Investment requires a commitment now against a future outcome, or a future set of outcomes that are thought to be consistent with the wealth maximization of the investor. The predictability of future outcomes varies depending on the nature of the outcome, the stock of available information about it, the party with influence upon the outcome, and the background and clairvoyance of the investor.

Two states of the world may be distinguished: uncertainty and risk. Uncertainty is a state in which the investor simply has no knowledge whatever about the future outcomes or their probabilities of occurrence. In a state of risk, the investor knows the probability distribution of future outcomes. Complete uncertainty means that the individual does not know and cannot guess the probability of occurrence of an event; complete certainty means a probability of occurrence equal to one.

Armed with the probability distribution, investors are able to speak of, for example, the expected return on a given security. Their risk stems from the deviation of the realized return from the expected return. In this chapter, we focus on risk and on the attitude of investors towards risk.

5.2 TYPES OF RISKS

An investor is subject to a variety of risks. Among them are the following.

Interest-Rate Risk

This risk stems from the variability in the level of interest rates. As rates change, bonds with fixed coupon payments experience price changes, as is demonstrated in Chapter 10.

Default Risk

The probability of failure by the debt insurer to meet interest and/or principal obligations represents default risk. Stocks may also experience price-level changes to the extent that their rates of return are correlated with those on bonds.

Price-Level Risk

Changes in the inflation rate produce uncertainty about the real income from an investment and, consequently, about its present or market value and its future value as well. Since all interest rates have an inflation component, unpredictable rates of inflation would mean unpredictable rates of interest as well. Chapter 16 also demonstrates the impact of inflation on currency values.

Business Risk

Business risk is inherent in the operations of a firm or industry. The steel industry is more susceptible to changes in economic conditions than the food industry is. This "cyclicality" is inherent in the steel industry and can thus have an impact on its rate of return and on the value of securities it issues.

Financial Risk

Financial risk is the risk resulting from leverage. The higher the percentage of a firm's assets financed by debt, the greater the probability of insolvency or bankruptcy and the greater the riskiness of the firm. This riskiness is compensated for by higher rates of return on the securities issued by the firm.

Liquidity Risk

Liquidity risk results from poor synchronization (either unanticipated or due to inefficient management) of a firm's cash flows.

Market Risk

Market risk results from the impact of market conditions on the operations of a firm or on the value of its securities. The higher the correlation between the rates of return on a given security and those on an index representative of the market, the greater the market risk. This is discussed in great detail in Chapter 6.

Operating Risk

Operating risk is a function of the fixed charges in the firm's operations. The higher fixed costs are, the higher the operating leverage and the higher the operating risk. This is so because a firm with high operating leverage would require higher sales levels in order to reach its break-even point (zero profit point).

5.3 MEASUREMENT OF RISK

Risk is measured using semivariance, variance, covariance, and other methods.

Semivariance

Semivariance is the weighted sum of squared negative (−) deviations of a random variable X from a chosen value A. If $X_1, \ldots , X_n$ are the possible values of X, with probabilities $P_1, \ldots , P_n$ respectively of occurring, then

$$S_A = \sum_i ((X_i - A)^-)^2 \cdot P_i$$

or alternatively:

$$S_A = \sum_{X_i < A} (X_i - A)^2 \cdot P_i \tag{5.1}$$

The emphasis on negative deviation is consistent with the concept of risk aversion. An investor with a targeted rate of return of 20 percent is concerned with the realized rate X falling short of 20 percent $= A$. Any return in excess of 20 percent is an unexpected pleasure.

Semivariance suffers from lack of recognition and the arbitrariness of A. Also, some investors may wish to know the upside potential of their investment (realizing a rate of return in excess of the expected rate) in addition to its downside risk. Semivariance does not afford this result, for it concentrates on the left side of the distribution.

Variance

The variance of a random variable X is the weighted sum of its squared deviations from its mean value μ. That is, we define the variance of X to be

$$\sigma_X^2 = \sum_i (X_i - \mu)^2 P_i$$
$$= E[(X_i - \mu)^2] \tag{5.2}$$

where μ = mean value of the distribution of returns
  = first moment of the probability distribution
  $= E(X) = \sum_i X_i P_i$

An equivalent formula for the variance derived from Equation 5.2 is:

$$\sigma_X^2 = E(X - \mu)^2$$
$$= E(X^2 - 2\mu X + \mu^2)$$
$$= E(X^2) - 2\mu E(X) + E(\mu^2)$$
$$= E(X^2) - 2\mu^2 + \mu^2$$
$$= E(X^2) - \mu^2$$

$$= E(X^2) - [E(X)]^2 \qquad (5.3)$$

= expected value of the squared random variable minus the square of the expected value

The square root of σ_X^2 is known as the standard deviation σ_X.

Example

Calculate the variance of the rates of return on a common stock with the following outcomes and associated probabilities.

Rates of Return (R)	P_i
8%	0.25
10%	0.50
12%	0.25

Solution

(1)	(2)	(3) = (1)(2)	(4) = (1)²	(5) = (4)(2)
R_i	P_i	$E(R)$	R^2	$E(R^2)$
8	0.25	2	64	16
10	0.50	5	100	50
12	0.25	3	144	36
		10	**308**	**102**

$$\sigma_R^2 = E(R^2) - [E(R)]^2$$
$$= 102 - (10)^2 = 2$$
$$\sigma_R = \text{standard deviation} = \sqrt{\sigma_R^2}$$
$$= \sqrt{2} = 1.414\%$$

If we assume that the random variable R is not limited to just three values but instead can vary over an interval of possibilities, then it likely has the well-known "normal" (bell-shaped) probability distribution, shown in Figure 5.1.

$$\mu \pm 1\sigma = 8.586 \text{ to } 11.414$$

If σ_R is still 1.414 percent, then about 68 percent of the total probability distribution is contained in the range 8.586 to 11.414.

A flatter distribution indicates greater risk (that is, a larger value for σ_R); and a tighter distribution, lower risk, as in Figure 5.2. There, C is riskier than B which is riskier than A.

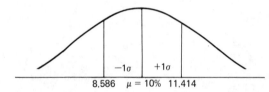

FIGURE 5.1 Normal or bell-shaped probability distribution.

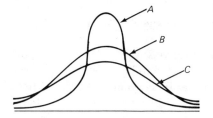

FIGURE 5.2 Tighter distribution, indicating lower risk.

Variance of bX

The variance of bX where b is a constant is, as the student should be able to verify using Equation 5.3, equal to

$$\sigma^2(bX) = b^2\sigma_X^2 \qquad (5.4)$$

Variance of $(X_1 + X_2)$

Using Equation 5.3, we calculate the variance of two random variables X_1 and X_2 as follows:

$$
\begin{aligned}
\sigma^2_{(X_1+X_2)} &= E\{[(X_1 + X_2) - E(X_1 + X_2)]^2\} \\
&= E[(X_1 - \mu_1) + (X_2 - \mu_2)]^2 \\
&= E[(X_1 - \mu_1)^2 + (X_2 - \mu_2)^2 + 2(X_1 - \mu_1)(X_2 - \mu_2)] \\
&= E(X_1 - \mu_1)^2 + E(X_2 - \mu_2)^2 + 2E[(X_1 - \mu_1)(X_2 - \mu_2)] \\
&= \sigma_1^2 + \sigma_2^2 + 2E[(X_1 - \mu_1)(X_2 - \mu_2)] \qquad (5.5)
\end{aligned}
$$

$\sigma^2_{(X_1+X_2)} =$ the variance of X_1
           + the variance of X_2
           + twice the covariance of X_1 with X_2

This derivation leads us to the discussion on covariance.

Covariance

Covariance is a measure of the extent to which two variables move together or in opposite directions. If two variables are independent, their covariance is equal to zero. A positive covariance means that the two variables tend to move in the same direction; a negative covariance means that they tend to move in opposite directions. We define the covariance between X_1 and X_2 as follows:

$$\sigma_{12} = E[(X_1 - \mu_1)(X_2 - \mu_2)] \qquad (5.6)$$

Rewriting Equation 5.5, we get

$$
\begin{aligned}
\sigma^2_{(X_1+X_2)} &= \sigma_1^2 + \sigma_2^2 + 2\sigma_{12} \\
&= \sigma_1^2 + \sigma_2^2 + 2\rho\sigma_1\sigma_2
\end{aligned}
$$

where $\rho = $ correlation coefficient

= a measure of the strength of the relationship and its nature

By definition, $\rho = \sigma_{12}/\sigma_1\sigma_2$. It can be proven mathematically that ρ always lies in the interval from -1 to 1. If $\rho = +1$, the two variables are said to be perfectly positively correlated. This happens if and only if X_2 is an exact linear function of X_1, with positive slope $X_2 = aX_1 + b$ where $a > 0$. In this (extreme) case, X_2 is completely determined by X_1, and an increase of 5 percent in X_1 produces an increase of 5 percent in the quantity $X_2 - b$. If $\rho = -1$, the two variables are said to be perfectly negatively correlated, which occurs when X_2 is an exact linear function of X_1, with negative slope $X_2 = aX_1 + b$ where $a < 0$. If the two variables are independent, then $\rho = 0$ and Equation 5.5 reduces to

$$\sigma^2_{(X_1+X_2)} = \sigma_1^2 + \sigma_2^2 \tag{5.7}$$

Similarly, if we have n independent variables, then

$$\sigma^2_{(X_1+X_2+\ldots+X_n)} = \sigma_1^2 + \sigma_2^2 + \ldots + \sigma_n^2 \tag{5.8}$$

The general formulation for the variance of the sum of n random variables is:

$$\sigma_Y^2 = \sum_{ij} \sum \sigma_{ij} = \underset{i=J}{\sum_i \sigma_i^2} + \underset{i \neq J}{\sum_i \sum_j \sigma_{ij}} \tag{5.9}$$

where $Y = X_1 + X_2 + X_3 + \ldots + X_n$

If $Y = W_1X_1 + W_2X_2 + \ldots + W_nX_n$ where the W's are constants, then Equation 5.9 can be rewritten, based on the principle established in Equation 5.5, as follows:

$$\sigma_Y^2 = \sum_{i=1}^n W_i^2\sigma_i^2 + 2\sum\sum_{i<j} W_iW_j\sigma_{ij} \tag{5.10}$$

$$\sigma_Y^2 = \sum_{i=1}^n W_i^2\sigma_i^2 + 2\sum\sum_{i<J} W_iW_j\rho\sigma_i\sigma_j \tag{5.11}$$

If $\rho = 0$ for each pair X_i, X_j $(i \neq j)$, then

$$\sigma_Y^2 = \sum_{i=1}^n W_i^2\sigma_i^2$$

Other Risk Measures

Other risk measures that have been utilized are as follows:

1. Probability of occurrence of an event. An investor focuses in this case on the probability of realizing a negative rate of return, or a rate of return below the desired rate of return.

2. The semiinterquartile range. The semiinterquartile range, occasionally referred to as the quartile deviation (QD), is a measure of dispersion between the upper and lower quartiles of a distribution. It is the difference between the seventy-fifth percentile (Q_3) of a distribution and the twenty-fifth percentile (Q_1) divided by 2.

$$QD = \frac{1}{2}(Q_3 - Q_1)$$

If the distribution is normal, the range values of the QD covers the middle half of the distribution, that is, 25 percent of the observations will fall below the mean and 25 percent above the mean.

3. Skewness measure. Skewness represents the case of a nonsymmetric distribution about the mean value of a random variable. When the mean of the distribution is greater than the median, the distribution is said to be skewed to the right; that is, the mean gives an exaggerated measure of the location of the "center" of the distribution (Fig. 5.3).

If, on the other hand, the median is larger than the mean, the distribution is said to be skewed to the left (Fig. 5.4); that is, the observations are bunching above the mean.

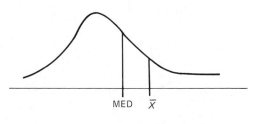

MED $\overline{X}$

FIGURE 5.3 Distribution skewed to the right.

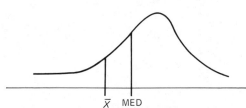

$\overline{X}$ MED

FIGURE 5.4 Distribution skewed to the left.

These risk measures are useful, but cannot be easily incorporated in a comprehensive risk evaluation model.

Portfolio Risk

A portfolio represents a collection of securities. Our discussion will concentrate on portfolios made up of only two securities, so that the mathematics as well as the graphic presentations are made easier.

Consider an investor with $\$A$ to invest. Two securities are available to him. The percentage of A he would commit to each security is represented by W_i (where $i =$

1,2). If he chooses to invest all of A in the first security, then $W_1 = 1$. If A is invested in the second security, than $W_2 = 1$. In any case, the constraint is that:

$$W_1 + W_2 = 1 \qquad\qquad (5.12)$$

We shall also assume that short sales are permitted (see Chapter 3). Therefore, W_1 or W_2 can assume negative values. If $W_1 = -3$, assuming short sellers have access to the proceeds from the short sale, then W_2 must equal 4 if the constraint $W_1 + W_2 = 1$ is binding. The feasible combinations of securities 1 and 2, therefore, if $W_1 + W_2 = 1$, lie along line ab (Figure 5.5), with a short position in one of the securities possible. The line segment designated by 1, 1 represents the feasible set if $0 \leq W_1 \leq 1, 0 \leq W_2 \leq 1$ and if $W_1 + W_2 = 1$; that is, a short position in neither security is possible.

Assume now that the expected rate of return from the first security is equal to $E(R_1)$ and that from the second security to $E(R_2)$. Let R_P be the rate of return on the entire portfolio. Then it is easy to see that $R_P = W_1R_1 + W_2R_2$. It follows that the expected rate of return on the portfolio is equal to

$$E(R_p) = \sum_i W_i E(R_i) = W_1 E(R_1) + W_2 E(R_2) \qquad\qquad (5.13)$$

FIGURE 5.5 **Graphic representation of an investment portfolio.**

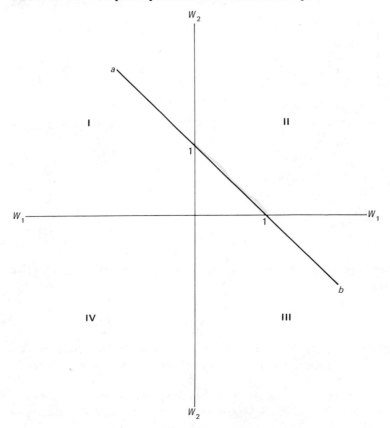

The variance of the portfilio would equal to:

$$\sigma_p^2 = W_1^2\sigma_1^2 + W_2^2\sigma_2^2 + 2W_1W_2\sigma_{12}$$
$$= W_1^2\sigma_1^2 + (1 - W_1)^2\sigma_2^2 + 2W_1(1 - W_1)\,\rho\sigma_1\sigma_2 \qquad (5.14)$$

since $W_1 + W_2 = 1$, $W_2 = 1 - W_1$, and $\sigma_{12} = \rho\sigma_1\sigma_2$.

Armed with Equations 5.13 and 5.14, we calculate $E(R_p)$ and σ_p assuming that

$$\sigma_1^2 = 16, \sigma_1 = 4 \qquad \sigma_2^2 = 9, \sigma_2 = 3$$
$$E(R_1) = 12\% \qquad E(R_2) = 8\%$$

These calculations are made under three assumptions for the value of ρ: $\rho = 0$, $\rho = -1$, and $\rho = +1$. The results are shown in Table 5.1.

For values of $\rho = +1$ and $\rho = -1$, the relationship between $E(R_p)$ and σ_p is linear (here, $E(R_1)$, $E(R_2)$, σ_1, and σ_2 are fixed; W_1 varies, $W_2 = 1 - W_1$). The proof of this when $\rho = +1$ is as follows:

$$\sigma_p^2 = W_1^2\sigma_1^2 + (1 - W_1)^2\sigma_2^2 + 2W_1(1 - W_1)\sigma_1\sigma_2$$

$$\sigma_p = \sqrt{[W_1\sigma_1 + (1 - W_1)\sigma_2]^2} = W_1\sigma_1 + (1 - W_1)\sigma_2 \qquad (5.15)$$

Therefore $W_1 = (\sigma_p - \sigma_2)/(\sigma_1 - \sigma_2)$.

Replacing W_1 in $E(R_p) = W_1E(R_1) + (1 - W_1)E(R_2)$ by its value, we get

TABLE 5.1

	No Short Position Permitted							Short Position Is Possible				
$\rho = 0$												
W_1	0	.2	.4	.428	.6	.8	1.0	−.5	−1	−3	2	1.5
W_2	1	.8	.6	.572	.4	.2	0	+1.5	+2	+4	−1	−.5
$E(R_p)$	8%	8.8	9.6	9.71	10.4	11.2	12	6	4	−4	16	14
σ_p	3	2.53	2.41	2.42	2.68	3.25	4	4.92	7.21	16.97	8.54	6.18
$\rho = -1$												
W_1	0	.2	.4	.428	.6	.8	1.0	−.5	−1	−3	2	1.5
W_2	1	.8	.6	.572	.4	.2	0	1.5	+2	+4	−1	−.5
$E(R_p)$	8%	8.8	9.6	9.71	10.4	11.2	12	6	4	−4	16	14
σ_p	3	2.77	.20	0	1.2	2.95	4	6.5	10	16.97	7	7.5
$\rho = +1$												
W_1	0	.2	.4	.428	.6	.8	1.0	−.5	−1	−3	2	1.5
W_2	1	.8	.6	.572	.4	.2	0	1.5	+2	+4	−1	−.5
$E(R_p)$	8%	8.8	9.6	9.71	10.4	11.2	12	6	4	−4	16	14
σ_p	3	3.2	3.4	3.428	3.6	3.8	4	2.5	2	0	9.85	4.5

$$E(R_p) = E(R_1)\left(\frac{\sigma_p - \sigma_2}{\sigma_1 - \sigma_2}\right) + E(R_2)\left[1 - \left(\frac{\sigma_p - \sigma_2}{\sigma_1 - \sigma_2}\right)\right]$$

$$E(R_p) = \left[E(R_2) - \frac{E(R_1) - E(R_2)}{\sigma_1 - \sigma_2}\sigma_2\right] + \left[\frac{E(R_1) - E(R_2)}{\sigma_1 - \sigma_2}\right]\sigma_p \qquad (5.16)$$

The relationship between $E(R_p)$ and σ_p is, therefore, linear. The proof of the linear relationship where $\rho = -1$ is more difficult:

$$\sigma_p^2 = W_1^2\sigma_1^2 + (1 - W_1)^2\sigma_2^2 - 2W_1(1 - W_1)\sigma_1\sigma_2$$
$$\sigma_p^2 = (W_1\sigma_1 - (1 - W_1)\sigma_2)^2$$
$$\sigma_p = \pm[W_1\sigma_1 - (1 - W_1)\sigma_2]$$

Therefore:

$$\sigma_p = W_1\sigma_1 - (1 - W_1)\sigma_2, \text{ so } W_1 = \frac{\sigma_p + \sigma_2}{\sigma_1 + \sigma_2} \qquad (5.17)$$

or

$$\sigma_p = -W_1\sigma_1 + (1 - W_1)\sigma_2, \text{ so } W_1 = \frac{\sigma_2 - \sigma_p}{\sigma_1 - \sigma_2} \qquad (5.18)$$

Replacing the W_1's by their values in $E(R_p)$, we get

$$E(R_p) = W_1E(R_1) + (1 - W_1)E(R_2)$$

(1) $E(R_p) = E(R_1)\left(\dfrac{\sigma_p + \sigma_2}{\sigma_1 + \sigma_2}\right) + \left[1 - \left(\dfrac{\sigma_p + \sigma_2}{\sigma_1 + \sigma_2}\right)\right]E(R_2)$

(2) $E(R_p) = E(R_1)\left(\dfrac{\sigma_2 - \sigma_p}{\sigma_1 + \sigma_2}\right) + \left[1 - \left(\dfrac{\sigma_2 - \sigma_p}{\sigma_1 + \sigma_2}\right)\right]E(R_2)$

or, alternatively,

(1) $E(R_p) = \left[E(R_2) + \dfrac{E(R_1) + E(R_2)}{\sigma_1 + \sigma_2}\sigma_2\right] + \dfrac{[E(R_1) - E(R_2)]}{\sigma_1 + \sigma_2}\sigma_p \qquad (5.19)$

(2) $E(R_p) = \left[E(R_2) + \dfrac{E(R_1) - E(R_2)}{\sigma_1 + \sigma_2}\sigma_2\right] + \left[\dfrac{E(R_2) - E(R_1)}{\sigma_1 + \sigma_2}\right]\sigma_p \qquad (5.20)$

Therefore, when $\rho = -1$, two linear relationships prevail between $E(R_p)$ and σ_p. Since $E(R_1)$, $E(R_2)$, σ_1, and σ_2 are observable, the calculation of σ_p and $E(R_p)$ becomes very easy.

The linear relationship between $E(R_p)$ and σ_p is further confirmed by Table 5.1. When $\rho = 1$, the portfolio standard deviation is simply the weighted average of the standard deviation of the individual securities. There are no diversification effects.

Plotting $E(R_p)$ against σ_p for $\rho = \pm 1$ and $\rho = 0$, we get (assuming no short position) Figure 5.6.

When $\rho = 0$, the relationship between $E(R_p)$ and σ_p is curvilinear.

It is left as an exercise to the reader to extend Table 5.1 for cases where $\rho = 0.5$ or any other value between -1 and $+1$ (except 0). The reader would find that if $\rho = 0.5$, the relationship would be approximated by the dotted curve in Figure 5.6.

From Table 5.1, we can also observe the following:

1. Every short position in the first security ($W_1 < 0$) yields rates of return that are dominated by any of the expected rates of return where a short position is not permitted. Additionally, the standard deviations of the short position are higher than those of the no-short position when $\rho = 0$ and $\rho = -1$. The lower standard deviations when $\rho = +1$ (short positions are permitted) produce very low expected rates of return—indeed, negative expected rates of return in some cases. The exceptions to this occur when the short position is established in the security with the lower expected rate of return and when $W_1 \geq |W_2|$. This is illustrated by the $W_1 = 1.5$, $W_2 = -0.5$ case. Note, however, that while succeeding in improving the expected rate of return on the portfolio, the short position ($W_2 = -0.5$) produces higher risk than otherwise would be the case if both $1 \geq W_1$ and $W_2 \geq 0$. The impact of a short position is shown in Figure 5.7, assuming $\rho = 0.5$.

Point 1 represents the case where $W_2 = 0$ and $W_1 = 1$. Point 2 represents the case where $W_2 = 1$ and $W_1 = 0$. Point 2 represents also the minimum risk for the 8 percent expected return. No combinations of W's can produce a superior tradeoff. Indeed, certain combinations of long and short positions would produce simultaneously higher risk and lower rates of return (segment 2–a in Figure 5.7).

It can be concluded, therefore, that certain short positions could improve returns only if the investor accepts the higher risk (segment 1–b). There is no free lunch.

2. If short positions are not permitted, the maximum return, regardless of the values of W_1 and W_2, is that rate on the higher yielding security. The minimum portfolio variance is achieved when $\rho = -1$, $\sigma_p = 0$.

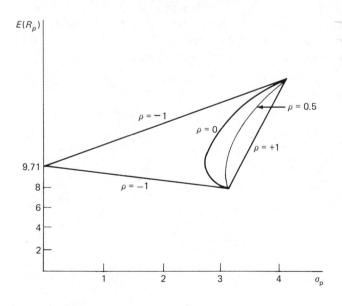

FIGURE 5.6 **Graphic representation of an investment strategy.**

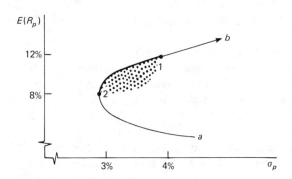

FIGURE 5.7   **The effect of a short position.**

3. Segment 2–1 in Figure 5.7 represents that combination offering the best risk/return tradeoff for a given value of ρ ($\rho = 0.5$ in this case); for certain known values of σ_1, σ_2, $E(R_1)$; $E(R_2)$; and for all conceivable combinations of W_1 and W_2 with $W_1 \geq 0$, $W_2 \geq 0$ and $W_1 + W_2 = 1$. This is the *efficiency frontier* for the no-short case.

An efficiency frontier is that locus of points where for a given level of risk the investor receives the highest rate of return and for a given level of return the investor assumes the lowest possible risk.

4. Segment 2–1–*b* in Figure 5.7 represents the efficiency frontier where combinations of long positions or of short and long positions are possible.

The reason for choosing a value of $\rho = 0.5$ is because the extreme values of $\rho = \pm 1$ or zero used in Table 5.1 are rarely if ever observed in the real world. The efficiency frontier we shall use henceforth is illustrated in Figure 5.8.

The shape of the efficiency frontier is concave, as we shall elaborate later in this chapter. Must its surface be smooth without any faults in it, as illustrated in Figure 5.9?

The answer is yes. Point T is not efficient because there exists a feasible combination of W_1 and W_2 that would produce a higher return for that given level of risk (σ_{p_1}). That combination is represented by point K (a combination of efficient portfolios a and b). Line akb would be straight if a and b were perfectly correlated. Otherwise, it follows the curvature of the efficiency frontier. The straight line does not destroy the concavity requirement, for it is considered both concave and convex.

Figure 5.8   **Efficiency frontier.**

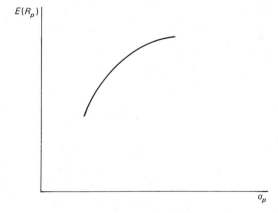

FIGURE 5.9 Variant of efficiency frontier.

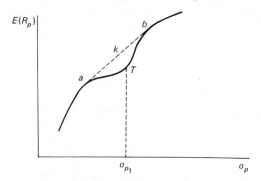

Minimum Variance Portfolios

The risk/return profile of a risky portfolio (a portfolio made up of only risky securities) is determined by the market and by the investor. The market determines $E(R_i)$ and σ_i for each security. Faced with these values, the investor decides only on how to distribute her wealth among the preferred securities, that is, she decides on the values of W_i. A rational investor would choose those W_i's which guarantee her a position on the efficiency frontier. For a two-security portfolio case, the determination of the optimal values of the W_i's proceeds as follows:

$$\sigma_p^2 = W_1^2 \sigma_1^2 + W_2^2 \sigma_2^2 + 2W_1 W_2 \sigma_{12} \tag{5.21}$$

where $\sigma_p^2 =$ variance of portfolio

$\sigma_{12} =$ covariance between the rates of return on the first and on the second security

Replacing W_2 with $1 - W_1$, we get:

$$\sigma_p^2 = W_1^2 \sigma_1^2 + (1 - W_1)^2 \sigma_2^2 + 2W_1(1 - W_1) \sigma_{12} \tag{5.22}$$

Differentiating Equation 5.22 with respect to W_1, we get:

$$\frac{d\sigma_p^2}{dW_1} = 2W_1 \sigma_1^2 - 2(1 - W_1) \sigma_2^2 + 2\sigma_{12} - 4W_1\sigma_{12} \tag{5.23}$$

Setting Equation 5.23 equal to zero and solving for W_1, we get:

$$W_1 = \frac{\sigma_2^2 - \sigma_{12}}{\sigma_1^2 + \sigma_2^2 - 2\sigma_{12}}$$
$$W_2 = 1 - W_1 \tag{5.24}$$

Equation 5.24 allows for the calculation of those values of W_1 and W_2 which produce the minimum variance portfolio

$$\frac{d^2\sigma_p^2}{dW_1^2} > 0$$

Referring back to the data in Table 5.1 and using the same values for σ_1^2, σ_2^2, and σ_{12}, we can calculate W_1 and W_2. In the case where $\rho = 1$ we get:

$$W_1 = \frac{9 - 12}{16 + 9 - 2\,(12)} = -3$$

$$W_2 = 1 - (-3) = 4$$

for $\rho = -1$, then $W_1 = \dfrac{9 + 12}{16 + 9 + 24} = 0.429$

$$W_2 = 1 - 0.429 = 0.571$$

therefore $\sigma_p^2 = (0.429)^2\,(16) + (0.571)^2\,(9) - 2\,(0.429)\,(0.571)\,(4)\,(3) = 0$

thus a correlation coefficient of -1 eliminates risk totally if the proper weights are assigned.

If, instead, the value of ρ is 0, then

$$W_1 = \frac{\sigma_2^2}{\sigma_1^2 + \sigma_2^2}$$

$$W_2 = 1 - W_1$$

The values of W_1 and W_2 (-3 and 4, respectively), where $\rho = +1$ are clearly undesirable, as was demonstrated in Table 5.1, for they yield a negative rate of return. This complication arises from unconstrained maximization. It can be avoided by minimizing portfolio risk subject to a given (or desired) level of return.

Having determined those combinations of W_1 and W_2 that produce minimum variance portfolios (MVP), the exact point where the investor chooses to be is yet unsettled. That combination of $E(R_p)$ and σ_p on the efficiency frontier which is preferred by the investor is determined by individual preferences, which are summarized by the utility curve.

5.4 UTILITY THEORY

The seeds for the concept of utility were planted by Jeremy Bentham, a British philosopher, during the early 1800s. The first development of the theory came during the latter part of that century in the work of Francis Y. Edgeworth, who developed the indifference curve technique.

The section to follow looks at the concept of utility under conditions of certainty and under conditions of risk, at the theoretical and practical implications of various type utility curves, and at the optimum combination of return and risk consistent with the preferences of an investor.

Utility Under Certainty

We begin our analysis by defining utility as a measure of psychic gain derived from the consumption (current or prospective) of a good or a combination of goods. As such, it provides a rationale for choice among goods competing for the interest and hence the dollars of the consumer.

FIGURE 5.10 Utility curve.

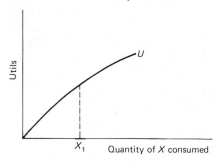

Classical economists felt that utility is measurable. The unit of measurement used was the util.

Figure 5.10 shows a utility curve. The bend in the curve represents the logical case of having had too much of a good thing. While the consumer would not cease accepting more of good X (that is, marginal utility dU/dX is positive), each additional unit of X beyond X_1 brings less and less additional satisfaction. This is the concept of diminishing marginal utility.

If, on the other hand, the consumer is faced with a choice between two combinations of goods X and Y, he may choose to consume only X, only Y, or a combination of X and Y. Figure 5.11 illustrates the case where both X and Y are being consumed.

The solid curve represents those combinations of X and Y that yield constant level of utility U_2 to the consumer. The consumer is indifferent to a choice between any two points along the curve. Hence, the designation of U_2 as an *indifference curve*. Points (X, Y) lying below the curve correspond to combinations that have utility less than U_2 to the consumer, such as U_1. Points above the curve have utility higher than U_2; that is, they lie on higher indifference curves (U_3, U_4 in Fig. 5.11).

The shape of U_1 or U_2 suggests that there exists some degree of substitution between X and Y. The reader should be able to verify that if X and Y were perfect substitutes or perfect complements, the indifference curves would appear as in Figure 5.12a and 5.12b respectively. The degree of substitutability or complementarity is determined by the slope of the indifference curve.

The shape of the solid curve in Figure 5.11 further indicates that while X and Y are substitutable, they are so at a decreasing rate. This is the concept of decreasing *marginal rate of substitution* (MRS) of X for Y. The MRS is defined to be the absolute value of the slope of the indifference curve. Roughly, it is the amount of Y the consumer

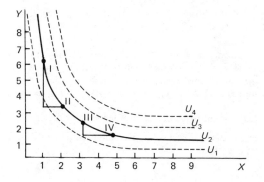

Figure 5.11 Case where both X and Y are being consumed.

FIGURE 5.12   **Indifference curves.**

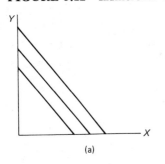
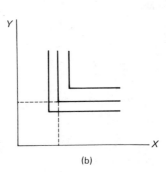

(a)   (b)

is willing to give up to get an extra unit of X. Thus, in Figure 5.11, for example, movement from I to II along the curve requires giving up 1.5 units of Y for 1 extra unit of X. Thus the MRS at point I is equal to 1.5. By contrast, at point III the consumer has very little of Y and lots of X, so he is willing to give up only about ½ unit of Y for 1 extra unit of X; thus the MRS at point III is 0.5.

In the language of calculus, MRS is obtained by multiplying the slope dY/dX by -1 to change its sign from negative to positive (the quantity dY/dX is negative because Y is a decreasing f^n of X). That is,

$$\text{MRS} = (-1)\ dY/dX$$

We have just argued that MRS should itself be decreasing. This means that

$$\frac{d}{dX}\text{MRS} < 0$$

so $$\frac{d}{dX}\left(-1\frac{dY}{dX}\right) < 0$$

and thus $$(-1)\frac{d^2Y}{dX^2} < 0$$

which implies that $d^2Y/dX^2 > 0$. As is well known, a positive second derivative indicates a convex[1] curve, which is consistent with Figure 5.9.

Readers will find it instructive to argue for themselves that a concave curve of the type shown in Figure 5.13 cannot be a sensible indifference curve.

In Figure 5.13 the investor gives up less of Y when it is plentiful to receive one

---

[1] A convex curve is one where every straight line connecting any two points on the curve lies on or above the curve. By contrast, in a concave curve, the line connecting and two points on the curve lies on or under the curve. A straight line is both concave and convex.

Stated in mathematical terms, the convexity argument reduces to the sign of the second derivate of a function. For $Y = f(X)$, if $(\partial^2 Y)/(\partial X^2) < 0$, the curve is concave from below. If $(\partial^2 Y)/(\partial X^2) > 0$, the curve is convex. For further details, see **R. G. D. Allen,** *Mathematical Analysis for Economists.* St. Martin's Press, New York, 1938.

FIGURE 5.13   Concave utility curve.

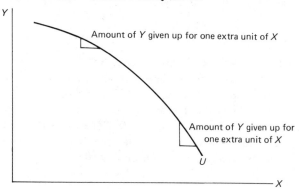

extra unit of X and more of Y when it is dear to receive one extra unit of X. This is not rational. The utility curve in Figure 5.13 is concave. In discussing utility theory, therefore, we rule out concave curves or portions of an indifference curve that are concave.

What we have thus far observed about *indifference curves* is that:

1. They are convex to the origin.
2. Marginal utility is always positive.
3. They are continuous and increase at a decreasing rate.
4. In the two-or-more-good case, the MRS is decreasing.

These properties are the result of various assumptions about the behavior of individuals.

Utility theory is a prescriptive theory intended to ensure rational and consistent behavior by consumers. Its prescriptions, called axioms of choice, are intended to transform the individual into the perfectly rational being. Its axioms of choice are as follows:

1. *Axiom 1—comparability.* This axiom requires an individual to make a choice between any two combinations of goods. That is, given a choice between a combination X_1, Y_1 and a different combination X_2, Y_2, he prefers X_1, Y_1 to X_2, Y_2 (i.e., the first has higher utility than the second) or he prefers X_2, Y_2 to X_1, Y_1, or he is indifferent (that is, X_1, Y_1 and X_2, Y_2 lie on one of our curves of constant utility).

2. *Axiom 2—transitivity.* This axiom guarantees consistency in choice. If $X_1, Y_1 \succ\succ X_2, Y_2$ and $X_2, Y_2 \succ\succ X_3, Y_3$, then $X_1, Y_1 \succ\succ X_3, Y_3$. Transitivity prevents two indifference curves from intersecting.[2]

3. *Axiom 3—nonsatiation.* This axiom serves to rule out cases where the marginal utility of any good in the choice set is nonpositive. The consumer always wants more of both goods in a two-good world.

4. *Axiom 4—convexity.* This axiom requires us to assume that the indifference curves are convex. This is equivalent to assuming that if an individual is indifferent between two combinations X_1, Y_1 and X_2, Y_2, she can be moved to a higher indifference curve if a new combination X_3, Y_3 is constructed in the following way:

---

[2] The symbol $\succ\succ$ stands for "preferred to." This originated in the work of **Eugene Fama** and **Merton Miller,** *The Theory of Finance.* Holt, Rinehart and Winston, New York, 1972.

$$(X_3, Y_3) = \alpha(X_1, Y_1) + (1 - \alpha)(X_2, Y_2) = [\alpha X_1 + (1 - \alpha)X_2, \alpha Y_1 + (1 - \alpha)Y_2]$$

where $0 \leq \alpha \leq 1$.

In order to see how these axioms yield convex, nonintersecting indifference curves, imagine utility as a mountain. The greatest satisfaction realizable is derived from reaching the apex of the mountain. The mountain plateaus are shown in Figure 5.14.

The lowest plateau in Figure 5.14 represents the lowest level of utility ($U = 5$); the highest plateau represents the highest level of utility ($U = 40$). The lines VV' and HH' represent artificial dividing lines. The intersection at 0 splits the "mountain" into four quadrants. The nonsatiation axiom constricts the area of utility maximization process

FIGURE 5.14 Utility contours. Higher U values mean higher utility. The highest contour ($U = 40$) represents the highest level of utility.

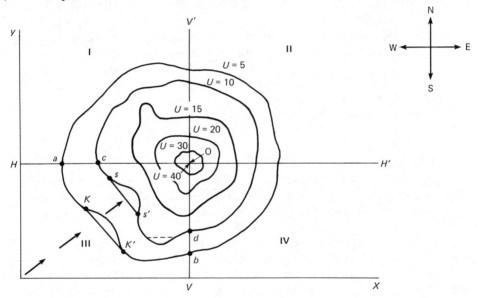

to the southwest region, that is, to quandrant III. The relevant portion of the first plateau ($U = 5$) is line *ab*. The rest of the plateau, referred to in the economic literature as utility contour, is not useful. The reason is that as the consumer moves from one utility contour to another in quadrants I, II, and IV, toward the apex of the mountain, he ends up with less of one of the goods or with less of both. This is inconsistent with the nonsatiation hypothesis. Only in quadrant III can a movement from one utility contour to a higher one translate into more of both goods.[3] The ascent to the top should be confined to the southwest quadrant and should proceed in the direction of the arrows.

Readers should verify that a voyage along a given plateau will allow them to see every side of the mountain but move them no closer to the apex. The level of satisfaction

---

[3] The proof had already been provided in the discussion of Figure 5.11.

remains constant. This is precisely the reason for referring to indifference curves as iso-utility curves (the prefix *iso* means "constant").

Utility and Risk

Investment opportunities present choices involving a desirable good (the expected rate of return) and an undesirable good (risk). The typical investor wishes to maximize the expected rate of return and minimize risk. In this context, utility or, more precisely, expected utility $E(U)$, is maximized by moving in a northwesterly direction, as shown in Figure 5.15.

The slope of the indifference curves indicates the extent to which the investor is concerned with avoiding risk. Stated differently, the slope indicates the extent to which the investor wishes to be compensated for assuming one additional unit of risk.

Investors who derive unlimited joy from risk or have unlimited fear of it have utility curves that are horizontal and vertical respectively (Fig. 5.16).

The steeper the slope of the utility curve, the greater the risk aversion—that is, the greater the compensation demanded per unit of risk. The concept of risk aversion will be treated more rigorously below. We now proceed with the statement of the axioms of choice under conditions of risk.

Axiom 1—comparability. This axiom is as stated in the certainty case.

Axiom 2—transitivity. This axiom is as stated in the certainty case.

Axiom 3—independence. Suppose an investor is indifferent between two certain (risk-free) outcomes X and Y. Then, given any outcome Z, the investor is indifferent between a gamble involving X and Z and one involving Y and Z. The new choice is between:

1. Outcome X occurring with probability P and Z (the third outcome) with probability $1 - P$. This gamble is represented by $g(X, Z : P)$.
2. Outcome Y occurring with probability P and outcome Z with probability $1 - P$. This is represented by $g(Y, Z : P)$.

FIGURE 5.15   Indifference curves.

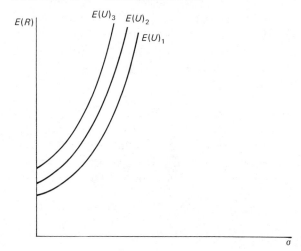

FIGURE 5.16 Low- (a) and high-risk (b) utility curves.

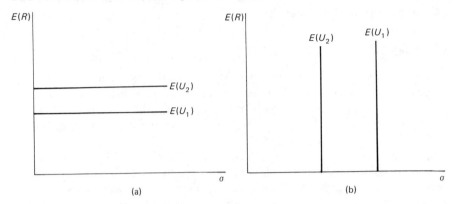

Axiom 4—certainty equivalent. Every gamble has a certainty equivalent that makes the investor indifferent between it and the certainty equivalent.

From these axioms and assuming rationality (more is preferred to less), von Neumann and Morgenstern were able to prove that in the case of risk, utility maximization requires the maximization of expected utility of wealth, which is achieved by taking the expected value of an ordinary utility function.

$$E[U(W_i)] = \sum_i P_i U(W_i) \qquad (5.25)$$

The proof is shown in the appendix to this chapter.

Utility Functions and Attitudes Toward Risks

Figure 5.17 shows some of the shapes utility curves (for wealth W) can assume. Each of these curves has different implications on the attitude towards risk. We shall attempt to point out ways for gauging the risk-aversiveness of an investor.

Consider an investor with the linear utility function. His current wealth is $10,000. He is offered a fair gamble which pays $15,000 if heads show on a coin and $5,000 if tails show. The investor has a choice of holding on to his current wealth or taking the fair gamble. Graphically, the choice can be represented as follows (Figure 5.18).

The expected payoff from the gamble is equal to:

$$E(W) = \$15,000 \ (0.50) + (5,000)(0.50) = \$10,000$$

The utility corresponding to $E(W) = \$10,000$ is read off the utility axis and is equal to 2.4. $U[E(W)] = 2.4$. (The utility values on the vertical axis are assumed values.)

The expected utility of wealth $E[U(W)]$ is calculated as follows:

$$E[U(W)] = U(5,000)[P(5,000)] + U(15,000)[P(15,000)]$$

where P = probability of an outcome. Thus

$$E[U(W)] = 1.2\,(0.5) + 3.6\,(0.5)$$
$$= 0.6 + 1.8 = \mathbf{2.4}$$

Therefore $U[E(W)] = E[U(W)] = 2.4$

Here, the investor experiences a level of satisfaction from taking the gamble equal to that of the certainty case (holding on to current wealth). This is a risk neutral investor. A linear utility function represents, therefore, the risk-neutral case.

Consider the same example for an investor whose utility curve is logarithmic. $U[E(W)]$ and $E[U(W)]$ are easily calculated with Figure 5.19 used as a reference.

First note that $E(W)$ and E[U(W)] are calculated using the same weighted average

FIGURE 5.17 Different forms of functional relations.

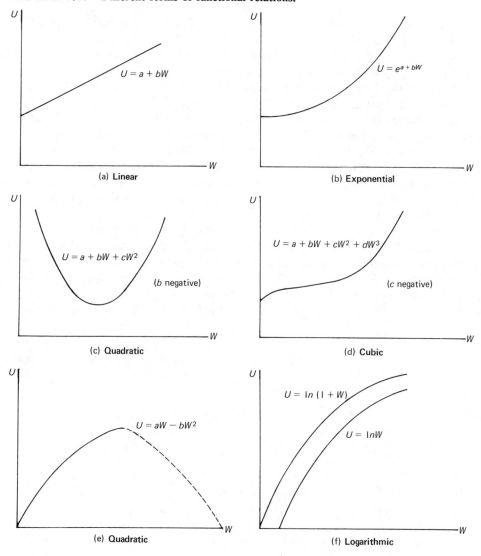

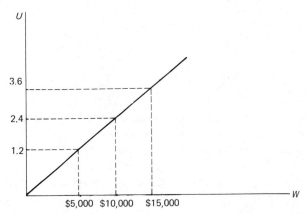

FIGURE 5.18   Graphic display
of alternative strategies.

of values of W and of $U(W)$; that is, $E(W) = (15,000)(0.5) + (5,000)(0.5) = \$10,000$ and $E[U(W)] = (3.6)(0.5) + (1.2)(0.5) = 2.4$.

The mathematical consequence of this is that the point with coordinates ($10,000, 2.4$) lies on the line segment connecting the points $a = (5,000, 1.2)$ and $b = (15,000, 3.6)$ shown in Figure 5.19. However, the utility of $E(W)$ is $U(10,000)$, and this number is taken from the utility curve itself: $U[E(W)] = U(10,000) = 2.8$.

To summarize this example, even though the investor's present wealth ($10,000) is equal to his expected wealth $E(W)$ from the gamble, the utility of his present wealth is 2.8 while the utility he can expect from the gamble (in the actuarial sense) is only $E[U(W)] = 2.4$. This is because a loss of $5,000 causes him more pain (1.6 lost utility units) than a gain of $5,000 causes him joy (0.8 gained utility units). This investor is obviously risk-averse, and the same will be true of any investor whose utility curve is concave downward.

Note that the expected utility 2.4 in the gamble corresponds on the utility curve to $W = \$7,500$. The difference between this and the $10,000 present wealth is $2,500, and this amount has the following interesting interpretation: It represents the maximum amount of funds the investor is willing to commit to an insurance policy to protect himself in the event he is *forced* to take a gamble.

The reader should be able to verify that if $U[E(W)] < E[U(W)]$, the investor would

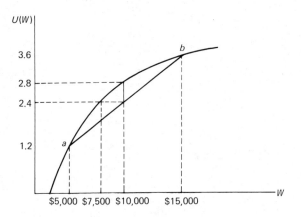

FIGURE 5.19   Logarithmic utility
curve.

be considered a risk seeker. An exponential function of the type shown in Figure 5.14 is suggested for the analysis.

Pratt-Arrow Measure of Risk Aversion

The measurement of the risk characteristics of a utility function requires more than the observation of the "curvature" of the function if precise conclusions are to be drawn.

J. W. Pratt[4] and later Kenneth Arrow[5] developed a measure for gauging the risk characteristics of a utility function. The measure was called local risk premium or π.

$$\pi = (\tfrac{1}{2})\ \sigma_Z^2 \left[-\frac{U''\ (W)}{U'\ (W)} \right] \qquad (5.26)$$

where σ_Z^2 = variance of an actuarially neutral gamble of Z dollars $[E(Z) = 0]$

$U''(W)$ = rate of change in marginal utility

= second derivative

$U'(W)$ = marginal utility

In Equation 5.26, the term $(\tfrac{1}{2})\sigma_Z^2$ is constant, and $U'(W)$ is assumed positive. Thus the sign of π depends on the sign of $U''(W)$. A negative $U''(W)$ shows risk aversion, a positive $U''(W)$ means risk preference, and $U''(W) = 0$ means risk neutrality.

The term in parentheses in equation (5.26) is referred to as *absolute risk aversion* (ARA).

$$\text{ARA} = -\frac{U''(W)}{U'(W)} \qquad (5.27)$$

ARA measures risk aversion corresponding to a given level of wealth. The question of interest is what happens to ARA as wealth changes. Does an investor invest more in risky assets as a result of an increase in wealth or does she invest less? That is, is $[d(\text{ARA})]/dW \lesseqgtr 0$? If $[d(\text{ARA})]/dW > 0$, the investor is said to exhibit increasing absolute risk aversion, that is, she invests less of her total wealth in risky assets than she did prior to the increase in her wealth (if she had invested $10,000 prior to an increase in wealth, she now invests less than $10,000). If $[d(\text{ARA})/dW < 0$, the investor is said to exhibit decreasing absolute risk aversion, that is, she invests more funds in risky assets after an increase in wealth. If $[d(\text{ARA})]/dW = 0$, absolute risk aversion is constant, that is, the same amount of total wealth is invested in risky assets before and after the increase in wealth.

In order to determine how the percentage of total wealth invested in risky assets changes as a result of a change in wealth, we simply multiply ARA by W to arrive at relative risk aversion (RRA):

---

[4] **J. W. Pratt,** "Risk Aversion in the Small and in the Large." *Econometrica,* January–April 1964, pp. 122–136.

[5] **K. J. Arrow,** *Essays in the Theory of Risk Bearing.* North-Holland, Amsterdam, 1971.

$$\text{RRA} = -W \frac{U''(W)}{U'(W)} \tag{5.28}$$

If the percentage of wealth in risky securities decreases as wealth increases, that is, $[d(\text{RRA})]/dW > 0$, relative risk aversion increases; if $[d(\text{RRA})]/dW < 0$, relative risk aversion decreases; and if $[d(\text{RRA})]/dW = 0$, relative risk aversion is constant.

The empirical evidence of ARA and RRA is mixed, with the latter (RRA) being most problematic. Intuition tells us that ARA should be decreasing. The wealthier an investor is, the more funds he is likely to commit to risky assets. Evidence in support of decreasing ARA is provided by Friend and Blume[6] and by Cohn et al.[7] Friend and Blume also argued that RRA is constant, while Cohn et al. suggests that RRA is decreasing. Other works, such as that by H. Latane,[8] argue that RRA is increasing.

Let us investigate whether a quadratic utility function of the type shown in Figure 5.17e is consistent with the findings of Friend and Blume.

Let $U(W) = aW - bW^2$ where $a > 0$ and $b > 0$.
Therefore $U'(W) = a - 2bW$

Since marginal utility is assumed to be positive,

$$U'(W) = a - 2bW > 0$$

then

$$U''(W) = -2b < 0$$

Therefore

$$\text{ARA} = -\frac{-2b}{a - 2bW} = \frac{2b}{a - 2bW} > 0$$

We now look at how ARA changes with W.

$$\frac{d(\text{ARA})}{dW} = \left(\frac{2b}{a - 2bW} \right)' = \frac{(a - 2bW)0 - (2b)(-2b)}{(a - 2bW)^2} = \frac{4b^2}{(a - 2bW)^2} > 0$$

because $(a - 2bW) > 0$

$$\text{Therefore RRA} = \frac{2b}{\dfrac{a}{W} - 2b}$$

---

[6] Irwin Friend and Marshall Blume, "The Demand for Risky Assets." *American Economic Review*, December 1975, pp. 900–922.

[7] R. A. Cohn, R. W. G. Lewellen, R. C. Lease, and G. G. Schlarbaum, "Individual Investor Risk Aversion and Investor Portfolio Composition." *Journal of Finance*, May 1975.

[8] Henry Latane, "Income Velocity and Interest Rates: A Pragmatic Approach." *Review of Economics and Statistics*, 1960.

And $\dfrac{d(\text{RRA})}{dW} > 0$

This shows that the properties that a quadratic utility function possesses are inconsistent with intuition and with the findings of Friend and Blume. As wealth increases, an investor with a quadratic utility function becomes more risk-averse. She places less of her wealth in risky assets, both in absolute and in proportional terms.

Friend and Blume suggested that the utility function with the correct properties is the power function[9] $U(W) = -W^{-1}$.

Therefore $U'(W) = W^{-2} > 0$

$$U''(W) = -2W^{-3} < 0$$

$$\text{ARA} = \frac{2}{W}, \ \frac{d(\text{ARA})}{dW} < 0$$

$$\text{RRA} = 2, \ \frac{d(\text{RRA})}{dW} = 0$$

Then why do most researchers persist in using a quadratic utility function? The reason is that it is the only function that is completely and easily specified by its mean and variance regardless of the underlying distribution (whether normal or not).

$$U(W) = aW - bW^2$$
$$E[U(W)] = aE(W) - bE(W^2)$$
$$E[U(W)] = aE(W) - b\{\sigma^2 + [E(W)]^2\}$$

Note: $\sigma^2 = E(W^2) - [E(W)]^2$ \hfill (5.29)

$$E[U(W)] = aE(W) - b\sigma^2 - b[E(W)]^2$$
$$E[U(W)] = f[E(W), \sigma^2]$$

This function is positively related to $E(W)$ and negatively related to σ^2.

A rate of return can be looked upon as the change in wealth over a one-year holding period:

$$R = \frac{W_t - W_0}{W_0}, \ E(R) = \left[\frac{1}{W_0} E(W)\right] - 1$$

Thus, the relationship between $E(R)$ and $E(W)$ is linear. $E[U(W)]$ can, therefore, be expressed as a function of $E(R)$ and σ^2 as shown in Figure 5.20.

---

[9] A logarithmic utility function has the same qualities. $U(W) = \ln W$, $U'(W) = 1/W > 0$, therefore $U''(W) = -1/W^2 = 0$; $\text{ARA} = \frac{1}{W}$, $[d(\text{ARA})]/dW = -\frac{1}{W^2} < 0$, $\text{RRA} = 1$, $[d(\text{RRA})]/dW = 0$.

FIGURE 5.20

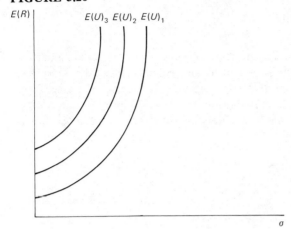

Looking back at Equation 5.29, we find that:

$$\sigma^2 = \frac{1}{b}\left\{-\text{constant} + a\,E(W) - b[E(W)]^2\right\}$$

$$\frac{\partial \sigma^2}{\partial[E(W)]} = \frac{1}{b}\,[a - 2bE(W)] > 0 \text{ if } 2bE(W) < a \tag{5.30}$$

Equation 5.30 explains the shape of the utility function in Figure 5.20.

Where along the efficiency frontier in Figure 5.8 would an investor then choose to be? Superimposing Figure 5.20 on Figure 5.8, we get Figure 5.21.

Point S is the optimal point consistent with a minimum-variance portfolio theory and with utility maximization.

It is precisely this point S that necessitated all the preceding analysis, and lays the foundation for further study of portfolio theory.

FIGURE 5.21

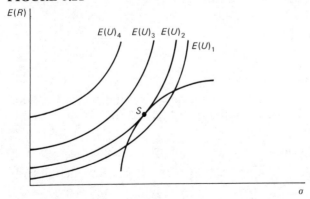

CONCLUSION

Decision making under conditions of risk can be systematized, as was demonstrated in this chapter. The reader must note, however, that the assumptions made are not as restrictive as they appear and that the theory is quite robust. In the next chapter, we show how portfolio theory can be used as a foundation for a model to price securities.

QUESTIONS

1. Distinguish between uncertainty and risk.

2. What does risk aversion mean? How is it best measured? Are people risk-averse by nature? If so, why do you suppose this is true?

3. What is the strength of the semivariance technique of measuring risk? What is its weakness?

4. What correlation would you expect to find between the earnings per share of a firm and the price of that firm's stock?

5. Why must the relationship between $E(R_p)$ and $\sigma(p)$ be linear when $\rho = 1$ (assuming a two-security portfolio)?

6. When is variance an adequate measure of the riskiness of a stock?

7. Two securities (A and B) have the following rates of return and risk:

	A	B
Return $E(R)$	10%	12%
Risk σ	8%	9%

   Which investment would a risk averse person choose? Why? What must be considered before A or B is added to an existing portfolio of securities?

8. Look at Table 5.1; where $W_1 = 1.5$, $W_2 = -.5$ (a short position in security 2), and $E(R_p) = 14\%$, how is this higher rate of return justified?

9. Look at Table 5.1; if $\rho = 0$, would a rational investor ever set $W_1 = -.5$ (short security 1)? Explain.

10. What does the efficiency frontier represent?

11. Under what conditions might the marginal rate of substitution between two goods be constant at 1?

12. What does the slope of an investor's indifference curve represent? What does the second derivative represent?

13. Will two investors always demand the same certainty equivalent sum when presented with the same gamble?

14. Why is the risk-neutral investor's utility function linear?

15. "The Markowitz model cannot be used to price risky securities." Comment in detail. If you agree with the statement, then of what value is the model?

16. Concave utility functions are ruled out in utility analysis. Why?

17. What are the benefits/shortcomings of a quadratic utility function?

18. Why is it important to know an investor's utility function?

19. Does the Pratt-Arrow measure of risk aversion make sense to you? That is, is it intuitive? Why? (Look at the graph of the logarithmic function $f(x) = \ln x$ as you contemplate your answer.)

PROBLEMS

1. Calculate the variance of MES stock given the following possible outcomes:

R_i (return)	10%	12%	14%
P_i (probability)	.3	.4	.3

2. Extend Table 5.1 for the $\rho = .5$ case. Plot the results. Compare your graph with Figure 5.4.

3. A lady provides the following information about her cigarette-smoking habit:

Cigarette	0	1	2	3	4	5	6	7	8	9
Utils		0	5	12	20	28	35	41	44	45	46

    After which cigarette does she experience diminishing marginal utility? (Hint: Graph her marginal utility)

4. Joe Investor is risk-averse. His utilities for various levels of wealth are given below:

Wealth ($000)	40	47	48	49	50	60
Utils	4.0	4.9	5.0	5.1	5.2	6.0

    He is faced with a fair gamble which will either raise his wealth to $60,000 from $50,000 or drop it to $40,000 each outcome has a 50 percent chance of occurring.
    a. Graph his utility function.
    b. If presented with the choice, will he accept the gamble?
    c. If he were forced to take the gamble, what is the maximum amount he would be willing to pay an insurance company to assume the risk?

5. Jane Investor's utility function is known to be:

    $$U = 4w - 2w^2$$

    a. Calculate her absolute risk aversion (ARA).
    b. What is her relative risk aversion (RRA)?

Utility and Risk—The Nature of the Relationship

Consider the case of an investor faced with choosing one of the following:

1. A gamble $G(W,0;P)$ with two possible payoffs:

   $G = W$ with probability P

   $G = 0$ with probability $1 - P$

   where G is the payoff random variable, that is, the gain.

2. Certain sum.

The first alternative could be represented by the expected (actuarial) value of the payoff variable:

$$E(G) = WP + 0\,(1 - P) = WP$$

By axiom 4 (the certainty equivalent axiom), every gamble $[G(W,0;P)]$ must have a certainty equivalent (CE).

Note that two gambles $g(W,0;P)$ and $\tilde{g}(\tilde{W},0;\tilde{P})$ might have the same expected value but different certainty equivalents. For example, suppose $W = 500,000$, $P = \frac{1}{50}$, and $\tilde{W} = 20,000$, $\tilde{P} = \frac{1}{2}$. Then $E(G) = 10,000 = E(\tilde{G})$. Now suppose the investor is neither extremely fearful of nor recklessly prone to risk. Then he may judge that gamble G is very unlikely to pay off and thus be willing to accept a small certainty equivalent, say \$500, while gamble $\tilde{g}$ has an even chance of paying off, so that the certainty equivalent he would demand would be much higher, say \$5,000. The reader will find it instructive to verify that the standard deviation of the payoff random variable G is 7×10^4, while that of $\tilde{G}$ is only 10^4.

The choice between g and CE depends on the value of P. The higher P is, the higher the certainty equivalent must be. For a given CE, the lower P is, the more preferred the certainty equivalent becomes. For some value of P, however, the investor is indifferent between g and CE. If another gamble offers a higher P for the same W or the same P for a higher W, the new G would be preferred to the CE.

In real life, the investor is faced with a portfolio of gambles that must be compared with their certainty equivalent. Therefore:

$$g(W_1, \ldots, W_n; P_1, \ldots, P_n) = \left\{ \begin{array}{l} W_1 \text{ with probability } P_1 \\ \vdots \\ W_n \ldots \ldots \ldots \ldots \ldots P_n \end{array} \right\}$$

Then, if $G = G_1 + \ldots + G_n$, we have

$$E(G) = \sum_i E(G_i) = \sum_i W_i P_i \qquad (1)$$

One portfolio yielding $E(G_i)_1$ would be preferred to another yielding $E(G_i)_2$ if $E(G_i)_1 > E(G_i)_2$.

In utility terms, Equation i can be written as follows:

$$E[U(G_i)] = E[U(W_i)] = \sum_i P_i U(W_i) \qquad (2)$$

where $E[U(W_i)] = $ expected utility of wealth

Rational investors seek to maximize Equation 2 by computing its value for each separate portfolio, knowing that one of the alternative portfolios is that with zero risk (a savings certificate with a known interest rate).

CHAPTER 6 | Modern Portfolio Theory

6.1 INTRODUCTION

The preceding chapter firmly established the fact that the analysis of a security or a portfolio in terms of its rate of return is an incomplete if not a misguided analysis. Risk analysis must be an integral part of portfolio analysis. The riskiness of a security in a portfolio context was shown to be different from that of the same security held in isolation. The contribution a security makes to the riskiness of the portfolio to which it is being added assumes a dominant role.

We have also demonstrated that the determination of the optimal combinations of rates of return and risk (measured by the standard deviation of the portfolio) represents only partial analysis, which can be completed by looking at the investor's own risk/return tradeoffs and by matching them with the available market opportunities.

In this chapter we continue with the development of portfolio analysis and formally introduce the Markowitz model, the capital asset pricing model (CAPM), and the arbitrage pricing theory (APT).

6.2 THE MARKOWITZ MODEL

The foundations of the Markowitz model were laid down in Chapter 5. It is built on the following assumptions:

1. Investors focus on the expected rate of return and on the variance of a security.
2. Investors prefer more returns and less risk.
3. Investors wish to hold efficient portfolios: those yielding maximum expected return for a given level of risk or minimum risk for a given level of expected return.
4. Investors agree on the probability distribution of rates of return on securities. This ensures a unique efficiency frontier.

Based on these assumptions, Markowitz was able to derive, as was shown in Chapter 5, the efficiency frontier—that locus of points where every risky portfolio is efficient.

121

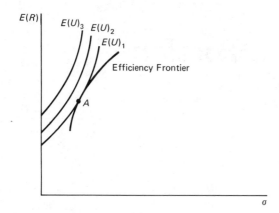

FIGURE 6.1   **Efficiency frontier showing optimum point.**

In a Markowitz world, the investor proceeds systematically in selecting securities that are less than perfectly positively correlated. The construction of the efficiency frontier is not based on a random selection of securities. Where along this efficiency frontier an investor chooses to be is determined by his or her utility function. Point *A* in Figure 6.1 is the optimum point for an investor whose preferences are summarized by the designated utility curves.

Another investor, with different preferences, may find another point along the efficiency frontier most suitable. The combination of risky securities preferred by investors is, therefore, not unique. Each investor may allocate his or her wealth differently among risky securities. That is why a general equilibrium asset pricing model could not be derived by Markowitz. An explicit equilibrium expected return on a risky asset could not be predicted in the Markowitz framework. The model could only describe the tradeoff between return and risk in the market for securities and in the mind of the individual.

The development of a capital asset pricing model began with the work of Sharpe,[1] followed by that of Lintner.[2] Sharpe introduced a risk-free asset in the analysis, and the effects of his work are still being felt. This study and others that followed it are currently the subject of a heated debate, the basic elements of which will be discussed below.

6.3 CAPITAL ASSET PRICING MODEL

The capital asset pricing model requires, in addition to the assumptions of the Markowitz model, the following assumptions:

1. That there is equilibrium in the securities markets. (The equilibrium is only partial. The effects of the securities markets on the production sector, for example, are ignored.)

---

[1] **William Sharpe,** "Capital Asset Prices: A Theory of Market Equilibrium Under Conditions of Risk." *Journal of Finance,* vol. 19, no. 3 (September 1964), pp. 425–442.

[2] **John Lintner,** "The Valuation of Risky Assets and the Selection of Risky Investments in Stock Portfolios and Capital Budgets." *Review of Economics and Statistics,* vol. 47, no. 2 (February 1965), pp. 13–37; **J. Lintner,** "Security Prices, Risk and Maximal Gains from Diversification." *Journal of Finance,* vol. 20, no. 12 (December 1965), pp. 587–615.

2. That investments are divisible and any size investment is feasible.
3. That there is a risk-free asset yielding the risk-free rate and that investors can borrow or lend at this rate.
4. That there are either no transactions costs or taxes or identical transactions costs and taxes for all investors.
5. That ex ante expectations about the market as a whole are homogeneous and all investors agree on the distribution of rates of return (the market is efficient).
6. That the market portfolio is a convex combination of individual portfolios.
7. That investors are risk-averse and maximizers of mean/variance utility functions. They are one-period expected-utility-of-wealth maximizers, and the length of the period (the investment horizon) is identical for all investors.

Let $E(R_M)$ = expected return on portfolio M made up of only risky securities

σ_M^2 = variance of portfolio M made up of only risky securities.

The introduction of the risk-free asset affords the investor several previously unavailable choices:

1. To invest 100 percent of available funds in the riskless asset.
2. To issue risk-free securities; that is, borrow at the risk-free rate and invest in risky assets.
3. To invest in any combination of risky and riskless assets.

These choices will be explored in detail in arriving at the new efficiency frontier.

Portfolio M made up of a collection of risky assets on the one hand and of a riskless asset on the other has an expected rate of return and a variance of

$$E(R_p) = W_1 R_F + W_2 E(R_M) \tag{6.1}$$

$$\sigma_p^2 = W_1^2 \sigma_F^2 + W_2^2 \sigma_M^2 + 2 W_1 W_2 \sigma_{F,M} \tag{6.2}$$

But for the risk-free asset $\sigma_F^2 = 0$, thus

$\sigma_{F,M} = \rho \sigma_F \sigma_M = 0$, and σ_p^2 reduces to

$\sigma_p^2 = W_2^2 \sigma_M^2$ or $W_2 = \dfrac{\sigma_p}{\sigma_M}$

Equation 6.1 can be rewritten as

$$E(R_p) = (1 - W_2) R_F + W_2 E(R_M)$$

because

$$W_1 + W_2 = 1$$

Therefore, replacing W_2 by its value σ_p / σ_M, we get

$$E(R_p) = \left(1 - \frac{\sigma_p}{\sigma_M}\right) R_F + \frac{\sigma_p}{\sigma_M} E(R_M)$$

$$E(R_p) = R_F + \left(\frac{E(R_M) - R_F}{\sigma_M}\right) \sigma_p \tag{6.3}$$

Thus, from Equation 6.3, one can observe that the relationship between $E(R_p)$ and σ_p is linear. This is depicted in Figure 6.2 (segment $R_F M$).

If a short position in the risk-free security is established, the line $R_F M$ can be extended as shown by the dotted line. If unlimited borrowing is possible, the extension is infinite in length.

A short position in the risky securities with the proceeds used to increase the position in the riskless asset $W_1 > 1$ yields distinctly inferior results shown by line $R_F V$.

Point M in Figure 6.2 represents a point where $W_2 = 1$, that is 100 percent of the investable funds are committed to risky securities. Point R_F represents 100 percent investment in the riskless asset. Any point between R_F and M represents a combination of risky and of riskless securities: $1 > W_1 > 0, 1 > W_2 > 0, W_1 + W_2 = 1$.

Going back to the efficiency frontier in Figure 6.1, we observe that every point along the frontier represents a commitment of 100 percent of the investable funds to the risky assets. Thus, line $R_F M$ in Figure 6.2 must touch the efficiency frontier in Figure 6.1 at point M, where $W_2 = 1$. This is shown in Figure 6.3.

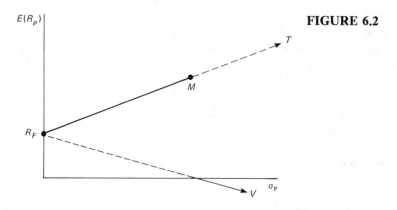

FIGURE 6.2

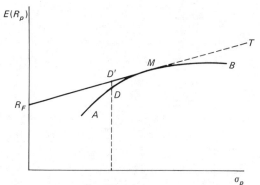

FIGURE 6.3 Key: M = Market portfolio; AB = efficiency frontier without the risk-free asset; $E(R_P)$ = expected portfolio rate of return; σ_P = standard deviation of portfolio rate of return; $R_F MT$ = efficiency frontier with borrowing and lending at the risk-free rate.

The efficiency frontier is no longer *AMB* but rather R_FMT. The reason is very simple. Every point along *AMB* is either matched or dominated by a feasible point along R_FMT. For example, point *D* is dominated by point *D'*, for *D'* offers a higher rate of return for the same level of risk. If shorting the risk-free security (borrowing at the risk-free rate) is ruled out, the new efficiency frontier is R_FMB. Otherwise the efficiency frontier is R_FMT.

The slope of R_FMT is equal to $[E(R_M) - R_F]/\sigma_M$, which represents the market price per unit of total risk. $E(R_M) - R_F$ represents the risk premium—that rate of return on a risky portfolio in excess of the risk-free rate. Line R_FMT is referred to as the *capital market line*. If all investors have homogeneous expectations, they would have the same capital market line.

The reader should observe that point *M* is unique. That is, the choice of a portfolio of risky securities is limited strictly to portfolio *M* if the choice is to be consistent with the efficiency objective. Efficient portfolios will plot along R_FMT, assuming the homogeneity assumption holds, and would consist of a combination of risk-free assets (long or short) and of portfolio *M*. This is so regardless of the shape of the individual's utility curve. Of what use are utility curves, then, in the capital asset pricing framework? Utility curves help the investor decide where along the efficiency frontier he or she must be—that is, how much to borrow or lend at the risk-free rate and consequently how much to commit to portfolio *M*. This is referred to as the *separation theorem* and is illustrated in Figure 6.4. The allocation of wealth between risky assets and risk-free assets is separated from the wealth allocation among risky assets.

Utility curve U_1 indicates that the investor wishes to combine risky securities with the riskless asset. The closer the tangency point with the efficiency frontier is to R_F, the larger the percentage of funds invested in riskless assets; the farther it is from R_F, the larger the percentage of funds invested in risky assets. The tangency point between U_2 and the efficiency frontier indicates that the investor is borrowing funds at the risk-free rate to invest in risky securities. Risk-averse investors would choose a point along the efficiency frontier to the left of *M*. The greater the degree of risk aversion, the closer to R_F would the combination be. Those who wish to assume more risk will choose points beyond *M*.

Let us now look at the composition of portfolio *M*, that unique portfolio that anyone wishing to own risky securities must hold. Portfolio *M* is optimal for any investor *independent* of that investor's utility function. That is, the optimality of portfolio *M* is determinable *separately* from anything we might know or do not know about the investor. Portfolio *M* is made up of every security in the market. If it were not, then arbitrage would become possible. That is, if one security were not included in *M*, there would

FIGURE 6.4   Separation theorem.

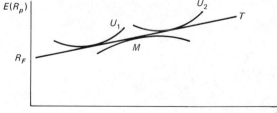

be a way to assign the distribution of weights such that the inclusion of the security in M produces a higher rate of return for that given level of risk. This would imply that portfolio M is not efficient and would contradict the assumption and subsequent proof that every portfolio lying on the efficiency frontier must be efficient. Thus portfolio M must include every security in the market. The proportion W_i of funds invested in each security in the market portfolio M is equal to the ratio of the market value of all the shares outstanding for that particular firm to the market value of all shares in the market. That is, if the market value of IBM accounted for 10 percent of the market value of all stocks in the market, then 10 percent of all funds invested in portfolio M must be in IBM stock.

Generally

$$W_{i,M} = \frac{N_i MP_i^s}{V_M}$$

where $W_{i,M}$ = the weight of security i in the market portfolio

N_i = number of company i shares outstanding

MP_i^s = market price of share i

V_M = total value of all publicly traded shares

Since investors have homogeneous expectations, by assumption they would all hold the exact distribution of $W_{i,M}$. Otherwise, the movements of portfolio M would not correspond to those of the whole market.

The Security Market Line (SML)

The preceding discussion centers on the relationship between risk and return on *portfolios*. The securities market, however, prices securities individually. Thus the value of the portfolio is the collective value of all securities in the portfolio.

Consider a portfolio made up of a risky asset i and the market portfolio. The expected return on this portfolio and its variance are calculated as follows:

$$E(R_p) = W_i E(R_i) + (1 - W_i)E(R_M) \tag{6.4}$$

$$\sigma_p = \sqrt{W_i^2 \sigma_i^2 + (1 - W_i)^2 \sigma_M^2 + 2W_i(1 - W_i)\sigma_{iM}} \tag{6.5}$$

Using the fact that

$$\frac{\delta E(R_p)}{\delta \sigma_p} = \frac{\delta E(R_p)/\delta W_i}{\delta \sigma_p/\delta W_i} \tag{6.6}$$

we find that

$$\frac{\delta E(R_p)}{\delta \sigma_p} = \frac{E(R_i) - E(R_M)}{\{1/2[W_i^2 \sigma_i^2 + (1 - W_i)^2 \sigma_M^2 + 2W_i(1 - W_i)\sigma_{iM}]^{-1/2}\}}$$

$$\times \frac{1}{[(2W_i \sigma_i^2 + 2W_i \sigma_M^2 - 2\sigma_M^2 + 2\sigma_{iM} - 4W_i \sigma_{iM})]} \tag{6.7}$$

Security i, however, could not exist outside portfolio M if M is the market portfolio. Security i is already included in portfolio M, thus, W_1 must equal zero. With $W_1 = 0$,

$$\frac{\delta E(R_p)}{\delta \sigma p} = \frac{E(R_i) - E(R_M)}{1/2[\sigma_M^2]^{-1/2}[2\sigma_{iM} - 2\sigma_M^2]}$$

$$= \frac{E(R_i) - E(R_M)}{1/2\left[\dfrac{1}{\sigma_M}\right]\left[2\sigma_{iM} - 2\sigma_M^2\right]}$$

$$= \frac{E(R_i) - E(R_M)}{(\sigma_{iM} - \sigma_M^2)/\sigma_M} \qquad (6.8)$$

This represents a new price of risk which must be equivalent to that derived earlier, $[E(R_M) - R_F]/\sigma_M$, because we are talking about the same point M.

Therefore

$$\frac{E(R_M) - R_F}{\sigma_M} = \frac{E(R_i) - E(R_M)}{(\sigma_{iM} - \sigma_M^2)/\sigma_M} \qquad (6.9)$$

Multiplying both sides of Equation 6.8 by $1/\sigma_M$ and solving for $E(R_i)$, we get

$$E(R_i) = R_F + [E(R_M) - R_F]\frac{\sigma_{iM}}{\sigma_M^2} \qquad (6.10)$$

where $E(R_M) - R_F$ = marketwide risk premium

$\dfrac{\sigma_{iM}}{\sigma_M^2} = \beta$ = measure of systematic nondiversifiable risk (This risk cannot be eliminated through portfolio diversification.)

= measure of the extent to which the security rate of return moves with that of the market

$[E(R_M) - R_F]\dfrac{\sigma_{iM}}{\sigma_M^2}$ = asset i risk premium

An asset with a $\beta > 1$ is referred to as an aggressive stock; a stock whose rate of return improves or falls faster than that of the market. If the stock's beta is equal to 1.5, for example, then an excess return on the market of 1 percent will result in a 1.5 percent excess return on the stock. An asset with $\beta < 1$ is referred to as a defensive stock—one whose rate of return improves or falls slower than that of the market.

The linear relationship between the rate of return on a security and β shown in Equation 6.10 holds even if a risk-free asset does not exist. Black[3] showed the linear relationship to hold, with zero beta portfolios replacing the risk-free asset.

---

[3] **F. Black,** "Capital Market Equilibrium with Restricted Borrowing." *Journal of Business,* July 1972, pp. 444–455.

The comments of Professor Stephen Ross on Equation 6.10, the *capital asset pricing equation* (or model), are most adequate to repeat here:

> *The CAPM theory . . . not only "explains" asset prices, but it does so by providing an analytic basis for a brilliant, if not entirely reliable, intuition. Asset risk premia depend not on the total risk of the asset, but rather on the relationship of the asset to the overall market. Since* m *aggregates all risk borne by the market portfolio, only the relationship between the asset and the market portfolio, its beta, can determine the premium for an individual asset.* [4]

The reader should note that the rate of return on a security is no longer wholly determined by its total risk σ_i but by the correlation of that security's rate of return with the market rate of return, as seen in the equation

$$\beta = \frac{\rho_{i,M}\sigma_i\sigma_M}{\sigma_M^2} = \frac{\rho_{i,M}\sigma_i}{\sigma_M}$$

where $\rho_{i,M}\sigma_i =$ marginal risk of asset i—that is, that extra risk which security i adds to the portfolio if incorporated in it.

FIGURE 6.5   Security market line.

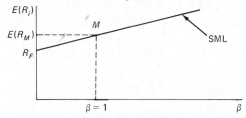

Figure 6.5 depicts the security market line (SML). Securities with rates of return lying above the SML are undervalued securities; they have too high a return given their level of risk. Those with rates of return plotting below the line are considered overvalued securities; they have too low a return given their level of risk.

The rate of return on the market portfolio is equal to

$$E(R_M) = R_F + \frac{E(R_M - R_F)}{\sigma_M^2}\,\sigma_{M,M}$$

The covariance of the market with itself is equal to its variance, thus:

$$E(R_M) = R_F + [E(R_M) - R_F]\frac{\sigma_M^2}{\sigma_M^2} = R_F + [E(R_M) - R_F] \tag{6.11}$$

[4] **Stephen A. Ross,** "The Current Status of the Capital Asset Pricing Model (CAPM)." *Journal of Finance,* vol. 33, no. 3 (June 1978), p. 886.

Since an efficient portfolio is some combination of a market portfolio and a risk-free asset, its beta would equal:

$$\beta_{\text{efficient},p} = W_M \beta_M = W_M(1) = W_M$$

Thus, a portfolio with $\beta > 1$ would lie to the right of point M ($W_M > 1$) and one with $\beta < 1$ would lie to the left of point M ($0 \leq W_M < 1$).

The point at which $\beta = 1$ is represented by M along the SML. Thus the market portfolio lies on the SML. In equilibrium, every security and portfolio will be on the SML.

The reader should observe that the capital market line represents a special case of the security market line. Rewriting Equation 6.10, we get

$$E(R_i) = R_F + \frac{E(R_M) - R_F}{\sigma_M^2} \rho \sigma_i \sigma_M$$

If i is an efficient portfolio, then $\rho = 1$ and therefore

$$E(R_i) = R_F + \frac{E(R_M) - R_F}{\sigma_M} (\sigma_i) \tag{6.12}$$

The reader should recognize Equation 6.12, which was developed earlier. It represents the capital market line.

The Characteristic Line

Equation 6.10 can be written as follows:

$$E(R_i) - R_F = \beta_i [E(R_M) - R_F] \tag{6.13}$$

Equation 6.13 is referred to as the *characteristic line* (CL) and is based on the assumption that all securities are efficiently priced; that is, the characteristic line has no intercept as shown in Figure 6.6. Stated differently, the excess return on a given security is strictly a function of the excess return on the market portfolio and the relationship between the rate of return on the security and that on the market portfolio (β).

If no relationship exists between the security and the market, $\rho_{i,M} = 0$, then $E(R_i)$

FIGURE 6.6 **The characteristic line.**

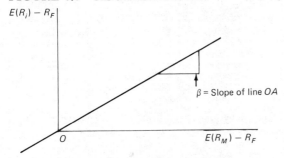

$- R_F = 0$ and $E(R_i) = R_F$. If $\rho_{i,M} > 0$, then the asset would earn a risk premium that is equal to $E(R_i) - R_F$ in an efficient market.

It is instructive to note at this stage one relationship between the security market line and the characteristic line. In the SML equation, β is the independent variable while it is the *slope* of the characteristic line.

All securities that are efficiently priced have a characteristic line passing through the origin; therefore all combinations of these securities, all portfolios, must have characteristic lines going through the origin as well. Such securities and portfolios plot on the SML. Returns exceeding those implied in Figure 6.6, or $E(R_i) - R_F$ occur frequently in the marketplace, however. Markets do get out of equilibrium, only to be brought back to equilibrium quickly through arbitrage. Thus the characteristic market line representing general market conditions at a point in time can be written as follows:

$$E(R_i) - R_F = \alpha_i + \lambda_i[E(R_M) - R_F] \tag{6.14}$$

where $\alpha_i =$ expected excess returns on security i if $E(R_M) - R_F = 0$.[5]

FIGURE 6.7   The market model.

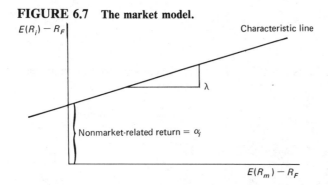

Equation 6.14 is illustrated in Figure 6.7 and is referred to as the *market model*. The characteristic line, therefore, represents a special case of the market model—a case where the security markets are efficient, $\alpha_i = 0$, and where $\lambda = \beta_i$.

The slope of the market model is equal to β_i, with $\beta_i \times [E(R_M) - R_F]$ representing the market-related excess return and the α_i the non-market-related excess return.

It bears repeating that the β coefficient (the slope of the characteristic line) measures the volatility of the individual asset in relation to the market (a measure of systematic risk).

Assuming that the "ex-post distribution from which returns are drawn is the ex-ante one perceived by investors,"[6] that is, the expected rate of return on a security is equal to the realized rate of return, the testable equation would be, rewriting Equation 6.13,

$$R_{i,t} = R_F + b_i(R_{M,t} - R_F) + \epsilon_{i,t} \tag{6.15}$$

---

[5] The alpha or α factor is used to evaluate the performance of portfolio managers, that is, to measure their ability to beat the market ($\alpha > 0$).

[6] **Ross**, p. 886.

where R_F = rate of return on the riskless asset if one exists or rate of return on a portfolio uncorrelated with the market portfolio

$\epsilon_{i,t}$ = portion of the security rate of return not explained by its relationship with the market rate of return

$b_i = \beta_i$ = slope of the regression equation

$E(\epsilon_{i,t}) = 0$

$\text{cov}(\epsilon_{i,t}, R_{M,t}) = 0$

$\sigma(\epsilon_{i,t}, \epsilon_{J,t}) = 0$

The proxies used for the variables in Equation 6.15, the nature of the data used, and the results of the regression analysis have produced an intense controversy in financial circles. We shall explore the foundation of this controversy after a brief discussion of the beta factor.

6.4 BETA

The estimable function for β can be arrived at by rewriting Equation 6.15,

$$R_{i,t} = (1 - b_i)R_F + b_i R_{M,t} + \epsilon_{i,t} \tag{6.16}$$
$$R_{i,t} = a + b_i R_{M,t} + \epsilon_{i,t} \tag{6.17}$$

To see how Equation 6.17 is estimated, we use a simple example. Assume that we wish to estimate the beta of Owens-Illinois (O-I). To do so, we regress the rate of return of O-I on the rate of return of a proxy for a market portfolio like the Standard & Poor's Composite Index. Using the percentage change in the end-of-month S&P index[7] as a measure of its rate of return for the period January 1977 to December 1980 and the percentage change in the end of month price of O-I (adjusted for stock splits) as a measure of the rate of return on O-I (columns X1 and Y respectively in Table 6.1), we ran a regression using Minitab.[8] The regression equation was linear of the following form:

$$Y = a + bX1 + \epsilon \tag{6.18}$$

The regression results appear partially in Table 6.1. The resulting estimates of the regression coefficients were

$$Y = -0.049 + 0.9934\ X1 \qquad \overline{R}^2 = 30.1\% \tag{6.19}$$
$$(-0.51) \quad (4.56)$$

The values in parentheses are t values. Therefore, O-I's beta is approximately one. The $\overline{R}^2$ indicates the credibility of the estimated beta.

---

[7] The source for these data is *Standard & Poor's Statistical Service Security Price Index Record,* Standard & Poor's Corporation, New York.

[8] See **Thomas A. Ryan, Brian L. Joiner,** and **Barbara Ryan,** *Minitab Student Handbook.* Duxbury, North Scituate, Mass., 1976.

TABLE 6.1
Estimating Beta for Owens-Illinois

ROW	X1 C1	Y C2	PRED. Y VALUE	ST.DEV. PRED. Y	RESIDUAL	ST.RES.
1	-2.0	-1.650	-2.527	1.118	0.877	0.14
2	-1.7	3.850	-2.140	1.075	5.990	0.94
3	-0.6	3.240	-1.077	0.985	4.317	0.68
4	-1.2	-0.450	-1.693	1.031	1.243	0.19
5	3.4	4.950	2.926	1.117	2.024	0.32
6	-1.5	-14.160	-1.941	1.055	-12.219	-1.91
7	-1.9	-7.000	-2.378	1.101	-4.622	-0.72
8	-1.5	-0.540	-1.991	1.059	1.451	0.23
9	-3.4	6.490	-3.839	1.295	10.329	1.63
10	4.8	-5.580	4.248	1.296	-9.828	-1.55
11	-1.8	2.690	-2.279	1.090	4.969	0.78
12	-5.7	-10.470	-6.114	1.676	-4.356	-0.70
13	-2.0	-4.090	-2.527	1.118	-1.563	-0.25
14	2.4	-1.220	1.873	1.013	-3.093	-0.48
15	8.0	4.940	7.466	1.852	-2.526	-0.41
16	0.4	1.760	-0.064	0.946	1.824	0.28
17	-1.9	-1.730	-2.368	1.099	0.638	0.10
18	3.9	4.120	3.344	1.169	0.776	0.12
19	4.5	1.130	3.940	1.250	-2.810	-0.44
20	-1.7	-1.120	-2.219	1.083	1.099	0.17
21	-4.3	-11.860	-4.783	1.444	-7.077	-1.12
22	-3.7	-1.920	-4.127	1.339	2.207	0.35
23	3.1	-6.540	2.589	1.079	-9.129	-1.43
24	3.4	4.200	2.867	1.110	1.333	0.21
25	-3.6	4.030	-4.117	1.337	8.147	1.29
26	6.0	7.740	5.509	1.499	2.231	0.35
27	0.4	-2.990	-0.104	0.946	-2.886	-0.45
28	-3.3	-2.470	-3.779	1.286	1.309	0.21
29	3.2	-2.530	2.708	1.092	-5.238	-0.82
30	0.8	10.390	0.284	0.944	10.106	1.58
31	5.7	4.710	5.191	1.445	-0.481	-0.08
32	0.9	-4.490	0.423	0.945	-4.913	-0.77
33	-7.4	-16.470	-7.892	2.011	-8.578	-1.39 X
34	4.8	9.150	4.387	1.302	4.863	0.77
35	1.0	4.520	0.532	0.947	3.988	0.62
36	6.9	15.430	6.324	1.642	9.106	1.45
37	-2.4	16.580	-2.925	1.167	19.505	3.06R
38	-12.2	-19.720	-12.601	2.963	-7.119	-1.24 X
39	7.7	9.710	7.168	1.796	2.542	0.41
40	5.4	-1.040	4.903	1.398	-5.943	-0.94
41	4.2	-2.630	3.642	1.208	-6.272	-0.99
42	4.7	10.270	4.198	1.288	6.072	0.96
43	1.1	-2.940	0.562	0.947	-3.502	-0.55
44	1.6	-7.070	1.069	0.963	-8.139	-1.27
45	1.6	12.500	1.099	0.964	11.401	1.78
46	10.2	3.380	9.682	2.284	-6.302	-1.04 X
47	-3.4	-5.610	-3.859	1.298	-1.751	-0.28

R DENOTES AN OBS. WITH A LARGE ST. RES.
X DENOTES AN OBS. WHOSE X VALUE GIVES IT LARGE INFLUENCE.

DURBIN-WATSON STATISTIC = 2.28

Beta and the Decomposition of Total Risk

The variance of Equation 6.17 is equal to:

$$\sigma_i^2 = b_i^2 \sigma_M^2 + \sigma_\epsilon^2 \tag{6.20}$$

Total variance of the rate of return on a security is, therefore, separable into systematic risk $b_i^2 \sigma_M^2$ and unsystematic risk σ_ϵ^2. A sufficiently diversified portfolio should have a

$\sigma_\epsilon^2 = 0$. Thus, the concern of investors should logically focus on systematic risk, for which they seek compensation in the form of higher rates of return.

The systematic risk of a portfolio is measured by the weighted average of the betas of each of the stocks in the portfolio.

$$b_p = \sum_i b_i W_i \qquad (6.21)$$

Beta and the Estimation of SML

The estimation of the capital asset pricing model (the security market line) ordinarily proceeds as follows:[9]

1. Estimate β_i using time series data and Equation 6.17. (The time series data are referred to by the subscript t.) This is done for several stocks.
2. Form portfolios based on the magnitude of their β.
3. Compute the average R_i's for each portfolio.
4. Regress the R_i's on the β_i's "in a cross-sectional test on the basis of data occurring after the formation period (period used to estimate β_i's)."[10]

The model used is a special form of Equation 6.14.

$$R_i = \pi_i + (R_M - R_F)\beta_i + \epsilon_i \qquad (6.22)$$

The estimated intercept of the regression equation is then compared with the risk-free rate and the slope with the excess rate of return ($R_M - R_F$).

The accumulated evidence indicates that the estimate of π_i in Equation 6.22 is significantly different from the T-bill rate used as a proxy for R_F and that the slope of the regression equation is less than $R_M - R_F$. A high intercept indicates that the compensation for market risk is lower than that for the market portfolio suggested by the capital asset pricing model and that low-β securities outperform the market (as predicted by the CAPM) and high-beta securities underperform the market. The return corresponding to a value of $\beta = 0$ has been dubbed by Fisher Black the *zero beta return*.

This estimation process makes clear that the characteristics and the behavior of beta are of considerable importance.

Stability and Biasedness of Beta?

The problem with the resulting β values is their biasedness. Also, the evidence suggests that β values are unstable. D. Levhari and H. Levy[11] argued that the length of the investment horizon underlying the estimation of the β value could produce biased results. The idea is simple. Empirical studies use different time periods in testing the CAPM.

---

[9] See **James M. Johnson** and **Howard P. Lanser**, "Dividend Risk Measurement and Test of the CAPM." *Journal of Portfolio Management*, Winter 1981, pp. 50–54.

[10] Ibid., p. 51.

[11] **David Levhari** and **Haim Levy**, "The Capital Asset Pricing Model and the Investment Horizon." *Review of Economics and Statistics*, vol. 59, no. 1 (February 1977), pp. 92–104.

Some use weekly, some use monthly, some use quarterly, and others use annual data. The CAPM is, however, a single-period model, with all investors having the same time horizon. To the extent that the time horizon (the time period used in the empirical analysis to define the data set) differs from the "true" time horizon (that time horizon over which all investors calculate their true rate of return on securities), the resulting beta could be biased upward or downward. The results of these studies are summarized in Table 6.2.

TABLE 6.2

	"True Beta"	>1	=1	<1
Estimated	Shorter period	smaller	same	larger
beta	Longer period	larger	same	smaller

Source: Quoted from Michael D. Carpenter and David E. Upton, "Trading Volume and Beta Stability." *Journal of Portfolio Management,* Winter 1981, p. 60.

Haim Levy[12] later also confirmed that the length of the holding period has an effect on beta: "The systematic risk of aggressive stocks [$\beta > 1$] increases with the investment horizon and that of defensive stocks [$\beta < 1$] decreases."[13]

The biasedness issue was extensively documented by M. Blume.[14] The beta of securities tended toward *one,* the average beta of all securities. Estimates of $\beta > 1$ tended to be overestimates, and those of $\beta < 1$ tended to be underestimates. This bias led to various adjustment techniques. In this chapter we discuss two of the adjustment techniques: Merrill Lynch beta, and Value Line beta.

The instability of beta also derives from changes in company fundamentals and in capital structure. Some of the evidence regarding the instability of beta was provided by Sharpe and G. Cooper[15] who, using CRSP data, estimated the betas of securities using the past 60 months of rates of return for each year from 1931 to 1967. The resulting betas were ranked and divided into ten risk classes. The procedure was repeated each year and the consistency of the membership of securities in risk classes was checked. A high percentage of securities (65 percent) did not remain in their risk class in certain cases. Sharpe and Cooper concluded that the instability of beta is significant.

M. Carpenter and D. Upton[16] suggested that the instability of the beta may be due to the "chronological time as an index in the return computation."[17] Using trading volume as a proxy for information flows into the market, Carpenter and Upton calculated

---

[12] **Haim Levy,** "The CAPM and the Investment Horizon." *Journal of Portfolio Management,* Winter 1981, pp. 32–40.

[13] Ibid., p. 39.

[14] **M. E. Blume,** "Betas and Their Regression Tendencies." *Journal of Finance,* June 1975, pp. 785–795.

[15] **W. F. Sharpe** and **G. M. Cooper,** "Risk-Return Classes of New York Stock Exchange Common Stocks, 1931–67." *Financial Analyst's Journal,* March–April 1972, pp. 46–54.

[16] **Michael D. Carpenter** and **David E. Upton,** "Trading Volume and Beta Stability." *Journal of Portfolio Management,* Winter 1981, pp. 60–64.

[17] Ibid., p. 60.

the rates of returns for periods with high volume and for periods with low volume of trading. A high volume would indicate "that operational time is passing more rapidly than chronological time."[18] and the opposite for low volume. Operational time is best understood in terms of rate generation. If high returns are generated in a week, say, then this week is operationally longer than a week with low returns.

The test results indicated that high volume volatility produced high beta volatility and low volume volatility produced low beta volatility. The results also showed that "volume effects" do exist and that by "controlling for the volume effect by using constant-volume periods, the relative betas of the assets will be more accurate, exhibiting less variance for a given set of data than they would without correction."[19]

Merrill Lynch Beta

The Merrill Lynch beta is computed using Equation 6.17:

$$R_{i,t} = a + b_i R_{M,t} + \epsilon_{i,t}$$

The $R_{i,t}$ and $R_{M,t}$'s are computed using only capital gains (ignoring dividends and the risk-free rate) as follows:

$$R_{i,t} = \frac{\Delta P_{i,t}}{P_{i,t}} \text{ and } R_{M,t} = \frac{\Delta P_{M,t}}{P_{M,t}}$$

where $P_{i,t}$ and $P_{M,t}$ are the prices for a given time period of a common stock and the values of a market index, respectively.

The dividends are ignored because empirical evidence presented by Sharpe and Cooper[20] has shown dividends to have no impact on the estimation of beta. The S&P 500 is used as a proxy for the market index.

Using 60 monthly observations, Merrill Lynch estimates beta using Equation 6.17 and adjusts it for the bias reported by Blume as follows:

$$\beta_{ML} = 0.33743 + 0.66257b \tag{6.23}$$

The Merrill Lynch estimate of O-I's beta would be $\beta_{ML} = 0.33743 + 0.66251(1) = 1$.

Value Line Beta

Value Line, on the other hand, uses weekly data covering 260 periods (weeks). The proxy for the market is the NYSE Composite Index. Dividends are ignored once again. The Value Line adjusted beta is calculated as follows:

$$\beta_{V.L.} = 0.35 + 0.67b \tag{6.24}$$

---

[18] Ibid., p. 61.

[19] Ibid., p. 64.

[20] **Sharpe and Cooper,** 1972.

Meir Statman[21] tested the relationship between $\beta_{M.L.}$ and $\beta_{V.L.}$ for 195 firms with the highest market value of common stock. The results were

$$\beta_{M.L.} = 0.127 + 0.879\beta_{V.L.} \tag{6.25}$$

While the intercept was significant (t-statistic = 2.13), Statman concludes that it is ". . . not strong that the difference is indeed systematic."[22]

Other Factors Influencing Beta

There are many factors influencing beta. Hamada[23] showed that financial leverage is one. The higher financial leverage is, the higher beta, and the greater the volatility of the stock.

Lev[24] found that the higher operating leverage is, the larger the volatility of the stock returns. This is true across the industries tested. This thesis was basically the subject of an analysis by Rubinstein,[25] who found beta to be a function of operating risk.

The more comprehensive analysis was produced by Rosenberg and McKibben.[26] Beta was hypothesized to be a function of various "descriptors" W_{Jit}, 32 in total initially. The subscript Jit refers to the J descriptor for the ith firm at time t. Beta was estimated using the following equation:

$$\beta_{it} = \sum_{J=1}^{n} b_J W_{Jit} + \epsilon_{it} \tag{6.26}$$

The descriptors were primarily accounting-related. Twenty were "accounting-based" (such as the acid-test ratio), seven were "market-based" (such as share turnover), and five were "market valuation-related" (such as earnings/price ratio). The selection of these descriptors was made:

> *Without any prior fitting of the data, on the basis of studies reported in the literature and the authors' intuition. . . .The regressions were conducted in a predesigned sequence. First, all 32 descriptors were included in regressions.*

---

[21] **Meir Statman,** "Betas Compared: Merrill Lynch vs. Value Line." *Journal of Portfolio Management,* Spring 1981, pp. 41–44.

[22] Ibid., p. 43.

[23] **R. S. Hamada,** "Portfolio Analysis, Market Equilibrium and Corporate Finance." *Journal of Finance,* March 1969, pp. 13–31.

[24] **B. Lev,** "On the Association Between Operating Leverage and Risk." *Journal of Financial and Quantitative Analysis,"* September 1974, pp. 627–641.

[25] **M. E. Rubinstein,** "A Mean-Variance Synthesis of Corporate Financial Theory." *Journal of Finance,* March 1973, pp. 167–181.

[26] **B. Rosenberg** and **W. McKibben,** "The Prediction of Systematic Risk in Common Stocks." *Journal of Financial and Quantitative Analysis,* March 1973, pp. 317–334.

> *Those descriptors insignificant at the 90 percent level were deleted. This cutoff was selected on the basis of the results.*[27]

A more ambitious study using 80 descriptors was later undertaken by Rosenberg and Marathe,[28] which again combined accounting and nonaccounting variables in forecasting beta and indirectly the required rate of return on a security.

Rosenberg was later to set up an investment service corporation selling Rosenberg betas to institutions. The exact procedure for arriving at these beta is somewhat of a mystery. The success of Rosenberg and his strong advocacy of the validity (both theoretical and empirical) of the CAPM have placed him at the center of the controversy regarding the value of beta.

Beta: Dead or Alive?

The controversy over the validity of beta as a measure of risk has become very profound and has polarized academicians and practitioners. The seeds of the controversy were planted by an article authored by Richard Roll.[29] In this article, Roll questions the very foundation of the CAPM. His fundamental point is that for a theory that acquired its reputation on the base of easy testability, the CAPM has never been correctly and unambiguously tested and "there is practically no possibility that such a test can be accomplished in the future."[30] The logic is the following:

1. The development of the CAPM requires that the market portfolio M is mean variance efficient. The linearity between the expected rate of return and beta summarized in the SML "follows from the market portfolio's efficiency and are not independently testable."[31]

2. The market portfolio M in the CAPM includes all invested assets. The use of proxies like the S&P 500 composite index is inadequate. Those proxies may be mean-variance efficient while the market is not and mean-variance inefficient while the market is. Unless the composition of the market portfolio is known and is measurable, Roll argues, the testability of the theory is not possible. S. Ross tempers this view a bit:

> *Roll's analysis does not say that we must observe* m *to test the theory. For example, we can all agree that* m *has only positive components, and this means that the CAPM could be refuted by refuting the existence of a positive (ex ante) efficient portfolio. This is a testable proposition, but as Roll's second point shows, the construction of suitable powerful tests will be difficult. More generally, even though* m *is unobservable, a proxy* P *can be used for testing*

---

[27] Ibid., p. 325.

[28] **B. Rosenberg,** and **V. Marathe,** "The Prediction of Investment Risk: Systematic and Residual Risk," *Proceedings of the Seminar on the Analysis of Security Prices.* Center for Research in Security Prices, Graduate School of Business, University of Chicago, November 1975, pp. 85–159.

[29] **Richard Roll,** "A Critique of the Asset Pricing Theory's Tests." *Journal of Financial Economics,* vol. 4, 1977, pp. 129–176.

[30] Ibid., p. 130.

[31] Ibid., p. 130.

if we know something about m − P. *By bounding the difference between* m *and* P—*for instance, by bounding the total wealth not included in our sample— it might be possible to construct tests of the efficiency of* m *by using* P. *This will not be easy, but it should be possible.*[32]

Roll proved his point by showing that different proxies against which portfolio performances are measured yield different rankings.[33] The value of the beta is thus questionable if not nil.

3. The exclusive attention to β as a measure of riskiness excludes much important information. This point was made clear by Robert Vandell.[34] The essence of his argument is that "Given two stocks with the same beta, but one with a high positive alpha (the vertical distance between the stock point and the security market line) and the other with a high negative alpha, can one really say, ex ante, that the two have equal risk? Then why do we?"[35] The riskiness of a stock may well be comprised of several risk premiums instead of just one, β, as claimed by the CAPM.

4. While the above criticism concentrates on the empirical aspects of the CAPM, Ross finds problems with the fundamental assumptions[36] of the theory, specifically with:

a. The normality of the distribution of rates of return, or

b. The quadratic preferences of investors.

The limitations of the CAPM led Stephen Ross to seek an alternative. He developed his model in the early 1970s at the University of Pennsylvania, but it was not published until 1976 in the *Journal of Economic Theory*.

The theory developed by Ross is the arbitrage pricing theory (APT). This theory represents the multifactor case of the CAPM; that is, factors other than the market rate of return and the covariance between that market rate of return and the rate of return on a security influence the price of a security. The CAPM, a one-factor model,

---

[32] **Ross,** 1978, p. 893.

[33] **Richard Roll,** "Ambiguity When Performance Is Measured by the Securities Market Line." *Journal of Finance,* September 1978, vol. 33, no. 4, pp. 1051–1069.

[34] **Robert F. Vandell,** "Is Beta a Useful Measure of Security Risk?" *Journal of Portfolio Management,* Winter 1981, p. 24.

[35] Ibid., p. 24.

[36] It must be noted that the other assumptions of the theory have been relaxed without a significant impact on the validity of the CAPM.

Fama (**Eugene Fama,** "Portfolio Analysis in a Stable Paretian Market." *Management Science,* January 1965, pp. 404–419.) investigated the normality assumption and found that returns were not normally distributed. The validity of the CAPM is preserved, however, if the distribution (not the variance) is used.

Mayers (**D. Mayers,** "Non-Marketable Assets and the Capital Market Equilibrium under Uncertainty," in M. C. Jensen, ed., *Studies in the Theory of Capital Markets.* Praeger, New York, 1972, pp. 223–248.) showed that the validity of the CAPM is unaffected by the presence of nonmarketable assets.

In a continuous (as opposed to a discrete) time framework, Merton (**R. Merton,** "An Intertemporal Capital Asset Pricing Model," *Econometrica,* September 1973, pp. 867–888.) showed that the CAPM is robust. The expected rate of return is replaced by an instantaneous rate of return.

Lintner (**J. Lintner,** "The Aggregation of Investors' Diverse Judgements and Preferences in Purely Competitive Security Markets." *Journal of Financial and Quantitative Analysis,* December 1969, pp. 347–400.) showed that heterogeneous expectations can be adjusted for mathematically, but the testability of the CAPM is severely impaired.

is, therefore, a special case of APT derived under much more restrictive assumptions. We shall discuss the basic tenets of APT next.

6.5 THE ARBITRAGE PRICING THEORY[37]

An arbitrage situation is one involving no commitment of capital and yielding a positive rate of return.

For arbitrage to work effectively, capital markets must be perfectly competitive and investors must be rational (prefer more wealth to less wealth).

Assume that returns are generated by the following linear relationship:

$$\tilde{x}_i = E_i + \beta_i \tilde{\delta} + \tilde{\epsilon}_i \tag{6.27}$$

where $\sim$ = a random variable

   E_i = ex ante expected return

   β_i = ex ante beta coefficient

   $\tilde{\delta}$ = Zero *common* (to all securities) factor representing the deviation of the market return from its trend

   $\tilde{\epsilon}_i$ = error term

Of the n assets available for investment, we pick the arbitrage portfolio η. Eta (η) is a vector of weights, that is, the proportions invested in each security. Since the arbitrage portfolio used zero wealth, the wealth invested in the long positions must be offset by the amount derived from the short sales. Thus the components of the vector η are positive and negative.

$$\eta = [\eta_1, \ldots, \eta_n]$$

where $|\eta_i| \approx 1/n$

For convenience introduce $\phi = \begin{bmatrix} 1 \\ \vdots \\ 1 \end{bmatrix}$

Since the arbitrage portfolio uses no wealth,

$$\eta\phi = 0$$

the return on the arbitrage portfolio is now equal

$$\eta\tilde{x} = \eta E + (\eta\beta)\tilde{\delta} + \eta\tilde{\epsilon} \tag{6.28}$$

---

[37] The discussion relies heavily (also uses the same notations) on the following two papers: **Stephen A. Ross,** "The Arbitrage Theory of Capital Asset Pricing. *Journal of Economic Theory,* vol. 13, 1976, pp. 341–360; and **Richard Roll** and **Stephen A. Ross,** "An Empirical Investigation of the Arbitrage Pricing Theory." *Journal of Finance,* vol. 35, no. 5 (December 1980), pp. 1073–1103.

where $\tilde{x} = \begin{bmatrix} \tilde{x}_1 \\ \tilde{x}_2 \\ \vdots \\ x_n \end{bmatrix}$, $E = \begin{bmatrix} E_1 \\ \vdots \\ E_\eta \end{bmatrix}$, $\beta = \begin{bmatrix} \beta_1 \\ \vdots \\ \beta_\eta \end{bmatrix}$, $\tilde{\epsilon} = \begin{bmatrix} \epsilon_1 \\ \vdots \\ \epsilon_\eta \end{bmatrix}$

By the law of large numbers, $\eta\,\tilde{\epsilon} \approx 0$. Thus $\eta\tilde{x} \approx \eta E + (\eta\beta)\tilde{\delta}$.

If the arbitrage portfolio is chosen to have no systematic risk, that is $\beta = 0$, then,

$$\eta\tilde{x} \approx \eta E \qquad (6.29)$$

Equation 6.29 effectively transforms random returns $\tilde{x}$ into certain returns E.

If the securities markets are in equilibrium (or not significantly out of equilibrium), ηE cannot materialize. Thus $\eta E = 0$.

Since $\eta E = \eta\phi = \eta\beta = 0$, the vectors E, ϕ, and β are in the same vector space and E is "spanned" by (is a linear combination of) ϕ and β.

$$E_i = \mu + \lambda\beta_i \qquad (6.30)$$

where μ and $\lambda =$ constants.

Equation 6.27 is depicted in Figure 6.8.

From Figure 6.8, we can see that μ represents the zero beta portfolio (see Black) or the risk-free rate if a riskless asset exists. For any portfolio m with a positive β, λ must represent the excess return on that portfolio over the zero beta rate or the risk-free rate. Thus Equation 6.30 can be written (very similarly to the SML) as

$$E_i = \mu + (E_m - \mu)\beta_i \qquad (6.31)$$

where $E_m =$ rate of return on the portfolio. In this case, E_m represents the rate of return on the market portfolio.

Equation 6.31 obtains, the reader must observe, whether the market is in equilibrium or is out of equilibrium (extreme disequilibrium cases can be problematic, however) and without concern for the market portfolio per se.

FIGURE 6.8   **Graphic depiction of Equation 6.27.**

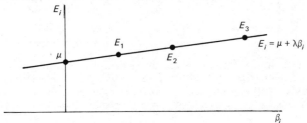

Then what basically are the differences between CAPM and APT? We let Roll and Ross explain:

> *The APT is a particularly appropriate alternative because it agrees perfectly with what appears to be the intuition behind the CAPM. Indeed, the APT is based on a linear return generating process as a first principle, and requires no utility assumptions beyond monotonicity and concavity. Nor is it restricted to a single period; it will hold in both the multiperiod and single period cases. Though consistent with every conceivable prescription for portfolio diversification, no particular portfolio plays a role in the APT. Unlike the CAPM, there is no requirement that the market portfolio be mean variance efficient.*
>
> *There are two major differences between the APT and the original Sharpe (50) "diagonal" model, a single factor generating model which we believe is the intuitive grey eminence behind the CAPM. First, and most simply, the APT allows more than just one generating factor. Second, the APT demonstrates that since any market equilibrium must be consistent with no arbitrage profits, every equilibrium will be characterized by a linear relationship between each asset's expected return and its return's response amplitudes, or loadings, on the common factors. With minor caveats, given the factor generating model, the absence of riskless arbitrage profits—an easy enough condition to accept a priori—leads immediately to the APT. Its modest assumptions and its pleasing implications surely render the APT worthy of being the object of empirical testing.* [38]

Testing APT

The first empirical test of APT was done by Gehr[39] using a methodology which was later adopted and expanded on by Roll and Ross.[40] The testable equation requires the generalization of the arbitrage model to the K-factor case using weighted beta coefficients with the constraint that the number of common factors does not exceed the number of assets.

When the generating model has the form $\overline{X}_i = E_i + \beta_{i1} \tilde{\delta}_1 + \cdots + \beta_{ik} \tilde{\delta}_k + \tilde{\epsilon}_i$ the basic arbitrage condition takes the form of

$$E_i = \mu + (E_m - \mu)(V_1 \beta_{i1} + \cdots + V_k \beta_{ik}) \tag{6.32}$$

where the V_i's are nonnegative constants such that $\Sigma V_1 = 1$ and $\mu = R_F$ in Equation 6.14.

Equation 6.32 reduces to the CAPM if only one β is operating, where $\beta = (\sigma_{i,m})/\sigma_m^2$.

What all of the β's represent is not quite clear. The APT model leaves them unspecified. It appears that each investor faces his or her own set of β's, which may be valued differently from one to another.

Using daily data from the Center for Research in Security Prices (CRSP) of the

---

[38] **Roll** and **Ross**, 1980, p. 1074.

[39] **Adam Gehr, Jr.,** "Some Tests of the Arbitrage Pricing Theory." *Journal of Midwest Finance Association,* 1975, pp. 91–105.

[40] **Roll** and **Ross**, 1980.

University of Chicago on 1,260 securities covering the period July 3, 1962, to December 31, 1972, Roll and Ross proceeded to test APT using a maximum likelihood factor analysis. The data were split into 42 groups (30 securities in each) with some groups having more observations than others. While admitting the weakness of the tests used, Roll and Ross were able to conclude that the empirical evidence supports APT "against both an unspecified alternative—a very weak test, and the specific alternative that own variance has an independent explanatory effect on excess returns.[41]

The most recent test of APT was conducted by M. Reinganum.[42] Using factor analysis on 1,457 firms beginning in 1963 with the sample size increasing to 2,500 by the mid-1970s (1978), Reinganum found the evidence to be "inconsistent with the APT."[43] His conclusion was that "the evidence indicates that a parsimonious APT fails [the] test."[44] APT was unable to account for the "empirical anomalies that arise within the CAPM."[45]

CONCLUSIONS

The controversy over the CAPM is far from over. The reader must keep in mind that the assault on the CAPM is not intended to deny its validity but mainly to show its limitations. However, the proposed alternative, APT, has yet to pass a rigorous test.

QUESTIONS

1. State the assumptions and the basic results of the CAPM. Compare and contrast the CAPM with the Markowitz model. Of what value is the CAPM?

2. A portfolio which lies on the efficiency frontier is said to be "efficient." What does this mean?

3. What does the slope of the capital market line (CML) represent?

4. If an investor chooses point X on the graph below and M is the point where 100 percent of assets are invested in risky securities, what does this indicate?

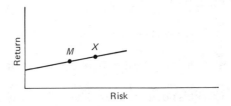

[41] Ibid., p. 1100.

[42] **Marc R. Reinganum,** "Empirical Tests of Multi-Factor Pricing Model, The Arbitrage Pricing Theory: Some Empirical Results." *Journal of Finance,* vol. 36, no. 2, May 1981, pp. 313–321.

[43] Ibid., p. 317.

[44] Ibid., p. 320.

[45] Ibid., p. 320.

5. What securities are in portfolio *M*? In what proportions?

6. Show every step for estimating the security market line (SML). How would you use the SML?

7. Compare the SML to the CML.

8. "Utility functions and their shapes are of critical value in the security valuation process." Comment.

9. If portfolio *M* is optimal for any investor, why doesn't every investor construct such a portfolio?

10. What risk does the CAPM consider when pricing an asset?

11. What is the slope of the characteristic line? Assign different likely values to it and interpret their meanings.

12. If nonmarket returns were zero, where would the characteristic line intercept the vertical axis $E(R)$?

13. A portfolio contains unsystematic risk. What does this imply?

14. What does empirical evidence reveal about the volatility or stability of betas? What are the implications of this evidence to investors?

15. What is the beta of the market portfolio *M*? Could a stock have a negative beta?

16. Mr. Investor owns a portfolio which has a beta of 0.5. What does this imply about his strategy.

17. Suggest a way, based on the CAPM, to evaluate the performance of a portfolio manager.

18. According to Stephen Ross, is the CAPM theoretically unsound or empirically intractable?

19. A speculator is bearish on the market. Would he pick a stock with a high or low beta? Why?

20. What return should a zero-beta portfolio offer if markets are efficient?

PROBLEMS

1. What would the β_{ML} (Merrill Lynch beta) equal if estimates of the characteristic lines indicate that $\beta = 0$, $\beta = 1$, $\beta = 2$?

2. The T-bill rate is 6 percent and the market portfolio is expected to return 12 percent with a standard deviation of return of 15 percent. A portfolio which is sufficiently diversified has a standard deviation of return of 10 percent.
a. What is the beta of the portfolio?
b. What is the SML equation?
c. What is the $E(R)$ of the portfolio?

3. The market is expected to return 10 percent above the risk-free rate of 8 percent. JAK stock has a beta of 0.8 while stock MSO has a beta of 1.2.

a. Write the SML equation.
b. What should JAK return?
c. What should MSO return?
d. What is the excess return of MSO over JAK, and how is it justified?

4. The following information is available on several instruments:

Instrument	E(R)	Risk (beta)
T-bill	10%	0.0
XYZ Corp. stock	12%	0.4
SAO Corp. stock	13.8%	0.6
AMO Corp. stock	15.5%	1.0
SHV Corp. stock	17.3%	1.4

a. Graph the SML using R_f and the coordinates $\beta = 1$, $E(R_m) = 15\%$.
b. Which instruments are over/underpriced?

5. Given the following information, use the Markowitz and Sharpe models (given below) to calculate the expected return and risk (variance) of five two-security portfolios. The proportion of funds to be placed in the two securities, SMO and TMH, is:

	(1)	(2)	(3)	(4)	(5)
SMO	0.0	.25	.50	.75	1.0
TMH	1.0	.75	.50	.25	0.0

	SMO	TMH	Market (S&P 500)
Beta (β)	.60	.40	1.00
Alpha (α)	.01	−.01	0.00
E(R)	.12	.08	0.10
Variance	.04	.025	0.01

The covariance between SMO and TMH is 0.005.

MARKOWITZ'S EQUATIONS

1. Expected return

$$E(R_p) = \sum_{j=1}^{n} w_j E(R_j) = w_1 E(R_1) + w_2 E(R_2)$$

2. Risk (variance)

$$\sigma_p^2 = \sum_{i=1}^{n} \sum_{j=1}^{n} w_i w_j \, \text{COV}\,(R_i, R_j)$$
$$= w_1^2(\sigma_{R_1}^2) + w_2^2(\sigma_{R_2}^2) + 2 w_1 w_2 \, \text{COV}(R_1, R_2)$$

SHARPE'S EQUATIONS

1. Expected return

$$E(Rp) = \sum_{j=1}^{n} w_j \alpha_j + \left[\left(\sum_{j=1}^{n} w_j \beta_j \right) E(R_m) \right] = \sum_{j=1}^{n} w_j [\alpha_j + \beta_j E(Rm)]$$

2. Risk (variance)

$$\sigma_p^2 = \sum_{j=1}^{n} w_j^2 (\sigma_j^2) + \left[\left(\sum_{j=1}^{n} w_j \beta_j \right)^2 (\sigma_m^2) \right]$$

PART
THREE

Equity Securities

CHAPTER
7

Valuation of Common Stocks

7.1 DEFINITION

A common stock is evidence of ownership in a corporate entity.

7.2 TYPES OF COMMON STOCK

Three types of common stock are issued:

1. *Class A common stock.* This type stock is issued to the public and ordinarily pays dividends. Class A common stocks carry full voting rights.
2. *Class B common stock.* This type stock is "bought" by the organizers of the corporation and does not pay dividends until the earning power of the corporation is proven.
3. *Founders' shares.* Founders' shares resemble class B stocks except that they carry sole voting rights. This type share guarantees that the control over the corporation remains in the hands of the founders.

7.3 RIGHTS OF STOCKHOLDERS

Common stockholders hold the ultimate power over the destiny of the corporation. Their rights and responsibilities are set by the laws of the state in which the firm is incorporated. Among their rights* are the following:

1. The right to vote for the directors of the corporation, to amend the corporate charter or bylaws, to sell the assets of the corporation or to merge with another

---

* Stockholders' rights are expanding. *The Wall Street Journal* reported in its October 10, 1981, issue that Berkshire Hathaway Inc. had given its stockholders the right to determine the recipient(s) of a designated corporate charitable contribution.

entity, and to issue new securities (additional common stock, bonds, preferred stock, etc.). This right is transferable through an instrument called a proxy.
2. The right to sell their securities whenever they deem it in their interest.
3. The right to inspect the corporate books and to share proportionately in the residual value of the corporation in the event of liquidation.

7.4 VALUATION OF COMMON STOCK

The valuation of a common stock requires consideration, as in the case of every capital asset, of the net benefits to be derived from its ownership. Unfortunately, the net benefits are not specified at the time ownership is established. Corporations do not have to pay dividends on common stocks and common stocks do not always appreciate in price despite the best wishes and prayers of their holders.

A holder of a common stock usually expects to receive the net benefits in the form of dividends and/or capital gains, neither of which is very predictable, capital gains in particular. The present value of these net benefits represents the intrinsic value of the common stock. Given efficient equity markets, that intrinsic value should equal the market value of the stock. With an expected holding period of one year, the market price of a stock should equal:

$$MP_0^s = \frac{D_1}{(1 + K_e)} + \frac{E(MP_1^s)}{(1 + K_e)} \tag{7.1}$$

where: MP_0^s = market price of stock at time zero

D_1 = end-of-year dividend payment

$E(MP_1^s)$ = market price expected to prevail at the end of the first period

K_e = cost of equity to the firm or the required rate of return on a stock that prevents its market value from falling (K_e will be assumed to remain constant in multiperiod models.)

Most investors, however, hold a stock for periods longer than a year. In this case:

$$MP_0^s = \sum_{t=1}^{n} \frac{D_t}{(1 + K_e)^t} + \frac{E(MP_n^s)}{(1 + K_e)^n} \tag{7.2}$$

If, on the other hand, the holding period is infinite (i.e., the investor has no plans ever to sell the stock), the market price is calculated as follows:[1]

$$MP_0^s = \sum_{t=1}^{\infty} \frac{D_t}{(1 + K_e)^t} \tag{7.3}$$

---

[1] The model summarized in Equation 7.3 is not extensively used by financial analysts. In fact, according to Ralph A. Bing [*Financial Analyst's Journal*, vol. 27 (May–June 1971), pp. 55–60] only 6 percent of the analysts used this model. The overwhelming majority (75 percent) of analysts simply multiply expected earnings (normalized to reflect the prevailing economic cycle) by an appropriate (to industry and risk) class.

Predicting the values of D_t is not an easy task, however. A convenient tool that theorists use, not without historical justification, is to assume that dividends grow at a steady rate g ad infinitum. Therefore

$$MP_0^s = \sum_{t=1}^{n} \frac{D_0(1+g)^t}{(1+K_e)^t}$$

$$= D_0 \sum_{t=1}^{\infty} \frac{(1+g)^t}{(1+K_e)^t} \tag{7.4}$$

The term

$$\sum_{t=1}^{n} \frac{(1+g)^t}{(1+K_e)^t}$$

represents the sum of a geometric series. Let $r = (1+g)/(1+K_e)$, then the sum of the series is equal to

$$S = D_0 r + D_0 r^2 + D_0 r^3 + \cdots + D_0 r^n \tag{7.5}$$

Multiplying both sides of Equation 7.5 by r, we get

$$rS = D_0 r^2 + D_0 r^3 + \cdots + D_0 r^{n+1} \tag{7.6}$$

Subtracting Equation 7.6 from Equation 7.5, we get:

$$rS - S = D_0 r^{n+1} - D_0 r$$
$$S(r-1) = D_0 r(r^n - 1)$$

Therefore

$$S = \frac{D_0 r(r^n - 1)}{r - 1}$$

and

$$\lim_{n \to \infty} S = \frac{-D_0 r}{r - 1} \quad \text{if } g < K_e$$

Thus

$$MP_0^s = \frac{D_0[(1+g)/(1+K_e)]}{1 - [(1+g)/(1+K_e)]} = \frac{D_0[(1+g)/(1+K_e)]}{(K_e - g)/(1+K_e)}$$

$$MP_0^s = \frac{D_1{}^*}{K_e - g} \quad \text{if } K_e > g \tag{7.7}$$

---

* If currently declared dividends payable at the end of the period represented the first term in Equation 7.5, then

Dividing Equation 7.7 by earnings per share, we get

$$\frac{MP_0^s}{e} = \frac{D_0}{e} \times \frac{(1+g)}{K_e - g} \tag{7.8}$$

where $(MP_0^s)/e$ = price/earnings ratio.

The drawbacks of the model represented by Equation 7.8 have been pointed out by B. Malkiel and J. Cragg.[2] The model is not applicable if the corporation does not pay dividends, its solution is infinity if $g \geq K_e$, it requires the constancy of both K_e and g, and it does not account for risk. The model is thus not useful in estimating the cost of equity of companies with highly variable dividend payout or of companies with very high growth rates, where g is likely to be higher than K_e. The alternative formulation suggested by Malkiel and Cragg is

$$\frac{MP_0^s}{e_0} = \sum_{t=1}^{n} \frac{D_0}{e_0} \times \frac{(1+g)^t}{(1+K_e)^t} + (m_s)_0 \frac{(1+g)^n}{(1+K_e)^n} \tag{7.9}$$

where $(m_s)_0$ = average current price/earnings ratio for the market as a whole.

If $D_0 = 0$, Equation 7.9 can be written as

$$MP_0^s = e_0 \times (m_s)_0 \frac{(1+g)^n}{(1+K_e)^n} \tag{7.10}$$

Equation 7.9 uses a finite time horizon. A linear approximation to Equation 7.9 was arrived at by Malkiel and Cragg, with n equal to 5 or more periods. It must be noted, however, that Equation 7.10, unless properly interpreted, applies only if e_0 is positive. Firms currently losing money ($e_0 < 0$) still command positive market values. Alternatively, e_0 could be conceived as those earnings in the first year of profitability, or the average expected earnings over a reasonable time horizon.

$$P = D_0\left(\frac{1}{1+K_e}\right) + D_0 \frac{(1+g)^2}{(1+K_e)^2} + D_0 \frac{(1+g)}{(1+K_e)^3} + \cdots + D_0 \frac{(1+g)^{n-1}}{(1+K_e)^n}$$

$$= D_0\left(\frac{1}{1+K_e}\right)(1 + r + r^2 + r^3 + \cdots + r^n)$$

The sum of the values in bracket is equal to $(1 - r^n)/(1 - r)$.

Therefore

$$P = \frac{[(D_0)/(1+K_e)]\,[1 - (1+g)^n/(1+K_e)^n]}{[1 - (1+g)/(1+K_e)]}$$

and as $n \to \infty$

$$P = \frac{D_0}{K_e - g} \qquad \text{(not } D_1\text{)}$$

[2] **Burton G. Malkiel** and **John G. Cragg**, "Expectations and the Structure of Share Prices." *American Economic Review*, vol. 60 (September 1970), pp. 601–617.

In all the equations above it *appears* that stock prices are determined to one degree or another by dividend policy. Do dividends determine stock prices or are they a proxy for another variable?

Before we answer this question, let us look at alternative but equivalent (although they appear different) methods.

The Wall Street Journal reported in its March 25, 1981, issue that the method for valuing firms that is gaining increasing acceptance involves the projection of "free" *cash flows* over a 10- or 20-year period:

> *the method first projects into the future a dozen or so important financial variables, including production, prices, non-cash deduction from income such as depreciation and depletion, taxes and capital outlays, all adjusted to reflect inflation. Then analysts reduce that total by an amount representing the buyer's accumulated return, at a specified rate target, on investment. The remainder represents the price the buyer is willing to pay for the . . . company. To take a simple example, if the . . . company is expected to accumulate cash at $1 million a year for 20 years and the buyer's rate-of-return objective is 15%, the buyer would be willing to pay about $6.25 million for the . . . company.*

Is the discounting of cash flows to arrive at the market price of the firm or equivalently at the market price of the stock any different from the discounting of dividends? The answer is no. In order to see why, we take a glimpse at the next section and find out what dividends are a proxy for.

The seminal work of Modigliani and Miller (M&M)[3] showed that the value of the firm *under certain conditions* is independent of its dividend policy. Assuming infinite life, the value of the firm, as is demonstrated in the next section, is equal to

$$MV = \sum_{t=1}^{\infty} \frac{e_t - I_t}{(1 + K_e)^t} \qquad (7.11)$$

where MV = market value of firm

e_t = net earnings

I_t = required investment to maintain the earning power of the firm and to meet target earning growth rate

Therefore

$$MP_0^s = \frac{MV}{n}$$

where n = number of shares outstanding.

In Equation 7.11, $e_t - I_t$ could produce either dividends to stockholder or additional issuance of stock and/or borrowing.

---

[3] **M. H. Miller** and **F. Modigliani**, "Dividend Policy, Growth, and the Valuation of Shares." *Journal of Business,* October 1961, pp. 411–433.

$e_t - I_t > 0 \rightrightarrows$ dividend is paid out
$e_t - I_t < 0 \rightrightarrows$ difference is made up by issuance of stock and/or borrowing

$e_t - I_t$ represent the "true economic earnings" of the firm—that is, the ability of the firm to add to its total valuation and hence to the wealth of the stockholder.

This concept is equivalent to the cash flow concept because net cash flows equal cash inflows minus cash outflows. Simply derived, cash inflows are equal to net earnings after taxes plus depreciation d_t. Cash outflows represent gross investment requirements— that is net investment I plus replacement investment (to make up for depreciation).[4]

$$\text{Therefore net cash flows} = (e_t + d_t) - (I_t + d_t) = e_t - I_t \qquad (7.12)$$

Thus, the concept of net cash flow is under certain conditions (see below) equivalent to the concept of true economic earnings and consequently to that of dividend.

We now discuss in greater detail the concept of discounted cash flow.

The Discounted Cash Flow Models

The common stock valuation formula—assuming dividend is growing indefinitely at a constant rate—is

$$MP_0^s = \frac{D}{K_e - g} , \; K_e < g \qquad (7.13)$$

where K_e = cost of equity.

As we have already shown, the discounting of dividends yields exactly the same valuation results as the discounting of cash flows. The discounting of future earnings was ruled out because of double counting. The problem of double counting is best understood if one focuses on the uses of earnings. A corporation has only two choices with regard to its earnings: (1) to pay dividends or (2) to retain earnings and invest to yield some rate r.

If all earnings are paid out in the form of dividends, then discounting earnings *or* dividends produces the same results. If all or part of the earnings are retained, the firm can invest them at R and realize RI_t (I_t = amount invested). The increased future earnings from the new investment will eventually be paid out in dividends. Thus higher future earnings translate into higher dividends at some time in the future. To discount earnings, therefore, is to discount both of its components $D_t + be_t$, where b represents the retention ratio. In so doing we discount be_t today and the same be_t and earnings thereon which will be paid at some time in the future, thus the double counting.

The double counting problem, however, in no way makes earnings irrelevant to the determination of the value of the firm. Indeed, if financial analysts agree on anything, it is the key role future earnings play in the determination of the value of a security. The foundation of this belief was laid down unmistakably by Irving Fisher.[5]

---

[4] The structure of this discussion is found in **Seha Tinic** and **Richard West,** *Investment in Securities: An Efficient Market Approach.* Addison-Wesley, Reading, Pa., 1979.

[5] **Irving Fisher,** *The Theory of Interest.* A. M. Kelley, Publishers, New York, 1965.

The key issues related to earnings and stock prices are discussed in Chapter 8. We present here some variations of Equation 7.13.

Dividing both sides of Equation 7.13 by e, we get

$$\frac{MP_0^s}{e} = \frac{D/e}{K_e - g} \tag{7.14}$$

Since b is the retention ratio, then D_1/e (payout ratio) is by definition equal to $1 - b$. Earnings at any point in time e_t are equal to

$$e_t = e_{t-1} + RI_t \tag{7.15}$$

where RI_t represents the incremental earnings accruing from the investment of retained earnings.

Equation 7.15 can also be written as

$$e_t = e_{t-1} + R(be_{t-1}) = e_{t-1} + Rbe_{t-1}$$

Thus, Rb must be equal to g_e (growth in earnings) simply because the reinvestment of earnings be_{t-1} represents the only source of growth. Since b is assumed constant, then g_e must equal g, and Equation 7.14 can now be written as:

$$\frac{(MP_0^s)}{e} = \frac{(1-b)}{(K_e - bR)} \tag{7.16}$$

The constancy of $bR(g)$ over an infinite time horizon is a rather extreme assumption, however. Few if any companies can maintain a constant growth rate indefinitely, considering the life-cycle of firms' product lines (pioneering stage, maturity stage, and stable stage). Some adjustment is therefore needed.

The Two-Period Growth Model

B. Malkiel[6] saw the corporation growing initially at a high rate g for a certain time period N and then falling off to the average (normal) growth rate of its industry g_I. The price of the stock can be looked upon as having two components:

$$MP^s = MP_1^s + MP_2^s$$

where MP_1^s = discounted value of the dividends from time zero to N

MP_2^s = discounted value of the dividends from time N to ∞

$$MP_1^s = \sum_{t=0}^{N} \frac{D_0(1+g)^t}{(1+K_e)^{t+1}} \tag{a}$$

$$MP_2^s = \frac{D_{N+1}}{K_e - g_I} \times \frac{1}{(1+K_e)^N} \tag{b} \quad (7.17)$$

---

[6] **Burton Malkiel**, "Equity Yields, Growth, and the Structure of Share Prices." *American Economic Review*, vol. 53 (December 1963), pp. 1004–1031.

Equation 7.17a is the sum of a geometric progression.

$$S = \frac{r(1 - r^N)^*}{(1 - r)}$$

Let $r = \dfrac{(1 + g)}{(1 + K_e)}$

then $MP_1^s = D \left[\dfrac{1 - (1 + g)^N/(1 + K_e)^N}{K_e - g} \right]$

Therefore

$$MP^s = D \left[\frac{1 - (1 + g)^N/(1 + K_e)^N}{K_e - g} \right] + \frac{D_{N+1}}{(K_e - g_I)(1 + K_e)^N}$$

$$MP^s = \frac{D}{K_e - g} \left[\frac{(1 + K_e)^N - (1 + g)^N}{(1 + K_e)^N} \right] + \frac{D_{N+1}}{(K_e - g_I)(1 + K_e)^N} \tag{7.18}$$

The term $(D_{N+1})/(K_e - g_I)$ in Equation 7.18 is equal to the price of the security at time N; that is

$$\frac{D_{N+1}}{K_e - g_I} = MP_N^s \tag{7.19}$$

Multiplying both sides of Equation 7.19 by e_N and dividing both by same, we get

$$\frac{[(D_{N+1})/(e_N)]e_N}{K_e - g_I} = \frac{MP_N^s}{e_N} \times e_N$$

letting $(MP_N^s)/(e_N)$ = price/earnings multiple m, then $(D_{N+1})/(K_e - g) = me_N$, and if earnings and dividends are growing at the same rate,

$$\frac{D_{N+1}}{K_e - g} = m \times e(1 + g)^{N-1}$$

and therefore

---

* Let $S = r + r^2 + \cdots + r^N$ (i)

Therefore

$rS = r^2 + r^3 + \cdots + r^{N+1}$ (ii)

Subtracting (ii) from (i), we get

$S - Sr = r - r^{N+1} = r(1 - r^N)$

Therefore

$S = \dfrac{r(1 - r^N)}{(1 - r)}$

$$MP^s = \frac{D}{K_e - g} \frac{(1 + K_e)^N - (1 + g)^N}{(1 + K_e)^N} + \frac{me(1 + g)^{N-1}}{(1 + K_e)^N} \tag{7.20}$$

where $m = [1 - b)_N]/(K_e - g_I)$.

The earnings multiple used, since the firm's characteristics have become quite similar to those of the industry, is the industry's multiple expected to prevail at time N.

Example

XYZ Corporation has a current dividend of $1.00, a cost of equity of 15 percent, and a dividend growth rate (earnings growth rate) of 10 percent, which is expected to continue for the next ten years ($N = 10$). Calculate the market price of XYZ common stock if the industry earnings multiple is expected to be 8 in ten years (assume $g_I = 6$ percent) and if current earnings are $3.60:

Answer

$$MP^s = \frac{1.00}{0.15 - 0.10} \times \frac{(1 + 0.15)^{10} - (1 + 0.10)^{10}}{(1 + 0.15)^{10}} + \frac{8(3.60)(1 + 0.10)^9}{(1 + 0.15)^{10}}$$

Using the compound value tables in the appendix, we get the CVIF for each term in the brackets and the value of $(1 + 0.10)^9$:

$$MP^s = \frac{1.00}{0.05} \times \frac{4.046 - 2.594}{4.046} + \frac{67.91}{4.046}$$

$$MP^s = \$23.96$$

Yet another variation of Equation 7.13—a three-period growth model—was developed by Molodovsky and associates.[7] The reader can see that the number of periods that can be considered is quite large. Indeed, one can construct a model where each year has a different growth rate—an n-period model.

7.5 DIVIDENDS AND STOCK PRICES

An Overview

Dividends have presented a serious challenge to academicians and practitioners alike. The complexity of the dividend issue has left many unanswered questions regarding the impact of dividends on the value of the firm and the conditions under which that impact is felt.

In an article titled "The Dividend Puzzle," Professor Fisher Black[8] summarized the fundamental issues regarding dividends. These issues deal with the reasons for corporate payment of dividends, the reasons for investors' (some, if not all) interest in dividend-

---

[7] **N. Molodovsky, C. May** and **S. Chottinger,** "Common Stock Valuation." *Financial Analyst's Journal,* vol. 21 (March–April 1965), pp. 104–123.

[8] **Fisher Black,** "The Dividend Puzzle." *Journal of Portfolio Management,* Winter 1976, pp. 5–8.

paying stocks, the reasons why corporations pay dividends with one hand and borrow with the other, the impact of dividends on stock prices, the impact of taxes (corporate and individual) on dividend policy and the value of the firm, and the impact of dividends on portfolio strategy. Professor Black concluded his article with a pessimistic note, however, asking "What should the individual investor do about dividends in his portfolio? We don't know. What should the corporation do about dividend policy? We don't know."[9]

Efforts to resolve many of the issues relating to dividends have continued since Professor Black published his article. We are considerably more sure about some of the answers today than we ever were.

Relevancy of Dividends

Two schools of thought dominate dividend theory: one claims that dividends do not matter and the other claims that they do. Our analysis will focus on the major studies in this controversy and will draw heavily on the comprehensive and elegant work of Louis Hobeika.[10]

Dividends as Active Decision Variable

The school advocating the relevancy of dividends was founded by Graham and Dodd.[11] They argue that a dollar of dividend has four times the impact on stock prices as a dollar of retained earnings. This hypothesis, although to a lesser degree, was supported by Gordon,[12] who found that there exists an optimum (one that minimizes the firm's cost of equity and thus maximizes the value of the firm) dividend payout ratio independent of the variability in earnings. This ratio, however, was found to vary inversely with the rate of return on investments.

Further support for the target payout policy was offered, among others, by John A. Brittain.[13] He observed that between 1946 and 1962, dividends steadily rose by 6 percent, despite periods of profit squeeze. Brittain concluded that management is, in effect, concerned with dividend policy and pays considerable attention to the stability and growth of dividends.

John Lintner[14] also argues in favor of the relevancy of dividends. Management decides on the amount of dividends to be paid and assesses investment opportunities thereafter. If internally generated funds are insufficient, external financing is always possible. Management is thought to feel that the declaration of dividends contains substantial information about the performance of management and constitutes a basis for job security.

---

[9] Ibid., p. 77.

[10] **Louis Georges Hobeika,** *Dividend Policy.* Unpublished doctoral dissertation, University of Pennsylvania, Department of Economics, Philadelphia, 1980.

[11] **Benjamin Graham** and **David L. Dodd,** *Security Analysis; Principles and Techniques.* McGraw-Hill, New York, 1934.

[12] **M. J. Gordon,** "Dividends, Earnings, and Stock Prices." *Review of Economics and Statistics,* May 1959, pp. 99–105.

[13] **J. A. Brittain,** "The Tax Structure and Corporate Dividend Policy." *American Economic Review,* May 1964, pp. 272–287.

[14] **John Lintner,** "Distribution of Incomes of Corporations Among Dividends, Retained Earnings and Taxes." *American Economic Review,* May 1956, pp. 97–113.

The Irrelevancy of Dividends

The first major challenge to the dividend relevancy school was offered by James Walter,[15] who argued that the decision to pay dividends depends on the profitability of investment opportunities available to the firm. Dividends in this context are no longer an active decision variable but rather a residual sum. Walter offered the following stock valuation formula:

$$MP^s = \frac{D_t + (R_t/K_t)(e_t - D_t)}{K_t} \qquad (7.21)$$

where R_t = rate of return at time t

K_t = market capitalization rate at time t

The other variables are as defined earlier.

Walter argues that if $R_t > K_t$, the firm would distribute no dividends, because any positive distribution would not maximize MP^s. If $R_t < K_t$, then no investment would be undertaken and all the earnings would be distributed to the stockholders. If $R_t = K_t$, the price of the stock would be independent of dividend payouts.

To better understand Walter's position, consider a firm with $e = \$5$ and $K_t = 10\%$. The rate of return on available investments $R_t = 14\%$. Therefore with

$$D = \$2 = MP_0^s = \frac{2 + (0.14/0.10)(5 - 2)}{0.10} = \$62$$

$$D = \$0 = MP_0^s = \frac{0 + (0.14/0.10)(5 - 0)}{0.10} = \$70$$

$$D = \$5 = MP_0^s = \frac{5 + (0.14/0.10)(5 - 5)}{0.10} = \$50$$

Thus, when $R_t > K_t$, the firm should pay no dividends ($D = 0$), for this maximizes the value of its shares. Had $R_t < K_t$, the optimal dividend payout (the dividend payout that maximizes the value of the firm) would have been the full value of earnings ($D = 5$).

The implication of the Walter model is that the firm is most likely to pay no dividends or 100 percent dividends depending on the relationship between R_t and K_t. If the dividend pattern were such that in one year the investor received 100 percent of earnings, the next 0 percent of earnings followed by 100 percent, and so on, the stability of the dividend policy and the effect this might have on the value of the firm would be called into question. Walter's important contribution is, however, in the fact that the investment decision represents the active decision variable regardless of the relationship between R_t and K_t. This laid the groundwork for Modigliani and Miller (M&M), who effectively argued that neither the level nor the stability of dividends matters.

---

[15] **James Walter,** "Dividend Policies and Common Stock Prices." *Journal of Finance,* March 1956, pp. 29–41.

The major breakthrough came in the study by Modigliani and Miller,[16] who argue that dividends are irrelevant. The assumptions of the model are as follows:

1. Perfect capital markets characterized by free and equally available information
2. No transactions costs
3. Equal tax rates on dividends and capital gains
4. A fixed capital investment schedule for the firm
5. Perfect certainty regarding the investment schedules and the rates of return derived therefrom

The model developed by M&M is a simple one-period model, almost a tautology given the assumptions.

Consider the value of one stock with an expected one-year holding period—its market price is then equal to

$$MP_0^s = \frac{D_1 + (MP_1^s)}{1 + K_e}$$

The value of an equity firm with n shares outstanding is therefore equal to

$$n \times MP_0^s = \frac{1}{1 + K_e} [nD_1 + n \times (MP_1^s)] \tag{7.22}$$

Given a fixed investment schedule for the firm, its one year profits are determined. Let I be the size of the investment to be undertaken. If the firm elects to pay D_1 in dividends, its total dividend payments would then equal nD_1. Therefore, the one-period financial requirements are equal to $I + nD_1$. If expected one-period profits do not equal the total financial requirements, the firm would, we assume, have to raise capital by issuing new shares.[17] The value of the new issue is $m \times MP_1^s$, where m is equal to the number of newly issued shares.

$$m \times MP_1^s = I - (e - nD_1) \tag{7.23}$$

where $e - nD_1 =$ the earnings available for investment purposes.

Equation 7.22 can, therefore, be rewritten as follows:

$$n \times MP_0^s = \frac{1}{1 + K_e} [nD_1 + (n + m) MP_1^s - m MP_1^s] \tag{7.24}$$

or equivalently, replacing $m \times MP_1^s$ by its value,

$$n \times MP_0^s = \frac{1}{1 + K_e} [nD_1 + (n + m) MP_1^s - I + e - nD_1]$$

---

[16] **Franco Modigliani** and **Merton Miller,** "Dividend Policy, Growth and the Valuation of Shares." *Journal of Business,* October 1961, pp. 411–433.

[17] The firm can also borrow funds, however. Modigliani and Miller have proven in an earlier study that the value of the firm is independent of the financing decision.

$$n \times MP_0^s = \frac{1}{1 + K_e} \left[(n + m) MP_1^s - I + e \right] \tag{7.25}$$

Modigliani and Miller conclude from Equation 7.25 that since dividends no longer appear in the valuation equation, they do not matter. There is no optimum dividend policy in an M&M world. The firm simply makes its investment decision, uses its earnings to finance it, and distributes the excess $(e_t - I_t)$, if any, to the shareholders in the form of dividends. It can be seen from Equation 7.23 that an increase in D_1 would lead to a higher $m \times MP_1^s$ and necessarily to an issuance of new shares given fixed earnings; m is, therefore, a function of D_1. An increase in m leads to an increase in claims by stockholders (old and new) on a fixed income e; therefore, MP_1^s must drop by the exact value of D_1 if securities markets are efficient (an assumption of the model).

$$\Delta D_1 = -\Delta MP_1^s$$

Therefore, what the investor misses in dividend payments, he or she will make up in the form of price appreciation, and vice versa. The relationship is one to one. Investors who have a need for income can, in a world of no transactions costs, liquidate enough of their shares to make up for the dividend payments.

The M&M hypothesis implies, therefore, that the value of the firm is independent of whether dividends are paid or not. Given that two firms have the same set of available investment opportunities, their value would be identical even if one paid no dividends and the other paid all its earnings in dividends provided that the two firms belong to the same risk class.

The irrelevancy hypothesis also holds, so reasoned M&M, under conditions of uncertainty. The argument is rather presumptuous and is based on the assumption of "symmetric market rationality"; that is, by acting rationally, an investor imputes rationality to the market. This market rationality prevents two substitutes—two firms in the same risk class—from selling at different prices given identical expected future streams of investments and earnings.

If leverage is included in the model, the validity of the hypothesis is preserved given that all debt issued by the firm is default-free or that the bondholders are wise enough to insist on the "me-first" rule. In other words, it is assumed that bondholders will insist on clauses in the indenture agreement preventing expropriation of any of their wealth by common stockholders—an expropriation achievable through the distribution of dividends. E. Fama[18] showed later (1978) that the me-first rule is not necessary to prove the irrelevancy of dividends in the valuation process provided the firm issues bonds that do not have perfect substitutes and that the capital markets are perfect.

The inclusion of taxes (personal) leads to a breakdown in the irrelevancy argument because of the differential in tax rates that apply to dividends and capital gains. The preferential treatment of capital gains argues for retention of earnings by the firm if the intent of management is to maximize the wealth of stockholders. Then why do firms continue in the payment of dividends while simultaneously (in certain cases) issuing debt securities to finance their investments? Litzenberger and Ramaswamy (1979)[19] found

---

[18] **Eugene Fama,** "The Effects of a Firm's Investment and Financing Decisions on the Welfare of Its Security Holders." *American Economic Review,* June 1978, pp. 272–284.

[19] **R. H. Litzenberger** and **K. Ramaswamy,** "The Effect of Personal Taxes on Capital Asset Prices; Theory and Empirical Evidence." *Journal of Financial Economics,* 1979, pp. 163–195.

a significant relationship between before-tax expected returns and dividend yields on common stocks; they also note an attraction by investors in high tax brackets to low-yield stocks and by investors in low tax brackets to high-yield stocks.

The attraction by investors to certain securities with certain payout ratios is characterized by M&M as "the clientele effect"; that is, retired persons may choose AT&T stock over that of IBM because of AT&T's dividend policy. But this choice, systematic as it may be, will not influence the price of the stock; as far as IBM and AT&T are concerned, one investor's funds are good as those of another. Further empirical evidence will be presented below.

The combination of debt and *corporate* taxes was shown by Copeland and Weston to have no effect on the irrelevancy of dividend argument. Copeland and Weston[20] derived the following valuation formula for the leveraged firm:

$$V = \frac{e_1(1 - T_c)}{K_e} + T_c B + K[e_1(1 - T_c)]t\left[\frac{r - K_0}{K_0(1 + K_0)}\right]$$ (7.26)

where $K_0 = K_e\left[1 - \frac{T_c B}{B + S}\right] = $ weighted average cost of capital

$e_1 = $ end-of-year net operating profit

$B = $ market value of debt

$K = $ rate of return on investment

$t = $ number of years that $r > K_0$

$r = $ average rate of return on investment

$K_e = $ cost of equity to an all-equity firm

Equation 7.26 shows the value of the firm to be independent of dividend payments.

The Empirical Evidence

The empirical evidence we shall present here is that offered by Hobeika. The reason is that Hobeika's work is the most recent as well as the most comprehensive and it deals with the validity of several earlier studies.

Using annual data on 214 firms from 1957 to 1976, Hobeika tested the predictive powers of 13 models (7 price models and 6 dividend models). Regression coefficients were estimated using data from the first 18 years and were in turn used to predict the prices and the dividends for the years 1975 and 1976. The 13 models represent a summary of all serious attempts in the dividend theory. The equations were as follows:

$$P_{it} = a + bD_{it} + cR_{it}$$ (7.27)

$$P_{it} = a + bD_{it} + cR_{it} + d(e/P)_{i,t-1}$$ (7.28)

$$P_{it} = a + bD_{it} + cR_{it} + dP_{i,t-1}$$ (7.29)

[20] T. E. Copeland and J. F. Weston, *Financial Theory and Corporate Policy*. Addison-Wesley, Reading, Mass., 1979.

$$P_{it} = a + bD_{it} + cR_{it}^n \tag{7.30}$$

$$r_{it} = a + b(D_{it}/P_{it}) + c(R_{it}/P_{it}) \tag{7.31}$$

$$r_{it} = a + b(D_{i,t-1}/P_{i,t-1}) + c(R_{i,t-1}/P_{i,t-1}) \tag{7.32}$$

$$r_{it} = a + b(D_{it}/P_{i,t-1}) + c(R_{it}/P_{i,t-1}) \tag{7.33}$$

$$D_{it} = a + fD_{i,t-1} + ge_{it} \tag{7.34}$$

$$D_{it} = a + fD_{i,t-1} + ge_{it} + hA_{it} \tag{7.35}$$

$$D_{it} = a + fD_{i,t-1} + ge_{it} + he_{i,t-1} \tag{7.36}$$

$$D_{it} = a + fD_{i,t-1} + ge_{it}^n \tag{7.37}$$

$$D_{it} = a + fD_{i,t-1} + ge_{it} + hP_{i,t-1} \tag{7.38}$$

$$D_{it} = a + fD_{i,t-1} + ge_{it} + h(e/P)_{i,t-1} \tag{7.39}$$

where
P_{it} = price of stock i at time t
D_{it} = dividend of stock i at time t
$(e/P)_{i,t-1}$ = inverse of price/earnings ratio of stock i lagged by one period
R_{it} = retained earnings of firm i at time t
$A_{i,t}$ = per share depreciation of firm i at time t
a,b,c,d,h = regression parameters

The regression results showed Equation 7.29 to be the superior predictor of the price equations, confirming the results of Friend and Puckett,[21] and Equation 7.33 to be the best predictor in the rate-of-return subset of the price equations. The superior dividend model was represented by Equation 7.34, which was advanced by Lintner.[22]

Hobeika attempted to estimate the dividend and price equations simultaneously, using two-stage least squares. The system of equations tested was

$$P_{it} = a + bD_{it} + cR_{it} + dP_{i,t-1} \tag{7.29}'$$
$$D_{it} = e + fD_{i,t-1} + ge_{it} + hP_{it} \tag{7.34}'$$
$$e_{it} = D_{it} + R_{it}$$

The regression results showed that the simultaneous-equation models did not show superior predictive powers over single-equation models. Similar conclusions were reached when Equation 7.33 was estimated simultaneously with Equation 7.34.

---

[21] **I. Friend** and **M. Puckett**, "Dividends and Stock Prices." *American Economic Review,* September 1964, pp. 656–681.

[22] **J. Lintner**, "Distribution of Incomes of Corporations Among Dividends, Retained Earnings and Taxes." *American Economic Review,* May 1955, pp. 97–113.

Tests of the Various Issues in Dividend Policy

Four major issues in dividend theory have been identified in the earlier discussion. They are summarized below.

Are Dividends More Important to Investors Than Capital Gains (Retained Earning)? The answer lies in the estimation of Equation 7.27

$$P_{it} = a + b\,D_{it} + c R_{it}$$

If both b and c are significant and if c is greater than b, then retained earnings are more important to investors than dividends. Tests conducted by Hobeika confirm this ($c > b$) for the 1967–1972 period but not for the 1973–1976 period. Hobeika attributes this to the weak, lethargic market between 1973 and 1976, leading investors to place greater emphasis on dividends. This is natural for risk-averse investors. As uncertainty about the future increases, investors become more oriented toward short-term performance, and with a lethargic market, the only rewards come in the form of dividends.

The aberration cited above was confirmed when Equation 7.29 was tested. Again, dividends were preferred to retained earnings during the period 1973–1976.

Do Dividends Convey Information? Are companies increasing their dividends, signaling the investors that the future prospects for the company have become brighter (and conversely if dividends were reduced)? The empirical evidence on the information content of dividends is mixed. R Pettit[23] found evidence that changes in dividend payments did affect the performance of securities. R. Watts[24] found that the effects of unexpected changes in dividends on share prices were very small. R. Watt's results were not confirmed by a later study by G. Charest.[25] The author concluded that investors could have realized above-average rates of return by trading dividend-changing stocks. Aharoni and Swary,[26] using quarterly data on 149 firms between January 1963 and April 1976, found evidence in favor of dividends as valuable information in the evaluation of equity securities. The authors also noted, as did Charest, that the isolation of the dividend effects is not easy, for other factors (such as earnings announcements), can coincidentally influence the price of the stock.

The issue of the information content of dividends has yet to be fully resolved.

The Clientele Effect. The concern here is with whether more affluent investors are systematically attracted to low-yield stocks. Smaller firms—because of their lesser access to external financing, their greater probability of growth, and their tendencies to be managed by their high-tax-bracket owners—would retain more of their earnings.

---

[23] **R. R. Pettit,** "Dividend Announcements: Security Performance, and Capital Market Efficiency." *Journal of Finance,* December 1972, pp. 993–1007.

[24] **R. Watts,** "The Information Content of Dividends." *Journal of Business,* April 1973, pp. 191–211.

[25] **G. Charest,** "Dividend Information, Stock Returns and Market Efficiency—II." *Journal of Financial Economics,* 1978, pp. 297–330.

[26] **J. Aharoni** and **I. Swary,** "Quarterly Dividend and Earnings Announcements and Stockholders' Returns: An Empirical Analysis." *Journal of Finance,* March 1980, pp. 1–11.

It is, therefore, instructive to measure whether investors in higher tax brackets tend to purchase shares of smaller companies.

The data set was divided by Hobeika into ten classes, each representing a certain level of total sales and for each of which Equation 7.27 was tested. The retained-earnings regression coefficient was found to be higher than that of dividends for smaller firms and lower than that of dividends for larger firms, providing support for the clientele effect. Hobeika then tested Equation 7.34:

$$D_{it} = a + bD_{i,t-1} + ce_{i,t}$$

to find out whether the coefficient c tended to increase or decrease with size. The results were that c (the marginal propensity to distribute dividends in the short run) was not affected by the size of the firm. The long-run propensity to distribute dividends did increase with size, however.

$$D_{i,t} - bD_{i,t-1} = a + ce_{i,t}$$

Because, in the long run, $D_{i,t} = D_{i,t-1}$, then

$$D_{i,t}(1 - b) = a + ce_{i,t}$$

then

$$D_{i,t} = \alpha + \frac{c}{1-b} e_{i,t}$$

where $c/(1 - b)$ = long-run propensity to distribute dividend.

We can conclude that the clientele effect appears to be as originally hypothesized.

Dividends and Investors'/Managers' Rationality.
The concern here is with two rationalities: the investor's and the manager's.

In a world of taxes, a rational investor (an individual) would have a preference for capital gains over dividends, since capital gains are taxed at the preferred rate. The earlier results by Hobeika showed investors to prefer dividends over capital gains during the 1973–1976 period. Can this be considered as evidence of investors' irrationality? Not necessarily. Before offering a conclusive answer, however, we should be mindful of the other market participants and their preferences. Corporations with portfolio investments in domestic unaffiliated corporations have a preference for dividends because 85 percent of the dividends received are not taxable. Pension funds and tax-exempt organizations in general are indifferent between capital gains and dividends on tax grounds, since no tax is owed on either form of distribution. Pension funds may have a preference for dividends, however, because of their risk-aversiveness and their need for a regular stream of income. The impact on stock prices will, therefore, depend on what group (the group that pays higher or lower—or zero—taxes on dividend income) dominates the market.[27]

---

[27] It is instructive to note that individuals own the largest shares of equity securities in the United States. By the end of 1980, individual investors owned 62 percent of all stocks outstanding.

Hobeika rationalized that if the sample of firms used in testing the relevancy of dividends is split into groups in accordance with the percentage ownership by pension funds and the investment of individuals in each group is carefully scrutinized, then investors' rationality can be tested. Investors owning shares in corporations with low pension fund equity participation should prefer retained earnings to dividends, and investors in corporations with high pension fund equity participation should prefer dividends to retained earnings.

The data (reduced to 195 firms) were divided into ten classes according to the proportion of equity outstanding owned by pension funds. Equations 7.27, 7.32, and 7.34 were estimated. The results did not support the hypothesis that investors with preference for capital gains buy shares in firms with low pension fund equity participation. The results did show, however, that firms with high pension fund equity participation tended to have a high marginal propensity to distribute dividends both in the short and in the long run.

Unable to reach definite conclusions based on the above results, Hobeika rationalized that the preference for dividends during the 1973–1976 period could be due to the uncertainties about economic conditions that led investors to favor a certain income in the form of dividends over an uncertain income in the form of capital gains. Hence, there is no evidence of irrationality.

As to the rationality of managers, one would expect them to follow policies that maximize the welfare of stockholders. This necessitates, therefore, that earnings be retained when profitable investment opportunities are available and be distributed otherwise. Retained earnings are a cheaper source of capital than external financing. Managers would not be rational if they paid dividends simply because a large percentage of their shares were owned by pension funds and if dividend payments were made independent of earnings expectations. Once again, Hobeika found no evidence of irrationality.

7.6 OTHER FACTORS INFLUENCING STOCK PRICES

Depending on the school of thought an investor adheres to, every event—whether economic, political, sociological, or even spiritual in nature—could have an influence on stock prices. We shall be content, in this chapter, to identify some of the factors that directly influence stock prices, leaving others with direct and indirect effects to Chapter 8. We begin by restating the stock-valuation equation:

$$MP_0^s = \sum_{t=1}^{n} \frac{D_t}{(1 + K_e)^t} \tag{7.40}$$

As is evident from Equation 7.40, dividends (a proxy for earnings) do influence stock prices, as do K_e (the cost of equity) and the length of the holding period t (assumed to be very long here). The capital asset pricing model is ordinarily used to arrive at a value for K_e:

$$K_e = E(R_i) = R_F + [E(R_M) - R_F]\beta \tag{7.41}$$

where

R_F = risk-free rate

$E(R_M)$ = expected rate of return on a market index

$[E(R_M) - R_F]$ = price of risk

$$\beta = \text{measure of systematic (nondiversifiable) risk}$$

$$[E(R_M) - R_F]\beta = \text{security's risk premium; that is, market risk premium}$$
$$\text{weighted by the relative risk of a given security}$$

Changes in $R_F, E(R_M)$ and/or in β will have an effect on K_e and hence on the stock price. Various factors can cause a change in R_F and $E(R_M)$—ranging from monetary policy, to fiscal policy, to balance-of-payments problems, to the health of the President, to the opinion of an investment guru, and so on.

The changes in β can be caused by factors endogenous to the firm, namely, by changes in the firm's business or financial risk. Business risk is that risk inherent in the operations of the firm. It depends on the products sold by the firm and the degree of operating leverage. Financial risk, on the other hand, depends on the leverage (debt) used to finance the assets of the firm.

Business risk can be changed by changing the product mix of the company (dropping or adding products), by mergers and acquisitions, or by divestiture of certain plants or product lines. Also, the firm can change its business risk by affecting changes in operating leverage through changes in the capital/labor mix that affect the relationship between variable and fixed costs.

Financial risk is modified through the debt/equity ratio of the firm. The effect of debt financing on the systematic risk of the firm was analyzed by R. Hamada,[28] who arrived at the following new measure of systematic risk for leveraged firms:

$$\beta_L = \left(\frac{V_{s,u}}{V_{s,u} - (1 - T_c)V_B} \right)\beta_u \tag{7.42}$$

where β_L = systematic risk of a leveraged firm

β_u = systematic risk of an unleveraged firm

$V_{s,u}$ = market value of stock of unleveraged firm

V_B = market value of bonds outstanding

T_c = corporate tax rate

The new β is then incorporated in the capital asset pricing model:

$$E(R_i)_L = R_F + [E(R_M) - R_F]\beta_L \tag{7.43}$$

where $E(R_i)_L$ = expected rate of return on a leveraged firm i.

These adjustments help improve the capital asset pricing model but do not significantly reduce the fundamental reservations expressed in Chapter 6.

CONCLUSIONS

The valuation of common stocks requires considerable technical competence. In this chapter we analyzed the effects of dividends on stock prices and found that dividends do have an influence in a world of taxes. The announcement effects of dividends were

---

[28] **R. Hamada,** "The Effect of the Firm's Capital Structure on the Systematic Risk of Common Stock." *Journal of Finance,* May 1972, pp. 435–452.

not resolved. Both investors and managers appear to be rational in making their decisions. In addition, we looked at the factors that influence the cost of equity of the firm and concluded that both business risk and financial risk as well as "environmental" factors influence systematic risk.

The next chapter deals more extensively with the subject of stock valuation and offers a systematic approach to this subject; it also considers other important factors that influence the rate of return on stocks.

QUESTIONS

1. If capital gains and dividend income were taxed at the same rate, would the universality of the M&M dividend hypothesis be upheld?

2. Outline the various types of common stock. How would valuation of these shares differ?

3. What, in theory, determines the value of common stock?

4. DGO company is 100 percent financed by equity. If the company is losing money and prospects to reverse that trend are bleak, how could shares of DGO company retain any value?

5. What is the role of dividends in the valuation of common equity according to M&M?

6. Does the net cash flow concept give a different market price of a stock from discounting a stream of dividends?

7. Regression on a stock price yields the following values for the coefficients b and c:

$$P_{it} = a + b(D_{it}) + c(R_{it})$$
$$P_{it} = a + .4(D_{it}) + 0.2(R_{it})$$
$$\quad\quad\quad [2.1] \quad\quad [2.0]$$

   What is the significance of the b and c coefficients? (Values in brackets [ ] are t values.)

8. For a reason beyond management control, CJK company will suffer a loss this year. If CJK management expects to reverse the situation next year, why might the company choose to pay dividends this year despite the loss?

9. What were Hobeika's conclusions about the clientele effect? Does this make sense to you?

10. Discuss the major issues relating to dividend policy and the associated empirical evidence.

11. What events might alter a firm's cost of equity? How quickly would you expect changes in a firm's cost of equity to be reflected in the price of the firm's stock?

12. Could sociopolitical factors affect stock prices? Need these factors change the expected cash flows of the firm to change the price of the stock? Explain.

13. The stock valuation equation $MP_0^s = D/(K_e - g)$ is based on several assumptions. What are these assumptions? When does this formulation cease to be of value?

14. Many stock-valuation equations are based on steady growth rates in earning or in dividends. How valuable are these models for high-growth stocks? For very volatile stocks?

PROBLEMS

1. Given that
   a. Dividends are $3.50 per share and are expected to grow 6.5 percent annually,
   b. The cost of equity is 10 percent,
   what is the theoretical value of a share of RGH stock?

2. The following is known about NAS stock:

   $$a = \$15, \ b = 0.4, \ c = 0.2, \ D_{it} = \$2.50, \ R_{it} = 3(D_{it})$$

   Use Equation 7.27 to estimate P_{it}, the market price of NAS stock.

3. WJM stock trades at $50 per share, pays $3 annually in dividends, and has a beta of 1.5. The market as a whole is forecast to rise 6.7 percent this year. What is the implied K_e, if the investor's time horizon is one year? (Use Equation 7.1.)

4. DGO stock just paid a $2 per share dividend; the cost of equity is 10 percent. If the P/E (price/earnings) ratio were 7 and EPS for the past year were $4, determine:
   a. The current market price for DGO stock
   b. The implied dividend growth rate

5. AJC corporation currently pays a dividend of $1.50. It has a dividend growth rate (earnings growth rate) of 12 percent which is expected to continue for the next 12 years and a cost of equity of 14 percent. Calculate the market price of AJC common stock if the normal growth rate of the industry (g_I) is 5 percent and AJC's current earnings are $5.

6. EBS corporation currently retains 60 percent of its earnings. The firm's expected dividend growth rate (earnings growth rate) is 10 percent for the next eight years and its cost of equity is 13 percent. Calculate the expected industry earnings multiple in eight years if the normal growth rate of the industry (g_I) is 11 percent.

7. On Nov. 1, 1978, the common stock of Steady Nerves, Inc., was priced at $50. The following information is given: β of Steady Nerves = 0.8, standard deviation of stock's monthly returns = 0.09, standard deviation of S&P 500 returns = 0.04, 90-day T-bill monthly yield = 0.01, expected return on S&P 500 for November 1978 = 0.015. Find the expected return for the stock during November and the correlation between the returns of Steady Nerves and the S&P 500. If the stock was expected to pay a dividend of $0.75 per share on Nov. 30, 1978, what was the expected price of Steady Nerves stock at the end of November?

Where Do You Get Your Information?

When's the last time
you sat in the
bleachers?
When's the last time
you heard a
Jefferson Starship record?
(More than a million
were sold last year.)
Did you see
Superman II?
(It did $14 million
its first weekend.)
Do you read
Reader's Digest?
(The circulation is
31 million worldwide.)
Have you seen the top
10 TV shows?
When's the last time
you took a trip on
a Greyhound bus?
How many times
each month do you
shop in a supermarket?
Have you seen
evangelists on TV?
(Viewers send them
millions of dollars.)
Have you browsed through
a card shop?
(Hallmark sells one billion
cards a year.)
Have you stood on an
assembly line?
Gone down into a
coal mine?
Spent time on
a farm?
If you don't know
what's happening in other
people's worlds,
you can't make good decisions
in the business world.

CHAPTER 8 | Financial Analysis

8.1 INTRODUCTION

The corporation is like a living organism functioning in a dynamic world. Its operations cannot be insulated from its environment, and its control over that environment is never complete.

The balance sheet and the income statement of a corporation are, respectively, summary statements of where a corporation stands at a point in time and how it has performed over a period of time. As such, they report on the results of the interactions among people within the corporate structure, between people and machines, and between the corporation and its environment. While the results do contain a considerable amount of information, they say little about the process that brought them about or about the future prospects of the company.

While accountants are preoccupied with the accurate recording of *historical* transactions, the financial analyst, using history as a guide, looks to the future. The futurity of the analysis makes the task quite arduous because of the uncertainties the future embodies.

To understand the future, the financial analyst must be able to identify major trends in the business environment while also estimating the extent to which a specific corporation is aware of these trends, is attempting to cope with them, and—possibly—is managing to exploit them to its own advantage. In addition, the financial analyst examines closely the internal dynamics of the corporation, the degree and extent of care exercised in the development of future plans, and—most particularly—the types of individuals at the helm.

Financial analysis is a prospective tool. It recognizes the fact that to look simply at numbers (balance sheet and income statement) without understanding their source and the environment in which they were created and still draw conclusions is quintessentially the same as to ignore the condition of the major organs of the human body and still pronounce it fit.

Financial analysis, by the sheer requirements of sanity and logic, involves much more than we will discuss in this chapter. It is infinitely more than the generation and interpretation of numbers from existing or prospective data. It is people, interaction among people, leadership quality, dynamic and comprehensive planning (or lack thereof), understanding the markets for input factors and for outputs, realizing the subtle and the not-so-subtle changes in the environment, realizing the interdependence among nations, understanding the nature of current and expected competition, understanding the power and the influence labor unions have on motivation and wages, understanding fundamental societal changes that could have profound impact on productivity and the business order, and certainly understanding the role governments (at all levels and across national boundaries) play in determining the fate of organizations.

8.2 THE CHANGING EXTERNAL ENVIRONMENT

In this section we briefly outline some of the fundamental changes in the environment with respect to technology, politics, and social attitudes.

The pace of technological innovation is dizzying. The knowledge accumulated in the last 15 years alone represents 70 percent of knowledge accumulated throughout human history, and there is every indication that the pace of invention and innovative change is increasing. A silicon chip the size of a thumbnail is capable of storing a million bits of information. Some computers are currently capable of conducting research without human assistance. Robots are currently performing many skilled functions with an efficiency and durability far exceeding human capacities. Recombinant DNA technology is developing at a rapid pace, with wide-ranging implications on the makeup of living things (plants, animals, and even humans) and on the cure of various diseases. Oil companies are using ever more sophisticated seismological instruments to help find oil without drilling. These are but a few of the remarkable developments that are currently observable.

Futurists see many more dramatic developments. They foresee "sailing cities" to relieve urban congestion, the development of many more artificial organs to replace parts of the human body, the successful use of nuclear fusion in relieving energy shortages, the development of artificial high-protein diets, the development of food supplements that can improve memory and intelligence, doctors who can make house calls using electronic means, computers with artificial intelligence exceeding that of humans, various processes for molding metals and improving their strength and resistance, and the spread of complex communications systems, making the office as we know it today obsolete. These are but a few of the dramatic things that we may witness in the future. The question for the financial analyst with regard to technology is how well the corporation has internalized all this information, what is it doing to cope, and how this will affect future profitability and risk.

On the political front, people's attitude toward government is shifting drastically. The decline in voting participation at all levels of government is but one sign of public apathy. Government has, at the same time, increased its reach into the corporate and personal lives of individuals. Government regulations play a very important role in determining levels of efficiency in corporate entities and influence considerably capital budgeting decisions and the environment in the workplace. How all this comes to bear on a specific industry and company is of importance to a financial analyst. Also of concern is the stability of the government and its ability to influence world events. The position a country occupies in world affairs is of considerable importance, for it speaks for that country's ability to protect both supply routes of raw materials and markets for home products.

On the social front, some of the concerns are with the rights of women and minorities in the work force; the increasing call for "meaningful" jobs; the effects of the spread of drugs, alcoholism, and crime on the performance of business entities; the safety of the workplace; and the changing character and attitude of labor unions.

No successful financial analyst can hope to ignore the issues cited above and still produce adequate forecasts about the future. Lest the reader be misled, a clear distinction between awareness and feasibility must be drawn. The analyst may well be aware of relevant variables, but only some of them, if any, can be incorporated in a forecasting model regardless of its level of sophistication. Some variables are just not measurable, and a proxy for them may not be available.

The discussion above portrays the very complex world in which the financial analyst must operate. Some analysts have chosen simply to extrapolate from past data to predict the future, and others have taken some major steps forward in order to systematize the approach to financial analysis. In the pages to follow, we shall examine some of the prevailing techniques used in determining the future prospects of a corporation and thus its current market value.

8.3 DIRECTION OF ANALYSIS

A financial analysis can follow either of two directions: economy level → industry level → firm level or firm level → industry level → economy level. Our preference is for the first direction. The reasons are these:

1. The economy is part of the corporate environment and thus can influence its performance.

2. About half the security's risk is systematic on the average. To the extent that the return on the market portfolio is correlated with the health of the economy, the economy influences the performance of the stock.

Richard Brealey[1] measured the effects of the economy and of the industry on the earnings movement of the firm and found the results reported in Table 8.1. As the reader may observe, the economy has varying effects on different industries. The greater the effect, the more cyclical an industry is; that is, its earnings are influenced by the economic cycle to a larger extent.

The relationship between economic performance and industry and firm performance was also documented by N. Gonedes.[2] Using a sample of 99 firms, Gonedes found that the industry effect on the performance of the firm was insignificant, while the impact of the economy accounted for 50 percent of the variation in the total income of the firm. R. Ball and P. Brown found that both industry and economy effects are significant,[3] however.

---

[1] **Richard Brealey,** *An Introduction to Risk and Return from Common Stocks.* MIT Press, Cambridge, Mass., 1969.

[2] **Nicholas Gonedes,** "A Note on Accounting—Based on Market-Based Estimates of Systematic Risk." *Journal of Financial and Quantitative Analysis,* no. 2 (June 1975), pp. 355–357.

[3] **R. Ball** and **P. Brown,** "Some Preliminary Findings on the Association Between the Earnings of the Firm, Its Industry and the Economy," in *Empirical Research in Accounting: Selected Studies. Journal of Accounting Research,* vol. 5, suppl. (1967), pp. 55–77.

TABLE 8.1
Impact of Economy and Industry on Corporate Earnings

Industry	Economy Influence (Percent)	Industry Influence (Percent)
Aircraft	11	5
Autos	48	11
Beer	11	7
Cement	6	32
Chemicals	41	8
Cosmetics	5	6
Department stores	30	37
Drugs	14	7
Electricals	24	8
Food	10	10
Machinery	19	16
Nonferrous metals	26	25
Office machinery	14	6
Oil	13	49
Paper	27	28
Rubber	26	48
Steel	32	21
Supermarkets	6	33
Textiles and clothing	25	29
Tobacco	8	19
All companies	21	21

Source: Richard Brealey, *An Introduction to Risk and Return from Common Stocks.*
      MIT Press, Cambridge, Mass., 1969.

3. To proceed in the opposite direction is susceptible to double counting and inconsistency of assumptions. Furthermore, it would be very hard to incorporate the effects of the overall economy on each firm going from the micro to the macro level.

The recommended process moves in accordance with the steps suggested in Figure 8.1. Before discussing the contents of Figure 8.1 and elaborating on the various methods for forecasting stock prices, it is advisable to advance certain measures for evaluating the current status of the firm and the trends (if any) its operations have exhibited through recent history.

8.4 MEASURING PERFORMANCE

The technique used for measuring performance depends to some extent on who is doing the measuring. Management measures performance in terms of the difference between the actual (realized) and the expected (budgeted). The expectations of management are not necessarily consistent with those of the market. A financial analyst, therefore, measures the deviation between realized values and expected values or between realized values and the consensus (or median) of the expectations of all analysts.

If expectations are excluded, then performances can be measured in relation to the

FIGURE 8.1 Analytic system of stock evaluations. The methodology in Step Four is an abbreviated version of the Wells Fargo stock-evaluation system.

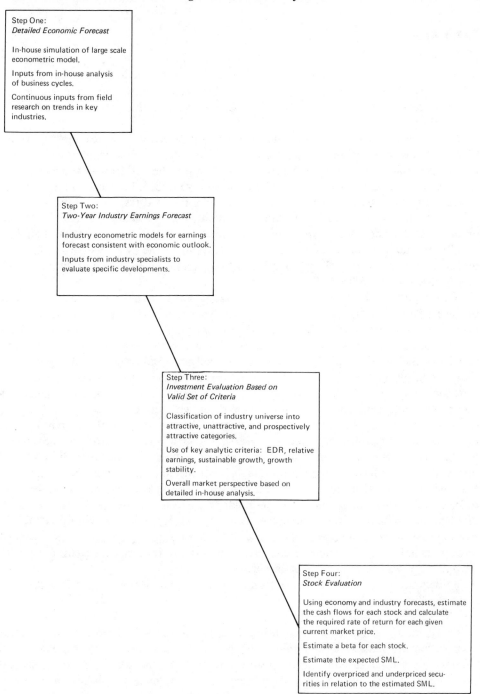

From *Industry Evaluations.* The Boston Company Investment Research and Technology, Inc., Boston, 1975. Used with permission.

history of the firm and in relation to the industry to which the firm belongs. This is done using ratio analysis.

Ratio Analysis

Ratio analysis is a device used to shed light on (put more meaning into) the results of the operations of the firm and its status reported in the income statement and the balance sheet. The meaningfulness of the analysis is enhanced by comparing the current performance of the firm with past performance and with that of other firms in the same industry.

Ratios can be divided into four broad categories: profitability ratios, activity ratios, liquidity ratios, and indebtedness or leverage ratios. Profitability ratios measure the overall effectiveness and efficiency of management in the utilization of capital and human resources. Activity ratios measure the effectiveness of resource utilization. Liquidity ratios measure the short-term solvency of the firm, with the acid-test ratio being the most effective of the ratios. The acid-test ratio excludes inventory, which is usually less liquid or has a high transaction cost (in terms of price discounts) attached to its liquidity. Finally, the leverage ratios measure the extent to which the firm's assets are financed by debt and by the firm's ability to meet long term commitments. A list of the frequently used ratios appears in Table 8.2.

With regard to all the ratios, the reader should take notice that ratios that ignore the fine print of the balance sheet and income statement footnotes could be seriously misleading. Another caution deals with the classification of certain transactions. Take the case of long-term debt, which figures prominently in the leverage ratios. Long-term debt *must* include the capitalized value of financial leases and the unfunded portion of the pension plan. Financial leases represent long-term obligations to the firm and are cancelable only if both the lessor and the lessee agree. They practically represent a 100 percent financing option. Another issue deals with the classification of preferred stocks: are they debt obligations or equity issues? The answer is, in the current opinion of the accounting profession, that they are equity. If a preferred stock is convertible, it is surely more equity than debt; if it is nonconvertible, the fact that the preferred dividend does not have to be paid (although it is considered a de facto obligation) and that the preferred stock does not have a maturity date makes it more like equity than debt; if it is participating—that is, if the holder may receive not only the stated annual dividend but a share of the earnings as well—it is surely more like equity. Thus, the opinion of the accounting profession is in favor of counting preferred stock as equity and/or including that portion of convertible bonds that can be converted during the current fiscal year in the equity of the firm.

While ratio analysis can be quite informative, as we shall demonstrate below, it suffers some weaknesses:

1. All ratios are based on accounting data, which are influenced by many factors even within the domain of "generally acceptable accounting principle." An example of the size of variance resulting from the utilization of various accounting methods was provided by Leonard Spacek,[4] who found that reported earnings per share of a company,

---

[4] **Leonard Spacek,** in **J. Lorie** and **M. Hamilton,** *The Stock Market: Theories and Evidence.* Irwin, Homewood, Ill., 1973, p. 146.

TABLE 8.2
Frequently Used Ratios

Profitability Measures

1. Net profit after taxes/net sales
2. Return on equity = net profit after taxes/net worth
3. Return on fixed assets = net profit/fixed assets
4. Return on total assets = net profit/total assets
5. Gross profit margin = gross margin/net sales

Activity and Turnover Measures

6. Sales/net worth
7. Sales/net working capital
8. Inventory turnover = sales/inventory
9. Tangible assets turnover = sales/tangible assets
10. Average collection period = receivable/sales per day

Liquidity Measures

11. Current ratio = current assets/current liabilities
12. Acid-test ratio = (current assets − inventory)/current liabilities
13. Inventory/net working capital
14. Net liquid assets = short-term securities (held) − short-term debt
15. Cash flow/total debt[a]

Indebtedness Measures

16. Fixed assets/net worth
17. Current debt/net worth
18. Total debt/net worth
19. Interest coverage = gross income (earning before interest and taxes)/interest charges
20. Fixed-charge coverage = $\dfrac{\text{gross income}}{\dfrac{\text{lease payments} + \text{rent} + \text{interest} + \text{principal}}{(1 - \text{corporate tax rate})}}$
21. Total debt/total assets
22. Long-term debt/total capitalization (stockholder's equity + preferred stock + long-term bonds)
23. Cash flow/total debt[a]

---

[a] This ratio was found by Beaver to be a good predictor of firm failure and is currently being reviewed by the SEC and the AICPA with regard to the need and nature of its disclosure.

---

using various combinations of accounting methods, varied from $0.80 to $1.79. The reasons for the variance are many, among them:

a. Inventory valuation methods. *The Wall Street Journal* in its January 19, 1981, issue carried an article by Gary Biddle in which he showed the considerable impact a change from FIFO (first in, first out) to LIFO (last in, first out) inventory valuation could have on profits and hence tax liability. For example, as a result of using FIFO, Minnesota Mining and Mfg. Co. paid $118 million more in taxes than it would have using LIFO, and Eastman Kodak saved $204 million as a result of using LIFO.

b. The choice of which items are to be capitalized (treated as assets to be written off over several fiscal periods) as opposed to being expensed exerts influence over the value of many ratios.

    c. The depreciation method used (declining balance vs. straight-line method) influences many of the ratios, the most watched ratios—profitability ratios—in particular.

    2. Ratios ignore time as an element in the maturity cycle of the firm. A new entrant into a market is usually compared, without sufficient consideration for its age, to a mature, well-established group within the industry.

    3. Ratios can give conflicting signals, the net effects of which are hard if not impossible to discern. Is a low profitability ratio bad per se? Is it a reflection of bad management? Is a low profitability ratio compared with industry averages a reflection of bad management? The answer to all of these questions is not necessarily. It all depends on the reasons (tornadoes, heavy outlays on research and development, etc.) for low profits, on the time period over which they were realized (thc short vs. the long-run view of profitability), and on whether or not they are expected to continue. Are high profitability ratios desirable per se, regardless of all else? Are high profitability ratios desirable concurrently with high leverage ratios if a soft economy is expected?

The development of an integrated picture of the corporation using ratio analysis—despite the difficulties cited above—is possible, as Altman and associates[5] and Dambolena and Khoury[6] have shown. We shall discuss their findings later in this chapter.

    It can be said, therefore, that ratios, while useful, must be used with care and must be balanced by industry conditions.

    We now proceed with an example on ratio analysis. First a few words of caution:

1. The comparison of the firm's current performance with past performance requires great care because:

    a. The accounting methods used may have changed.

    b. The character of the corporation may have changed through mergers or through significant expansions into new areas of business.

    c. The corporate environment may have shifted considerably, for example, from little interference by government to heavy government regulation.

2. The comparison of a firm's operations with the industry require the definition of that industry. Some companies are so diversified that it is impossible to assign one firm into an industry category, and some firms may be so new as to constitute the industry. In addition, there is a problem with the determination of the appropriate geographic area where competition with other firms in a similar line of business is in fact taking place. Is a department store in Chicago competing with every department store in Chicago, or in Chicago and its suburbs, or in the nation? Are national data of any significance to regional or local department stores? The answers to these questions are not very easy.

    The determination of the industry category is ordinarily made using one of the following methods:

    a. Cross elasticity of demand for products.

---

    [5] **E. I. Altman, Robert G. Haldeman,** and **P. Narayanan,** "Zeta Analysis: A New Model to Identify Bankruptcy Risk of Corporations." *Journal of Banking and Finance,* Spring 1977.

    [6] **Ismael G. Dambolena** and **Sarkis J. Khoury,** "Ratio Stability and Corporate Failure." *Journal of Finance,* vol. 35, no. 4, (September 1980), pp. 1017–1026.

$$\theta_{xy} = \frac{(\Delta X)/(X)}{(\Delta P_y)/(P_y)}$$

where X = quantity of X purchased

P_y = price of commodity y

θ_{xy} = percentage change in the quantity of X purchased given a percentage change in the price of y

$\theta_{xy} > 0 \rightarrow$ goods are substitutes for each other

$\theta_{xy} < 0 \rightarrow$ goods are complementary

The closer to perfect substitute goods are, the better the definition of the industry.[7]

b. Use Standard Industrial Classification (SIC) numbers published by the Office of Management and Budget. The larger the number of digits in the SIC classification, the more specific the breakdown. The first two digits stand for a major industry grouping (78–motion pictures); the three-digit number represents a further breakdown in the group (781—motion picture production and allied services); and the four-digit number represents a specific sector of the industry group (7813—motion picture production except for television).

c. Classify industry by product and geographic location similarities.

Our preference is for the SIC classification method, for it is the simplest and the most consistent.

A wealth of information is available on almost all industries. The industry surveys by Standard & Poor's and by several brokerage houses are particularly helpful. Each industry has its own trade publication, which provides considerable information. As to industry data in forms of ratios, two sources are particularly helpful: Dun & Bradstreet's *Key Business Ratios* and Robert Morris Associates. Both these services use the median value of ratios of firms within the industry as representative of the industry.

Example

The JAK Corporation is a maker of sporting goods. Its balance sheet and income statements for the periods ending in December 31, 1979, 1980, and 1981 are shown in Table 8.3.

Using the data in Table 8.3, we calculated some key ratios for the designated periods (Table 8.4), plotted the results against the industry average for the three years to identify trends (Figure 8.2), and then performed a percentage analysis of income statement—both horizontal and vertical—for the years 1980 and 1981 to get an idea about relative efficiency (Table 8.5).

Integrating Ratios

A major breakthrough in the integration of financial ratios to measure the well-being of the corporation was realized by E. Altman.[8] Using the multiple discriminant analysis technique, he was able to develop a model for forecasting corporate failure. Firms were

---

[7] **J. S. Bain,** *Price Theory.* Wiley, New York, 1956.

[8] **E. I. Altman,** "Financial Ratios, Discriminant Analysis and the Prediction of Corporate Bankruptcy." *Journal of Finance,* vol. 23 (September 1968), pp. 589–609.

classified as likely to fail or likely to succeed depending on how high their Z score was:

$$Z = 0.012X_1 + 0.014X_2 + 0.033X_3 + 0.006X_4 + 0.999X_5 \qquad (8.1)$$

where $X_1 =$ working capital/total assets

$X_2 =$ retained earnings/total assets

$X_3 =$ earnings before interest and taxes/total assets

$X_4 =$ market value of equity/book value of total debt

$X_5 =$ sales/total assets

TABLE 8.3
The JAK Corporation

		Balance Sheet *December 31, 1979–1981* (*in $1,000s*)				
Assets		1979		1980		1981
Cash		$ 2,100		$ 1,800		$ 1,600
Accounts receivable		1,400		1,800		1,500
Raw materials & supplies	800		1,000		1,200	
Work in process	2,600		3,500		4,600	
Finished goods	200		300		500	
Inventory		3,600		4,800		6,300
Total current assets		7,100		8,400		9,400
Fixed assets at cost	22,900		27,000		34,500	
Less: accumulated depreciation	6,300		6,600		6,900	
Net fixed assets		16,600		20,400		27,600
Goodwill		12,000		12,000		12,000
Total assets		**35,700**		**40,800**		**49,000**
Liabilities						
Line of credit		2,400		2,600		2,400
Accounts payable		700		1,000		1,600
Accruals		300		500		800
Total current liabilities		3,400		4,100		4,800
Bank loan (due Oct. 1982)		2,000		2,000		2,000
Long-term debt		—		—		7,500
Preferred stock[a]		12,000		12,000		12,000
Common stock[b]		4,000		5,000		5,000
Paid-in surplus		10,000		13,000		13,000
Retained earnings		4,300		4,700		4,700
Total stockholders' equity		30,300		34,700		34,700
Total liabilities & equity		**35,700**		**40,800**		**49,000**

TABLE 8.3 (*Continued*)

Income Statements for the Years Ending
December 31, 1979–1981
(*in $1,000s*)

	1979	1980	1981
Net sales	$20,600	$24,200	$25,700
Cost of goods sold	14,700	17,300	18,400
Gross profit	5,900	6,900	7,300
Selling general & administrative expenses	993	1,828	2,233
Depreciation	650	650	650
Earnings before interest & taxes	4,257	4,422	4,417
Interest expense	200	200	950
Earnings before taxes	4,057	4,222	3,467
Taxes	1,907	1,984.5	1,629.5
Net profit after tax	2,150	2,237.5	1,837.5
Dividends paid:			
Common	750.	937.5	937.5
Preferred	900.	900.	900.

[a] On Aug. 31, 1981 there were 625,000 shares of common outstanding.

[b] On Aug. 31, 1981 there were 120,000 shares of preferred stock outstanding with a par value of $100 each and yielding 7.5 percent.

Source: Scott/Martin/Petty/Keown, *Cases in Finance,* © 1977, pp. 13–14. Reprinted by permission of Prentice-Hall, Inc. Englewood Cliffs, N.J.

The discriminating score was 1.8.

If $Z < 1.8$, the firm will fail.
If $1.8 \leq Z \leq 3$, the firm will not likely fail.
If $Z > 3$, the firm will not fail.

Altman was later to improve on his model by capitalizing leases and including them in the corporate debt structure.[9] The new model was dubbed the zeta model and predicted corporate failures five years prior to their occurrence with a success rate of 69.8 percent.

Dambolena and Khoury,[10] using Altman's work as a foundation, noted that the variability of ratios prior to failure increased significantly. Using ratio levels and ratio variability (measured by the standard deviation of the ratios, taking three years at a time from the sample data and dropping one year and adding another as they moved away from the failure date), Dambolena and Khoury developed a bankruptcy model

---

[9] **E. I. Altman, Robert B. Haldeman,** and **P. Narayanan,** "Zeta Analysis: A New Model to Identify Bankruptcy Risk of Corporations." *Journal of Banking and Finance,* Spring 1977, pp. 29–54.

[10] **I. Dambolena** and **S. Khoury,** "Ratio Stability and Corporate Failure." *Journal of Finance,* vol. 35, no. 4 (September 1980), pp. 1017–1026.

TABLE 8.4
The JAK Corporation

Ratio	Formula for Calculation	Calculations			Industry Average
		1979	1980	1981	
Liquidity					
Current	current assets / current liabilities	2.09	2.05	1.96	1.943
Acid-test	current assets − inventory / current liabilities	1.03	.88	.65	.969
Leverage					
Total debt to net worth	total debt / net worth	.295	.268	.629	.636
Long-term debt to capitalization	long-term debt / total capitalization	.062	.054	.215	.487
Interest coverage	gross income / interest charges	21.285 times	22.11 times	4.65 times	4.533 times
Activity					
Average collection period	receivables / sales per day	24.5 days	26.8 days	21.0 days	40.3 days
Inventory turnover	sales / inventory	5.72 times	5.04 times	4.08 times	3.877 times
Tangible-asset turnover	sales / tangible assets	.869 times	.840 times	.695 times	.826 times
Profitability					
Gross profit margin	gross margin / net sales	28.6%	28.5%	28.4%	23.4%
Net profit margin	net profit after taxes / net sales	10.44%	9.25%	7.15%	9.64%
Return on tangible assets	net profits after taxes / tangible assets	9.07%	7.77%	4.97%	7.96%

FIGURE 8.2 The JAK Corporation—trend analysis. (Instead of the average, the analyst may wish to plot each observation on industry ratios.)

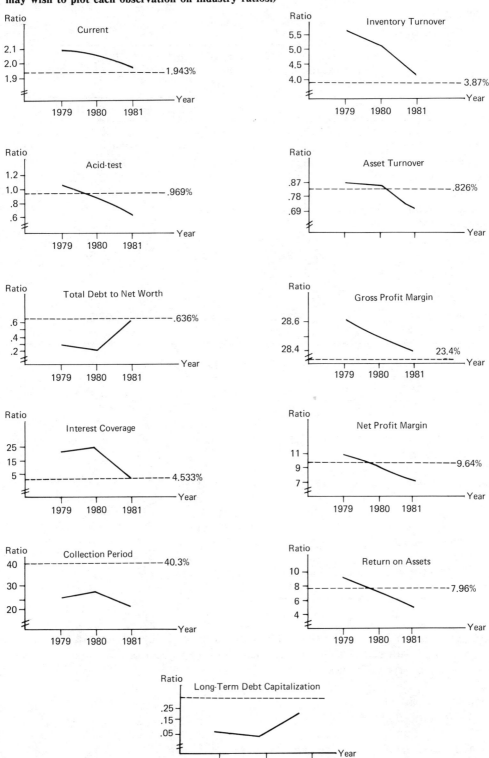

TABLE 8.5
The JAK Corporation

Percentage Analysis of Income Statement (Vertical)
Period Ending December 31, 1980, 1981
(in $1,000's)

	1980		1981	
Net sales	24,200.	100.0%	25,700.	100.0%
Cost of goods sold	17,300.	71.5	18,400.	71.6
Gross margin	6,900.	28.5	7,300.	28.4
Selling general & admin.	1,828.	7.5	2,233.	8.7
Depreciation	650.	2.7	650.	2.5
Earnings before int. & tax	4,422.	18.3	4,417.	17.2
Interest expense	200.	.8	950.	3.7
Earnings before taxes	4,222.	17.5	3,467.	13.5
Taxes	1,984.5	8.2	1,629.5	6.3
Net profit after taxes	2,237.5	9.3	1,837.5	7.2
Dividends paid				
Common stock	937.5	41.9	937.5	51.0
Preferred stock	900.0	40.2	900.0	49.0

Percentage Change from Previous Year (Horizontal)

Account	1980	1981
Net sales	17.5	6.2
Cost of goods sold	17.7	6.4
Gross profit	16.9	5.8
Selling general & admin.	84.1	22.2
Depreciation	.0	.0
Earnings before int. & taxes	3.9	(0.1)
Interest expense	.0	3.75
Earnings before taxes	4.1	(17.9)
Taxes	4.1	(17.9)
Net profit after taxes	4.1	(17.9)
Dividends paid		
Common stock	25.0	.0
Preferred stock	.0	.0

using multiple discriminant analysis. The model predicted failed firms five years prior to bankruptcy with a success rate of 78 percent. The independent variables of the discriminant function were as follows:

1. Net profit/sales (X_1)
2. Net profit/total assets (X_2)
3. Fixed assets/net worth (X_3)
4. Funded debt/net working capital (X_4)
5. Total debt/total assets (X_5)
6. Standard deviation of inventory/net working capital (X_6)

FIGURE 8.3 **Predicting share prices using ratios.**

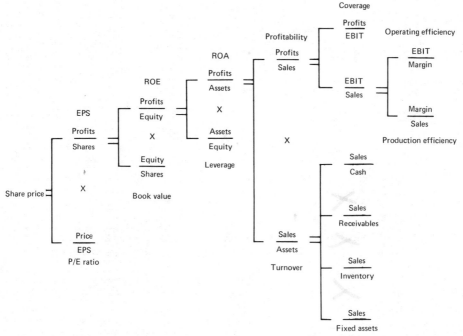

From Samuel E. Stewart, Jr., "Corporate Forecasting," in Sumner N. Levine, ed., *Financial Analyst's Handbook.* Dow Jones-Irwin, Homewood, Ill., 1975, p. 912.

7. Standard deviation of fixed assets/net worth (X_7)

$$Z = 1.189 - 8.436\ X_1 + 18.850 X_2 + 1.955 X_3 + 0.739 X_4$$
$$- 4.921 X_5 - 1.588 X_6 - 6.330 X_7 \quad (8.2)$$

Financial Ratios to Predict Stock Prices

Financial analysts also use ratios to predict share prices, as shown in Figure 8.3. Using a combination of leverage, turnover, and profitability ratios, the analyst can easily and systematically proceed to estimate the price of a common stock. The product of the ratios in each bracket is equal to that ratio preceded by the equality sign until the share price is arrived at.

The usefulness of ratios is even greater than the discussion above indicates. Ratios have also been used to predict the systematic risk of a security as well as in the development of proforma balance sheets, income statements, and cash flow statements; all these are critical to the valuation of securities, as we shall demonstrate later in this chapter.

Having just introduced a simple forecasting technique, we proceed with the development of the overall forecasting model summarized in Figure 8.1.

8.5 ECONOMIC FORECAST

The models used to forecast the future course of the economy are becoming increasingly complex. In many cases, the solution to the model requires solving over a hundred simultaneous equations. A simple model for the U.S. economy might look as follows:

$$Y_t = C_t + I_t + G + X_t \tag{8.3}$$

$$C_t = a_0 + a_1 Y_t + a_2 C_{t-1} \tag{8.4}$$

$$I_t = b_0 + b_1 i + b_2 Y_{t-1} \tag{8.5}$$

$$G = \overline{G} \tag{8.6}$$

$$i = \overline{\imath} \tag{8.7}$$

$$X_t = \overline{X} \tag{8.8}$$

where Y = gross national product (GNP)

  C = consumption

  I_t = investment expenditures

  G = government expenditures $\overline{G}$ assumed to be exogeneously determined, that is, determined outside the model, in this case by act of Congress

  X_t = net foreign exports

  $\overline{\imath}$ = interest rate assumed to be exogeneously determined

  t = time

Equations 8.4 and 8.5 are behavioral equations that describe how consumers and producers behave. The remaining equations are identities. By appropriate estimating procedures (usually regression analysis), Equations 8.4 and 8.5 are estimated and the values of C_t and I_t along with the exogenous G_t and X_t are used in Equation 8.3 to arrive at the predicted value of GNP.

Financial analysts, however, almost never make their own forecast of the economy. They rely on estimates based on the models of various university-affiliated organizations or commercial enterprises such as the Wharton School at the University of Pennsylvania, the Federal Reserve–MIT, Data Resources Incorporated, Chase Econometrics, Townsend-Greenspan and Company, as well as leading banks and investment banking institutions.

Data on the components of GNP are also available from a multitude of sources, as summarized in Table 8.6. The sources indicated in this table are quite reliable and have proven their worthiness over time.

Yet another alternative to arriving at a forecast of the *direction* of the U.S. economy is to use the barometric approach. The Bureau of Economic Analysis (BEA) of the U.S. Department of Commerce publishes on a monthly basis sets of cyclical indicators that fall into three categories:

1. *Leading indicators.* Time series data on 12 variables that have historically reached their peaks and their troughs in advance of economic activity are provided. The leading indicators are shown in Figure 8.4.

2. *Roughly coincident indicators.* BEA has identified four such indicators (employees on nonagricultural payrolls, personal income less transfer payments, industrial production, and manufacturing and trade sales) that reach their peaks and troughs coincidentally with economic activity.

TABLE 8.6
Sources of Data on the Components of GNP

Component of GNP	Type of Information	Source and Date	Uses of the Information
	Nonresidential construction contracts (F. W. Dodge Index).	*Survey of Current Business* (monthly) and *Business Conditions Digest* (monthly).	Since construction awards should normally lead actual construction, this series suggests potential changes in the building of factories, office buildings, stores, etc.
Residential construction	Family formation.	Intermittent projections by the Bureau of the Census.	Provides information of a key segment of the potential market for new housing.
	Residential construction contracts awarded or housing starts.	*Survey of Current Business* (monthly) and *Business Conditions Digest* (monthly).	Provides an indication of potential changes in housing construction before those changes take place.
	Mortgage terms and ease of securing loans (down payments, interest rates, monthly payments).	Newspapers provide intermittent reports. *Federal Reserve Bulletin* (monthly).	Information on the terms of FHA, VA, and regular mortgages indicates the financial restraints on the purchase of new homes.
	Vacancy rate.	Bureau of Labor Statistics.	Indicates the extent of saturation of the housing market.
	Home-building survey.	*Fortune* magazine (monthly).	Indicates developments in residential construction.
Inventory investment	Ratios of inventories to sales on the manufacturing, wholesaling, and retailing levels (requires computations involving series on inventories and series on sales).	*Survey of Current Business* (monthly).	Indicates whether inventories are high or low in relation to a "normal" ratio. Must be interpreted with caution in the light of recent changes in final sales and the attitude of business toward inventories.
	Manufacturers' inventory expectations.	*Survey of Current Business* (monthly).	Indicates extent to which businesses expect to expand or contract inventories.

TABLE 8.6
Sources of Data on the Components of GNP (Continued)

Component of GNP	Type of Information	Source and Date	Uses of the Information
	Inventory surveys.	*Fortune* magazine (monthly).	On the basis of sales expectations and assumed inventory-sales ratios, estimates amount of inventory change.
Consumer durable goods	Surveys of consumers' intentions to spend and save (including intentions to buy automobiles).	Survey Research Center, University of Michigan and Federal Reserve Board. *Federal Reserve Bulletin* (quarterly).	Indicates intentions to purchase durable goods. There is considerable correlation between these intentions and actual purchases.
	Rate of housing construction.	*Survey of Current Business* (monthly).	The building of new houses has an important influence on sales of furniture and appliances.
	Installment credit outstanding (in relation to the disposable personal income).	*Federal Reserve Bulletin* (monthly).	A high level of installment credit already outstanding may mean a lower willingness to incur new debt or a lower willingness to lend.
	Buying-plan surveys.	National Industrial Conference Board *Business Record.*	Suggests potential changes in the purchase of consumer goods.
	Projected consumer outlays on durable goods and housing.	*Consumer Buying Indicators* (quarterly).	Covers surveys of plans of consumers to purchase automobiles, appliances, furniture, and housing.
Nondurable consumer goods and services	Regression lines relating the past consumption of nondurable goods and services to the past disposable personal income.	Past issues of the *Survey of Current Business* provide the necessary data. Special articles in the *Survey of Current Business* review findings on such relationships.	Past relationships to disposable personal income show considerable stability, though the rate of sales to income rises in recession.
Comprehensive collection of indicators	Charts covering most of the best-known indicators.	*Business Conditions Digest* (monthly).	A compact collection of charts covering indicators of income, production, prices, employment, and monetary conditions.

Source: W. Haynes and W. Henry, *Managerial Economics: Analysis and Cases*, ed. 4. Business Publications, Inc., Dallas, 1978.

3. *Lagging indicators.* These number six in all (average duration of unemployment, manufacturing and trade inventories, labor costs per unit of output, average prime rate charged by banks, commercial and industrial loans outstanding, and the ratio of consumer installment debt to personal income); they reach their peaks and troughs after economic activity has reached its own.

Economic indicators, while useful, are not without handicaps. Leading indicators, for example, suggest only the direction of the economy and say nothing about the magnitude or length of the recovery or slowdown. Leading indicators may also give conflicting

FIGURE 8.4   Leading components of composite indexes.

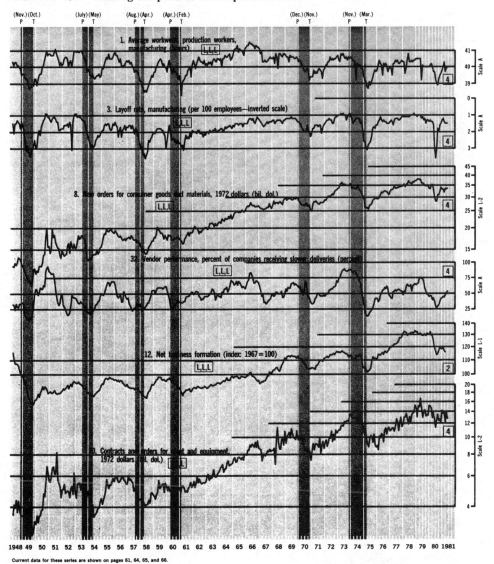

From *Business Conditions Digest,* Bureau of Economic Analysis, U.S. Department of Commerce, May 1981.

FIGURE 8.4 (*Continued*)

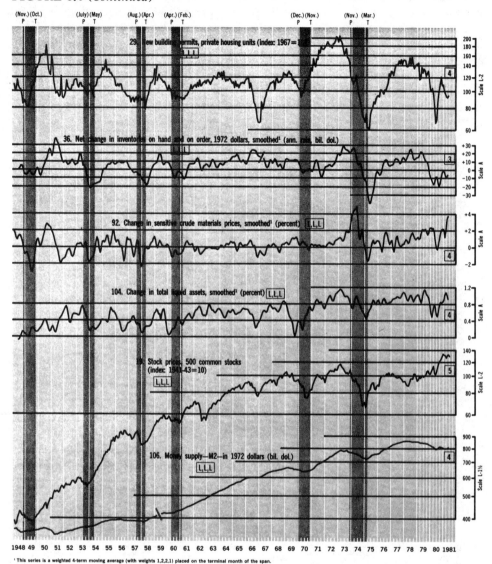

signals, which must be weighed in accordance with the significance of each of the indicators. Also, the same indicator may give conflicting signals from one month to another. This is why economists wait for a confirmation of a trend (successive increases or decreases in an indicator over a three-month period, on the average) before deciding on the direction of economic activity.

To resolve the conflicting signals from the various indicators, BEA developed diffusion indexes that combine various indicators into one and indicate the percentage of the total moving up or down in a given month.

8.6 INDUSTRY FORECASTS

Industry forecasts are the second step in the stock evaluation process. We present once again the approach used by The Boston Company for two industries, one in the manufacturing sector and the other in the financial sector.

The integration of the economic forecast in the industry forecast and the steps involved in arriving at a net income industry forecast are illustrated in Figure 8.5. The process, which involves a series of five equations, is illustrated at the top of Figure 8.5.

The forecast of earnings for the banking industry is illustrated in Figure 8.6. Once again, the economic outlook is incorporated in the industry analysis.

Based on the relationship (or lack thereof) between the industry profits and economic activity, industries can be classified into three basic groups:

FIGURE 8.5 Forecasting model for auto manufacturers. Industry earnings forecasts are generated by a series of five equations. Truck, bus, and auto factory unit sales projections reflect the determinants of demand—aggregate consumer financial position, durable goods consumption, demographics, and price levels—and are adjusted for inventory changes. Industry profitability is forecast from pricing and cost trends, operating leverage effects, and strike incidence. The margin and sales estimates are then combined to yield projections of industry net income.

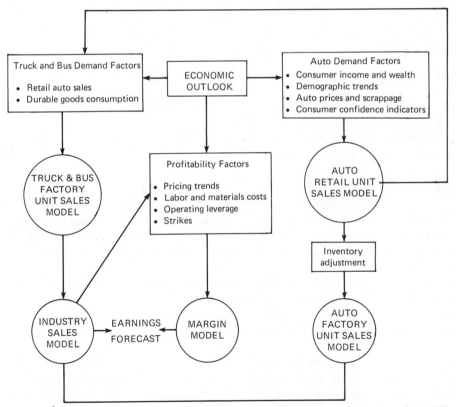

From *Industry Evaluation,* The Boston Company Investment Research and Technology, Inc., 1975.

FIGURE 8.6   Forecasting model for New York City banks. Our forecasting model integrates the supply and demand factors affecting loan portfolios, the implications of international financial conditions, and the monetary policy environment as bases for earnings projections.

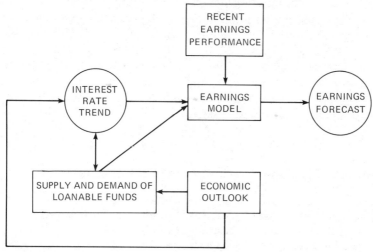

From *Industry and Evaluation,* The Boston Company Investment Research and Technology, Inc., 1975.

1. *Growth industries.* Industries whose activity is not influenced by the economic cycle (computers, some drugs, etc.).
2. *Cyclical industries.* Industries whose performance is influenced by the economic cycle (steel, rubber, autos, etc.).
3. *Defensive industries.* Industries that are not significantly affected by an economic downturn (food, hospitals, etc.).

In addition the forecaster attempts to incorporate in the model (or in the interpretation of the results of the model) as many as possible of the expected developments that are likely to have a significant impact on a specific industry. These may include changes in government policy (the windfall profits tax imposed on oil companies in 1980 is one example), changes in the labor climate, changes in the technology, and changes in inflationary expectations.

In addition, the analyst looks at the level of concentration in the industry, at its position relative to other industries with respect to technology and maturity of its product line, and at how the market has reacted to industry growth in the past. One measure of market reaction is the average price/earnings ratio the market attaches to one industry relative to another.

In order to keep up with industry developments, the reader should consult various government publications (census of manufacturers, for example), Standard & Poor's, Value Line, Chestnut Corporation, and the Funk and Scott Index on Industry and Company. *Business Week* and *Fortune* also report frequently and provide valuable data on a range of issues affecting various industries.

8.7 VALUATION OF COMMON STOCK

The importance of including economy and industry prospects in the evaluation of common stock was documented in Section 8.3 of this chapter (Brealey, Gonedes, Ball, and Brown). In this section, the various methods of forecasting critical variables for the valuation of stocks and of incorporating industry and economy effects will be discussed.

Earnings and Stock Prices

In Chapter 7, we demonstrated that there is a strong link between dividends and earnings. We also argued that dividends per se do not determine the price of a stock but are simply a proxy variable. The relevant questions,[11] therefore, are the following:

1. Do earnings determine the price of a stock?
2. If they do, what is the best measure of earnings?
3. Are earnings predictable? Do they follow identifiable patterns?
4. Having answered question 3, then what is the best predictive model to apply to the data?

Earnings and Stock Prices

The influence of earnings on stock prices is uniformly accepted by financial analysts. The difference of opinion centers on the extent and speed with which earnings are reflected in stock prices.

The skepticism about earnings is increasing, however. An article in the March 1, 1982, issue of *The Wall Street Journal* explains why and suggests an alternative:

> *In an earlier published study of the Standard & Poor's 400 industrial companies, I found that 16% of those achieving annual EPS growth of 15% or more from 1974 to 1979 provided negative rates of return to shareholders, while for 35% of the same companies, rates of return were inadequate to compensate shareholders for inflation.*
>
> *Some of the stock price drops for high EPS growth companies may reflect lower market expectations about a company's investment opportunities. A company's shares are likely to appreciate over time if the market expects management to earn a rate of return on new investments greater than the rate investors can expect to earn by investing in alternative, identically risky securities. But a company can maintain EPS growth even when it is investing below the market discount rate, and thereby decreasing the value of common shares.*
>
> *There are several important reasons why EPS fails to measure economic value for shareholders. First, earnings figures vary with the use of different accounting methods, for example LIFO vs. FIFO inventory costing. Second, earnings numbers do not reflect differences in business and financial risk faced by various companies or divisions within a single company. Third, earnings do not account for relative rates of investment in working capital and fixed capital needed to support sales growth. Some companies invest as little as 25*

---

[11] These questions are based on the excellent work of **Baruch Lev,** *Financial Statement Analysis: A New Approach.* Prentice-Hall, Englewood Cliffs, N.J., 1974.

cents to produce an incremental dollar of sales, while others require investment rates two or three times as large. Finally, reported earnings do not incorporate changes in a company's cost of capital due to either shifts in inflationary expectations or changes in business or financial risk.

The suggested alternative owes its origin to the Financial Accounting Standards Board (FASB), which recommends the utilization of a comprehensive cash-flow concept in equity valuation.

Stock-valuation models have predominantly used earnings or a proxy for earnings as an explanatory variable in equity valuation. The Value Line model arrives at stock prices as $P = f$(average stock price, D_1, e_1, Market Sentiment Index). (P is used here instead of MP^s.)

For the market value index, the average annual yield on about 50 stocks is used. The predictive power of the model was certified by F. Black.[12]

Whitbeck and Kisor[13] developed a rather interesting model in which the risk of a security is explicitly recognized:

$$P/e = f(g, \ \sigma, \ D/e)$$

where g = expected growth in earnings

σ = standard deviation of the earnings

D/e = expected dividend payout ratio

Their estimated function was[14]

$$P/e = -0.2 + 1.50g + 0.067D/e - 0.2\sigma \tag{8.9}$$

Thus P/e is related positively to g and D/e and negatively to risk. The negative sign on the coefficient of σ is consistent with the assumption that investors on the average are risk-averse. The P/e predicted by Equation 8.9 can be used to identify overpriced or underpriced securities. If predicted P/e is higher than the actual (observable), then the security is underpriced (buy); if the opposite is true, then the security is overpriced (sell and/or sell short).

Other models[15] also confirmed the importance of earnings in a stock-valuation model. Gordon's model showed that

$$P = f\left[e_0, \frac{e - D}{e}, r, K\right]$$

[12] **F. Black,** "Yes, Virginia, There Is Hope: Tests of the Value Line Ranking System." Paper presented at the Seminar on the Analysis of Security Prices, University of Chicago, May 1971.

[13] **V. S. Whitbeck** and **M. Kisor, Jr.,** "A New Tool in Investment Decision-Making." *Financial Analyst's Journal,* vol. 19 (May–June 1963), pp. 55–62.

[14] The estimated P/e from the Whitbeck-Kisor model is used by financial analysts as a measure for "normal" P/e, against which the prevailing P/e ratio is measured.

[15] See **M. J. Gordon,** *The Investment Financing and Valuation of the Corporation.* Irwin, Homewood, Ill., 1962, chap. 4. **B. G. Malkiel,** "Equity Yields, Growth, and the Structure of Share Prices." *American Economic Review,* vol. 53 (December 1963), pp. 1004–1031.

where $(e - D)/e$ = retention rate = b (earlier)

$\quad\quad\quad r$ = return on investment

$\quad\quad\quad K$ = rate of return required by investors

B. Malkiel showed that the *P/e* ratio is simply a function of the growth rate in earnings and in the dividend payout ratio.

Additional evidence comes in daily as financial analysts prove to themselves time and again that earnings are indeed important.

What Earnings?

The Financial Accounting Standards Board (FASB) in its Statement No. 33 issued in September 1979 requires that certain financial disclosures based on constant-dollar and current-cost accounting be submitted in addition to those traditionally developed using historic costs.

Constant-dollar accounting requires that data be adjusted to reflect changes in the general price level. Current-cost accounting requires that financial statements and other disclosures reflect inflation affecting specific balance-sheet or income statement items.

All three types of financial disclosures must be submitted by certain large, publicly held corporations. The obvious set of questions emanating from these new requirements deals with the basic premise behind inflation accounting: is there significant additional information that can result from inflation accounting? Specifically:

1. Can inflation accounting allow the financial analyst to predict future earnings better?
2. Can inflation accounting allow the financial analyst to predict systematic risk better?
3. Does inflation accounting lead to a more accurate prediction of stock prices?

The answers to all these questions are not yet conclusive.

Predicting Future Earnings. The question here is whether earnings data determined by using inflation accounting allow for a better forecast of future accounting income. W. Frank,[16] Simmons and Gray,[17] and D. Buckmaster and colleagues[18] all answer in the negative. All three studies have shown that current-cost and/or constant-dollar accounting will *not* improve the predictive power of income series. The analyst should not go farther than the publicly available data using historical costs.

Accounting Data and Beta. Several studies have attempted to measure whether β's arrived at using accounting data are superior to those using the naive (market data

---

[16] **W. Frank,** "A Study of the Predictive Significance of Two Income Measures." *Journal of Accounting Research,* vol. 7 (Spring 1969), pp. 123–136.

[17] **J. K. Simmons** and **J. Gray,** "An Investigation of the Effect of Differing Accounting Frameworks on the Prediction of Net Income. *Accounting Review,* vol. 44 (October 1969), pp. 757–776.

[18] **Dale A. Buckmaster, Ronald M. Copeland,** and **Paul Dascher,** "The Relative Predictive Ability of Three Accounting Income Models." *Accounting and Business Research,* Summer 1977, pp. 177–186.

only) forecasts discussed in Chapter 6. Beaver et al.,[19] using the ordinary least squares regression techniques, found that accounting-based prediction of systematic risk, represented by β, were superior to those based on market data. Beaver's work did not take the biasedness of the predicted beta values into consideration (see Chapter 6), however. Eskew[20] made explicit adjustments for biasedness and still found accounting-based data to be superior.

A later study by P. Elgers[21] contradicts the findings of Beaver and those of Eskew. Elgers concluded that:

> *Accounting-based predictions of beta do not improve our naive (market data only) forecasts. . . .*
> *Attempts to generalize over time about the predictive ability of accounting risk numbers, or about the relevance of specific accounting ratios to explanations or predictions of equity beta, should be done with extreme caution. The evidence reported here indicates that individual regression coefficients and the entire regression plan relating accounting numbers and betas are unstable over time.*[22]

D. Short[23] studied whether ratios using constant-dollar accounting data had better explanatory power of beta values than those based on historical costs. His findings confirmed that constant-dollar ratios had higher explanatory powers.

Short's findings were later supported by Arie Baran and associates,[24] who examined the value of general price level (GPL) adjusted earnings using data from 1957 to 1974. Their conclusion was as follows:

> *. . . the results obtained in this study appear to support the hypothesis that price level data contain information which is not included in the financial reports currently provided. The association between market beta and GPL adjusted betas was significantly higher than those observed between market and historical cost betas. For the total 18 year period examined, the GPL adjusted betas outperformed the historical-cost betas in every single comparison made."*[25]

Michael Morris[26] studied the difference in the explanatory powers of ratios based on historical costs and those based on current costs. The tests used were

---

[19] **W. H. Beaver, P. Kettler,** and **M. Scholes,** "The Association Between Market Determined and Accounting Determined Risk Measures." *Accounting Review,* October 1970, pp. 654–682.

[20] **R. K. Eskew,** "The Forecasting Ability of Accounting Risk Measures: Some Additional Evidence." *Accounting Review,* January 1979, pp. 107–118.

[21] **P. Elgers,** "Accounting Based Risk Predictions: A Re-Examination." *Accounting Review,* vol. 55, no. 3 (July 1980), pp. 389–408.

[22] Ibid, p. 403.

[23] **Daniel G. Short,** "The Usefulness of Price Level Adjusted Accounting Numbers in the Context of Risk Assessment." Unpublished doctoral dissertation, University of Michigan, Ann Arbor, 1977.

[24] **Arie Baran, Josef Lakonishok,** and **Aharon Ofer,** "The Information Content of General Price Level Adjusted Earnings: Some Empirical Evidence." *Accounting Review,* January 1980, pp. 22–35.

[25] Ibid, p. 34.

[26] **Michael H. Morris,** "A Study of the Potential Relevance of Replacement Cost Accounting Data in the Assessment of Systematic Risk." Unpublished doctoral dissertation, University of Cincinnati, June 1980.

$\beta = f$ (four variables) $\rightarrow$ using historical data
$\beta = f$ (four variables) $\rightarrow$ using current cost

The four variables used by Morris were

Leverage ratio
Dividend payout ratio
Earning variability ratio
Earning covariability

The last of these is an accounting β equal to the following ratio:

$$\frac{\text{Covariance between a company's earnings and average earnings of the market}}{\text{Variance of the average earnings of the market}}$$

The performance of current cost data was found to be not significantly different from that of historical cost data.

Stock Prices and Accounting Data. Two major studies have addressed the impact of accounting data on stock prices: one by A. Rashad Abdel-Khalik and James C. McKeown[27] and the other by William Hillison.[28]

Abdel-Khalik and McKeown found that replacement cost accounting did not contain information not already impounded in stock prices and that the market assessment of systematic risk was not altered by the disclosure of estimates of replacement-cost-based income.

W. Hillison attempted to show that the association between traditional earnings-per-share numbers and the movement in stock prices[29] held when general-purcashing-power-adjusted (GPPA) earnings per share were used. Using data from Compustat and CRSP for the period 1970–1974, Hillison concluded that the impact of GPPA data on stock prices was generally insignificant.

The *Journal of Accounting and Economics* devoted the entire August 1980 issue to the relationship between stock prices and replacement-cost disclosures. The conclusion of all papers in the issue was unanimous: replacement-cost disclosures have no effect on security prices. A summary of the issue is provided in the first article by R. Watts and J. Zimmerman (pp. 95–106).

Behavior of Earnings

The understanding of the behavior of earnings over time helps determine whether forecasting of any kind is possible or necessary, and if so, which is the optimal forecasting

---

[27] **A. Rashad Abdel-Khalik** and **James C. McKeown,** "Disclosure of Estimates of Holding Gains and the Assessment of Systematic Risk." *Journal of Accounting Research,* vol. 16, suppl., 1978, pp. 46–77.

[28] **William Hillison,** "Empirical Investigation of General Purchasing Power Adjustments on Earnings per Share and the Movement of Security Prices." *Journal of Accounting Research,* Spring 1979, pp. 60–73.

[29] See **R. Ball** and **P. Brown,** "An Empirical Evaluation of Accounting Income Numbers." *Journal of Accounting Research,* Autumn 1968, pp. 159–177; **N. Gonedes,** "Capital Market Equilibrium and Annual Accounting Numbers: Empirical Evidence." *Journal of Accounting Research,* Spring 1974, pp. 26–62.

technique. Kenneth Lorek and his colleagues best summarized the reasons for understanding earning patterns:

> *. . . the issue of forecasting annual earnings which has repeatedly been raised by the SEC has provided the impetus for assessment of the information content of accounting earnings numbers via the predictive ability criterion. . . . If in fact accounting income numbers do exhibit patterns through time, then the construction of a forecasting model which ignores these dependencies is clearly suboptimal. . . .*
>
> *Can a single parsimonious time-series model for earnings represent all firms adequately or should firm-specific earnings expectation models be employed? . . . the Financial Accounting Standards Board (FASB) has recently required supplementary general price level data (see FASB Statement of Financial Accounting Standards, No. 33, "Financial Reporting and Changing Prices"). We are currently ignorant of what effect (if any) these transformations might have on the time-series properties of earnings. Perhaps the nominal increase in sales and earnings due to inflation over the last two decades have introduced noise in the data making identification of the underlying generating accounting earnings difficult. . . .*[30]

Looking at earnings behavior from a slightly different perspective, Ball and Watts further justify the concern:

> *The interpretation of growth and decline (and their extreme counterparts, survival and failure) depends heavily on the income generating process. . . . A constant expectation finite-variance process implies the relative insignificance of variability in income. Deviations of income from the expectation are then once-and-for-all increments or decrements in the value of the firm. . . . In contrast, a process whose expectation is not constant or a deterministic function of time implies the importance of variability. For a martingale . . . [the] expectation of all future incomes is changed with each observation.*[31]

The evidence of the behavior of earnings over time is mixed. Before we review the literature, we discuss a few earnings-generating processes, some of which were referred to in the quotations above.

Martingales. Martingales are a special case of a random walk. They show that the best predictor of tomorrow's earnings are today's. Let e_t equal earnings and E the expected value operator, then

$$E(e_{t+1}/e_0, \ldots, e_t) = e_t \text{ (martingale)}$$
$$\text{If } E(e_{t+1}/e_0, \ldots, e_t) \geq e_t \text{ (submartingale)}$$
$$E(e_{t+1}/e_0, \ldots, e_t) \leq \text{ (supermartingale)}$$

[30] **Kenneth S. Lorek, Robert Kee,** and **William Vass,** "Time-Series of Annual Earnings Data: The State of the Art." *Quarterly Review of Economics and Business,* vol. 21, no. 1 (Spring 1981), pp. 98–99.

[31] **R. Ball** and **R. Watts,** "Some Time-Series Properties of Accounting Income," *Journal of Finance,* vol. 27 (June 1972), p. 665.

A martingale process requires the following:

1. $\rho[(e_{t+1} - e_t), (e_t - e_{t-1})] = 0$

That is, the first-order (and even higher-order) serial correlation must be equal to zero or, equivalently, the data must be independently distributed (i.e., behave as a series of random numbers).

2. The mean of the first difference ($\overline{\Delta e_t} = e_t - e_{t-1}$) is equal to zero; that is, deviations of earnings from the mean value of the process cancel out.

The submartingale and the supermartingale require that

a. $\rho[(e_{t+1} - e_t), (e_t - e_{t-1})] = 0$
b. $\overline{\Delta e_t} \neq 0$

These processes are martingales with a drift (some direction) in the data.

Mean Reverting Processes. Earnings generated by mean reverting processes tend to fluctuate around the mean (normal) earnings.

$$E(e_{t+1}/e_0, \ldots, e_t) = \mu$$

where μ = mean (normal) earnings.

$$e_t = \mu + \epsilon_t$$

where $E(\epsilon_t) = 0$
$\sigma^2(\epsilon_t) = \sigma^2$

These processes have the following characteristics:

$$\rho[(e_{t+1} - e_t), (e_t - e_{t-1})] < 0 \tag{a}$$

that is, earnings changes are dependent and serially correlated.

$$\overline{\Delta e_t} = e_t - e_{t-1} = 0 \quad \text{if no trend is present} \tag{b}$$
$$\overline{\Delta e_t} = e_t - e_{t-1} \neq 0 \quad \text{if trend is present}$$

Moving Average Processes. A moving average process incorporates all (over a limited time horizon) past unexpected earnings. The data are not independently distributed. A general moving average model looks like the following:

$$e_t = \epsilon_t - \phi_1\epsilon_{t-1} - \phi_2\epsilon_{t-2} - \cdots - \phi_k\epsilon_{t-k}$$

where ϵ = error term
ϕ_k = weight of the kth component of past unexpected earnings.

With this brief introduction to earnings-generating processes, we proceed to look at the evidence.

Evidence. The evidence in support of various types of earnings-generating processes is considerable and in many cases not very conclusive.

The earliest evidence came from I. M. D. Little,[32] followed by Little and Rayner.[33] Both studies, using U.K. firms, showed that the earnings-generating process is essentially random. Lintner and Glauber,[34] using data on 323 U.S. companies, found low and insignificant serial correlations among growth rates but were unwilling to draw general conclusions about the randomness of the earning-generating process. The exceptions to the results were sufficient reasons for the caution. The results and the caution of Lintner and Glauber were essentially similar to those of Little and Rayner. Additional evidence on randomness was provided by Brealey[35] and by the often quoted and extensive study of Ball and Watts.[36] Leroy D. Brooks and D. Buckmaster[37] produced mixed results depending on the model used. Their results could be consistent with a submartingale model if a single exponential smoothing model (see below) were used for all the firms in the sample. Additional strong support for the randomness hypothesis came from Watts and Leftwich,[38] who concluded that little confidence could be placed in the earlier studies showing departure from randomness.

Brealey,[39] in the same study cited above, found that the most successful and the least successful firms in the sample he studied had earnings patterns that deviate systematically from randomness. Beaver found, using rate of return (EPS/net worth per share) instead of earnings, that "much of the behavior of accounting rates of return is consistent with these measurements coming from a moving average model."[40] Beaver's findings were generally supported by L. Lookabill.[41] Further evidence on nonrandomness was provided by G. Foster. Using a sample of 69 NYSE firms, Foster found that the time series behavior of *quarterly* earnings is not adequately described by a random walk model; in fact, quarterly earnings had "(1) an adjacent quarter to quarter component and (2) a seasonal component."[42] Foster's results were confirmed independently by P. Griffin.[43]

[32] **I. M. D. Little,** "Higgledy Piggledy Growth." *Bulletin of the Oxford Institute of Economics and Statistics,* November 1962, pp. 389–412.

[33] **I. M. D. Little** and **A. C. Rayner,** *Higgledy Piggledy Growth Again.* A. M. Kelley, Publishers, New York, 1966.

[34] **John Lintner** and **Robert Glauber,** "Higgledy Piggledy Growth in America," in James Lorie and Richard Brealey, eds., *Modern Developments in Investment Management.* Praeger, New York, 1972, pp. 645–662.

[35] **Brealey,** pp. 94–95.

[36] **Ray Ball** and **Ross L. Watts,** "Some Time Series Properties of Accounting Income." *Journal of Finance,* vol. 27 (June 1972), pp. 663–81.

[37] **Leroy Brooks** and **Dale Buckmaster,** "Further Evidence of the Time Series Properties of Accounting Income." *Journal of Finance,* vol. 31 (December 1976), pp. 1359–1373.

[38] **Ross Watts** and **Richard Leftwich,** "The Time Series of Annual Accounting Earnings." *Journal of Accounting Research,* vol. 15 (Autumn 1977), pp. 253–271.

[39] **Brealey,** pp. 98–100.

[40] **William H. Beaver,** "The Time Series Behavior of Earnings," in *Empirical Research in Accounting: Selected Studies. Journal of Accounting Research,* Autumn 1970, suppl., p. 86.

[41] **Larry L. Lookabill,** "Some Additional Evidence on the Time Series Properties of Accounting Earnings." *Accounting Review,* vol. 51, no. 4 (October 1976).

[42] **G. Foster,** "Quarterly Accounting Data: Time Series Properties and Predictive Ability Results." *Accounting Review,* January 1977, pp. 1–2.

[43] **P. A. Griffin,** "The Time Series Behavior of Quarterly Earnings: Preliminary Evidence." *Journal of Accounting Research,* Spring 1977, pp. 71–83.

It can be said, therefore, that in attempting to determine the appropriate forecasting technique for sales, earnings, or any other variable of the firm, the first step must deal with the randomness issue. Plotting the data points is ordinarily sufficient in identifying whether or not there is a trend in the data. The blind application of forecasting techniques that presume a trend in the data must be avoided, although experience shows that students naturally tend to adopt such methods.

Selection of Forecasting Technique

A multitude of techniques are used to forecast earnings, whether over the short term (less than one year), the intermediate term (one to five years), or the long term (more than five years). Ordinarily, the longer the time horizon, the less accurate a given technique will be; and the higher the level of desired accuracy, the more expensive forecasting gets (taking into consideration some initial economies of scale). The adequacy of any technique depends on the nature of the data, the quality of the data, and the costs/benefits of various levels of accuracy.

Forecasting techniques can be divided into three categories:[44]

Qualitative techniques (like the Delphi technique)
Time series
Causal models

The Delphi Technique. The Delphi technique is best explained by an example. Assume you want to forecast the earnings of IBM. You ask "experts" in the computer industry to make a forecast of IBM earnings. Their forecasts are informal, subjective estimates based on experience and/or historical data. Once all the forecasts are in, they are summarized and the summary is sent out to all the participants in the initial forecast. On the basis of the summary, some forecasters may revise their original estimates. The process may be repeated several times until a clear consensus of opinion emerges.

Time-Series Analysis. Time-series analysis "focuses entirely on patterns and pattern changes, and thus relies entirely on historical data. . . ."[45]

Time-series analysis is too complex a subject to be treated in one chapter or even in a book. There is a wealth of information on the various techniques and the reader is urged to consult them.[46] We shall satisfy ourselves here with a skeletal outline of the analysis.

A time-series model assumes that the future is like the past; it typically contains an average value, a trend, cyclical factor(s), and an error term. Two often used techniques (members of the smoothing methods family) are the single (double) moving averages and exponential smoothing.

Moving averages. Suppose one wanted to forecast 1983 earnings of the ABC Corpora-

---

[44] The reader is strongly advised to read **John C. Chambers, Satinder K. Mullick,** and **Donald Smith,** "How to Choose the Right Forecasting Techniques." *Harvard Business Review,* July–August 1971.

[45] Ibid., p. 49.

[46] One of my favorite texts is **Spyros Makridakis** and **Steven Wheelwright,** *Forecasting Methods and Applications.* Wiley, New York, 1978.

tion. The objective is merely to arrive at an earnings figure for 1983 without any regard to the factors (causes) that bring them about. The assertion of a time series model is:

$$e_{1983} = f(\underbrace{e_{1982}, e_{1981}, e_{1980}, \ldots,}_{\text{pattern}} \underbrace{\epsilon_t)}_{\text{error term}}$$

A single moving average uses a changing subset (with a fixed number of components) from a data set with a fixed number of observations. As we move from one period to another, the subset changes by dropping the earliest observation and adding a new one.

Assume that the earnings of the ABC Corporation are as shown in Table 8.7.

TABLE 8.7
Earnings of the ABC Corporation

Year	t	SMA	DMA
1976	$2.00		
1977	$2.10		
1978	$2.15		
1979	$2.10	2.08	
1980	$2.20	2.11	
1981	$2.25	2.15	
1982	$2.30	2.18	2.11
1983		2.25	2.15

The moving average is calculated using the following equation:

$$\text{SMA} = 1/N \sum_{i=t-N+1}^{t} e_i \tag{8.10}$$

where e_i = earnings at time i
       N = length of the subperiod

Assuming $N = 3$, the forecasts using a single moving average are shown the column headed SMA (Table 8.7). The earnings forecast for 1983 is $2.25. Different values of N could have been used to produce different forecasts.

Despite its ease and low cost of application (or maybe because of them), SMA has a poor record of accuracy, can only be applied to stationary data (no trend), ignores observations preceding $t - N + 1$ and assigns equal weight to all the components of the subset, and never predicts a turning point.

As the reader may have observed, the earnings data contained in Table 8.7 show a trend. Thus, to improve on the SMA, a double (linear) moving average is calculated (DMA) using the same value for N. It is simply the moving average of a moving average. Using DMA, the forecasted earnings for 1982 are $2.15.

Exponential smoothing. Exponential smoothing recognizes the fact that not all past information is of equal importance in making a forecast and requires only two data points to forecast.

$$e_{1983} = \alpha e_{1982} + (1 - \alpha)(\text{previous E.S. forecast})$$
$$= \alpha e_{1982} + \alpha(1 - \alpha)e_{1981} + \alpha(1 - \alpha)^2 e_{1980} +$$
$$\alpha(1 - \alpha)^3 e_{1979} + \cdots + \alpha(1 - \alpha)^n e_n \tag{8.11}$$

The reader will observe that the weights applied to historic data decrease exponentially; hence the name of this forecasting technique.

The value of α in Equation 8.11 is arrived at by simulation. The chosen α is that which minimizes the size of the error resulting from the difference between actual and forecasted values.

Double (linear) exponential and other techniques based on exponential smoothing are also used for various types of data and various levels of accuracy. These techniques include Brown's one-parameter linear exponential smoothing, Winter's linear and seasonal exponential smoothing, the Box-Jenkin's model, and others. The ambitious reader should explore the details of these worthwhile models.

Causal Models. Causal models also rely on past information and seek to isolate those variables with significant impact on the dependent variable (earnings in our case) and to determine the degree of that impact.

The regression models discussed earlier with regard to stock prices (F. Black, M. J. Gordon, B. G. Malkiel) are examples of causal models.

One method for forecasting earnings and cash flows that is very popular with accountants involves the following steps:

1. Forecast sales using time-series analysis or regression analysis.
2. Develop proforma income statements and balance sheet using the percent-of-sales method and historically determined relationships within the balance sheet and the income statement and across them. New information about any balance sheet or income statement items is adjusted for.
3. From step 2, develop a proforma cash flow statement which yields an estimate of cash flows.

The process is repeated for several years, and the resulting cash flows are discounted at the appropriate discount rate to arrive at the value of the firm. This value is then divided by the number of shares outstanding to arrive at the market price of the stock.[47]

The forecast of sales using regression analysis begins with the selection of those variables that have been known to influence sales or that could have a logical (theoretical) influence on sales and on which reliable data over a sufficient number of periods are available. For example, the sales of a firm can be hypothesized to be a function of the following variables:

$$\text{Sales} = f\left(\text{GNP, } P_F, P_C, \frac{\text{Adv}_F}{\text{Adv}_I}, S_{t-1}\right) \tag{8.12}$$

where P_F = firm's price structure

P_C = competitor's price structure

---

[47] An example of the process is illustrated in **Sarkis J. Khoury,** *Transnational Mergers and Acquisitions in the United States.* Heath, Boston, 1980, chap. 5.

$\dfrac{\text{Adv}_F}{\text{Adv}_I}$ = advertising expenditures by firm relative to industry

S_{t-1} = sales of preceding period

Equation 8.12 can be rewritten assuming a linear relationship among the variables:

$$S = a + b_1 X_1 + b_2 X_2 + b_3 X_3 + b_4 X_4 + b_5 X_5 + \epsilon \qquad (8.13)$$

where the X's represent, respectively, each of the variables shown in parenthesis in Equation 8.12.

Before regression analysis is applied, the forecaster should be able to justify a priori the signs of the regression coefficients (b's)—that is, whether b is positive or negative.

Regression analysis is then used to estimate the value of a and of the b's. The relationship indicated in Equation 8.13 is vindicated if and only if all the b's are significant (their t-values exceed 1.96), the R^2 of the equation exceeds 80 percent (generally accepted), and there is no evidence of autocorrelation and multicollinearity.[48]

Having estimated a and the b's and armed with values for each of the independent variables (forecasted or expected values), the analyst proceeds with the calculation of S. This is the forecasted level of sales for the coming period.

Using the percent-of-sales method with percentages derived from historical data such as those shown in Table 8.8, a balance sheet and an income statement are developed. Very special care must be taken, however. A blind application of the percent-of-sales method can literally lead to ridiculous results: outrageous debt/equity ratios, assets $\neq$ liabilities plus stockholder's equity, very low or excessively high liquidity ratios, and so on.

From the proforma (estimated) balance sheet and income statement, a cash flow statement is developed using standard accounting techniques.

The sequence of cash flows using the above sequence repeatedly is then discounted at the cost of equity generated from the security market line. The sum of the discounted cash flows is the value of the firm:

$$V = \sum_{t=1}^{n} \dfrac{CF_t}{(1 + K_e)^t} \qquad (8.14)$$

where V = value of the firm

CF_t = cash flows at time t

Several leading banks and investment banking firms have developed their own models for estimating the market price of a stock. Some are extremely complex, others are simple, and a few are simplistic. These models have varying track records, and no one model has emerged as the clear leader (if it did and if its contents were public information, then a new model would be needed to beat a market in which all the participants were using the "leading" model).

_____

[48] The reader is urged to consult a basic book on multiple regression analysis, such as **Damodor Gujarati,** *Basic Econometrics,* McGraw-Hill, New York, 1978.

TABLE 8.8
Historical Data of a Hypothetical Firm

1. Purchases = (.23) (sales)
2. Ending inventory$_t$ = (.22) (sales$_t$)
3. Labor + burden costs$_t$ = (.24) (sales$_t$) (with special adjustments if necessary)
4. Depreciation$_t$ = (.125) (fixed assets$_t$)
5. Energy-related costs$_t$= (.03) (sales$_t$) (with special adjustments if necessary)
6. Selling + administrative costs$_t$ = (.21) (sales$_t$)
7. Royalties$_t$ = \$500,000 (assumed constant over time)
8. Interest expense$_t$ $\approx$ (.12) (borrowing)
9. Other expenses$_t$ = (.12) (sales$_t$)
10. Fixed assets$_t$ = (.175) (sales$_t$)
11. Cash$_t$ = (.03) (sales$_t$)
12. Receivables$_t$ = (.21) (sales$_t$)
13. Allowance for doubtful accounts$_t$ = (.016) (receivables$_t$)
14. Accounts payable$_t$ = (.28) (purchases$_t$)
15. Current liabilities
    Notes payable to banks$_t$ = (.06) (total assets$_t$)
    Current maturities of long-term debt$_t$ = (.01) (total assets$_t$)
    Accrued liabilities$_t$ = (.13) (total assets$_t$)
    Income taxes payable$_t$ = (.04) (total assets$_t$)

In the next section we present one of the more successful models developed and used by the Wells Fargo Bank.

Wells Fargo Model

The Wells Fargo model is one that combines the discounted cash flow technique with modern portfolio theory.

Wells Fargo analysts are required to forecast:

1. Dividends and earnings for the next five years.
2. Expected earnings per share, growth rate, and dividend payout ratio for the fifth year.
3. The length of period between the fifth year and the moment when "normal" earnings growth rate begins. *Normal* is used to mean long-run (permanent, steady-state) growth rate, a rate consistent with an economy in midcycle (between bust and boom) and/or an industry/firm midway through its life cycle.
4. The expected growth rate and payout ratio for the steady-state period and for the intervening period (after five years and before the steady-state period begins).

Armed with these values (which yield dividend flows over an infinite time horizon) and with the current market price of the stock, the analyst calculates that value of K_e which equates the present value of the dividend flows to the market price of the stock. This is done for every stock Wells Fargo follows.

In order to develop a security market line (SML), an estimate of beta is needed. This is done using historical data and whatever pertinent information the analyst possesses about current and future operations of the firm. The resulting beta values are expected and not actual values.

Stocks are then divided into risk classes in accordance with certain beta (expected) ranges. For each beta range an *expected* SML is estimated by fitting a straight line through the data points (K_{e_i}, β_i). This line suggests the average rate of return the market expects for that level of risk.

The recommendation of the analyst is then based on where a given stock plots in relation to the expected SML. A stock plotting above the SML would be considered underpriced and one below the SML overpriced.

This method of evaluating securities has proven useful and profitable, although not universally so.

We now look at the effect of a specific economic variable, inflation, on stock prices.

8.8 SECURITY PRICES AND INFLATION

The effect of inflation on debt securities was eloquently discussed by the legendary I. Fisher.[49] The nominal rate of interest consists, Fisher argues, of the real rate of interest and an inflation factor. Recent studies, however, show that the rate of inflation affects not only the nominal rate of interest but the real rate as well. These and other issues related to debt securities are discussed in Chapter 9.

Common stocks have traditionally been considered an excellent hedge against inflation. Figure 8.7 illustrates the relationship between inflation measured by the Consumer Price Index (CPI) and earnings yield (earnings/price). Rising inflation appears to have had a negative effect on earnings yield. Salomon Brothers reports that the average annual growth rate on investments between 1968 and 1978 was 2.8 percent. The average rate of inflation during the same period was 9.8 percent. This explains the rising skepticism about the merits in investing in common stock during inflationary periods.

The impact of inflation on stock prices has been analyzed under two states of the world: (1) the inflation rate is fully anticipated and (2) the inflation rate is not correctly anticipated. Correctly anticipated inflation has been shown to have an adverse effect on the nominal rate of return on common stock.[50] Uncertain or unanticipated inflation has been shown also to have a negative effect on stock yields. Nelson,[51] Bodie,[52] Jaffe and Mandelker,[53] and Fama and Schwert[54] have all shown that nominal yields on NYSE-listed stocks are negatively related to both anticipated and unanticipated inflation. A recent study by G. W. Schwert[55] examined the effects of CPI announcements on the

---

[49] **Irving Fisher,** *The Theory of Interest.* Macmillan, New York, 1930.

[50] See **Thomas J. Sargent,** *Some New Evidence on Anticipated Inflation and Asset Yields.* National Bureau of Economic Research, New York, 1970.

[51] **Charles R. Nelson,** "Inflation and Rates of Return on Common Stock." *Journal of Finance,* vol. 31 (May 1976), pp. 471–483.

[52] **Zvi Bodie,** "Common Stocks as a Hedge Against Inflation." *Journal of Finance,* vol. 31 (May 1976), pp. 459–470.

[53] **Jeffrey Jaffe and Gershon Mandelker,** "The 'Fisher' Effect of Risky Assets: An Empirical Investigation." *Journal of Finance,* vol. 31 (May 1976), pp. 447–458.

[54] **Eugene F. Fama** and **G. William Schwert,** "Asset Returns and Inflation." *Journal of Financial Economics,* vol. 5 (November 1977), pp. 115–146.

[55] **G. William Schwert,** "The Adjustment of Stock Prices to Information about Inflation." *Journal of Finance,* vol. 36, no. 1 (March 1981), pp. 15–29.

FIGURE 8.7 **Comparison of earnings, yields, long-term bond rates and inflation, 1957–1981.**

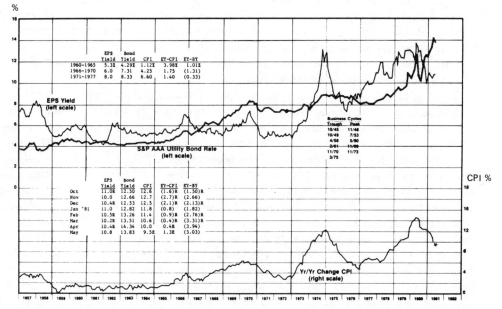

General Comment: The earnings yield of the stock market (earnings divided by price) and long-term bond rates move generally together, although the earnings yield is more subject to change with the economic environment. That is, it rises in recessionary times (e.g. 1957–1968, 1966–1967, 1970, and 1973–1974) and falls during economic recoveries. Otherwise, the earnings yield and the bond rate move very much with the inflation rate — earnings yield being relatively more negatively affected by rising inflation. In addition, the relationship between the earnings yield of the market and the long-term bond yield measures the relative willingness of investors to reinvest the cash flow from their investments versus having the companies reinvest it through retained earnings at the company's return on equity rate. Finally, the earnings yield and bond yield should provide a real rate of return to investors or the yields should be higher than the inflation rate.

From *Investment Strategy Highlight Update,* Goldman Sachs, June 1981.

daily returns on the S&P Composite Index and found no overwhelming evidence "that the stock market reacts strongly to unexpected inflation."[56] The data period covered 1953–1978. The adverse effects of inflation are not uniform across all common stocks, however, as Reilly and associates[57] have shown. Another recent study by R. Olsen using a modified version of the capital asset pricing model concludes:

> *On balance it would appear that inflation has an unfavorable effect on common stock investments. If inflationary expectations are held with certainty, real and nominal yields decline. If inflationary expectations are uncertain, real and nominal yields rise. However, this rise appears to reflect the greater risk*

---

[56] Ibid., pp. 27–28.

[57] **Frank K. Reilly** *et al.,* "A Correction and Update Regarding Individual Common Stocks as Inflation Hedges." *Journal of Financial and Quantitative Analysis,* December 1975, pp. 871–880.

being assumed by investors because common stock is an inferior hedge against unanticipated inflation.[58]

The adverse effects of inflation on stock prices is not confined to the U.S. market. Using data covering the decade of the 1970s for Canada, France, Germany, Japan, Netherlands, and the United Kingdom, Cohn and Lessard[59] found that stock prices in these countries did not keep up with the general price level. Cohn and Lessard noted that "the results do serve to challenge the traditional view that equities are real instruments whose values are unaffected by inflation."[60]

The effect of inflation on stock prices is seen through its effects on the balance sheets and the income statements of the firms.[61] Inflation distorts the "true" earnings of the firm when earnings are calculated in accordance with generally accepted accounting principles. Reported profits are based on historical data. Thus, in an inflationary period depreciation expenses are understated (and profits overstated) because the underlying assets are valued at cost and not at replacement value; interest costs are overstated because the inflation component (a dominant one) of nominal interest rates "should be viewed as a repayment of real principal rather than interest";[62] wages and salaries, to the extent that they are not indexed to inflation through explicit contracts or implicitly, are likely to be understated (and profits are overstated); and inventories recorded at historic costs and sold at inflated prices produce inventory profits, thus overstating overall profits. On the revenue side, long-term contracts not indexed to inflation preclude upward price adjustments and thus reduce total revenue. Indexed contracts, on the other hand, allow for the necessary price adjustments and produce, therefore, a nominal increase in revenue. On balance, it can be said that profits in an inflationary period are overstated, thus more corporate taxes must be paid. Net after-tax cash flows would increase, however. The additional cash flows available for investment *could,* however, prove inadequate for the expensive new investment projects intended not only to preserve the current level of vitality in the firm but also to add to its growth potential.

---

[58] **Robert A. Olsen,** "An Empirical Investigation of the Association Between Common Stock Returns and Uncertain Inflation." *Review of Business and Economic Research,* vol. 16, no. 2 (Winter 1980–81), p. 65.

[59] **Richard A. Cohn** and **Donald R. Lessard,** "Are Markets Efficient?" Tests of Alternative Hypotheses. The Effect of Inflation on Stock Prices: International Evidence." *Journal of Finance,* vol. 36, no. 2 (May 1981), pp. 277–289.

[60] Ibid., p. 287.

[61] The reader should consult the following sources:
   Eric Noreen and **James Sepe,** "Market Reactions to Accounting Policy Deliberations: The Inflation Accounting Case." *Accounting Review,* vol. 56, no. 2 (April 1981), pp. 253–269.
   H. J. Aaron, *Inflation and the Income Tax.* Brookings Institution, Washington, D.C., 1976.
   R. W. Kopcke, "Current Accounting Practices and Proposals for Reform." *New England Economic Review,* September–October 1976.
   R. W. Kopcke, "The Decline in Corporate Profitability." *New England Economic Review,* May–June 1978.
   Surendra P. Agrawal, "Accounting for the Impact of Inflation on a Business Enterprise." *Accounting Review,* vol. 52, no. 4 (October 1977), pp. 789–809.
   Arie Baran, Josef Lakonishok, and **Aharon Ofer,** "The Information Content of General Price Level Adjusted Earnings: Some Empirical Evidence." *Accounting Review,* vol. 55, no. 1 (January 1980), pp. 22–35.

[62] **Cohn** and **Lessard,** p. 281. Also see **F. Modigliani** and **R. Cohn,** "Inflation, Rational Valuation and the Market." *Financial Analyst's Journal,* vol. 35, no. 2, (March–April 1979), pp. 24–44.

FIGURE 8.8 Comparison of real profits and the S&P 400, 1969–1981.

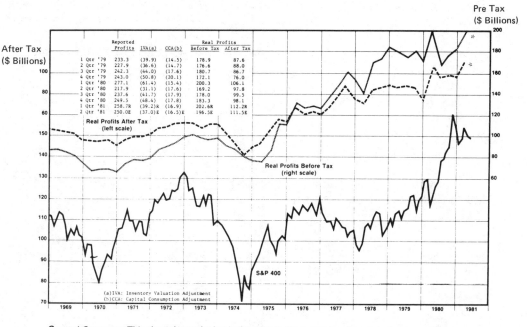

General Comment This chart shows the level of profits in the economy after excluding inventory profits and adjusting for the underdepreciation of assets. These real profits are more indicative of the corporate sector's ability to finance growth and pay dividends. After the 1974 acceleration in inflation, investors began to focus more attention on real profits — while reported earnings increased in 1974, real profits and the S&P 400 declined.

From *Investment Strategy Highlight Update,* Goldman Sachs, June 1981.

The concern with inflated profits has led many investors to focus on real instead of nominal earnings. The relationship between real earnings and the S&P 400 Industrial Price Index is shown in Figure 8.8.

The discussion thus far included only corporate taxes. When personal taxes are accounted for, inflation translates into lower value for securities. The reason is simple. Inflation is a *tax* which is collected by government in the form of real goods and services against the issuance of paper currency. Since it is a tax, the higher inflation is, the lower the real rate of return on investment. This is so for two reasons:

1. Because of "bracket creep," which means that as investors earn more (in nominal terms) they move into higher tax brackets and their effective tax rate rises (the 1981 Economic Recovery Tax Act eliminates this problem by 1985).
2. As inflation rises, the real return on securities falls when the additional income from securities in the form of capital gains are subject to taxation, even if the capital gains tax rate is constant. An investment yielding a 3 percent real rate of return has an after-tax real rate of 2.4 percent [3(1 − 0.20)] at today's 20 percent maximum capital gain rate. This same investment will yield a lower real rate if inflation is 5 percent:

Real after-tax rate $= 8\%(1 - 0.20) - 5\% = 1.4\%$

Falling real rates would require lower securities prices if investors expected wealth to remain constant. That is, the nominal rate of return must increase to account not only for the higher rate of inflation but to compensate for the increase in the other tax (personal income tax).

From a CAPM perspective, the adjustment to inflation would require the development of an SML based on a real rate of return and a real β:[63]

$$E(R_i^r) = E(r_Z) + \beta_i^r[E(R_M^r) - E(r_Z)] \tag{8.15}$$

where superscript r = real

$E(r_Z)$ = Expected real return on a zero real β portfolio

From Equation 8.15, and assuming that α = purchasing power factor with $\alpha < 1$ indicating inflation and $\alpha > 1$ deflation, Olsen arrived at a new formulation for the CAPM.

$$E(r_i) = E(R_Z) + \frac{\text{cov}(\alpha, R_Z - R_i)}{E(\alpha)} + b_i\left[E(R_M) - E(R_Z) - \frac{\text{cov}(\alpha, R_Z - R_M)}{E(\alpha)}\right] \tag{8.16}$$

where

$$b_i = \frac{E(\alpha^2)\,\text{cov}\,(R_i, R_M) + E\,(\alpha^2 R_i R_M) + E(\alpha^2)\,E\,(R_i)\,E\,(R_M)}{\text{var}\,(R_M)[\text{var}\,\alpha\,(l + \rho^2)]} \tag{8.17}$$
$$+[E(R_M)^2\,\text{var}\,\alpha + E(\alpha^2)\,\text{var}\,(R_M) + 2E(R_M)E(\alpha)\,\text{cov}\,(\alpha, R_M)]$$

and R_i, R_Z, R_M = nominal rates.

Differentiating Equation 8.16 with respect to $E(\alpha)$ and σ_α, we get

$$\frac{\partial E(R_i)}{\partial E(\alpha)} = -\left[\frac{\text{cov}(\alpha, R_i - R_Z)}{[E(\alpha)]^2}(1 - b_i)\right] \tag{8.18}$$

$$\frac{\partial E(R_i)}{\partial \sigma_\alpha} = \left[\frac{(\sigma_{z-i})(\rho_{\alpha, z-i})}{E(\alpha)}(1 - b_i)\right] \tag{8.19}$$

where $E(\alpha)$ = expected (certain) inflation

σ_α = uncertain inflation

σ_{z-i} = standard deviation of $R_Z - R_i$

$\rho_{\alpha, z-i}$ = correlation coefficient between α and $(R_Z - R_i)$

From Equations 8.18 and 8.19 we can see that if

$$b_i > 1,\ \text{cov}\,(\alpha, R_i - R_Z) < 0 \rightarrow \frac{\partial E(R_i)}{\partial E(\alpha)} < 0$$

---

[63] See **Olsen**, p. 57.

That is, the expected return on security i varies inversely with the expected rate of inflation.

$$b_i > 1, \text{ then } \frac{\partial E(R_i)}{\partial \sigma_\alpha} > \text{ or } < 0$$

depending on the sign of $\rho_{\alpha,z-i}$.[64]

Adjusting β may not be the complete answer to the impact of inflation. Other methods have been used to acquire a greater insight into the effects of inflation.

Another Measure

A measure of the differential impact of inflation on firms in different industries has been developed by Goldman Sachs Research. The measure gauges the ability of the firm (industry) to index its earnings to inflation. Goldman Sachs refers to the measure as the inflation passthrough index (IPI).

An IPI of 0.30 means that for every one percentage point increase in the underlying inflation rate, the earnings growth will only be 0.3 percent. The IPIs for some industries appear in Table 8.9.

TABLE 8.9
IPIs for Various Industries

Industry	1968–1973	1973–1979
Airlines	1.61	1.22
Cosmetics/Soaps	1.71	0.95
Brewers	0.92	(0.91)
Drugs	1.27	1.15
Office equipment	1.95	1.55
Retail/department stores	1.05	0.70
Soft drinks	2.02	1.30
Tire and rubber	0.25	(1.42)
Tobacco	1.54	1.13
S&P 500	0.15	1.02

Source: Portfolio Strategy. Goldman Sachs, New York, February 1982.

The IPI is arrived at by log regressions of respective industry earnings on the index of secular inflation. Industry earnings are arrived at using a five-year moving average with unequal weights. The earnings are adjusted to exclude inventory profits and underdepreciation from carrying fixed assets at historical costs.

Goldman Sachs argues that there are two major benefits from IPI. One is that IPI "can be helpful in assessing the long-term earnings prospects of industries and companies—a critical ingredient in most security valuation techniques," [65] and another is that it is useful as a measure of investment risk. The use of IPI as a measure of investment

---

[64] See **Olsen,** p. 58.

[65] *Portfolio Strategy.* **Goldman Sachs,** New York, July 21, 1980.

risk is suggested as an alternative or at least as a complement to beta. To make the IPI comparable with other risk measures, Goldman Sachs transforms the IPI values to arrive at an inflation risk index (IRI) using the following equation:

$$\mathrm{IRI} = 1 - \left[\frac{(X_i - \overline{X})}{S_i} \cdot S_b \right]$$

where X_i = industry IPI

$\overline{X}_i$ = mean value for X_i

S_i = standard deviation of X_i

S_b = standard deviation of the beta distribution

The IPI and the IRI do represent a step in the right direction in terms of improving financial analysis and in particular the quantification of risk.

It can be said, in conclusion, that inflation generally increases the riskiness of securities and, consequently, the need for better information and for professional portfolio management. The issue of whether professional managers have been able to provide a refuge for confused or busy investors is the subject of the next section.

8.9 THE RECORD OF FORECASTERS

Two stock price forecasts deserve analysis: those made by analysts and those made by the corporation itself. In an efficient labor market, analysts must be able to outperform forecasts using time-series models or they could not justify their salary. Investors could rely, alternatively, on the forecasts made by the firm or on their own forecasts, for no one really has the necessary insight that commands a positive market value.

The evidence provided by Cragg and Malkiel[66] and by Elton and Gruber[67] argues that analysts have a zero marginal product. Their models and resulting forecasts are not particularly helpful to investors.

Lawrence Brown and Michael Rozeff[68] note that the conclusions above are inconsistent with "basic economic theory" and set out to prove that analysts deserve to hold jobs. Using data on 50 firms selected from *Moody's Handbook of Common Stocks* and sophisticated statistical techniques, they were able to show that:

> B. J. (Box Jenkins) models consistently produce significantly better earnings forecasts than martingale and submartingale models; (2) Value Line Investment Survey consistently makes significantly better earnings forecasts than the BJ and naive time series models. The findings are in accord with rationality in the market for forecasts and the long-run equilibrium employment of analysts.[69]

[66] **J. G. Cragg** and **B. G. Malkiel,** "The Consensus and Accuracy of Some Predictions of the Growth of Corporate Earnings." *Journal of Finance,* March 1968, pp. 67–84.

[67] **E. J. Elton** and **M. J. Gruber,** "Earnings Estimates and the Accuracy of Expectational Data." *Management Science,* April 1972, pp. 409–424.

[68] **Lawrence D. Brown** and **Michael Rozeff,** "The Superiority of Analyst Forecasts as Measures of Expectations: Evidence from Earnings." *Journal of Finance,* vol. 33 (March 1978), pp. 1, 16.

[69] Ibid., p. 13.

While Lawrence and Brown were unequivocal about their conclusions, W. Ruland[70] arrived at results that gave qualified support for analysts. Ruland compared the forecasts made by analysts and those made by the management of a firm to those arrived at by way of an extrapolative model. His conclusions:

> *while the management forecasts appeared to be more accurate than either group of analyst forecasts, differences were not confirmed at statistically significant levels. The comparison also showed that analyst forecasts announced prior to management forecasts are less accurate relative to management forecasts than those announced afterwards.*[71]

The contradictory evidence we have just cited must be tempered by reality. If analysts are useless, then the market is systematically and flagrantly being fooled; if not, then analysts must possess special qualities. The fact that thousands of analysts have held permanent jobs for a considerable period of time is one form of proof that cannot be ignored.

CONCLUSIONS

The evaluation of equity securities is a complex task under the most ideal circumstances. No forecaster is ever consistently accurate, hard as he or she may try. The tools offered in this chapter are but a few of many used by financial analysts as they strive to justify their substantial wages. The various considerations in financial analysis on the economy, industry, or firm level presented in this chapter should only encourage the reader to study further.

QUESTIONS

1. How effective and revealing is ratio analysis if used to study the financial reports of a young company given that it is the only company in an industry?

2. Discuss the weaknesses of ratio analysis in determining the status (actual or expected) of a business entity. Are these weaknesses sufficiently strong to warrant the discarding of ratio analysis for stock valuation?

3. Several analysts employ certain ratios, profitability ratios in particular, to measure the quality of management. Do these ratios represent an accurate gauge of management quality? Explain. Think in terms of ratios over a short period of time versus ratios calculated over a much longer period. Can the quality of management ever be completely and accurately measured solely on the basis of numbers from financial statements.

4. Financial analysts must be as much concerned with events outside the corporation as with those within. How might the "drug culture," for example, be of concern to a financial analyst?

---

[70] **William Ruland,** "The Accuracy of Forecasts by Management and by Financial Analysts." *Accounting Review,* vol. 53, no. 2, April 1978, pp. 439–447.

[71] Ibid., p. 446.

5. What ratios would you emphasize if you held debt securities issued by a corporate entity? Why?

6. "Equity holders are only concerned with profitability ratios and with how profits are distributed." Comment.

7. What factors determine the growth patterns of business entities?

8. Discuss a measure of risk you could use in addition to beta, or as a substitute for it.

9. Discuss the methods used by financial analysts to determine a firm's industry group for ratio comparison. Why is it imperative that a firm be accurately matched to its industry group?

10. If you reviewed data indicating that, over the past few months, housing starts and new orders for consumer goods and materials had increased, industrial production and manufacturing trade sales had remained steady, and the prime rate had increased slightly after recent rapid increases, what would be your forecast for economic activity? Why are such economic forecasts so important to fundamental analysts?

11. Why is it important for fundamental analysts to determine whether betas calculated on the basis of historic cost accounting data or constant-dollar accounting data are superior to betas calculated from market data?

12. What is the impact of the disclosure of replacement-cost-based income on stock prices? What does this signify about market efficiency?

13. Describe three of the earnings-generating processes presented in this chapter and their implications for stock valuation.

14. Why does inflation have such a significant impact on common stock investments?

15. Discuss the importance of inflation passthrough indexes.

16. If financial analysts are unable to better predict earnings per share, what implications does this have for the efficiency of the labor market and the stock market?

17. How can ratio analysis be used to predict stock prices?

18. Discuss and compare the methods for integrating ratios.

PROBLEMS

1. Given company XYZ's financial statements (which appear at the end of the problems), calculate:

   a. return on equity   f. inventory turnover
   b. return on fixed assets   g. average collection period
   c. return on total assets   h. current ratio
   d. gross profit margin   i. acid-test ratio
   e. return on sales   j. interest expense coverage

2. Calculate the Z score using Altman's equation for the XYZ Company (financial statements follow) if the firm has 39,000 shares of stock outstanding, currently selling at $15 per share. What are the implications of this Z score?

3. The earnings for the DDS Corporation are as follows:

Year	1974	1975	1976	1977	1978	1979	1980	1981
$EPS	3.10	3.20	3.20	3.15	3.25	3.30	3.25	3.25

a. Calculate a three-year single moving average for EPS.
b. Calculate a three-year double moving average for EPS.
c. How do you use these averages in forecasting?

XYZ Company
Balance Sheet

Assets

Cash	$ 77,000
Accounts receivable	98,300
Inventory	78,950
Supplies	7,200
Total current assets	261,450
Land	130,000
Building	198,000
less: accumulated depreciation	(97,000)
Equipment	85,000
less: accumulated depreciation	(61,000)
Total assets	**516,450**

Liabilities & Equity

Current liabilities	128,725
Long-term liabilities	42,590
Total liabilities	171,315
Common stock	195,000
Paid-in surplus	105,000
Retained earnings	45,135
Total stockholder's equity	245,135
Total liabilities & equity	**516,450**

XYZ Company
Income Statement

Net sales	753,000
Cost of goods sold	449,000
Gross profit	304,000
Operating expenses	178,450
Earnings before interest, taxes	125,550
Interest expense	3,870
Earnings before taxes	121,680
Taxes	48,672
Net income	**73,008**

CHAPTER

9 | Investment Companies

9.1 INTRODUCTION

The preceding chapters suggest that the management of portfolios requires more than nominal interest and knowledge. This will be strongly confirmed in the chapters to follow as well. While many investors have the financial resources and the necessary knowledge and time to achieve adequate risk diversification and to optimize returns, many have opted for the services of professionals. Investment companies, however, have many advantages and provide much more than professional portfolio management, as we shall discuss below.

9.2 DEFINITION

An investment company is a company or trust that uses its resources to invest in stocks and in other investment vehicles. Investors, with similar goals, buy shares in an investment company whose sole purpose is to purchase and trade securities in order to meet its announced goal. In so doing, investors hope to increase their returns and reduce their risk.

9.3 A HISTORICAL PERSPECTIVE

Investment companies originated in Belgium around 1840. They began to spread in the United States toward the end of the nineteenth century primarily in Boston, New York, and in Philadelphia. The growth continued well into the 1920s, until its sharp reversal during the Depression. By 1940, investment companies' assets stood at $1.06 billion. The growth in these assets since 1940 has been truly remarkable, particularly during the latter part of the 1970s. This period was marked by an explosive growth in money market funds and municipal bond funds as interest rates rose and as the volatility of interest rates magnified.

The growth of investment companies' assets between 1940 and 1980 is shown in Table 9.1. The growth rate clearly favors mutual funds over the closed-end companies.

216

TABLE 9.1
Growth of Investment Company Assets Since 1940

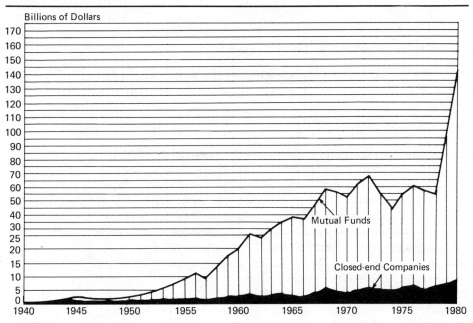

Year	Mutual Funds	Closed-End Companies[a]	Total
1980	$138,333,100,000	$8,053,201,000	$146,386,301,000
1979	97,053,100,000	6,873,179,000	103,926,279,000
1978	58,144,400,000	6,116,700,000	64,261,100,000
1977	51,479,800,000	6,283,700,000	57,763,500,000
1976	54,174,600,000	6,639,046,000	60,813,646,000
1975	48,706,300,000	5,861,300,000	54,567,600,000
1974	38,545,599,000	5,294,000,000	43,839,599,000
1973	49,310,700,000	6,622,700,000	55,936,700,000
1972	62,456,500,000	6,742,800,000	69,199,300,000
1971	58,159,800,000	5,324,300,000	63,484,100,000
1970	50,654,900,000	4,024,200,000	54,679,100,000
1969	52,621,400,000	4,743,700,000	57,365,100,000
1968	59,953,600,000	5,170,800,000	62,124,400,000
1967	44,701,302,000	3,777,100,000	48,478,402,000
1966	36,294,600,000	3,162,900,000	39,457,500,000
1964	30,370,300,000	3,523,413,000	33,893,713,000
1962	22,408,900,000	2,783,219,000	25,192,119,000
1960	17,383,300,000	2,083,898,000	19,467,198,000
1958	13,242,388,000	1,931,402,000	15,173,790,000
1956	9,046,431,000	1,525,748,000	10,572,179,000
1954	6,109,390,000	1,246,351,000	7,355,741,000
1952	3,931,407,000	1,011,089,000	4,942,496,000
1950	2,530,563,000	871,962,000	3,402,525,000
1948	1,505,762,000	767,028,000	2,272,790,000
1946	1,311,108,000	851,409,000	2,162,517,000
1944	882,191,000	739,021,000	1,621,212,000
1942	486,850,000	557,264,000	1,044,114,000
1940	447,959,000	613,589,000	1,061,548,000

Source: Reprinted by permission from The Wiesenberger Investment Companies Service 1981 Edition, p. 12. Copyright © 1981, Warren, Gorham and Lamont Inc., 210 South Street, Boston, Mass. All rights reserved.

[a]Including funded debt and bank loans.

The various types of investment companies, the reasons for their expansion, their performance records, and other investment-company-related considerations are the subject of this chapter.

9.4 TYPES OF INVESTMENT COMPANIES

There are two principal types of investment companies: closed-end and open-end or mutual fund.

Closed-End Companies

Closed-end companies have a *fixed* number of shares outstanding. They neither sell nor buy shares upon demand. Some closed-end companies have shares listed on the exchanges; others trade their shares over the counter. In this respect, stocks of closed-end companies resemble those of any other publicly owned firm. Prices of closed-end shares do not necessarily equal the net value of the investment portfolio held by the closed-end fund divided by the number of shares outstanding (net asset value). Prices are determined by supply and demand. The market price may exceed (closed-end share selling at a premium) or fall short of (closed-end share selling at a discount) net asset value. Some substantial discounts have been observed over long periods of time. During 1979, for example, discounts ranging from 3 to 35.1 percent were experienced by closed-end funds. The basic reason is that the expectations of the fund owners differ from those of the market. The market expectations, we must note, are reflected in the prices of securities. A closer analysis of premiums and discounts on closed-end shares was conducted by Hans Stoll, who concluded:

> two explanations . . . tax liability and past performance . . . tend to be supported by the data. Funds which do not accumulate unrealized gains as their net assets appreciate tend to sell at lesser discounts than funds which accumulate gains. This appears to reflect the reluctance of investors to purchase funds with a built-in capital gains tax liability. Funds with superior investment performance in the preceding year tend to sell at lesser discounts. This appears to reflect the market's belief (unsupported by the evidence) that past performance is a predictor of future performance.[1]

Closed-end funds were the first investment companies to come into being and, prior to the stock market crash of 1929, were the strongest. Many closed-end funds were heavily leveraged and heavily committed to speculative investments; therefore they lost considerably during the Depression. With their reputation tainted, they have yet to recover fully. Of the total of $146.4 billion in investment company assets on December 31, 1980, only $8.05 billion or 5.5 percent are invested in closed-end companies.

Types of Closed-End Companies

There are various types of closed-end investment companies with different objectives and levels of attractiveness. These are described below.

---

[1] **Hans R. Stoll,** "Discounts and Premiums on Shares of Diversified Closed-End Investment Funds." Working Paper No. 11–73, The Wharton School, University of Pennsylvania, Philadelphia, 1978, p. 13.

Diversified Closed-End Funds

Diversified closed-end companies invest their assets in a wide array of securities with no special emphasis on geographic area or on an industry or industries. These companies currently utilize practically no leverage and rely primarily on equity capital.

Dual-Purpose Funds

Dual-purpose closed-end funds, sometimes referred to as leveraged funds, were introduced in 1967. They originally issued an equal number of income and capital shares. The holders of income shares were to receive all the income generated by the portfolio, and the holders of capital shares were to receive (bear) all the capital gains (capital losses). Effectively, capital shares holders use the funds contributed by income shares holders to leverage their positions without payment of interest. The only cost is the foregone income. There are currently six dual-purpose funds, five of them listed on the New York Stock Exchange and the shares of the sixth (Putnam Duofund) traded over the counter. All these funds have a self-destruct feature. That is, on the maturity dates shown in Table 9.2, the income shares can be redeemed at a set price or converted into shares in an open-end investment company; the capital shares will also be converted into open-end shares. The market price of the capital shares will no longer be determined by supply and demand for the closed-end fund shares but rather by the net asset value of the mutual fund.

As closed-end funds approach their maturity dates, income shares move closer and closer to their redemption price and capital shares move toward the underlying net asset value. The farther from maturity the shares are, the more market factors determine their price. The price of income shares is largely determined by the yield on income securities (bonds for example) of comparable risk and the price of capital shares by investors' expectations.

Specialized Closed-End Companies

Specialized closed-end companies limit their portfolios to certain industries, industry groups, geographic areas, a certain investment vehicle (convertible funds, for example),

TABLE 9.2

	Income Shares				Capital Shares	
	Maturity date	Maturity price	Market price	NAV	Market price	Dis- counts
1. Gemini	12/31/84	$11.00	15⅛	$39.84	34⅛	14%
2. Hemisphere Fund	6/30/85	$11.44	8⅛	$ 2.49	3⅜	26%
3. Income & Capital	3/31/82	$10.00	9⅝	$11.98	10¼	14%
4. Leverage Fund Boston	1/4/82	$13.725	13⅞	$27.79	25½	8%
5. Putnam Duofund	1/3/83	$19.75	17¾	$15.61	12	23%
6. Scudder Duo-Vest	4/1/82	$ 9.15	9	$14.10	12⅛	14%

Source: General Media Financial Weekly, November 1981.

TABLE 9.3
Relation of Mutual Fund Assets to New York Stock Exchange
Market Value of All Listed Shares, Annually, 1951–1980 (Dollar
Figures in Millions)

Year	Market Value of all NYSE– Listed Shares	Mutual Fund Assets Total	Mutual Fund Assets In NYSE– Listed Stocks (estimated)	Mutual Fund Assets As Percentages Total	Mutual Fund Assets As Percentages In NYSE– Listed Stocks (estimated)
1951	$ 109,484	$ 3,130	$ 2,222	2.86%	2.03%
1952	120,536	3,931	2,791	3.26	2.32
1953	117,257	4,146	2,944	3.54	2.51
1954	169,149	6,109	4,337	3.61	2.56
1955	207,699	7,838	5,565	3.77	2.68
1956	219,176	9,046	6,423	4.13	2.93
1957	195,570	8,714	6,187	4.46	3.16
1958	276,665	13,242	9,408	4.79	3.40
1959	307,708	15,818	11,231	5.14	3.65
1960	306,967	17,026	12,088	5.55	3.94
1961	387,841	22,789	16,179	5.88	4.17
1962	345,846	21,271	15,102	6.15	4.37
1963	411,318	25,214	17,902	6.13	4.35
1964	474,322	29,116	20,672	6.14	4.36
1965	537.481	35,220	24,992	6.55	4.65
1966	482,541	34,829	27,100	7.22	5.62
1967	605,817	44,701	37,200	7.38	6.14
1968	692,337	52,677	44,100	7.61	6.37
1969	629,453	48,291	39,100	7.67	6.21
1970	636,380	47,618	39,000	7.48	6.13
1971	741,827	55,045	46,800	7.42	6.31
1972	871,540	59,831	46,090	6.86	5.29
1973	721,012	46,519	34,143	6.44	4.74
1974	511,100	34,062	23,902	7.00	4.68
1975	685,110	42,179	30,544	6.16	4.46
1976	858,300	47,582	34,032	5.54	3.97
1977	796,640	45,049	28,286	5.65	3.55
1978	822,740	44,980	29,145	5.47	3.54
1979	960,610	49,297	32,618	5.18	3.40
1980	1,242,800	58,400	39,483	4.70	3.18

Source: 1981 Mutual Fund Fact Book. Investment Company Institute,
Washington, D.C., p. 16.

Note: Comparison of open-end assets to market value of shares listed on the New York
Stock Exchange has been made to utilize available uniform data in illustration of the
relative size of investment companies. These investment companies also invest in
issues traded on other exchanges and over the counter markets, which are not listed
on the New York Stock Exchange and may purchase or sell issues listed on the New
York Stock Exchange in other securities markets.

or certain special situation investments such as investing in restricted (unregistered) securities.

These funds do not always achieve complete diversification of unsystematic risk, and because of their narrow focus they have a limited appeal.

9.5 MUTUAL FUNDS (OPEN-END INVESTMENT COMPANIES)

The first mutual fund was created in 1924. Investors' interest and confidence in this new phenomenon did not build up until the passage of the Investment Company Act of 1940, which regulates the operations of investment companies.

Mutual funds are characterized by an open capitalization structure in which the total number of shares outstanding constantly fluctuates. Shares are sold and redeemed on demand. The price is equal to the net asset value per share of the fund after the closing hours of the exchanges on the trading day. Shares of mutual funds are traded over the counter or are bought and sold from the fund.

The relative size of the mutual fund industry has fluctuated over time (between 1951 and 1980), never reaching more than 7.7 percent when measured by the value of all the assets held by mutual funds relative to the market value of all NYSE-listed shares (Table 9.3).

The most explosive growth in mutual funds occurred in the second half of the 1970s, fueled by the growth of the assets of funds with income-generation objectives such as money market funds and limited maturity municipal bond funds. By the end of October 1981, the distribution of the assets of the mutual funds industry was as follows: $54.4 billion in funds other than short-term funds, $169.6 billion in money market funds, and $3.72 billion in limited maturity municipal bond funds. The reach of mutual funds other than short term funds extends across almost all industries. As Table 9.4 shows, their investment funds are committed to industries ranging from agricultural equipment to oil to tobacco.

The various objectives of mutual funds are discussed below. We begin, however, by differentiating between two broad categories of funds: load and no-load funds.

No-load funds charge no sales commissions at the time of purchase and are sold through advertising and direct mail. However, they incur operating expenses and management advisory fees just as load funds do, thus reducing the effective rate of return on the fund's shares. The management advisory fee is 0.50 percent of the fund's assets. The recently formed No-Load Mutual Fund Association is intended to promote public awareness of these funds by pointing to their record and their advantages both in absolute and in relative terms (relative to load funds in particular). As of December 1981, there were 330 mutual funds of the no-load variety. Load funds, as their name implies, charge a load—a sales charge upon purchase. The trend distinctly favors no-load funds, as load funds regularly convert into no-load funds. Investors, having realized that there is no significant difference in performance between load and no-load funds, continue to buy load funds despite the saving of the hefty sales charge through no-load funds. This effectively reduces the net realized rate of return. The implications of this phenomenon for market efficiency are dramatic, for it suggests that investors are grossly misinformed. A discussion of these implications is beyond the scope of this chapter, however. The distribution of the net assets of mutual funds between load and no-load funds during the 1975–1980 period is shown in Table 9.5.

TABLE 9.4
Mutual Funds' Portfolio Diversification—Common Stock Holdings by
Industries: 1970, 1975, 1980 (in Millions of Dollars)[a]

	Market Value 1970	Market Value 1975	Market Value 1980
Agricultural equipment	$ 33,104	$ 82,216	$ 177,351
Aircraft mfg. & aerospace	221,670	346,481	456,891
Air transport	361,867	385,770	267,703
Auto & accessories (excl. tires)	778,348	489,027	204,214
Building materials & equipment	1,063,665	487,707	374,161
Chemicals	1,348,168	1,647,192	1,115,084
Communications (TV, radio, motion pictures)	221,202	383,733	317,902
Containers	108,220	92,062	56,262
Drugs & cosmetics	1,470,904	1,625,643	1,409,598
Elec. equip. & electronics (excl TV & radio)	1,590,472	901,701	1,724,872
Foods & beverages	1,182,362	785,819	509,899
Financial (incl. banks & insurance)	2,252,237	1,457,360	1,530,945
Machinery	351,116	347,812	315,816
Metals & mining	889,161	629,692	607,728
Office equipment	1,858,795	1,590,536	1,510,997
Oil	2,570,483	2,870,657	4,532,213
Paper	417,872	613,086	377,875
Public utilities (incl. telephone & natural gas)	2,597,020	1,107,512	976,728
Railroad	353,888	314,321	245,150
Railroad equipment	74,553	60,374	116,459
Retail trade	1,301,329	699,969	727,831
Rubber (incl. tires)	430,343	227,826	65,292
Steel	59,017	417,612	246,551
Textiles	119,157	93,559	25,795
Tobacco	506,503	488,044	328,672
Miscellaneous[b]	2,571,573	2,068,392	2,015,525
TOTALS	$24,683,029	$20,214,103	20,237,514

Source: 1981 Mutual Fund Fact Book, Investment Company Institute, Washington, D.C., p. 16.

[a]Composite industry investments drawn from the portfolios of 40 of the largest investment companies as of the end of calendar year 1980 whose total net assets represented 410% of total net assets of all institute member companies excluding all short-term funds.

[b]Includes diversified industrial companies not readily assignable to specific industry categories.

Categories of Mutual Funds

Today there is a mutual fund to suit almost every investment objective. The announced objectives of mutual funds range from the very conservative to the very speculative. Some investment houses offer a range of funds under one umbrella organization, allowing investors in one category of funds to shift (without penalty) to another as tastes and

TABLE 9.5
Total Net Assets of Mutual Funds by Investment Objective Within Method of Distribution, 1975–1980 (in Millions of Dollars)

	Load		
Year	Broker–Dealer	Direct Sellers	No-Load
1975	27,296.1	9,305.8	4,601.6
1976	30,088.4	10,168.3	6,026.9
1977	25,745.1	9,136.9	8,988.8
1978	26,233.8	8,852.1	9,612.2
1979	32,032.4	8,720.2	12.729.6R[a]
1980		9,176.7	15,647.5

Note: Prior to 1976 figures for aggressive growth funds are included in the growth-fund category and figures for bond funds are included in the income-fund category.

Source: 1981 Mutual Fund Fact Book. Investment Company Institute, Washington, D.C., p. 67, 1981.

[a] R = revised

preferences shift. An example of the choices available from one company is shown in Table 9.6. We shall now discuss the various categories of funds.

Capital Gains (Aggressive Growth) Funds

Capital gains funds accept high risk (including leverage) in the pursuit of their objectives. The companies in which these funds invest are relatively unknown and relatively young. The distribution, if any, to shareholders is mostly in the form of capital gains. Little in the form of dividends (from the underlying investments) is distributed to shareholders. These funds also use options to magnify gains or to hedge against losses.

Capital gains funds accounted for 9 percent of all the assets of mutual funds excluding short-term funds as of October 1981 (Table 9.7). Their high liquidity ratio (14 percent) is not reflective of risk aversion but of the condition of the stock market, whose performance was lethargic during the latter part of 1981. High liquidity allows fund managers considerable flexibility as they wait for major turns in the market, new companies to emerge, and new investment opportunities to develop.

Growth and Growth-Income Funds

These funds stress capital gains, but to a lesser degree than the capital gains funds. Income is generally a secondary objective, providing some degree of share price stability. These types of funds accounted for 61.2 percent of the assets of all mutual funds excluding short-term mutual funds in October 1981.

Funds for Relative Price Stability

The majority of the assets of this type of fund are invested in defensive instruments like secured bonds. These funds offer stability without sacrificing long-term capital appreciation.

TABLE 9.6

Merrill Lynch
Group of Funds

Merrill Lynch Ready Assets Trusts
offer high current income, liquidity, and
stability of principal, investing in short-
term money market securities.

Merrill Lynch High Income Fund
generates high yields from selected corporate bonds primarily rated BBB or below.
The Fund has elicited a growing response from investors seeking to cope
with inflation.

Merrill Lynch Municipal Bond Fund
produces tax exempt income—through
three different portfolios.
Insured Portfolio generates consistent
income from its conservatively invested
portfolio, insured as to the timely payment of principal and income, and not
to the net asset value of shares.
High Yield Portfolio offers high income from medium to lower grade
long-term municipals.
Limited Maturity Portfolio offers relative stability of principal with commensurate income, from investment
grade short to intermediate term
municipals.

Merrill Lynch Basic Value Fund
seeks capital appreciation, then income,
through investments in equities perceived as temporarily undervalued.
The Fund maintains a diversified portfolio of investments in companies
whose stocks generally sell at substantial discounts from their underlying
assets, have above average dividend
growth, and have relatively low price/
earnings ratios.

Merrill Lynch Capital Fund
seeks highest total return through flexible investments primarily in high quality stocks and short-term interest
bearing securities.
Investment efforts are directed toward companies perceived to have
greater-than-average profitability and
lower-than-average market valuations.

Merrill Lynch Special Value Fund
invests in lesser-known companies expected to achieve above average gains
over time.
The Fund's portfolio of small and
"emerging growth" companies is designed
to provide greater-than-average long-
term growth potential to those who
can assume greater-than-average risk.

Source: Merrill Lynch Pierce Fenner & Smith, Inc., New York, 1981.

Balanced Funds

Balanced funds are concerned with risk reduction consistent with long-term growth
and high current income. They attempt to "balance" their portfolios by committing
funds to bonds, preferred stock, and common stock. Balanced funds accounted for 5.1
percent of the assets of all mutual funds excluding short term mutual funds in October
1981.

Income Funds

As their name implies, income funds stress current income and not capital appreciation.
These funds invest primarily in high-dividend-paying stocks and in bonds. They are
very suitable for retirees and those investors with high risk aversion and a strong need
for current income.

TABLE 9.7
Total Assets, Liquid Assets, and Liquidity Ratios Classified by Method of Distribution and Investment Objective (Excluding Short-Term Funds)[a] (Millions of Dollars)

	Total Assets			Liquid Assets			Liquidity Ratios[b]		
	October '81	September '81	October '80	October '81	September '81	October '80	October '81	September '81	October '80
Totals for ICI reporters	$54,334.9	$51,659.4R[a]	$56,152.9	$5,799.4	$5,408.5R	$5,456.9	10.7%	10.5%	9.7%
Method of distribution									
Broker-dealer	30,111.1	28,494.6R	30,715.5	2,952.4	2,726.6	3,069.4	9.8%	9.6%R	10.0%
Direct selling	8,425.8	8,012.0	8,856.0	1,307.8	1,212.7R	986.8	15.5	15.1R	11.1
No-load	14,381.1	13,781.4	15,079.7	1,485.4	1,402.7	1,331.8	10.3	10.2	8.8
Others[c]	1,416.9	1,371.5	1,501.7	53.8	66.5	69.0	3.8	4.8	4.6
Investment objective									
Aggressive growth	4,915.2	4,573.8	4,172.5	685.7	547.5	494.0	14.0%	12.0%	11.8%
Growth	15,160.8	14,090.7R	15,764.0	1,735.9	1,575.5	1,457.3	11.4	11.2	9.2
Growth & income	18,096.8	17,368.8R	18,635.2	1,785.5	1,704.1	1,863.0	9.9	9.8	10.0
Balanced	2,780.5	2,692.2	3,338.8	237.5	191.3	257.7	8.5	7.1	7.7
Income	4,331.7	4,203.2	4,557.8	329.2	277.6	397.7	7.6	6.6	8.7
Corporate bond	5,424.0	5,216.8	5,745.5	616.6	610.1R	591.1	11.4	11.7R	10.3
Long-term municipal bond	3,089.6	2,996.6R	3,390.5	380.2	429.0R	341.2	12.3	14.3	10.1
Option/income	536.4	517.5	548.6	28.9	73.3	54.9	5.4	14.2	10.0

Source: Trends in Mutual Fund Activity. Investment Company Institute, Research Department, October 1981.

[a] Excludes money market and limited-maturity municipal bond funds.

[b] Liquid assets—Holdings of cash and short-term securities—as a percent of total assets.

[c] Exchange funds not offering new shares

[d] R = revised.

Income funds accounted for 8 percent of the assets of all mutual funds excluding short-term mutual funds in October 1981.

Corporate Bond Funds

Corporate bond funds, as their name implies, commit their funds primarily to corporate bonds. Their emphasis is on income generation. On Oct. 30, 1981, corporate bond funds accounted for 10.11 percent of the assets of all mutual funds excluding short-term mutual funds.

Option/Income Funds

Option/income funds seek high current income from high-dividend-paying stocks and from the option premiums on call options sold on the stocks held. Realized short-term gains, if any, are primarily options-related (see Chapters 12 and 13).

Option/income funds accounted for about 1 percent of mutual funds assets excluding short-term mutual funds. As of Oct. 30, 1981, they represented a new phenomenon in the mutual funds industry.

Money Market Funds

Unable and/or unwilling to settle for the returns realized on bank deposits or to deal with the complexities of the financial markets, many investors have found refuge in money market funds, which represent a pool of professionally managed short-term income assets in which the investor owns a share.

The emergence of money market funds toward the end of 1972 and their subsequent phenomenal growth can be ascribed to the complex regulatory system of reserve requirements and interest rate ceilings imposed on the U.S. banking system. As of Oct. 30, 1981, there were 147 money market funds with record total assets of $169.6 billion, up from about $90 billion at the beginning of February 1981. The average annual yield on these funds (October 1981) was 15.5 percent, compared with 12.52 percent on six-month certificates sold by banking institutions. Banks could not compete against money market funds because of the reserve requirements on their deposits, which effectively increase their cost of funds, and because of the limit set by federal law on the rate that can be paid on certificates of deposit. This rate cannot exceed by more than 0.25 percent the average rate on 26-week T-bills auctioned each Monday. Barring any changes in the laws affecting money market funds or banks, and many are being contemplated, and barring a substantial drop in interest rates, the growth in the assets of these funds is expected to continue.

The attractiveness of money market funds lies in:

1. Their relatively high yield.
2. Their professional management.
3. Their high level of liquidity, since price of shares is computed daily by dividing the fund's total net asset value by the number of outstanding shares.
4. Their flexibility. Income from the fund's assets can be received by the investor or automatically reinvested. Income and principal can be withdrawn in a lump

sum or on a periodic basis, which is very suitable to many pension plans. Early withdrawal of funds is subject to penalty in the case of savings certificates.

5. Their smaller denominations. Some investors do not have the funds to participate even in the smallest denominations of certain corporate or government debt issues but can easily meet the minimum investment required by money market funds.

6. Their risk diversification. The funds under the control of money market funds are invested in different types of debt securities from different issuers and from different parts of the country and the world. This allows for considerable risk diversification, which is not attainable by many investors.

Most of these benefits are typical of mutual funds, as we shall demonstrate below.

The explosive growth in money market funds continued throughout 1981 and part of 1982. Between Oct. 30, 1981, and Dec. 16, 1981, alone, money market funds added $16.36 billion more to their assets, for a total of $185.96 billion, and the trend appears to be continuing. Almost a third of money market funds assets were invested in commercial paper. The next most important instrument in their portfolio is certificates of deposits issued by commercial banks, followed by Eurodollar certificates of deposits. The average maturity of the portfolio held at the end of October 1981 equaled 35 days (Table 9.8).

Municipal Bond Funds

Tax-exempt bond funds become more and more popular as yields on municipal bonds increase, as inflation pushes people into higher and higher tax brackets, and as rates on time deposits fail to adjust sufficiently to reflect market rates. In February 1981, tax-exempt municipal bonds were yielding 13 to 14 percent while high-grade taxable utility bonds were yielding 15 percent.

Municipal bond funds come in two forms: unit trusts and open-end funds.

Unit Trusts. This is the older of the two forms and it resembles a closed-end investment company. It was first offered in 1961.

The investor's share in a unit trust municipal bond fund consists of a "unit" in an unmanaged portfolio of tax-exempt securities. The initial value of a unit is determined by the value of the underlying securities. Subsequently, the value of the units is determined primarily by prevailing market rates relative to the average rate on the underlying securities. Municipal bond units are sold over the counter. Their secondary market is not very active, however.

Open-End Municipal Bond Fund. The first open-end municipal bond fund was offered in 1976. These funds resemble most other mutual funds in the flexibility open to management and in the way they are sold and redeemed. The funds' assets are invested in tax-exempt securities. Some of these funds invest primarily in long-term municipal bonds and the others in short-term maturities.

The assets of long-term municipal bond funds amounted to $3.1 billion at the end of October 1981 (Table 9.7). Those of limited-maturity municipal bonds amounted to $3.72 billion on the same date.

We now look at the advantages of mutual fund ownership.

TABLE 9.8
Monthly Statistics of Money Market Funds (Dollar Figures in Millions)

	October '81	September '81	October '80
Change in net assets during the month	$8,736.5	$11,410.7	$36.0
Total net assets[a] (at month end)	169,576.5	160,840.0	77,467.8
Distribution of assets (*at month end*)			
U.S. treasury bills	12,231.6	10,071.3R[f]	4,810.5
Other treasury securities	1,733.8	1,347.4R	1,435.5
Other U.S. securities	11,543.3	9,655.2	4,861.1
Repurchase agreements	11,463.0	10,114.4	3,732.3
Commercial bank CD[b]	34,707.9	36,234.9	18,894.9
Other domestic CD[c]	4,362.8	3,830.1	992.0
Eurodollar CD[d]	19,198.2	17,072.3	8,358.6
Commercial paper	60,032.8	58,424.5	24,327.8
Bankers' acceptances	12,435.7	12,707.7	8,669.2
Cash reserves	−612.9	−820.6R	154.1
Other	2,480.2	2,202.8R	1,231.8
Average maturity of portfolio[e] (number of days)	35	31	37
Number of accounts outstanding	9,717,245	9,278,527R	4,169,667
Number of funds	147	145	95

Source: Trends in Mutual Fund Activity. Investment Company Institute, Research Department, Washington, D.C., October 1981.

[a] Estimates of total net assets are as of the end of the month. Funds reporting to the institute account for approximately 98 percent of assets of all money market funds.

[b] Commercial bank CDs are those issued by American banks located in the United States.

[c] Other domestic CDs include those issued by S&Ls and American branches of foreign banks.

[d] Eurodollar CDs are those issued by foreign branches of domestic banks and some issued by Canadian banks; this category includes some one-day paper.

[e] Maturity of each individual security in the portfolio at end of month weighted by its value.

[f] R = revised.

9.6 ADVANTAGES OF MUTUAL FUND OWNERSHIP

There are many advantages (actual or perceived) that fund shareholders enjoy. Among them are the following.

Professional Management

The record of most mutual funds does not offer sufficient justification for considering professional management as a real and consistent advantage. The fundamental premise is that professional managers, because of their knowledge and continuous involvement in financial matters, should ostensibly turn in a superior performance. This must be so, otherwise the labor market would be inefficient, for it would be paying a wage rate higher than the value of the manager's marginal product. Professional management is thought, and correctly so, to reduce (1) transactions costs incurred in the search for and assimilation and digestion of information and (2) commission costs incurred on securities transactions. One simple yearly statement is all the investor has to contend with, instead of coping with a multitude of companies and doing the exhaustive research necessary to achieve an adequately diversified portfolio and a sufficiently high rate of return. Also, the investor would hold a mutual fund share, which represents ownership in several corporations instead of holding the corporations' securities themselves.

Long-Term Planning

The low minimum contributions required by mutual funds encourage investors to make periodic contributions to the fund (purchase a number of shares on a regular basis) in their drive to fulfill a long-range goal such as retirement. These savings may not otherwise be realized.

The systematic approach to investing (saving) can be achieved in either of two forms: the voluntary plan and the contractual plan. Under the voluntary or informal plan, the individual makes regular or irregular purchases of funds shares at prevailing net asset value. This plan does not have a specified duration or a set goal. It can be started with an investment as low as $100. The contractual plan, on the other hand, requires the investor to make regular purchases of a set value at set intervals over a specified number of years. These type plans are ordinarily used to meet retirement objectives, child-education objectives, or certain estate objectives. They are best utilized for long-term purposes and carry a built-in penalty in the form of proportionately high sales charges when used for short-term purposes.

Risk Diversification

This factor alone accounts for most of the reasons behind the popularity of mutual funds. It is very hard for an investor with, say, $1,000 to construct a properly diversified portfolio without incurring excessive transactions costs. Limited funds may produce portfolios with too many odd lots or with an insufficient number of securities. The pooling of funds through a mutual fund permits the investor an efficient (least costly) way of diversifying unsystematic risk.

The diversification we speak of is one achieved in a Markowitz sense; that is, it minimizes risk for a given level of return or maximizes return for a given level of risk.

Liquidity

Mutual funds shares are redeemable at the option of the shareholder. Minimum transactions costs are charged. Shares of closed-end companies are either listed or have a sufficiently large number of market makers to ensure their liquidity.

Mutual funds stand ready to purchase their shares at net asset value, determined after the closing hours of the New York Stock Exchange on the day the order is placed.

Information

Extensive and complete information regularly flows from mutual funds to their shareholders. This is required by law. The investor knows the composition of the fund's portfolio as well as the changes therein and thus can make a more educated decision. This information is supplied at least twice annually, with some funds providing quarterly reports.

Flexibility

The mutual funds industry affords investors a range of options that make investing a lot more convenient and more rewarding. Among these are regular or lump-sum accounts, regular accounts with automatic dividend reinvestment, accumulation accounts, withdrawal accounts, exchange privileges, and other options permitting investors to tailor this investment program to their needs.

Buying into a regular account means paying a lump-sum for shares of the mutual fund. These shares are not bought at a set price but rather fluctuate according to the market price of the underlying securities. No saving is achieved by buying in round lots, but most firms will lower the sales charge on large purchases. Upon receiving the cash payment for shares, a mutual fund usually sends stock certificates for the amount purchased, or the fund may merely issue a statement on the shares held on deposit for the investor. This second method is more convenient for the shareholder, since it reduces the time and expense needed to safeguard the stock certificate.

Dividends are received quarterly, semiannually, or annually, depending on the fund's policy. This dividend is usually a cash payment, but most funds offer an alternative method: a regular account with automatic dividend reinvestment. Instead of mailing out dividend payments, the fund credits the dividend to the investor's account as representing additional shares of the mutual fund. In either case the dividend payment is taxed as if the investor had earned it on his or her own, as we shall discuss in detail below.

Most funds also distribute realized capital gains to their shareholders either in cash or through the reinvestment plan. One of the advantages of a reinvestment plan is the saving on sales charges. The reinvestment is done at net asset value for the amount of the distribution.

The various accumulation plans available through the mutual fund industry were discussed in the preceding section.

Withdrawal accounts have proven their utility to many investors, particularly to those contemplating retirement or actually retired. Withdrawal plans can call for fixed or for variable payments. They can call for the distribution of invested capital or merely for payment of income thereon. In either case the payments are made at regular intervals. Withdrawal plans ordinarily require a minimum level of investment ($10,000 in most cases). As funds are withdrawn from the account, the remaining investment continues accumulating income (or realizing losses). The distribution of shareholders accounts by type during the 1976–1980 period is shown in Table 9.9.

Mutual funds, aware of the fact that investor preferences shift over time, permit them to shift from one fund with a certain goal to another within the same fund group. This exchange privilege has proven to be very useful and does not require the payment of a sales charge. A small fee is charged when the exchange is made, however. Under the exchange program, people approaching retirement may exchange their shares in a

TABLE 9.9
Types of Shareholder Accounts (in Thousands) 1976–1980[a]

Year End	Total Shareholder Accounts	Regular Accounts	Accounts with Automatic Dividend Reinvestment	Contractual Accumulation Plans	Contractual Single-Payment Plans	Withdrawal Accounts
			Number			
1976						
Mutual funds	8,879	2,322	5,325	930	112	190
Money market funds[b]	155	30	124	—	—	1
1977						
Mutual funds	8,515	2,008	5,387	844	101	175
Money market funds[b]	141	16	124	—	—	1
1978						
Mutual funds	8,068	1,766	5,314	757	75	156
Money market funds[b]	381	47	333	—	—	1
1979						
Mutual funds	7,486	1,704	4,901	677	64	140
Money market funds[b]	1,691	147	1,541	—	—	3
1980						
Mutual funds	7,212	1,605	4,879	554	45	129
Money market funds[b]	4,746	228	4,515	—	—	3
Limited-maturity municipal bond	17	6	11	—	—	—
			Percent			
1976						
Mutual funds	100.0	26.1	60.0	10.5	1.3	2.1
Money market funds	100.0	19.4	80.0	—	—	0.6
1977						
Mutual funds	100.0	23.6	63.3	9.9	1.2	2.0
Money market funds	100.0	11.4	87.9	—	—	0.7
1978						
Mutual funds	100.0	21.6	64.9	9.2	2.4	1.9
Money market funds	100.0	12.3	87.4	—	—	0.3
1979						
Mutual funds	100.0	22.8	65.5	9.0	0.8	1.9
Money market funds	100.0	8.7	91.1	—	—	0.2
1980						
Mutual funds	100.0	22.2	67.7	7.7	0.6	1.8
Money market funds	100.0	4.8	95.1	—	—	0.1
Limited-maturity municipal bond	100.0	35.3	64.7	—	—	—

Source: 1981 Mutual Fund Fact Book. Investment Company Institute, Washington, D.C., p. 20.

[a] Automatic dividend reinvestment accounts do not include accumulation plans and contractual single-payment plans, the great bulk of which also reinvest all distributions. Minor adjustments in prior years have been made as between types of accounts.

[b] Prior to 1980, total money market shareholder accounts shown above will be slightly less than total accounts in force, as not all of the funds supply a breakdown by type of account.

TABLE 9.10
Fiduciary, Business, and Institutional Investors of Mutual Funds Excluding Money Market Funds—Value of Holdings, 1974, 1976, 1978, and 1980 (in Thousands of Dollars)

	1974	1976	1978R	1980
Fiduciaries (banks and individuals serving as trustees, guardians and administrators)	$2,896,796	$ 4,133,157	$3,623,262	$ 6,690,185
Business corporations	815.554	964,166	617,983	1,506,531
Employee pension and profit sharing funds[b]	1,894,820R	3,691,619	3,861,559	7,139,023
Insurance companies and other financial institutions	627,784	576,343	636,719	1,093,426
Unions	16,295	26,388	26,514	30,719
Total business organizations	$3,354,453	$ 5,258,516	$5,142,775	$ 9,769,699
Churches and religious organizations	82,802	102,433	72,433	147,195
Fraternal, welfare, and other public associations	85,711	129,343	66,678	262,167
Hospitals, santariums, orphanages, etc.	37,220	70,398	37,119	94,291
Schools and colleges	33,640	68,066	57,491	155,040
Foundations	N/A	N/A	21,738	67,218
Total institutions and foundations	$ 239,373	$ 370,240	$ 255,459	$ 725,911
Other institutional investors not classified[c]	625,479	957,775	569,036	479,038
Total	$7,116,101	$10,719,688	$9,590,532	$17,664,833

Source: 1981 Mutual Fund Fact Book, Investment Company Institute, Washington, D.C., p. 55.

[a]Reporter of Institutional data represented 75.4% of total net assets in 1974, 77.3% in 1976, 82.4%. in 1978 and 77.7% in 1980. N.A: not available; R: reversed to exclude money market funds.

[b]The data for this category prior to 1974 are not comparable due to an understatement of Keogh figures.

[c]Includes institutional accounts which do not fall under other classifications and those for which no determination of classification can be made.

[d]This figure includes $5.9 billion of institutional assets invested in money market funds.

growth fund, for example, with those in an income fund or in a money market fund, depending on availability and conditions. It must be noted, however, that this transaction, while representing an exchange from the fund's point of view, is a sale and a purchase in the opinion of the Internal Revenue Service and thus has tax consequences. Other conveniences that have become prevalent in the mutual fund industry are bank-draft investing, which permits direct transfer of a predetermined sum from the investor's checking account to the mutual fund, and the salary deduction plan, whereby investors belonging to a qualified group may have their periodic contributions to a mutual fund accumulation plan deducted from their salaries or wages.

The expected high growth rate in Individual Retirement Accounts (IRAs) as a result of the liberalization of eligibility under the Economic Recovery Tax Act of 1981 coupled with the prevalence of Keogh plans for the self-employed, the large number of corporate pension and profit-sharing plans, and the Simplified Employee Pension (SEP) plans have necessitated accommodating policies by the mutual funds industry. All these plans call for regular contributions and for the management of substantial amounts of resources. Through the various deduction or direct contribution schemes the mutual funds industry has offered, an individual or a corporation can simply set up the transfer mechanism for the investment funds and shift the burden of fund management onto the mutual fund. Indeed, corporations, nonprofit organizations, foundations, and fiduciaries of different types have been substantial investors in mutual funds, as Table 9.10 shows. The various types of retirement plans are discussed in Chapter 18.

9.7 EVALUATING MUTUAL FUNDS

The evaluation of mutual funds must be in terms of return and risk. Some funds, like the Merrill Lynch funds, stress only returns—total returns. Total return represents the change in net asset value during the performance period, assuming the reinvestment of dividend income and any capital gains distributions. The performance measured in total rate of return can be gauged in relation to the preceding period or to a base period (an index form). If the index form is used, a value exceeding 100 (assigned to the base period) indicates a positive performance and one below 100 indicates a negative performance. An example of the index form is the following:

Asset value 12/31/80 including $3,500 value of shares accepted as capital gains distribution	$12,500
+	
1970–1980 dividends from investment income	3,600
Total adjusted asset value 12/31/1980	$16,100
Asset value 1/1/1970 (10,000 − load of 8.5 percent)	**$ 9,150**

Total return = (16,100/9,150) − 1.00 = 76 percent gain

The performance of mutual funds with differing objectives—measured using the percentage change in net asset value per share or using the index form—is shown in Table 9.11. For the year 1980, the various types of growth funds performed well, with the maximum capital gains funds realizing an impressive 41.5 percent change in net asset value per share.

The results reported in Table 9.11 represent gross returns before taxes and do not

TABLE 9.11
Performance of Various Mutual Funds

Mutual Funds

No. of Funds		Total Net Assets ($ million)	% Change in Net Assets per Share				
			9 Mos. 1981	Year 1980	5¾ Years	10¾ Years	% Yield
78	Max Capital Gains	6,462.5	−11.4	42.0	192.9	190.0	2.3
112	Long-Term Growth	15,667.6	− 9.6	35.3	123.9	125.0	3.3
60	Growth & Income	14,499.4	− 9.0	28.9	95.4	128.9	4.7
19	Balanced	2,584.9	− 7.7	19.6	58.0	85.7	7.0
12	Income-Com Stk	638 4	1.0	19.1	109.6	172.4	5.5
48	Income-Flexible	4,495.9	− 3.8	11.6	63.8	111.8	10,6
51	Income-Sr Secs	5,129.9	− 4.5	3.9	33.2	81.4	13.3
12	Speclzd-Canadian	1,253.2	−10.4	46.1	178.8	350.1	5.7
3	Speclzd-Ins & Bank	132.0	4.0	7.8	124.8	158.5	4.7
2	Public Utilities	156.1	3.6	3.6	59.4	27.6	9.8
7	Speclzd-US Gov't	148.5	− 6.6	− 0.9	8.3	19.7	13.0
34	Tax-Exempt Bonds	2,955.4	− 9.0	−12.7	−	−	10.6

Closed-End Companies

No. of Funds		% Disc.	% Change in Net Assets per Share				
			9 Mos. 1981	Year 1980	5¾ Years	10¾ Years	% Yield
9	Diversifd Inv Co Avg	17.2	− 7.5	33.6	135.4	153.7	4.7

Market Indicators

		% Change		
	9 Mos. 1981	Year 1980	5¾ Years	10¾ Years
Dow Jones Industrial Avg*	− 7.5	21.4	32.9	55.7
S*P 500-Stock Index*	−10.8	31.5	62.7	105.3

*Adjusted to include dividends paid.

Wiesenberger Mutual Fund Indexes

	Value 9/30/81	9 Mos. 1981	Year 1980	Years 5¾	Years 10¾
Growth	625.80	−12.0	34.9	95.1	97.7
Growth/Income	497.89	− 7.8	27.9	84.5	112.2
Income	520.18	−12.0	15.4	73.2	125.9
Balanced	352.39	− 7.2	19.3	56.5	81.5

12/31/58 = 100.00; data on total return basis.

account for differential in sales charges, potential tax liability to the investor, and for whether dividends and/or capital gains are reinvested or not. The results do account, however, for all expenses incurred by the fund, including management fees, and they carry all the drawbacks any average does. They do not indicate the returns a particular individual was able to realize. A particular individual may have bought high and sold low or may have liquidated too soon or held the position too long. Furthermore, a certain level of returns is taxed differently for different investors, and investors may look differently at certain rates of return, depending on their needs and their risk profile. It should also be pointed out that Table 9.11 summarizes historical results, with no guarantee of recurrence. Different funds have different histories of varying length. Thus, investors must be careful not only to evaluate current fund management and investment policies in light of their expectations about the market or about the type security or industry a specific fund has traditionally emphasized but also to adjust reported results to account for sales charges and for factors peculiar to their own investment profiles, given a certain holding period.

Thus far we have concentrated on rates of return and have ignored the very important risk factor. A superior measure of performance would include risks in the evaluation of the record of a mutual fund. Some analysts use total risk measured by the standard deviation or the variance of the rates of return on the fund, others use systematic risk measured by beta that represents the nondiversifiable portion of total risk. A beta of 1.5 indicates that the fund's portfolio returns would tend to rise (or fall) 50 percent more than the return on a market index such as the NYSE Composite or the S&P Composite Index.

William Sharpe[2] used total risk to devise an index of portfolio performance:

$$S_i = \frac{\overline{R}_i - R_F}{\sigma_i} \qquad (9.1)$$

where S = portfolio i performance index

$\overline{R}_i$ = average return on ith portfolio

R_F = risk-free rate

$\overline{R}_i - R_F$ = risk premium for portfolio i = excess yield

σ_i = standard deviation of returns for portfolio i = ex post portfolio risk.

The higher the value of S_i, the better the performance of the fund—that is, the higher the risk premium per unit of total risk.

This performance method yields the absolute level of S_i. The relative performance of a fund is also of interest to investors. Thus, the expected return/total risk tradeoff observed for a given fund should be compared with the efficiency frontier—the market-observed tradeoff between expected return $E(R)$ and various levels of risk σ. An example of an efficiency frontier is shown in Figure 9.1.

The value of S represents the price per unit of total risk. The more risk-averse a person is, the higher the S_i he or she will require.

J. Treynor[3] proposed an alternative performance measure emphasizing systematic

[2] **William F. Sharpe,** "Mutual Fund Performances." *Journal of Business,* suppl., January 1966.

[3] **J. Treynor,** "How to Rate Management of Investment Funds," *Harvard Business Review,* January–February 1965, pp. 63–75.

FIGURE 9.1   An efficiency frontier.

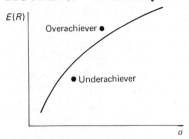

rather than total risk. He based his index on the characteristic line for a portfolio. His index is:

$$T_i = \frac{\overline{R}_i - R_F}{b_i} \qquad\qquad (9.2)$$

where b_i = slope of the characteristic line = measure of the fund's systematic risk.

Treynor argued that the first step in developing a performance measure is to estimate the characteristic line, which summarizes the relationship between the rate of return on a mutual fund (taking capital gains, interest, and dividends into consideration) and that on a market index (like the S&P).

The slope of the characteristic line measures the volatility of the fund's rate of return. The higher the slope (the value of b), the larger the volatility of the fund—that is, the greater the sensitivity of the fund's rate of return to changes in the rates of return on the market portfolio. An aggressive growth fund would, therefore, have a steeper characteristic line than a growth fund. This is shown in Figure 9.2.

An aggressive growth fund A would perform better than another aggressive growth fund B if the characteristic line of A were higher throughout than that of B, given that A and B had an equal slope.

The estimation of the characteristic line relies on time-series data to estimate the following equation:

$$R_{i,t} = h_i + b_i \, (R_{M,t}) + \epsilon_{i,t} \qquad\qquad (9.3)$$

where $R_{i,t}$ = rate of return on portfolio i at time t

$\qquad\quad R_{M,t}$ = rate of return on a market index at time t

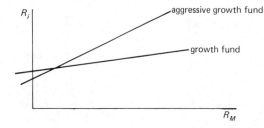

FIGURE 9.2 Comparison of two growth funds.

ϵ_t = error term

h_i, b_i = regression coefficients

The value of T_i represents the price per unit of systematic risk. This obviously assumes that unsystematic risk has been completely eliminated through portfolio diversification. In an efficient market, the risk/return tradeoff of mutual fund i should plot on the security market line.

The performance of the management of mutual funds is ranked by T_i values. The higher the value of T_i, the higher the ranking. The ranking order, Treynor demonstrated, is independent of the value of R_F.

Both Treynor and Sharpe use risk premium as a measure of the return on a portfolio. Their indexes represent the risk premium per unit of systematic and total risk, respectively, and assume that investors can borrow and lend at the risk-free rate. Most studies show considerable consistency between the two indexes in ranking mutual funds in accordance with either performance index. This is not surprising, because most mutual funds are sufficiently diversified so that total risk is equal to systematic risk. Were this not the case, the two performance measures could yield different rankings.

Another performance measure based on the market model introduced in Chapter 6 was advanced by M. Jensen in 1969.[4] The estimable function is

$$R_{i,t} - R_{F,t} = \alpha_i + \beta_i \, (R_{M,t} - R_{F,t}) + \epsilon_{i,t} \tag{9.4}$$

The ranking of mutual fund i would depend on the value of α. A positive and significant α value would indicate that the fund manager had consistently outperformed the market. A negative and significant α would indicate consistent underperformance. In either case, the implication is that the market is inefficient, for there is a manager or a group of managers who can consistently outperform a buy-and-hold strategy.

Using the performance measure, Jensen was able to demonstrate, for 115 open-end investment companies during the 1945–1965 period,

> *not only that these 115 mutual funds were on average not able to predict security prices well enough to outperform a buy-the-market-and-hold policy, but also that there is very little evidence that any individual fund was able to do significantly better than that which we expected from mere random chance. . . . Thus on average the funds apparently were not quite successful enough in their trading activities to recoup even their brokerage expenses.*[5]

Jensen's results were later questioned by Norman Mains.[6] The criticism centered on the methods used by Jensen to calculate rates of return and the risk of mutual funds.

Another problem with Jensen's performance measure and with those of Sharpe and Treynor is the biasedness of one-parameter estimates. I. Friend and M. Blume[7] reestimated the variables in the Jensen study and found that the risk-adjusted performance

---

[4] **Michael Jensen,** "The Performance of Mutual Funds in the Period 1945–1965." *Journal of Finance,* May 1968, pp. 389–416.

[5] Ibid., p. 415.

[6] **Norman Mains,** "Risk, the Pricing of Capital Assets, and the Evaluation of Investment Portfolios: Comment." *Journal of Business,* July 1977.

[7] **Irwin Friend** and **Marshall Blume,** "Measurement of Portfolio Performance Under Uncertainty." *American Economic Review,* vol. 60, no. 4 (September 1970), pp. 561–575.

was significantly inversely correlated with risk. That is, low-risk portfolios achieved higher risk-adjusted performance than high-risk portfolios. Friend and Blume attribute the results primarily to the assumption of equality of the borrowing and lending rates with the risk-free rate in the capital asset pricing model.

Robert Klemkosky[8] also examined the biasedness issue using quarterly data on 40 actual portfolios between the years 1966 and 1971. His results showed a bias in a positive direction (opposite that of Friend and Blume); that is, higher-risk portfolios have higher risk-adjusted performance.

F. Fabozzi and J. Francis[9] tested the performance of mutual funds managers using the stability of beta. The authors reasoned that "If beta does differ with market conditions, the use of beta estimated from the entire period can result in different conclusions about the skills of the fund manager under different market conditions."[10]

The fund manager, by adjusting his portfolio beta upward in a bull market and downward in a bear market, can improve investment performance; otherwise ". . . good investment performance in the bull period may be done solely to market timing ability rather than security selection ability."[11]

Using monthly data on 85 different type open-end investment companies covering the period from December 1965 to December 1971, Fabozzi and Francis tested the equality of portfolio systematic risk in bull and bear markets. Their conclusions were consistent with those offered earlier by Treynor and Mazuy,[12] namely, that mutual fund managers did not adjust their portfolios in order to change the value of their betas as market conditions changed and improve the risk-adjusted returns to fund shareholders.

The results of Fabozzi and Francis were later supported by the work of G. Alexander and R. Stover. Their findings were that "no fund classification had superior ability in altering its beta to reflect market conditions. Overall, mutual funds were unable to increase their beta when market conditions changed from bearish to bullish."[13]

It appears, therefore, that mutual funds managers have no special insight into the behavior of the market.

9.8 MUTUAL FUNDS AND ECONOMIC EFFICIENCY

The most ambitious study on the economic impact of the mutual fund industry was undertaken by I. Friend, M. Blume, and J. Crockett.[14] Their study used five different criteria for evaluating mutual funds:

[8] **Robert C. Klemkosky,** "The Bias in Composite Performance Measures." *Journal of Financial and Quantitative Analysis,* vol. 8, no. 3 (June, 1973), pp. 505–514.

[9] **Frank Fabozzi** and **Jack Francis,** "Mutual Fund Systematic Risk for Bull and Bear Markets: An Empirical Examination." *Journal of Finance,* vol. 34, no. 5 (December 1979), pp. 1243–1249.

[10] Ibid., p. 1243.

[11] Ibid., p. 1243.

[12] **J. L. Treynor** and **K. K. Mazuy,** "Can Mutual Funds Outguess the Market?" *Harvard Business Review,* July–August 1966.

[13] **Gordon J. Alexander** and **Roger Stover,** "Consistency of Mutual Fund Performance During Varying Market Conditions." *Journal of Economics and Business,* Spring 1980, p. 225.

[14] **Irwin Friend, Marshall E. Blume,** and **Jean Crockett,** *Mutual Funds and Other Institutional Investors: A New Perspective.* McGraw-Hill, New York, 1970.

TABLE 9.12
Systematic Risk and Performance

Systematic Risk			Performance Measures			
Risk Decile	Beta Range	Mean Beta	Monthly Excess Return (%)	Sharpe[a] Measure	Treynor[b] Measure	Jensen[c] Measure
10	1.22–1.46	1.24	.755	.122	.563	.128
9	1.09–1.21	1.14	.672	.130	.590	.144
8	1.02–1.07	1.04	.476	.107	.458	−.003
7	.97–1.02	.99	.454	.110	.458	−.003
6	.92– .96	.94	.458	.112	.487	.023
5	.88– .92	.90	.520	.120	.578	.103
4	.82– .87	.84	.442	.118	.526	.055
3	.73– .81	.77	.461	.128	.599	.105
2	.65– .72	.69	.291	.091	.420	−.028
1	.00– .64	.49	.213	.078	.435	−.014
Sample means		.92	.477	.112	.518	.051
Market-based portfolios				.133	.510	0

Source: John G. McDonald, "Objectives and Performance of Mutual Funds." *Journal of Financial & Quantitative Analysis,* June 1974, pp. 311–333.

[a] Reward-to-variability ratio: mean excess return dividend by the standard deviation of fund return.

[b] Reward-to-volatility ratio: mean excess return divided by beta.

[c] Alpha: estimated constant from least-squares regression of fund excess returns on market excess returns (Jensen's delta).

1. *Promotional efficiency.* Do mutual funds channel optimum savings to investors?
2. *Allocational efficiency.* Do mutual funds allocate savings to the most efficient users?
3. *Operating efficiency.* Do mutual funds perform their function at minimum cost?
4. *Freedom of choice.* Do mutual funds enhance the freedom of choice of investors in the financial markets?
5. *Equity.* Are mutual funds "fair" from a legal point of view?

The evidence reported by Friend and associates shows that because of their ability to diversify risk, mutual funds have succeeded in lowering the cost of capital to the firm and in raising the average return realized by the small investor who would have avoided the stock market because of high risk. This confirms that mutual funds have enhanced the promotional efficiency of the market.

The contribution by mutual funds to the allocational efficiency of the market has been negligible. Mutual funds were just as likely to invest in overvalued or undervalued securities as individual investors were. Furthermore, mutual funds tend to emphasize NYSE-listed stocks with large capitalizations, which does not help to inject funds into the smaller firms.

The evidence presented by Friend and associates on allocational efficiency was corroborated by J. McDonald.[15] Mutual funds can achieve a higher rate of return than the market only by assuming a higher proportional share of risk, as shown in Table 9.12.

---

[15] **John G. McDonald,** "Objectives and Performance of Mutual Funds." *Journal of Financial & Quantitative Analysis,* June 1974, pp. 311–333.

The performance of mutual funds (by type) relative to market indexes is shown in Table 9.11. Their performance is mixed.

The evidence on operational efficiency is negative. Mutual funds have not succeeded in bringing economies of scale in transactions costs. Indeed, the larger funds have had higher management and trading expenses.

Friend and colleagues argued that freedom of choice did increase as a result of the activities of mutual funds. This again is due to risk diversification and to the flexible investment programs mutual funds make available to investors—small investors in particular.

The risk diversification of portfolios and the attraction mutual funds have had for an increasing number of small investors have contributed to the equity of the market.

In summary, mutual funds have played a constructive role in the development of the financial markets in the United States and in helping investors, particularly small investors, to meet their investment needs.

9.9 REGULATION OF INVESTMENT COMPANIES

Investment companies are subject to regulations at various levels of government. The applicable laws are:

1. Individual state laws under which the investment company is formed as a business entity.
2. The "blue-sky" laws of states in which securities of investment companies domiciled in other states are being sold.
3. The Securities Act of 1933.
4. The Securities Exchange Act of 1934.
5. The Investment Company Act of 1940.
6. The Investment Company Amendments Act of 1970.

All the aforementioned laws except the Investment Company Act of 1940 and the Federal Investment Company Amendments Act of 1970 are discussed in Chapter 2. The 1970 amendment dealt with the standards for management fees and mutual fund sales charges. Shareholders of investment companies are empowered to initiate a court action if the management fee is unreasonable. In addition, this act requires that the offering price to the public shall not include "an excessive sales load" and that mutual fund shares shall not be sold at any price other than net asset value. Also, the 1970 act imposes a "fiduciary duty" on the investor advisor. A shareholder or the SEC may initiate legal action claiming "breach of fiduciary duty" under the act.

Investment Company Act of 1940

Part A of the Investment Company Act of 1940 provides for the registration of investment companies (with the SEC) and Part B, also called the Investment Advisors Act, for the regulation of investment companies and investment advisors. The act is administered by the SEC and supplements other federal and state laws. The intent of the act is to ensure maximum disclosure of information and fair treatment of the holders of investment companies' securities.

The provisions of the act include the following:

1. The definition of an investment company as a corporation or trust through which investors pool their funds under the supervision of professional management in order to diversify risk and improve returns.

2. The identification of three classes of investment companies:

    a. Face-amount certificate companies—investment companies issuing long-term (about 20 years) face-amount certificates guaranteeing a certain rate of return (3½ percent). Returns in excess of 3½ percent can be realized if the fund earns them. Only four such companies are currently active.

    b. Unit investment trusts—investment companies issuing redeemable securities each of which represents a unit of interest in a single portfolio (with specified components). The trust is managed by a trustee under a trust indenture agreement. The trust has no board of directors and does not guarantee rates of return on its portfolio. Investment banking companies are extensively involved in setting up these trusts. An example of a unit investment trust is in the tax-exempt bond fund.

    c. Management companies—the most common class of investment companies. A diversified investment company must have at least 75 percent of the value of its total assets in cash and securities, own no more than 5 percent of its total assets invested in the securities of a single issuer, and own no more than 10 percent of the voting stock of any one company. Management companies can be closed-end or open-end.

3. Restrictions on the capitalization of investment companies. The minimum capital requirement is $100,000 before any security can be issued to the public. (The minimum for a face-amount certificate company is $250,000). Open-end investment companies may issue only common stock. Closed-end investment companies may issue bonds only if the asset coverage is 300 percent. Similarly, the issue of preferred stock is restricted to half the assets (face-amount certificate companies may not issue preferred stock). Closed-end companies may issue only one class of bonds or preferred stock.

4. Membership in the board of directors is restricted as follows:

    a. No more than 60 percent of the board members can be officers or investment advisors to the company.

    b. A majority of the board must be independent from the underwriter of the company's securities, and a majority may not be officers or directors of one bank.

    c. Directors must be elected by the holders of the outstanding funds shares and two-thirds of them must be elected annually.

5. Investment advisors to the firm must be approved initially by a majority vote of the shareholders and reapproved annually thereafter by the board of directors or by a majority vote of shareholders.

It is important to note that while state and federal laws do offer protection against fraud and irresponsible actions, they in no way guarantee appreciation or a certain rate of return on investment. Investment vehicles still carry various levels of risk, which must be carefully scrutinized by the investor.

If initial approval was not given by the shareholders, the approval by the board of directors requires a majority vote by the "outside directors."

9.10 TAXATION OF INVESTMENT COMPANIES

Under the "conduit theory," mutual funds are not taxed as an entity if certain conditions are met. In order to receive the special tax treatment, a fund must be considered a regulated investment company and must meet the requirements of Subchapter M of the Internal Revenue Code. The requirements are as follows:

1. The fund must be a domestic corporation, taxable as a separate entity.
2. The fund must be registered with the SEC under the Investment Company Act of 1940. The registration must be continuous during the taxable year.
3. The fund must derive at least 90 percent of its gross income from dividends, interests, and gains from the disposition of securities.
4. The fund cannot derive more than 30 percent of its gross income from the sale of securities held for less than three months.
5. The fund must distribute at least 90 percent of its net investment income (excluding capital gains) to its shareholders.
6. The fund must have 50 percent of its assets in cash and securities at the end of each quarter of the tax year and must not have more than 5 percent of its assets invested in the securities of any one issuer or own more than 10 percent of the voting securities of that issuer.

A fund that qualifies as a regulated investment company would pay corporate income taxes only on the 10 percent or less of its income that was not distributed and pays capital gains taxes on the undistributed capital gains. The tax on the distributed income is paid by the investor; hence the conduit principle.

An investment company ordinarily sends a statement at the end of every tax year detailing the components of its distribution, that is, that portion of the distribution which is taxed as ordinary income and the other which is taxed as capital gains (or deductible as capital losses).

Whether the distributions made by an investment company are made in cash or in shares (reinvested in the fund), they are taxable to the investor in a qualified fund. If a qualified fund has already paid the tax on a distribution, the investor will not have to pay again.

When an investor decides to liquidate his or her shares in an investment company, the cost basis of the investment is calculated as follows:

$$\text{Cost basis} = \text{cost of initial investment} + \text{reinvested dividend income} + \text{capital gains accepted in shares form}$$

$$\text{Capital gains (losses)} = \text{proceeds from the sale of shares} - \text{cost basis}$$

If the shares were held for more than a year, the capital gains are taxed as long-term capital gains, otherwise as ordinary income (see Chapter 18).

Investors contemplating the purchase of mutual funds shares must carefully inspect the records of the fund in order to determine the size of unrealized gains on stocks likely to be liquidated. As soon as the liquidation takes place, investors would be faced with a tax liability which they otherwise did not anticipate.

CONCLUSIONS

Investment companies continue to prosper because they have proven their worth to the investor, the saver, and the financial planner. Investors owe it to themselves to take great care in checking the records of funds they are contemplating, regardless of management reputations. In addition, the risk profile and the objectives of the fund must match those of the investor.

QUESTIONS

1. "As interest rates subside, money market funds should experience a significant drop in assets and may, in fact, become an endangered species." Comment.

2. Discuss the major differences between closed-end and open-end investment companies.

3. "Mutual funds are primarily for the unsophisticated investor." Comment.

4. Why are there so many types of mutual funds on the market today?

5. Discuss the advantages (real or perceived) of investing in a mutual fund.

6. Discuss Jensen's method of evaluating mutual funds.

7. Why is it meaningless to evaluate the performance of mutual funds simply by looking at their rate of return? How do indexes (Sharpe, Treynor, Jensen) aid evaluation? How similar/dissimilar are these evaluation methods?

8. Explain how the inflexibility of an investment company's declared strategy (maximum capital gains, income, etc.) might restrict the company's performance.

9. "As investment company managers cannot outperform the market, it is senseless to invest in a mutual fund." Comment on this statement.

10. Why should an investor with a short time horizon avoid "load" funds?

11. Summarize the advantages of money market mutual funds. Evaluate the contention by commercial banks that these funds have enjoyed tremendous growth because of unfair competition.

12. Why is it essential that the income that investment companies earn be tax-exempt (if 90 percent of the income is distributed)? How does this reinforce the notion that these companies are merely conduits?

13. Closed-end funds have their own form of a sales charge; what is it? (Hint: How are these funds purchased?)

14. Under what conditions would the Jensen and the Treynor methods for evaluating performance give conflicting rankings of mutual funds?

15. How do mutual funds contribute to economic efficiency? How does the regulation of mutual funds enhance their contribution?

16. "Securities markets must be inefficient because investors continue to buy load funds instead of no-load funds despite the fact that there is no empirical evidence to suggest that load funds consistently outperform no-load funds." Comment.

17. What are the dangers of looking at funds' historical performances?

18. How is the net asset value per share of an investment company computed?

PROBLEMS

1. Mr. Jones puts $1,000 into a mutual fund whose load is 8 percent. How much will the fund have to increase for him to break even? He will need $2,000 in five years to pay his daughter's college tuition. On average, what percent return will the fund have to earn over the five years for him to achieve his goal? At what average rate would a no-load fund have doubled his money in the five years?

2. Three mutual funds (G, B, and I) have posted the following historical results.

Fund	Average Return	σ of Returns (Risk)
G	26%	25%
B	16%	10%
I	10%	3%

   The risk-free rate is 8 percent. Using Sharpe's index, evaluate the performance of each fund.

3. The systematic risks (betas) of the three portfolios G, B, and I (from problem 2) are known to be 1.8, 0.6, and 0.25 respectively. Given that the portfolios are sufficiently diversified, evaluate their performance using Treynor's index.

CHAPTER 10 | Debt Instruments

10.1 DEFINITION

A bond is evidence of indebtedness specifying the rights of the holder and the duties of the issuer.

10.2 TYPES OF ISSUER

Debt securities are issued by three major types of entities: (1) corporations, (2) the U.S. government, and (3) political subdivisions of the United States and nonprofit organizations.

Securities issued by these entities differ in liquidity, risk, coupon payments, size, maturity, taxability, and other features. The dominant types of bonds issued and traded will be discussed in detail in this chapter.

10.3 MARKETS FOR BONDS

Bonds are traded on the floor of organized exchanges or over the counter. Approximately 800 issues trade daily on the New York Stock Exchange, representing an average daily dollar volume of $160 million. Trading on the American Stock Exchange is much weaker. Average daily dollar volume is about $1 million for approximately 60 issues. The bulk of the bond transactions take place in the over-the-counter market. This market consists of bond dealers connected by a very sophisticated electronic network, allowing for quick price discovery and consummation of transactions.

10.4 PRICING BONDS

The market value of a bond is the discounted value of the cash flows expected from the bond. It is the present value of the coupon payments and that of the face value if the bond is held to maturity (or the selling price if the bond is sold prior to maturity). Specifically,

$$MP_0^B = \sum_{t=1}^{n} \frac{C_t}{(1+K_d)^t} + \frac{FV}{(1+K_d)^n} \tag{10.1}$$

where MP_0^B = market price of a bond at time zero

C_t = dollar value of the coupon = coupon rate $\times$ 1,000

FV = face value of the bond (usually \$1,000)

K_d = cost of debt = yield to maturity = assumed reinvestment rate

It should be obvious from Equation 10.1 that the value of the bond is also dependent on its life n and on K_d. The discount rate K_d is also the reinvestment rate; that is, as coupons are clipped and cashed in, it is assumed that they can be reinvested at K_d. This is the nature of interest compounding. The riskiness of the bond is taken as given here. Discussion on bond risk will appear in the next chapter.

Equation 10.1 assumes that coupon payments are made annually. If coupon payments were paid semiannually or m times a year, Equation 10.1 would become:

$$MP_0^B = \sum_{t=1}^{mn} \frac{C_t/m}{[1+(K_d/m)]^t} + \frac{FV}{[1+(K_d/m)]^{mn}} \tag{10.2}$$

The subscript t in C_t is dropped if all the coupons are equal in value.
An alternative formulation to bond valuation is[1]

$$MP_0^B = FV + PVDF_a \left[\frac{C}{m} - \left(\frac{K_d}{m} \right)(FV) \right] \tag{10.3}$$

where $PVDF_a$ = present value of an annuity of \$1 received every year for n years (Appendix, Table 4).

Example
Find the market value of a bond with a 5 percent semiannual coupon, a five-year life, and a \$1,000 face value. The market yield on bonds in the same risk class is 12 percent.

Answer
Using Equation 10.2:

$$MP_0^B = \sum_{t=1}^{5 \times 2} \frac{[(.05 \times 1,000)/2]}{[1+(0.12/2)]^t} + \frac{1,000}{[1+(0.12/2)]^{10}} =$$

$$MP_0^B = 25 \, PVDF_a + 1,000(PVDF)$$

$$= 25(7.360) + 1,000(0.558)$$

$$= 184 + 558 = \$742$$

where PVDF = present value of \$1 received n years from now (Appendix, Table 2).
Using Equation 10.3,

---

[1] The derivation of this equation can be found in **Sarkis J. Khoury** and **Torrence D. Parsons,** *Mathematical Methods in Finance and Economics.* Elsevier North-Holland, New York, 1981.

$$MP_0^B = 1,000 + 7.360\left[25 - \left(\frac{0.12}{2}\right)1,000\right]$$

$$= 1,000 - 258 = \$742$$

If bonds have an infinite life, the calculation of their market price becomes very easy:

$$MP_0^B = \frac{C}{K_d} \tag{10.4}$$

The derivation of this equation requires taking the limit of a geometric series. The reader is encouraged to derive Equation 10.4 from Equation 10.1.

10.5 BOND YIELDS

Three types of returns are considered when investing in a debt instrument:

1. *The coupon rate.* This rate represents the rate of return on the face value of the bond.
2. *The current yield.* This rate represents the rate of return on the actual investment (current price) of the bond.

$$CY = \frac{C}{MP_0^B}$$

3. *Yield to maturity.* This rate represents the rate of return on the face value of the bond adjusted for the amortization of the premiums (paid) or the discount (saved) on the bond at the time of purchase.

The yield to maturity can be calculated precisely using Equation 10.1, or it can be approximated. The use of Equation 10.1 requires an iterative process where various rates are plugged into the equation for K_d, given the observable market price. The process should begin with the current yield as an approximation of the yield to maturity, which is then adjusted upward or downward—upward when the bond is selling at a discount and downward when it is selling at a premium.

An approximation of the yield to maturity is provided by the following equation:[2]

$$K_d = \frac{[(FV - MP_0^B)/n] + C}{(FV + MP_0^B)/2} \tag{10.5}$$

where $(FV - MP_0^B)/n$ = periodic amortization of the premium ($MP_0^B > FV$) or the discount ($FV > MP_0^B$) on the bond

$(FV + MP_0^B)/2$ = average value of the investment in the bond

Example
Find the yield to maturity on a 10 percent coupon bond selling at a market price of $850 with a remaining life of five years.

---

[2] The approximation method becomes less reliable the higher the rates.

Answer

$$K_d = \frac{[(1,000 - 850)/5] + .10 \times 1,000}{(1,000 + 850)/2}$$

$$= \frac{[150/5] + 100}{925} = \frac{130}{925} = 14.05\%$$

This turns out to be a very good approximation of the yield to maturity, or the market yield on bonds in an equivalent risk class, or the assumed reinvestment rate for the coupon payments.

This example points out that the yield to maturity (14.05 percent) is always higher than the coupon rate (10 percent) and the current yield, 11.76 percent (100/850), when $MP_0^B < FV$. If the bond were sold at a premium, its yield to maturity would be lower than its coupon rate. Bonds selling at par ($MP_0^B = FV$) would, therefore, have a current yield equal to the yield to maturity equal to the coupon rate. If the bond is callable, the investor should calculate yield to call date instead of maturity date.

10.6 BOND DURATION

The concept of duration was introduced by Frederick Macaulay[3] in the late 1930s. Duration recognizes the fact that two bonds having the same maturity but different levels and patterns of coupon payments cannot be considered equivalent. The duration concept is best understood if one compares a pure discount (no coupon) bond with a coupon bond of the same maturity. The coupon payments allow for the realization of a portion of the expected wealth before the bond's maturity date. Hence its duration is less than its term to maturity. The pure discount bond would always have a duration equal to its term to maturity. Hence duration is always equal to or less than the term to maturity.

Duration (d), therefore, simply accounts for the difference in the cash flow streams between bonds of equivalent maturities. It is the weighted maturity of the bond. The life of the bond is weighted by some factor reflecting the size and timing of the coupon payment. The weights used by Macaulay are the present values of the coupon payments.

$$d = \frac{\sum_{t=1}^{n} t[(C_t)/(1 + K_d)^t] + [(FV \cdot n)/(1 + K_d)^n]}{\sum_{t=1}^{n} [(C_t)/(1 + K_d)^t] + [(FV)/(1 + K_d)^n]} \qquad (10.6)$$

The reader may have recognized that the denominator of Equation 10.6 represents MP_0^B as shown in Equation 10.1. Therefore,

$$d = \frac{\sum_{t=1}^{n} t[(C_t)/(1 + K_d)^t] + [(FV \cdot n)/(1 + K_d)^n]}{MP_0^B}$$

---

[3] **Frederick Macaulay,** *Some Theoretical Problems Suggested by the Movements of Interest Rates, Bond Yields, and Stock Prices in the United States Since 1938.* National Bureau of Economic Research, Columbia University Press, New York, 1956.

If the bond does not have coupons, d would equal

$$\frac{[(FV \cdot n)/(1 + K_d)^n]}{MP_0^B} = n$$

because

$$\frac{FV}{(1 + K_d)^n} = MP_0^B$$

M. Hopewell and G. Kaufman[4] showed that for a given change in the market yield, bond prices vary proportionately with duration; that is, the duration of a bond or a portfolio of bonds contains information about risk. The equation derived by Hopewell and Kaufman is

$$\frac{\partial MP_0^B}{MP_0^B} = -d(\partial K_d) \tag{10.7}$$

Therefore, for a given change in yields to maturity, say an increase of 1 percent, a bond with a duration equal to 4 would experience a higher change in its price (-4 percent) than a bond with a duration equal to 3 (-3 percent), other things being equal.

Example 1
Calculate the duration of a four-year bond with a 12 percent coupon rate payable semiannually. The bond is selling at par.

Answer
The duration is best calculated as follows:

(1) t	(2) C	(3) PVDF[a]	(4) (3)(2)	(5) (4)/1,000	(6) (5) × t
.5(6 mo.)	60	.9434	56.60	.0566	.0283
1.0(1 year)	60	.8900	53.40	.0534	.0534
1.5	60	.8396	50.38	.05038	.0756
2.0	60	.7921	47.53	.04753	.0951
2.5	60	.7473	44.84	.04484	.1121
3.0	60	.7050	42.30	.04230	.1269
3.5	60	.6651	39.91	.03991	.1397
4.0	1,060	.6274	665.04	.66504	2.6602
			1,000.00		**3.2913**

a $PVDF = \left(1 + \dfrac{K_d}{2}\right)^{-2t}$ where $K_d = 12\%$. See Appendix, Table 2.

The duration of this bond is equal to 3.2913.

---

[4] **M. Hopewell** and **G. Kaufman**, "Bond Price Volatility and Term to Maturity: A Generalized Respecification" *American Economic Review,* September, 1973.

Example 2

Calculate the duration of a five-year bond with a 10 percent coupon rate payable annually. The bond is selling for $862.68. Its yield to maturity is equal to 14 percent.

Answer

(1)	*(2)*	*(3)*	*(4)*	*(5)*	*(6)*
t	*C*	*PVDF (14%)*	*(3)(2)*	*(4)/862.68*	*(5) × t*
1	100	.8772	87.72	.1017	.1017
2	100	.7695	76.95	.0892	.1784
3	100	.6750	67.50	.0782	.2346
4	100	.5921	59.21	.0686	.2744
5	1,100	.5194	571.30	.6622	3.3110
			862.68		**4.1**

The duration of this bond is equal to 4.1.

The concept of bond duration is more powerful than that of bond maturity and is very useful in bond portfolio management, as will be shown in the next chapter in the discussion of bond immunization.

10.7 BOND PRICE THEOREMS

The bond price theorems owe their development to Burton Malkiel of Princeton Unviersity.[5] Five in all, they are most helpful in explicating bond price movements.

Theorem 1.   Bond prices are inversely related to bond yields.

This conclusion can be drawn from Equations 10.1 and 10.4. The presence of K_d in the denominator certifies the inverse relationship. More specifically, using Equation 10.4,

$$MP_0^B = \frac{C}{K_d}$$

$$\frac{\partial MP_0^B}{\partial K_d} = \frac{-C}{K_d^2}$$

Hence the inverse relationship.[6]

---

[5] **Burton G. Malkiel,** *The Term Structure of Interest Rates: Theory, Empirical Evidence, and Applications.* McCabb-Seiler, New York, 1970.

[6] The inverse relationship assumes that the coupon rate is fixed. Citicorp of New York, for example, issues floating rate notes, the rate on which is adjusted every six months to reflect higher or lower market yields. This reduces the potential for capital losses (eliminates it if the investor does not sell between the adjustment dates) but also that for capital gains. Other entities have come up with even more creative ways to reduce the size of capital loss. New York State's Municipal Assistance Corp (MAC) attached a warrant to its bonds permitting bondholders to buy an equal amount of their holdings at a later date at the same price and interest rate. If interest rates fall (bond prices rise), the investor would be able to buy additional bonds at below-market prices. Brevard County Housing Finance Authority in Florida issued 32-year bonds that could be sold back or redeemed at face value after 5 years.

Theorem 2. **Bond price changes are an increasing function of maturity *n* for any given difference between the coupon rate and the yield to maturity.**

Consider two bonds *a* and *b* of equivalent risk. Bond *a* offers a 10 percent semiannual coupon payment of $50 and matures in five years. Bond *b* offers a 10 percent semiannual coupon payment of $50 but matures in ten years. Both bonds are purchased at par. Calculate the price change in both bonds if the market yield on instruments of comparable risk increases to 11 percent.

Using Equation 10.1, one finds the following:

Bond	N	Sale Price at 11% Yield
a	5	$962.31
b	10	$940.25

The drop in the price of bond *a* is $1,000 − $962.31 = $37.69. That of bond *b* is $1,000 − $940.25 = $59.75. Different price changes are observed for the same increase in yield to maturity, 11 percent, with all other characteristics of the bonds being the same. Therefore, bond price changes are an increasing function of maturity.

Theorem 3. **The percentage change in the price of a bond increases at a diminishing rate as *n* increases.**

Consider five bonds each selling at par with a coupon rate equal to 10 percent payable semiannually. If market yields rise by 1 percent, from 10 to 11 percent, the following price changes result (using Equation 10.1.

Bond	Maturity	Price Drop	Percent Change in Price	Marginal Percent Price Change
1	5 years	37.69	3.77	3.77
2	10 years	59.75	5.98	2.21
3	15 years	72.67	7.27	1.29
4	20 years	80.33	8.03	.76
5	25 years	84.66	8.47	.44

So, the marginal percentage price changes are decreasing as *n* increases. That is, for a given maturity structure, the percentage price drop increases at a decreasing rate for a given rise in yields.

Theorem 4. **Given the maturity, the capital gains resulting from a decrease in yields are always higher than the capital losses resulting from an increase in yields.**

Using the same bonds in the previous example, we find the following:

Bond	11% Price	9% Price	11% Capital Loss	9% Capital Gain
1 yr. bond	990.77	1009.36	9.23	9.36
5 yr. bond	962.31	1039.56	37.69	39.56
10 yr. bond	940.25	1065.04	59.75	65.04
15 yr. bond	927.33	1081.44	72.67	81.44

In all cases, the capital gains resulting from a 1 percent decline in market yields is greater than the capital loss (in absolute terms) resulting from a 1 percent rise in yields.

Theorem 5. **The higher the coupon rate on a bond, the smaller the percentage price change resulting from a given change in yields.**

Compare two bonds, one with a 5 percent coupon and five years to maturity and the other with five years to maturity and a 10 percent coupon as the market yields fall from 10 to 9 percent. The bonds are otherwise equal. The coupon is paid semiannually. The original price (at 10 percent market yield) using Equation 10.1, is

5% bond = $806.96

10% bond = $1,000.00

New price at 9% market yield:

5% bond = $841.75

10% bond = $1,039.56

The price changes are as follows: for the 5 percent bond $841.75 − $806.96 = $34.79, or an increase of 4.31 percent, and for the 10 percent bond $1,039.56 − $1,000 = $39.56, or 3.96 percent.

So the bond with a higher coupon experiences a price change that is smaller in percentage terms (larger in absolute dollars) than the bond with the lower coupon.

Using these and other bonds with different coupons, we can develop the following table:

Bond Coupon Rate (percent)	Price at 10%	New Price at 9% Yield	Price Change	Percent Price Change
5	$ 806.96	$ 841.75	$34.79	4.31
7	884.17	920.87	36.70	4.15
10	1,000.00	1,039.56	39.56	3.96
12	1,077.22	1,118.69	41.47	3.85
15	1,193.04	1,237.38	44.34	3.58

The implications to the investor are quite clear. An aggressive investor would speculate using low-coupon bonds because their price fluctuations, in percentage terms, are larger than those of bonds carrying higher coupons.

We now look at various types of corporate, government, and municipal securities.

10.8 CORPORATE DEBT SECURITIES

Corporations issue debt instruments to finance investment projects. Debt issues reduce the cost of financing and improve the rate of return on equity capital when leverage is operating in the intended direction. The tax deductibility of interest expenses is the primary factor for the advantageous position debt occupies in relation to equity.

Corporate debt securities are issued by manufacturing, commercial, transportation, public utility, communication, real estate, and financial entities. The size of new corporate debt issues was $53.2 billion in 1980 (Table 10.1) and averaged about $40 billion in each of the preceding three years.

Corporate debt securities are sold through a public distribution in the primary market or through direct placement. In a public distribution, the underwriter typically buys

TABLE 10.1
New Security Issues of Corporations
(Millions of Dollars)

Type of Issue or Issuer or Use	1978	1979	1980	1981 Jan.	Feb.	Mar.	Apr.	May	June	July
1 **All issues**[a]	**47,230**	**51,533**	**73,688**	**5,581**	**4,157**	**6,423**	**6,835**	**5,457**	**9,536**	**4,013**
2 **Bonds**	**36,872**	**40,208**	**53,199**	**3,386**	**2,834**	**4,275**	**4,597**	**3,080**	**5,601**	**2,256**
Type of offering										
3 Public	19,815	25,814	41,587	2,928	2,408	3,778	3,668	2,520	4,603	1,925
4 Private placement	17,057	14,394	11,612	458	426	497	929	560	998	331
Industry group										
5 Manufacturing	9,572	9,678	15,409	1,635	1,140	1,064	1,459	1,269	1,313	497
6 Commercial and miscellaneous	5,246	3,948	6,688	231	356	212	342	138	566	206
7 Transportation	2,007	3,119	3,329	353	45	172	142	49	584	131
8 Public utility	7,092	8,153	9,556	800	593	594	904	1,063	996	383
9 Communication	3,373	4,219	6,683	62	272	958	554	56	470	767
10 Real estate and financial	9,586	11,094	11,534	306	430	1,276	1,197	506	1,672	273
11 **Stocks**	**10,358**	**11,325**	**20,490**	**2,195**	**1,323**	**2,148**	**2,238**	**2,377**	**3,935**	**1,757**
Type										
12 Preferred	2,832	3,574	3,632	364	149	298	85	164	188	67
13 Common	7,526	7,751	16,858	1,831	1,174	1,850	2,153	2,213	3,747	1,690
Industry group										
14 Manufacturing	1,241	1,679	4,839	609	204	735	531	903	382	335
15 Commercial and miscellaneous	1,816	2,623	5,245	603	589	816	477	958	1,024	437
16 Transportation	263	255	549	124	81	17	146	47	18	29
17 Public utility	5,140	5,171	6,230	562	260	414	717	173	843	308
18 Communication	264	303	567	14	31		56		1,036	73
19 Real estate and financial	1,631	12,931	3,059	284	159	167	310	296	632	574

Source: Federal Reserve Bulletin, October 1981, p. A36.

[a] Figures, which represent gross proceeds of issues maturing in more than one year, sold for cash in the United States, are principal amount or number of units multiplied by offering price. Excludes offerings of less than $100,000, secondary offerings, undefined or exempted issues as defined in the Securities Act of 1933, employee stock plans, investment companies other than closed-end, intracorporate transactions, and sales to foreigners.

the bond issue for resale to institutions or individual investors. This form of disposal accounted for 78 percent of new issues in 1980. Direct or private placement, on the other hand, avoids the details of public offerings and allows for greater flexibility in structuring the terms of the issue and for earlier access to the funds. The issuer in this case sells the bonds to institutions, mostly life insurance companies. Investment bankers, if they play any role, would act as brokers for the transaction. Direct placement is the domain of industrial bonds, because railroad and utility bonds must be sold under competitive bidding. Of the $53.2 billion in new bond issues in 1980, 22 percent were sold through direct placement.

Types of Corporate Bonds

There are various types of corporate bonds, among them the following:

1. *Mortgage bonds.* Mortgage bonds are debt instruments secured by real property (land and buildings).
2. *Debenture bonds.* Debenture bonds are securities backed by the creditworthiness of the issuing corporation and by any asset not otherwise pledged by the issuing corporation. In the event of liquidation, the holders of debenture bonds are placed ahead of holders of common and preferred stocks.
3. *Subordinated debentures.* Subordinated debentures are unsecured debt instruments that rank behind bank loans and regular debentures but ahead of common and preferred stock.
4. *Income bond.* An income bond is an unsecured debt instrument that pays interest only if it is earned. These bonds typically arise from corporate reorganization.
5. *Collateral trust bond.* A collateral trust bond is a debt instrument generally backed by securities pledged to the trustee, who is empowered to liquidate them in the event of default.
6. *Equipment trust certificate.* Equipment trust certificates are secured debt instruments typically issued by railroads to finance their rolling stock.
7. *Convertible bonds.* Convertible bonds are debt instruments that are convertible into common stock under specified terms. We shall discuss these bonds in great detail later in the chapter.

Bond Features

All the important facts dealing with the rights of the holder and the obligations of the bond issuer are contained in the indenture agreement. Every detail relating to the bond issue is contained in this agreement. Among these details are the following:

1. The callability of the bond. A callable bond is one that can be called away from the holder by the issuing corporation at a specified price after a certain period of time. The call price is higher than par value by a sum referred to as the *call premium.*
2. The coupon rate.
3. The frequency of the coupon payments.

Some indenture agreements require that the issuer maintain a sinking fund to facilitate the retirement of the bond issue. Under this provision the firm may buy and retire a certain percentage of its outstanding bonds on an annual basis.

We now look at other corporation-issued financial instruments that occupy prominent positions in many portfolios.

Bankers' Acceptances

To understand bankers' acceptances requires some knowledge of the financing of international trade. Bankers' acceptances typically arise from international trade.

Start with a U.S. importing firm that wishes to assure the exporter of the quality of its credit. The importer asks its bank to issue a letter of credit as evidence of availability of funds to pay for the imports. The letter of credit represents a payment guarantee by the bank if certain specific conditions are met. It effectively substitutes the bank's credit for that of the importer. The exporting firm receives payment from its local bank by drawing a draft against the letter of credit and discounting it at its local bank. To receive payment, the exporter must present appropriate documents as indicated in the letter of credit (e.g., bill of lading, invoice, insurance form, etc.). The exporter's bank forwards the discounted draft to its correspondent bank in the United States which, in turn, presents it to the bank that issued the letter of credit. The "acceptance" of the draft by the latter is what is referred to as a *bankers' acceptance.*

The accepting bank may purchase the acceptance. In this case, its position is equivalent to that of extending an outright loan to the importer. The practice of accepting banks is not to purchase their own acceptances but rather to buy the acceptances of other banks. These have much higher liquidity because they bear three signatures—that of the exporter, that of the bank that discounted the draft, and that of the accepting bank. Accepting banks ordinarily trade their own acceptances for those of other banks in order to improve the marketability of their portfolios.

Bankers' acceptances range in maturity from 30 to 180 days, with 90 days maturity being the most common.

The market for bankers' acceptances is made up primarily of foreign banks and financial institutions (the most active being the Federal Reserve banks, particularly in New York; large banks and non-bank dealers; and other private investors).

The Federal Reserve banks participate in the acceptance market by purchasing or discounting acceptances. Their participation is limited to "eligible" acceptances—maturities of not more than six months for discounting and nine months for purchasing. Acceptances arising from letters of credit are almost always eligible. Non-bank dealer participation in the acceptance market is summarized in the activity of 10 to 15 dealers in New York City. Their trades are done on a negotiated basis, with dealers' profits resulting from the spread between the buy and sell prices.

The size and the ownership distribution of bankers' dollar acceptances are shown in Table 10.2. The growth of this financial instrument has been very impressive. Outstanding dollar bankers' acceptances increased by 154 percent between December 1977 and August 1981, with others (primarily foreign financial institutions) leading the way. At the end of August 1981, there was $64.6 billion in bankers' dollar acceptances outstanding. Foreign financial institutions are attracted by the quality, liquidity, breadth, and depth of the market for bankers' acceptances.

Commercial Paper

A commercial paper is an unsecured note issued by a business to dealers, institutional investors, and other businesses in return for funds.

TABLE 10.2
Commercial Paper and Bankers' Dollar Acceptances Outstanding
(Millions of Dollars, End of Period)

Instrument	1977 Dec.	1978 Dec.	1979[a] Dec.	1980 Dec.	1981						
					Feb.	Mar.	Apr.	May	June	July	Aug.
				Commercial Paper (Seasonally Adjusted)							
1 All issuers	65,051	83,438	112,154	123,703	128,252	130,548	132,052	139,224	145,652	150,945	157,081
Financial companies[b]											
Dealer-placed paper[c]											
2 Total	8,796	12,181	16,722	18,186	18,805	20,489	22,029	22,819	24,442	24,497	26,370
3 Bank-related	2,132	3,521	2,874	3,561	3,742	4,163	4,437	4,800	4,750	5,267	6,037
Directly placed paper[d]											
4 Total	40,574	51,647	64,748	67,888	68,936	69,461	69,537	71,842	74,952	79,571	80,769
5 Bank-related	7,102	12,314	17,598	22,382	22,331	21,604	22,858	23,880	24,107	26,104	25,153
6 Nonfinancial companies[e]	15,681	19,610	30,684	37,629	40,511	40,598	40,486	44,563	46,258	46,877	49,942

Bankers' Dollar Acceptances (Not Seasonally Adjusted)

7 Total	25,450	33,700	45,321	54,744	58,084	60,089	62,320	60,551	63,427	63,721	64,577
Holder											
8 Accepting banks	10,434	8,579	9,865	10,564	9,911	10,117	10,781	10,132	11,595	10,505	9,959
9 Own bills	8,915	7,653	8,327	8,963	8,770	8,735	9,626	9,049	10,207	9,437	9,214
10 Bills bought	1,519	927	1,538	1,601	1,141	1,382	1,155	1,082	1,389	1,068	745
Federal Reserve banks											
11 Own account	954	1	704	776	0	298	0	0	0	453	0
12 Foreign correspondents	362	664	1,382	1,791	1,399	1,372	1,383	1,255	1,272	1,459	1,451
13 Others	13,700	24,456	33,370	41,614	46,779	48,303	50,156	49,164	50,560	51,303	53,167
Basis											
14 Imports into United States	6,378	8,574	10,270	11,776	12,976	13,292	13,634	12,775	12,996	13,059	13,313
15 Exports from United States	5,863	7,586	9,640	12,712	12,979	13,451	13,368	13,057	13,388	13,296	13,774
16 All other	13,209	17,540	25,411	30,257	32,129	33,347	35,319	34,768	37,043	37,365	37,490

Source: *Federal Reserve Bulletin*, October 1981, p. A25.

[a] A change in reporting instructions results in offsetting shifts in the dealer-placed and directly placed financial company paper in October 1979.

[b] Institutions engaged primarily in activities such as, but not limited to, commercial, savings, and mortgage banking; sales, personal, and mortgage financing; factoring, finance leasing, and other business lending; insurance underwriting; and other investment activities.

[c] Includes all financial company paper sold by dealers in the open market.

[d] As reported by financial companies that place their paper directly with investors.

[e] Includes public utilities and firms engaged primarily in such activities as communications, construction, manufacturing, mining, wholesale and retail trade, transportation, and services.

Commercial papers are issued by large corporations with good credit standing, are denominated in multiples of $1,000, and have maturities ranging from 30 to 270 days. Commercial papers are sold at a discount.

Rates on commercial papers parallel T-bill rates and are generally below the prime rate, making them more desirable than bank credit (see Fig. 10.1).

The majority of commercial papers are "directly placed"; that is, the issuer sells the commercial paper directly to the lender. Directly placed paper has a secondary market, since the lender may resell the paper to a bank or dealer to receive funds. The remainder of the commercial paper market consists of "dealer paper," which is sold by the issuer to a dealer who, in turn, resells it in the market. There is no secondary market for this type of paper.

The commercial paper market is very large. By the end of August 1981, there was $157,081 million in commercial papers outstanding, with approximately half this total in directly placed paper (financial companies placing their paper directly with investors). See Table 10.2.

Certificates of Deposits

A certificate of deposit (CD) is a time deposit evidenced by a negotiable or nonnegotiable receipt. The full interest on a CD is realized if it is held to maturity. Early redemption of a CD is subject to substantial penalties.

Since 1961, security dealers have provided a secondary market for negotiable CDs.

FIGURE 10.1   Short-term interest rates—business borrowing (prime rate, effective date of change; prime paper, quarterly averages).

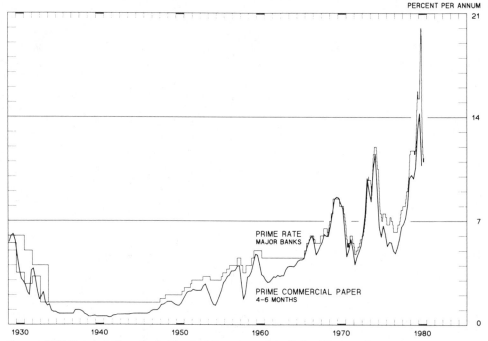

Source: 1980 Historical Chart Book. Board of Governors of the Federal Reserve System.

This increased their liquidity and hence their popularity with investors. Negotiable CDs are issued by banks to corporations, pension funds, and other large investors in $100,000 or $1 million denominations.

Negotiable CDs are issued in bearer form (not registered) and command yields that are similar (a bit higher) to those on T-bills. By Oct. 28, 1981, negotiable CDs issued by large weekly reporting commercial banks amounted to $123,300 million.

Federal Funds

The market for federal funds arises directly from the reserve requirements imposed on deposits in financial institutions. These funds are on deposit with Federal Reserve banks and do not earn interest. Commercial banks with insufficient reserves must borrow from those with surplus reserves and from other sources in order to meet their reserve requirements. Federal funds include " 'real' or one-day federal funds, repurchase agreements, term federal funds, and other forms of borrowing nonreservable immediately available funds."[7]

The sources of federal funds, as determined by a survey conducted by the Federal Reserve System in 1974, are summarized in Table 10.3. The interbank federal funds lending takes place because banks with excess reserves wish to transform idle funds into income-generating assets. The denominations in this market are generally multiples of $1 million. Smaller denominations are becoming increasingly common as smaller banks enter the market.

The manner in which the transaction is effected depends on many factors. If the banks belong to the same Federal Reserve District, the lending bank instructs the Federal Reserve Bank to transfer funds from its account to that of the borrowing bank. The following day the process is reversed.

The decision to borrow federal funds depends on the cost of alternative sources of funds. Banks with reserve deficiencies can alternatively raise funds by selling securities, calling a loan with a government securities dealer, raising dealer loan rates to discourage borrowing, or, if they are members of the Federal Reserve System, using the discount window (borrowing from the Federal Reserve bank).

On Sept. 30, 1981, one-day and continuing contract federal funds and repurchase agreements borrowed by commercial banks in the United States amounted to $45,275 million (Table 10.4).

Federal funds rates, which are very highly correlated with T-bill rates (Fig. 10.2), are good indicators of the level and direction of interest rates for the short run. Their level represents the pressures in the market for bank reserves, which ultimately determine the extent to which banking institutions can accommodate the financial needs of business institutions.

Considering the high levels of substitution and sometimes complementarity between federal funds and repurchase agreements, a brief discussion of repurchase agreements is warranted.

Repurchase agreements (or simply RPs) are contractual arrangements whereby a holder of securities sells them to a lender who, in turn, agrees to sell the securities back to the same party at the same price. For this the lender charges a fee—interest.

[7] **Jimmie R. Monhollon,** *Federal Funds in Instruments of the Money Market.* Federal Reserve Bank of Richmond, Va., 1979, p. 38.

TABLE 10.3

Gross Borrowings of Immediately Available Funds, Daily Average for Week Ending April 24, 1974—

45 Large Banks (Amounts in Billions of Dollars)

Borrowed from	Regular Federal Funds[a]	RP's on U.S. Gov't. and Agency Securities	Total	Amount Maturing in One Day[b]
I. Lenders from whom member banks may borrow "regular" federal funds	(1)	(2)	(3)	(4)
1. Member commercial banks	13.1	1.0	14.1	12.8
2. Nonmember commercial banks	3.9	.5	4.4	4.2
3. Domestic offices of foreign banks	3.2	*	3.2	2.4
4. Edge Act and Agreement Corp.	.1	*	.1	.1
Commercial bank subtotal	20.3	1.5	21.8	19.5
5. Savings and loan associations and cooperative banks	2.9	*	2.9	2.3
6. Savings banks	1.6	*	1.6	1.6
7. Federal Home Loan Banks and Board	1.2	*	1.2	.7
8. All other agencies of the U.S.	.5	.2	.7	.4
9. Securities dealers	c	.9	1.0	.2
Total	26.5	2.6	29.2	24.7
II. Lenders from whom member banks may not borrow "regular" federal funds				
1. Business corporations	—	2.1	2.1	1.2
2. State and local governments	—	3.0	3.0	1.4
3. Foreign banks and foreign official institutions	—	.6	.6	.5
4. All other	—	.2	.2	.1
Total	—	5.9	5.9	3.2
Grand total	26.5	8.7	35.3	27.9
MEMO: Noncommercial bank subtotal	6.2	7.2	13.5	8.4

Note: Totals may not add due to rounding.

Source: Board of Governors of the Federal Reserve System.

[a] May be secured or unsecured.

[b] Includes continuing contracts which have no maturity but can be terminated without advance notice by the lender or the borrower.

[c] * Less than $500 million.

This arrangement is similar to a bank loan, with the securities used as collateral. The maturity is usually a day, although it can be as much as 30 days or even indefinite.

The Federal Reserve System ("the Fed") enters into repurchase agreements with nonbank dealers in U.S. government securities. By buying the securities, the Fed is adding to the reserves of the banking system, for it credits the accounts of the sellers' banks and thus increases their reserves. This addition is temporary, for the agreements

TABLE 10.4
Federal Funds and Repurchase Agreements—Large Member Banks[a]
(Averages of Daily Figures, in Millions of Dollars)

By Maturity and Source	1981, Week Ending Wednesday								
	Aug. 5	Aug. 12	Aug. 19	Aug. 26	Sept. 2	Sept. 9	Sept. 16	Sept. 23	Sept. 30
One day and continuing contract									
1 Commercial banks in United States	47,895	51,567	47,237	45,287	47,564	53,070	54,730	47,157	45,275
2 Other depository institutions, foreign banks and foreign official institutions, and U.S. government agencies	15,092	15,522	16,048	15,841	15,414	15,234	16,375	16,742	16,890
3 Nonbank securities dealers	2,767	2,629	3,081	3,143	2,879	2,325	3,050	3,441	3,125
4 All other	20,888	20,998	20,224	21,365	21,194	20,431	20,564	19,693	19,107
All other maturities									
5 Commercial banks in United States	3,592	3,283	3,233	3,275	3,281	3,106	3,019	3,237	3,397
6 Other depository institutions, foreign banks and foreign official institutions, and U.S. government agencies	7,212	6,721	7,111	6,865	6,860	7,283	7,107	7,708	7,191
7 Nonbank securities dealers	4,887	4,479	4,573	4,328	4,485	4,470	3,987	4,216	4,676
8 All other	9,854	9,908	9,596	9,501	9,351	9,526	9,854	9,898	10,188
MEMO: Federal funds and resale agreement loans in maturities of one day or continuing contract									
9 Commercial banks in United States	16,389	15,347	16,247	14,111	16,550	17,103	19,335	16,151	17,432
10 Nonbank securities dealers	2,534	2,819	2,679	2,408	2,623	2,883	3,001	2,740	2,919

Source: Federal Reserve Bulletin, October 1981, p. A6.

[a] Banks with assets of $1 billion or more as of Dec. 31, 1977.

FIGURE 10.2 Short-term interest rates—money market (discount rate, effective date of change; all others quarterly averages).

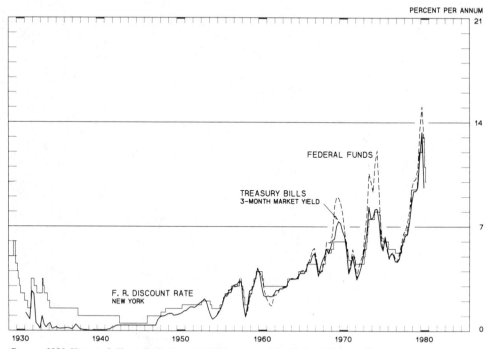

Source: 1980 Historical Chart Book. Board of Governors of the Federal Reserve System.

have a typical life of a single day with maximum maturity of 15 days. When a reduction in the level of bank reserves is desired, the Fed enters into a reverse repurchase agreement (the Fed is the original seller of securities), also known as a matched sale-purchase transaction, with a bank or with nonbank securities dealers.

Similarly, banks enter into RPs or reverse RPs with their clients or with securities dealers in order to utilize idle cash or generate reserves. In this case, the increase (decrease) in reserves is a decision for the bank to make. Total bank reserves for the banking system as a whole do not increase as a result of the initiative of the bank. New York banks typically use RPs to adjust actual reserves to desired reserve levels. RP transactions entered into by the Fed, however, increase or decrease the reserves of the banking system as a whole.

10.9 CONVERTIBLE BONDS

Convertible bonds are debt instruments that can be converted into equity securities at the option of the holder during a specified period of time. They are usually debenture bonds with no collateral pledged by the issuing corporation.

Elements of Convertible Bonds

A convertible bond represents a combination of a straight bond (nonconvertible) and a warrant, a long-term option to purchase common stock from the issuing corporation under specified terms.

An understanding of convertible bonds requires a knowledge of the following:

1. *Investment value* IV is the price at which a convertible bond would have to sell in order to provide a yield equivalent to that of a nonconvertible bond of equal maturity and risk. If the bond were to sell for this price, the value of the conversion privilege would be zero. Investment value represents a support level, a cushion in the event of excessive decline in the price of the common stock, assuming no accompanying changes in the bond risk.

2. *Conversion ratio N* is the number of shares to which a bond can be converted. This number is stated in the indenture agreement.

3. *Conversion price* CP is the reciprocal of the conversion ratio multiplied by face value (FV). It is equal to $1,000/N$.

4. *Conversion value* CV is the market value of the bond if conversion takes place. It equals the conversion ratio multiplied by the market value of the common stock:

$$CV = N \cdot MP^S$$

where MP^S = market price per common stock.

5. *Premium over conversion value* PC is the percentage difference between the conversion value and the market price of the convertible bond MP: $PC = (MP^B - CV)/CV$.

6. *Premium over investment value* is the percentage difference between the investment value and the market price of the convertible bond: $PI = (MP^B - IV)/IV$. PI measures the worth of the conversion privilege and concurrently the proportion of the market value of the convertible bond subject to risk resulting from the fluctuation in the price of the common stock.

7. *Price of latent warrant* represents the value of the conversion privilege per warrant— that is, per each share to which the bond can be converted: W = price per warrant = $(MP^B - IV)/N$ (or number of latent warrants).

Example

The JAK Corporation issued an 8 percent coupon bond at par convertible into 20 shares of common stock. The stock is currently trading at $40. Calculate the values of the relevant variables listed above, assuming the values shown in the first two rows of Table 10.5.

For the yield on this convertible bond to equal to the market yield 10.00% on a straight bond, the price must be $800: $80/$800 = 10.00\%$. This, however, assumes that the bond has an indefinite life. If, on the other hand, the bond had ten years to go before it matured, the market price (of a straight bond) should be determined using the following equation:

$$MP^B_0 = \sum_{t=1}^{10} \frac{C}{(1 + K_d)^t} + \frac{FV}{(1 + K_d)^{10}}$$

where C = value of coupon

K_d = yield to maturity = 10%

FV = face value of bond = $1,000

$$MP^B_0 = \sum_{t=1}^{10} \frac{80}{(1 + .1000)^t} + \frac{1,000}{(1 + .1000)^{10}}$$

$$= 80 \, (PVDF_a) + 1,000 \, (PVDF)$$

$$MP^B_0 = 80(6.145) + 1,000(0.386) = 878$$

TABLE 10.5
Relevant Data on a Convertible Bond

Variable Name	Symbol	Values at Time of Purchase	Values if Stock Price Appreciates by 25%	Values if Stock Price Appreciates by 87.5%	Values if Stock Price Drops by 50%
Market price of bond	MP^B	$1,000	$1,200 (an assumed value)	$1,500 (an assumed value)	$878
Current yield	C/MP^B	$\dfrac{8\% \times 1,000}{1,000} = 8\%$	$\dfrac{8\% \times 1,000}{1,200} = 6.66\%$	$\dfrac{8\% \times 1,000}{1,500} = 5.33\%$	$\dfrac{8\% \times 1,000}{878} = 9.11\%$
Conversion ratio	N	20	20	20	20
Conversion price	CP	$\dfrac{1,000}{20} = 50$	$\dfrac{1,000}{20} = 50$	$\dfrac{1,000}{20} = 50$	$\dfrac{1,000}{20} = 50$
Market price of stock	P	$40	$50	$75	$20
Conversion value	CV	$40 × 20 = $800	$50 × 20 = $1,000	$75 × 20 = $1,500	$20 × 20 = $400
Premium over conversion value	PC	$\dfrac{1,000 - 800}{800} = 25\%$	$\dfrac{1,200 - 1,000}{1,000} = 20\%$	$\dfrac{1,500 - 1,500}{1,500} = 0\%$	$\dfrac{878 - 400}{400} = 94.5\%$
Investment value	IV	878	878	878	878
Premium over investment value	PI	$\dfrac{1,000 - 878}{878} = 13.9\%$	$\dfrac{1,200 - 878}{878} = 36.7\%$	$\dfrac{1,500 - 878}{878} = 70.8\%$	$\dfrac{878 - 878}{878} = 0\%$
Price per warrant	W	$\dfrac{1,000 - 878}{20} = \$6.1$	$\dfrac{1,200 - 878}{20} = \$16.1$	$\dfrac{1,500 - 878}{20} = \$31.1$	0 (The price never actually drops this low unless the bond is approaching maturity.)

We observe from Table 10.5 that the premium over conversion value moves in the opposite direction as premium over investment value. As the premium over conversion value PC shrinks toward zero, the convertible bond would behave (at zero) exactly like a common stock. Conversely, as PC rises, the convertible bond would approach its investment value and its behavior would correspond exactly, when PI = 0%, to that of a straight bond.

A conservative investor would, therefore, choose a convertible bond with a higher PC and a low PI, because the behavior of the bond under these conditions is less dependent on the behavior of the stock. An aggressive investor would choose a convertible bond with a low PC and a higher PI because its price more closely follows that of the common stock.

The following observations are also worth making:

1. The percentage increase in the market price of the bond lags behind that of the stock. The reasons for this and the extent of the lag will be explained below.

For a 25 percent increase in the price of the stock, the premium over conversion value dropped by only 5 percent. For an additional 62.5 percent increase in the price of the stock, $87.5 - 25\%$, PC dropped by 20 percent or a ratio of $20/62.5 = 0.32$, as compared with an earlier ratio of $5/25 = 0.2$. This simply indicates that the faster the price of the stock rises, the more quickly the behavior of the bond corresponds to that of the stock until the one-to-one correspondence is achieved. Again, aggressive investors would be most interested in convertible bonds with low PC because they offer higher appreciation potential.

2. The lower the premium over conversion value, the lower the yield.

3. The investment value represents a cushion of considerable importance in a bear market. When the market price of the bond is equal to its investment value, the convertible bond behaves exactly like a straight bond and its price is then determined by market rates of interest, supply and demand, and the financial position of the issuing company.

Our discussion, thus far can be summarized diagramatically as shown in Figure 10.3 (assuming $MP^B < FV$).

The heavy line from **IV** through *S* to CV' represents the minimum market price of the bond. The bond cannot sell below its conversion value, otherwise investors would buy bonds, convert them immediately, and sell the stocks in the market. The conversion value curve CV to CV' is sloped as such because of the assumed constant geometric growth rate in the price of the underlying stock, $P_t = P_0 (1 + g)^t$. This obviously excludes the 50 percent decline in the price of the stock discussed in Table 10.5.

The curve from MP^B to $MP^{B'}$ represents the bond market value curve over a portion of the bond's life. This value is higher than the conversion value curve, initially because of the protection convertible bonds provide (in a bear market) through their investment value. The difference between MP^B and CV represents the value of the "safety net" that convertible bonds provide. This protection diminishes in significance as the price of the stock rises in value.

At $t = 5$, in this particular case, the market value of the bond is equal to its conversion value (premium over conversion value is equal to zero) and the bond is equivalent to holding 20 shares of the underlying security. The investment value of the bond is shown in Figure 10.3 to converge linearly to the face value of the bond as the maturity date of the bond approaches.

FIGURE 10.3   Relationships among the various values of a convertible bond.
MP^B = market price of a convertible bond; IV = investment value of a convertible bond; CV = conversion value of a convertible bond.

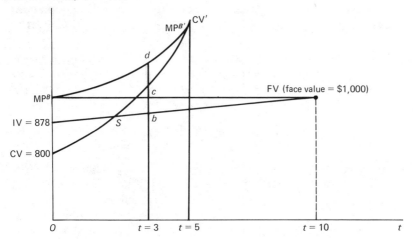

Determinants of the Market Price of a Convertible Bond

The pricing of a convertible bond is considerably more involved than that of a straight bond. The complications result from the unpredictability of future stock prices (and consequently the conversion value) and from the relationship between the conversion value and the investment value. If the convertible bond is callable, the pricing mechanism is complicated further. The mathematical development of a pricing model appears in the appendix of this chapter.

The problem in pricing convertible bonds results primarily from the asymmetric effects on the convertible bond price when different conditions hold. This asymmetry can best be understood through a reexamination of Figure 10.3. The market price of the bond equals or exceeds the investment value because of the equity aspect of the convertible bond—that is, because of the price appreciation potential the convertible bond offers. This is observed at $t = 0$, where $MP^B > IV > CV$. The difference $MP^B - IV$ represents the value of the conversion privilege. Beyond point S, the market price MP^B of the convertible bond would exceed the conversion value. At $t = 3$, the difference $MP^B - CV$ is equal to cd and represents the value of the safety net provided by the investment value. This safety factor is nonexistent if the convertible bond is replaced by an equivalent number of common stocks; it becomes meaningless when the conversion premium equals zero. A stock position could theoretically fall to zero, but an equivalent convertible bond position would fall to the investment value. It is important to note, however, that the investment value is not constant. It is affected by changes in market yields and in the riskiness of the firm. A falling stock price is generally reflective of a deteriorating position within the firm. This increases the risk of default and of bankruptcy. As this risk increases, the investment value falls. The safety net is not as strong as it may appear to be.

J. Walter and A. Que[8] attempted to improve on the conventional model developed

---

[8] **James E. Walter** and **Augustin V. Que,** "The Valuation of Convertible Bonds." *Journal of Finance,* vol. 28 (June 1973), pp. 713–733.

in the appendix by using the Monte Carlo simulation to forecast rates of return on convertible bonds conditional upon "the simulated behavior of the underlying stock." Their conclusion was that

> *Behavioral input derived for the simulation model attested to the powerful influence of the relationship between conversion values and straight bond values upon convertible bond premiums and to the asymmetry of premiums, depending on whether conversion values or straight bond values dominated.* [9]

If the range of expectations about the course of future stock prices is restricted to certain dimensions and if discrete time intervals are used, the calculation of market value will be considerably simpler.

An investor expecting the conversion value of the bond always to exceed its investment value and the stock price to grow at a constant rate g, would calculate the market price of a bond as follows:

$$\text{MP}^B = \sum_{t=1}^{n} \frac{C}{(1 + K_c)^t} + \frac{\text{MP}_0^S(1 + g)^n \cdot N}{(1 + K_c)^n} \tag{10.8}$$

where $n =$ length of holding period

$\text{MP}_0^S =$ market price of stock at time of purchase

$C =$ value of coupon = coupon rate $\times$ \$1,000

$K_c =$ cost of capital of the firm

$\quad = W_d K_d + W_e K_e$

$W_d, W_e =$ the weights of long-term debt and equity in the capital structure, respectively.

$K_d, K_e =$ cost of debt and equity, respectively

$N =$ number of shares to which the bond can be converted

The deficiencies of this method should be obvious, we hope. However, it is very useful and easy to use.

Features of Convertible Bonds

Convertible bonds are characterized by the following:

1. Fixed income set by the size of the coupon rate.
2. Appreciation possibilities resulting from increases in the price of the underlying stock and from a decline in interest rates.
3. Maximum downside risk defined by the investment value of the bond.
4. Generally lower commission costs than those incurred on an equal-size investment in the underlying stock.
5. Generally higher yields than those on common stock.

---

[9] **Walter** and **Que,** p. 730.

6. Dividend on common stock is earned only if the investor is holder of record when dividends are paid. The interest on convertible bonds, on the other hand, accrues from the day of purchase.

Investors holding convertible bonds must be alert to changes in the conversion privilege (e.g., different conversion price) and to the expiration date of this privilege. Also of great importance is the call date if the convertible bonds held are callable.

10.10 U. S. GOVERNMENT SECURITIES

We shall examine here those U.S. government and U.S. agency securities with substantial investor participation.

Treasury Bills

Treasury bills (T-bills) are short-term obligations of the U.S. government. They do not carry a coupon and are sold at a discount from par value under competitive and noncompetitive bidding. They generally are not redeemable before maturity.

Features

Income on T-bills is calculated as the difference between the purchase price and the sale price. Two rates are of concern to T-bill holders, the discount rate and investment yield or coupon equivalent.

The Discount Rate. This is based on a 360-day period and on the face value of the bill.

$$\text{Discount rate} = \frac{\text{face value} - \text{actual issue price}}{\text{face value}} \times \frac{360}{\text{days to maturity}} \qquad (10.9)$$

Example
A T-bill selling at 97 and maturing in 90 days would have a discount rate of

$$\text{DR} = \frac{100 - 97}{100} \times \frac{360}{90} = \textbf{12\%}$$

Investment Yield or Coupon Equivalent. This yield allows the investor to compare the yield on a T-bill with that on a coupon-bearing financial instrument. It is calculated using the initial purchase price of the bill and 365 days to maturity. It is expected, therefore, to be larger than the discount rate.

$$\frac{\text{Investment}}{\text{yield}} = \frac{\text{face value} - \text{actual issue price}}{\text{actual issue price}} \times \frac{365}{\text{days to maturity}} \qquad (10.10)$$

Example

Using the same example as above, the investment yield would be

$$IY = \frac{100 - 97}{97} \times \frac{365}{90} = \mathbf{12.54\%}$$

T-bills are issued with maturities of 13 weeks, 26 weeks, and 52 weeks and are sold in minimum amounts of $10,000 and in multiples of $5,000 over this minimum. Investors in T-bills do not receive certificates from the treasury; instead, their ownership is recorded as a book entry at the treasury. This reduces the issuance costs to the treasury as well as the probability of theft, loss, or counterfeit.

Competitive bids are submitted to the treasury on the basis of a 100 price with not more than three decimals (98.753) using a tender (a special form used for submitting a bid; see Fig. 10.4). Noncompetitive bidders do not specify the price in their bid. They simply agree to purchase a certain number of T-bills at the weighted average price of accepted competitive bids. An investor may submit only one noncompetitive bid for a maximum of $500,000. All competitive tenders for a T-bill issue must be made before 1:30 P.M. of the deadline day.

Offering Schedule

The offering schedule for T-bills depends on the maturity period; 13-week and 26-week maturities are offered every week. The offering is announced on Tuesday, the bills are auctioned the following Monday, and the bills are issued (recorded) on the Thursday after the auction. The 52-week maturity is offered every four weeks. The offering is announced every fourth Thursday, the auction takes place the following Wednesday, and the bills are recorded (issued) the following Tuesday.

Settlement of Treasury Bills

Bidders for T-bill issues must have a check (certified if a personal check), cash, or T-bills maturing on or before the issue date of the new T-bill series accompanying their bids. The amount should equal the face value of the bills. The difference between the face value and the eventual issue price will be refunded the bidder. Owners of maturing T-bills may elect to receive a check from the treasury or roll over (reinvest) the proceeds into new bills. Roll-over requests can only be made on noncompetitive bids when the issue date on the new bills coincides with that of the maturing bills.

Bids are submitted to Federal Reserve banks and their branches throughout the United States. Although issued by the U.S. Treasury, T-bills are sold by the Federal Reserve System.

Market for Treasury Bills

The value of T-bills outstanding at the end of October 1981 was $229.1 billion, with approximately $10 billion in new six-month and three-month T-bills coming to the market on a steady basis.

The secondary market is equally deep. Average daily dealers' transactions in T-bills was $15.5 billion measured by par value as of September 16, 1981 (Tables 10.6a, b),

FIGURE 10.4 Application form for noncompetitive bidding on government securities.

FORM PD 4632-2
Dept. of the Treasury
Bur. of the Public Debt

TENDER FOR TREASURY BILLS
IN BOOK-ENTRY FORM AT THE
DEPARTMENT OF THE TREASURY
26-WEEK BILLS ONLY

FOR OFFICIAL USE ONLY

FRB Request No. ____

Issue Date ____

Due Date ____

Cusip No. 912793 ____

MAIL TO:
☐ Bureau of the Public Debt, Securities Transactions Branch
Room 2134, Main Treasury, Washington, D. C. 20226
☐ Federal Reserve Bank or Branch
of your District at: ____

BEFORE COMPLETING THIS FORM READ THE ACCOMPANYING INSTRUCTIONS CAREFULLY

ACCOUNT NO.

ALPHA-CROSS-REF.

Pursuant to the provisions of Department of the Treasury Circular, Public Debt Series No. 27-76, the public announcement issued by the Department of the Treasury, and the regulations set forth in Department Circular, Public Debt Series No. 26-76, I hereby submit this tender, in accordance with the terms as marked, for currently offered U.S. Treasury bills for my account. (Competitive tenders must be expressed on the basis of 100, with three decimals. Fractions may not be used.) I understand that noncompetitive tenders will be accepted in full at the average price of accepted competitive bids and that a noncompetitive tender by any one bidder may not exceed $500,000.

TYPE OF BID
NONCOMPETITIVE ☐ or COMPETITIVE ☐ at: Price ____

AMOUNT OF TENDER $ ____
(Minimum of $10,000. Over $10,000 must be in multiples of $5,000.)

ACCOUNT IDENTIFICATION: (Please type or print clearly using a ball-point pen because this information will be used as a mailing label.)

Depositor(s) ____

Address ____

PRIVACY ACT NOTICE
The individually identifiable information required on this form is necessary to permit the tender to be processed and the bills to be issued, in accordance with the general regulations governing United States book-entry Treasury bills (Department Circular PD Series No. 26-76). The transaction will not be completed unless all required data is furnished.

DEPOSITOR(S) IDENTIFICATION NUMBER

FIRST NAMED — SOCIAL SECURITY NUMBER ☐☐☐ – ☐☐ – ☐☐☐☐

OR EMPLOYER IDENTIFICATION NO. ☐☐ – ☐☐☐☐☐☐☐

SECOND NAMED — SOCIAL SECURITY NUMBER ☐☐☐ – ☐☐ – ☐☐☐☐

DISPOSITION OF PROCEEDS

The par amount of the account will be paid at maturity unless you elect to have Treasury reinvest (roll-over) the proceeds of the maturing bills. (See below)

☐ I hereby request noncompetitive reinvestment of the proceeds in book-entry Treasury bills.

METHOD OF PAYMENT
TOTAL SUBMITTED$ ____ Cash $ ____ Check $ ____ Maturing Treasury Securities $ ____

DEPOSITOR'S AUTHORIZATION

Signature ____ Date ____ Telephone Number During Business Hours (____) ____ Area Code

FOR OFFICIAL USE ONLY

Received by ____ Date ____

STATEMENT OF ACCOUNT	Issue Discount Price $		Amount of Discount $		
Date	Transaction	Par Amount Transacted		Account Balance	Authority Reference	Validation
		Decrease	Increase			
		$	$	$		

A: DEPARTMENT OF THE TREASURY COPY

Source: Buying Treasury Securities at Federal Reserve Banks. Federal Reserve Bank of Richmond, Dec. 1976.

and dealers' position for approximately the same date (August 6, 1981) was $4.42 billion measured by par value. The secondary market is characterized by very high liquidity at very low transaction costs.

Treasury Notes and Bonds

U.S. Treasury notes and bonds are, respectively, medium and long-term obligations of the U.S. government. They are coupon bearing instruments issued with one- to ten-year maturity (notes) and a maturity of ten years or more for bonds. The longest maturity in T-bonds is thirty years, with usually a five-year-before-maturity call provision. The treasury calls back the bond by paying principal and interest to the bondholder.

Features

U.S. Treasury notes and bonds pay interest semiannually until the call date or the maturity date. Interest on notes and bonds is figured using 365 days. Yield to call is calculated (instead of yield to maturity) using the call date in the bond pricing equation.

Treasury bonds are quoted as percentage of par value (100) with changes expressed in thirty-seconds of a percentage point.

Notes may be issued in $1,000, $5,000, $10,000, $100,000, and $1 million denominations. The minimum denomination is at the discretion of the treasury. The $1,000 minimum denomination is not always issued.

Bonds generally have the same denominations as notes and are available, like notes, in registered or bearer forms. Registered notes or bonds bear the owner's name and are recorded on the treasury's book. Transfer of ownership requires the owner's written assignment (certified by a commercial bank or a trust company) on the back of the certificate. Bearer notes/bonds, on the other hand, do not bear the name of their owner. They are, therefore, easier to transfer but more susceptible to theft because of the presumption that the holder is the owner. Bearer bonds and notes have coupons attached to them. When the coupons become due, the owner submits them to a savings or commercial bank or to a Federal Reserve bank and collects the semiannual interest payment.

Sales Procedure

The treasury sells its notes and bonds through the Federal Reserve System using an auction system similar to that used to sell T-bills. The auction may be on a price basis or on a yield basis. Investors, as in the T-bill case, may submit a competitive or a noncompetitive bid. A noncompetitive bid does not require the specification of a percentage yield. The noncompetitive bidder agrees, however, to accept the average yield or equivalent price determined by the accepted competitive bids. A commercial bank or a primary security dealer may submit, for a fee, a bid on behalf of the investor. Buyers of bearer notes or bonds should expect to pick up their notes or bonds on any of the five business days following the issue date or expect to receive them (if this is their choice as noted in the tender form) by registered mail three to four weeks after the issue date. Buyers of registered notes or bonds are encouraged to opt for the mail delivery because of the increased processing time.

Treasury notes and bond offerings are not as regular as those of T-bills. *The Wall Street Journal* and other financial publications report on current treasury offerings and on the results of the auction.

TABLE 10.6a
U.S. Government Securities Dealers Transactions—Par Value, Averages of Daily Figures (Millions of Dollars)

Item	1978	1979	1980	1981 June	July	Aug.	1981, Week Ending Wednesday Aug. 12	Aug. 19	Aug. 26	Sept. 2	Sept. 9	Sept. 16[p]
Immediate delivery[a]												
1 U.S. government securities	10,285	13,183	n.a.	23,195	21,615	23,901	26,241	20,011	23,604	25,147	22,193	25,221
By maturity												
2 Bills	6,173	7,915		13,769	13,873	14,188	14,847	11,996	14,739	14,577	14,881	15,545
3 Other within 1 year	392	454		480	584	516	352	848	375	563	450	902
4 1–5 years	1,889	2,417		3,983	3,139	3,990	4,374	2,983	4,347	3,351	2,546	3,471
5 5–10 years	965	1,121		2,392	2,084	2,410	2,315	1,525	1,865	4,321	2,375	3,033
6 Over 10 years	867	1,276		2,571	1,937	2,797	4,353	2,659	2,278	2,336	1,942	2,221
By type of customer												
7 U.S. government securities dealers	1,135	1,448		1,378	2,171	1,767	1,853	1,650	1,604	1,864	1,517	1,597
8 U.S. government securities brokers	3,838	5,170	n.a.	11,173	10,222	11,555	13,343	9,271	11,720	12,025	10,959	13,414
9 All others[b]	5,312	6,564		10,644	9,223	10,579	11,046	9,091	10,279	11,258	9,717	10,211
10 Federal agency securities	1,894	2,723		3,621	3,060	3,136	3,485	3,257	3,215	2,858	2,578	3,964
11 Certificates of deposit				4,352	4,290	4,161	4,432	3,827	4,031	4,530	3,757	6,413
12 Bankers acceptances				1,822	1,655	1,420	1,564	1,109	1,272	1,570	1,344	1,978
13 Commercial paper				6,323	5,918	5,942	5,685	5,804	6,199	6,714	6,514	6,424
Futures transactions[c]												
14 Treasury bills	n.a.	n.a.		3,359	3,893	3,619	3,519	3,721	3,716	3,722	3,280	4,249
15 Treasury coupons				904	1,160	1,337	1,138	901	1,367	1,534	1,766	1,664
16 Federal agency securities				197	143	237	216	243	227	147	78	125
Forward transactions[d]												
17 U.S. government securities				227	369	612	1,110	380	377	637	445	228
18 Federal agency securities				1,377	911	1,123	1,744	694	720	1,313	1,420	2,056

[a] Before 1981, data for immediate transactions include forward transactions.

[b] Includes, among others. all other dealers and brokers in commodities and securities, nondealer departments of commercial banks, foreign banking agencies and the Federal Reserve System.

[c] Futures contracts are standardized agreements arranged on an organized exchange in which parties commit to purchase or sell securities for delivery at a future date.

[d] Forward transactions are agreements arranged in the over-the-counter market in which securities are purchased (sold) for delivery after 5 business days from the date of the transaction for government securities (Treasury bills, notes, and bonds) or after 30 days for mortgage-backed agency users.

Notes. Averages for transactions are based on number of trading days in the period. Transactions are marked purchases and sales of U.S. government securities dealers reporting to the Federal Reserve Bank of New York. The figures exclude allotments of, and exchanges for, new U.S. government securities, redemptions of called or matured securities, purchases or sales of securities under repurchase agreement, reverse repurchase (resale), or similar contracts.

TABLE 10.6b
U.S. Government Securities Dealers: Positions and Financing—Averages of Daily Figures (Millions of Dollars)

Item	1978	1979	1980	1981 June	1981 July	1981 Aug.	1981, Week Ending Wednesday July 29	Aug. 5	Aug. 12	Aug. 19	Aug. 26	Sept. 2
							Positions					
Net immediate[a]												
1 U.S. government securities	2,656	3,223		8,975	6,270	6,635	6,104	5,048	7,210	6,722	7,147	6,791
2 Bills	2,452	3,813		5,713	2,953	4,322	2,741	2,985	4,215	4,711	5,021	4,417
3 Other within 1 year	260	-325		-487	-1,419	-2,181	-1,414	-1,972	-1,995	-2,227	-2,303	-2,598
4 1–5 years	-92	-455		1,075	1,754	2,531	2,282	2,380	3,083	2,157	2,443	2,501
5 5–10 years	40	160	n.a.	466	815	72	487	83	164	144	-172	466
6 Over 10 years	-4	30		2,209	2,167	1,892	2,008	1,573	1,743	1,938	2,158	2,005
7 Federal agency securities	606	1,471		2,480	3,041	2,984	3,132	2,889	2,236	2,132	1,972	1,987
8 Certificates of deposit	2,775	2,794		3,947	4,880	3,925	4,391	4,811	4,754	3,920	3,149	3,214
9 Bankers acceptances				2,088	1,927	1,475	1,523	1,681	1,642	1,441	1,186	1,498
10 Commercial paper				3,061	2,309	2,171	2,099	2,477	2,263	1,991	1,998	2,397
Future positions												
11 Treasury bills		n.a.		-9,723	-8,352	-9,939	-10,744	-7,667	-8,932	-10,809	-11,009	-11,106
12 Treasury coupons				-2,448	-2,480	-2,598	-2,394	-2,248	-2,691	-2,650	-2,638	-2,551
13 Federal agency securities				-1,039	-946	-807	-887	-782	-733	-873	-719	-724
Forwards positions												
14 U.S. government securities		n.a.		-715	-523	-509	-683	-488	-86	-525	-897	-662
15 Federal agency securities				256	91	-206	-60	-186	-262	-274	-218	-85
							Financing[b]					
Reverse repurchase agreements[c]												
16 Overnight and continuing		n.a.		12,193	15,371	16,087	16,464	15,617	16,176	16,151	16,494	
17 Term agreements				29,785	29,519	29,414	29,230	29,348	29,438	29,086	29,808	n.a.
Repurchase agreements[d]												
18 Overnight and continuing		n.a.		33,748	36,175	36,719	34,752	36,705	36,765	36,858	36,594	
19 Term agreements				27,684	26,122	27,213	25,708	26,353	27,435	27,147	28,139	

Source: Federal Reserve Bulletin, Oct. 1981, p. A34.

[a] Immediate positions are net amounts (in terms of par values) of securities owned by nonbank dealer firms and dealer departments of commercial banks on a commitment, that is, trade-date basis, including any such securities that have been sold under agreements to repurchase (RPs). The maturities of some repurchase agreements are sufficiently long, however, to suggest that the securities involved are not available for trading purposes. Securities owned, and hence dealer positions, do not include securities to resell (reverse RPs). Before 1981, data for immediate positions include forward positions.

[b] Figures over financing involving U.S. government and federal agency securities, negotiable CDs, bankers acceptances, and commercial paper.

[c] Includes all reverse repurchase agreements, including those that have been arranged to make delivery on short sales and those for which the securities obtained have been used as collateral on borrowings, i.e., matched agreements.

[d] Includes both repurchase agreements undertaken to finance positions and "matched book" repurchase agreements.

Note. Data for positions are averages of daily figures, in terms of par value, based on the number of trading days in the period. Positions are shown net and are on a commitment basis. Data for financing are based on Wednesday figures, in terms of actual money borrowed or lent.

Settlement of Treasury Notes and Bonds

Bids on treasury notes and bonds must be accompanied by cash, federal funds checks (checks drawn by a commercial bank on its Federal Reserve account), certified personal checks, official bank checks, or government securities maturing on or before the issue date of the new notes or bonds; they must be equal to at least 5 percent of the face amount of the securities being purchased.

Notes and bonds are not redeemable by the treasury prior to maturity. They can, however, be sold in the secondary markets. Upon maturity, notes or bonds may be redeemed at any Federal Reserve bank free of charge or by a commercial bank or securities dealer for a fee. A treasury check is issued for the value of the securities tendered to the Federal Reserve System.

Market for Treasury Notes and Bonds

The market for treasury notes and bonds is characterized by depth (size of issues), breadth (various maturities), and low transactions costs. As Table 10.6 shows, the average daily volume of dealers' transactions in treasury issues as of Sept. 16, 1981 was $6.5 billion with maturities between one and ten years and $2.22 billion with maturities over ten years. The average daily size of dealers' position for treasury issues was $2,967 million as of Sept. 2, 1981 for those maturing between one and ten years and $2,005 million for those with a maturity exceeding ten years.

The riskiness of these securities emanates from changes in market yields. Interest income from T-notes and T-bonds is taxable as ordinary income; profits (losses) from their sale are taxed at capital gains (losses) rates if the securities are held for more than a year. However, interest on T-notes and T-bonds is exempt from state and local income taxes.

Federal Agency Securities

The volume of securities issued by agencies of the federal government and involving federal sponsorship or guarantees has expanded at a substantial rate. By July 1981 the outstanding debt of federal and federally sponsored agencies totaled $214 billion (Table 10.7). If the indebtedness of the Federal Financing Bank is added to this figure, the size of debt outstanding reaches $316.8 billion (July 1981).

The Federal Financing Bank was created in 1974 to borrow funds for federal agencies. The hope was to increase the efficiency of the market by increasing the size of the issue. The use of the facilities of the Federal Financing Bank (FFB) is voluntary, however.

We shall concentrate our discussion on debt instruments issued by the Government National Mortgage Association (GNMA) and by the Federal National Mortgage Association (FNMA).

Federal National Mortgage Association

The Federal National Mortgage Association (FNMA or "Fannie Mae") is a profit-making corporation wholly owned by its stockholders. FNMA is supervised by a fifteen-member board of directors, five of whom are appointed by the President of the United States; the remaining ten are elected annually by the stockholders.

FNMA was formed in 1954 under the FNMA Act. Its function is to provide liquidity in the secondary market for mortgages and to provide special assistance in the mortgage area as may be requested by the President or the Congress.

FNMA's 56 million outstanding shares are actively traded on the New York Stock Exchange. Institutions servicing mortgages on behalf of FNMA must own FNMA stock.

Although classified as Federal Agency Securities (Table 10.7), debt instruments issued by the FNMA are *neither* federal government obligations *nor* federally guaranteed. However, FNMA has authority to borrow up to $2.25 billion from the U.S. Department of the Treasury. Interest on these securities are taxable on the federal, state, and local levels.

The primary function of FNMA is to supplement the secondary market for residential mortgages. It does so by injecting funds into the mortgage market when conditions are not very accommodating to home buyers, home builders, and mortgage lenders. The funds used to increase the availability of mortgage money are raised by borrowing from private sources. These funds would not have flowed to the mortgage market otherwise.

FNMA buys outstanding mortgages from approved lenders at yields determined by auction. The approval of lenders by FNMA is based on their financial positions and their ability to service residential mortgage loans. The major suppliers of mortgages to FNMA are savings and loan associations, commercial banks, mutual savings banks, life insurance companies, and mortgage bankers. Total FNMA debt outstanding equaled $55.4 billion; this represents 25.9 percent of all debt outstanding for federal and federally sponsored agencies in July 1981. The FNMA mortgage and loan portfolio accounts for approximately 5 percent of total residential mortgage debt in the United States.

FNMA issues various types of securities, among them FNMA discount notes (30- to 360-day maturity tailored—as to maturity date—to the specific need of investors); secondary-market notes and debentures with maturities ranging from 1.5 to 25 years and with denominations of $10,000, $25,000, $50,000, $100,000, and $500,000; and mortgage-backed bonds secured by mortgages, some guaranteed by the Government National Mortgage Association (a U.S. government agency). The minimum denomination on mortgage-backed bonds is $25,000.

Government National Mortgage Association

The Government National Mortgage Association (GNMA or "Ginnie Mae") was created in 1968 to assume programs that were originally part of FNMA: (1) special assistance functions like the extension of financial aid to certain types of housing programs of the federal government and (2) management functions relating to existing FNMA mortgage portfolios. GNMA made possible the origination of federally insured and guaranteed mortgages at below-market rates; that is, it allowed for the subsidization of home ownership.

Securities issued by GNMA are taxed on the federal, state, and local levels.

Three types of securities are issued by GNMA:

1. *Mortgage-backed securities.* These securities are backed by a pool of FHA or VA-insured mortgages.
2. *Participation certificates.* These certificates are issued against loan assets of government agencies whose mortgage management was taken over by GNMA from FNMA.

TABLE 10.7
Federal and Federally Sponsored Credit Agencies—Debt Outstanding (Millions of Dollars, End of Period)

Agency	1978	1979	1980	1981					
				Feb.	Mar.	Apr.	May	June	July
1 Federal and federally sponsored agents[a]	137,063	163,290	193,229	194,926	198,828	200,434	205,020	208,961	213,990
2 Federal agencies	23,488	24,715	28,606	28,596	29,397	29,502	29,311	29,945	29,978
3 Defense Department[b]	968	738	610	591	576	566	556	546	536
4 Export-Import Bank[c,d]	8,711	9,191	11,250	11,201	11,881	11,868	11,850	12,423	12,401
5 Federal Housing Administration[e]	588	537	477	468	464	459	449	448	443
6 Government National Mortgage Association participation certificates[f]	3,141	2,979	2,817	2,817	2,817	2,775	2,775	2,715	2,715
7 Postal Service[g]	2,364	1,837	1,770	1,770	1,770	1,770	1,538	1,538	1,538
8 Tennessee Valley Authority	7,460	8,997	11,190	11,550	11,680	11,845	11,930	12,060	12,130
9 United States Railway Association[g]	356	436	492	199	209	219	213	215	215
10 Federally sponsored agencies[a]	113,575	138,575	164,623	166,330	169,431	170,932	175,709	179,016	184,012
11 Federal Home Loan Banks	27,563	33,330	41,258	42,275	43,791	44,357	47,121	49,425	52,431
12 Federal Home Loan Mortgage Corporation	2,262	2,771	2,536	2,514	2,409	2,409	2,409	2,409	2,408
13 Federal National Mortgage Association	41,080	48,486	55,185	54,110	54,666	54,183	54,430	54,657	55,362
14 Federal Land Banks	20,360	16,006	12,365	11,507	11,507	10,583	10,583	10,583[c]	10,317
15 Federal Intermediate Credit Banks	11,469	2,676	1,821	1,388	1,388	1,388	1,388	1,388[c]	1,388
16 Banks for Cooperatives	4,843	584	584	584	584	220	220	220[c]	220
17 Farm Credit Banks[a]	5,081	33,216	48,153	50,675	51,689	54,345	56,061	56,932	57,784
18 Student Loan Marketing Association[h]	915	1,505	2,720	3,275	3,395	3,445	3,495	3,400	4,100
19 Other	2	1	1	2	2	2	2	2	2
MEMO:									
20 Federal Financing Bank debt[a,i]	51,298	67,383	87,460	89,444	94,101	96,489	98,297	100,333	102,853
Lending to federal and federally sponsored agencies									
21 Export-Import Bank[d]	6,898	8,353	10,654	10,654	11,346	11,346	11,346	11,933	11,933
22 Postal Service[g]	2,114	1,587	1,520	1,520	1,520	1,520	1,288	1,288	1,288

23 Student Loan Marketing Association[h]	915	1,505	2,720	3,275	3,395	3,445	3,495	3,400	3,800
24 Tennessee Valley Authority	5,635	7,272	9,465	9,825	9,955	10,120	10,205	10,335	10,405
25 United States Railway Association[g]	356	436	492	199	209	219	213	215	215
Other Lending[j]									
26 Farmers Home Administration	23,825	32,050	39,431	39,851	41,791	43,456	44,746	45,691	47,396
27 Rural Electrification Administration	4,604	6,484	9,196	10,212	10,443	10,652	10,988	11,346	11,604
28 Other	6,951	9,696	13,982	13,908	15,442	15,731	16,016	16,125[c]	16,212

Source: *Federal Reserve Bulletin*, October 1981, p. A35.

[a] In September 1977 the Farm Credit Banks issued their first consolidated bonds, and in January 1979 they began issuing these bonds on a regular basis to replace the financing activities of the Federal Land Banks, the Federal Intermediate Credit Banks, and the Banks for Cooperatives. Line 17 represents those consolidated bonds outstanding, as well as any discount notes that have been issued. Lines 1 and 10 reflect the addition of this item.

[b] Consists of mortgages assumed by the Defense Department between 1957 and 1963 under family housing and homeowners assistance programs.

[c] Includes participation certificates reclassified as debt beginning Oct. 1, 1976.

[d] Off-budget Aug. 17, 1974, through Sept. 30, 1976; on-budget thereafter.

[e] Consists of debentures issued in payment of Federal Housing Administration insurance claims. Once issued, these securities may be sold privately on the securities market.

[f] Certificates of participation issued prior to fiscal 1969 by the Government National Mortgage Association acting as trustee for the Farmers Home Administration; Department of Health, Education, and Welfare; Department of Housing and Urban Development, Small Business Administration, and the Veterans Administration.

[g] Off-budget.

[h] Unlike other federally sponsored agencies, the Student Loan Marketing Association may borrow from the Federal Financing Bank (FFB) since its obligations are guaranteed by the Department of Health, Education, and Welfare.

[i] The FFB, which began operations in 1974, is authorized to purchase or sell obligations issued, sold, or guaranteed by other federal agencies. Since FFB incurs debt solely for the purpose of lending to other agencies, its debt is not included in the main portion of the table in order to avoid double counting.

[j] Includes FFB purchases of agency assets and guaranteed loans; the latter contain loans guaranteed by numerous agencies with the guarantees of any particular agency being generally small. The Farmers Home Administration item consists exclusively of agency assets, while the Rural Electrification Administration entry contains both agency assets and guaranteed loans.

3. *GNMA modified passthroughs.* These securities are created when a mortgage originator, often a mortgage banker or a savings and loan association, assembles a pool
($500,000 minimum) of mortgages insured by the Federal Housing Administration (FHA)
or the Farmers Home Administration, or guaranteed by the Veterans Administration
(VA) with identical maturities and interest rates and consisting of mortgages on homes
in one geographical area, and deposits them at a custodial bank. Upon submission of
all necessary documents by the originator to GNMA and approval by the latter, the
originator issues securities against the mortgage pool and assumes the responsibility
for making monthly payments of interest *and* principal to holders of GNMAs. If the
payments date coincides with that of the underlying mortgages, the securities are referred
to as straight GNMA passthroughs. If, on the other hand, the payments date does
not coincide with that of the underlying mortgages—that is, the originator makes payments on GNMA securities prior to or after the receipt of payments from the underlying
mortgages—the securities are referred to as GNMA modified passthroughs. What GNMA
guarantees, therefore, is the payment of interest and principal on a given date. The
guarantee against default by the mortgage is provided by the VA or FHA.

Yields on GNMA passthroughs are closely tied to mortgage interest rates. They
offer great opportunities for investors interested in the mortgage market while increasing
the liquidity of the market and the participating financial institutions. Since their introduction in 1970, GNMA passthroughs have been most popular with thrift institutions,
which currently hold about 30 percent of outstanding securities.

GNMA mortgage-backed securities are quoted in terms of percentage of unpaid principal balance, with fractions quoted in increments of thirty-seconds of a percentage point.
The average life of the pool of mortgages underlying the GNMA securities is about
12 years. Yield quotations on GNMA certificates are based on the assumption of prepay-
ment in the twelfth year. The minimum denomination on GNMA modified passthroughs
is $25,000.

The advantages associated with ownership of GNMA passthroughs are as follows:

1. Participation in the mortgage market without the paperwork and the service requirements associated with mortgage investing.
2. Practically risk-free assets.
3. Monthly cash-flows of interest and principal payments guaranteed regardless of
   whether payments on the underlying mortgages are made or not.
4. The collateral value of the securities, since GNMA passthroughs qualify as a
   real estate asset and meet the regulations of the FSLIC.
5. High liquidity.

10.11 MUNICIPAL BONDS

Introduction

The increasing size of state and local governments, the increased need for synchronization
of receipts and payments, and the political realities requiring the distribution of the
cost of major capital projects over many tax years have led to very substantial increases
in the outstanding debt of these political entities. During the year 1980, total borrowing
by state and local governments amounted to $48.5 billion, of which $46.7 billion was
new capital and the remainder used for refunding old bond issues.

Little, if any, problems were encountered by municipalities in the sale of their bonds. Municipal bonds have several attractive features that encourage their ownership. We shall discuss those features in detail.

Definition

Municipal bonds are debt obligations issued by a state, territory, or possession of the United States; by any municipality or political subdivision of the United States (city, county, school district, etc.); or even by a university.

Features of Municipal Bonds

Municipal bonds possess several attractive features; these are outlined below.

Tax Exemption

Interest on municipal bonds is exempt from federal income taxes, from the taxes of the issuing state, and usually from the taxes of the political entity in which the bondholder resides.

The exemption from federal income taxes derives from the constitutional doctrine of reciprocal immunity. State and local governments do not tax federal property, and the federal government reciprocates in kind. However, appreciation in the value of municipal bonds is subject to capital gains taxes.

The yield equivalence for a taxable bond can be easily calculated and is obviously dependent on the bondholder's tax bracket, as shown in Table 10.8. Investors who buy municipal bonds on credit should note that the margin interest is not tax deductible under the rules of the Internal Revenue Service.

Safety

Municipal bonds enjoy an excellent safety record. The recent New York and Cleveland scares put many investors on guard, however. Under adverse economic conditions, the full taxing power of New York City did not help, because taxing powers also have a maximum level of tolerance. Nevertheless, municipal bonds are still considered second only to U.S. government bonds in terms of safety. All municipal bonds have collateral value. Owners of municipal bonds may borrow against their bond holdings from financial institutions.

While municipal bonds are generally considered safe, different bonds have different levels of safety. Three major financial services companies rate municipal bonds, as shown in Table 10.9. Fitch's Investors' Service also rates some municipal bonds. Not all municipal bonds are rated, and a rating should not be considered an absolute standard of quality. Rating services do not always agree on the creditworthiness of the issuers.

Fixed Income and Capital Appreciation Potential

Municipal bonds provide a steady source of income to their holders in the form of semiannual (sometimes annual) interest payments.

Municipal bonds purchased at a discount from face value offer an opportunity for

TABLE 10.8
Tax-Exempt vs. Taxable Income

TAX-EXEMPT YIELDS

% Tax Bracket	24	27	30	34	39	42	45	48	52	54	57	59	62	65	67	69	71	73	74	75	
4.50%	5.92	6.16	6.43	6.82	7.38	7.76	8.18	8.65	9.38	9.78	10.47	10.98	11.84	12.86	13.64	14.52	15.52	16.67	17.31	18.00	4.50%
4.75	6.25	6.51	6.79	7.20	7.79	8.19	8.64	9.13	9.90	10.33	11.05	11.59	12.50	13.57	14.39	15.32	16.38	17.59	18.27	19.00	4.75
5.00	6.58	6.85	7.14	7.58	8.20	8.62	9.09	9.62	10.42	10.87	11.63	12.20	13.16	14.29	15.15	16.13	17.24	18.52	19.23	20.00	5.00
5.10	6.71	6.99	7.29	7.73	8.36	8.79	9.27	9.81	10.63	11.09	11.86	12.44	13.42	14.57	15.45	16.45	17.59	18.89	19.62	20.40	5.10
5.25	6.91	7.19	7.50	7.95	8.61	9.05	9.55	10.10	10.94	11.41	12.21	12.80	13.81	15.00	15.91	16.94	18.10	19.44	20.19	21.00	5.25
5.40	7.11	7.40	7.71	8.18	8.85	9.31	9.82	10.38	11.25	11.74	12.56	13.17	14.21	15.43	16.36	17.42	18.62	20.00	20.77	21.60	5.40
5.50	7.24	7.53	7.86	8.33	9.02	9.48	10.00	10.58	11.46	11.96	12.79	13.41	14.47	15.71	16.67	17.74	18.97	20.37	21.15	22.00	5.50
5.75	7.57	7.88	8.21	8.71	9.43	9.91	10.45	11.06	11.98	12.50	13.37	14.02	15.13	16.43	17.42	18.55	19.83	21.30	22.12	23.00	5.75
6.00	7.89	8.22	8.57	9.09	9.84	10.34	10.91	11.54	12.50	13.04	13.95	14.63	15.79	17.14	18.18	19.35	20.69	22.22	23.08	24.00	6.00
6.10	8.03	8.36	8.71	9.24	10.00	10.52	11.09	11.73	12.71	13.26	14.19	14.88	16.05	17.43	18.48	19.68	21.03	22.59	23.46	24.40	6.10
6.25	8.22	8.56	8.93	9.47	10.25	10.78	11.36	12.02	13.02	13.59	14.53	15.24	16.45	17.86	18.94	20.16	21.55	23.15	24.04	25.00	6.25
6.40	8.42	8.77	9.14	9.70	10.49	11.03	11.64	12.31	13.33	13.91	14.88	15.61	16.84	18.29	19.39	20.65	22.07	23.70	24.62	25.60	6.40
6.50	8.55	8.90	9.29	9.85	10.66	11.21	11.82	12.50	13.54	14.13	15.12	15.85	17.11	18.57	19.70	20.97	22.41	24.07	25.00	26.00	6.50
6.75	8.88	9.25	9.64	10.23	11.07	11.64	12.27	12.98	14.06	14.67	15.70	16.46	17.76	19.29	20.45	21.77	23.28	25.00	25.96	27.00	6.75
7.00	9.21	9.59	10.00	10.61	11.48	12.07	12.73	13.46	14.58	15.22	16.28	17.07	18.42	20.00	21.21	22.58	24.14	25.93	26.92	28.00	7.00

Note: These tabulations emphasize the fact that the tax exempt income means *more keeping dollars.*
For example, in a 30% tax bracket, you must find a taxable investment with a return of 8.57 to equal a tax-exempt security with a return of 6.00.

TABLE 10.9
Municipal Bond Ratings

	Moody's	Standard & Poor's	Dun & Bradstreet
Prime	Aaa	AAA	01
			02
			03
Excellent	Aa	AA	04
			05
			06
Good	A[a]	A	07
			08
			09
Average	Baa[a]	BBB	10
			11
			12
Fair	Ba	BB	13
			14
			15
Poor	B	—	16
			17
			18
Marginal	Caa	B	19
			20
			21
Default	Ca	D	22
	C		

[a] Those bonds in the A and Baa groups which Moody's believes possess the strongest investment attributes are designated by the symbols A-1 and Baa-1 within their groups.

capital gains, as do other municipal bonds as their prices react to changes in interest rates.

Flexibility and Marketability

The municipal bond market is one with considerable depth and breadth. A steady stream of new issues comes into the market, offering the investor a wide variety of choices. The over-the-counter dealing in municipal bonds is extensive, allowing the investor to buy and sell at minimum spread levels (difference between bid and ask). The diversity of the issues allows investors to best tailor the bonds to their own needs and to diversify the risk of their bond portfolios. More than a thousand municipal bond dealers ready to buy and sell securities operate throughout the United States. During August of 1980 alone, municipal bonds valued at $3.79 billion were issued by state and local governments. New issues for 1981 totaled $47.7 billion, with approximately 58 percent of this sum going to special district and statutory authority.

Municipal bonds are generally traded in $5,000 denominations and occasionally in $1,000 denominations. Some municipal bonds are "term" bonds (all bonds in a given issue mature at the same time) and others are serial bonds (a certain amount of the issue matures every year through maturity, which can be as long as 30 years and sometimes longer). Some municipal bonds are callable and others are not. Callable bonds are bonds that can be withdrawn (bought back at a stated price after a certain date) by the issuer before the expiration date. Investors, therefore, can enjoy considerable flexibility in their bond portfolios.

Types of Municipal Bonds

There are basically four types of municipal bonds: (1) general obligation bonds, (2) revenue bonds, (3) authority and agency bonds, and (4) double-barreled bonds. These are described below.

General Obligation Bonds

General obligation bonds are bonds guaranteed (interest and principal) by the full faith, credit, and taxing power of the issuing authority. If the general tax is subject to a ceiling or if the obligation is to be discharged using a specific tax (e.g., gasoline tax) or by using a fixed portion of a certain type of tax, then the general obligation bond is referred to as a *limited-tax bond*.

Revenue Bonds

Revenue bonds are payable from the revenue generated by the facilities they financed or by other facilities owned by the issuer. Water, sewer, electric, and gas systems as well as port authorities, toll bridges and the like are primary issuers of this type of bond. The yield on this type of bond is generally higher than that on a general obligation bond.

Authority and Agency Bonds

Authorities and agencies of political subdivisions constructed for the purpose of performing specific functions issue bonds that are backed by the revenues generated by the authority and at times the faith and the taxing power of another political body. An example of such a bond is that of the New Housing Authority. These bonds are backed by the net rental revenue from the housing units built and by periodic contributions from the Public Housing Administration of the United States and the local public housing authority. This bond is essentially a tax-exempt U.S. government security.

Double-Barreled Bonds

Double barreled bonds are secured by a pledge of two or more sources of payment. Many special assessment or special tax bonds are additionally backed by the full faith, credit, and taxing power of the issuer.

Form of Municipal Bonds

Municipal bonds are sold in a bearer or coupon form or in a registered form. The coupon bond is presumed owned by the holder, who periodically clips the coupon and submits it for collection. Coupon bonds are more liquid and generally command a higher price.

Registered bonds are registered in the name of the owner. The registrar pays interest and principle to the owner, whose name appears on the bond certificate. These bonds are less marketable than coupon bonds and are thus most suitable for those who intend to hold them until maturity.

Pricing Municipal Bonds

Municipal bonds maturing serially are usually offered on a yield basis plus accrued interest (interest accruing from the last coupon payment). Yield-basis pricing means setting the price of a bond so that the yield to maturity is equal to a certain percentage.

If the yield to maturity is higher than the coupon rate, the bond will sell at a discount; if the opposite is true, the bond will sell at a premium.

When the price of a bond is stated in a dollar amount, the bonds are referred to as *dollar bonds.* Dollar bonds are frequently term bonds with one maturity date.

At the time of purchase, accrued interest (the portion of the semiannual interest income that belongs to the seller) is added to the market price of the bond. This sum is "returned" to the investor when the next coupon payment is made. Therefore, the accrued interest is not included in the cost basis of the bond. This basis is used to determine the capital gain (loss) on the bond. The difference between the cost basis and the selling price or redemption price is taxable as a capital gain (long-term if the holding period exceeds one year).

Mathematics of Municipal Bonds

The mathematics of municipal bonds is basically the same as that of other straight bonds. The critical value is the yield to maturity which is approximated by the following equation:

$$K_d = \frac{\text{value of coupon} \pm \text{annual amortization}}{(\text{purchase price} + \text{redemption value})/2} \tag{10.11}$$

Example
What is the yield to maturity on a municipal bond with 15 years to maturity, a coupon rate of 10 percent, and a market price of $900?

$$K_d = \frac{(10/100) \times 1{,}000 + [(1{,}000 - 900)/15]}{(1{,}000 + 900)/2} = \frac{106.66}{950} = 11.23\%$$

If the bond is callable, then a yield to call is calculated. The life of the bond would shrink and its redemption value would rise.

Municipal bonds should be selected to best fit the investor's needs. The need for high current income requires a higher initial investment and produces no capital gains. A discount bond (coupon rate below market yields) would not offer high periodic income but would produce capital gains taxable at the preferred tax rate if the bond were held to maturity. Investors should be careful in the selection of municipal bonds.

The reader should note that the calculation of the basis on a municipal bond is made easy through "basis books" available in any library or bank office.

Tax-Exempt Bond Funds

Tax-exempt bond funds are pooled resources of investors committed to tax-exempt securities.

Tax-exempt bond funds are becoming more and more popular as yields on municipal bonds increase, inflation pushes people into higher and higher tax brackets, and rates on time deposits fail to adjust sufficiently to reflect market rates. In February 1981, tax-exempt municipal bonds were yielding 13 to 14 percent while high-grade taxable utility bonds were yielding 15 percent.

The attractiveness of municipal bond funds lies in their tax-exempt income; relative stability of capital; risk diversification in terms of issuer, quality, and geography; convenience in terms of collecting income and safeguarding the underlying securities (kept by the trustee in safekeeping); and liquidity (units are usually redeemed without a charge by the issuer at at least the net asset value). These and other funds are discussed in Chapter 9.

CONCLUSIONS

The existing variety of debt issues increases the opportunity for maximizing returns and minimizing risks of portfolios. Although the markets are becoming increasingly complex, they are providing greater opportunities. Investors should realize that there is no substitute for thorough homework and for good judgment.

QUESTIONS

1. What factors could cause two bonds issued by firms in the same risk class to sell at different prices?

2. Given bond theorem 2, what maturities of bonds should speculators prefer? Explain. Modify your answer to the first part in terms of bond theorem 3.

3. Should speculators prefer low- or high-coupon bonds? Explain.

4. How does a bond's duration relate to its maturity? To its coupon?

5. What is the duration of a six-month T-bill? Why?

6. How do bankers' acceptances enhance international trade?

7. Why might corporations issue commercial paper instead of seeking bank financing? Which types of corporations can issue commercial paper?

8. Why is a secondary market for negotiable CDs important to maintain their popularity?

9. How do repo's (repurchase agreements) and Fed funds increase banks' liquidity?

10. What factors influence the price of a convertible bond?

11. If the market price of a share of RJC stock exceeds the conversion price of shares available to holders of RJC convertible bonds, how would you expect the price of the bond to behave?

12. Which estimate of return, the discount rate or the investment yield, is more accurate? Why?

13. What factors must an investor consider before investing in municipal bonds?

14. Convertible bonds are hybrid securities that can play interesting roles in many portfolios. Their valuation is a problem, however. Why? What are the advantages of owning convertible bonds? What characteristics must they have before you recommend them to, say, your grandmother? Be specific.

15. Discuss conditions (company/market) under which a corporation might issue a convertible bond instead of a straight bond or convertible bonds instead of common stock.

16. Discuss the factors that might reduce the conversion premium on a convertible bond to zero.

17. Under what conditions would a company choose to call a bond issue?

18. "FNMA securities are just like U.S. government bonds: they are issued by the federal government and are fully guaranteed by the faith and taxing power of the U.S. Treasury." Comment.

19. John Dunno wishes to participate in new treasury issues. How can he accomplish this?

20. The yield to maturity can be approximated by Equation 10.11. This equation suffers from many weaknesses. What are they? Why?

PROBLEMS

1. Use Equation 10.1 to derive the market value of a three-year bond that has a $1,000 face value and pays $35 semiannually in coupon payments. Similar instruments yield 8 percent.

2. A bond pays $50 semiannually in coupon payments, sells for $900, and matures in one year. Calculate:
   a. Coupon rate
   b. Current yield
   c. Yield to maturity

3. A bond maturing in four years pays interest annually, is selling for $850, and has a yield to maturity of 12 percent. Calculate its coupon rate and annual coupon payment.

4. Calculate the duration of a two-year bond that is selling for $964.53, pays $40 twice a year, and has a yield to maturity of 10 percent.

5. Recalculate the duration of the bond described in problem 4 if yields were 8 percent. (Hint: What would be the bond's new market price?)

Valuation of Convertible Bonds

We begin the pricing process by assuming that future stock prices are normally distributed and equivalently the conversion value $CV = P \cdot N$, as shown in Figure 10A.1.

If the conversion value is larger than the investment value, the convertible bond would behave like a group of common stocks without their level of riskiness because of the downside protection offered by the investment value. If, on the other hand, the investment value is larger than the conversion value, the value of the bond would depend on the expectations regarding stock prices.

At any point in time, therefore, the investor holding a convertible bond can expect to receive the higher of conversion value or investment value. Which value is received depends on the value of P and its probability of occurrence.

Using the convertible bond valuation model developed by Otto Poensgen[1] and expanded by James Walter and Augustin Que,[2] we find that the expected market value of a convertible bond can be derived as follows:[3]

$$E(\mathrm{MP}^B) = y \int_0^y f\left(\frac{P}{y}\right) dP + \int_y^\infty Pf\left(\frac{P}{y}\right) dP$$

where y = investment value and the other variables are as defined before

$f(P/y)$ = conditional probability = probability of P occurring given that y has occurred

Equation 1 can be rewritten to allow for bond yield variability as follows:

---

[1] **Otto H. Poensgen,** "The Valuation of Convertible Bonds." *Industrial Management Review,* Fall, 1965, pp. 72–92 and Spring, 1966, pp. 83–98.

[2] **James E. Walter** and **Augustin V. Que,** "The Valuation of Convertible Bonds." *Journal of Finance,* vol. 28 (June 1973), pp. 713–733.

[3] The reader may choose to skip the mathematical derivation and concentrate on Equation 4.

FIGURE 10A.1

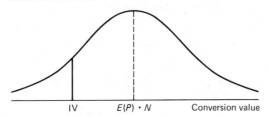

IV $E(P) \cdot N$ Conversion value

$$E(\text{MP}^B) = \int_0^\infty \left[y \int_0^y f\left(\frac{P}{y}\right) dP + \int_y^\infty Pf\left(\frac{P}{y}\right) dP \right] f(y) \, dy$$

$$= \int_0^\infty \left[\int_0^y yf\left(\frac{P}{y}\right) dP + \int_y^\infty Pf\left(\frac{P}{y}\right) dP \right] f(y) \, dy \qquad (2)$$

$$= \int_0^\infty \left[\int_0^y yf\left(\frac{P}{y}\right) dP + \int_0^\infty Pf\left(\frac{P}{y}\right) dP - \int_0^y Pf\left(\frac{P}{y}\right) dP \right] f(y) \, dy$$

$$= \int_0^\infty \left[\int_0^\infty pf\left(\frac{P}{y}\right) dP + \int_0^y (y - P) f\left(\frac{P}{y}\right) dP \right] f(y) \, dy$$

but $f\left(\dfrac{P}{y}\right) f(y) = f(P,y) =$ joint probability of P and y occurring at the same time.

$$= \int_0^\infty \left[\int_0^\infty Pf(P,y) \, dP + \int_0^y (y - P) f(P,y) \, dP \right] dy \qquad (3)$$

$$= \int_0^\infty \left[\int_0^\infty Pf(P,y) \, dP + \int_0^\infty (y - P) f(P,y) \, dP - \int_y^\infty (y - P) f(P,y) \, dP \right] dy$$

$$= \int_0^\infty \left[\int_0^\infty yf(P,y) \, dP - \int_y^\infty (y - P) f(P,y) \, dP \right] dy$$

$$= \int_0^\infty \left[\int_0^\infty yf(P,y) \, dP + \int_y^\infty (P - y) f(P,y) \, dP \right] dy$$

$$= \int_0^\infty \left[\int_0^\infty yf(y) f\left(\frac{P}{y}\right) dP + \int_y^\infty (P - y) f(P,y) \, dP \right] dy$$

$$= \int_0^\infty \left[yf(y) \int_0^\infty f\left(\frac{P}{y}\right) dP + \int_y^\infty (P - y) f(P,y) \, dP \right] dy$$

$$= \int_0^\infty \left[yf(y) + \int_y^\infty (P - y) f(P,y) \, dp \right] dy$$

Therefore

$$E(\text{MP}^B) = \int_0^\infty yf(y) \, dy + \int_0^\infty \int_y^\infty (P - y) f(P,y) \, dP dy \qquad (4)$$

where $\displaystyle\int_0^\infty yf(y) \, dy = E(\text{IV}) =$ expected investment value

$\qquad\qquad\qquad$ = the minimum price the investor would receive for a convertible bond

$$\int_0^\infty \int_y^\infty (P - y) f(P,y) \, dP dy = \text{expected value of the conversion option}$$

Before we explain further, we rewrite Equation 3 as follows:

$$E(\text{MP}^B) = \int_0^\infty P f(P) \, dP + \int_0^\infty \int_0^y (y - P) f(P,y) \, dP dy \tag{5}$$

where $\displaystyle\int_0^\infty P f(P) \, dp = \text{expected conversion value}$

$$\int_0^\infty \int_0^y (y - P) f(P,y) \, dP dy = \text{value of the floor guarantee}$$

Equations 4 and 5, although mathematically equivalent, carry different implications. In simpler terms, the bond premium may be expressed as follows:

$$\text{Bond premium} = \begin{matrix} \text{market value of} \\ \text{convertible bond} \end{matrix} - \max \left\{ \begin{pmatrix} \text{conversion} \\ \text{value} \end{pmatrix}, \begin{pmatrix} \text{straight} \\ \text{debt} \\ \text{bond} \\ \text{value} \end{pmatrix} \right\}$$

If $P \geq y$, then

$$\begin{aligned} \text{Bond premium} &= \text{market value} - \text{conversion value} \\ &= \text{value of the floor guarantee} \end{aligned}$$

Therefore Equation 5 applies.
If $y \geq P$, then

$$\begin{aligned} \text{Bond premium} &= (\text{market value}) - \text{straight debt bond value} \\ &= \text{value of the conversion privilege} \end{aligned}$$

Therefore Equation 4 applies.
It is this "asymmetry" that makes for the difficulty in evaluating convertible bonds.

Market Interest Rates and Bond Portfolio Strategy

11.1 INTRODUCTION

The wide variety of debt instruments discussed in Chapter 10 offers many opportunities and much flexibility in the structuring of an efficient portfolio—a portfolio that maximizes the rate of return for a given level of risk or minimizes risk for a given level of return. The market rate of interest influences the rate of return on a bond as well as the variability of that rate of return. It is for these reasons that we shall examine the determinants of the market rate of interest, the impact of the changes in market rates of interest on the performance of bond portfolios, and the opportunities or special problems to which these changes may give rise.

11.2 FACTORS INFLUENCING BOND PRICES

The bond price theorems discussed in Chapter 10 allow for the conclusion that bond prices are influenced by the coupon rate, the length of the maturity, and the market rate of interest on comparable securities. The yields on other securities (such as common stock) may also influence the price of bonds.

Since all bonds do not have homogeneous characteristics and all investors do not have homogeneous needs, different bonds would sell at different prices—that is, at different yields.

The factors leading to the different observed prices for bonds can be summarized as follows:

1. The frequency of the coupon payments and the number of days in a year over which interest is accrued. Also of importance is the size of the coupon payment on a bond.

2. The quality of the bond, that is, the probability of default on interest and/or principal payments. This quality is reflected in the rating given the bond by the various rating services. Default risk is nondiversifiable risk, as Hickman and Atkinson have shown.[1] This indicates that the default risk of a portfolio is simply the weighted average of the default risk of the securities making up the portfolio.

3. The liquidity of the bond. The broader the market for the bond, the less the transactions costs (commission or spread between bid and ask prices) to be paid by the investor.

4. The yield on a bond. This is thought to be positively related to the maturity of the bond. Some argue that the longer the maturity the larger the liquidity premium investors would demand, the higher the yield. This and other arguments on this issue will be discussed below.

5. The peculiar features of the bond, which can also influence the price. A callable bond (a bond that can be bought back by the issuing corporation at a specified price after a certain period of time) may not be as attractive as a noncallable bond. Other influential factors include the taxability of interest on a bond; the conversion feature, if any; the nature of the collateral behind the bond; the nature of the provisions in the indenture agreements, like the sinking funds provision or restrictions on payment of dividend or on further issuance of debt; the currency in which the bond is denominated; and the newness and size of the bond issue. All these have an impact on the yield of the bond and should explain the differential in bond yields.

6. The investor's personal preference for a certain type of bonds, issuer, or maturity. This can also influence the bond price.

All these factors are reflected in the yield on every bond. However, the extent of the influence of each of the factors cited above is not very easy to discern.

11.3 FACTORS INFLUENCING INTEREST RATES

We present in this section those factors that have repeatedly been documented to have a significant impact on interest rates. We begin by defining *interest,* which represents the price paid for exchanging future dollars for current dollars. It is the price of credit— the nominal rate of interest.[2]

The components of the nominal rate of interest are the real rate of interest—the exchange rate between future consumption of goods and services and current consumption—and the expected rate of inflation. Developments in the 1981–1982 period have created doubt about the extent to which inflation rates influence nominal rates of interest, however.

The interest rates reported in the financial papers are nominal ex ante rates of interest. Their real-rate component must be positive, otherwise the lender would willingly be transferring wealth to the borrower. Thus:

---

[1] **W. Braddock Hickman,** *Corporate Bond Quality.* National Bureau of Economic Research, New York, 1967; **T. R. Atkinson,** *Trends in Corporate Bond Quality.* National Bureau of Economic Research, New York, 1967.

[2] For an excellent discussion on this matter, consult **G. J. Santoni** and **Courtenay C. Stone,** "Navigating Through the Interest Rate Morass: Some Basic Principles." *Review,* vol. 63, no. 3 (March 1981), pp. 11–18.

$$R = \lambda + E\left(\frac{\Delta P}{P}\right)$$

where R = nominal rate of interest expected

λ = real rate of interest > 0

$E(\Delta P/P)$ = expected change in the price level

We note here that λ may turn out to be negative ex post. This is so whenever the lender has incorrectly anticipated the rate of inflation. Our discussion will not deal with the nominal/real and ex ante/ex post issues per se (important as they are) but will, instead, address interest rates as nominal rates.

Supply and Demand

In the absence of credit controls, with the elimination of the power of government to set maximum rates on some deposits through the Monetary Control Act of 1980, and with the relaxation of the state usury laws (which set ceilings on interest rates to be charged borrowers), the determination of the price of credit is largely a function of supply and demand.

The influence of the Fed on the money supply is direct and powerful in the short run (on a month-to-month basis). The Fed influences the supply of money primarily in four ways: (1) by changing the discount rate it charges its member banks, (2) by changing the reserve requirements on various deposits held by member banks or by subjecting to or exempting some types of deposits from reserve requirements, (3) by buying and selling securities in the open market—open-market operations—with the intent of influencing the level of excess reserves of depository institutions, and (4) by moral suasion. The first two options are infrequently used. Before we discuss the third policy option, a word on excess reserves.

Excess reserves are those reserves held in excess of the required reserves on some liabilities of financial intermediaries. They are reserves which can be used to expand the loans made to businesses, individuals, or to governments both in the United States and abroad. Algebraically, total reserves for the banking system equal[3]

$$TR = RR + ER \tag{11.1}$$

where TR = total reserves

RR = required reserves

ER = excess reserves

Total reserves can belong to the banking system or can be borrowed from the Fed. Therefore

---

[3] For an extensive discussion, see **Polakoff et al.,** *Financial Institutions and Markets.* Houghton Mifflin, Boston, 1970.

$$UR + BR = RR + ER$$

where UR = unborrowed reserves $\qquad$ (11.2)

$\qquad$ BR = borrowed reserves

or

$$UR = RR + (ER - BR)$$
$$UR = RR + FR \qquad (11.3)$$

where FR = free reserves.

Since borrowed reserves are very short term and cannot be relied on exclusively to expand the loan portfolios of banks, the focus may as well be on the excess reserves of the banking system. The size of these reserves are reported on a regular basis in the *Federal Reserve Bulletin.* A negative ER that is becoming more negative over time is a strong indication of tight credit conditions because it indicates that the ability of the banking system to expand credit is being stretched further and further toward its limits. If, on the other hand, ER is positive and the Fed wishes to reduce the ability of banks to extend credit, the Fed would sell government securities to the banks, reducing their excess reserves in the process (because banks pay for the bonds in reserves). If the Fed wishes to reduce excess reserves on a very temporary basis, it may enter into reverse repurchase agreements with nonbank dealers; thus the Fed might sell securities to government bond dealers with the intention of buying them back at a specified price after a specified time period (usually 1 to 15 days).

The reserves of the banking system imply a certain level of deposits in the banking institutions. Those deposits plus the currency held by the public represent the level of the money supply. It is the control of the growth rate in monetary aggregates and the control of the size and growth rates of excess reserves that motivate the open-market operations. The problem in controlling (if at all possible) the growth in the money supply lies partially in deciding on the variable to be controlled. There are many definitions of money and many money supply figures reported by the Fed. These figures are published by the Fed on a weekly basis and on a regular monthly basis in the *Federal Reserve Bulletin* (the reader is strongly urged to consult this publication.) The growth patterns and definitions of the various money supplies appear in Figure 11.1. The definition of money that seems most consistent, predictable, and reflective of economic activity[4] is M1-B (referred to as M1 beginning in 1982), which includes currency plus commercial bank checking accounts plus checking type deposits in banks, thrift institutions, credit unions, and mutual savings banks.

After a long period of trying to control interest rate levels, the Fed switched on Oct. 6, 1979, to the management of the money supply, with only cursory attention to interest rates. This was to be achieved by "placing greater emphasis on day-to-day operations on the supply of bank reserves and less emphasis on confining short-term fluctuations in the federal funds rate."[5]

---

[4] **Keith M. Carlson** and **Scott E. Hein,** "Monetary Aggregates as Monetary Indicators." *Review,* Federal Reserve Bank of St. Louis, November 1980.

[5] "Announcements: Monetary Policy Actions." *Federal Reserve Bulletin,* October 1979, p. 830.

FIGURE 11.1 Growth patterns and definitions of money supplies.

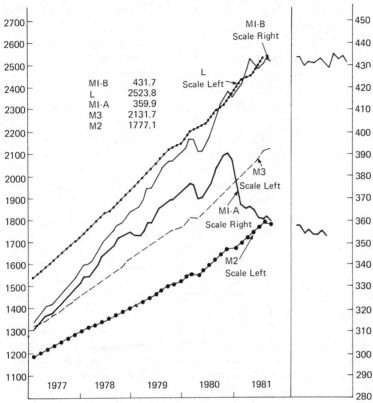

Source: Media General Financial Weekly, Nov. 9, 1981.

During 1980, the Federal Open Market Committee specified "its objectives in terms of ranges of growth rates for several monetary aggregates . . . and ranges for the federal funds rate."[6] The monetary targets which were chosen were M1-A, M1-B, M2, M3, and commercial bank credit.

The results of the new policy during 1980 were mixed:

> *Over the year 1980, the Federal Reserve achieved a small reduction in the trend rate of money growth relative to recent years. Growth rates of M1B and M2, however, exceeded their annual target ranges. Thus, the Federal Reserve did not achieve the degree of deceleration in money growth that it announced as its objectives for the year. Money growth was highly variable during the year, falling below the annual target range during April and July, and rising above the annual range in September through part of December.*[7]

The policy shift by the Fed, having not always produced the intended results, have led some prominent economists to argue that there has not been a policy shift at all. For example, the unprecedented rise in interest rates during the first part of 1980 was

---

[6] **R. Alton Gilbert** and **Michael Trebing,** "The FOMC in 1980: A Year of Reserve Targeting." *Review,* vol. 63, no. 7 (August/September 1981), p. 2.

[7] Ibid., p. 16.

untenable, the Fed discovered, both in economic and political terms. Consequently, as soon as the interest rate "ceiling" is reached (the maximum tolerable limit before monetary policy has an unacceptable impact on economic activity), the Fed expands the growth in the money supply in order to keep interest rates from rising further. Many economists, having examined the record of the Fed under both the new and the old policy, have concluded that the only way to manage the money supply is to insist on a steady growth in money supply without undue emphasis on interest rates. This would allow the Fed greater control over monetary policy or, more accurately, would transform monetary policy into a passive policy and thus reduce inflationary expectations. This policy, to the extent that it revises and stabilizes expectations, should reduce the rate of inflation and/or make it more predictable. This translates into a more predictable interest rate. Neither the old nor the new policy of the Fed has made the job of interest rate forecasters easier, however. An unpredictable course by the Fed makes for the embarrassing situations in which forecasters have found themselves.

The efforts of the Fed are frequently frustrated by fiscal policy. An ever-expanding federal budget without the tax base to support it has often forced the Fed to monetize the deficit and consequently to increase the growth of the money supply beyond the intended target. The federal government, being a necessitous borrower, enters the financial markets regardless of the level of interest rates. In so doing, the government crowds out private borrowers by pushing interest rates to levels unacceptable to business firms.

It is, therefore, recommended that despite the Fed's relatively weak hold on the money supply, any forecast of interest rates takes the activities of the Fed and those of the U.S. Treasury Department into consideration. Open-market activities, repurchase agreements entered into by the Fed, and changes in the discount rate that signal substantive policy moves as opposed to moves to offset other factors (such as seasonal fluctuations) not under the control of the Fed must be followed carefully. A harder task yet is to figure out how policy changes by the Fed affect the expectations of economic agents. An expansionary monetary policy may well result in higher rather than lower rates of interest if it increases inflationary expectations. Precisely how Fed policies affect expectations has not been resolved satisfactorily.[8]

Also influencing the supply of loanable funds are tax incentives, as provided for in the Economic Recovery Tax Act of 1981. The provisions of this act should have a considerable impact on savings. It created, albeit temporarily, the all savers certificate, which allows for a lifetime exclusion of $1,000 ($2,000 for joint returns) of interest generated on certificates purchased before Dec. 31, 1982. The act also decreased the maximum tax rate on personal income and on capital gains, thus further increasing the incentive to save and invest.

Demand for Money

In attempting to predict the level and/or the direction of interest rates, the demand side of the financial markets must also be watched carefully.

The Federal Reserve System (the Fed), whose policies have considerable (if not exclusive, as some may argue) impact on interest rates, can influence the demand for credit and money in several indirect and direct ways.

---

[8] For a discussion of the issues involved, see **Rachel Balbach,** "The Effects of Changes in Inflationary Expectations." *Review,* Federal Reserve Bank of St. Louis, April 1977, pp. 10–15.

The indirect influence of the Fed over the demand for money comes in two forms: (1) through the actual imposition or the threat of imposition of credit controls or (2) through the pursuit of other policies that affect the expectations of borrowers in the marketplace. The Fed can also affect the demand for money (e.g., transactions demand) by changing the interest rate and by influencing the level of economic activity. An unduly expansionary monetary policy—and accommodating monetary policy to the treasury operations—can stoke inflationary expectations, which, in turn, can influence the level as well as the direction of interest rates because of the high inflation component in the nominal rate of interest. The demand for funds comes from primarily three sources: government, business, and consumers.

The demand by government consists of (1) demand by the federal government to include that by federal agencies included in the budget, (2) demand by agencies indirectly sponsored by the federal government but not included in the U.S. budget or in the national debt figures (FNMA, Banks for Cooperatives, Federal Intermediate Credit Bank, Federal Land Bank, Federal Home Loan Bank, Federal Home Loan Mortgage Corporation), (3) demand by the Federal Financing Bank, and (4) demand by state and local governments.

Information on the federal government's borrowing plans is embodied in the budget of the United States. Large budget deficits require large borrowings. The timing of these borrowings is quite predictable in view of past patterns of behavior by the federal government. The borrowing plans of federal agencies are contained in the "Forward Calendar" published in *The Wall Street Journal.* The amount of borrowing by state and local governments is contained in the placement ratio published in the *Bond Buyer.* This ratio reveals the percentage of municipal bonds underwritten and sold by underwriters. Additionally, the forecaster should watch for announcements by state and local governments on their intent to borrow. Government borrowing must also depend on the condition of the economy, which is not always predictable with great accuracy.

The demand by business firms for funds is a function of the size of internally generated funds (mainly profits and depreciation) relative to expansion plans and of business expectations about future refinancing costs. The ratio of internal cash flow less inventory valuation adjustment to manufacturers' plant and equipment expenditures (Fig. 11.2) is a good indicator of borrowing pressures by corporate entities.

Other strong indicators of business borrowing are new orders of capital equipment and nonresidential construction contracts, all of which require outlays that may exceed the size of internally generated funds. Data on these variables are readily available (Fig. 11.3) and can easily be incorporated in the forecast of interest rates. The Securities and Exchange Commission publishes what is called the *Corporate Debt Calendar,* which tells the size and timing of debt securities to be issued by corporate firms to finance plant and equipment expenditures.

Borrowing by consumers is very much a function of their current debt burden in relation to their saving and current and expected income and of their expectations with regard to the future course of the economy and their own welfare. The higher the income coverage of debt (gross income/total debt payments), the greater the potential for borrowing by consumers (Fig. 11.4). On the other hand, the greater the delinquency and repossession rate on outstanding loans, the lower the potential for borrowing by consumers (Fig. 11.4). These indicators occasionally give conflicting signals, as shown in Figure 11.4. Consumer sentiment or expectations about the future and hence willingness to make commitments today is measured by the University of Michigan on a periodic

FIGURE 11.2   **Manufacturers' capital spending indicators.**

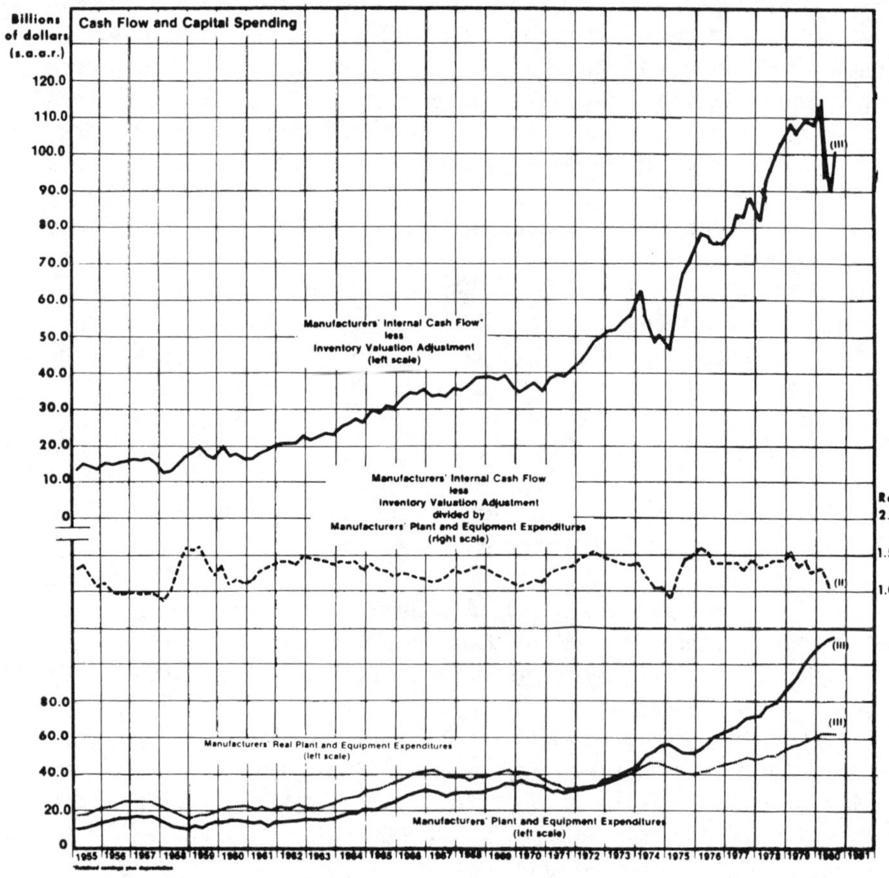

Source: The Pocket Chartroom. Goldman Sachs, New York, March 1981.

basis (Fig. 11.5). A drop in these indicators is a sign of pessimism and consequently of lower spending and borrowing levels.

It must be noted at this juncture that while demand for funds by business and by consumers may influence interest rates, they are also influenced by the level and direction of interest rates. This interdependence must not be overlooked in the development of interest rate models.

In general, it can be said that a multitude of factors, some too complex to be incorporated neatly in a forecasting model, influence the level and direction of interest rates. Economists Peter Goldsmith and James Kochan of Merrill Lynch Pierce Fenner & Smith, Inc., have identified six economic series with considerable value in identifying turning points in short-term rates. These series, which are available on a timely basis, are (1) index of spot prices of industrial raw materials, (2) index of industrial production, (3) business demand for short-term credit (commercial plus industrial loans plus nonfinancial papers), (4) unemployment rate, (5) annual growth rate in money (M1), and (6) the producer price index.

Some interest rates forecasting techniques will be discussed later in this chapter.

FIGURE 11.3a New orders for capital equipment.

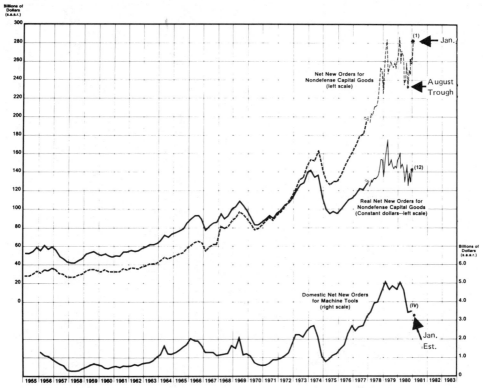

Source: U.S. Department of Commerce.

11.4 THE TERM STRUCTURE OF INTEREST RATES

The term structure of interest rates is summarized by the yield curve, which represents the relationship at a point in time between time to maturity and yield to maturity on fixed-income securities[9] within a given risk class. The yield curves have taken on various shapes in the last decade, as shown in Figure 11.6. On Aug. 30, 1974, the yield curve was essentially a descending yield curve. On March 13, 1979, the yield curve was a humped yield curve with low yields for very short-term maturities and higher yields for medium-term maturities followed by lower yields for longer-term maturities. The yield curve constructed on March 15, 1977, is an ascending yield curve with higher yields to maturity for successively longer maturities. Flat yield curves (not shown in Fig. 11.6) were observed during the 1901–1905 period.

---

[9] Several texts, indeed, every text we have examined, treat term structure and yield curves as being exactly equivalent. Well, they are if and only if the debt instruments are pure discount bonds. The term structure is the yield curve for pure discount bonds (bills). The term structure is not the yield curve for coupon-bearing bonds. The yield on a coupon bond maturing in two years, for example, is some weighted average of the term structure. The calculation of the weights requires a rather complex mathematical formulation, which we shall avoid. The distinction we make here should become clearer as the reader digests the full contents of this section.

FIGURE 11.3b   **Nonresidential construction contracts.**

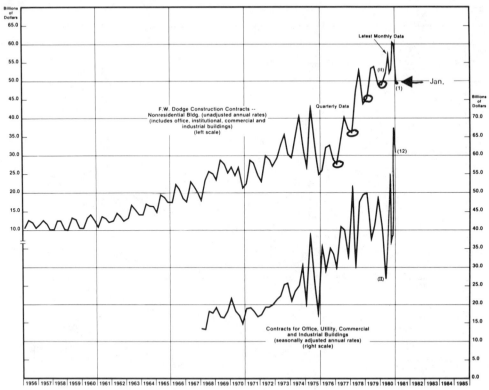

Source: U.S. Department of Commerce.

11.5 CONSTRUCTION OF YIELD CURVES

The yield curve is a snapshot of the term structure at a point in time. The yield curve may later shift upward or downward and/or change its slope. The accurate forecasting of changes in the yield curve can pay handsome dividends, as we shall demonstrate later in this chapter.

The construction of yield curves is an art to some and a science to others. Most typically, yield curves are constructed using the methodology of the U.S. Treasury. This construction, like any other, requires, as a first step, a collection of homogeneous securities, that is, securities that have the same characteristics in terms of riskiness and type (callable/when, or noncallable, convertible or nonconvertible, debentures or mortgage bonds, etc.) and differ only in the length of time to maturity (the difference in the coupons is usually, although mistakenly, ignored, as we explain below). The second step is to plot, on a given day or hour, the yield to maturity (dependent variable, Y axis) against the time to maturity (independent variable, X axis). The scatter of points usually exhibits a pattern through which a curve is fitted. The procedure used by the treasury locates "the yield curve in the middle of the data scatter for Treasury

FIGURE 11.4   Indicators of the consumer debt burden.

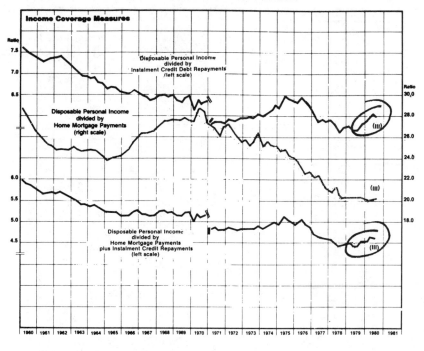

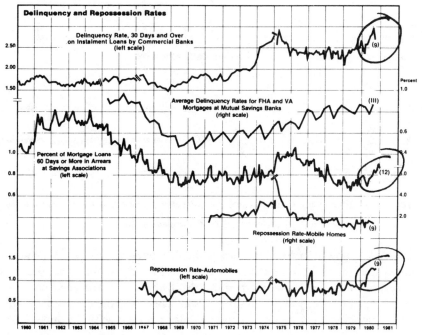

Source: The Pocket Chartroom. Goldman Sachs, New York, March 1981.

FIGURE 11.5   Consumer psychology.

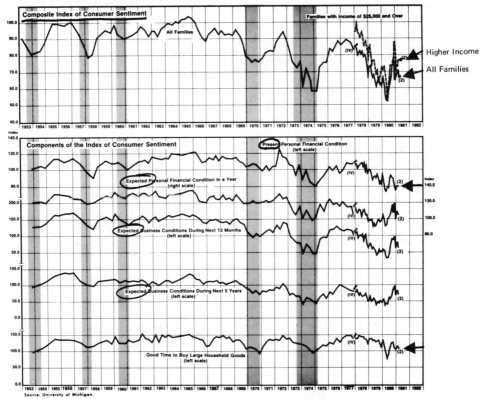

Source: The Pocket Chartroom. Goldman Sachs, New York, March 1981.

bonds, bills and notes."[10] The criticism from the academic community focuses on this last step.

The term structure identity, which holds if expectations are unbiased, requires that

$$(1 + {}_tR_N) = [(1 + {}_tR_1)(1 + {}_{t+1}r_1) \cdots (1 + {}_{t+N-1}r_1)]^{1/N} \tag{11.4}$$

where ${}_tR_N$ = current yield to maturity at time t on a bond with N years to maturity

${}_{t+N-1}r_1$ = one-period rate expected to prevail at time $t+N-1$

Equation 11.4 shows that the long rate is the geometric average of short-term rates. This implies that the yield to maturity on long-term bonds should equal that resulting from consecutive investments in one-period debt instruments. The yield on a two-year bond should equal to that yield from investing in a one-year bond and then reinvesting the proceeds (principal plus interest) in another one-year bond with the same characteristics.

---

[10] **Martin E. Ecols** and **Jan Walter Elliott,** "A Quantitative Yield Curve Model of Estimating the Term Structure of Interest Rates." Journal of Financial and Quantitative Analysis, March 1976, p. 88.

FIGURE 11.6   Yields on U.S. government securities.

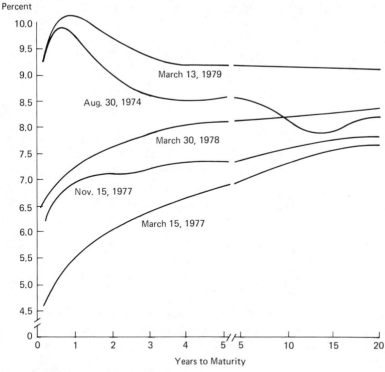

Source: Federal Reserve Bank of St. Louis.

Starting with Equation 11.4, M. Ecols and J. Elliott (E&E) set out to test the efficiency of the treasury method for constructing yield curves. They derived testable equations which were used to fit the curve using econometric techniques instead of the treasury's freehand approach. The treasury method ignores the impact of coupon rate differentials on the shape of the yield curve.
The equation E&E tested follows:

$$1n(1 + R_N) = \frac{1}{t}\left[1n(1 + R_1) - 1nY_1\right] + t\left[\frac{Y_2}{2}\right] + \left[1nY_1 - \frac{Y_2}{2}\right] \qquad (11.5)$$

or

$$1n(1 + R_N) = a\left(\frac{1}{t}\right) + b(t) + c + \xi_t \qquad (11.5)'$$

where $a = 1n(1 + R_1) - 1nY_1$
       $b = Y_2/2$
       $c = [1nY_1 - Y_2/2]$

Y_1 and Y_2 are constants in the exponential term structure model used by E&E: $(1 + {_t}r_1) = Y_1 e^{Y_2 \cdot t}$

E&E added one variable to Equation 11.5 to account for the very important fact that bonds with different coupon rates are not homogeneous. The new testable equation is:

$$1n(1 + R_t) = a\frac{1}{t} + b(t) + d(x) + c + \xi_t \qquad (11.6)$$

where x = value of bond coupon.

Equation 11.6 was tested using various measures of goodness of fit and other measures dealing with autoregression and multicollinearity. Equation 11.6 was also tested against a model proposed by Cohen and his colleagues.[11] Cohen's model uses a quadratic structure to estimate the yield curve.

$$(1 + R_t) = a + b(t) + c(\log t)^2 + \xi_t \qquad (11.7)$$

E&E added a coupon variable to Cohen's to arrive at

$$(1 + R_t) = a + b(t) + c(1nt)^2 + d(x) + \xi_t \qquad (11.8)$$

The results using data from the 1964–1972 period confirmed the superiority of Equation 11.6 and with it the importance of including the coupon rate. Therein lies the main contribution of E&E. Equation 11.6 explains the various shapes of the yield curves depending on the values of a and b:

Condition	Curve Shape
(1) $a < 0, b < 0$	Humped
(2) $a < 0, b > 0$	Rising
(3) $a > 0, b < 0$	Falling
(4) $a > 0, b > 0$	Flat

The issue of differing coupon rates and the implication it has on the estimation of the term structure was further explained by Deborah H. Miller.[12]

The difficulty in the estimation of the term structure results from two factors, Miller argued: "(1) Most observable securities are not pure discount bonds, (2) The maturities of observable securities are scattered throughout the future and not necessarily at points in time for which term structure estimates are needed."[13]

The first factor mentioned by Miller corroborates the findings of E&E. It deals with differential impact bonds or a set of bonds have on yields to maturity depending on whether the bonds carry coupons or not and on the size of the coupon payment. Pure

---

[11] **Kalmon J. Cohen, Robert L. Kramer,** and **W. Howard Waugh,** "Regression Curves for U.S. Government Securities." *Management Science,* vol. 13, no. 4 (December 1966), pp. 168–175.

[12] **Deborah H. Miller,** "Estimating the Yield Curve: Alternatives and Implications." Unpublished doctoral dissertation, University of Pennsylvania, Philadelphia, 1979.

[13] Ibid., p. 10.

discount (Zero coupon) bonds have only one cash flow equal to the face value of the bond.

$$MP_0^B = \frac{CF_n}{(1 + K_d)^n} = \frac{FV}{(1 + K_d)^n} \tag{11.9}$$

where K_d = yield to maturity.

A coupon bond, on the other hand, has one or many cash flows prior to the payment of face value. Its present value or its market price is equal to

$$MP_0^B = \frac{C_1}{(1 + {}_tR_1)} + \frac{C_2}{(1 + {}_tR_2)^2} + \frac{C_3}{(1 + {}_tR_3)^3} + \cdots + \frac{C_n}{(1 + {}_tR_N)^n} + \frac{FV}{(1 + {}_tR_N)^n} \tag{11.10}$$

where ${}_tR_N$ = current (spot) market rates making up the term structure at time t.

Equation 11.10 can be viewed as the present value of a series of pure discount bonds. The first coupon payment represents the maturity value of a one-period pure discount bond. The second coupon represents the maturity value of a two-period discount bond, and so on until the last payment (the balloon payment consisting of principal and interest payments).

Using the yield to maturity (a unique rate) as a discount factor in Equation 11.10, Miller argues, distorts the effective rate of return on the bond. Only if all the ${}_tR_N$'s were equal to each other and to K_d would the yield to maturity equal the effective rate of return on the bond. If the yield curve were rising, the expected return on a debt security would be higher than the yield to maturity, and the opposite would material-ize if a descending yield curve were observed. This is so because of higher reinvestment rates in the first case and lower reinvestment rates in the second. These problems, it must be noted again, would not occur if the bonds did not carry coupons which may have to be reinvested at a rate different from the yield to maturity.

A utilization of K_d in Equation 11.10 instead of ${}_tR_N$ would effectively deny the existence of a term structure unless the yield curve were flat. The larger the coupon payments, the greater the distortion, as D. Miller points out.

> *If interest rates are expected to change over the life of a bond, then the size and timing of coupon payments can greatly affect the return from a bond. The more of a bond's return which comes from its coupon payments rather than from a payment of principal at maturity, the more important reinvestment rates become in determining a bond's return. Thus yield to maturity has the potential of causing greater distortions as a spot rate estimator when coupons are large.[14]*

The increasing functional relationship between the differential between the spot rate and the yield to maturity and the size of the coupon has been discussed in the preceding chapter, in the sections on duration and bond price theorems.

While the issues discussed by E&E and D. Miller are of considerable importance,

---

[14] Ibid., pp. 15–16.

most practitioners still ignore them and use the freehand approach in fitting the yield curve, which works well in many cases.[15]

11.6 THEORIES OF TERM STRUCTURE

There are various theories to explain the term structure of interest rates. Some overlap and the others have little in common. We shall focus our attention on three major theories: the expectations theory, the liquidity preference theory, and the market segmentation theory.

Expectations Theory

The expectations theory is a demand-based theory. The expectations of investors about the future course of interest rates determine their demand for certain maturities. The theory asserts that no supplier of securities not even the federal government, is large enough to exert influence over the structure of interest rates.

The assumptions of the expectations theory are as follows:

1. Zero transactions costs, allowing for a high cross elasticity between maturities.
2. No taxes.
3. Complete certainty about future rates and homogeneity in expectations across the majority of well-financed investors.
4. Perfect capital markets, allowing for the necessary flexibility in interest rates to reflect the competitive forces in the U.S. economy.
5. Universality of markets—no segmentation. Investors are indifferent as to maturity.
6. Rational investors operating so as to maximize the expected return over the investment horizon.

Based on these assumptions, the expectations theory argues that the long rate is the geometric average of short rates (as indicated earlier by Equation 11.4):

$$(1 + {}_tR_N) = [(1 + {}_tR_1)(1 + {}_{t+1}r_1)\cdots(1 + {}_{t+N-1}r_1)]^{1/N} \tag{11.11}$$

or

$$(1 + {}_tR_N) = [(1 + {}_tR_1)(1 + {}_{t+1}F_1)\cdots(1 + {}_{t+N-1}F_1)]^{1/N} \tag{11.12}$$

where ${}_{t+1}r_1$ = expected one-period spot rate to prevail at the beginning of period $t+1$

${}_{t+N}F_N$ = forward rate of interest to prevail at time $t + N$ over period N (Therefore, ${}_{t+5}F_5$ would represent the forward 5 period rate to prevail at the beginning of period $t + 5$. This is the rate embodied in the yield curve.)

---

[15] The ambitious reader should carefully examine Deborah H. Miller's comprehensive work on the problems of estimating the term structure of interest rates and the methods of estimation.

What distinguishes Equation 11.11 from Equation 11.12 is the presence of the expected spot rate instead of the forward rate. The expectations hypothesis argues that the two are perfect substitutes, that is,

$$_{t+N-1}F_1 = {}_{t+N-1}r_1.$$

To illustrate how the forward rate is calculated, assume that the investor is concerned with the one-year yield expected to prevail a year from now. Given the one-year yield to maturity and the two-year yield to maturity, the forward one-year rate can easily be calculated.

From Equation 11.12, the two-period rate is equal to

$$(1 + {}_tR_2) = [(1 + {}_tR_1)(1 + {}_{t+1}F_1)]^{1/2} \tag{11.13}$$

therefore

$$_{t+1}F_1 = \frac{(1 + {}_tR_2)^2}{1 + {}_tR_1} - 1 \tag{11.14}$$

and in general

$$_{t+N-1}F_1 = \frac{(1 + {}_tR_N)^N}{(1 + {}_1R_{N-1})^{N-1}} - 1 \tag{11.15}$$

This forward rate represents, in line with what appears to be the consensus of opinion, the spot rate to prevail in that period (plus a liquidity premium;[16] see next section).

In the two-period case, the forward rate would equal 9 percent assuming $_tR_2 = 8$ percent and $_tR_1 = 7$ percent. The forward rate is calculated as follows:

$$_{t+1}F_1 = \frac{(1 + 0.08)^2}{(1 + 0.07)} - 1 = 9\%$$

The forecasted one-year rate beginning with the next period is 9 percent. Thus we have a rising yield curve. The reader must be careful to choose rates covering the correct period. If the three-month forward rate to prevail three months from now is to be calculated, the six-month rate and the three-month rate will have to be chosen. If, on the other hand, the three-month rate to prevail one year from now is to be calculated, then the investor must use the one-year and three-month rates as well as the one-year rate. We present first the general equation:

$$_{t+(N\cdot m-1)}F_1 = \frac{[1 + (R_N/m)^{Nm}]}{[1 + (R_{N-1}/m)^{Nm-1}]} - 1$$

---

[16] **Richard W. Lanz** and **Robert H. Rasche,** "A Comparison of Yields on Futures Contracts and Implied Forward Rates." *Review,* Federal Reserve Bank of St. Louis, December 1978, pp. 21–30.

where subscript 1 after F = subperiod (a quarter, a month, etc.)

$\qquad\qquad\qquad$ m = number of subperiods in a year (four in the case of quarters)

Therefore, the one-quarter rate to prevail one year from now is calculated as follows:

$$_4F_1 = \frac{[1 + (R_N/4)]^{1.25 \times 4}}{[1 + (R_{N-1}/4)]^{5-1}} - 1$$

If R_N (five-quarter rate) = 10.5 percent and R_{N-1} (four-quarter or one-year rate) = 10 percent, the one-quarter rate to prevail one year from now is equal to:

$$_4F_{1\mathrm{qtr}} = \frac{(1 + 0.02625)^5}{(1 + 0.025)^4} - 1 = \frac{1.13832}{1.1038} - 1$$

$$= .0313 = 3.13 \text{ percent/quarter}$$

The expectations theory explains every type of yield curve. If rates are expected to rise in the future, the yield curve would be rising; if rates are expected to fall, yield curves would be descending; if rates are expected to remain at their current level, the curves would be flat; and if rates were expected to rise in the near future and fall later on, the yield curve would be humped.

In practical terms, the expectations theory is asserting that investors should be indifferent between investing in long-term securities or in a series of short-term securities. This indifference is very dependent on the absence of transactions costs and of a preference function for certain maturities (by assumption). Any changes in the supply of bonds of a given maturity would not affect the term structure unless it somehow affected expectations.

Empirical Evidence

The most serious of the early attempts at testing the validity of the expectations hypothesis was made by D. Meiselman.[17] The model proposed by Meiselman is the "error-learning" model. As investors observed that the actual rate of interest is different from the forward rate, which they have anticipated, they would revise their forecast of the next one-period rate by a fraction of the previous error.

The test conducted by Meiselman purported to show that forward rates do, in fact, conform to the error-learning model. The equation he tested was

$$_{t+N}F_{1,t} - _{t+N}F_{1,t-1} = a_N + b_N(R_{1,t} - _tF_{1,t-1}) + \xi \qquad (11.16)$$

or

$$\Delta_{t+N}F_{1,t} = a_N + b_N(E_t) + \xi \qquad (11.17)$$

---

[17] **David Meiselman,** *The Term Structure of Interest Rates.* Prentice-Hall, Englewood Cliffs, N.J., 1962.

where $_{t+N}F_{1,t}$ = forecasted one year rate to prevail at time $t + N$ (The forecast is made at time t.)

$_{t+N}F_{1,t-1}$ = forecasted one year rate to prevail at time $t + N$ (The forecast is made at time $t - 1$.)

E_t = size of the error = difference between the actual and the forecasted rate.

The error-learning model would be vindicated if $a \approx 0$ and if $0 < b_i < b_{i-1} < 1$ for $i = 2, \ldots, n$. Using data covering the 1901–1954 and the ordinary least square technique, Meiselman found that the results were in support of the hypothesis confirming the validity of the expectations theory.

The Achilles' heel of Meiselman's test was the data used. Meiselman used the "basic yield" curves of Durand,[18] which by Durand's own admission do not lend themselves to "refined" analysis or precise computation.

J. Grant[19] tried to duplicate Meiselman's results with British data and found that the error-learning model is not supportable using unsmoothed data (as opposed to Durand's smoothed data).

A. Buse,[20] using smoothed yield curves for British and U.S. government securities, found the constant term to be positive and significant, which contradicts the error-learning model.

A. Santomero,[21] using Eurodollar spot rate observations—which bypasses the problems of yield to maturity and the differential in coupon rates—found substantial support for the error-learning model.

In summary, the evidence on the error-learning model is mixed. Expectations alone do not determine the shape of the yield curve. Furthermore, and more fundamentally, the argument that the yield curve allows for the discovery of expected rates does not lead to the conclusion that expectations are the sole determinant of the shape of the yield curve. Moreover, observable yield curves are "market" yield curves that do not necessarily coincide with those of individual investors.

The Liquidity Preference Theory

The fundamental assertion of the liquidity preference theory is that Equations 11.12 and 11.11 are not perfect substitutes. Restating Equation 11.12:

$$(1 + {}_tR_N) = [(1 + {}_tR_1)(1 + {}_{t+1}F_1) \cdots (1 + {}_{t+N-1}F_1)]^{1/N} \tag{11.18}$$

where $_{t+N-1}F_1 = {}_{t+N-1}r_1 + {}_{t+N-1}LP_1$

---

[18] *Economic Almanac,* The Conference Board of the National Industrial Conference Board, New York City, 1944–1966.

[19] **J. A. G. Grant,** "Meiselman on the Structure of Interest Rates. A British Test." *Economica,* February 1967.

[20] **A. Buse,** "Interest Rates, the Meiselman Model and Random Numbers." *Journal of Political Economy,* February 1967.

[21] **Anthony M. Santomero,** "The Error-Learning Hypothesis and the Term Structure of Interest Rates in Eurodollars." *Journal of Finance,* June 1975.

and

$$_{t+N-1}\text{LP}_1 > {_{t+N-2}}\text{LP}_1 > {_{t+N-3}}\text{LP}_1 > \cdots > {_{t+1}}\text{LP}_1$$

and where LP = liquidity premium.

The liquidity premium, Hicks[22] argued, is necessary to compensate the risk-averse speculators in the financial markets. Borrowers have a propensity to borrow long to lock in the interest rate costs and ensure the availability of funds. Lenders are more interested in lending short term; they require compensation for assuming longer-term maturities because of the probability that the bonds will be called before their maturity or that interest rates will rise in the interim and investors will be unable to take advantage of the higher rates as their capital is locked in. Risk-averse investors also tend to view distant dates with greater uncertainty (about interest and principal payments) and hence require compensation for the additional risk. The size of the premium, its value over time, its sign, and even its very existence are subject to much controversy.

The expectations theory, in contrast, assumes that speculators are risk neutral. Their utility function is linear:

$$U(W) = aW + b$$
$$E[U(W)] = E[aW + b]$$
$$E[U(W)] = aE(W) + b \tag{11.19}$$

By maximizing the expected utility of wealth, investors maximize their expected wealth. This conclusion does not hold if the utility function is a quadratic function (or of different forms), representing the attitude of a risk-averse person. In a Meiselman world, borrowers and lenders are indifferent between long and short maturities. If interest rates deviate from expectations, arbitrageurs (a sufficient number of them) would enter the market on the demand side or on the supply side to ensure equality between the expected and the forward rate.

$$\text{If} _{t+n-1}r_1 < {_{t+n-1}}F_1 = \frac{(1 + {_t}R_N)^N}{(1 + {_t}R_{N-1})^{N-1}} - 1$$

Arbitrageurs (or speculators) would borrow for $n - 1$ periods and lend for n periods. An opposite strategy would be employed if

$$_{t+N-1}r_1 > {_{t+N-1}}F_1$$

In equilibrium, the expectations hypothesis asserts that the liquidity premium is equal to zero, while the liquidity preference theory asserts that the value is positive. It is the "size, sign and behavior of the term premiums"[23] that distinguishes one theory from another.

The immediate implication of the liquidity theory, some may superficially argue, is that it can only explain rising yield curves. The shape of the yield curves may well be determined by factors that offset the rising liquidity premium. If the expected-rate portion

---

[22] **John R. Hicks,** *Value and Capital.* Oxford: Clarendon Press, 1946.

[23] **Miller,** p. 116.

of the forward rate is expected to fall by a value larger than the rise in the liquidity premium, the forward rate would be falling and consequently also the yield curve. These and other factors explaining a downward-sloping yield curve were documented by A. Reuben, R. H. Scott, and J. Gray.[24] R. Kessel offered evidence that accounting for the liquidity premium substantially contributes to the explanatory power of the yield curve.

The Market Segmentation Theory

The fundamental argument of the market segmentation theory is that both supply and demand—which are determined by many factors, including expectations—determine the yield to maturity. The elasticity of substitution, (or the extent to which bonds of differing maturities are substitutes) is assumed to equal to zero for bonds with substantially different maturities. The elasticity of substitution between close maturities (three months with six-month bills) may be nonzero, however. This stems from the fact that institutions, because of the nature of their business and because of their attempts to match the maturity structure of their liabilities with that of their assets in order to reduce if not eliminate exposure to interest rate fluctuations (risk), would have a natural affinity for securities with certain maturities. Insurance companies would thus, demand longer term bonds to match their long-term obligations, and commercial banks may have a preference for short-term securities to invest time or demand deposits and ensure a certain level of liquidity. This implies, therefore, that the bond market is "segmented" by maturity. For each maturity there are identifiable demand curve and supply curves which determine the yield and, consequently, the liquidity premium, which can be positive, zero, or negative. Changes in the yield structure are, therefore, determined by changes in the supply and/or the demand for a given maturity.

Figure 11.7 shows how the yield to maturity is determined by the intersection of supply and demand.

The supply of funds as well as its components are identifiable and allow for the determination of the equilibrium yield for a given term to maturity.

This theory has considerable currency among practitioners in the field of managing fixed-income securities portfolios. Academicians, however, have not emphasized this theory as much as the expectations theory. Nonetheless, the practioners persist in their belief. Bankers Trust Co. of New York, for example, publishes on a regular basis a flow-of-funds statement showing in detail the sources and uses of funds for the entire U.S. economy (Table 11.1a and b). Statements of sources and uses of funds per term to maturity are also made, allowing for the prediction of the corresponding interest rates. The effects of changes in the supply and demand for funds would depend on the elasticity of the supply and demand curves. For a given change in supply, the resultant change in yield will be greater the less elastic the demand curve.

The supply of funds basically comes from three sources: savings; changes in the money supply, those which impact bank reserves in particular; and changes in the money

---

[24] **A. Reuben Kessel,** "The Cyclical Behavior of the Term Structure of Interest Rates." Occasional Paper 91, National Bureau of Economic Research, New York, 1965.

R. H. Scott, "A 'Liquidity' Factor Contributing to Those Downward Sloping yield Curves, 1900–1916." *Review of Economics and Statistics,* August 1963, pp. 328–329.

Jean M. Gray, "New Evidence on the Term Structure of Interest Rates, 1884–1900." *Journal of Finance,* vol. 28 (June 1973), pp. 635–646.

FIGURE 11.7 Yield to maturity.

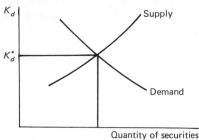

balances held for speculative purposes (hoarding, dishoarding). The demand for loans comes from government (federal, state, and local), business, and consumers. The correct anticipation of the size and direction of the supply and demand components translates itself into an accurate forecast of interest rates, as we shall discuss later.

The empirical evidence does not support the extreme cases of the segmentation hypothesis. E. Kane and B. Malkiel examined the issue of whether markets are indeed segmented by surveying banks, insurance companies, and nonfinancial corporations. They concluded: "Our various findings each support a single conclusion: that the demands for various maturities of debt are not infinitely elastic at going rates, and, therefore, that changes in the relative supplies of different maturities . . . can alter the term structure."[25]

W. Trudgian and R. Scott[26] also found evidence of market segmentation in their survey of government securities dealers. Supply and demand factors were closely monitored by the dealers in the formulation of investment strategies.

Modigliani and Sutch[27] attempted to reconcile the three theories discussed above by suggesting an alternative theory that relies on all three. They dubbed it the *preferred habitat* theory. Their hypothesis states that investors, who are not as risk-averse as their counterparts under the segmentation hypothesis, can be induced out of their preferred maturity, the one that minimizes their risk, by paying them a positive or a negative premium, depending on the relationship between their time horizon and the time to maturity of the bond. An investor with a two-year liability would be interested in two-year investments because shorter maturities increase reinvestment risk and longer maturities increase exposure to changes in market rates. To get this investor interested in securities with one-year maturity, a negative risk premium must be paid.

The reason for the negative risk premium can be explained by restating Equation 11.13:

$$(1 + {}_1R_2) = [(1 + {}_1R_1)(1 + {}_2r_1)]^{1/2}$$

The concern of the investor is with the probability that his expectations (summarized by ${}_2r_1$) would not materialize. In particular, the concern is that the actual one-period

[25] **Edward J. Kane** and **Burton G. Malkiel,** "The Term Structure of Interest Rates: An Analysis of a Survey of Interest Rate Expectations." *Review of Economics and Statistics,* August 1967, p. 354.

[26] **William Trudgian** and **R. H. Scott,** "A Survey of Maturity Pattern of Yields. *University of Washington Business Review,* Spring 1971, pp. 65–76.

[27] **Franco Modigliani** and **Richard Sutch,** "Innovations in Interest Rate Policy." *American Economic Review,* May 1966.

rate prevailing at the beginning of the record period, $_2R_1$, would fall short of $_2r_1$. This is so because of risk aversion. Against this background, the investor would demand a risk premium L_1. Therefore, for the investor with a two-year horizon to be interested in a one year bond, the following must be true:

$$(1 + {_1R_2}) < [(1 + {_1R_1})(1 + {_2r_1} + L_1)]^{1/2}$$

If $_2r_1 < {_2R_1}$, the investor is much better off than expected. If, on the other hand $_2r_1 > {_2R_1}$, the investor would be worse off; thus the compensation for risk. For equilibrium to be reestablished, the following equation must hold:

$$(1 + {_1R_2}) = [(1 + {_1R_1})(1 + {_2r_1} + L_1)]^{1/2}$$

which can only be obtained if L_1 is negative, for in the certainty case,

$$(1 + {_1R_2}) = [(1 + {_1R_1})(1 + {_2R_1})]^{1/2}$$

Simply stated, for $_2R_1 = {_2r_1} + L_1$, L_1 must be negative if $_2r_1 > {_2R_1}$. Using logic opposite that of the above, a positive risk premium would be required for a bond with a maturity exceeding two years.

Therefore, provided risk is adequately compensated for, there can be a cross elasticity in maturities. Risk-averse investors do not necessarily have a preference for short maturities but do hedge by staying in their preferred maturity habitat unless other maturities (longer or shorter) offer a sufficient inducement through a risk premium. Thus, the "liquidity premium" can assume positive, zero, or negative values, depending on the nature of the supply and demand factors for a given maturity and across maturities. The empirical tests conducted by Modigliani and Sutch did not confirm that changes in the supply of government securities affect the term structure of interest rates.

It can be said, in conclusion, that to understand the behavior of interest rates one must pay attention to expectations, liquidity premiums, and supply and demand factors.

11.7 FORECASTING INTEREST RATES

The analysis thus far should confirm the importance of forecasting interest rates. An accurate forecast should enable an investor to adjust the maturity of his or her portfolio so as to avoid the adverse effects of interest rate changes. To illustrate this point and summarize the issues, we distinguish between yield to maturity on a bond and one-period return on a bond R.

We define R as

$$R = \frac{C + MP_1^B}{MP_0^B} - 1 \tag{11.20}$$

where C = coupon rate $\times$ face value of bond

MP^B = market price of bond

Yields and returns move in the opposite direction, as shown in Figure 11.8.

A rising yield curve (curve A, Fig. 11.8a)—assuming that the bond is bought at the beginning of the period and sold at the end of it and that the yield curve is properly constructed and has a sufficiently steep slope—shows falling returns due to capital losses. If, on the other hand, yields are falling, returns on bonds would rise due to capital

TABLE 11.1a
Summary of Financing—Total Funds (in Billions of Dollars)

	1975	1976	1977	1978	1979	1980 (est.)	1981 (proj.)
Funds Raised							
Investment funds	119.3	143.9	192.6	219.7	228.7	210.0	228.2
Short-term funds	2.7	58.6	94.8	125.1	121.0	71.1	89.3
U.S. government and budget agency securities, privately held	78.1	59.4	51.5	46.8	29.9	74.3	79.9
Total uses	200.1	261.9	338.9	391.6	379.7	355.4	397.4
Funds Supplied							
Insurance companies and pension funds							
Life insurance companies	19.0	26.7	29.4	33.7	33.6	34.3	32.6
Private noninsured pension funds	14.1	12.5	16.5	16.0	22.8	25.3	28.3
State and local retirement funds	11.5	12.4	13.9	14.9	19.6	23.9	28.2
Fire and casualty insurance companies	6.0	12.4	19.2	19.2	17.3	17.0	16.7
Total	50.6	64.1	79.0	83.8	93.4	100.5	105.8
Thrift institutions							
Savings and loan associations	36.6	51.9	64.9	57.1	49.7	43.1	51.7
Mutual savings banks	10.9	12.5	11.7	7.9	3.8	5.5	7.9
Credit unions	5.0	6.6	8.2	8.3	2.4	3.5	6.6
Total	52.5	71.1	84.8	73.4	55.9	52.1	66.2
Investment companies	3.1	1.4	2.9	5.2	22.1	24.4	18.5
Other financial intermediaries							
Finance companies	2.0	8.3	16.2	17.7	21.0	8.8	13.3
Mortgage companies	1.2	2.7	3.0	2.8	.7	-2.1	—
Real estate investment trusts	-4.8	-3.8	-2.4	-1.0	-.3	—	—
Total	-1.6	7.2	16.8	19.5	21.4	6.7	13.3

Commercial banks	31.5	66.3	89.9	125.9	120.3	96.5	102.3
Business							
Business corporations	12.4	14.9	11.4	9.7	14.6	12.7	21.3
Noncorporate business	.8	1.4	1.6	1.6	1.7	1.0	1.0
Total	13.2	16.3	13.0	11.3	16.3	13.7	22.3
Government							
U.S. Government	6.2	–.8	2.0	3.2	6.3	6.2	6.2
Nonbudget agencies	6.6	6.9	2.8	13.5	19.7	16.8	16.3
State and local general funds	8.6	8.8	8.2	15.2	6.0	13.3	15.2
Total	21.4	14.9	13.0	32.0	32.1	36.3	37.7
Foreign Investors	10.4	17.9	42.1	40.1	–4.9	20.8	28.0
Individuals and others	24.3	17.9	25.9	47.7	73.8	41.6	43.1
Total gross sources	205.4	277.1	367.4	438.9	430.3	392.6	437.2
Less: Funds raised by financial intermediaries							
Investment funds	4.4	8.2	10.9	9.0	10.0	10.5	10.3
Short-term funds	–.8	5.0	11.6	14.4	17.1	4.3	10.2
Nonbudget agency securities privately held	1.8	2.0	6.0	23.9	23.6	22.4	19.3
Total	5.3	15.2	28.5	47.3	50.7	37.2	39.8
Total net sources	200.1	261.9	338.9	391.6	379.7	355.4	397.4

TABLE 11.1b
Summary of Financing—Investment Funds (in Billions of Dollars)

	1975	1976	1977	1978	1979	1980 (est.)	1981 (proj.)
Funds Raised							
Corporate securities							
Bonds	27.2	22.8	21.0	20.1	21.2	32.5	31.5
Stocks	10.7	10.0	2.7	2.6	3.5	9.0	11.0
Total	37.9	32.8	23.7	22.7	24.7	41.5	42.5
State and local securities	16.1	15.7	23.7	28.4	22.4	26.3	24.5
Real estate mortgages	57.2	87.1	134.0	149.0	158.6	125.3	143.0
Foreign securities	6.5	9.1	5.5	3.5	4.8	3.9	3.7
Term loans							
Commercial banks	1.3	−1.2	5.2	15.7	17.7	12.5	14.0
Banks for cooperatives	.3	.5	.5	.4	.6	.5	.5
Total	1.6	−.7	5.7	16.1	18.3	13.0	14.5
Total	119.3	143.9	192.6	219.7	228.7	210.0	228.2
Funds Supplied							
Insurance companies and pension funds							
Life insurance companies	15.1	23.6	26.3	28.4	25.9	24.0	25.0
Private noninsured pension funds	11.8	11.3	13.5	15.2	19.4	20.5	23.1
State and local retirement funds	9.8	9.6	10.2	9.5	13.3	16.7	19.6
Fire and casualty insurance companies	3.3	9.0	15.7	18.3	16.1	12.5	12.7
Total	40.0	53.5	65.7	71.5	74.7	73.7	80.4
Thrift institutions							
Savings and loan associations	32.6	47.0	60.7	55.7	48.6	36.4	46.5
Mutual savings banks	7.8	10.3	11.1	8.8	4.2	2.8	4.3
Credit unions	.1	.9	1.8	.5	.4	.3	.5
Total	40.5	58.2	73.6	65.0	53.1	39.5	51.3

Investment companies	2.6	1.9	2.2	.9	2.2	6.8	8.5
Other financial intermediaries							
Mortgage companies	1.2	2.7	3.0	2.8	.7	-2.1	—
Real estate investment trusts	-4.8	-3.8	-2.4	-1.0	-.3	—	—
Total	-3.6	-1.1	.6	1.8	.4	-2.1	—
Commercial banks	8.9	16.4	43.8	61.5	60.7	45.7	46.7
Business corporations	-.2	-1.1	—	.2	—	-.1	—
Government							
U.S. Government	6.2	-.8	2.0	3.2	6.3	6.2	6.2
Nonbudget agencies	5.6	3.4	4.0	12.6	15.0	13.1	12.7
State and local general funds	4.0	3.7	.8	3.6	4.4	9.5	11.2
Total	15.9	6.3	6.7	19.4	25.7	28.8	30.1
Foreign investors	5.3	3.1	3.5	2.7	1.7	5.5	5.5
Individuals and others	14.2	14.9	7.4	5.6	20.3	22.7	16.0
Total gross sources	123.7	152.1	203.5	228.7	238.7	220.5	238.5
Less: Funds raised by financial intermediaries							
Bonds	4.7	7.1	10.0	7.5	7.8	8.7	8.3
Stocks	-.3	1.1	.9	1.5	2.2	1.8	2.0
Total	4.4	8.2	10.9	9.0	10.0	10.5	10.3
Total net sources	119.3	143.9	192.6	219.7	228.7	210.0	228.2

Source: *Credit and Capital Markets 1981.* Bankers Trust Company, New York, 1981.

FIGURE 11.8 Various yield (a) and return (b) curves.

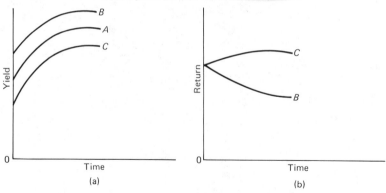

gains. If the yield curve shifts upward or downward with or without changing its slope, it would have an effect on the return curve. Figure 11.8 shows that an upward shift from *A* to *B* (Fig. 11.8a) translates itself into a new return curve (*B* in Fig. 11.8b). The shift of the yield curve from *A* to *C* translates itself into the rising return curve *C*.

The implications of these relationships for the investor are to shift the maturity of the portfolio toward the short end of the term structure if an upward shift in the yield curve is expected and to shift the maturity of the portfolio to the long term if a downward shift in the yield curve is anticipated. Both strategies, if expectations do materialize, would maximize the return on the bond portfolio.

The correct anticipation of the direction of interest rates is most valuable in the management of fixed-income securities. The ideal state, however, is to forecast not only the direction but the exact level of interest rates to prevail in the future. Most portfolio managers have learned over time to settle for knowing the direction of change in interest rates. To forecast the level of interest rates accurately has been all but impossible for economists on a consistent basis. In fact, no economist on record predicted the exact or even the approximate size of the historic rise in the prime rate between the middle of 1979 and early 1980 (up from 11.54 percent in July 1979 to 20 percent by April 2, 1980). This experience did not dampen the desire to forecast levels of interest rates, as economists continued to do for 1981 (Table 11.2). To give a range of 11 to 20 percent for the prime rate in 1981 is meaningless operationally and is not even entertaining. Despite this dismal record, the forecasting of interest rates continues unabated.

If the prime is currently 15 percent, the investment strategy would vary considerably depending on whether the prime rate were judged to be on the lower end of the range or on its upper end. One might just as well flip a coin. To repeat the words of George W. McKinley, Jr., chairman of the economic advisory committee of Irving Trust Co., as quoted in *The Wall Street Journal* of Jan. 5, 1981: "Anybody who can go out and say what interest rates will be at the end of the year has rocks in his head."

We now discuss a few of the forecasting techniques used by money managers and academicians. They range from the simple to the very complex.

Simple Forecasting Techniques

The payoffs from using any forecasting techniques depend on the nature of the financial markets. To forecast or not to forecast depends on the efficiency of the market. If the financial markets were strongly efficient, no amount of forecasting skill would produce yields higher than those obtained by buying a bond and holding it to maturity. That

TABLE 11.2
A Sampling of 1981 Prime Rate Forecasts

	'81 Average (percent)	High (percent)	Low (percent)	Year end (percent)
Irwin Kellner *Manufacturers Hanover*	14½	20	11	11
Donald Maude *Merrill Lynch*	15	22	12–13	13–14
Francis Schott *Equitable Life*	14–15	21½	13–14	15–16
George McKinney *Irving Trust*	12	21½	9–10	9–10
Leif Olsen *Citibank*	11½–12½	21½	11½	No forecast
David Jones *Aubrey G. Lanston*	14	21½	11	14
Alan Greenspan *Townsend-Greenspan*	15	21½	10–12	10–12
John O. Wilson *Bank of America*	18	22	14	14
Timothy Howard *Wells Fargo*	13½	21½	11	12–14
Norman Robertson *Mellon Bank*	16	21½	14	16
Allen Sinai *Data Resources*	15.36	21½	13	15
Albert Sindlinger *Sindlinger & Co.*		18–20	28–30	18½ "No idea"

Source: The Wall Street Journal, Jan. 5, 1981.

is, successive trades based on forecasts of interest rates would not outperform the naive buy-and-hold strategy in an efficient market.

An efficient market is one in which all publicly available information is impounded in the observed yield curve. The best predictor of the future course of interest rates is the yield curve, which represents all the investors' expectations—that is, the collective wisdom of the market. The evidence presented earlier in this chapter showed the deficiencies in the expectations hypothesis. Investors do not have homogeneous expectations and bonds of differing maturities are not perfect substitutes for each other. Thus, the forecasted rate implied in the yield curve

$$_{t+N-1}F_1 = \frac{(1 + {}_tR_N)^N}{(1 + {}_tR_{N-1})^{N-1}} - 1$$

is at best an approximation of yields that will prevail at the suggested time period in the future. An equally simple forecasting technique is the futures rate discussed in Chapter 14.[28]

---

[28] For a thorough analysis of the relationship between forward and future notes, the reader should consult **John C. Cox, J. E. Ingersoll, Jr.** and **S. Ross**, "The Relation Between Forward Prices and Futures Prices." Center for the Study of Futures Markets, Columbia University, New York, May 1981.

The arguments in Chapter 4 with regard to market efficiency and its implications are very relevant here. The technology of information gathering employed by portfolio managers, the employment of an army of financial analysts, and the existence and prosperity of forecasting services like Wharton Econometric Forecasting Associates, Inc., could be indicators of inefficient markets. The models employed by the various advisory or in-house services range from the very simple to the very complex.

Some of the simple models are of the following form:

$$K_{d,L} = a + \sum_{i=0}^{t} b_i (K_{d,s})_{-i} + \xi \tag{11.21}$$

or

$$K_{d,s_t} = a + b_1 K_{d,s_t-1} + b_2 \left(\frac{\Delta P}{P}\right)_t + \xi \tag{11.22}$$

where $K_{d,L}$ = long-term yield to maturity
$K_{d,s}$ = short-term yield to maturity
$(\Delta P/P)_t$ = current rate of inflation
ξ = error term

The coefficients a and b_i are estimated using regression techniques. A technique that is gaining popularity involves the usage of *expected* inflation and *expected* short rates (ordinarily estimated using rational expectations theory) to predict long rates of interest.

Another frequently used method is that of developing a table showing the source and use of funds for each maturity and/or for the economy as a whole. Having arrived at the expected level of supply and demand for the period under consideration, the next step would involve the determination of that level of the interest rate that would equate supply to demand, given some assumptions about the elasticities of the supply and demand.

An interesting method used by Morgan Guaranty Trust Co. of New York (and described by Irwin Kabus in the May–June 1976 issue of the *Harvard Business Review*) is called *histogramming*. A histogram is a graphic presentation of the probability distribution of certain ranges of the variable under examination; its height represents the probability of occurrence. For example, assume that a committee of three were charged with the investment strategy of an institution and that each member were asked (1) to forecast the ranges of the prime rate and (2) to estimate the probability that this forecast would prove accurate. The results might appear as in Figure 11.9a.

Each individual would turn in his or her interest rate estimates based on personal judgment and/or analysis. If each had equal weight in the organizational structure, a simple arithmetic average of the histograms would be taken. (Perfect mathematical accuracy in terms of the range and the associated probability is not absolutely necessary; both qualitative and quantitative factors are important.)

Figure 11.9b presents the average of the histograms in Figure 11.9a. The base of each histogram here covers 0.5 percent. The consensus is that the probability that interest

FIGURE 11.9

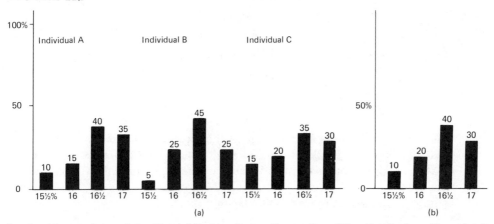

(a)   (b)

rates will exceed 16 percent is 70 percent. The expected rate $E(R)$ is, therefore, equal to $E(R) = 15.5 \,(0.10) + 16 \,(0.20) + 16.5 \,(0.40) + 17 \,(0.30) = 16.45\%$.

From Figure 11.9 a cumulative probability distribution can be developed, allowing for the calculation of the probability that a certain interest rate will prevail or that values below a certain rate will obtain. The histogram technique spreads the burden of predicting interest rates and makes it more manageable. We now turn our attention to a much more complex forecasting technique.

The Wharton Model[29]

Wharton Econometric Forecasting Associates, Inc. (WEFA) makes available to subscribers forecasts on various interest rates. The latest version of the model completed in the autumn of 1981, follows these steps:

1. Forecast excess reserves
2. Calculate total bank reserves

    TR = RR + FR + currency held by nonbank public

    = adjusted monetary base

    = high-powered money

    where RR = required reserves

    FR = free reserves

3. Using the money multiplier, estimate the money supply. A money multiplier has the following form:

$$MR = \frac{1 + c + t}{e_{td}t + e_{dd} + c + f(r, r^d)}$$

---

[29] Supplied and partially developed by **Ed Friedman,** Financial Economist, Wharton Econometric Forecasting Associates, Inc., January 1982.

where c = currency/demand deposits

t = time deposits/demand deposits

e_{td} = required reserves on time deposits

e_{dd} = required reserves on demand deposits

f = free reserves/demand deposits = $f(r, r^d)$

r = market rate of interest

r^d = discount rate

4. Using the money supply figures, estimate the three-month T-bill rate.
5. On the basis of the T-bill note, estimate the other short-term rates, using single-equation models. This is possible because of the high correlation among short-term rates.
6. Estimate long rates using distributed lag models.

The following equation is used by WEFA to forecast free reserves:

$$
\begin{aligned}
\text{LHS} = {}&3.5104 + 0.4876X1 - 0.3966\,X2 - 0.3775X3 \\
&(4.75)\quad\;\,(7.19)\qquad\;(-6.93)\qquad\;(-7.52) \\
&+ 0.5736X4 - 0.2173\,D1 - 0.5144\,D2 \\
&\quad(6.98)\qquad\;(-0.66)\qquad\;(-1.96) \\
&-0.5664\,D3 - 0.8412X5 \\
&\quad(-2.15)\qquad(-5.88)
\end{aligned}
$$

(11.23)

adjusted R^2 = 0.941   SEE = 0.95889   DW = 1.01
Period of fit = 1960/01 (first quarter) to 1976/04

where $\text{LHS} = \dfrac{\text{free reserves of member banks} \times 1{,}000}{\text{four-quarter moving average of lagged demand deposits}}$

$X1 = \dfrac{(\text{free reserves of member banks})_{t-1} \times 1{,}000}{\text{four-quarter moving average of lagged demand deposits}}$

$X2$ = change in commercial loan demand

$X3$ = change in reserve requirements

$X4$ = change in nonborrowed reserves

$X5$ = three-month T-bill rate

$D1$ = dummy variable (First quarter seasonal; all first quarters = 1, zero otherwise.)

$D2$ = dummy variable (Second quarter seasonal; all second quarters = 1, zero otherwise.)

$D3$ = dummy variable (Third quarter seasonal; all third quarters = 1, zero otherwise.)

Variables $X2$, $X3$, and $X4$ are dynamic variables that affect excess reserves. Their impact vanishes with time. The estimation of the three-month T-bill rate (using quarterly data) is calculated as follows:

$$RTB = -1.7407 + 0.1935\ Y1 - 2.1373\ Y2$$
$$\qquad\ (-2.21)\qquad (.44)\qquad\ (-2.91)$$
$$\qquad -0.1526\ D4$$
$$\qquad\quad (-1.13)$$

$\overline{R}^2 = 0.919 \qquad SEE = 0.1206 \qquad DW = 1.393$

Period of Fit: 1960/01 $-$ 1980/04 $\hfill$ (11.24)

where $RTB = $ log of the three-month T-bill rate

$$Y1 = \log \left[\frac{\text{private domestic assets: U.S. govt. sec., treasury issues}}{\text{gross national product} - \text{federal government purchases}} \right]$$

where the numerator also includes "including savings bonds" and the denominator "of goods and services":

$$Y1 = \log \left[\frac{\begin{array}{c}\text{private domestic assets: U.S. govt. sec., treasury issues}\\ \text{including savings bonds}\end{array}}{\begin{array}{c}\text{gross national product} - \text{federal government purchases}\\ \text{of goods and services}\end{array}} \right]$$

$$Y2 = \text{Money} = \log \left[\frac{\begin{array}{c}\text{money supply, M1-A plus other checkable deposits} -\\ \text{currency in the hands of the public}\end{array}}{\begin{array}{c}\text{gross national product-federal government purchases}\\ \text{of goods and services}\end{array}} \right]$$

$D4 = $ Dummy variable, 0 before 1975/02, 1 after 1975/02.

The estimation of other short rates such as the commercial paper rate (CP) is then calculated as follows:

$$CP = -\ 0.1299\ + 1.1835\ TB$$
$$\qquad\ (-0.53)\qquad (25.61)$$

$\overline{R}^2 = 0.972 \qquad SEE = 0.33091 \qquad DW = 1.76$

Period of Fit: 1960/01 $-$ 1978/04 $\hfill$ (11.25)

where $TB = $ three-month T-bill rate.

We now look at one method used by portfolio managers to "insulate" their portfolios from interest rate risks. In this case, it is no longer necessary to forecast interest rates.

11.8 BOND IMMUNIZATION

The forecasting of interest rates is, as we have just argued, an inexact science if not an art form. Bond portfolio managers faced with the uncertainty of interest rates have devised a method for immunizing their bond portfolios from interest rate changes. In this case, the word *immunization* does not have the same meaning as it does in a biological context. The eradication of interest rate risk is realized only under certain circumstances, as we shall demonstrate below.

Equation 10.1 in Chapter 10 shows one way of calculating the market price of a bond:

$$MP_0^B = \sum_{t=1}^{n} \frac{C}{(1 + K_d)^t} + \frac{FV}{(1 + K_d)^n} \qquad (11.26)$$

The assumptions underlying Equation 11.26 are vital for an understanding of the bond immunization principle. They are as follows:

1. Constant coupon value $C_1 = C_2 = C_3 = \cdots = C_n$
2. Fixed time horizon $= n$
3. K_d is constant.
4. $K_d = $ yield to maturity and the reinvestment rate

The first two assumptions reflect reality in the marketplace. Bonds do have a fixed coupon and a fixed maturity. The yield to maturity K_d is realizable if and only if the coupon payments are invested at K_d. If interest rates change after the coupon payment is made, the realized yield RY would be lower or higher than K_d depending on the relationship between the duration of the bond d and the holding period H. Guilford Babcock[30] devised a simple formula for calculating the value of RY:

$$RY = \left(\frac{d}{H}\right)(K_d) + \left(1 - \frac{d}{H}\right)RR \qquad (11.27)$$

[handwritten: When d = H, realized yield = yield to mat]

where RR $=$ average reinvestment rate.

Commenting on Equation 11.27, Richard McEnally[31] observed that the realized yield is a weighted average of the yield to maturity and the reinvestment rate and that the realized yield would equal the yield to maturity if the duration of the bond were equal to the time horizon of the investor.

An increase in the reinvestment rate increases the income from reinvested coupons but decreases the value of the bond (unless held to maturity) given the inverse relationship between the market price of the bond and yield. The impact on the realized yield depends, therefore, on the extent to which the income effects offset the capital loss effects. A falling reinvestment rate produces a lower income from coupon investments but an appreciation in the market price of the bond. The impact on the realized yield depends, once again, on whether or not the capital gains offset the negative (less positive revenue from reinvestment) income effects. Equation 11.27 clearly suggests that the capital gains effects offset the income effects exactly when the duration of the bond purchased is equal to the time horizon of the investor (the expected holding period). The reasons for this conclusion should become clear in the example provided below. By the way of introduction, we offer Figure 11.10 as an illustration of the value of duration in the management of bond portfolios.

At d, the loss accumulation from coupon reinvestment due to a decrease in the reinvestment rate is exactly offset by the price gain. The desired yield to maturity is thus achievable if the investor chooses a bond whose duration is equal to his or her time horizon.

[30] **Guilford Babcock,** "A Modified Measure of Duration." Paper presented at the annual meeting of the Western Finance Association, San Francisco, June 1975.

[31] **Richard W. McEnally,** "How to Neutralize Reinvestment Rate Risk." *Journal of Portfolio Management,* vol. 6, no. 3 (Spring 1980), pp. 59–63.

FIGURE 11.10 Decrease in reinvestment rate.

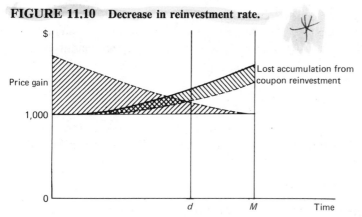

Reprinted with permission from Richard McEnally, "How to Neutralize Reinvestment Rate Risk," *Journal of Portfolio Management*, vol. 6, no. 3 (Spring
1980), pp. 59–63.

Immunization at Work

Immunization is a technique that allows for the transformation of a coupon bond into
a pure discount bond.

A pure discount bond trades at a price below face value and pays face value upon
maturity. The difference between face value and market price is the interest earned.
No income is collected in the interim, hence the reinvestment rate is of no concern.
The investor knows exactly the rate of return (provided the bond is held to maturity)
on the bond at the time of purchase. An example of such an instrument is the T-bill.
Unfortunately, longer-term instruments carry coupons that must be reinvested upon
collection.[32] The elimination of the risk resulting from a change in the reinvestment

---

[32] *The Wall Street Journal* disclosed in its April 15, 1981, issue plans by J. C. Penney to
offer "zero-coupon" long-term bonds. This followed an earlier private placement of a similar
bond by PepsiCo., Inc. Many foreign bond issues are pure discount issues, however. The popularity
of zero-coupon bonds in the United States is increasing. The Manufacturer's Hanover Corporation
issued deep discount bonds toward the end of 1981, which sold at $360 each. Upon maturity,
each bond will be worth $1,000. The difference ($640) is interest income and is taxed as such.
The interest income is allocated over the life of the bond (eight years in this case) and is taxable
each year as ordinary income. The actions of Manufacturer's Hanover followed that of Barclay's
American Co., which sold $200 million of zero-coupon notes maturing in 1990. The sale price
was $266.42.

The Wall Street Journal reported on Feb. 18, 1982, a new fund introduced by Paine Webber,
Inc., consisting solely of zero-coupon bonds. E. F. Hutton followed in March, with a zero-coupon
municipal bond fund. Also, in March 1982, Bank America announced a $500 million face amount
zero-coupon "money-multiplier notes" with three maturities. Unless held in a qualified retirement
account, the increase in the value of the zero-coupon bond is taxable in the year it accrues.

American corporations were also active in 1982 in the Eurobond markets, issuing various
types of zero-coupon bonds. Companies like Gulf Oil, General Motors, General Electric, and
Sears, Roebuck led the way.

A new method devised by Wall Street allows for the creation of a zero-coupon bond out of
a coupon bond, which are referred to as *strips*. A *strip bond* is a bond stripped of its coupons.
The principal and the coupons are then sold separately to investors with differing objectives.
The U.S. Department of the Treasury has expressed serious reservations about this innovation,
however. (*Continued*)

rate is thus of great importance to portfolio managers. In achieving this result, portfolio managers may well be foregoing favorable changes in the reinvestment rate—an outcome they are willing to live with given the risk-aversiveness that characterizes their investment strategies.

Example

Consider a four-year noncallable bond (call it bond A) bearing a 12 percent semiannual coupon. The bond is selling at par and has a duration of 3.2913 years, calculated as follows:

(1) t	(2) C	(3) PVD[a]	(4) (3 × 2)	(5) (4)/1,000	(6) (5)t
0	0	1	0	0	0
.5	60	.9434	56.60	.0566	.0283
1.0	60	.8900	53.40	.0534	.0534
1.5	60	.8396	50.38	.05038	.0756
2.0	60	.7921	47.53	.04753	.0951
2.5	60	.7473	44.84	.04484	.1121
3.0	60	.7050	42.30	.04230	.1269
3.5	60	.6651	39.91	.03991	.1397
4.0	1060	.6274	665.04	.66504	2.6602
			1000.00		**3.2913**

[a] Present value discount factor.

A pension fund manager with $1 million to invest over 3.2913 years (time horizon) would, beginning on Sept. 15, 1980 (the current date), invest in a security yielding a sufficiently high rate to guarantee the receipt of $1,467,500 on Jan. 1, 1984, when pension payments come due. The necessary rate for the target sum to be realized is 12 percent compounded semiannually.[33]

$$FV = \$1,000,000\left(1 + \frac{0.12}{2}\right)^{2\times3.2913} = \$1,467,500$$

Assume that the only two investments available to the pension fund manager are bond A and bond B. The latter bond is a 12 percent semiannual coupon bond maturing on January 1, 1984 and selling at par. Thus, the maturity of bond B coincides with

Another form of protection against changing interest rates was devised by Kidder Peabody & Co. and Citibank. Early in 1981, they issued put or option bonds which permit the holder to put (tender or sell back) bonds to the issuer at face value plus interest on the fifth anniversary of the issue and every anniversary thereafter.

While the ingenuity of investment bankers is becoming increasingly apparent, the instruments they have devised are still in their infancy and do not yet constitute a significant hedging mechanism.

[33] The use of yield to maturity here is slightly misleading. The rate to use should be the spot rate, that is, the yield on the term structure corresponding to five years. We chose yield to maturity in order to simplify the presentation.

the time horizon of the investor, while the duration of bond A coincides with the investor's time horizon.

In order to assure himself of the 12 percent required rate of return, the pension fund manager would select bond A because under certain circumstances it guarantees him 12 percent, while bond B does not necessarily do that as the reinvestment rate changes over time. This is demonstrated below.

We now examine the effects of reinvestment rate changes on the $1 million investment.

Case 1. The reinvestment rate falls to 11 percent on Dec. 1, 1980 (before the first coupon payment is received), and remains at that level for the rest of the manager's time horizon.

The reinvestment income from bond *A* per $1,000 is:

Income from first coupon	$(3/15/81) = 60(1.055)^{2 \times 2.791} =$	$ 80.90
Income from second coupon	$(9/15/81) = 60(1.055)^{2 \times 2.291} =$	76.68
Income from third coupon	$(3/15/82) = 60(1.055)^{2 \times 1.791} =$	72.68
Income from fourth coupon	$(9/15/82) = 60(1.055)^{2 \times 1.291} =$	68.90
Income from fifth coupon	$(3/15/83) = 60(1.055)^{2 \times 0.791} =$	65.30
Income from sixth coupon	$(9/15/83) = 60(1.055)^{2 \times 0.291} =$	61.90
	Total reinvestment income	**$426.36**

On Jan. 1, 1984, bond A will sell for $1,006.64, a capital gain of $6.64. The manager would receive $1,006.64 per bond and accrued interest of (3.5 months/6 months) 60 = $35.

Total income on Jan. 1, 1984, is equal to ($1,006.64 + 35 + 426.36) 1,000 = $1,468,000, or a yield of 12.01 percent calculated as follows:

$$1468 = 1,000\left(1 + \frac{Kd}{2}\right)^{2 \times 3.2913}$$

Therefore $K_d = 12.01\%$

If bond B were purchased instead of bond A, the investor would receive 3.5 months/ 6 months of the first coupon payment, which he or she can invest at 11 percent. The reinvestment income is equal to:

$35(1.055)^{2 \times 3}$	$= $ 48.26
$60(1.055)^{2 \times 2.5} =$	78.42
$60(1.055)^{2 \times 2} =$	74.33
$60(1.055)^{2(1.5)} =$	70.45
$60(1.055)^2 =$	66.78
$60(1.055)^{2 \times 0.5} =$	63.30
Total $=$	**$401.54**

Total cash received on Jan. 1, 1984 is equal to [1,000 + 60 (last coupon) + 401.54] [1,000 (bonds)], or $1,461,540, or a yield of 11.87 percent, 0.13 percent short of the 12 percent target.

So if market yields fall by one percentage point prior to the first coupon payment, if the fall is a one-time fall throughout the investment horizon, if the manager buys bond A (with a duration matching the time horizon), and if the manager follows the naive buy-and-hold strategy, the 12 percent yield is assured and the bond portfolio is immunized.

Case 2.   The reinvestment rate falls to 11 percent after the first coupon payment. The result of this fall in the reinvestment rate is additional interest income:

$$\text{From investment of first coupon } 60(1.06)^{2(2.791)} = \$83.06 \left\} \begin{array}{l} \text{at 6\% per} \\ \text{half a year} \end{array} \right.$$

$$\text{Previous income level } 60(1.055)^{2(2.791)} = \underline{\quad 80.90\quad} \left\} \begin{array}{l} \text{at 5.5\% per} \\ \text{half a year} \end{array} \right.$$

$$\text{Net difference } \$ \ \textbf{2.16}$$

Total cash received at the end of the hold period is therefore equal to $1,468 + 2.16 = $1,470.16.
The overall yield is now equal to

$$1,000\left(1 + \frac{K_d}{2}\right)^{2 \times 3.2913} = \$1,470.16$$

Therefore $K_d = 12.06\%$.
    Under similar conditions, bond B yields only 11.9 percent, 10 basis points below the targeted 12 percent rate of return.

Case 3.   The reinvestment rate falls twice; on Dec. 1, 1980, to 11 percent and on May 1, 1981, to 10 percent. The bond portfolio manager maintains the same naive buy-and-hold strategy; that is, he keeps the same bond he started out with.
    The reinvestment income from bond A is now equal to:

Income from first coupon (3/15/81)	$60(1.055)^{2 \times 2.791} =$	$ 80.90
Income from second coupon (9/15/81)	$60(1.05)^{2 \times 2.291} =$	75.03
Income from third coupon (3/15/82)	$60(1.05)^{2 \times 1.791} =$	71.46
Income from fourth coupon (9/15/82)	$60(1.05)^{2 \times 1.291} =$	68.06
Income from fifth coupon (3/15/83)	$60(1.05)^{2 \times 0.791} =$	64.81
Income from sixth coupon (9/15/83)	$60(1.05)^{2 \times 0.291} =$	61.73
	Total reinvestment income	**$421.99**

On Jan. 1, 1984, the market price of the bond should be $1,013.37, allowing a capital gain of $13.37. Again, the accrued interest received will be $35 (3.5/6 × 60). Total cash received on Jan. 1, 1984, would be $1,013.37 + 35 + 421.99 = $1,470.36.
    The yield is calculated as follows:

$$1,000\left(1 + \frac{K_d}{2}\right)^{2 \times 3.291} = \$1,470.36$$

Therefore $K_d = 12.06\%$ and the yield on holding bond B is equal to 11.76%.
    We can thus conclude that with one or more rate drops, the bond portfolio manager will earn at least the desired (required) rate of return if bond A is held to its duration with no portfolio revision. Bond B, whose maturity is equal to the time horizon, will fall short of the targeted rate of return.

Case 4. In this case we deal with rate increases.

If the market rates rise to 13 percent on Dec. 1, 1980, the reinvestment income for bond A would equal:

$$60(1.065)^{2 \times 2.791} = \$\ 85.27$$
$$60(1.065)^{2 \times 2.291} =\ \ \ \ 80.07$$
$$60(1.065)^{2 \times 1.791} =\ \ \ \ 75.18$$
$$60(1.065)^{2 \times 1.291} =\ \ \ \ 70.59$$
$$60(1.065)^{2 \times 0.791} =\ \ \ \ 66.29$$
$$60(1.065)^{2 \times 0.291} =\ \ \ \ \underline{62.24}$$

Total reinvestment income   **$439.64**

On Jan. 1, 1984, the bond will sell for $993.43, creating a capital loss of $6.57. The accrued interest received will still be $(3.5/6) \times 60 = \$35$. The total cash received on Jan. 1, 1984, would equal $993.43 + $439.64 + $35 = $1,468.07, or a yield of 12.01%.

The realized yield on bond B would have been 12.16%, however.

Case 5. Here there are two successive interest rate increases, to 13 percent on Dec. 1, 1980, and then to 14 percent on May 1, 1981. The exact dates, the reader must note, are not important as long as the increases occur between the coupon payments.

The reinvestment income from bond A is:

$$60(1.065)^{2 \times 2.791} = \$\ 85.27$$
$$60(1.07)^{2 \times 2.291} =\ \ \ \ 81.81$$
$$60(1.07)^{2 \times 1.791} =\ \ \ \ 76.45$$
$$60(1.07)^{2 \times 1.291} =\ \ \ \ 71.45$$
$$60(1.07)^{2 \times 0.791} =\ \ \ \ 66.78$$
$$60(1.07)^{2 \times 0.291} =\ \ \ \ \underline{62.41}$$

Total reinvestment income   **$444.17**

The total sum received on Jan. 1, 1984, is equal to 444.17 + 35.00 + 986.94 (prevailing market price) = $1,466.11. The yield corresponding to this receipt is $K_d = 11.97$ percent. The yield on bond B would have equaled 12.28 percent.

The results of all the cases discussed above can be summarized as follows:

Bond Market Events	Yield on Bond A in Percent	Yield on Bond B in Percent
Rates rise to 13 % immediately.	12.01	12.16
Rates rise to 13% on December 1 and then to 14% on May 1.	11.97	12.28
Rates rise to 13% on May 1.	11.964	12.13
Rates fall to 11% immediately.	12.01	11.87
Rates fall to 11%, then to 10%.	12.06	11.76
Rates fall to 11% on May 1, 1981.	12.06	11.90

It can therefore be said that for a *one-time immediate* rate increase or decrease in the reinvestment rate, the strategy of investing in a bond whose duration is equal to the time horizon guarantees the required rate of return. This rate will also be obtained if the reinvestment rate falls and would not be realized (by no more than three basis points in this case) if interest rates rose. In the latter case, the increase in interest income would not exactly offset the capital loss.

The impact of changes in the reinvestment rate on total wealth and on the realized yield if the sale of the bond is considered whenever a coupon payment is made is demonstrated in Table 11.3.

The values in Table 11.3 are plotted in Figure 11.11. The important factor to keep in mind is the time period at which the curves cross. The reader must note that the value 3.2913 years is the duration of bond A and is equal to the investment horizon of the portfolio manager. At the crossover point, the capital gains resulting from a decline in the market rate of interest exactly offset the reduction in interest income from coupon reinvestment. Similarly, at the crossover point, the capital losses resulting from a rise in the market rate of interest are exactly offset by the higher income realized by reinvesting the coupons received at the higher prevailing rate. Figure 11.11 illustrates the impact of an immediate 1 percent rise (or drop) in the market rate of interest and equivalently a rate change prior to the first coupon payment.

The inability of duration to immunize the bond portfolio completely lies in the fact that duration is not perfectly correlated with the passage of time. That is, with the passing of one month, duration will decrease by something less than one month, hence the need for frequent portfolio revision. The duration of bond A is 3.2913 years as calculated at purchase (four-year maturity and 13 percent coupon paid semiannually).

After the passage of six months, the new duration is 2.9588, which is not equal to $3.2913 - 0.5 = 2.7913$, the remaining time horizon. Bond A is no longer suitable for immunization.

TABLE 11.3
Impact of Changes in the Reinvestment Rate

Time Period (*T*)	11% Interest		13% Interest		12% Interest	
	Total Wealth	Yield if Sold	Total Wealth	Yield	Total Wealth	Yield
.0	1,031.67	—	969.56	—	1,000.	12
.5	1,088.41	17.68	1,032.58	6.52	1,060.	12
1.0	1,148.28	14.32	1,099.69	9.73	1,123.6	12
1.5	1,211.43	13.20	1,171.17	10.82	1,191.02	12
2.0	1,278.06	12.65	1,247.30	11.36	1,267.48	12
2.5	1,348.35	12.32	1,328.38	11.69	1,338.23	12
3.0	1,422.51	12.10	1,414.73	11.91	1,418.52	12
3.291	1,468.00	12.01	1,468.07	12.01	1,467.95	12
3.5	1,500.75	11.94	1,506.69	12.06	1,503.63	12
4.0	1,583.29	11.82	1,604.62	12.18	1,593.85	12

FIGURE 11.11   **Immunization with different reinvestment rates.**

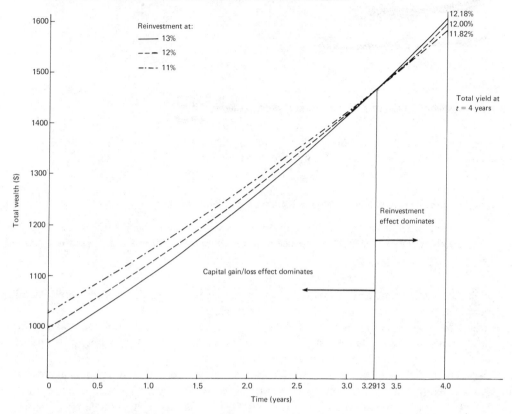

The new duration is calculated as follows:

(1) t^a	(2) $Cash^b$	(3) $PVDF^c$	(4) (3)(2)	(5) (4)/1,000	(6) (5)(1)
.0	0	0	0	0	0
.5	60	.9434	56.60	.05660	.0283
1.0	60	.8900	53.40	.05340	.05340
1.5	60	.8396	50.38	.05038	.07557
2.0	60	.7921	47.53	.04753	.09506
2.5	60	.7473	44.84	.04484	.1121
3.0	60	.7050	42.30	.04230	.1269
3.5	1,060	.6651	705.00	.70501	2.4675
			1,000.00	Duration	2.9588

^{a} Time from six months after purchase.

^{b} Receipt of the first coupon.

^{c} $[1 + (K_d/2)]^{-2t}$ = present value discount factor.

The new duration can also be calculated as follows:

$$(3.2913 - 0.5)\frac{1}{\text{PVDF}} =$$

$$(3.2913 - 0.5)\frac{1}{0.9434} = 2.9588$$

which is

$$\text{New duration} = (\text{old duration} - \text{actual time passed})\left(\frac{1}{\text{PVDF}}\right)$$

The assumptions of a one-bond portfolio and a naive buy-and-hold strategy must, therefore, be examined more closely. We do this next.

Bond Immunization—A More Realistic Approach

The discussion in the preceding section dealt with a one-bond portfolio. The fact is that portfolio managers do not utilize a single bond in immunizing their portfolios. The reasons are as follows:

1. The size of the pool of investable funds may well exceed the size of a given bond issue. The inclusion of another bond is, therefore, necessary.

2. Risk diversification is achievable only through the inclusion of more than one bond in the portfolio. The bonds' returns must be less than perfectly positively correlated to allow for the reduction of unsystematic risk.

3. The inclusion of more than one bond in the portfolio allows for greater flexibility and efficiency. One bond does not permit, as we have shown earlier, the necessary periodic adjustments to keep the bond portfolio immunized from interest-rate fluctuations. As interest rates change and as bonds move closer towards their maturity date, the immunization as originally set up would be unshackled. With more than one bond, the portfolio manager can adjust the weights (proportion of funds invested in each bond) in such a way as to ensure that the weighted duration is exactly equal to the remaining time horizon.

The structuring of such a bond portfolio is not very difficult. The process is as follows:

1. Select bonds with maturities equal to or exceeding the investor's time horizon. The type (government, corporate, etc.) and the quality (AAA, AA, A, etc.) of the bonds selected must correspond to the needs of the investor.

2. Combine the bonds in such a way as to maximize the yield to maturity on the portfolio and simultaneously immunize it.

Example

Using the same data from the preceding examples where duration $d = 3.2913$ years, the investor, wishing to invest exclusively in U.S. government securities, picks five T-notes listed in the Jan. 15, 1981, issue of *The Wall Street Journal*. The notes selected are described below.

Description of Note	Price (Asked)	Value of Semiannual Coupon Payment	Yield to Maturity	Remaining Time to Maturity (Years)
9¼ S 1984 May	91 7/32 = $912.19	46.25	12.57	3.2917
7¼ S 1984 August	85 13/32 = $854.06	36.25	12.43	3.5417
8 S 1985 February	86 6/32 = $861.88	40.00	12.41	4.0417
10 3/8 S 1985 May	93 21/32 = $936.56	51.88	12.31	4.2917
9 S 1985 August	90 10/32 = $903.13	48.13	12.46	4.5417

The immunization of the bond portfolio would require that the weighted duration $d = \sum_i X_i d_i$ be equal to the time horizon. The weight X_i is equal to the funds invested in a given bond divided by total investable funds.

The durations of these T-notes, as the reader should be able to verify, are respectively equal to 2.881 years, 3.155 years, 3.486 years, 3.541 years, and 3.738 years.

Solution

The immunization of the bond portfolio would require the solution of a linear program for the values of X_i, that is, the proportion of investable funds to be committed to each bond.

Maximized portfolio yield: $Y = \sum_i X_i Y_i$

$$
\left.
\begin{array}{l}
\text{Subject to } \sum_i X_i d_i = d_0 = t = \text{time horizon} \\[2ex]
\sum_i X_i = 1 \\[2ex]
\text{all } X_i \geqslant 0
\end{array}
\right\}
\qquad 11.28
$$

where X_i = proportion of funds invested in bond i
Y_i = yield to maturity of bond i
d_0 = desired (equal to time horizon) weighted duration

In terms of the data presented in the example, the linear program would be as follows:

Maximize $Y = 12.57\, X_1 + 12.43\, X_2 + 12.41\, X_3 + 12.31\, X_4 + 12.46\, X_5$

Subject to

1. $2.881\, X_1 + 3.155\, X_2 + 3.486\, X_3 + 3.541\, X_4 + 3.738\, X_5 = 3.2913$
2. $X_1 + X_2 + X_3 + X_4 + X_5 = 1$
3. $X_1 \geq 0,\ X_2 \geq 0,\ X_3 \geq 0,\ X_4 \geq 0,\ X_5 \geq 0$

The solution of the linear program results in the following values:

$X_1 = 0.521$
$X_2 = 0$
$X_3 = 0$
$X_4 = 0$
$X_5 = 0.479$

With $1 million to invest and given the market prices of notes 1 and 5, the portfolio manager would purchase 530 units of note 5 and 571 units of note 1 for a total investment of $479,000 in note 5 and $521,000 in note 1.

The weighted duration is equal to

$$(0.479)(3.738) + (0.521)(2.881) = \mathbf{3.291}$$

The yield on the portfolio is equal to

$$(12.46)(0.479) + (12.57)(0.521) = \mathbf{12.517\%}$$

The portfolio yield will therefore exceed the target yield of 12 percent while the immunization holds.

Our assumption that the portfolio manager wishes to concentrate on U.S. government securities can easily be modified to accommodate different types of bonds, such as corporate or municipal bonds, with the associated probable increase in the riskiness of the portfolio.

As interest rates change and as the weighted duration shifts with the passage of time, the portfolio manager shifts the investment in each bond in such a way as to keep the new duration equal to the remaining time horizon and thus keep the portfolio immunized. The portfolio revision may well include a substitution of one bond for another or others as conditions warrant. The strategy of frequent portfolio examination and revision, when necessary, is superior to naive immunization and to holding bonds the maturities of which are equal to the investor's time horizon.

More sophisticated immunization strategies intended to deal with several interest-rate changes have been devised by G. Bierwag.[34] The interested reader should examine this paper.

In conclusion, it can be said that immunization is a worthwhile strategy if and only if its limitations are kept in mind.

The various investment strategies using yield curves are discussed next.

11.9 USES OF THE YIELD CURVE

Yield curves have proven their usefulness in several cases:

1. As a tool for forecasting interest rates
2. As a tool for identifying overpriced, underpriced, or correctly priced debt instruments
3. As a strategy tool in helping the investor decide on the appropriate maturity for his security or portfolio of debt securities
4. As a tool for improving the realized rate of return by simply "riding the yield curve"

---

[34] **G. O. Bierwag,** "Immunization, Duration, and the Term Structure of Interest Rates." *Journal of Financial and Quantitative Analysis,* December 1977, pp. 725–742.

Yield Curves as a Forecasting Tool

From *The Wall Street Journal* and other daily business publications, the investor can observe the actual yields to maturity for various time horizons. From these quotations, using Equation 11.15, one can derive the expected rate of interest for any intervening time period, as was demonstrated earlier in this chapter.

Yield Curves and Bond Prices

Figure 11.12 best illustrates how yield curves allow for the identification of overpriced or underpriced debt securities.

Security *A* (assumed to have exactly the same characteristics as those securities utilized in the construction of the yield curve) has a lower yield (a higher price) than the security that plots on the yield curve. The investor should avoid security *A* in a long position or should (the intelligent route) establish a short position in *A*. Security *B* is, on the other hand, underpriced in relation to the market. Buying this security will allow for a higher rate of return than is generally available in the marketplace.

Yield Curves and Maturity Structure

Yield curves are useful tools for policy makers, corporations contemplating the issuance of debt, and bond portfolio managers.

Policy makers frequently attempt, though with infrequent success, to manipulate the term structure of interest rates through changes in the supply of securities in the designated maturities. The most ambitious undertaking of this type was "Operation Twist," whereby the Kennedy administration attempted to increase the short-term rates in order to increase the flow of funds into the United States and thus improve the balance of payments, and reduce the long rates in order to encourage investment.

This policy would have changed the yield curve from an upward-sloping curve to a descending curve (dashed line), as shown in Figure 11.13. The existing shape of the yield curve, it was thought, was not consistent with national policy objectives. The Federal Reserve System issued short-term securities and bought long-term securities,

FIGURE 11.12 Evaluative yield curves.

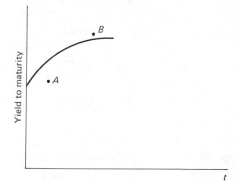

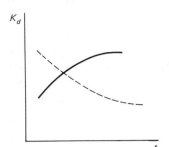

FIGURE 11.13   **Rising and descending yield curves.**

thus raising short-term rates and lowering long-term rates. The degree of success that this policy achieved is the subject of controversy. The accepted wisdom, however, is that government was reaching beyond its limits of influencing conditions in the financial markets.

The U.S. Treasury does, however, use the yield curves successfully in deciding on the appropriate maturity to issue. That maturity with the lowest number of outstanding securities, given a yield, may well be the one capable of withstanding a new issue without significant impact on the structure of yields.

From the corporation's point of view, the yield curve is of great value in timing the issuance of debt instruments and in deciding on the maturity structure of the debt issue. A corporate treasurer looking at a flat yield curve but expecting yields on long-term securities to rise would issue long-term securities now in order to "lock-in" the cheaper borrowing rate. Corporate treasurers expecting a drop in yields from the high indicated by the observed yield curve may well choose to borrow short term and then roll over the debt into long term debt when and if rates do in fact drop.

To a portfolio manager, a continuously rising yield curve, for example, indicates higher and higher expected yields, that is, successively lower and lower bond prices. The appropriate strategy may well be, assuming that the yield curve reflects the investor's own expectations (the investor's expectations coincide in this case with those of the market), to purchase longer-term bonds. If the investor disagrees with the expectations of the market and expects interest rates to rise farther than indicated by the yield curve, he or she may well invest in short term securities in order to avoid the capital losses resulting from the drop in the price of bonds. Some financial theorists claim, however, that the length of the maturity of a bond portfolio depends on the special characteristics of the business the investor is in and is not dependent on the relationship between short-term and long-term rates; that is, they maintain that insurance companies will always opt for long-term securities and commercial banks for shorter-term securities with considerable liquidity because of the nature of their businesses. We shall further scrutinize this issue later in this chapter.

Riding the Yield Curve

Riding the yield curve is a strategy intended to capitalize on certain shapes of the yield curve that are expected to hold over a period of time. Given the shape of the yield curve, the question for an investor with a certain time horizon t is whether to

FIGURE 11.14 Yield curves positions.

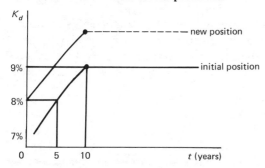

purchase a security maturing at time *t* or to purchase a longer-term security and sell it at time *t*.

Consider the yield curve shown in Figure 11.14. Assume that this curve is expected to hold for a period of time. An investor with a five-year horizon can invest in a five-year security; in a security with a maturity longer than five years and sell it after five years; in shorter-term securities (say one year) and reinvest the proceeds every year for five years; and so on.

We assume that the ten-year bond (Fig. 11.14) is selling at par ($1,000) with a 9 percent semiannual coupon and yield to maturity. As the bond moves closer to maturity ($t \rightarrow 0$, that is, moving from right to left down the yield curve), its price will increase as the yield on similar bonds decreases. At $t = 5$, the price of the ten-year bond with five years remaining life to maturity would equal $1,040.55 (using Equation 11.26), producing a capital gain of $40.55. The annual yield on this bond can now be approximated as follows:

$$K_d = \frac{90 + (40.55/5)}{(1,000 + 1,040.55)/2} = 9.65\%$$

This 9.65 percent yield is achievable by investing in a bond with maturity equal to *t* at the point of inflection in the yield curve (ten years in our case). The underlying assumption to the calculation of K_d above is that the reinvestment rate is equal to 9 percent. However, as the yield curve makes clear, the reinvestment rate for the coupons is decreasing continuously between the tenth and the fifth year, which implies that the realized yield will be less than 9.65 percent but certainly higher than the 8 percent that could have been earned on a five-year bond, on five consecutive investments in one-year bonds, or on other consecutive investments in shorter maturities.

Once again, the reader is reminded that riding the yield curve—that is, taking advantage of the structure of rates as bonds move closer to maturity without any trading in the portfolio—is dependent on the assumption that the shape and the position of the yield curve remains intact or does not move unfavorably. If the yield curve shifts upward and its slope remains the same as in Figure 11.14, if the yield curve shifts upward and changes slope, or if the curve just changes slope, the investor could have been better off—depending on the magnitude and the timing of the shift—investing in a series of shorter-term maturities. A downward shift in the yield curve would not affect the outcome or the conclusions of the example above, as the reader should be able to verify.

Since yield curves rarely stay in a fixed position, the common strategy is to revise the portfolio frequently.[35] As the yield curve changes position or slope, it may become advantageous to shift from long maturities to successive investments in short maturities. The investor should also consider the impact of transactions costs, which have been ignored thus far.

11.10 BOND SWAPS

Bond swaps involve the exchange of equivalent bonds selling at different prices; or the exchange of bonds with different coupons, different maturities, different risk characteristics, different types and belonging to different categories. The intent is to improve the rate of return on the bond portfolio by taking advantage of unjustifiable relationships between yields on debt securities, to reduce the tax burden, or to adjust the cash flows and/or the riskiness of the investment to the needs of the investor.

Swapping Equivalent Bonds Selling at Different Prices

Two bonds of exactly the same characteristics (same coupon, rating, maturity, liquidity, and other features such as sinking fund and call provisions) must sell at the same price whether issued by the same party or by different issuers of a similar profile. Securities issued, for example, by government agencies are excellent candidates for swaps if they sell at different prices. The strategy is to sell the overpriced bond and buy the underpriced bond.

	Price	K_d
Sell 20-year maturity of X agency	100	10%
Buy 20-year maturity of Y agency	99	10.10%
Net cash addition	1	

The net cash addition is $10 per $1,000, which can be used for other purposes. Simultaneously, an additional 0.10 percent in yield to maturity is earned. As soon as this aberration in market yields is corrected through arbitrage, the capital gain on the lower-priced bond would be larger than that on the overpriced bond for a given drop in market yields. This is an additional advantage of swaps. Ordinarily, this is not realized because swaps are typically short-lived.

A swap of agency X bond, if already owned by the investor, for agency Y bond is referred to as a substitution swap.

---

[35] It is instructive here to review the case of Institutional Liquid Assets Money Fund. The fund's advisor, the First National Bank of Chicago, thinking that interest rates were at an all-time high, recommended purchase of long-term government securities. Interest rates went higher and there were substantial capital losses (see *The Wall Street Journal,* Oct. 9, 1980). If you cannot predict the shape and position of the yield curve, invest in bonds with short maturities so as to keep maximum flexibility.

The profitability of swaps depends largely (if not exclusively) on the quality of the analysis before the swap transaction is entered into. Among the issues to consider are the following: (1) Is the yield differential truly unwarranted or is it justified by apparent (or "hidden") characteristics of the bonds? (2) Is the relationship between the expected yield adjustment period and the investor's time horizon favorable? (3) Are the transactions costs within reason or so high as to reduce or even eliminate any potential profits? (4) What are the tax consequences? and (5) Is the swap indeed the best one available?

Swapping Bonds with Differing Coupon and Maturity (Bond Spreads)

Swapping two bonds with very similar issuers but different coupons and a slightly different maturity is illustrated in Table 11.4. The Export Development Corporation of Canada is a federally owned commercial enterprise fully backed by the credit, faith, and the taxing power of the Canadian government.

On May 10, 1980, the differential in basis points was too large to be justified by the three-month difference in maturity, hence the designated transaction. The transaction entered into on May 10, 1980, was reversed on June 30, 1980, as yields shrank to a "normal" level. The resulting price differential in points was 0.625, or $18,750 on the $3 million transaction.

Major banks and bond dealers continuously monitor the debt markets for such opportunities and respond very quickly upon their discovery.

The reasons for the differential in yield between bonds with different coupon rates (all other characteristics being the same) have been partially explained in Chapter 10. Higher-coupon bonds experience less price volatility than lower-coupon bonds for a given change in yields. Furthermore, lower-coupon bonds realize a larger percentage of their total return in the form of capital gains instead of coupon income, while total income from higher-coupon bonds is distributed differently, with a larger share coming from the coupon payments. The significance of the differing distributions lies in the provisions of the tax laws, which give a preferential treatment to long-term capital gains (asset is held for more than a year).

Swaps of bonds with different coupons are consummated in the direction of the higher coupon (the long position) or of the smaller coupon (the long position) depending on the investor's expectations with regard to future rates of interest. If interest rates are expected to rise, a higher-coupon bond may be more desirable, for it will experience a

TABLE 11.4
Results of Swapping Two Bonds

Date	Trans-action	Amount	Issue	Coupon	Maturity	Quality	Price	Yield	Differential in Basis Points	Price Differential in Points	Price Differential in Dollars	
May 10, 1980	Sell	3,000,000	Government of Canada	9%	10/15/83	AAA/AAA	94.00	11.03			2,820,000	
	Buy	3,000,000	Export Dev. Corp. of Canada	9.85%	1/15/84	AAA/AAA	95.50	11.30	+27	−1.50	2,865,000	−45,000
June 30, 1980	Sell	3,000,000	Export Dev. Corp. of Canada	9.85%	1/15/84	AAA/AAA	91.75	12.58			2,752,500	
	Buy	3,000,000	Government of Canada	9%	10/15/83	AAA/AAA	89.625	12.63	+5	+2.125	2,688,750	+63,750
					Net Cash Addition					+0.625		+18,750

lower depreciation in its value than a bond with a lower coupon. Conversely, if market yields are expected to fall, the bond with the smaller coupon would be the most desirable, for it will realize the larger price appreciation.

Swapping Different Quality Bonds

The quality of the bond is reflected, to a large degree, in the rating given the bond by the various rating firms. Bonds with different ratings do not earn the same yield because of the risk differential, ceteris paribus. The yield spread normally falls in a range known to hold over long periods of time. If the yield spread between A-rated bonds and AAA-rated bonds has historically equaled 75 basis points and the investor observes that it is currently at 40 because of an undue appreciation in the price of the A-rated bond, he or she would sell the A-rated bond and buy the AAA-rated bond and reverse the transactions when the yield spread moved back to the normal range. Spreads of this type require considerable knowledge of the behavior of yields over time. Yield spreads tend to be smaller during periods of expansionary monetary policy and wider during contractionary monetary policy. If yield spreads are expected to widen, a swap from low-quality securities to high-quality securities is advisable; the opposite is true if yield spreads are expected to narrow.

Other Yield-Based Swaps

Other swaps may involve the sale (purchase) of a government security and the purchase (sale) of a corporate security with similar characteristics or the sale (purchase) of a straight debt bond and the simultaneous purchase (sale) of a convertible bond. Intimate knowledge of the yield-spread patterns under differing credit and economic conditions is essential. The intent here is to capitalize on yield spreads that are not considered normal for the period and the securities under consideration.

Tax Swaps

Tax swapping is a technique used ordinarily to establish a capital loss at the end of the tax year. Tax swaps are also used to update a portfolio or to consolidate holdings in certain issues.

For tax losses to be allowed on a swap, the acquired bonds must differ from those sold in two of the following three characteristics: coupon, maturity, and issuer. Often a slightly different coupon or a slightly different maturity is sufficient to appease the IRS. If the two bonds are not sufficiently distinct, the IRS would not permit the tax deduction on the basis that the swap constitutes a wash sale (see Chapter 18).

Capital losses realized from bond swaps can be used to offset capital gains, if any, or to reduce taxable income up to a maximum of $3,000. Long-term capital losses offset taxable income on a two-to-one basis; that is, it takes $6,000 in capital losses to qualify for the maximum $3,000 deduction.

The most often heard about tax swaps involve municipal bonds. These swaps often take place solely for tax reasons and are independent of the expectations of the investor with regard to future interest rates.

An example of a municipal bond swap might have an investor with $25,000 JAK County bonds swapping them for Gabriel County bonds at the end of the tax year.

The transaction results would be as follows:

Original purchase price of JAK bonds	(7½S'92)	$25,000
Sale price (12/25/81)		19,700
Capital loss		**$ 5,300**

Purchase of 7.65S'96 Gabriel bonds on 12/25/81 at 81. The total commitment is $25,000 × 0.81 = **$20,250.**

The capital loss can be applied against capital gains and current income as prescribed in Chapter 18.

In this swap, the investor reduced the tax burden for the current year, if not for future years, and increased cash flows (7.65 percent coupon rate on new bond vs. 7.5 percent on the old bond) while not increasing risk. Both bonds have an equal rating in this example.

Cash Flow Swaps

Cash flow swaps are intended to increase the cash flow from the bond portfolio. This is achieved by swapping low-coupon bonds for higher-coupon bonds. The swapped bonds are similar in every respect except for coupon rates.

The investor enters this transaction independent of the expected changes in interest rates. Some additional risk is being assumed, however. Higher-coupon bonds are more likely to be called by the issuer and are more susceptible to changes in the reinvestment rate. But high-coupon bonds experience a lower percentage change in price than lower-coupon bonds do as a result of a given change in yields. This last feature could be considered an advantage or a disadvantage depending on the risk profile of the investor.

Cash flow or "yield pick-up" swaps are popular with investors who are ready to retire. In this case they swap low-coupon bonds for higher-coupon bonds in the hope of increasing retirement income. Taxes and other considerations such as those discussed in substitution swaps are of paramount importance.

Upgrade Swaps

An upgrade swap is intended to improve the quality of the securities in the portfolio. This reduces the yield on the portfolio but decreases the risk of default and increases the marketability of the bonds held. Upgrade swaps are usually undertaken when poor economic conditions are expected. Conversely, switching to lower-grade bonds is done when a strong economy is anticipated because the spread between lower-quality bonds and higher-quality bonds narrows. This and the other swaps discussed earlier are but a confirmation that periodic reviews of the bond portfolio, taking market conditions and the investor's attitude into consideration, can pay handsome dividends.

CONCLUSIONS

The management of portfolios made up partially or totally of fixed-income securities is a rather complex process. There is considerably more to it than we have covered in this chapter. The basic considerations and relationships presented here should prove to be a superior foundation, however. While returns on bonds and stocks may be positively correlated, there is considerable opportunity to diversify risk by including bonds in any portfolio.[36] Thus, careful attention to the details presented here should prove rewarding.

QUESTIONS

1. The forecasting of interest rates—their direction and level—is of critical importance to portfolio managers. Attempts at accurately forecasting the level of interest rates have not been successful; indeed, they have failed miserably in many cases. Yet many forecasting services continue to try. Why?

2. The segmentation hypothesis is capable of explaining every shape of yield curve. What does a rising yield curve suggest under this hypothesis? A falling curve?

3. The expectations hypothesis is based on rather restrictive assumptions and denies the importance of supply factors. How does the segmentation hypothesis differ from the expectations hypothesis in these regards?

4. What does the "real rate of interest" component of nominal interest rates represent?

5. "The current policy which the Federal Reserve Board pursues will have the effect of driving up interest rates, for it increases the uncertainty about the level of interest rates." Comment.

6. What might happen if government "crowds out" business borrowers from capital markets?

7. "Flipping a coin is the best way to forecast interest rates." Do you agree? Why?

8. How are interest-rate forecasts embodied in the yield curve? Are the forecasts accurate? When do these forecasts change?

9. With which shape of the yield curve is the liquidity preference theory consistent?

10. Why might an investor be satisfied with a correct forecast of the direction of change in interest rates?

11. What might you conclude about market efficiency if a sophisticated model such as the Wharton model were shown to forecast interest rates with consistent accuracy?

12. "A bond portfolio manager who immunizes his portfolio guarantees himself that he will earn his desired rate of return." Comment.

13. What is the duration of a bond with a perpetual life (for example, a British consul)?

14. Does the duration of bonds increase or fall with increases in coupon rates? Why?

---

[36] See **William F. Sharpe**, "Bonds vs. Stocks: Some Lessons from Capital Market Theory." *Financial Analyst's Journal,* vol. 29 (November–December 1973), pp. 74–80.

15. An investor has decided to ride the yield curve by purchasing one-year T-bills (*P*) and selling them 9 months after purchase (*S*). Under what conditions will the strategy succeed or fail?

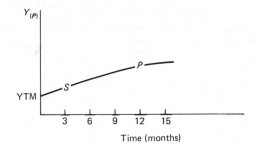

16. "Since yield curves change daily, they are of little use to investors as a forecasting tool." Do you agree? Explain.

17. How do yield curves help corporations time debt issues? How do they help investors structure the maturity of their debt portfolios?

18. What factors determine the yield that investors will demand on a bond?

19. What characteristics of duration are relevant to immunization?

20. A portfolio manager, aware of an upward-sloping yield curve, wishes to alter the maturity structure of her portfolio. How would you advise her?

21. What factors must a pension fund manager consider in constructing an "immunized" portfolio?

22. The method used by the treasury to construct yield curves is deficient. Why? Explain in detail.

PROBLEMS

1. A lender forecasts that inflation will average 5 percent per year over the life of a three-year loan. He seeks a real return of 3.5 percent on his money. What rate would he charge a no-default risk borrower?

2. An investor observes that a six-month T-bill currently yields 11.8 percent while a three-month bill offers a 10.5 percent return. Calculate the three-month rate expected to prevail three months hence.

3. A three-year bond issued by SMO Corp., selling at par, offers two $65 coupon payments semiannually. Calculate the bond's duration.

4. Use the shortcut formula to recalculate the duration of the SMO bond in problem 3 after three months have passed.

5. Estimate the yield to maturity of a five-year bond selling for $895 which offers $80 annually ($40 semiannually) in interest. What should a similar bond, selling at par, pay in interest semiannually?

6. If the return on three-month T-bills is 8.25 percent and the return on six-month T-bills with four months remaining is 8.55 percent, find the one-month rate expected to prevail three months hence.

7. An arbitrageur notices that his FHA bond yields 9.8 percent while FHLB bonds yield 10.2 percent. Under what conditions would he consider a bond swap? If he undertook the transaction, what would his expectation be?

Stock Options— Introductory Analysis

12.1 INTRODUCTION

The explosive growth in the number of stock options contracts traded and in the number of participants in the options market is but a reflection of the increased sophistication of financial instruments and of investors trying to deal in an increasingly complex and uncertain economic environment.

Since the Chicago Board Options Exchange (CBOE) pioneered the concept of listed options on April 26, 1973, the number of stocks whose options traded on the CBOE increased from 32 to 141 (both calls and puts) by the end of June 1982. The number of organized exchanges handling options contracts increased from one in 1973 to four in 1982 to include CBOE, the American Stock Exchange, Inc., the Philadelphia Stock Exchange, Inc., and the Pacific Stock Exchange, Inc. The dominant role is played by the CBOE, which accounted for 53.0 percent of the total volume of options contracts in May 1982. The options volume in shares as a percent of the volume of shares traded on the New York Stock Exchange reached 76.7 percent in May 1982, up from only 38.6 percent in 1975.

12.2 DEFINITIONS

Option. An option is a contract that carries privileges and obligations and is executed at the discretion of its holder.

Call option. An American call option gives its buyer, for a price called a premium, a right (option) to purchase at any time during the specified life of the contract 100 shares of the underlying security at a set price—the striking price (or exercise price). A European call has the same characteristics as an American call except that it is exercisable only upon expiration.

Put option. A put option gives its buyer, for a price called a premium, the right to sell at any time during the specified life of the contract 100 shares of the underlying security at a set price—the striking price.

12.3 THE OPTIONS CLEARING CORPORATION

The Options Clearing Corporation (OCC) is owned equally by its clearing members: the Chicago Board Options Exchange, Inc.; the American Stock Exchange, Inc.; the Philadelphia Stock Exchange, Inc.; and the Pacific Stock Exchange, Inc.

The OCC serves as a clearing agency by interposing itself between the buyer and the seller of the option without interfering in the market mechanism for price determination. Buyers and sellers, through their brokers, arrive at the option price (premium) on the floor of the participating exchange. What the OCC does is, in effect, to make the buyer's contract not with the seller but rather with the OCC. The same applies to the seller, whose commitments are now to the OCC and not the buyer.

Options contracts traded by clearing members are issued by the OCC with set expiration time and exercise price (striking price). The market price of the option as well as the transactions costs are determined by the market. Each type of option is assigned to one of three expiration month cycles: the January–April–July–October cycle, the February–May–August–November cycle, or the March–June–September–December cycle. A contract expiring in any of these months requires that the notice of exercise be given to the OCC by 11:59 P.M. eastern standard time on the Saturday immediately following the third Friday of the expiration month. Each option has one striking price (price at which the underlying stock could be bought in a call or sold in a put), and one expiration date. A common stock can, therefore, have many options with different striking prices and different expiration dates written on it.

The standardization of the terms of the options issued by the OCC, as well as the issuance of the option contract by the OCC which substitutes its ability to deliver on its commitments for that of the issuer, were intended to facilitate trading in the secondary market. Investors with option positions can choose to close out their positions at any time before the expiration date of their options simply by reversing the original position (sell if they had bought, buy if they had sold [written]).[1]

The OCC determines the exercise price of an option in the following manner: for a given expiration month, OCC selects two exercise prices surrounding the market price (e.g., 35 and 40 for a stock selling at 38). It then introduces new contracts with different striking prices as warranted by the movements of the market price of the stock—a new contract with a striking price of 30 if the market price of the stock falls to 32. New exercise prices may be set for one or every month of the expiration month cycle.[2] The usual intervals between striking prices are 5 points ($5) for stocks trading below $50 a share, 10 points for stocks trading between $50 and $200, and 20 points for securities trading above $200.

Upon receipt of an exercise notice from an option holder, the OCC, with a pool of options it can call on to answer the notice, selects at random from among all clearing member accounts with outstanding obligations on options with the exact characteristics as those being exercised. The clearing member, in turn, selects at random from the accounts of its clients with outstanding obligations on the option being exercised. The

---

[1] Selling an option is frequently referred to as writing an option. In this case, the option writer stands ready to buy the stock from the option holder in case of a put and to sell the stock to the options holder in case of a call at a fixed price during a specified period of time.

[2] For additional information on this and many issues relating to options, the reader should consult the prospectus of the OCC.

chosen client (the option seller or writer) would, therefore, have to deliver a security (100 shares per option contract) in the case of a call or buy a security in the case of a put. The terms for delivery are exactly as specified on their contract except for adjustments due to dividends, distributions, stock splits, recapitalizations, or reorganizations with respect to the underlying security. No adjustment is made for the declaration or payment of cash distributions. Stock splits, stock dividends, and other stock distributions increase the number of underlying shares and accordingly reduce the striking price of the option. If the underlying security were split two for one, a call option covering 100 shares with a striking price of 30 would turn into two options of 100 shares each at a striking price of $15. The number of options was adjusted in this case because the adjustment in the underlying security resulted in a new round lot. If not, the number of outstanding options would remain the same, with a different number of underlying shares and a different striking price. If a three-to-two stock dividend is declared, an option on 100 shares of stock with a $60 striking price becomes an option on 150 shares with a striking price of $40.

Investors with interest in the options market are limited by the OCC as to the size of their position. No single investor or group of investors acting in concert may own more than an aggregate (on all clearing member exchanges combined) of 1,000 puts and calls on the same side of the market in the underlying security. A call sold is on the same side of the market as a put purchased.

We advise the reader to examine the OCC prospectus for additional details on the issues covered above and other pertinent issues. The prospectus is available free of charge from any brokerage house.

12.4 BUYING CALL OPTIONS

Call options are traded on four different exchanges, all of which are members of the OCC. Call options transactions are reported regularly in *The Wall Street Journal,* as shown in Table 12.1. The first column refers to the underlying security and the closing price of the stock; the second column refers to the exercise or striking price—the price at which the options buyer may acquire the stock from (in the case of a call) or may sell the stock to (in the case of a put) the options writer; the December heading refers to the options expiration month (as does March); and so on. *Last* refers to the options price per one underlying share, but since options normally cover 100 shares, the price should be multiplied by 100 to arrive at the market price per call. An *r* entry in a column indicates that an options contract for that expiration month did not trade. An *s* entry indicates that the option is not available. An *o* indicates that the old last is the purchase price. The GM call option (indicated by ↔ in Table 12.1) has a striking price of $35, with a market price of $325 for the December contract and $500 for the March contract; no June GM call contract with a striking price of $55 or $60 was available on Dec. 4, 1981. The December GM put with a $35 striking price could be purchased for $12.50 on Dec. 4, 1981, while the underlying stock is selling for $38⅛.

In-the-Money Call

A call is in the money if the market price of the stock exceeds the striking price, that is, if the call can be profitably exercised. The investor will gain by calling the stock at the striking price and selling it in the marketplace for a higher sum. The higher the differential, the deeper in the money the call option is.

TABLE 12.1
Listed Options Quotations

Option & NY Close	Strike Price	Calls–Last Dec	Calls–Last Mar	Calls–Last Jun	Puts–Last Dec	Puts–Last Mar	Puts–Last Jun
Apache	15	r	r	r	1-16	r	r
20⅜	20	⅞	2¾	3¼	½	1 11-16	r
20⅜	25	1-16	13-16	1⅝	r	r	4½
20⅜	30	r	7-16	s	r	r	s
BrisMy	45	11½	r	r	r	r	1
56	50	6¼	7½	9	1-16	13-16	1¾
56	55	1½	4⅛	r	⅜	1 15-16	3
56	60	1-16	1¾	r	r	4¼	r
Bruns	15	4	4⅝	5	r	r	r
19⅛	20	¼	1 9-16	2¼	1¼	2	2⅜
19⅛	25	r	7-16	13-16	r	r	r
Chamln	15	6¾	r	r	r	r	¼
21⅞	20	1¾	2¾	r	3-16	¾	r
21⅞	25	r	¾	1¼	r	r	r
CompSc	10	r	2¾	3½	r	⅝	1
11½	15	r	11-16	1 5-16	3⅛	r	r
11½	20	r	5-16	r	r	r	r
CornGl	45	11½	r	s	r	r	s
56½	50	6½	8	s	1-16	⅞	s
56½	55	1¾	4½	s	⅝	2⅜	s
56½	60	¼	1¾	s	3¼	r	s
56½	70	r	½	s	r	r	s
Dow Ch	20	7	7¼	r	r	¼	r
27⅜	25	2½	3¼	3⅝	1-16	¾	1⅛
27⅜	30	1-16	⅞	1½	3	3⅜	r
27⅜	35	r	¼	s	r	r	s
Esmark	50	3¾	r	r	⅜	2⅞	r
53⅜	55	3-16	3⅜	r	r	r	r
Evans	20	⅝	r	s	⅜	1⅛	s
20¼	25	1-16	½	s	r	r	s
20¼	30	r	¼	s	r	r	s
Ford	15	4	4½	5	r	½	15-16
19⅛	20	5-16	1 5-16	2	15-16	2⅛	2⅝
19⅛	25	1-16	⅜	⅝	6¾	r	r
FptMcM	20	6	r	s	r	9-16	s
26	25	1 9-16	3¼	s	7-16	1⅞	s
26	30	⅛	1½	s	4⅛	4⅞	s
26	35	r	9-16	s	9½	r	s
26	40	1-16	5-16	s	r	r	s
Gen El	50	9⅞	11	12½	r	⅝	15-16
59⅞	55	4⅞	7	r	1-16	1⅛	r
59⅞	60	13-16	3¼	4¼	1 1-16	2⅞	4
59⅞	65	s	1	1⅞	s	r	r
G M	30	8¼	9⅜	10⅛	r	⅜	11-16
38⅛ ↔	35	3¼	5	5¾	⅛	1 9-16	2
38⅛	40	¼	2⅛	3¼	2	3⅝	4½
38⅛	45	1-16	11-16	1½	7⅛	7	7
38⅛	50	1-16	¼	11-16	12⅛	12	r
38⅛	55	r	3-16	s	r	r	s
38⅛	60	r	1-16	s	r	r	s
Glf Wn	10	7¼	r	r	r	r	r
17⅛	15	2¼	2¾	3	r	5-16	9-16
17⅛	20	1-16	½	13-16	3	r	r
17⅛	25	1-16	r	s	r	r	s
HughTl	25	r	r	r	r	1-16	r
42⅞	30	r	r	r	r	⅜	¾
42⅞	35	8⅛	9½	11¼	1-16	⅞	1⅞
42⅞	40	3¼	5½	7⅛	5-16	2	3¼
42⅞	45	7-16	2¾	4¾	2½	4¼	r
42⅞	50	1-16	1 5-16	s	r	r	s
I T T	25	4⅞	5⅝	r	r	5-16	r
30	30	½	1 9-16	2⅜	⅜	1⅛	r
30	35	r	7-16	¾	r	r	r
K mart	15	1⅝	2⅝	3	r	⅜	r
16⅝	20	1-16	⅝	1 1-16	3⅞	4	r
16⅝	25	r	¼	s	r	r	s
Litton	45	r	13⅛	r	r	⅜	r
57¼	50	7⅜	9⅞	12	1-16	1¼	r
57¼	55	3⅛	6⅛	8½	½	2⅜	r
57¼	60	9-16	3⅜	5¼	2⅞	4⅝	r
57¼	65	1-16	1⅝	r	r	r	8½
Lttn o	49	8½	10½	s	r	15-16	s
57¼	53⅞	4¼	r	s	5-16	2⅛	s
57¼	58⅞	15-16	4	s	2⅛	4¼	s
57¼	63¾	⅛	r	s	r	r	s
57¼	68⅝	1-16	r	s	r	r	s
57¼	78⅜	1-16	r	s	r	r	s
Mc Don	55	11	12¾	r	1-16	r	r
66	60	6	8¾	r	1-16	1⅞	r
66	65	2	5¼	7½	1¼	3⅜	5
66	70	¼	2⅝	5¼	4¾	6	6
66	80	r	11-16	r	r	r	r
Mid SU	10	3⅜	3⅜	3⅜	r	r	r
13½	15	r	3-16	⅜	r	r	r
N C R	35	s	8	r	s	r	r
42¼	40	2 5-16	4½	5⅞	5-16	2	3
42¼	45	3-16	2 1-16	3¾	3¼	4	r
42¼	50	r	⅞	1⅞	8½	8½	9
Nw Ind	40	35	36¼	s	r	1-16	s
76	45	30¾	31⅜	31½	r	1-16	⅛
76	50	26	26½	27¼	1-16	3-16	½
76	55	21	21½	22⅝	r	¼	⅝
76	60	15¾	16¾	18½	r	½	1 7-16
76	65	11	12¾	15	1-16	1⅜	r
76	70	s	9	10¾	s	2¾	3½
76	80	s	4	6½	s	7½	8¼
Ow Ill	25	4¾	r	s	r	⅜	s
30	30	⅝	1¾	s	⅝	1 7-16	s
30	35	r	⅜	s	r	r	s
R C A	15	3	3½	3⅞	r	⅜	⅝
18¼	20	1-16	¾	1 3-16	2 7-16	2⅝	3
18¼	25	r	3-16	s	r	7	s
RalPur	10	1⅝	1⅞	2⅜	r	¼	⅜
11¾	15	r	3-16	⅜	3⅜	r	r
Revlon	25	6¾	7⅝	7½	r	¼	9-16
31¼	30	1⅝	3	4½	5-16	1	r
31¼	35	1-16	1 1-16	2	3½	3½	r
31¼	40	r	7-16	1⅛	r	r	r
31¼	45	r	3-16	s	r	r	s
Rockwl	25	5⅛	5⅞	s	1-16	⅜	s
30⅛	30	1 1-16	2 13-16	s	¾	1½	s
30⅛	35	1-16	1	s	r	5¾	s
30⅛	40	r	½	s	r	10¾	s
30⅛	45	r	¼	s	r	r	s
Safewy	25	1¾	2⅝	s	r	⅜	s
26¾	30	r	11-16	s	r	r	s
Sears	15	1 15-16	2⅜	2⅞	r	⅜	r
16⅞	20	1-16	5-16	⅝	3¼	r	r
16⅞	25	1-16	1-16	s	r	r	s
SupOil	25	r	15	r	r	r	⅜
39⅝	30	9¾	10¾	12	1-16	⅝	15-16
39⅝	34	5¾	8	s	1-16	1¼	s
39⅝	35	4¾	7½	8¾	3-16	1¾	2 5-16
39⅝	36	3¾	6⅞	s	5-16	2	s
39⅝	38	2½	5⅜	s	13-16	3	s
39⅝	40	1 5-16	4⅜	6	1¾	4⅛	4½
39⅝	44	½	s	s	r	s	s
39⅝	45	⅜	2½	4¼	5¾	r	r
39⅝	48	3-16	s	s	r	s	s
39⅝	50	⅛	1½	s	r	r	s
Syntex	45	r	15¼	16¼	r	⅜	r
60¼	50	11	13¼	13¾	1-16	⅝	r
60¼	55	5⅛	8¼	11	⅛	1¼	r
60¼	60	1 11-16	5	8	1⅜	3¼	4
60¼	65	s	2¾	4⅝	s	r	r
60¼	70	1-16	1¾	s	r	r	s
Tektrn	50	4⅜	7⅛	r	¼	2⅛	r
55	55	1	4	r	1¼	3½	r
55	60	1-16	2	r	5½	r	r

Option & NY Close	Strike Price	Calls–Last Jan	Calls–Last Apr	Calls–Last Jul	Puts–Last Jan	Puts–Last Apr	Puts–Last Jul
Alcoa	20	6⅞	r	r	r	r	r
26¾	25	2⅝	3⅜	4¼	⅜	1	r
26¾	30	[illegible]	1⅛	1 9-16	r	r	r
26¾	35	⅛	s	s	r	s	s
26¾	40	1-16	s	s	r	s	s
Am Tel	50	10	10⅝	s	r	r	s
59⅜	55	5¼	5⅞	r	3-16	¾	r
59⅜	60	1⅜	2½	3⅝	1¼	r	2⅞
59⅜	65	⅛	11-16	1 5-16	r	r	r
Atl R	40	9	r	r	⅛	r	1
48½	45	4⅝	6	r	11-16	1⅝	r
48½	50	1½	3	4⅜	2½	r	r
48½	55	7-16	1⅜	2¼	r	r	r
48½	60	⅛	¾	s	r	r	s
Avon	30	3⅜	r	r	5-16	15-16	r
32⅝	35	¾	1⅜	2⅜	2½	r	r
32⅝	40	1-16	5-16	r	r	r	r
BankAm	20	4¼	r	r	r	r	r
24	25	½	1¼	r	r	r	2½
24	30	1-16	5-16	s	r	r	s
Beth S	20	3½	3¾	r	r	⅝	r
23	25	7-16	1⅛	1¾	1 15-16	r	r
Burl N	40	15½	17¾	s	1-16	⅝	s
55⅛	45	11	13	14¼	5-16	1½	r
55⅛	50	6⅝	9⅛	11⅜	1	3	3⅞
55⅛	55	3½	6⅛	r	3	5⅛	r
55⅛	60	1 5-16	3⅝	5¼	5⅝	7⅜	r
55⅛	70	3-16	s	s	r	s	s
55⅛	80	r	s	s	24⅞	s	s
Burrgh	30	5	r	r	r	r	r
Citicp	20	r	r	7¼	1-16	r	r
26⅝	25	1¾	2¾	3⅝	⅜	1	r
26⅝	30	5-16	⅞	1⅛	r	4	r
26⅝	35	1-16	s	s	r	s	s
Delta	22½	1 5-16	2¼	r	1½	r	r
27	25	2¾	4	r	½	1⅜	r
27	27½	r	r	r	5¾	r	r
27	30	7-16	1½	2¼	3½	r	r
27	32½	4¾	r	r	⅛	r	r
27	35	1-16	½	s	r	r	s
27	40	1-16	¼	s	r	r	s
Dig Eq	80	r	r	r	¾	2⅝	r
du Pnt	40	r	r	r	1½	r	r
Eas Kd	60	11⅝	13	r	⅛	13-16	1½
70¾	65	7	9	10½	7-16	1¾	2½
70¾	70	3⅜	5⅝	7¼	1⅞	3½	4¼
70¾	80	3-16	1⅝	2⅞	9¼	10	r
70¾	90	1-16	s	s	r	s	s
Exxon	30	3¼	3⅞	4⅜	3-16	⅝	15-16
32⅝	35	5-16	1	1 11-16	2½	2½	2⅝
32⅝	40	1-16	5-16	s	7½	r	s
FedExp	45	13½	r	s	⅛	r	s
57⅞	50	9	12	s	¾	2¼	s
57⅞	55	5½	8¾	r	2 3-16	4¼	r
57⅞	60	2¾	6	9¼	4⅝	6⅝	6¾
57⅞	65	1¼	3⅝	6½	8	10	r
57⅞	70	⅜	2¼	4¼	12¾	13¼	13¾
57⅞	80	⅛	s	s	22¾	s	s
F N M	10	¼	13-16	s	s	s	s
Fluor	25	r	6⅞	r	3-16	11-16	1⅜
30⅛	30	2	3⅝	4¾	1⅞	2⅞	3⅜
30⅛	35	11-16	1⅞	2⅞	r	r	r
30⅛	40	3-16	15-16	s	r	r	s
30⅛	45	⅛	½	s	r	r	s
Gt Wst	10	r	5¼	r	r	r	r
14⅞	15	1	1⅞	2¼	r	1⅜	r
14⅞	20	1-16	⅜	⅝	r	r	r
Halbtn	40	20	22	s	r	¾	s
59½	45	15¼	17¼	r	¼	⅞	r
59½	50	10¼	12¾	r	⅜	1⅝	3
59½	55	5¾	r	r	1¼	3¼	r
59½	60	2⅞	5	r	3⅛	r	r
59½	65	1	3	s	6	r	s
59½	70	7-16	1⅞	s	r	r	s
59½	80	1-16	⅝	s	r	r	s
Homstk	35	6⅝	8⅜	r	9-16	1⅝	r
40¾	40	3⅛	5¼	7½	2 1-16	3⅝	4⅜
40¾	45	1⅛	3¼	4½	5⅜	6¼	6¾
40¾	50	⅜	1¾	2⅞	9¼	9¾	9¾
40¾	55	⅛	1	2	14¼	14¼	14½
40¾	60	⅛	¾	s	19⅛	19½	s
40¾	70	1-16	s	s	29	s	s
I N A	45	3⅜	5	r	r	r	r
47	50	¾	r	r	r	r	r
47	60	r	s	s	13¼	s	s
I B M	45	9¾	10⅝	12½	1-16	½	⅝
54⅝	50	5½	6½	8⅛	⅜	1¼	2
54⅝	55	1¾	3¼	4⅞	1 11-16	3¼	3¼
54⅝	60	¼	1 7-16	s	5½	5¾	s
54⅝	65	1-16	s	s	10½	s	s
In Har	10	5-16	1	1¼	2⅛	2⅛	r
8⅛	15	r	⅜	r	r	r	r
In Min	30	4⅜	5⅜	r	r	r	r
34⅜	35	1½	2⅜	r	r	r	r
34⅜	40	½	1⅛	s	r	r	s
34⅜	45	¼	½	s	r	r	s
34⅜	50	⅛	r	s	r	r	s
In Pap	35	7⅛	r	r	⅛	r	⅝
41¾	40	3	r	4¾	⅝	1½	1⅞
41¾	45	9-16	1⅞	r	3½	r	r
41¾	50	⅛	r	s	r	r	s
John J	30	6¾	r	r	r	r	r
36⅜	35	r	4	r	1	1½	3
36⅜	36⅝	1⅝	s	s	r	s	s
36⅜	40	⅝	1¾	r	r	4⅜	5½
Kerr M	30	9⅞	10⅝	s	r	r	s
39⅝	32½	7⅝	9¾	r	⅛	r	r
39⅝	35	7	r	9¼	7-16	1½	1¾
39⅝	40	2¾	4⅞	6	2½	r	r
39⅝	45	⅞	2⅞	3¾	r	r	r
Merck	70	15	r	r	3-16	r	r
84⅞	80	7	9½	r	1½	3⅛	r

Option & NY Close	Strike Price	Calls–Last Jan	Calls–Last Apr	Calls–Last Jul	Puts–Last Jan	Puts–Last Apr	Puts–Last Jul
84⅞	90	1¼	4	6½	5¾	7	r
84⅞	100	½	1½	s	15⅛	r	s
M M M	45	r	r	r	r	r	1
54½	50	5⅜	6½	r	⅜	1⅜	r
54½	55	1 7-16	3	r	1½	2⅝	r
54½	60	3-16	1 3-16	s	r	r	s
Monsan	55	r	r	s	1-16	r	s
72	60	12⅝	13¾	r	⅛	r	r
72	65	r	r	r	½	r	r
72	70	4⅛	6⅝	r	1⅝	3¼	r
72	80	9-16	2⅛	3½	r	r	r
72	90	⅛	r	s	r	r	s
Nw Air	25	4½	r	r	½	1⅛	r
28¾	30	1¼	2⅞	4	2¼	3⅛	r
28¾	35	⅛	r	r	6¼	6⅞	r
28¾	40	⅛	s	s	r	s	s
Pennz	35	13¾	15	17	1-16	9-16	1 5-16
48⅝	40	9⅜	11½	13⅛	9-16	2	2½
48⅝	45	5⅞	8¾	10¼	2	3⅞	4½
48⅝	50	3⅜	6½	8	4½	6¼	r
48⅝	55	2 3-16	4¾	6¼	7⅞	r	r
48⅝	60	1⅜	3⅝	4¾	r	r	r
Pepsi	30	7½	8½	r	r	r	r
37⅜	35	2⅞	4	5	⅝	1	1½
37⅜	40	½	1⅜	2¾	r	r	3¼
Polar	15	7¼	7⅝	r	r	r	r
22	20	2½	3½	4¼	⅜	1	1¼
22	25	⅜	1¼	1 15-16	3⅛	3½	3½
22	30	1-16	⅜	s	r	r	s
Sperry	25	r	10¾	r	r	⅛	r
35⅜	30	6	6⅜	r	r	r	r
35⅜	35	1 13-16	3⅜	4⅝	1¼	2¼	3
35⅜	40	5-16	1¼	2½	r	r	6
35⅜	45	1-16	7-16	s	r	r	s
Squibb	25	r	r	r	1-16	r	r
31⅞	30	2⅝	3½	4⅜	⅜	r	1⅝
31⅞	35	7-16	1 1-16	1¾	r	r	r
31⅞	40	1-16	s	s	r	s	s
StorTec	25	12⅝	13⅞	s	1-16	⅜	s
37⅜	30	8	9¾	11⅝	5-16	1 1-16	1⅝
37⅜	35	4⅛	6¼	8	1½	2¾	3¼
37⅜	40	1 9-16	4	5½	4	4⅞	5⅝
37⅜	45	⅜	2⅛	3⅝	6¾	r	r
Teldyn	120	16¾	23	s	1	3⅜	s
134¼	130	9⅝	16	22¾	3⅝	6½	7⅝
134¼	140	4½	11½	18	8½	10¾	11¾
134¼	150	1 13-16	7½	12⅝	16	17½	17½
134¼	160	⅝	4¾	10	25¾	26	23
134¼	170	3-16	3	s	32	35¼	s
134¼	180	⅛	s	s	41	s	s
Tex In	70	12¾	r	r	7-16	1⅞	r
82⅛	80	5¼	9	r	3	5½	r
82⅛	90	1⅜	4¼	6¾	9¼	10¼	r
82⅛	100	⅜	1⅝	s	r	19¼	s
82⅛	110	⅛	s	s	r	s	s
Upjohn	50	4¾	6¼	r	½	r	r
54	55	1½	3½	4¼	2¼	3½	r
54	60	½	r	r	r	r	r
54	70	1-16	s	s	r	s	s
Weyerh	25	6	6½	r	3-16	¾	r
30¾	30	1¾	2¾	3½	¾	1⅝	2¼
30¾	35	¼	15-16	1⅝	r	r	r
Xerox	35	5⅜	7⅛	7½	¼	1	1¼
39⅜	40	1¾	3¼	4⅜	1 13-16	2¾	r
39⅜	45	7-16	1⅜	2¼	5½	6	6
39⅜	50	⅛	13-16	s	10⅜	10⅛	s
39⅜	55	1-16	⅜	s	15	r	s
39⅜	60	r	¼	s	20	r	s

r—Not traded. s—No option offered. o—Old. Last is premium (purchase price)

[a]Friday; December 4, 1981; Closing prices of all options. Sales unit usually is 100 shares. Security description includes exercise price. Stock close is New York.

Source: The Wall Street Journal. Monday, Dec. 7, 1981.

At-the-Money or Close-to-the-Money Option

A call is close to the money when the striking price approximates the market price of the stock.

Out-of-the-Money Calls

Calls are out of the money if the striking price of the call is higher than the market price, that is, if an exercise of the call will result in a loss. The greater the differential, the deeper out of the money the option is.

The differential between the striking price and the market price of the security is of considerable importance. An out-of-the-money option commands a lower price. The deeper the out-of-the-money condition is, the lower the market price of the option. Conversely, the deeper in the money an option is, the higher its price. The differential between the prices also affects the risk profile of the option and the movement in the price of the option in relation to the movement in the price of the underlying stock. A closer examination of these and related issues follows later in this chapter.

Puts are in or out of the money for reasons opposite those of calls.

Why Buy Calls?

Call options are bought for several reasons, primarily for leverage and risk limitation.

Calls for Leverage

A call option on JAK (a hypothetical company) stock expiring in July with a striking price of $50, JAK/July/50 call, selling for $500 allows for substantial leverage potential. If the market price on the underlying stock is $55, the purchase of 100 shares will require a total commitment of $5,500 or the equivalent of the cost of 11 options. If the stock advances to $60 and the option to $10, the profits are:

Stock Position		Call Position	
Loss	Profit	Loss	Profit
	$6,000 - 5,500 = 500$		$(1,000 - 500) \times 11 = 5,500$

To simplify the presentation, the profit figures ignore taxes and transaction costs. The rate of return on the stock position is 500/5,500 or approximately 9 percent. That on the option position is 5,500/5,500 or 100 percent. Clearly the investor should prefer the option position under those circumstances. If, on the other hand, the share price remains constant or actually falls during the life of the option, the loss on the option position is 100 percent of the invested capital, while it is much smaller or negligible on the stock position. The leveraged position must, therefore, be looked at very carefully.

The reader may already have observed that call buyers have a more complex task with regard to future predictions of movements in stock prices. Not only must they predict the direction of the market price of the underlying security but also the timing of the appreciation in the value of the security. The accretion in the value of the security must occur during the life of the option and must be substantial enough to cover the cost of the option and ensure the desired rate of return.

Calls to Limit Trading Risk

A JAK/July/50 call purchased for $500 becomes profitable if the stock trades at over $55, say $58 (Fig. 12.1). An investor watching the charts on JAK may arrive at the conclusion that the stock has hit a resistance level and decide to sell his or her call and simultaneously short the stock. Using this strategy, however, the investor stands to lose a considerable sum if the price of JAK continues to rise instead of falling. The extent of the loss is theoretically unlimited. If, instead, the investor keeps the call option and goes short, the risk is reduced considerably. If the stock continues to appreciate, the call will appreciate in value, offsetting the loss on the short position. Once the price of the stock pierces the resistance level, the short position is closed. If the stock drops in price, the loss on the call is limited by its premium at the time of purchase ($500). The $500 is the maximum loss. Therefore, if the stock falls below 50, the gains on the short position will more than offset the losses on the call. The real value of the call, however, is increased through repeated trades against the protection it provides.

A short position at 58 followed by a cover and a simultaneous long position at 51, a sale of the long position and a short sale at 60 followed by a cover and a long position at 52, and finally a sale of the long position (optimal) and a sale of the option contract for 54 at its expiration date for $200 would produce considerable profits. This obviously assumes almost perfect foresight on the part of the investor. Needless to say, the presence of the call emboldens the investor to a great degree.

Calls to Release Cash

An investor with 20-point appreciation in a security may wish to sell the security because of a cash need and replace his or her long position in the stock with a call in order to continue participating in the expected upside potential (Fig. 12.2). At 70 the stock is sold for $7,000 (assume 100 shares). Simultaneously, a call is purchased for $800, reducing the gross proceeds (before deduction of taxes and commissions) to $6,200. If the stock continues to appreciate, the investor would hope to recover the cost of the premium and even make a profit. If the stock price declined instead, the maximum loss would be the price of the call.

FIGURE 12.1

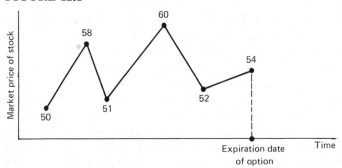

FIGURE 12.2

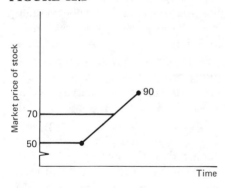

Calls to Protect Principal

A call is a substitute, although potentially an expensive one, for a long position in the stock. Instead of going long on 100 shares of JAK selling at 50, an investor may choose to buy a JAK/December/50 contract for $500. The difference, $4,500, will be kept in a bank, invested in money market instruments like T-bills, or used for other purposes. This advantage must be balanced by the following sobering considerations:

1. Unless the stock price rises by more than 5 points, there would be no profit in the call position if an irrational decision to exorcise the option is made, while a positive return would have been realized in a long position in the stock.

2. If the stock price stays at 50 during the life of the call option, the call position would expire and be worthless, incurring a loss of $500. A long position in the stock would have zero loss unless the opportunity cost of tying up the principal (funds committed to the purchase of a stock) were accounted for.

3. If a stock price falls by more than 5 points by the option expiration date, the loss on the call position is the maximum $500, but the loss limit on the long position in the stock could theoretically reach $5,000. An investor wishing to limit this loss could, however, place with his or her broker a stop-loss order at 45, which means that if this stock trades at or through 45, the order becomes a market order and the stock will be sold at the next bid. This is true for securities listed on the New York Stock Exchange. Stocks listed on the American Stock Exchange will trade at the limit of the stop order. If that limit is passed and the stock is not sold, the investor would have to adjust the price limit if the stock were to be sold. Therefore the stop order, while it offers considerable downside protection, does not limit the maximum loss the investor would suffer. Given the trading rules on the floor of the New York Stock Exchange, however, a trade significantly below 45 is not likely. Hence our conclusion that a stop order does offer a reasonable level of protection when compared to a call.

Calls to Protect Short Positions

As discussed earlier in this section, a call is useful in keeping the loss in a short position to a maximum set by the call premium. The profit on the short position is reduced, however, by that premium. The profit on a 100-share unprotected short position in

XYZ at 60 will be $2,000 if the stock trades at 40 but $1,400 if the position is protected by a call costing $600. With an uncovered position, the loss is theoretically unlimited if the XYZ appreciates in value (the limit defined by the investor's level of rationality and wealth does exist, however). The call limits the loss to the size of the premium. The reader should note that the options market permits various levels of protection at obviously different costs depending on the striking price of the call, the life of the call, and the relationship between the market price of the underlying security and the striking price of the call—that is, on whether a given call is out of the money, at the money, or in the money. Referring back to Table 12.1, an investor with a short position in GM in December 1981 can protect it by purchasing GM/March/30 (in the money call because the market price of GM, 38⅛, is higher than the striking price of the option, 30), or by purchasing a GM/March/35, which is less in the money and closer to being at the money; or a GM/March/40, which is almost at the money; or a GM/March/45, which is out of the money. The investor can also consider the June and December 1982 maturities with different striking prices. Given the maturity date, the less in the money the option is, the lower its cost. Therefore the higher the level of the desired protection the higher the cost ceteris paribus. The purchase of an in-the-money option and particularly a deep in-the-money option is consequently not a desirable hedging strategy. The more risk-averse an investor is, the closer to the money he or she would want to be, particularly when the striking price is equal to that price at which the short position was established. The reader should be better able to conceptualize this discussion after reading the section on the determinants of call-option premia.

Calls for Psychological Sustenance

An investor with a long position in the JAK Corporation established at 60 may panic and sell the stock if the market price drops to 50, for example. The worst psychological pains would be felt if the stock were sold only to return back to 60 and beyond. A call position, established on the basis of expectations at the time of purchase, would permit the investor to ride out downward slumps in the price of the underlying security for two major reasons:

1. The maximum loss that the investor can sustain regardless of how low the price of the underlying security falls is limited to the price of the option (the premium).
2. The fact that the price of an option does not fall to zero if the stock drops substantially in price—provided that a considerable portion of the life of the option has not expired—is an added advantage. The time premium (more on this later) will provide a cushion.

The investor is therefore, more likely to "stick it out" if he or she owns a call option instead of a long position in the underlying security.

Calls to Fix the Price of a Security to Be Purchased in the Future

An investor expecting a dramatic rise in the price of a security but unable to purchase it now would buy a call on the security with a maturity coinciding with the date of receipt of expected funds. If the investor's price expectations materialized, he or she would purchase the underlying security for a total cost equal to the striking price plus the call premium plus the additional transactions costs. If the expectations did not materialize, the investor would simply sell the call option at a loss or allow it to expire.

Vector Representation of a Call Position

One easy way to track the effect of price movements in the underlying security on the profitability (or lack thereof) of a security or an option position is through the utilization of a vector notation. The vector here is a column vector with two of three possible entries: $+1$, 0, and -1. The first entry in the vector (the first row) represents the effect of a price rise in the underlying security and the second or last row represents the effect of a price drop in the security. A long position in a stock is, therefore, represented by the vector $\begin{bmatrix} 1 \\ -1 \end{bmatrix}$, since the investment rises by 1 point when the stock appreciates by 1 point and falls by 1 point when the stock falls by one point. A short position in a stock has the opposite signs of a long position $\begin{bmatrix} -1 \\ 1 \end{bmatrix}$.

A long call position is represented by $\begin{bmatrix} 1 \\ 0 \end{bmatrix}$. If the market price of the underlying security increases, the call will realize a profit (gross profit), but a decrease in the price of the security will result only in a loss of the cost of the call (zero gross loss) without any further liability. The cost of the call is considered here as a sunk cost. The vector representation ignores the premium paid in any of the instruments. Alternatively and more accurately, the vector notation for a call looks at profits in a call position resulting from a change in the price of the stock before accounting for the premium.

The vector representation should prove a very useful tool, as we shall later see, in the analysis of the consequences of various option combinations and strategies.

12.5 WRITING (SELLING) CALL OPTIONS

The call writer is on the opposite side of a call buyer in terms of attitude toward risk and expectations about the future. Call writers seek a reasonable rate of return (in addition to that earned on the security alone) on their capital and are willing to sell options only on securities for which price movements are not expected to be substantial. Otherwise, call writers would be better off maintaining a long position in the security. A security with considerable upside potential will realize a greater return if held long instead of being held as an underlying security to an option. Call option writers seek to capitalize on the option price and particularly on the time premium that favors them and not the option buyer.

The preceding presupposes that the call writer owns the underlying security; that is, he or she has a "covered" position. Call options can also be written "naked" (no underlying security). The writer of a naked option would be assuming a greater risk if the price of the underlying security rose substantially. To deliver against the naked call, the writer would purchase the security at a higher price than that prevailing at the time the contract was sold. In the event of a price decline, the writer of a naked option would realize the full premium on the call because the option holder would choose not to exercise his or her option. A covered option writer, on the other hand, would see the premium received reduced (if not eliminated) by the loss on the long position in the underlying security in the event of a price decline. Later on, we shall examine other alternatives to owning the underlying security in a covered option—alternatives consisting of owning a warrant, a call option, or a security convertible into the underlying stock. What is important to remember, however, are the risk characteristics faced by the writer of a naked call. His or her income is limited to the size of the call premium, but the possible losses are theoretically limitless.

We now examine the motives for writing a call.

Writing a Call Option for Income

An investor (individual, corporation, pension fund, mutual fund, etc.) with a long position in JAK Inc. could choose to write a call on the stock in order to improve dividend income. Many possibilities exist. The investor can frequently choose from many maturity dates and striking prices. Given JAK's market price, the size of the premium will be determined, among other things, by the investor's choice of maturity and of the striking price.

Consider the following case:

JAK's market price	$50
Call striking price	$55
Call maturity	three months
Call premium	$ 2

If the market price of JAK $\leq$ $55, the call premium will be realized in full because the call buyer would simply not exercise the call. If the market price exceeds $55, but is less than $57 (55 + 2), the call buyer would exercise the call (or sell it on the options exchange) in order to recoup portions of the call premium. If the market price exceeds $57, the option buyer will exercise the option (or sell it) and realize a profit (gross profits before commissions).

From the perspective of the option writer, the possibilities are as follows:

1. Stock remains at $50. The return on the sale of a call contract is equal to the premium received: $200. The annualized rate of return = (200/5,000) $\times$ 4 = 16%.
2. Stock advances beyond $55 to $70. The return is still $200 if commissions, dividends, and taxes are ignored. The investor, however, no longer owns the stock, for it was called away. The opportunity loss is enormous. If a call had not been written on JAK, the investor would have realized a gain equal to 70 − 50 = $20 per share.
3. The stock declines to $40. The investor, though still realizing the $200 in premium, now holds an asset that has depreciated by $1,000 (based on 100 shares). The $200 received merely cushions the loss.

In conclusion, the covered call writer would forego the possibility of price appreciation and assume the risk of a price decline against the receipt of the call premium. This conclusion must be tempered by the nature of the investor's expectations. The investor expected little movement in the price of the security at the time the contract was sold, was not averse to losing the stock at a price higher than market value, 50 + 2 (premium), and is content to hold on to the stock even if it dropped to $40. If at $40 or anywhere below $50 the investor revises his or her expectations and decides the stock is no longer worth holding onto, the stock can be sold and the investor can assume a naked position. Another conclusion worth remembering comes from Fischer Black:

> *It is not correct to say that an investor can increase his rate of return by writing call options against his stock. In fact, he reduces his "expected return" because he creates a position that is equivalent to selling some of his stock. He creates a position in which he will come out ahead only if the stock doesn't move very much. He will come out behind if the stock moves a lot.*
>
> *The only way the writer can improve expected return and retain the same exposure to small stock movements is to buy more stock and write overpriced options against his dated stock position. The hedge ratio tells how much more stock to buy. If this hedge ratio is 0.50, then writing options against a stock position cuts its exposure in half; so the investor should double his stock position and write overpriced calls on all of it.[3]*

A discussion of the hedge ratio follows later in the chapter.

When the same data are used for the writer of a naked option, the results are as follows:

1. Stock remains at $50. The returns are $200 but no funds are tied up in the purchase of the underlying security. However, brokerage houses require that a sum set by the margin requirement (established by the Federal Reserve Board) be maintained in the account of the naked option writer. In the JAK's case, this sum will be $5,000 × 30% (current margin requirement) = $1,500.[4] This is less than the sum that would have been tied up had the stock been purchased outright on margin (the margin requirement in this case is 50 percent). An additional saving is realized from the commission that would have been owed in the long position. The returns on the stock must be reduced by the interest costs on the borrowed funds ($5,000 − $1,500) and by the commissions (on the sale of a call).

2. The stock goes up to $70. The writer of a naked option would have to purchase the stock at $70 in order to deliver it against the call when exercised or equivalently buy a call similar to the one sold to offset the open position. The loss is $2,000 − $200 = $1,800. The call writer may choose to close his position considerably earlier than the $70 level on the underlying security. This decision may be enhanced by the marking to the market required by the brokerage house. This simply means that whenever the price of the stock rises, the brokerage house would ask the option writer to deposit more funds in his or her margin account so as to keep the value of the deposit at 30

---

[3] **Fischer Black,** "Fact and Fantasy in the Use of Options." *Financial Analyst's Journal,* July–August 1975, p. 3.

[4] Actually the margin requirement is calculated as follows: 30 percent of the value of the underlying stock ± amount in the money minus premium received (margins for exchange members are significantly less). Example:

5,000 × 30%	$1,500
Less out-of-the-money credit	−500
	$1,000
Less premium received	−200
Total commitment	$ 800

It must be noted that 80 percent of the naked margin can be posted in interest-yielding T-bills.

percent of the market value of the security. A naked call writer may get fed up with frequent requests for additional funds and decide to close the position.

3. Stock goes down to $40. This is the best of all worlds for the writer of a naked option. The return is $200, there are excess funds in the margin account, and there is no book or real loss on the underlying security.

In conclusion, an investor with limited financial resources should avoid writing naked options.

Writing a Call Option to Hedge

The premium received from writing a call option serves as a cushion against a price decline in the underlying security. The larger the premium, the greater the cushion.

Writing a Call Option to Improve on Market

An investor with little hope of an upward price movement in a given stock may sell a call on the stock. The current market price on the stock plus the option premium constitute a new price that is only realizable through the option market. If the stock price advances, the investor happily sells the stock. If the price remains the same, the investor is even happier. Gloom sets in with a price decline. The stock will not be called away from the investor. However, the premium received provides a cushion. The investor with a depreciated security may choose to sell yet another call on it, further cushioning the loss or reducing the cost of the security.

One additional advantage to be elaborated on later stems from tax considerations. The premium received on an exercised option is added onto the price of the security and is, therefore, subject to capital gains taxes. If the option is not exercised or is closed out on the option exchange, then the premium is taxed as ordinary income. This represents an additional incentive to use the option market as a mechanism for selling at above the current market price. The premium from an exercised option is equivalent, from a tax point of view, to an appreciation in the market value of the security.

Vector and Graphic Representations

The vector representation for writing a call is $\begin{bmatrix} -1 \\ 0 \end{bmatrix}$. An increase in the price of the security results in a loss on the sale of a call, while a decline results in no loss. The loss on the sale of the call represents the call writer's foregone gain on the long position or, more accurately, the realized loss on a naked position.

Graphically, buying and writing a call can be shown as in Figure 12.3.

In Figure 12.3a, the call buyer will lose the premium (before commissions and other charges) in its entirety until the market price of the stock reaches the striking price. Beyond that point, the call buyer begins to recoup the premium on a one-to-one basis (one point appreciation in the market price of the security means a one-point reduction in the cost of the premium). Once K is reached, profits continue to accumulate.

The writer of the call (Fig. 12.3b) will earn the premium and will continue in an

FIGURE 12.3 Buying and writing a call.

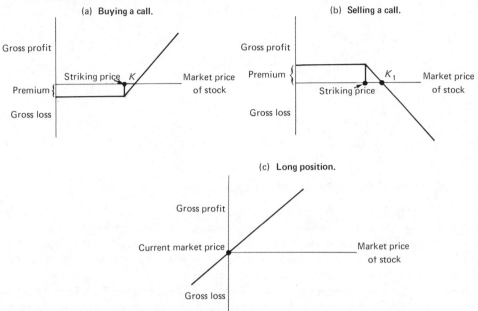

advantageous position until the stock price falls below K_1. At that point, the investor wishes that the option had never been sold or simply that the long position in the stock had been sold.

Both option strategies should be compared with the long position in the stock market depicted in Figure 12.3c.

12.6 THE DETERMINANTS OF THE CALL PREMIUM

The major theoretical breakthrough in the identification and quantification of the determinants of call premiums did not come until 1973, in a study by Fischer Black and Myron Scholes in the May–June issue of the *Journal of Political Economy.* The paper, entitled "The Pricing of Options and Corporate Liabilities," presented a theoretical valuation formula for options and laid the foundation for a deluge of literature on option pricing, efficiency of option markets, and trading strategies in the marketplace. We shall examine the Black-Scholes (B&S) model in considerable detail. We will first look at some of the intuitive determinants of option pricing.

Option Premium Determinants

The connection between options and the underlying stock is of considerable importance in the determination of options premiums. More specifically, the current market price of the stock in relation to the striking price is a major determinant. The lower the market price in relation to the striking price—that is, the more out of the money the option is—the less valuable it is. The more in the money the option is, the more valuable it is and the higher the premium.

FIGURE 12.4   Relationship between market price and option premium.

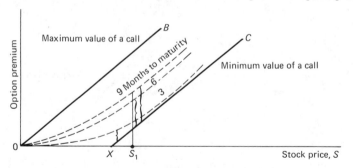

Market Price of Stock and Call Premium

The relationship between the market price of the stock and the option premium is shown in Figure 12.4. The maximum price for an option is shown by O*B*, because an option with an infinite life would be equivalent to a common stock. Along O*B*, every point of appreciation in the price of a stock brings a point of appreciation in the value of the call. This is the maximum appreciation possible.

The lower limit, the minimum value of a call, is shown by *XC* (parallel to O*B*) in Figure 12.4. Every point along *XC* represents the difference between the market price of the stock *S* and the striking price *X*. *S* − *X* is referred to as the *relative price* or *intrinsic value*. The price of an option is always greater than or equal to zero even if the intrinsic value is negative. No one is going to pay you for buying his or her option.

The option price must therefore be somewhere between O*B* and *XC*, as shown by the broken lines in Figure 12.4. These lines show that the price of an option is greater than the intrinsic value and is always tending towards it. To the left of *X*, *S* − *X* < 0 and the option is out of the money. At or around *X*, the option is at the money. To the right of *X*, the option is in the money. The farther to the right of *X* the stock price, the deeper in the money the option. The outstanding issue still is: What determines the shape of the broken lines? A few theorems should aid in providing the answer.

Theorem 1.[5]   **The rate of increase in the price of an option *W* is approximately half that of the underlying security when *S* = *X*.**

Theorem 2.   **The excess of market price of an option over its intrinsic value *W* − (*S* − *X*) increases with the price of the underlying security *S* when *S* < *X* and decreases with the price of the underlying security when *S* > *X*.**

This theorem is best explained using Figure 12.5.

Up to *X*, the excess *W* − (*S* − *X*) is rising (excess equals *W* if S − X ≤ 0). Beyond *X*, the excess decreases. Correspondingly, the option premium rises at a slow

---

[5] This and the theorems to follow are based on the work of **Claude G. Henin** and **Peter J. Ryan,** *Options,* Lexington Books, Lexington, Massachusetts, 1977. (Differentiating the Black and Scholes model with respect to stock price shows that the rate would be exactly one half only when *S* is slightly less than *X*, as we shall present later).

FIGURE 12.5   **Graphic depiction of Theorem 2.**

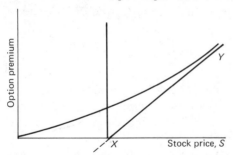

rate up to X and at a faster rate beyond X when the option is in the money. At point Y, when the option is well in the money, the option premium rises on an almost one-to-one basis with the stock price. This is the nature of the beast. When the stock price is close to zero, it is far from the striking price. That is, a large appreciation in the price of the security must take place before the option buyer expects to break even.

Theorem 3.   **The excess on an option is symmetrical about the striking (exercise) price.**

Theorem 4.   **The option on a stock commands a higher price than another option on the same stock if the striking price is lower. The difference in the price of the options is lower than that in the striking prices.**

Time and Call Premium

The three courses shown by the broken lines in Figure 12.4 illustrate the relationship between time and the call premium. From the perspective of the option buyer, the longer the life of the option, the larger the probability that the stock price will move sufficiently to allow a profit on the position to be realized. Hence the willingness to pay more for an option that has a longer maturity, ceteris paribus. From the perspective of the option seller, the longer the life the larger the probability that the option will be exercised and a loss on the underlying security incurred. The option writer will therefore demand a higher premium.

The option price can therefore be generalized, although incompletely, as follows:

$W =$ intrinsic value (relative price) + time premium

An out-of-the-money option with a zero or close to zero relative price would have a positive value. The longer the remaining life of the option, the larger the time value and the larger the price of the option. The brackets in Figure 12.4 corresponding to a stock price of S_1 represent the time premium. The longer the remaining life, the larger the time premium. The further to the left of X the market price travels, the larger the share of the time premium in the call premium. As $S - X$ approaches zero, the time premium approaches W. From Figure 12.4 we can also observe that the shorter the remaining life of the option, the more the price of the option moves in congruence with the stock price. Another conclusion to be drawn from Figure 12.4 is that the rate of decrease in the option price accelerates as the option approaches the date of expiration.

Call Premium and Stock Volatility

Common stocks that have a history of wide price fluctuations (Polaroid and Teleprompter, for example) command higher call premiums because the probability of those options becoming profitable is that much higher. Table 12.2 shows the differences in price volatility among three NYSE-listed securities.

The covariance between the rate of return on a stock and that on a market index normalized by the variance of the rates of return on the market index is a measure of volatility referred to as the beta (β) coefficient. This concept was covered in Chapter 6. The importance of this measure lies in the fact that in times of generally rising stock prices, there is an increased interest in option ownership; consequently prices for options are higher, since option writers are less interested in supplying option contracts. If stock prices are generally falling, option writers are ready to supply larger numbers of option contracts, while option buyers are not so interested. The result is lower option prices. Stocks with high variances, therefore, command higher prices for options written on them than those with lower variances if stock market prices are generally rising, and vice versa.

It is instructive at this point to differentiate between the volatility of the underlying security and that of the option itself. The volatility of the option is usually larger than that of the underlying stock because of the leverage offered by options. The further in the money an option is, the more consistent its volatility with that of the stock. Figure 12.6 shows the volatility of the option market as measured by the CBOE Call Option Index. A comparison of Fig. 12.6 with Fig. 12.7 (with slight adjustment) will show the volatility of the options market relative to that of the stock market as measured by the Standard & Poor's Composite Index.

Call Premium and Interest Rates

The risk/return tradeoff in the option market must be compatible with the tradeoffs on alternative investment opportunities with similar profiles. When interest rates are rising, options premiums tend to move upward; when interest rates are falling, options premiums move downward.

F. Black and M. Scholes (B&S) argue that the option premium is a function of the risk-free rate.[6] The basis of the argument is that option buyers, by following a certain hedging strategy, can establish a risk-free position. This is done by taking a long position in the stock and a short position in a certain number of options. This number is equal to

$$\frac{1}{W_1\,(S,t)}$$

Where $W_1\,(S,t)$ is the partial first derivative of the option price with respect to the

[6] **Fischer Black** and **Myron Scholes**, "The Pricing of Options and Corporate Liabilities." *Journal of Political Economy,* vol. 81 (May–June 1973), pp. 637–654.

price of the stock S. The option price is expressed here as a function of the price of the underlying security S and the life of the option t.

For a change equal to ΔS in the price of the stock, the price of the options will change by $W_1\,(S,t)\,\Delta S$. The changes offset each other and the net position is risk-free.

B&S calculated the value of $W_1\,(S,t)$ to equal $N\,(d_1)$. $N(d_1)$ is the cumulative

TABLE 12.2
Price Volatility Differences Among Three NYSE-Listed Securities

Polaroid Corp. (PRD)

		Quarter I	II	III	IV
1979	high	56	40 1/4	31 3/8	29
	low	38 1/4	29 1/2	26 1/8	22 3/8
1978	high	26 1/4	41 5/8	60 1/4	54 1/8
	low	23 3/8	25 1/4	35 3/8	43 1/2
1977	high	38 5/8	34 3/4	32	30 7/8
	low	32 3/8	29	27 5/8	25
1976	high	42 1/8	41 1/8	45 1/8	44 1/4
	low	31 1/4	31 7/8	36 3/4	34 1/8
1975	high	26 1/8	38	43 1/2	41 1/4
	low	15	23 3/8	30 1/4	28 1/4

General Foods (GF)

		Quarter I	II	III	IV
1979	high	36 3/4	33 3/8	37	36 7/8
	low	31 7/8	28 1/4	31	31 7/8
1978	high	31 1/2	33	35	35 1/4
	low	26 1/2	27 1/4	31 3/8	30 3/8
1977	high	33	35 1/2	36 1/8	33 7/8
	low	29	31	32 1/4	29
1976	high	31 1/4	29 7/8	34 3/4	34 1/4
	low	27	26 1/8	27 1/2	29 5/8
1975	high	26	27 1/2	26 7/8	29 3/8
	low	18 3/8	21	21	22 7/8

Gulf & Western Industries (GW)

		Quarter I	II	III	iV
1979	high	12 1/4	12 1/4	14 1/2	15 3/4
	low	11 1/8	11 1/2	11 1/2	10 7/8
1978	high	10 5/8	12 5/8	13	12
	low	8 3/4	10	10 7/8	9
1977	high	14 3/4	11 7/8	11	9 7/8
	low	11 1/8	10 1/4	8 7/8	8
1976	high	17 1/4	16 1/2	16 5/8	14 3/4
	low	12 5/8	13 7/8	13 1/4	11 3/4
1975	high	9 1/2	11 1/2	12 3/4	13
	low	6 3/4	8 1/4	10 1/2	11 1/8

Source: Moody's Industrial, Spring 1980, and Market Statistics 1980, CBOE, Chicago.

FIGURE 12.6   CBOE call option index.

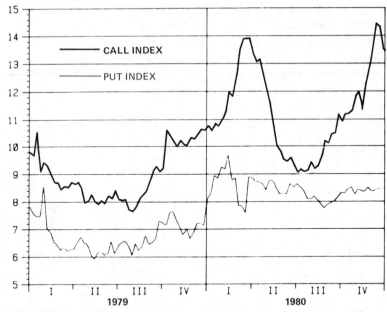

The indices are designed to provide investors with a concise and consistent measure over time of average premium levels on all call and put classes traded on the CBOE, Amex, Philadelphia and Pacific exchanges. For each class, the market price of a six-month, at-the-money option is estimated and expressed as a percentage of the underlying stock price. The index value is the simple average of these percent premiums.

Source: Market Statistics 1981, Chicago Board Options Exchange, Ill., 1981.

FIGURE 12.7   Standard & Poor's price index—quarterly averages.

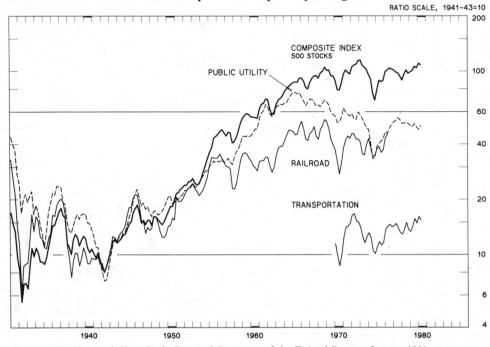

Source: 1980 Historical Chart Book, Board of Governors of the Federal Reserve System, 1981.

normal density function with respect to the first argument of the function *S*. For a normal probability distribution with mean zero and a standard deviation equal to one, $N(d_1)$ gives the probability that a deviation less than *S* will take place.

The hedge ratio is, therefore, the ratio of the change in the option value to that in the value of the underlying stock. A partial first derivative equal to 0.19 means that if the price of the stock goes up or down by $1, the value of the option goes up or down by $0.19. Therefore, a long position in the stock combined with a short position of $1/0.19 = 5.26$ options (the hedge ratio) result in a neutral hedge—a hedge that is risk free and should earn the risk-free rate if the option market is operating efficiently. The reader should note that the amount expended on the long position is not necessarily equal to that committed to the short position.

It must be noted and emphasized that the neutral hedge strategy is merely a theoretical possibility. The hedge ratio requires continuous hedging as the price of the underlying stock changes. Very few investors follow their portfolios that closely. Transaction costs can become prohibitive if a continuous hedging strategy is pursued. Furthermore, the hedge ratio requires divisibility that is not present in the options market; no one is going to sell 26 percent of an option. These realities have led to the utilization of the call-money rate instead of the risk-free rate in the price determination equation of a call option. The call rate[7] is deemed more representative of arbitrageurs' costs and incomes.

From the preceding discussion and based on the assumptions above, it can be concluded that the price of an options contract is determined as follows:

$$W = f(S, X, \sigma^2, t, r, D)$$

where W = option price

        S = price of the underlying stock

        X = striking price of the stock

        σ^2 = volatility of the stock price measured by the instantaneous variance of the rate of return on the stock.

        t = life of the options contract

        r = the risk-free rate of interest

        D = dividend yield on the stock

$$\frac{\delta W}{\delta S} > 0, \ \frac{\delta W}{\delta X} < 0, \ \frac{\delta W}{\delta \sigma^2} > 0, \ \frac{\delta W}{\delta t} > 0, \ \frac{\delta W}{\delta r} > 0, \ \frac{\delta W}{\delta D} < 0$$

The B&S model conveniently drops dividends as a determinant of the options price and deals with non-dividend-paying stocks or with stocks on which the options expire prior to the ex-dividend date.

12.7 THE BLACK-SCHOLES CALL-VALUATION MODEL

The development of the B&S model requires considerable mathematical sophistication. We shall, therefore, content ourselves with a discussion of the main features of the model and pay little attention to the details.

---

[7] The call rate is the rate paid by brokerage firms to their bankers.

Assumptions of the B&S Model

1. Efficient securities markets.
2. No dividends on the underlying stock.
3. No transactions costs.
4. No restrictions on short selling.
5. The option is of the European type—exercisable only at maturity.[8]
6. Stock prices follow a random walk. Stock prices are log-normally distributed so that the continuously compounded one-periods rates of return are normally distributed with a known constant variance. The variance rate is proportionate to the square of the stock price.
7. A known and constant rate of interest.

Starting with the value of a hedged portfolio,

$$V_H = SQ_s + WQ_w \tag{12.1}$$

where Q_s = number of shares in the hedged position

$\quad\quad Q_w$ = number of option contracts in the hedged position

Black and Scholes took the total derivative of Equation 12.1 and, using techniques borrowed from physics, arrived at the call-valuation equation:

$$W(S,t) = S \cdot N(d_1) - e^{-r\tau} X \cdot N(d_2)$$
$$d_1 = \frac{\ln(S/X) + r\tau}{\sigma \sqrt{\tau}} + 1/2\, \sigma \sqrt{\tau}$$
$$d_2 = d_1 - \sigma \sqrt{\tau} \tag{12.2}$$

When all the variables are as previously defined except

$\tau = t - T$ = time to maturity = life of the option − time elapsed

$\quad N(\cdot)$ = cumulative standard normal distribution

$\quad N(-\infty) = 0$, $N(0) = 0.5$, and $N(\infty) = 1$

Note: If t were equal to infinity, the price of the option should equal that of the underlying stock—an option on the assets of the corporation.

Example
Calculate the theoretical value of an option on a security with a market price of $40, a striking price of $35, and a maturity of three months ($\tau = 3$ mo $= \frac{1}{4}$ year). The

---

[8] **R. C. Merton,** "Theory of Rational Option Pricing." *Bell Journal of Economics and Management Science,* vol. 4 (1973), pp. 141–183. In this article Merton shows that if the underlying security pays no dividend, the option on it will never be exercised prior to the expiration date. This makes the B&S model applicable to American options on stocks that do not pay dividends. Whether exercised at expiration date or before, the value of the American option can only be equal or greater than that of a European call option. The American option offers an additional advantage—that option is the expiration date.

FIGURE 12.8 **Plot of call prices.**

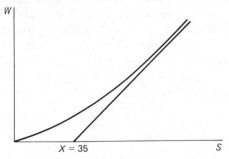

annual risk-free rate is 8 percent and the instantaneous variance of the stock price is equal to 20 percent.

Answer

$$d_1 = \frac{\ln{(40/35)} + 0.08\,(0.25)}{\sqrt{0.2}\,\sqrt{0.25}} + 1/2\,(\sqrt{0.2})\,(\sqrt{0.25})$$

$$= \frac{0.13348 + 0.02}{(0.447)\,(0.5)} + 1/2\,(0.447)\,(0.5)$$

$$= 0.799$$

$$d_2 = 0.799 - 0.447\,\sqrt{0.250} = 0.5755$$

$$N(d_1) = \text{cumulative probability from} -\infty \text{ to } 0.799$$

$$= 0.7881 \text{ (using Table 12A.1 in the appendix to this chapter)}$$

$$N(d_2) = 0.7174 \text{ (interpolating from Table 12A.1)}$$

Therefore

$$W(S,t) = 40\,(0.7881) - e^{-0.08\,(0.25)}\,35\,(0.7174)$$

$$= 31.52 - 24.61 = \$6.91 \text{ per share}$$

The value of the call contract on 100 shares is therefore equal to \$691 (6.91 × 100).

The reader may wish to calculate option prices for various stock prices with the values of the remaining variables held constant. If the resulting call prices are plotted, we get Figure 12.8.

In the preceding example, all the values are available in the financial press with the exception of the instantaneous variance. One way of estimating the size of the variance is to set the right-hand side of Equation 12.2 equal to the actual current market price of the option and calculate the implied variance.[9] The accurate gauging of the size of the variance is important, for the B&S option model is very sensitive to the volatility

---

[9] **Parkinson M.,** "Option Pricing: The American Put." *Journal of Business,* January 1977, pp. 21–36. **H. Latane** and **R. J. Rendleman, Jr.,** "Standard Deviations of Stock Price Ratios Implied in Option Prices." *Journal of Finance,* May 1976, pp. 369–382.

variable. One additional comment worth making relates to the risk-free variable. It is customary to use the average bid-and-ask price on a U.S. Treasury bill with equivalent maturity date. It is our experience that this method does not always yield a satisfactory answer.

It must further be noted once again that the B&S model applies to non-dividend-paying stocks. Many attempts[10] have been made to adjust the model for dividend payouts. The mathematics are complex and the efforts did not produce a neat, closed-form solution.

Investment Implications

The B&S model is of considerable help in the setting of investment strategy. The model can be used in identifying options that are overpriced (market price > B&S option price) or underpriced. Black cautions us, however, that:

> *The actual prices on listed options tend to differ in certain systematic ways from the values given in the formula. Options that are way out of the money tend to be overpriced, and options that are way into the money tend to be underpriced. Options with less than three months to maturity tend to be overpriced.*[11]

Black offered three possible explanations for this observation: (1) the volatility variables, (2) taxes, and (3) leverage. None of the possible explanations was satisfactory to Black, nor are they to us.

Empirical Tests

The first test of the B&S option pricing model was conducted by Black and Scholes[12] using the diaries of an option broker from 1966 to 1969 (a period predating the CBOE). They were able to select 2,039 six-month calls and 3,052 straddle contracts. Using the commercial paper rate continuously compounded (for r), their own estimate of σ, and assuming no transactions costs, they calculated W and the hedge ratio on a daily basis. Based on this, Black and Scholes were able to calculate the "realized excess dollar return" on each hedge for each day and sum over 766 trading days to arrive at a "portfolio excess dollar return." Four portfolios were developed using accurately (according to the model) priced options as well as overpriced and underpriced options. Overpriced options were sold and underpriced options were bought.

Regressing the excess dollar portfolio return on the returns on the S&P Composite Index, they were able to verify that β, systematic risk of the hedged portfolio, was

[10] **M. Brennan** and **E. Schwartz,** "The Valuation of American Put Options." *Journal of Finance,* vol. 32, no. 2 (May 1976), pp. 449–462. **R. J. Rendleman** and **B. J. Bartter,** "Two State Option Pricing." Working paper, Northwestern University, Evanston, Ill., 1978. **R. Roll,** "An Analytical Valuation Formula for Unprotected Call Options With Known Dividends." *Journal of Financial Economics,* vol. 5, 1977, pp. 251–258. **R. Geske,** "The Pricing of Options with Stochastic Yield." *Journal of Finance,* May 1978, pp. 617–625.

[11] **Fischer Black,** *Financial Analyst's Journal,* p. 8.

[12] **Fischer Black** and **Myron Scholes,** "The Valuation of Option Contracts and a Test of Market Efficiency." *Journal of Finance,* vol. 27, May 1972.

not "significantly different from zero"; that is, the actions are uncorrelated. Whether or not a profit were realized in the options market depended on whether ex post variances (using past stock prices) or ex ante variances (estimate the variance over the holding period) were used. The profits realized using the ex post estimate of the variance were insignificant and, in fact, disappeared when transactions costs were introduced.

Black and Scholes concluded that "the model tends to overestimate the value of an option on a high variance security and . . . tends to underestimate the value of a low variance security."[13]

Dan Galai, following in the footsteps of his professor, tested the B&S model using a different and better data base from the CBOE.[14] Galai used the same type of test as Black and Scholes but adjusted the hedged option position on a daily basis. Again, overpriced options were sold and underpriced options were bought. Two tests were conducted using an ex post hedging test (using end-of-day option prices—to establish option positions) and an ex ante hedging test (using end-of-previous-day closing prices to establish option positions) and various estimates of the volatility variable were made. Each estimate was assumed to remain constant during the life of the option. Galai's tests resulted in the following conclusions:

1. Significant excess returns can be earned using ex post data.
2. Transactions costs (1 percent) eliminate any excess returns.
3. Nonmembers of the CBOE cannot consistently beat the market.
4. The B&S model performed best when its specifications were adhered to.

Both tests, that of Black and Scholes and Galai's, show that the B&S model does price options accurately and that the options markets were efficient.

A more recent test of the B&S model was made by J. Macbeth and L. Merville.[15] The authors' conclusions were exactly the opposite of those of Black.[16] Macbeth and Merville found—using daily closing prices for CBOE-traded options on AT&T, Avon Products, Eastman Kodak, Exxon, IBM, and Xerox between Dec. 31, 1975, and December 1976—that

1. *The B-S model predicted prices are on average less (greater) than market prices for in-the-money (out-of-the-money) options.*
2. *With the lone exception of out-of-the-money options with less than ninety days to expiration, the extent to which the B-S model underprices (overprices) an in-the-money (out-of-the-money) option increases with the extent to which the option is in the money (out of the money), and decreases as the time to expiration decreases.*
3. *B-S model prices out-of-the-money options with less than ninety days to expiration are, on average, greater than market prices, but there does not*

---

[13] Ibid, pp. 415–417.

[14] **Dan Galai,** "Tests of Market Efficiency of the Chicago Board Options Exchange." *Journal of Business,* vol. 50 (April 1977), pp. 167–197.

[15] **James D. Macbeth** and **Larry J. Merville,** "An Empirical Examination of the Black-Scholes Call Option Pricing Model." *Journal of Finance,* vol. 34, no. 5 (December 1979), pp. 1173–1186.

[16] **Black,** *Financial Analyst's Journal.*

appear to be any consistent relationship between the extent to which these options are out of the money or the time to expiration. [17]

The conflicting results were attributed by the authors largely to the nonstationary variance (σ^2 changing through time) used in the B&S model (the σ used in calculating d_1).

The evidence presented thus far suggests that great care should be exercised in arriving at option prices, particularly in arriving at a definite conclusion as to whether or not an option contract is overpriced.

12.8 PUTS

Definitions

A put is an option to sell 100 shares of an underlying security at a designated price (the striking price) during a specified period of time.

In-the-Money Put

A put is in the money, that is, it is profitable to exercise, if the market price of the underlying stock is below the striking price. The put holder can purchase the underlying security on the market and sell it at the higher striking price to the put writer.

Out-of-the-Money Put

A put is out of the money if the market price of the underlying security is higher than the striking price. The exercise of the put will result in a loss.

Why Buy Puts?

Put trading did not become prevalent on the CBOE until 1980. Prior to this date, only a handful of puts were listed on the CBOE. To understand the usefulness of puts, the trader has to shift into reverse from the call option case.

Puts for Leverage

An investor expecting the price of JAK Inc. to fall can either sell the stock short or buy a put on the security. If the stock price were $50, the investor would have to commit either the required minimum for a margin account ($2,000), for short sales are usually affected in the margin account, or 30 percent of the value of the stock, whichever is higher.

If the stock goes down to $40 after one month, the profits from the short position, assuming 100 shares, would be

Original market price	$5,000
Current market price	4,000
Gross profits	$1,000

---

[17] **Macbeth** and **Merville**, p. 1185.

The return on the invested capital is $1,000/$2,000 = 50 percent. Annualized, it is equal to 50 × 12 = 600 percent. This obviously assumes no transactions costs.

If, instead, the investor bought 5 puts at $400 each for a total commitment of $2,000, the profits would be as follows:

Gross profit per option: $1,000 − $400 = $600
Total gross profit: $600 × 5 = $3,000

The return on the invested capital is $3,000/$2,000 = 150 percent, an annual return of 1,800 percent. The numbers would double if the total commitment were $4,000, the full price of the shares.

This illustrates the tremendous leverage possibilities of puts. Lest our enthusiasm for puts lead us astray, we must examine the opposing side. Leverage is great when the market forces lead prices in the desired direction, but it is disastrous if things go wrong. Consider the situation of the stock rising to $55 in three months.

The investor with five puts would lose $2,000—that is, 100 percent of his or her investment. The loss in the short position in the stock would have been 50 percent of investment capital ($1,000/$2,000).[18]

The preceding assumes that the investor does not initiate a closing sale transaction prior to the expiration date of the option. The investor may well decide to sell the puts prior to expiration in order to reduce the loss. The puts can also be exercised. The preferred way for closing out the position is a function of transactions costs, taxes, and margin requirements.

Puts to Protect a Long Position

An investor with a long position in JAK Inc. (actual or contemplated) may choose to buy a put to eliminate the downside risk on the stock. The maximum loss if the stock falls in price is the price of the put. If the put is purchased, profits begin to accrue only after the price of the put is earned. If stock is selling at $50 when a put is purchased against it for $400, profits begin to accrue after the stock price reaches $54. This protection is usually sought on volatile securities and is the only effective protection against a long position. No insurance company sells policies protecting investors against the whims of the market. The investor buying a put to protect an existing long position in the stock may negate certain tax benefits. This issue will be discussed later in the chapter.

Puts to Protect Book Profits

An investor owning a security with a cost basis of $50 and a market value of $80 may choose to purchase a put in order to lock in the book profit (minus the put premium). If the stock price continues to move upward, the put may be sold or be allowed to expire. Taxes are an important consideration here. As we shall explain later, the purchase of the put will eliminate the holding period on the stock for tax purposes. The holding period begins again when the put position is closed.

---

[18] The loss in percentage terms would be lower because additional margin would have been required of the investor as the market moved in an unfavorable direction. The additional margin is required because the investor is "marked to market."

FIGURE 12.9

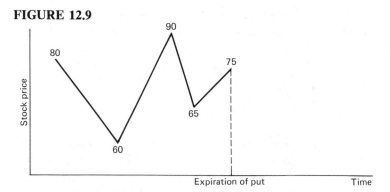

Puts for Limited-Risk Trading

An investor wishing to trade a volatile security but wary about the probability of not being able to guess the turns in the market price accurately may purchase a put for protection.

At 80 (Fig. 12.9), the investor may wish to buy a put. At 60 he or she will go long. An appreciation in the price of the stock is offset by the loss of book profit on the put up to 80. Beyond 80, a net profit is realizable. At 90, sell the long position and go short. The short position is unprotected, however. This may lead the investor to a decision simply to close out the long position at 90 and wait for the stock to come back down to 65. At 65, the investor goes long once again, protected by the put position in the event the stock continues to depreciate. And so the process continues until the option expires. The preceding assumes that the investor has guessed the turns in the stock prices correctly. Furthermore, as we shall later see, many other strategies are also possible.

Puts for Psychological Sustenance

An investor with a short position in a security may panic if its price appreciates by a certain number of points and may therefore decide to close out the position. A put owner, knowing the maximum size of the loss (the put premium), would wait out the stock until, with luck, its trend were reversed. The closing of the short position may occur and the investor may only later discover that the stock price has dropped considerably. Additional pressure is put on the short position in the security by the brokerage house. As the price of the stock appreciates, the short seller is marked to the market— that is, asked to deposit more money, further increasing the commitment and the pressure to close the position.

Vector Representation

A put buyer position is represented by the vector $\begin{bmatrix} 0 \\ 1 \end{bmatrix}$. If the stock appreciates, there is no loss on the put. The cost of the put is a sunk cost. If the price of the underlying security drops by one point, the put will appreciate by a point $(+1)$.

A long put position, it must be observed, is equivalent to a short position in the stock and a long position in a call option.

short stock   buy call   buy put

$$\begin{bmatrix} -1 \\ 1 \end{bmatrix} \ + \ \begin{bmatrix} 1 \\ 0 \end{bmatrix} \ = \ \begin{bmatrix} 0 \\ 1 \end{bmatrix}$$

Put vs. a Stop-Loss Order

Protection against a loss in a newly established long position and the protection of book profits in a long position is securable through the purchase of a put. The market, however, affords the investor another avenue for protection requring no initial commitment of funds. This avenue is the stop-loss order. An investor with a long position, for example, may ask his or her broker to place a stop-loss order at five points below the current market price. If the market price falls to five points below market or through this threshold, the stop order becomes a market order (remains a limit order for stocks listed on the American Stock Exchange) and is sold at the bid, which can be much lower than the price limit set by the investor. The investor will obviously be distraught if the stock price rebounds back up immediately after the stop order is executed. By contrast, the put gives the trader a considerable amount of flexibility, but at a price. The stop order is more rigid but does not require the commitment of funds. The additional advantages of a stop order stem from the fact that its time horizon can be indefinite, while a put has a fixed and short life, and that can be used against odd-lot security holdings. Puts are available on round lots only.

We can, therefore, conclude that the choice between puts and stop orders is a matter of investor biases, risk preferences, and other considerations.

12.9 WRITING PUTS

The put writer, like the call writer, is primarily interested in earning premium income. Against the premium, he or she is committed to purchasing the underlying security at the striking price any time it is "put" to him or her by the option buyer during the life of the contract.

Puts to Earn Premium Income

The put writer must be bullish on the underlying stock or, at worst, expect it not to decline in price before a commitment is made. Otherwise the losses in the event of a price decline will equal those realized on a long position adjusted for the put premium received.

Consider the case of an investor who sold a three-month put on JAK Inc. for $250 with a striking price of $45. The current market price of JAK is $45. The investor does not hold a long position. Three situations are possible:

Situation 1—Stock Appreciates (Assume to $55)
The holder of the put will obviously not exercise it. The put writer realizes the full premium. The rate of return is equal to (assuming a 30 percent margin requirement):[19]

---

[19] This is the amount the investor must keep on deposit with his broker. The exact amount actually equals 30 percent of the value of the stock plus the amount in the money or minus the amount out of the money less the proceeds from the sale of the put.

$$\frac{250}{(4,500 \times 30\%)} = \frac{\text{call premium}}{\text{funds committed}} = 18.51\% \text{ per quarter}$$

or an annualized rate of $18.51 \times 4 = 74.04\%$.

These results must be compared with the outright ownership of the stock, a real alternative given that the investor is bullish on the security.

The returns on a long position (assuming 100 shares) are

$$\frac{5,500 - 4500}{(4,500 \times 50\%)} - \begin{array}{l}\text{interest costs on}\\ \text{borrowed funds}\\ \text{(assume market}\\ \text{rate} = 15\%)\end{array} = \left(\frac{1,000}{2,250} \times 100\right) - (15\% \times 1/4) = 40.69\%$$

or an annual rate of $40.69\% \times 4 = 162.76\%$.

Hindsight shows that the investor would have been better off holding a long position.

Situation 2—Stock Remains at $45

If the stock remained at $45, the put writer would simply realize the full amount of the premium.

Situation 3—Stock Falls to $35

At $35 the put holder will have a profitable option. Exercising the option means that the option writer would acquire a security with a $35 market value at the striking price of $45. There is a loss of $750 (1,000 − 250 premium received) on the position. The implications of these results for the put writer are not to write a put unless you are willing to own the security under those circumstances.

Puts to Acquire a Stock

The put writer here sells the put in the hope that it will be exercised—that the price of the underlying security will, in fact, drop. If the writer's expectations materialize, he or she would succeed in buying a stock at a price lower than that prevailing at the time the put was written. The obvious contradictions are that the investor who expects a temporary correction in the price of the stock would still go through with the sale of the option when it would have been wiser simply to wait. If the stock appreciated in price the put would not be exercised and the put writer collects the full put premium.

Vector and Graphical Representation

The put writer's position is summarized in the following vector $\begin{bmatrix} 0 \\ -1 \end{bmatrix}$, which indicates that the position would realize zero profit (before considering the put premium) if the stock appreciated by a point and would lose a point for every point depreciation in the value of the underlying security. This position is equivalent to a long position in the stock against which a call has been written.

long   write call   write put

$$\begin{bmatrix} 1 \\ -1 \end{bmatrix} + \begin{bmatrix} -1 \\ 0 \end{bmatrix} = \begin{bmatrix} 0 \\ -1 \end{bmatrix}$$

FIGURE 12.10   Graphic depiction of put position.

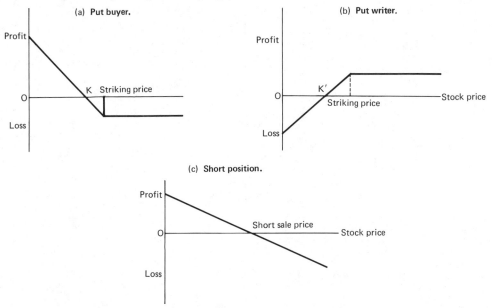

This vector presentation assumes that the put sold is naked, that is, the put writer does not own the security. If the put writer owns the underlying stock, a put may well be sold with the expectation of improving cash flow on a stock position held for long-term appreciation. The expectations are obviously that the stock will not drop in price or actually go up.

Graphically, the put position is illustrated by Figure 12.10.

Figure 12.10a shows the position of a put buyer. The buyer begins to recover the cost of the put when the striking price is reached. Profits are realized below K. The position of the option writer is shown in Figure 12.10b. Losses are incurred below point K' on the stock price axis. The writer would obviously be averse to a price decline—an event for which the options buyer is hoping if not praying.

The put positions are to be contrasted with the short position depicted in Figure 12.10c.

12.10 PRICING PUTS

The logic applied to the pricing of a call should be reversed if one is to understand the pricing of put options. Figure 12.11 shows how the put price is related to the stock price, the term to maturity, and the striking price.

The straight line beginning at point X on the horizontal axis represents the minimum value of a put. At X, the striking price is equal to the stock price. Below X, $S - X$ is negative, that is, put is in the money. The put holder can buy the stock at the market price and "put" it to the put writer at the higher striking price. At X, the put is just in the money. To the right of X, the put is out of the money. The put holder will not exercise the put; that is, the put writer will realize the full premium.

Figure 12.11 shows two curves for puts with differing maturities. The explanations

FIGURE 12.11 **Put price in relation to stock price, term to maturity, and striking price.**

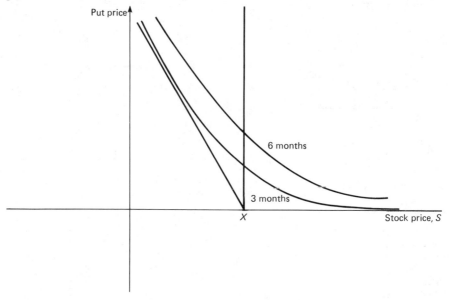

of the curvature are essentially similar to those of a call. The longer the life of the option, the higher the values of the put. The appreciation of the value of the put in relation to the price of the stock is closer to a one-to-one basis the more in the money the put option is and the closer it is to its expiration date. At X, the rate of increase in the put price is half the rate of depreciation in the price of the stock.

Put-Valuation Formula[20]

Consider an investor with a long position in the stock. In order to establish a riskless position in the security, the investor would sell a call and buy a put. Using the vector notation, the risk-free position is as follows:

long position   sell call   buy put   risk-free position[21]

$$\begin{bmatrix} 1 \\ -1 \end{bmatrix} + \begin{bmatrix} -1 \\ 0 \end{bmatrix} + \begin{bmatrix} 0 \\ 1 \end{bmatrix} = \begin{bmatrix} 0 \\ 0 \end{bmatrix}$$

---

[20] The discussion is based on **Hans R. Stoll,** "The Relationship between Put and Call Option Prices." *Journal of Finance,* vol. 24, no. 5 (December 1969), pp. 801–829; and **J. P. Gould** and **D. Galai,** "Transactions Costs and the Relationship between Put and Call Prices." *Journal of Financial Economics* 1, 1974, pp. 105–129. An alternative and more rigorous derivation was provided by **Michael Parkinson** ("Option Pricing: The American Put." *Journal of Business,* January 1977, pp. 21–35).

[21] A risk-free position can also be established starting with a short position in the stock.

short position   write put   buy call   risk-free position

$$\begin{bmatrix} -1 \\ 1 \end{bmatrix} + \begin{bmatrix} 0 \\ -1 \end{bmatrix} + \begin{bmatrix} 1 \\ 0 \end{bmatrix} = \begin{bmatrix} 0 \\ 0 \end{bmatrix}$$

The cash outlay required for the establishment of a risk-free position is equal to

$$C = V + P - W$$

where C = total cash outlay

V = price of stock × number of shares bought (assume 100)

P = put premium

W = call premium

Since the investor's position is risk-free, a broker or bank should be willing to loan him V dollars at the risk-free rate i, thereby avoiding the commitment of any of the investor's funds. The total interest cost is Vi. The present value of the interest costs is $Vi/(1 + i)$. Therefore the profit resulting from a risk-free arbitrage operation is equal to

$$W - \frac{Vi}{1 + i} - P = \Pi_f$$

where Π_f = risk-free profit.

In a perfect market, Π_f should equal zero. That is, as the arbitrage process starts and continues, $\Pi_f > 0$, the sale of the calls exerts downward pressure on their price, and the purchases of the puts places an upward pressure on their price, causing Π_f to move toward zero. Therefore,

$$W - \frac{Vi}{1 + i} - P = 0 \tag{12.3}$$

$$\text{and} \quad W - P = \frac{Vi}{1 + i} \tag{12.4}$$

dividing Equation 12.4 through by V, we get

$$\frac{W}{V} - \frac{P}{V} = \frac{i}{1 + i} \cong i$$

Therefore, the difference between the relative value of a call (W/V) and the relative value of a put (P/V) is approximately equal to the risk-free rate. In order to calculate the put premium, an investor only has to consider the call premium and the risk-free rate.

12.11 WARRANTS

A warrant is a long-term option to buy a certain number of shares of the issuing company stock at a specified price during a given period of time. This option is issued by the corporation.

Use of Warrants

Warrants are usually issued by corporations as "sweeteners" to debt and preferred stock issues. Their inclusion in debt issues is intended to lower the interest costs to the firm, reduce if not eliminate the restrictive covenants in the indenture agreement, and/or to facilitate the sale of the issue. A warrant attached to a bond is equivalent to a convertible bond. This equity feature allows bondholders to participate in the growth of the issuing corporation. If the growth is realized and reflected in a higher market price for the stock and hence the warrant, the warrant holder may be motivated to exercise the warrant. This exercise is equivalent to the corporation issuing new stock at the option price, a price higher than that prevailing at the time the warrant was issued.

From the point of view of the investor, a warrant allows for the following:

1. *Leverage.* The price of a warrant is a fraction of the price of the stock. The investor can, therefore, using the same dollar amount that would have been committed to the purchase of common stock, be able to participate in the growth of more shares by buying warrants. The extent of the leverage depends on the relationship between the price of the warrant and the price of the stock.

2. *Limited-risk trading.* This results from the lower financial commitment required for warrants versus common stock.

3. *Protecting a short position in the stock.* Warrants protect a short position against rising stock prices in a fashion not too dissimilar from call options. The protection comes from the fixed option price at which the stock can be purchased. Warrants, however, may be much more costly and less flexible than listed options. There is only one striking price and one maturity, and few companies have warrants outstanding.

Warrants vs. Calls

The supply of warrants is limited to the financial needs of a certain corporation in relation to the capital markets requirements. It exists, and it expands by corporate fiat. The supply of call options, on the other hand, is determined by market forces. The expansion of this supply has no impact on the number of shares outstanding. As calls are exercised, a mere transfer of ownership of existing shares from a stockholder to an investor occurs. The exercise of a warrant results in a net increase in the number of shares outstanding, with the attending issue of ownership distribution to existing stockholders.

Other differences lie in unequal margin requirements and commission costs and in the fact that warrants have a much longer maturity than any available call option. Indeed, warrants may have unlimited lives because the Internal Revenue Service provided the issuing corporations with the incentive to extend the warrant life. In 1971, the IRS ruled that the proceeds from the sale of warrants become taxable income to the issuing corporation if the warrants expire worthless. In order to escape payment of taxes, issuing corporations extended the expiration date on their warrants, leaving those with a long warrant position delighted and those with a short warrant position depressed. The extension breathes life into the warrant and hence value.

Valuation of Warrants

The theoretical value of a warrant is equal to:

$$Wt = (S - OP)N$$

where Wt = theoretical value of a warrant
S = market price of stock
OP = option price of stock
N = number of shares to which the
warrant can be converted

Wt would be negative if $OP > S$. This is not possible because a warrant selling at a negative price implies that the buyer is receiving money from the seller. We thus concentrate on warrants with positive prices.

The market price of a warrant is ordinarily larger than the theoretical value. Leverage and the life of the warrant account for this difference. As in the call case, the larger the price of the stock, the larger the price of the warrant. The relationship between the price of the warrant and the price of the stock intensifies beyond the option price, as shown in Figure 12.12. The reader may want to compare Figure 12.8 with Figure 12.12.

Warrants are transferable securities and are traded like stocks. Some warrants are listed on the major exchanges, others are traded over the counter. The popularity of warrants as financing vehicles seems to be waning. No research has yet been completed as to why or as to what impact, if any, the options market has had on the warrant market.

FIGURE 12.12   Theoretical vs. market value of a warrant.

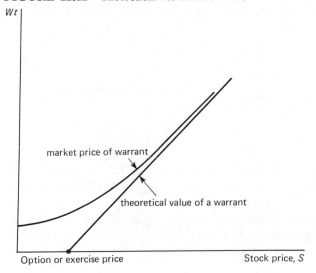

12.12 STOCK RIGHTS

A stock right is an option given existing stockholders to buy a certain number of shares of a new stock issue. Stock rights are technically referred to as "stock subscription warrants." A stockholder receives a right for every share held. Stock rights have a limited life and are transferable.

Use of Rights

Stock rights are used by the issuing corporation to induce existing stockholders to purchase new shares of stock, allowing them in the process to maintain their proportionate ownership in the company. The subscription price (price at which the right holder can purchase a new share of stock) is lower than the market price of stock.

An investor uses stock rights the same way warrants are used. Typically, stock rights have a much shorter maturity than warrants.

Value of Rights

The value of one stock right is derived as follows:

$$SR = \frac{S - SP}{M + 1}$$

where SR = price of a stock right

S = market price of one stock with rights on

SP = subscription price

M = number of rights required to purchase one share of stock

The 1 in the denominator is added because the numerator is inflated by the price of one stock right.

Example

What is the value of one right if the market price of one share (rights on) is $55, the subscription price is $50, and it takes four rights to acquire a new share of stock?

$$SR = \frac{55 - 50}{4 + 1} = \$1$$

The holder of one share of stock needs four rights valued at $4 and $50 in cash in order to acquire a share of stock valued at $55. The net saving is $1 or the price of one right. Hence, the addition of 1 in the denominator.

If the stock goes "ex-right" (the holder of the stock no longer receives a right for a share held), its price will drop by the theoretical value of a right, to $54. The theoretical value of one right remains the same as is calculated as follows:

$$SR = \frac{S' - SP}{M}$$

where $S' =$ market price of stock ex-rights.

$$SR = \frac{54 - 50}{4} = \$1$$

Some corporate statutes have preemptive rights clauses requiring the company to give existing stockholders preferential treatment (in terms of access and price). Rights, therefore, allow existing stockholders to keep their proportionate ownership in the corporation, if they so desire, and prevent management from selling new stocks at prices that would effectively disenfranchise existing stockholders. One additional benefit worth noting is that stock rights enjoy a lower margin requirement, hence they have an even larger leverage potential.

CONCLUSIONS

In this chapter we have provided the basics of stock options. Hedgers, investors, and speculators in the options market have found other means of using options successfully, however. These strategies and other options considerations are covered in the chapter to follow.

QUESTIONS

1. The April 2, 1982, issue of *The Wall Street Journal* gave the following option prices on IBM.

		Calls-Last			Puts-Last		
		Apr	Jul	Oct	Apr	Jul	Oct
IBM	45	16	16¾	s	r	$\frac{1}{16}$	s
61	50	11	11½	s	r	⅜	s
61	55	6⅛	7⅞	8⅞	$\frac{1}{16}$	⅞	1⅝
61	60	1$^{13}\!/_{16}$	4¼	6	1$\frac{1}{16}$	2$^{5}\!/_{16}$	3¼
61	65	⅛	1⅞	3½	4	4⅝	5½

a. Which options are in the money?
b. Which options are out of the money?
c. Which option would you use to protect a long position if you were very concerned about an adverse price movement in IBM? What type of risk does this put option protect you against?
d. Which option would you use to protect a short position if you were somewhat unsettled about market conditions?
e. Why would the July/45 put have a positive value?

2. How are intervals between striking prices set?

3. What function does the Options Clearing Corporation perform?

4. How can calls be used to limit trading risk (assuming an investor has gone short on a stock)?

5. The vector representation of a call is $\begin{bmatrix} 1 \\ 0 \end{bmatrix}$. What does this reveal about the potential loss of the option buyer?

6. From a risk perspective, what is the difference between "naked" and "covered" call option writing?

7. An option trader resells a call option that she bought in the money. If the price of the underlying stock has not moved, can she still lose out on the option investment? (Ignore transactions costs.)

8. Two calls have the same striking price but different maturities. How does one explain the additional value of the call with nine months to maturity over the call with three months to maturity? (Look at Fig. 12.2 as you contemplate your answer.)

9. Why would an option on a security with a high beta coefficient tend to have a higher premium than options written on securities with lower betas?

10. Many of the assumptions of the B&S model are questionable. What are their implications for the validity of the model itself?

11. How is writing a call similar to buying a put? How is it dissimilar? What are the vector representations of each position?

12. What are the costs/benefits of a put versus a stop-loss order to reduce downside risk on a long position in a stock?

13. An investor who is bullish on a stock may choose to write a put versus taking a long position in the stock. Why?

14. Compare and contrast a warrant to a call.

15. Delineate specifically the risk associated with writing put and call options to generate income.

16. You are a manager of a pension fund. Under what conditions would you add options to your portfolio? Justify your decision, given your fiduciary responsibility.

17. List the various ways of using call and put options.

18. Stagnant equity markets have historically dampened the investors' enthusiasm for committing funds to equity securities. How might the option market have changed this reluctance?

19. An investor has a long position in a stock and a long position in a put. Does he have a perfectly hedged position? If not, what would he need to do in order to achieve such a position?

20. "The relationship between the price of a call and that of a put is complex." Comment.

21. How does the size of dividends affect the price of call options? Why?

PROBLEMS

1. Mrs. Trader buys a call option for $400 on Oct. 1, 1981, and exercises it one month later to acquire a round lot of DGO stock at $45/share. Assume Mrs. Trader is in the 50 percent tax bracket. What is the cost of the stock for tax purposes? If she sells the stock for $5,500 on Oct. 10, 1982, what will her tax liability be? What if she waits to sell until Nov. 10, 1982?

2. Mr. Investor, optimistic about WJM stock (current price: $44/share) is considering these two strategies (assume no margin buying):
   a. Buy 100 shares of WJM
   b. Buy WJM/3 mo./40 selling for $500
   What is the profit and annualized return on each of these two strategies if WJM moves up to $50? WJM moves up to $45? WJM retreats to $40?

3. Mrs. Investor owns 100 shares of Kinnare Cube Company stock selling at $83/share; Mr. Speculator does not. They both write call options on KCC stock with a striking price of $85 and receive a $750 premium. Calculate the gain/loss for each if KCC stock moves to $88/share.

4. RGH stock is known to have a hedge ratio of 0.25. How could an investor who owns one round lot of the stock construct a "neutral hedge"? What would his return be if markets are efficient?

5. Use the B&S model to calculate the theoretical value of a MES/3 mo./40 call option. MES stock is selling at $50, has a dividend yield of 3 percent, and a σ^2 of 0.36. The risk-free rate is 6 percent.

6. Use the B&S model to estimate the σ^2 of a KWO/6 mo./45 call option; KWO is selling at $52 and has a dividend yield of 5 percent. The risk-free rate is 8 percent and the option sells for 12¼. (Hint: You will have to use trial and error.)

7. What is the value of one right if the market price of one share (rights on) is $31, the subscription price is $25, and it takes five rights to acquire one new share of stock?

APPENDIX

Cumulative Probability Distributions

Values of $N(x)$ for Given Values of x for a Cumulative Normal Probability Distribution with Zero Mean and Unit Variance

x	$N(x)$	x	$N(x)$	x	$N(x)$	x	$N(x)$	x	$N(x)$	x	$N(x)$
		−1.00	.1587	1.00	.8413	−2.00	.0228	.00	.5000	2.00	.9773
−2.95	.0016	−.95	.1711	1.05	.8531	−1.95	.0256	.05	.5199	2.05	.9798
−2.90	.0019	−.90	.1841	1.10	.8643	−1.90	.0287	.10	.5398	2.10	.9821
−2.85	.0022	−.85	.1977	1.15	.8749	−1.85	.0322	.15	.5596	2.15	.9842
−2.80	.0026	−.80	.2119	1.20	.8849	−1.80	.0359	.20	.5793	2.20	.9861
−2.75	.0030	−.75	.2266	1.25	.8944	−1.75	.0401	.25	.5987	2.25	.9878
−2.70	.0035	−.70	.2420	1.30	.9032	−1.70	.0446	.30	.6179	2.30	.9893
−2.65	.0040	−.65	.2578	1.35	.9115	−1.65	.0495	.35	.6368	2.35	.9906
−2.60	.0047	−.60	.2743	1.40	.9192	−1.60	.0548	.40	.6554	2.40	.9918
−2.55	.0054	−.55	.2912	1.45	.9265	−1.55	.0606	.45	.6736	2.45	.9929
−2.50	.0062	−.50	.3085	1.50	.9332	−1.50	.0668	.50	.6915	2.50	.9938
−2.45	.0071	−.45	.3264	1.55	.9394	−1.45	.0735	.55	.7088	2.55	.9946
−2.40	.0082	−.40	.3446	1.60	.9452	−1.40	.0808	.60	.7257	2.60	.9953
−2.35	.0094	−.35	.3632	1.65	.9505	−1.35	.0885	.65	.7422	2.65	.9960
−2.30	.0107	−.30	.3821	1.70	.9554	−1.30	.0968	.70	.7580	2.70	.9965
−2.25	.0122	−.25	.4013	1.75	.9599	−1.25	.1057	.75	.7734	2.75	.9970
−2.20	.0139	−.20	.4207	1.80	.9641	−1.20	.1151	.80	.7881	2.80	.9974
−2.15	.0158	−.15	.4404	1.85	.9678	−1.15	.1251	.85	.8023	2.85	.9978
−2.10	.0179	−.10	.4602	1.90	.9713	−1.10	.1357	.90	.8159	2.90	.9981
−2.05	.0202	−.05	.4801	1.95	.9744	−1.05	.1469	.95	.8289	2.95	.9984

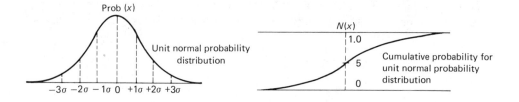

Prob (x)

Unit normal probability distribution

-3σ -2σ -1σ 0 $+1\sigma$ $+2\sigma$ $+3\sigma$

$N(x)$

1.0

.5

0

Cumulative probability for unit normal probability distribution

CHAPTER 13

Advanced Option Strategies and Considerations

13.1 INTRODUCTION

The options market is becoming increasingly complex, multiplying, in the process, potentially profitable opportunities. This chapter focuses on most of the strategies employed by options traders and on the necessary elements of an options program. We begin our discussion with combinations.

13.2 COMBINATIONS

The variety of investment opportunities available to the sophisticated investor in the options market is practically limitless. We begin the sorting out with the various combinations that can be developed using puts and calls. First, a few definitions.

A *combination* is the purchase or sale of a call and a put with different (or similar) striking prices or maturities or both.

A *straddle* is a combination of a put and a call with the same striking price and maturity. Both options are on the same side of the market (long or short).

13.3 BUYING STRADDLES

Call buyers are optimistic about the direction of the price of the underlying security. Unless their expectations materialize and their optimism yields a price appreciation larger than the cost of the option, they would not realize a profit on the long call position. The opposite is true for put buyers. A problem presents itself if the direction of the market price of the security is unpredictable or the news that could cause a certain price movement is unpredictable. An example of the latter would be, to pull an episode from corporate history, an announcement by Polaroid on the production of its own films used in its instant cameras (these films were previously bought from Eastman Kodak). If all the "bugs" in the production process and in the quality of the film have been worked out, the stock will experience a substantial price appreciation; if not, the stock will suffer a significant price decline. The question, therefore, is how an investor could bet on the outcome and simultaneously minimize the cost of the bet. Straddles offer just such an alternative. The call offers a profit potential if the price rises, and the put offers a profit potential if the price falls. We now summarize the various motivations for buying straddles.

Straddles for Leverage

An investor who is expecting a *major* change in the price of a security but is uncertain about the direction would purchase a straddle. A price change in *either* direction exceeding the price of a straddle would result in a profit. Such possibilities are not as rewarding and as risk-limiting outside the option market. Given the uncertainty about the direction of the price movement, a long position in the stock offers no downside protection; a short position offers no protection against price appreciation; and a combination of both a short and a long position offers a zero profit opportunity. The losses (gains) on the long position would offset the gains (losses) on the short position. An investor can, however, close out either of the positions as soon as the direction of the market is determined. In so doing the investor does not capitalize on the full increase or decrease in the price of the stock (a somewhat analogous position to that of a straddle) but, most importantly, remains open to the possibility of price reversals. These possibilities are very real if the evidence on the random walk theory is correct. There are no observable trends in the market that allow an investor to realize a gain from any filter rule, regardless of the nature of the filter. Protection, however, is not costless.

The leverage provided by a straddle results from the small financial commitment it requires when compared with a position in the underlying stock. A straddle on JAK/ Dec/50 selling for $7 requires a commitment of $700 plus commission costs. A commitment to a long, short, or combined position in the stock would require an investment of at least 50 percent of the price of the security. If the current market price is $50, the minimum commitment would be $2,500 on one side of the market, over three times that of a straddle. While leverage can be very lucrative in the event of a major price change, we must voice a caution about the negative side; mainly that if there is no movement in the price of the stock, the investor would lose the full premium or 100 percent of the capital invested in the straddle. The losses in percentage terms are large (small in dollar terms) up to the neighborhood of the break-even point. This point is determined by the striking price on the straddle ± the premium. A JAK/Dec/50 straddle selling at $700 has break-even points of 43 (50 − 7) and 57 (50 + 7). Below 43, the put is well in the money and hence profitable; beyond 57, the call is well in the money and is profitable. The extent to which an option is in the money or out of the money depends, as stated earlier, on the relationship between the striking price and the market price on the underlying security. If the straddle premium of $700 were distributed $300 and $400 for the put and the call respectively and the current market price of the stock is $55, then the call is $5 in the money ($S - X = 5$) and the put is $5 out of the money ($X - S = -5$). The profit on the call option is equal to $100; the loss on the put is $300 if the straddle is exercised. The put price does not drop to zero, however, if the straddle has some time left to run before expiring. The positive put premium in this case is time premium, as was suggested earlier.

An investor who is more optimistic than pessimistic about the prospects for a stock may wish to purchase a straddle with an in-the-money call and a put that is out of

FIGURE 13.1 **Hypothetical stock price pattern.**

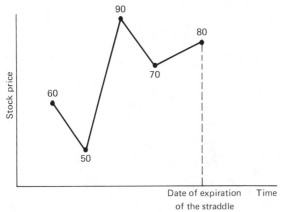

the money. A rather pessimistic investor may purchase a straddle with an in-the-money put and an out-of-the-money call. The length of the life of the straddle purchased would depend on the expected speed of adjustment in the stock price. The structuring of the straddle strategy depends on the investor's expectations, risk profile, and budget size.

Straddles for Aggressive Trading

An investor wishing to be protected against unexpected movements in the price of a stock, given a position in the stock, would buy a straddle. The option position would allow for a more aggressive posture.

Consider the hypothetical stock price pattern shown in Figure 13.1. An investor owning a straddle (premium = $1,200) with $S = 60$ would be protected by the put had he or she bet on a long position and the price dropped to 50.

A short position at 60 would result in a $1,000 gross profit (on 100 shares) excluding commission; it would bring a profit on the put and a loss on the call (equal to its cost) if the stock fell to 50. If at 50 the investor believed that the price of the stock were about to rebound and would be unlikely to return to this level, he or she would close out the short position, go long on the stock, and possibly decide to close out the put side of the straddle. This latter course is referred to as "lifting a leg." If this were done, the investor would have guessed the market correctly (Figure 13.1) and would reap substantial profits. Lifting a leg exposes the investor to downside risk, however, in the event of a continuing price decline. If the straddle position were kept intact, the appreciation from 50 to 90 would obviously cover the full cost of the straddle. Once this were achieved, the investor could trade with impunity. The investment is zero, and no matter what the direction of the stock, a profit will accrue on the straddle because its cost has been recovered. A long position will be doubly profitable (long + call) if the stock moves as expected; a short position will be doubly profitable (short + put). The ideal—an unrealistic expectation—based on Figure 13.1, is to lift a leg at 50, go long, sell at 90 and go short, cover at 70 and go long, and close out the long position and/or the call position at 80 when the option expires.

FIGURE 13.2 Position of the straddle buyer.

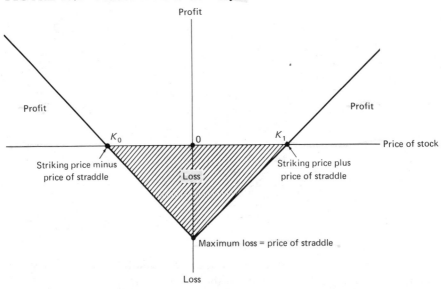

Vector and Graphic Representation

The vector representation of a straddle is as follows:

$$
\underset{\textstyle Call}{\begin{bmatrix} 1 \\ 0 \end{bmatrix}} + \underset{\textstyle Put}{\begin{bmatrix} 0 \\ 1 \end{bmatrix}} = \underset{\textstyle Straddle}{\begin{bmatrix} 1 \\ 1 \end{bmatrix}}
$$

A point appreciation in the price of the stock causes a point appreciation in the value of the call (before accounting for the premium); a point drop in the price of the stock brings about a point appreciation in the value of the put.

The position of the straddle buyer is shown graphically in Figure 13.2, which shows the straddle position realizing a gain beyond K_1 and below K_0. The maximum loss (100 percent of the premium) is realized at point O, where there is no movement in the price of the stock (striking price = market price).

13.4 WRITING STRADDLES

The straddle writer makes a commitment to purchase a stock at the striking price during the life of the option (against the put) and to sell a stock at the same striking price during the same time period (against the call).

The commitment of the straddle writer can be made against a position in the underlying security or against no position (a naked straddle). No matter the position in the stock, the straddle writer seeks a return, the ceiling on which is defined by the size of the straddle premium. The maximum return is realized if the market price of the underlying security is equal to the striking price. Any deviation (+ or −) from the striking price would mean a dollar return lower than the full premium (minus the *double* commission

TABLE 13.1
Straddle Opportunities in GM, Quoted Sept. 9, 1980[a]

| Option | Expiration Dates | | |
	September	December	March
GM 45	7⅝	8⅞	10¼
GM 45 P[b]	¹⁄₁₆	⅝	1⅛
GM 50	2¹⁵⁄₁₆	4⅞	6⅛
GM 50 P	⁵⁄₁₆	2	3
GM 60	¹⁄₁₆	1¹¹⁄₁₆	2³⁄₁₆
GM 60 P	7⅛	8⅛	8½

[a] GM market price = 52⅝

[b] P = put

incurred upon the sale of the straddle). A loss would result, however, if the price of the stock appreciated or depreciated by an amount greater than the size of the premium.

The option market currently allows for varied straddle writing opportunities on several securities. Turning to Table 13.1, we can see that in the case of General Motors, Inc., nine straddle writing opportunities present themselves.

The maximum premium could be earned on the longest maturity of GM 45. The straddle writer must be aware, however, of the fact that the longer the commitment is outstanding, the longer the position is exposed to price fluctuations which could lead to a loss in position.

In addition to the choice of maturity and striking price, given the security, the straddle writer has an additional choice between a covered position and a naked position.

Writing Covered Straddles

The writer of a covered straddle assumes a position with different risk/return features than that of the writer of a naked option. This, we shall examine in detail.

A covered straddle position should be assumed if and only if the writer is prepared to sell shares when the stock appreciates in price and the call is exercised and to buy additional shares when the stock drops in price and the put is exercised. A rise in the price of the stock could leave the writer with no position in the security and a decline could leave him or her with twice the original position. The possibility that both sides of the straddle could be exercised prior to expiration should not be discounted, however.

Consider a December straddle position involving the following (from Table 13.1):

Buy 100 GM at 52⅝
Sell GM/Dec/50 at 4⅞
Sell GM/Dec/50 P at 2

The proceeds from the sale of the straddle are $487.50 + $200 = $687.50.

The size of the capital committed (with 50 percent margin requirement on the stock and 30 percent on the put) is as follows:

For Stock

52⅝ × 100 = $5,262.50
Margin requirement = 5,262.50 × 50% = $2,631.25

For the Put Option

The margin requirement on the put is 30 percent of the market price of the underlying stock ± the difference between the market price and the striking price (+ if the put is in the money, − if the put is out of the money)

(5,262.50 × 30%) − ((52⅝ − 50) × 100) =	1,316.25
Total (2,631.25 + 1,316.25)	$3,947.50
Less premium received 6⅞ × 100	−687.50
Capital commitment (investment)	**$3,260.00**

The figures above do not account for the commissions; one on the stock, one on the call, and a third on the put.

If the stock appreciates in price, to 60 for example, the call will be exercised. The straddle writer would lose the stock and earn just the call premium or $487.50 (a lower sum than could have been earned on a straight long position) minus the loss on the stock due to the exercise of the call (52⅝ − 50 = 2⅝). If the appreciation continues during the life of the straddle, the put becomes worthless and the straddle writer could have earned a total of 4¼ (6⅞ − 2⅝) or $425/$3,260 ≅ 0.13 (from September 9 to the Saturday following the third Friday of December).

If the stock price reverses its upward direction and declines down to but not below 50, the put will not be exercised and the returns to the straddle writer are similar to the previous case.

If the stock price declines below 50, the put will be in the money and its holder will exercise it. The straddle writer is, once again, the owner of the stock which could produce more loss if the market continues to weaken.

If the stock price started out in a downward direction, the straddle writer would see the put exercised against him or her. If the stock price falls to 40 and the put is exercised at this level, the writer would now own a depreciated asset (the original stock) and an overvalued asset (the new shares of stock). The returns from the sale of the straddle are as follows:

Loss on old stock: 52⅝ (100) − 40 (100) =	$1,262.50
Loss on new shares: 50 (100) − 40 (100) =	1,000.00
Total loss	$2,262.50
Less the premium received	687.50
Loss	**$1,575.00**

This loss is a book loss (realized loss if the straddle expires with the stock trading at 40) on an investment of $3,260, or a rate of approximately 48 percent.

One way to reduce this loss is to close out the stock position before the stock price reaches 40. Another course, an optimum course for the minimization of a loss resulting from a decline in the price of the underlying security, is to write a naked straddle.

This strategy, however, could, as we shall demonstrate, backfire if the stock appreciates substantially over 52⅝.

Writing a Naked Straddle

Writing a naked straddle would obviously reduce the size of the total initial commitment, for the writer would not have to pay for a long position in the stock and for the commission thereon.

The capital commitment on a naked straddle is equal to 30% of the value of the underlying security:

$$(52⅝ \times 100) \times 30\% = \$1,578.75$$

± the larger of the amount in (out) of the money on the call or the put.

The put is 2⅝ out of the money; the call is 2⅝ in the money. Therefore an additional sum equal to 2⅝ × 100, or $262.50, would have to be deposited with the broker.

Additional sum	262.50
Total investment (1,578.75 + 262.50)	$1,841.25
Minus premium on straddle	687.50
Required initial commitment (before commission)	**$1,153.75**

The position of the naked straddle writer can best be shown as in Figure 13.3.

The best position for the writer of a naked straddle is when the stock price is at 50, the striking price. At 50, neither the call or the put are exercisable and the option writer realizes the full straddle premium. At another point, less than the full premium is realized and a loss is, in fact, possible depending on the size of the deviation from 50 in relation to the size of the premium received.

Consider the option writer's position if the stock appreciates to 60. The call, well in the money, will be exercised. The writer of a naked straddle would have to purchase the stock in the open market at 60 and deliver it to the option holder. This means buying a stock at 60 and simultaneously selling it at 50. The loss will exceed the premium received on the straddle. This position should be contrasted with that of a covered straddle. A stock price rise to 60 results in a realization of the full premium on the straddle (assume stock remains above 50 up to expiration date).

If the price of the stock falls to 40, the put will be exercised. The straddle writer now holds a $40 stock for which $50 was paid. The loss is equal to

Loss on acquired shares (put to the writer)	$1,000.00
Less premium received	$ 687.50
Loss	**$ 312.50**

The $312.50 loss is realized on an investment of $1,154 or a rate of 312.50/1,154 = 27%. This loss is significantly lower than that realized on the covered straddle position (48 percent). In addition, the writer of a naked straddle holds only 100 shares as opposed

FIGURE 13.3   **Position of writer of naked straddle.**

| Loss | Profit range | Loss |

43.125   56.875
[50 − (6 7/8)]   [50 + (6 7/8)]

to 200 shares for the writer of a covered option. This position reduces the risk associated with the naked option by one half in the event the market weakness persists.

We can, therefore, summarize by stating that a naked straddle position, while loss-minimizing in a lean market, could be devastating in a bullish market. The loss from an upward movement in the price of the security is theoretically limitless unless the straddle writer closes out the position at a certain "acceptable" loss level by either buying a call or buying the stock to deliver against the outstanding call commitment.

If the stock price remains at or around 50, the naked straddle position is superior to that of a covered straddle. These tradeoffs must be weighed carefully if the straddle writer is to realize any positive return on investment.

Vector and Graphic Representation

The vector representation of a straddle sale position is as follows:

$$\underset{\text{Write Put}}{\begin{bmatrix} 0 \\ -1 \end{bmatrix}} + \underset{\text{Write Call}}{\begin{bmatrix} -1 \\ 0 \end{bmatrix}} = \underset{\text{Short Straddle}}{\begin{bmatrix} -1 \\ -1 \end{bmatrix}}$$

A one-point movement (+ or −) in the price of the underlying stock would result in a one-point loss on a short straddle position (before accounting for the premium).

Graphically, the straddle writer position can be depicted as in Figure 13.4, in which the put is exercisable to the left of K_3. The loss that could result from the newly established long position is limited (the stock could fall only to zero). Beyond K_5, the loss which could result from an exercised call is theoretically limitless. There is no upward limit to the price of a security. The constraining forces are time, the nature of the market, and the psychology of the straddle writer (the ability to withstand the pressures to cover a given position). From Figure 13.4 we can also see that the maximum return is realized at K_4, the striking price. The straddle writer earns the full value of the premium at K_4. It is unrealistic to expect, we must stress, that a straddle-writing strategy would result in earning the full premium.

13.5 BUYING COMBINATIONS

A combination, once again, is made up of a call and a put with different striking prices, different lives, or both.

Referring back to Table 13.1, we can identify 81 possible combinations: nine calls each combinable with any of the nine puts ($9 \times 9 = 81$).

The combination buyer, like the buyer of a straddle, is seeking protection no matter the direction in the price of the underlying security. The nature of the protection is

FIGURE 13.4 **Straddle writer's position.**

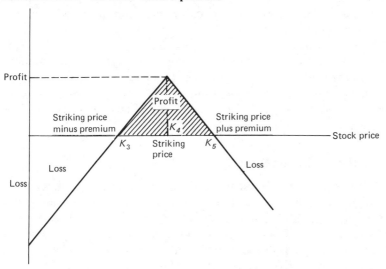

considerably different from that offered by the straddle and the range of choice is vastly superior (81 vs. 9; see Table 12.3).

A combination buyer uses a combination for the same purposes as a straddle buyer, but starting with a different prognosis. While straddle buyers admit to the inability (or unwillingness) to predict the direction of the market at the time the straddle is bought, combination buyers bet that the stock will go up or down with a certain probability in mind. Given that the probability is not equal to one, they would seek protection with a call (if they were betting on a stock price decline) or with a put (if they were betting on a stock price rise). The lower the probability that the direction of the market will be in accordance with expectations, the larger the sum the investor would be willing to commit to the protection. That is, the lower the probability is, the further in the money (or the less out of the money) a call option is bought to protect a short position, and the further in the money (or the less out of the money) a put is bought to protect a long position in the underlying security.

Consider the case of an investor who expects a considerable decline in the price of GM. The expected decline will be realized, he or she reasons, no matter the attitude of the U.S. government toward import quotas or tariffs. U.S. policymakers are expected to announce a new policy concerning the importation of cars into the United States. The policy, the investor expects, will not be very restrictive and consequently the investor will either sell GM short, buy a put, or do both. Concerned with the possibility that very restrictive measures on imports could be announced coupled with stimulative measures for the U.S. auto industry, the investor may wish to purchase protection using a long call position. The higher the probability of restrictive measures, the more the investor would pay for a call.

The investor may pick a GM/March/60 selling at $2\frac{3}{16}$ and a GM/Sept/60 P selling at $7\frac{1}{8}$. The call option is out of the money (GM is trading at $52\frac{5}{8}$) and the put is well in the money; hence, the movement in its price will roughly coincide with the movement in the price of the stock. If the policy announcement is made and is favorable to the investor's position, and if GM drops in price from $52\frac{5}{8}$ to 45, an investor holding a combination plus a short position in the stock would realize $7\frac{5}{8}$ points on the put portion of the combination and another $7\frac{5}{8}$ points on the short position. The only costs are the commissions, the cost of the call ($2\frac{3}{16}$), and the interest costs on the margined short position in the stock.

Opposite expectations would have produced an opposite strategy. An in-the-money call option and an out-of-the-money put option would have been purchased. The range of opportunities (in or out of the money) is quite substantial.

The reader should be able to produce various combination strategies to fit various expectations.

13.6 SELLING COMBINATIONS

A short combination position is established to earn a desired rate of return. The size of the return depends on the behavior of the underlying stock, on the distribution of the combination premium between the put and the call, and on how far the two options are in or out of the money. A combination writer unable to predict the direction of the market but willing to place a higher probability on a price decline would want a lower limit on the profit range (consult Fig. 13.2). This would obviously allow the writer to keep a larger portion of the premium if the price of the stock should follow the expected direction. The wide range of combination opportunities available in the marketplace does allow the combination writer to set the desired profit range. The lower profit limit on a combination (the break-even price on the downside) is equal to the striking price on the put minus the total premium received. The upper limit (the break-even price on the upside) is equal to the striking price on the call plus the premium on the combination.

The sale of GM/Dec/60 P and a GM/Dec/50 (Table 13.1) would produce the following range:

$$[60 - (4\frac{7}{8} + 8\frac{1}{8})] \quad \text{to} \quad (50 + 13)$$
$$\text{or} \qquad 47 \qquad\qquad \text{to} \quad 63$$

Below 47 or over 63 the investor loses money. The lowest possible limit that can be extracted from Table 12.3 is through the sale of a GM/March/45 P and the sale of GM/March/60. The lower limit in this case is $45 - 3\frac{5}{16}$ ($1\frac{1}{8} + 2\frac{3}{16}$) = $41\frac{11}{16}$. The upper limit is $63\frac{5}{16}$.

The resulting combination here consists of two out-of-the-money options and thus provides a considerable protection against small price fluctuations. If GM falls in price from $52\frac{5}{8}$, the combination writer would have $10\frac{15}{16}$ points ($52\frac{5}{8} - 41\frac{11}{16}$) before a loss in the short combination position. If the stock rises in price, there is a $10\frac{11}{16}$-point ($63\frac{5}{16} - 52\frac{5}{8}$) protection. The ideal situation, therefore, as in the case of a straddle, is for the price of the underlying security not to change at all or not to change substantially—either to remain within the range set by the striking call price and the striking put price if they are different.

In the case above where the maximum limit was established, it must be noted that only $2\frac{3}{16} + 1\frac{1}{8}$ or $3\frac{5}{16}$ was collected as premium. The writer could have picked another combination that would have yielded a much larger premium income. But there is no free lunch. The larger the premium, the smaller the profit range and the greater the

FIGURE 13.5   **Combination writer's position.**

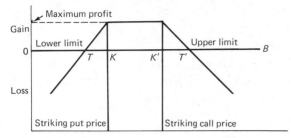

risk. This situation is depicted in Figure 13.5. *KK'* represents the maximum profit range and *TT'* the no-loss range.

A combination writer should therefore be very careful in selecting a combination. While the combination allows for a considerable room for error, it does not eliminate risk altogether.

We have thus far spoken of a naked short combination position. This position can obviously be covered by a long position in the underlying security. The considerations are very similar to those discussed under covered straddles, with the necessary adjustment to account for the added flexibility that combinations introduce in the investment process.

13.7 SYNTHETIC COMBINATIONS

If a put on a given security is not available on the option exchanges, a combination can still be created through the sale of two calls with different striking prices against a long position in the stock.

Consider the case of the investor interested in writing a combination on JAK Inc., but who is unable to sell the put side through the option exchanges. The resolution lies in the creation of a synthetic combination where two calls with different striking prices are written, as follows:

Market price JAK Inc.	46
JAK/Sept/45	4
JAK/Sept/50	2

As previously discussed, the maximum profit from this position is when the stock price remains between $45 and $50. Therefore, an investor expecting a considerable movement (more than five points, in this case) in the price of the stock should not consider writing a synthetic combination.

The synthetic combination position with a long position in the stock is equivalent to the conventional naked combination sale. Using the vector notation, we can see why:

Long Position	*Write Call*	*Sell Put*
$\begin{bmatrix} +1 \\ -1 \end{bmatrix}$ +	$\begin{bmatrix} -1 \\ 0 \end{bmatrix}$ =	$\begin{bmatrix} 0 \\ -1 \end{bmatrix}$

Sell Put		**Sell Call**		
$\begin{bmatrix} 0 \\ -1 \end{bmatrix}$	$+$	$\begin{bmatrix} -1 \\ 0 \end{bmatrix}$	$=$	naked combination

The margin requirement for the synthetic combination is equal to (using the current 50% margin requirement on a long stock position and a 30% margin requirement on a naked call) the following:

Long stock position

Stock margin requirement		
50% × 46 × 100 =	$2,300	
Less premium on covered call	400	
		$1,900

Naked call

30% of stock price (30% × 46) = $1,380		
Less out-of-the-money credit		
(50 − 46) × 100	= −400	
Less call option premium	−200	780
Total investment		**$2,680**

The maximum profit, as mentioned earlier, is realized if the price of the stock remains between $45 and $50. This profit is equal to the size of the premium collected, or $400 + $200 = $600. Let us now consider the results from a stock price decline or appreciation.

1. *Stock declines to 40.* Both calls will be worthless, hence not exercised, if the stock price is at $40. The writer of a synthetic combination earns the $600 in premiums but loses $600 on the long stock position.

2. *Stock appreciates to 50.* One call is profitable (that with a $45 exercise price) to the holder, and the other is at the money and hence not worth exercising. The call with the lower striking price will be exercised and the stock will be called away from the investor. His or her income is $600.

3. *Stock appreciates to 70.* Both calls are profitable at 70. The investor would have to deliver stock against one of the calls and purchase 100 shares of JAK Inc. at a $70 market price. Before calculating the profit/loss position, we must mention that as the price of JAK Inc. rises, the synthetic combination writer would be marked to the market for the naked call position and asked to deposit additional funds in the margin account. Also, the writer always has the option of closing the position either by buying a call on JAK Inc. or by purchasing another 100 shares of JAK Inc.

The profit/loss position at $70 is calculated as follows:

Loss on the covered call position (46 − 45) =	$ 100
Loss on the naked call position (70 − 50) =	2,000
Total loss	$2,100
Minus premium received	600
Loss	**$1,500**

This loss does not account for transactions costs, which are larger for synthetic combinations than for conventional combinations because of the additional commission charges on the long stock position. Also, the loss does not include the interest charges on the debit balance from the margin requirements on the stock and on the naked call position, with the debit balance on the latter position increasing as the price of the stock rises.

We can, therefore, observe that the combination writer is advised to stick with conventional combinations on stocks with minimum expected price movements and to use synthetic combinations only if conventional combinations are not possible.

13.8 SPREADS

Definitions

Spread

A spread is the simultaneous purchase and sale of option contracts of the same class (put *or* call) on the same underlying security. The option bought has a different striking price and/or a different expiration month from the option sold.

The spread is the difference between the premium received and the premium paid.

Bull Spread

A bull spread is established when the investor "buys" a spread, that is, paying more (less) premium for the call (put) option bought than is collected in premium on the option sold. As its name implies, a bull spread is established when an investor expects an advance in the price of the underlying stock. In the call case, the bull spread results in a debit to the investor's account; in the put case, in a credit to the investor's account. In both cases, however, the investor is buying the option with the lower striking price and is selling the option with the higher striking price.

Bear Spreads

A bear spread is established when the investor "sells" a spread, that is, paying less (more) premium for the call (put) option bought than is collected in premium on the option sold. As its name implies, a bear spread is established when an investor expects a decline in the price of the underlying stock. In the call case, the bear spread results in a credit to the investor's account; in the put case, in a debit to the investor's account. In both cases, however, the investor is buying the option with the higher striking price and selling the option with the lower striking price.

Vertical Call Spreads

Vertical (sometimes referred to as "price") call spreads involve the purchase of a call contract at one price and the simultaneous sale of a call contract on the same stock, with both option contracts having the same maturity but a different striking price. Referring back to Table 13.1, the reader can observe that for a given maturity, striking prices are listed vertically. Hence the designation "vertical."

Vertical call spreads can be bullish or bearish.

Vertical Bull Call Spread

The raison d'être of spreads is the establishment of a perfectly hedged position (*not* a riskless position, we must remember) that reduces the risk associated with a long or a short position and allows the investor a respectable rate of return with only minor movements in the price of the underlying security. The spread position is best understood using the vector notation:

$$\underset{\textit{Buy Call}}{\begin{bmatrix} 1 \\ 0 \end{bmatrix}} + \underset{\textit{Write Call}}{\begin{bmatrix} -1 \\ 0 \end{bmatrix}} = \underset{\textit{Spread}}{\begin{bmatrix} 0 \\ 0 \end{bmatrix}}$$

The zero entries in the spread vector represent profits before the premium is accounted for. The size of the premium paid in a vertical bull call spread is the maximum amount at risk. The call spread, therefore, limits the risk to the differential between premium received and premium paid.

On a given day we can observe all possible spread opportunities involving a certain stock, such as IBM, by merely inspecting *The Wall Street Journal*. Assume that the opportunities on IBM are as summarized in Table 13.2.

An investor bullish on IBM would, based on Table 13.2, have several vertical call spreads to choose from. The choice then would depend on the investor's level of risk aversion, on how bullish he or she is, and on the size of the financial commitment the investor wishes to make. With IBM trading at 64½, the investor settles on the following:

Buy IBM/Oct/55	$1,025
Sell IBM/Oct/60	−575
Investment (maximum loss)	**$ 450**

TABLE 13.2
Summary of Spread Opportunities

		October	January	April
IBM P[a]	45	r	⅙	s
IBM	50	15½	15¾	s
IBM P	50	¹⁄₁₆	r	s
IBM	55	10¼	11	s
IBM P	55	⅛	¹¹⁄₁₆	s
IBM	60	5¾	7¼	8¾
IBM P	60	⁹⁄₁₆	1¾	2⅜
IBM	65	2½	4½	6
IBM P	65	2³⁄₁₆	3⅝	4⅜
IBM	70	⅞	2½	3⅞
IBM P	70	6	6¾	7
IBM	75	⅛	s	s
IBM P	75	10¼	s	s

[a] P = put; r = not traded; s = no option offered.

Being bullish on IBM, the investor buys the option with the greater potential (the one more in the money) and sells the option with the lesser potential (the one less in the money), which requires a financial commitment. We now explore the impact of stock price movements on the spread position while ignoring commissions and tax considerations.

Stock Remains at 64½

Since both options are in the money, they will be profitable to exercise or to close out by entering a closing sale (purchase) transaction. The exercise would result in the following:

Profit in long call position (6,450 − 5,500) = $950
Loss on the short position (6,450 − 6,000) =   −450
Gross profit   **$500**

Profit = 500 − 450 = $50
    or a return of 50/450 = 11.11%

Stock Appreciates to 75

The results are as follows:

Exercise the long position at a cost of $5,500 (striking price) + 1,025 (option premium) = $6,525
Short position is exercised against us. (The stock we now own (from the exercise of the long call) is effectively being sold at the striking price + option premium)
6,000 (striking price) + 575 (option premium) =   6,575
Gross profit   **$50**
or a return of 11.11% (50/450)

Therefore, the maximum profit in a spread position is established in advance. It is simply equal to: [(striking price on short position) + (option premium received)] − [(striking price on long position) + (option premium paid)].

Stock Falls to 50

At 50, both the short and the call positions are out of the money (the market price is below both striking prices). Neither option will be exercised. The maximum loss is the differential in the premia or $450. The investor, therefore, by establishing a bullish vertical call spread position, knows in advance the maximum gain and the maximum loss. Since the investor expects the stock price to rise, he or she is therefore expressing satisfaction with the 11.11 percent return (for one month) on a $450 investment in a spread.

FIGURE 13.6   Graphic representation of vertical call option.

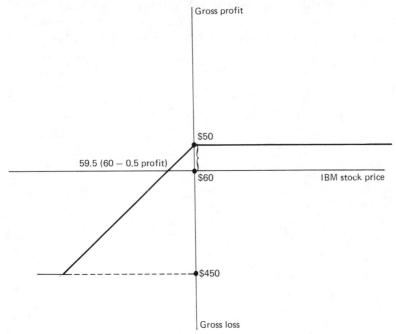

The Alternatives

A bullish investor on IBM has various options for participating in an upward stock price movement. He can establish a long position in the stock, which offers an unlimited upward potential, a maximum loss potential equal to the price of the stock, and requires a financial commitment equal to at least 50 percent of the market price of the stock—or $(64.5)(100) \times 50\% = \$3,225$. The investor can buy a call that would offer a substantial appreciation potential (limited by the movement in the price of the stock during the life of the option) and limits the potential loss to the size of the call premium ($1,025). The vertical call option spread position, while limiting the upside potential to only $50, also limits the downside loss to $450 (compared with $1,025 for the call position and $6,450 for the long stock position). The reduction of exposure is, therefore, not without its costs.

The maximum profit is $50 and the maximum loss is $450—the difference between the premium paid and the premium received (Figure 13.6). This assumes that both options are not exercised prior to maturity. If the investor receives an exercise notice against the short position in the spread, he or she would be left with a net long position in the call option. The maximum loss may obviously be larger in this case. The investor can meet an exercise notice in various ways: (1) by delivering a stock that is already owned, (2) by buying a stock in the open market, (3) by borrowing a stock and delivering it (establish a short position in the stock), or (4) by exercising the long side of the spread. The decision depends on the circumstances. If the long side of the spread is out of the money or is substantially less in the money than the short position, it would have a larger time-premium component, which will be lost immediately upon the exercise. The investor should, therefore, be very careful in assessing opportunities.

TABLE 13.3
Vertical Bull Call Spread Worksheet

		Option Price	Stock Price
Sell	IBM/Oct/60	5¾	64½
Buy	IBM/Oct/55	10¼	64½

A. Money at risk = 10¼ − 5¾ = 4½
B. Maximum profit potential = difference in exercise prices
    − money at risk = (60 − 55) − 4½ = ½
C. Risk/reward = (A)/(B) = 4½/½
D. Break-even point = Money at risk + exercise price of option
    bought = 4½ + 55 = 59½
E. Percent change in the price of the underlying security
    needed to reach break-even point [59½ (break even
    point) − 64½ (price of stock)]/64½ = 7.75% (decrease)

Closing one side of the spread is sometimes deliberately done by the investor. In this case, the strategy is referred to as "lifting a leg." This is done when the investor anticipates a weakness in the price of the stock after a dramatic move, resulting in a substantial profit in one side of the spread. An anticipated temporary weakness in the price of the stock may lead the investor to lift a leg on the long call position (in so doing he or she turns the short position into a naked short position, which requires the additional investment equal to 30 percent of the market price of the underlying security plus or minus the appropriate adjustment) and to reestablish the long call position once the market moves in the expected direction and reaches the desired level. In so doing, the investor is undoing the spread and automatically increases the chance of a loss. The investor is well advised not to forget the reasons for establishing the spread position in the first place. This, however, should not suggest that the optimal position is to remain wedded to the spread position no matter what the developments in the market may be.

Vertical Bull Call Spread Worksheet

A very convenient tool for evaluating and understanding spreads is the worksheet, as shown in Table 13.3.

Vertical Bear Call Spread

In a vertical bear call spread, the difference (+) between the premium received and the premium paid determines the profit limit (as compared with the loss limit in the vertical bull call spread). The maximum loss is determined as follows:

(Striking price on short position + premium received) − (striking price on long position + premium paid) = maximum loss

An investor, bearish on IBM, for example, would assume a position opposite that discussed in the previous section. For example:

Sell	IBM/Oct/55	$1,025
Buy	IBM/Oct/60	−575
Credit		**$ 450**

The $450 credit represents the maximum profit. The maximum loss = (5,500 + 1,025) − (6000 + 575) = (50).

Let us now examine the effects of changes in the price of the underlying stock.

Stock Remains at 64½

At 64½, both options are exercisable. The exercise of the short option against our investor results in a gain of:

$$(5,500 + 1,025) - \$6,450 = \$75$$

The exercise of the long call position by the investor would yield a loss equal to:

$$6,450 - (6,000 + 575) = (125)$$
The net loss = $75 - 125 = (50)$

Stock Appreciates to 75

At 75, both options are exercisable.

Loss on short position = (5,500 + 1,025) − 7,500 =	($975)
Gain on long position = 7,500 − 6,575 =	925
Net loss	**$(50)**

Stock Falls to 50

At 50, both options are out of the money and neither will be exercised. The spread holder would have earned the full premium differential, or $450.

The Alternatives

A bearish investor could have chosen to establish a short position in IBM, sell a naked IBM call, or buy a put on IBM instead of the spread. All these possibilities, while increasing the return, also increase the exposure by the investor. Hence the importance of establishing a position that carefully takes one's risk profile and financial resources into consideration.

Graphic Representation

The IBM vertical call spread can be visualized as shown in Figure 13.7. As it shows, the maximum loss is realized when the price of the underlying stock exceeds $60. The maximum gain is realized at or below the lower of the two striking prices in the spread.

FIGURE 13.7   IBM vertical call spread.

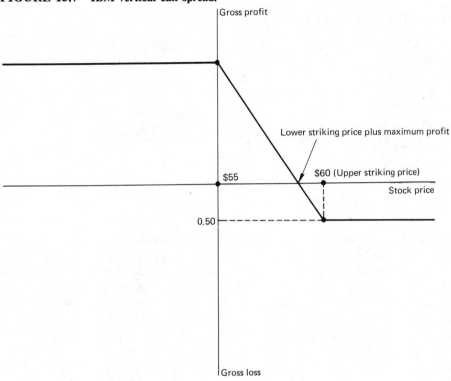

Vertical Bear Call Spread Worksheet

As in the case of the vertical bull call spread, a worksheet is of considerable usefulness to the investor. (See Table 13.4.)

TABLE 13.4
Vertical Bear Call Spread Worksheet

	Option Price	Stock Price
Buy IBM/Oct/60	5¾	64½
Sell IBM/Oct/55	10¼	64½

A. Maximum profit potential = difference in option premiums
$$= 10¼ - 5¾ = 4½$$

B. Money at risk = difference in exercise prices − (A)
$$= 5 - 4½ = ½$$

C. Risk/reward $= \dfrac{½}{4½}$

D. Break-even point = (A) + exercise price of option sold
$$= 4½ + 55 = 59½$$

E. Percent change in the price of the underlying security
needed to reach break-even point =
$$\frac{64½ \text{ (price of stock)} - 59½ \text{ (break-even point)}}{64½} = 7.75\%$$

Vertical Put Bull Spreads

To understand vertical put spreads, the reader must reverse the logic used in the case of vertical call spreads.

As in the vertical call bull spread, the vertical put bull spread involves the purchase of the option with the lower striking price and the sale of the option with the higher striking price. While this results in a debit balance in the call case, a credit balance would result in the put case. An example should make the point clear.

Referring to Table 13.2, an investor bullish on IBM would

Buy IBM P/Oct/50	$\frac{1}{16}$
Sell IBM P/Oct/70	6
Credit	$5^{15}\!/_{16}$

The reader should be able to verify, as is shown in detail in the preceding section, what the impact of expected and unexpected changes in the price of the underlying security would be. Briefly, if the price of the underlying security rises (to 80 from its current level of 64½), both put options will be worthless and the investor would earn the full $5^{15}\!/_{16}$. If the stock price remains at 64½, the put option with the 70 striking price is profitable, the other is worthless. The stock will be put to the investor at 70 while its market value is only 64½ (a loss of 5.5 practically wiping out the credit of $5^{15}\!/_{16}$). If the stock falls in price to 45, for example, then both options are in the money and the investor would lose $14^{1}\!/_{16}$, which is equal to the difference in the striking prices minus the credit, or the loss on the short position (70 − 45 = 25) minus the gain on the long position (50 − 45) and minus the credit $5^{15}\!/_{16}$.

Vertical Put Bear Spread

In a vertical put bear spread, the investor undertakes the opposite of the vertical put bull spread: buying the put with the high striking price and selling the put with the low striking price.

Buy IBM P/Oct/70	6
Sell IBM P/Oct/50	$\frac{1}{16}$
Debit	$5^{15}\!/_{16}$

The debit represents the maximum loss. The maximum gain is equal to the difference in exercise prices minus the debit, or $20 - 5^{15}\!/_{16} = 14^{1}\!/_{16}$, yielding a risk reward ratio of $5^{15}\!/_{16}/14^{1}\!/_{16}$. This ratio is much more advantageous than that of the vertical put bull spread, and the underlying strategy should be adopted if the probability of an appreciation in the price of the security is equal to that of a depreciation.

Horizontal Call Spreads

Horizontal call spreads are also referred to as "calendar" or "time" spreads. The "horizontal" connotation derives from the fact, as shown in Table 13.2, that the time to maturity is listed horizontally. The options bought/sold have the same striking price but different maturities. The investment considerations are essentially the same as those of vertical spreads with one *major* qualification: the time premium. Two options with equal striking prices but different maturities would have different premiums due to the time-premium component. The reader should recall the discussion earlier in this chapter, where it was shown that

W = relative price (intrinsic value) + time premium

As an option approaches its expiration date, the time premium approaches zero. The longer the maturity, the higher the time premium. The fundamental reason for using horizontal spreads is that the time value of the near option diminishes more rapidly than that of the distant option. That is why the investor is more likely to sell the near and buy the distant option and establish a bullish horizontal spread.

Horizontal Bull Call Spreads

From Table 13.2, we can see the various horizontal spread opportunities available on IBM. Once again, a bullish spread should result in a debit balance in the investor's account. Assume that the investor settles for the following:

Sell IBM/Oct/70	⅞
Buy IBM/Jan/70	2½
Debit	**1⅝**

With IBM trading at 64½, both options are out of the money; that is, an exercise would result in an immediate loss to the holder of a call spread. If, by the end of the third week in October, IBM is trading at 70, the short side is worthless but the long side still has three months to go and may be selling at, say, 3.5. If the stock advances to 75, both options are profitable. The short side would be exercised against the investor for a loss of $500 [(75 − 70)(100)] and the long side of the spread would realize a profit larger than $500 because the option still has three months to run and the spread has widened. If the IBM/Jan/70 is currently selling at 6¾ and the investor decides to close out the position, his or her profit would be as follows:

Profit on long position − loss on short position = (6¾ − 2½) − (5 − ⅞) = ⅛

The profit is ⅛ points on an investment of 1⅝ points.

The investment represents the amount at risk or the maximum loss, assuming the spread is kept intact until both options expire; that is, the investor does not decide to lift a leg temporarily or permanently. The maximum profit is realized at the striking price. Graphically, the horizontal call spread can be depicted as in Figure 13.8.

Horizontal Bear Call Spread

The strategy here is the opposite of a horizontal bull call spread. Two problems must be pointed out:

1. The time premium favors, as indicated earlier, the option with the longer life— the option sold in this case (the short position).

FIGURE 13.8   **Graphic representation of horizontal bull call spread.**

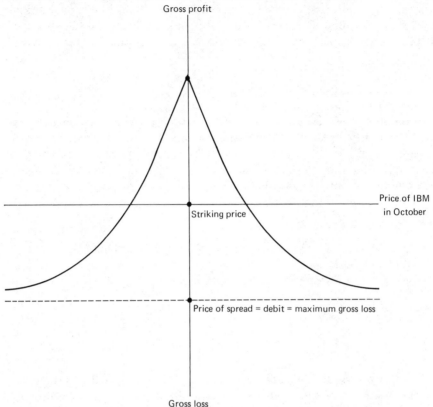

2. Since the option bought is shorter in life, its exercise or expiration would leave the investor with a short call position. This would require approximately a 30 percent margin and would leave the investor open to the risks discussed in Chapter 12, in the section on naked call options.

Graphically, the horizontal bear call option can be depicted as in Figure 13.9.

Diagonal Spreads

Diagonal spreads involve the purchase of an option and the sale of another on the same underlying stock, with the options having different striking prices and different maturities.

Diagonal spreads offer substantial additional flexibility to the investor in the formulation of strategy and in the determination of the risk/reward ratio. One possible diagonal spread that can be established on IBM, given bullish expectations, is:

Buy IBM/Jan/50	15½
Sell IBM/Oct/65	2½
Debit	**13**

FIGURE 13.9   **Graphic representation of horizontal bear call spread.**

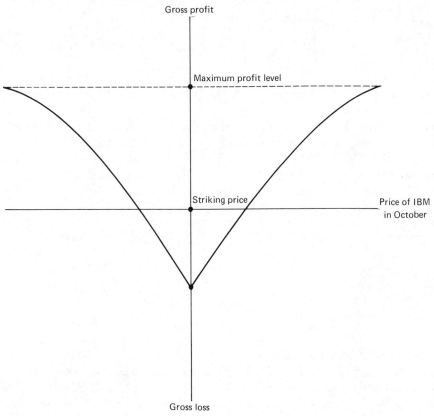

The call option sold has a shorter maturity. This is advantageous, because the opposite position would mean that towards the end of October, the spread position would reduce to a naked short call position, necessitating funds to meet the margin requirements.

Again, the debit represents the maximum loss. The maximum gain is equal to the difference in the exercise prices minus the debit, or 2 points. Needless to say, if the investor is not satisfied with this risk/reward ratio, he or she can easily find a diagonal spread on IBM or on another suitable stock to accommodate his or her needs.

Other Sophisticated Spreads

The spread opportunities in the marketplace are almost limitless. The more capable and imaginative the investor, the more interesting and complex the spread formations. We shall discuss a few of the more prevalent types of sophisticated spreads.

Sandwich Spreads

Sandwich spreads are a combination of bull and bear spreads on the same stock, having the same expiration month but different striking prices. These spreads necessarily involve four options: two on the long side at both ends of the striking price range and two on the short end sandwiched between the long positions. An example can be developed from Table 13.2:

Buy 1 IBM/Oct/50	15½
Sell 2 IBM/Oct/60	
(5¾ each)	11½
Buy 1 IBM/Oct/70	⅞
Debit	**4⅞**

On certain securities, sandwich spreads can be so structured that the out-of-pocket cost is zero (before commissions are accounted for).

The sandwich spread has a profit potential as long as IBM trades in the 50–70 range.

Consider a stock price at 60 toward the end of October. The short positions will be worthless. The IBM/Oct/50 earns 10 points. The IBM Oct/70 is worthless. The net profit (before commissions) is equal to $10 - 4⅞ = 5⅛$. This is the maximum profit.

If IBM falls in price to 45, none of the options is in the money. The investor has lost 4⅞.

If IBM rises in price to 80, then all the options are profitable to exercise (the profit is to the option holder; the option writer loses money). The profits could equal:

Profit on IBM/Oct/50	30
Loss on IBM/Oct/60	−40
Profit on IBM/Oct/70	10
Net profit	**0**

Again, the investor loses 4⅞, the cost of the sandwich spread (the debit).

Had the investor structured a sandwich spread requiring no investment, he or she could earn a substantial return—the maximum of which is realized at 60, the median point in the striking price range. There could be no better risk/reward ratio than this. Below the lowest striking price, losses are zero, as they are above the highest striking price. Anywhere between the low and the high striking price, profits are realized on a zero investment.

Butterfly Spread

The butterfly position is opposite that of a sandwich spread. Here the investor is short the options with striking prices on both ends of the spread range, and is long on the options with the median striking price. The expectations here are for a major movement in the price of the underlying security. Otherwise a net loss or a zero gain will result from the butterfly position.

It is left as an exercise to the reader to develop an example from Table 13.2 and to measure the consequences of a price decline below the lowest striking price, a price rise above the highest striking price, and a situation of no price change.

Words of Caution

Spreading, while potentially lucrative, has several disadvantages:

1. The most serious disadvantage lies in the execution of the spread order. Both sides of the spread must be executed simultaneously, otherwise there is no execution.

2. While our calculations show profits on certain positions under certain assumptions, those profits can disappear if commissions are accounted for.

Tests run by M. Gombola, R. Roenfeldt, and P. Cooley show that investors trying to beat the market using various spread strategies were not successful once commissions were subtracted from the anticipated arbitrage profits. The options market was, once again, shown to be efficient. In the authors' words, "For those arbitrage positions with available price information at expiration, profits were barely sufficient to cover commission costs at the rate of 0.25 per underlying share. Profits after commissions were sufficiently small to provide only a minimal return for the average investor."[1]

3. The market for certain options are thin. This means that the volume is not large enough to allow a spread to be executed.

4. Our preceeding calculations did not take another major transaction cost into consideration: taxes. The tax implications of a spread or any option position are serious enough to require consultation with competent tax attorneys or accountants. If taxes are accounted for, certain option positions may lose their attractiveness.

We now review the major tax considerations.

13.9 OPTIONS CONTRACTS AND THE TAX LAWS

The tax treatment of option positions is both straightforward and complex. The level of complexity depends on the nature of the position, its timing, its horizon, its intended purpose, and the method of closing it out.

We shall examine the tax implications for both sides of the market—the buy and the sell sides—and we shall examine techniques for deferring or reducing tax liability through the options market.[2]

Taxes on Long Option Positions

An option is a capital asset provided that the underlying stock (owned currently or prospectively) is treated as a capital asset. Options held for over a year qualify for the preferential long-term capital gain treatment. Otherwise, gains or losses are treated as short-term gains or losses. Such is usually the case, for options have maturities of less than one year.

---

[1] **Michael J. Gombola, Rodney L. Roenfeldt,** and **Philip L. Cooley** "Arbitrage Opportunities and Pricing Efficiency in CBOE Options." Unpublished paper, University of Connecticut School of Business, P. 11.

[2] The Economic Recovery Tax Act of 1981 includes in Title V, "Tax Straddles," provisions that significantly change the tax treatment of spreads and straddles in various kinds of personal property. (Title V also makes a number of changes that are not limited to straddles, such as requiring all "regulated futures contracts" to be marked to market at the end of each year, with unrealized gains or losses taken into account at a special tax rate; eliminating provisions that previously permitted securities dealers to defer for 30 days identifying those securities that are held in an investment account; and providing that certain short-term government obligations will be traded as capital assets.) The straddle provisions, together with the mark to market provisions applicable to regulated futures contracts, are designed to eliminate the opportunity for a taxpayer to use a loss to reduce taxes if the taxpayer has an unrealized gain in a position that is "offsetting" to the loss position. These provisions prevent the use of such losses either to defer income from year to year or to convert ordinary income to long-term capital gains. Another provision of the legislation disallows any deduction from carrying charges allocable to personal property that is part of a straddle. Offsetting positions, which are termed "straddles" for purposes of the legislation, are those where one or more positions substantially diminish the risk of another position. The reader is strongly advised to consult with a tax advisor with regard to straddles and spreads, and The Chicago Board Options Exchange memo to members, 8/19/81.

The tax treatment of options depends on whether they are exercised, sold, or allowed to expire.

Exercise

The call holder becomes the owner of the underlying stock upon the exercise of the option. The cost of the option is simply added to the striking price of the stock to determine the tax basis for the stock. The holding period on the stock begins with the acquisition of the stock and not with the acquisition of the option.

The put holder disposes of a stock upon exercising his or her option and receives the striking price. For tax purposes, receipts are the striking price minus the cost of the put. Put holders, however, must be careful of certain factors that could have a considerable impact on their tax liability.

The acquisition of a put is considered a short sale by the Internal Revenue Service because, like the short sale, the put buyer is contracting to sell a stock at a fixed price. If the put buyer establishes a long position in the underlying stock during the same day, that is, "marries" the stock to the put, the short sale rule will no longer apply. The tax implications of the latter case are that the exercise of the put option produces long- or short-term gains or losses on the stock position depending on the holding period. If a substantially identical stock is purchased during the holding period of the put or was held for one year or less prior to the acquisition of the put, then any gain from the exercise of the put is a short-term capital gain and any loss is a short-term capital loss. This is so even if the total holding period of the stock (holding period prior to purchase of the put plus the holding period beginning with the purchase of the put and ending with its exercise) exceeds one year. An owner of a long stock position between Jan. 1, 1980 and Jan. 5, 1981 would have a short-term capital gain (loss) if he or she purchased a put at any time between Jan. 1, 1980 and Jan. 1, 1981. Effectively, the purchase of the put eliminates the holding period of the underlying stock and transforms realized gains into short-term capital gains. The holding period on the underlying stock begins to run on the earliest of (1) the sale date of the stock, (2) the put exercise date, (3) the put sale date, or (4) the put expiration date.

Sale

The sale of a call will produce long term (short-term) capital gains or losses if the call is held for more than a year (a year or less). Considering the maturity distribution of listed options, capital gains or losses will always be short-term.

The sale of a put is equivalent to closing a short position if a substantially identical asset was held short-term prior to the acquisition of the put or was bought during its life. Resulting gains or losses are short-term capital gains or losses. If a put option in a "married" position is sold, then the gains or losses are also short-term capital losses, given the maturity schedule of listed options.

Expiration

A listed call expiring unexercised results in a short-term capital loss equal to the call premium. The same is true for a put. However, a "married" put that goes unexercised produces neither long- or short-term capital losses. Its cost is added to the tax basis of the stock.

Taxes on Short-Option Positions

The premium received by an option writer is not taxable income until the option is exercised or until it expires. If the option expires, the premium is treated as short-term capital gain. If the option is exercised, the premium is used to reduce the cost of the underlying stock in the put case or to add to the striking price received in the call case.

If the option writer chooses to close out a commitment by entering into a closing transaction, then the difference between the premium received and the premium paid is a short-term capital gain or loss.

The short-sale rule—section 1233(6) of the Internal Revenue Code—does not apply to a short option position. A call written against a long stock position does not change the holding period of the underlying stock.

Special Tax Considerations and Strategies

A straddle is taxed on the basis of each of its components, the put and the call, as it is for spreads. The special tax rules apply to spreads. The net tax liability is the sum of the liabilities of the component parts.

Investors adjusting their portfolios at the end of the tax year must be careful with the use of options. An investor who sells a security at a loss at the end of the tax year is disallowed the tax loss deduction if he or she reacquires the stock or an option thereon anytime during a period beginning 30 days prior to the sale and ending 30 days after the sale. This is considered a "wash sale."

Such are the special considerations. Investors can, however, use options to reduce their tax burden in any given tax year.

Options can be used to convert short-term gains into long-term gains. An investor wishing to sell a stock held for less than a year and wanting to avoid paying taxes on short-term capital gains would write a call option against his or her stock position. The life of the call will be long enough to ensure that the holding period on the stock is longer than a year. The premium received on the call would be added to the striking price of the stock when the option is exercised. The call writer obviously hopes that the call will not be exercised before the holding period on the stock (which begins with the purchase date of the stock) exceeds one year. The reader is reminded that the maximum tax on capital gains is 20 percent.

Another beneficial outcome can accrue to the investor from the above strategy. By writing a call against a long stock position, an investor is shifting taxable income from one year to the next. This may be predicated upon the expectation that next year some capital losses may be incurred to neutralize the capital gains and reduce, if not eliminate, the taxes due on the sale of capital assets.

The potential problem with this strategy lies in the fact that call options may be exercised well before their expiration date. The investor may still be better off than he or she was prior to writing the option. The sale of the option earned a premium that would have been foregone had the option market been overlooked. Moreover, if the investor wishes to hold on to shares so that gains will be realized in the following year, he or she would purchase shares in the marketplace and deliver them against the call. This produces a short-term capital loss, which can offset current capital gains or offset current income on a one-to-one basis up to $3,000.

Another tax strategy available to a put holder with a profit in the position involves the exercise of the put using borrowed stock for delivery. This is equivalent to a short sale. In so doing, the put holder postpones the payment of taxes on the profit in the put from one year to the next. The short sale, the reader may recall, can only produce short-term capital gains or losses.

Tax considerations and strategies can be quite complex. An option investor should seek competent professional help when in doubt.

13.10 FIDUCIARIES DISCOVER OPTIONS

Until recently, professional money managers have avoided options. Many believed, and some still do, that options are not consistent with prudent money management and are nothing more than a gimmick or a gamble similar to a poker game where the house gets the lion's share of the money gambled. It is believed by some that options are a tool invented by brokers in order to further line their pockets. Many new developments are beginning to win several converts to the options market. These developments were summarized in the Sept. 22, 1980, issue of *The Wall Street Journal:*

> . . . *In March, the Securities and Exchange Commission ended a long morato-rium on increasing the number of stock issues against which options can be traded on exchanges. The comptroller of the currency, who regulates national banks, and the Department of Labor, which oversees pension funds, have issued statements expressing no objections to options trading that is consistent with portfolio diversification and yield objectives.*
>
> *Last month, Gov. Edmund Brown of California signed an Act permitting insurance companies in the state to trade in options. Elsewhere, state insurance commissioners have removed some regulatory restrictions on options trading by insurance companies. . . .*

These developments follow two other major events that set the stage for the acceptance of options trading. The first was the passage of the Rostenkowski Bill (HR 3052) in 1976, which changed the definition of unrelated business to exclude premiums from options trading. The second was the clarification of the Employee Retirement Income Security Act (ERISA) provided by the courts, showing option writing to be prudent and desirable, and by the Department of Labor, which emphasizes the "whole portfolio" approach instead of the "single investment" approach in the evaluation of fiduciary conduct.

Money managers are well advised to consider selling call options on stocks they wish to continue holding but consider fully priced currently. Puts should also be considered by money managers expecting major weaknesses in the market. No wholesale recommendation can be made, however. Every portfolio manager has a different strategy or portfolio investment requirements. However, no portfolio manager should reject options as an element in the process of maximizing return on and minimizing risk of portfolios.

13.11 OPTION STRATEGY—BROAD OUTLINES

The development of an investment strategy requires the setting of investment goals and the full realization of one's financial position. An investor with little cash reserves, poor health and minimal life insurance, an inadequate housing arrangement, and other glaring shortages should avoid the stock and option markets.

With the needed financial resources justifying entry into the capital markets, an investor is well advised to adopt a portfolio strategy in which options have a constructive role to play. The ad hoc arrangements and the "looks good" approach inevitably lead to financial setbacks.

From a portfolio perspective and with a certain attitude towards risk, the investor can best devise the option strategy most suitable for his or her needs and tax bracket. The characteristics of the most prevalent options strategies are summarized in Table 13.5. The choice depends on the special circumstances of the investor and on the perceived risk of each position. The reader should remember from the discussions throughout the chapter that the options markets are so flexible as to allow the investor a wide range of possibilities in structuring the desired risk/return tradeoff. An income-oriented strategy would preclude the long side of the option market. The choice is between a combination, a short put, and/or a short call. A short-run speculative strategy could ordinarily restrict the investor to a long position in the call or in a put. There obviously exist other strategies, as indicated earlier.

These strategies, however, or the choice among them, constitute the second level in the investment decision-making process. As the reader is aware by now, there are several ways of acquiring an option on the stock. The first level in the choice process consists, therefore, of choosing between a long position in the stock (a stock being an option on the assets of the corporation), a long position in a convertible bond (an option—a much longer-term option than is available with the listed options—on the stock of the company), and a long position in a convertible preferred stock, a long position in a warrant or in a stock right. This obviously assumes that all or some of these instruments are available on each company being considered for investment purposes. Having mentioned this, we should not lose sight of the fact that options offer much flexibility as well as a high level of liquidity and that they are becoming available on an increasing number of stocks. Furthermore, options may be the least costly and the quickest if not the only way for hedging a stock position.

An investor seeking income from an investment should consider alternative income-producing vehicles such as government bonds, corporate bonds, dividend-paying stock, convertible stocks, and other that offer good if not better risk/return opportunities in certain cases.

Having settled on the options route, the investor must have a mechanism for surveying market opportunities. Many investment houses have devised both simple and very sophisticated techniques for sifting through the options market and identifying those options consistent with certain specifications. Tables 13.6 and 13.7 summarize the opportunities in straddles and bull spreads. The operator specifies the time range—that is, the acceptable range for the life of the option—the minimum and maximum price for the straddle (Table 13.6), and whether he or she wishes to have deviations from the theoretical value (as determined by the B&S model) included in the output. The outputs are shown in both tables, with the necessary footnotes. From all the stocks on which options are sold, those listed are the only ones that meet the specifications of the investor. The remaining decision requires a choice among those available opportunities.

These computer outputs are available to the public, generally at little or no cost. They are useful for certain purposes, but not for all. An investor wishing to hedge a long or a short position in a stock has little freedom in the choice of the option to be used.

No matter what the expressed purpose for using options, an investor is best advised

TABLE 13.5
Characteristics of Strategies

Strategy	Nature of Strategy	Desired Action of Stock at Expiration	Risk	Gain Potential
Write naked Puts	High risk/ high return	Up (above strike)	Substantial but limited to price of stock minus premium received	Limited to option premium
Write covered calls	Moderate risk/ moderate return	Down (below strike)	Substantial but limited to price of stock minus premium received	Limited to premium
Write naked call	High risk/high return	Down (below strike)	Unlimited	Limited to premium
Write covered Straddles	Moderate risk/ moderate return	Band between strike prices	Limited downside	Dual premium
Write naked Straddles	High risk/ moderate return	Band between strike prices	Unlimited upside but limited downside	Dual premium
Buy puts	High risk/ high return	Down	Limited but may lose entire premium	Limited but substantial
Buy calls	High risk/ high return	Up	Limited but may lose entire premium	Unlimited
Buy straddle	High risk/ moderate return	Above call or below put striking price	Limited but may lose entire premium	Unlimited

Source: *Financial World*, Jan. 15, 1979 p. 80.

TABLE 13.6
Straddles

Time range in days (min, max) 0, 190 (days)
Straddle price range (min, max) 0.25, 3
Theoretical values (yes = 1/no = 0) 1
6/30/80

Jan Series 1 Stock[a]		Exch[b]	Option		Price	In-COMM[c]	%-N-VAL[d]	Down[e]	Up[e]
ASH	38.500	NX	JLY	40.0	2.687	0.130	130.33	37.31	42.68
BOL	43.875	NA	JLY	45.0	2.187	0.496	82.65	42.81	47.18
STK	15.125	NX	OCT	15.0	2.906	0.236	130.81	12.09	17.90
Jan Series 2 Stock		Exch	Option		Price	In-COMM	%-N-VAL	Down	Up
ACD	48.125	NX	JLY	50.0	2.937	0.462	84.06	47.06	52.93
AH	25.687	NX	JLY	25.0	1.593	0.510	129.74	23.40	26.59

Source: E. F. Hutton & Co., New York, 1980.

[a] The stock symbol (ASH, etc.) is followed by the current stock price. ASH is the sticker tape symbol for Ashland Oil, BOL for Bausch & Lomb, STK for Storage Technology, ACD for Allied Chemical, and AH for Allis-Chalmers.

[b] Exchange is NX = New York Stock Exchange; NA = American Stock Exchange.

[c] In-COMM = commission cost = 0.13 × 100 = $13.

[d] %-N-VAL = percent duration from the theoretical value determined by the B&S model. Overvalue (>100%) indicates sell, undervalue (<100%) indicates buy.

[e] Down = stock price − price (premium); up = stock price + price (premium).

to consult his or her options broker, to do frequent homework, and to consult competent, professional tax advisors.

13.12 IMPACT OF OPTIONS MARKET

Several studies on the impact of options trading on the value of the underlying stock have been undertaken. The most extensive of which were done by Robert R. Nathan Associates.[3] These studies concluded that there were no systematic effects of options trading—including effects of the exercise of options during the expiration week—on the price behavior of the underlying stocks. In fact, these studies showed that optioned stocks had narrower bid/ask spreads and experienced less price volatility. G. N. Naider disputed the finding related to volatility and concluded that the decline in volatility

[3] **Robert R. Nathan Associates, Inc.,** *Review of Initial Trading Experience at the Chicago Board Options Exchange.* Chicago Board Options Exchange, December 1974; *Analysis of Volume and Price Patterns in Stocks Underlying CBOE Options from December 30, 1974 to April 30, 1975.* Chicago Board Options Exchange, July 1975; *Analysis of Volume and Price Patterns in Stocks Underlying CBOE Options from December 31, 1975 to January 16, 1976,* Chicago Board Options Exchange, February 1976.

TABLE 13.7
Bull Spread

Time range in days (min, max) 0, 115 (days)
Price range (min, max) 0, 7
Ratio of spread (buy, sell) 1, 1
In/out of the money (in, out) 105, 85
06/30/80

Stock[a]		Exch[b]	Long		Short		Debit[c]	B.E.[d]	In-COMM[e]
ACD	48.125	NX	JAN	45.0	JLY	50.0	6.56	52.08	0.520
ACD	48.125	NX	JLY	45.0	JLY	50.0	2.93	48.41	0.475
ACD	48.125	NX	OCT	45.0	JLY	50.0	5.06	50.56	0.504
ACD	48.125	NX	JAN	45.0	OCT	50.0	4.12	49.45	0.331
ACD	48.125	NX	OCT	40.0	OCT	50.0	5.87	46.22	0.349
ACD	48.125	NX	OCT	45.0	OCT	50.0	2.62	47.94	0.316
AH	25.687	NX	JAN	25.0	JLY	30.0	2.59	27.75	0.159
AH	25.687	NX	JLY	25.0	JLY	30.0	1.03	26.16	0.135
AH	25.687	NX	OCT	25.0	JLY	30.0	2.21	27.37	0.153
AH	25.687	NX	JAN	25.0	OCT	30.0	2.06	27.62	0.557
AH	25.687	NX	OCT	25.0	OCT	30.0	1.68	27.23	0.552

Source: E. F. Hutton & Co., New York, 1980.
[a] ACD is a stock symbol for Allied Chemical. AH is a stock symbol for Allis-Chalmers.
[b] NX = New York Stock Exchange.
[c] Debit = required financial commitment to the bull spread.
[d] B.E. = break-even point on the bull spread.
[e] In-COMM = required commission on a bull spread. For the first row, it equals 0.52 × 100 = $52.

on the stock examined by R. Nathan was due to cyclical market movements.[4] Furthermore, Naider formed evidence of increased relative volatility of CBOE stocks.

Many other studies have attempted to measure the effect of options trading on the capital markets' operational and allocational efficiencies. The studies we have surveyed suffer from lack of quality data and/or from deficiencies in the statistical techniques employed. We believe that the evidence is not conclusive and that further research is needed in this area as far as investors are concerned. A voluminous study undertaken by the SEC concludes by stating that:

> In general, the Options Study found that options can provide useful alternative investment strategies to those who understand the complexities and risks of options trading. . . .
> The Options Study found numerous instances of sales practice abuses in which registered representatives told investors of possible rewards they might expect from options without simultaneously warning them of the risks inherent to options trading. Often inadequately trained registered representatives recommended options strategies to their customers which it is doubtful that the salesmen, much less their customers, understood.[5]

---

[4] **G. N. Naider,** "The Effect of Option Trading on Variability of Common Stock Returns." Paper presented at the Annual Meeting of the Southern Finance Association, 1977.

[5] *Report of the Special Study of the Options Markets to the Securities and Exchange Commission.* Securities and Exchange Commission, Washington, D.C., Dec. 22, 1978.

These findings further point out the need for investors to have a strategy; to do their homework thoroughly, taking among other things, taxes and transactions costs into account; and to keep a watchful eye on developments affecting the underlying security.

CONCLUSIONS

Advanced options strategies are not for amateurs. Complex as they may seem, options strategies can be mastered with some effort. They represent yet another vehicle for improving return and lowering risk and should be used as part of an overall portfolio strategy and not to the exclusion of everything else.

QUESTIONS

1. (This question covers material from Chapters 12 and 13.) The Thursday, March 4, 1982, edition of *The Wall Street Journal* carried the following options quotations:

		Calls—Last			*Puts—Last*		
		Mar	*Jun*	*Sep*	*Mar*	*Jun*	*Sep*
GM	30	9¼	10	r	$\frac{1}{16}$	¼	⅝
39	35	4¼	5¾	6½	⅛	1⅛	$\frac{13}{16}$
39	40	⅝	$2\frac{7}{16}$	3⅝	1⅝	$2\frac{3}{16}$	3½
39	45	$\frac{1}{16}$	⅞	1⅝	6⅛	6¼	6⅝
39	50	$\frac{1}{16}$	$\frac{3}{16}$	s	r	11⅞	s

   a. Which puts and calls are in the money? Which are out of the money?
   b. Which of the call options would you purchase if you were very bullish? Which put options? Why?
   c. Which of the options would you pick if you held a long position about which you felt rather but not very comfortable?
   d. What combination (one) would be best to establish if you were very bullish on GM? Which combination would be best if you were very bearish?
   e. Do you see any spread (March) opportunities? How would you segregate between them depending on your expectations?
   f. How and when would you use the GM/Sep/45?
   g. Construct a butterfly spread. Explain your decision and the conditions under which it will work.
   h. Which option (one) would you choose to write if your outlook on GM were bearish between now and June? Why?
   i. Why does the GM/June/50 sell at a positive price?
   j. Which variables influence option prices? How? Why?
   k. Pick a straddle to write if you were mildly bullish on GM. Explain your selection.

2. What are the expectations of an investor who buys a straddle? Why could he or she not profit outside the options market? What are the straddle writer's expectations?

the chapter) by purchasing an IBM/Apr/60 for 8¾ and selling and IBM/Apr/65 for 6. IBM is selling for $64, what is her investment? What will she earn if the stock moves to $60? To $70?

3. An options trader constructs a vertical put bear spread by purchasing a DGO P/April/60 for $12 and writing a DGO P/April/45 for $1. DGO is currently selling for $50/share. What is the maximum potential loss? What is the maximum potential gain? What is the risk/reward ratio? Evaluate the ratio of this position.

4. Given: on Jan. 22, 1982, the current price of SRB stock was 61½ and cost of options (s.p. = strike price) was as follows:

	Call			Put		
s.p.	Apr	Jul	Oct	Apr	Jul	Oct
50	13¼	15½	16¼	¼	½	1
55	6½	8½	9½	¼	1¼	1½
60	4	5½	6¼	2	2½	3
65	1½	3¼	4½	5½	6¼	7

Develop strategies for two types of investors: a conservative (risk-averse) investor and a speculator. Present the potential profit for that investor with $2,500 in cash and $10,000 worth of government securities (remember capital requirements for option positions) if expectations develop under each of the following cases:
a. Expect SRB to increase to 70 by July.
b. Expect SRB to retreat to 50 by July.
c. Forthcoming R&D announcement will cause SRB either to advance sharply or decline sharply by July.
d. Expect SRB to remain static, near 60, until July.

3. A "strap" is a combination of two calls and one put with the same striking price and exercise date. What does the buyer of a strap believe about the movement of the underlying stock?

4. A options trader establishes a bull spread by purchasing a call (put) and by selling a call (put) on the same security. Which option will he or she buy (the one with the lower or higher striking price)? How will he or she profit?

5. Many brokerage houses now use what is known as a "reverse conversion strategy" to profit. It involves selling a stock short, investing the proceeds at money market rates, and hedging the short position by writing a put and buying a call in the option market. How does the investor hope to profit from the reverse conversion strategy? What potential drawbacks do you see to such a strategy? To which market participants is this strategy available? What type of stocks would best suit a reverse conversion? What is the vector representation for the investor?

6. What major drawbacks taint the allure of spreads?

7. What should a potential options trader consider before entering the options market?

8. R. R. Nathan Associates' studies show minimal impact of options upon the price of the underlying security. What would be the implications of opposite findings?

9. From the information in question 1, construct at least three combinations and show the profit and loss ranges for each.

10. The tax law treats a call option differently depending on whether it is exercised. What is that difference from the perspective of the option buyer and the option seller?

PROBLEMS

1. Construct a graph depicting possible profit/loss outcomes for an investor who writes a naked straddle on a stock selling at $45/share. He receives $450 for writing a 90 day call with a striking price of 45, and $350 for writing a 90 day put with the same striking price (ignore transactions costs). How much capital would he have to commit? What is the most he could hope to earn?

2. An options trader could have established a vertical call spread on IBM (see data in the chapter) by purchasing an IBM/Apr/60 for 8¾ and selling and IBM/Apr/65 for 6. IBM is selling for $64, what is her investment? What will she earn if the stock moves to $60? To $70?

3. An options trader constructs a vertical put bear spread by purchasing a DGO P/April/60 for $12 and writing a DGO P/April/45 for $1. DGO is currently selling for $50/share. What is the maximum potential loss? What is the maximum potential gain? What is the risk/reward ratio? Evaluate the ratio of this position.

4. Given: on Jan. 22, 1982, the current price of SRB stock was 61½ and cost of options (s.p. = strike price) was as follows:

	Call			Put		
s.p.	Apr	Jul	Oct	Apr	Jul	Oct
50	13¼	15½	16¼	¼	½	1
55	6½	8½	9½	¼	1¼	1½
60	4	5½	6¼	2	2½	3
65	1½	3¼	4½	5½	6¼	7

Develop strategies for two types of investors: a conservative (risk-averse) investor and a speculator. Present the potential profit for that investor with $2,500 in cash and $10,000 worth of government securities (remember capital requirements for option positions) if expectations develop under each of the following cases:
a. Expect SRB to increase to 70 by July.
b. Expect SRB to retreat to 50 by July.
c. Forthcoming R&D announcement will cause SRB either to advance sharply or decline sharply by July.
d. Expect SRB to remain static, near 60, until July.

CHAPTER
14 | Interest-Rate Futures

14.1 INTRODUCTION

Recent developments in the U.S. money and capital markets have been dramatic. The 1970s have witnessed, as never before, sustained sharp fluctuations in the rate of interest combined with occasional and at times caustic assaults on the ability of the Federal Reserve System to control the money supply. Changes in interest rates meant reciprocal changes in bond prices and hence changes in the wealth of investors. Bondholders watching their wealth shrinking and expanding frequently and unexpectedly had to seek refuge somewhere. The creation of the futures markets provided one answer.

Interest-rate gyrations are depicted in Figures 14.1, 14.2, 14.3, and 14.4. The largest average weekly fluctuation in 13-week T-bill auction rates was recorded in 1974. The size of the fluctuation was 33.4 basis points[1] following a 22.4-basis-point average weekly fluctuation in 1973. It is not a mere coincidence, therefore, that the Chicago Board of Trade began trading financial futures in the fall of 1975. Bondholders watching rising interest rates (falling bond values) are concerned with the value of their assets, although they may intend to hold the bonds until maturity and expect to receive face value. This is so because changing interest rates affect the reinvestment rate for coupon bonds. The face value to be received is also worth less in real terms as interest rates rise, due primarily to revised expectations about the price level.

Rising interest rates also affect decision makers who expect to be net borrowers in the future. They would seek protection against escalating interest costs through various hedging mechanisms, which we shall explore in detail.

Falling interest rates, on the other hand, are of concern to lenders and to bondholders wishing to roll over their investments. Their concern is with the reinvestment of their funds at advantageous rates (roughly equal to those prevailing currently in the marketplace). A hedging mechanism is needed in this case as well.

All the economic agents mentioned above and many others are concerned with stability

---

[1] A basis point is 0.01 percent.

and predictability. The following hedging avenues can be considered in the pursuit of these goals:

1. The purchase of insurance
2. A hedge in the cash market
3. The use of the repurchase agreement
4. The interest-rate futures markets
5. Debt options (not covered in detail in this chapter)

14.2 THE PURCHASE OF INSURANCE

Protection against various types of risks—theft, fire, explosion, and others—is provided by insurance companies against the payment of a premium. The losses and the operating costs of insurance companies are spread over the policyholders in the form of a premium. In so doing, the insurance company is not assuming the risk but rather functioning as an agent for spreading the incidence of the risk among the insured population so that one's premium pays for another's losses, and so on. In short, the losses have been "socialized" (spread out through the insured segment of the population).

Insurance companies have not yet devised a mechanism for socializing losses resulting from price changes or from changes in the creditworthiness of the issuer of a security. Not even Lloyd's of London sells insurance protecting investors against losses in a stock or a bond position. The insurance option is, therefore, not available to provide

FIGURE 14.1 Short-term interest rates—business borrowing (prime rate, effective date of change; prime paper, quarterly averages).

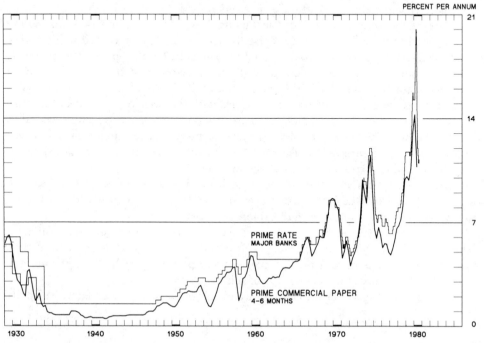

Source: 1980 Historical Chart Book. Board of Governors of the Federal Reserve System, Washington, D.C., p. 99.

FIGURE 14.2   **Short-term interest rates—money market (discount rate, effective date of change; all others, quarterly averages).**

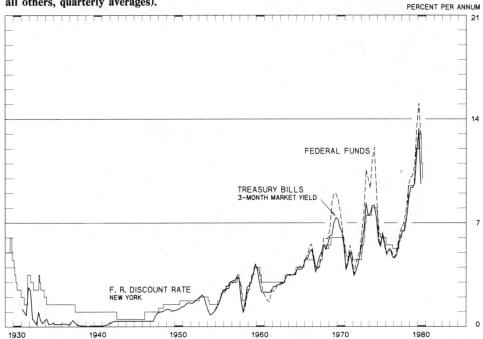

Source: 1980 Historical Chart Book. Board of Governors of the Federal Reserve System, Washington, D.C., p. 98.

FIGURE 14.3   **Long-term bond yields—quarterly averages.**

Source: 1980 Historical Chart Book. Board of Governors of the Federal Reserve System, Washington, D.C., p. 97.

FIGURE 14.4 Long- and short-term interest rates—annually.

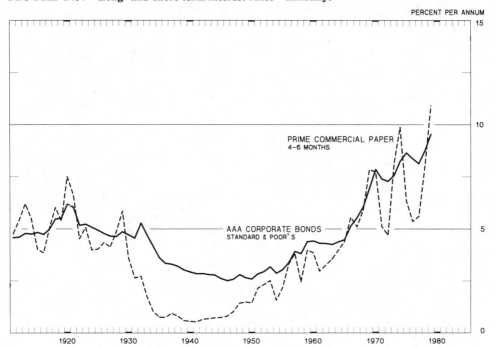

Source: 1980 Historical Chart Book, Board of Governors of the Federal Reserve System, Washington, D.C., p. 96.

investors with protection against changes in interest rates, although such changes can cause losses that are more devastating than those resulting from insurable casualties. However, option bonds guaranteeing a resale price and interest options that are available to investors represent two forms of insurance schemes.

14.3 THE CASH MARKET

Investors wishing to lock in the rate of interest implied in the yield curve—that is, to earn the forward rate—can achieve their goal in the cash (spot) market by an appropriate combination of bond purchase and sale. Wishing to realize the one-year forward rate to prevail one year hence, an investor would sell (short)[2] a one-year bond, and buy a two-year bond. The forward rate on this one-year investment to begin one year into the future is equal to

$$_1F_1 = \frac{(1 + R_2)^2}{(1 + R_1)^1}$$

where $_1F_1$ = one-year (second subscript) rate to prevail one year from now (first subscript)

---

[2] A short position begins with the sale of a borrowed security followed by a purchase of the same security. The securities bought are then returned to the party who initially loaned them. Profit accrues if the sale price is higher than the purchase price; losses accrue if the opposite is true.

$R_2 =$ current two-year rate (expressed in annual rates)

$R_1 =$ current one-year rate

The short one-year position offsets the one-year return on the long position in the two-year bond and the investor is left with the second-year interest on the two-year bond.

For this strategy to be of economic consequence, it must be possible. The facts are that

1. Only securities dealers can expect to assume short positions in the bond market on a reasonably consistent basis.

2. The short positions are not likely if the underlying bond is thinly traded. Dealers cannot do much about this. The alternative of going short on another bond whose returns are close to perfectly positively correlated with those on the thinly traded bond is not always possible.

3. No dealer can borrow bonds to deliver against a short position on a long-term basis. The argument that the dealer can enter the market continuously and establish a short position is not workable. Interest-rate differentials may shift and transactions costs can become prohibitive.

The argument by certain dealers that they could do in the cash market whatever one can do in the futures market is not very potent.

Hedging in the cash market, as the other hedging tools we shall discuss, is used as an alternative—and at times as a complement—to the classical hedging method, which consists of the matching up (in size and in maturity) of cash assets and liabilities on the balance sheet.

14.4 THE REPURCHASE AGREEMENT

An investor wishing to secure a certain rate of return on a T-bill beginning three months from now can do so in the cash market by entering into a repurchase agreement—that is, buying a six-month bill and selling it with a proviso that the buyer will sell it back three months to date at a specified price (yield). The difference in yields will be the cost of the hedge. The risk due to changes in interest rates is being borne by the buyer, otherwise known as the speculator. Risk has not been dissipated throughout society as in the insurance case; rather, it has been shifted from the investor to the speculator. The repurchase agreement is not very feasible, however.

1. The repurchase market is basically a dealer market. Small investors hardly participate, since brokerage houses do not provide such facilities to them.
2. The repurchase market is not a centralized market.
3. The repurchase market does not have a standardized contract backed by a third party. Transactions are consummated over the telephone, which is hardly reassuring to investors of a lesser market significance.
4. The repurchase market does not have a centralized agency capable of performing clearing functions for all transactions.

5. As Marcelle Arak[3] argues, the repurchase market offers lower after-tax rates of return than the equivalent position in the futures market.
6. The repurchase agreement does not offer the needed time flexibility for the establishment of a hedge.

14.5 THE INTEREST-RATE FUTURES MARKET

The interest-rate futures market is currently the most widely used avenue for hedging price and credit risks. The number of financial futures markets contracts traded on the various exchanges rose from 605,000 in 1977 to 10,213,000 in 1980, with no sign of abating. The financial futures market provides a centralized, orderly market where standardized contracts are traded in accordance with prescribed rules backed by the needed guarantees.

Financial Futures Contract

A financial futures contract is an agreement (an obligation) to buy or sell a specified amount of a financial instrument at some future date at a price determined today. The net effect is to lock in the price and the interest rate on the financial instrument for that period of time to begin sometime in the future. Simply, it is the purchase (sale) of a financial instrument to be received (delivered) at a specified time into the future at the agreed upon price. The results are a reduction in the investors' concerns about future bond price levels, which could have adverse effects on their welfare (financial as well as mental).

Historical Background

As the prices of financial instruments acquired the volatility of commodity prices, the emergence of a futures market in interest rates was inevitable. Building on its vast experience in dealing with futures contracts, the Chicago Board of Trade (CBT) became the first organization to provide an interest rate futures market in the fall of 1975. The trading vehicle was the Government National Mortgage Association (GNMA or Ginnie Mae) certificate, representing a pool of government-insured mortgages. The success of CBT with the Ginnie Mae futures encouraged other organizations to enter the interest-rate futures market. The first to follow was the International Monetary Market (IMM), a division of the Chicago Mercantile Exchange. Futures trading on the IMM in 90-day (13-week) T-bills began on Jan. 6, 1976. Buoyed by its immediate success (110,223 contracts changing hands between Jan. 6, 1976, and Dec. 31, 1976), the IMM introduced one-year T-bill futures contracts on Sept. 11, 1978, and contracts on four-year T-notes on July 10, 1979.

The success experienced by the IMM and the CBT in interest futures coupled with increasingly wider surges in interest rates (8.46 percent range between December 1976 and February 1980) brought on additional competitors to the marketplace. In September 1978, the American Stock Exchange began trading GNMA futures through its affiliate American Commodities Exchange (ACE). Its success was not impressive, and the ACE

---

[3] See **Marcelle Arak,** "Taxes, Treasury Bills, and Treasury Bill Futures." Federal Reserve Bank of New York, March 26, 1980.

stopped trading in interest-rates futures in August of 1980, transferring all its business to the newly formed New York Futures Exchange (NYFE), a wholly owned subsidiary of the New York Stock Exchange. In the fall of 1979, the Commodity Exchange Inc. (COMEX) inaugurated a three-month-bill futures contract, but was later to drop it because of insufficient volume. And on Aug. 7, 1980, the New York Futures Exchange inaugurated trading in 90-day T-bills (with January, April, July, and October delivery months) as well as in T-bonds having 20-year maturity (with February, May, August, and November delivery months).

Since 1975, the established exchanges have added several new instruments. The most versatile of the exchanges has been the Chicago Board of Trade, which currently (1981) trades six different types of financial futures contracts, as shown in Table 14.1.

Many new contracts are now under consideration for introduction some time in the near future. The IMM has applications pending to begin trading in three-month certificates of deposit, three-month Eurodollar contracts, and stock index futures contracts. The latter are the most exciting of the instruments (to speculators in particular) currently in existence or contemplated. The stock index contract works like the other contracts with few exceptions. The maturities obviously differ and the delivery against the contract will be made in cash. There will not be bits and pieces of stock certificates delivered to the contract holder. The Index the IMM will be using is Standard and Poor's 500 Index (S&P 500). An investor expecting a rise in the S&P 500 would buy a futures contract. If the S&P appreciates in value, the investor will receive cash in accordance with the level of the index times a constant multiplier. If the investor has a short position, a profit will accrue to him if the S&P drops. Once again, the delivery is made in cash. The clearinghouse commitment to honor the contract is the investor's only recourse. No stock certificates or company assets underlie the contract. This instrument, like others in the futures markets, should provide stock market investors with a hedge and a price "discovery" mechanism. Portfolio managers and securities underwriters should find the S&P futures contract to be a very useful tool to hedge their positions against stock market risk.

The CBT has even more ambitious plans for the stock index contract.[4] CBT invented its own stock index broken down by industry category. Delivery against the contracts will also be made in cash.

The Wall Street Journal reported in its Dec. 4, 1981, issue that the chairman of the Commodity Futures Trading Commission (CFTC), the federal regulatory agency that oversees futures exchanges and futures contracts and trades, expected stock index futures to begin trading in the first half of 1982. In fact, the Kansas City Board of Trade began trading a stock index contract based on the Value Line index on Feb. 24, 1982.

The introduction of these contracts should allow for a more efficient separation between systematic (market) risk and unsystematic risk. They accomplish this by increasing the value of information on systematic risk and by providing an effective hedge against it. Futures contracts have lower transactions costs and lower margin requirements than cash transactions, which further induce investors to enter the market and establish new positions based on newly acquired information. These futures contracts represent a signifi-

---

[4] Stock index futures contracts have met initial resistance from the Federal Reserve System because they effectively reduce the margin requirement on the purchase of stocks (Regulation T). As a result of Fed pressures the current margin requirements on stock index futures is rather high when compared with other futures contracts.

TABLE 14.1
CBT Financial Futures Contracts

	30-Day Commercial Paper	90-Day Commercial Paper	4- to 6-Year Treasury Notes	GNMA CDRs	Certificate Delivery GNMA	Long-Term Treasury Bonds
Basic trading unit	Commercial paper, $3 million face value.	Commercial paper, $1,000,000 face value.	U.S. Treasury notes and noncallable bonds $100,000 principal balance with a coupon rate of 8%.	$100,000 principal balance of GNMA 8% coupon or equivalent.	GNMA certificates $100,000 principal balance.	U.S. Treasury bonds with $100,000 face value.
Deliverable grade	Prime commercial paper rated both A-1 by Standard & Poor's and P-1 by Moody's and approved as deliverable by CBT. Maturity not more than 30 days from date of delivery.	Prime commercial paper rated both A-1 by Standard & Poor's and P-1 by Moody's and approved as deliverable by CBT with maturity not more than 90 days from the date of delivery.	U.S. Treasury notes and noncallable bonds. Maturity no less than 4 years and no greater than 6 years from the day of delivery.	Modified passthrough mortgage backed certificates guaranteed by GNMA. Yield equivalent coupons, based on the exchange's designated interest rate of 8% at settlement price under the assumptions of a 30-year certificate prepaid in the 12th year.	Modified passthrough mortgage backed certificates guaranteed by GNMA. Yield equivalent coupons, based on the exchange's designated interest rate of 8% at settlement price under the assumptions of a 30-year certificate prepaid in the 12th year.	U.S. Treasury bonds. Maturing at least 15 years from delivery day if not callable; if callable, are not so for at least 15 years from delivery day.
Delivery method	Financial receipt backed by	Financial receipt backed by	Federal Reserve book entry wire	GNMA collateralized	Actual GNMA certificate. Only	Federal Reserve book entry wire

	RP	P	TN	M	MC	US
	...paper in an approved vault.	...paper in an approved vault.	...system. Invoice is adjusted for coupon rates and maturity.	depository receipt (CDR).	one day per month, usually the 16th.	transfer system. Invoice is adjusted for coupon rates and maturity or call dates.
Price quotation	Index: 100 minus annualized discount, e.g., $100 - 6.54 = 93.46$.	Index: 100 minus annualized discount, e.g., $100 - 6.54 = 93.46$.	Percentage of par, e.g., 94-10 or 94 10/32.	Percentage of par, e.g., 94-01 or 94 1/32.	Percentage of par, e.g., 94-01 or 94 1/32.	Percentage of par, e.g., 94-01 or 94 1/32.
Minimum fluctuation	1/100 of 1% of $3 million on a 30-day basis or $25 per contract.	1/100 of 1% of $1 million on a 90-day basis or $25 per contract.	1/32 of a point or $31.25 per contract.[a]	1/32 of a point or $31.25 per contract.[a]	1/32 of a point or $31.25 per contract.[a]	1/32 of a point or $31.25 per contract.[a]
Daily price limit	50/100 ($1,250 per contract) above or below the previous day's settlement price.	50/100 ($1,250 per contract) above or below the previous day's settlement price.	64/32 ($2,000 per contract) above or below the previous day's settlement price.	64/32 ($2,000 per contract) above or below the previous day's settlement price.	64/32 ($2,000 per contract) above or below the previous day's settlement price.	64/32 ($2,000 per contract) above or below the previous day's settlement price.
Initial margin[b] (maintenance)	$1,500 per contract ($1,200).	$1,500 per contract ($1,200).	$900 per contract ($600).	$2,500 per contract ($2,000).	$2,500 per contract ($2,000).	$2,500 per contract ($2,000).
Hedging margin	$1,200 per contract.	$1,200 per contract.	$600 per contract.	$2,000 per contract.	$2,000 per contract.	$2,000 per contract.
Hours of trading (Chicago time)	8:30 A.M. to 1:45 P.M.	8:30 A.M. to 1:35 P.M.	8 A.M. to 2 P.M.	8 A.M. to 2 P.M.	8 A.M. to 2 P.M.	8 A.M. to 2 P.M.
Ticker tape symbol	RP	P	TN	M	MC	US
Date trading began	May 14, 1979	Sept. 26, 1977	June 25, 1979	Oct. 20, 1975	Sept. 12, 1978	Aug. 22, 1977

Source: Chicago Board of Trade.

[a] Changes to 1/64 ($15.625) approved by CFTC, pending implementation.

[b] Margins are subject to change and may not reflect actual margin deposits required by member firms.

Note: Future contracts in U.S. government debt are not obligations of the U.S. Treasury.

433

cant, rational, and practical alternative to a short position in an entire portfolio or a long position in a mutual fund in which assets consist of securities that make up a market index or are highly correlated with that index.

Another contract requiring "cash settlement" was approved on Dec. 8, 1981, by the CFTC for trading on the Chicago Mercantile Exchange. The new Eurodollar futures contract is based on an index referred to as the London Interbank Offered Rate, used to determine the interest rate on Eurodollar loans (dollar-denominated loans booked outside the United States). Upon expiration of the contract, Eurodollar contract holders will simply collect their profits in cash or pay their losses in cash.

A new contract that was expected to trade on the Chicago Board Options Exchange on October 30, 1981, is the GNMA option contract. This new vehicle for shifting financial risk offers protection both on the buy side (through the call option) and the sell side (through the put option). The option covers $100,000 of GNMA bonds. Its future is now (June 1982) in the hands of the courts.

The call GNMA option allows the holder to purchase GNMA securities at any time during the life of the option at a striking (exercise) price set today. The option holder does *not* have to exercise the option. For this right, the option holder pays a price called premium.

A put GNMA option, on the other hand, allows the holder to sell GNMA securities at any time during the life of the option at a striking price set today. The price of this right is the put premium.

The GNMA options should prove to be a major competitor to financial futures contracts. The main reasons are as follows:

1. The financial futures contract represents an obligation to deliver or to take delivery of a financial instrument unless the position is reversed prior to expiration date. The options contract allows its holder a choice. The holder of an options contract can simply let the contract expire.
2. The maximum loss of an option holder is limited to the premium paid, as we discussed in the stock option case. The loss on a futures contract does not have a maximum set limit.
3. The futures contract, as we discuss below, requires marking to market and daily settlement; that is, it releases or requires cash on a daily basis as interest rates fluctuate. The option buyer, on the other hand, has a fixed cash outflow limited to the size of the premium paid upon the purchase of the contract.

It remains to be seen whether financial futures contracts can live side by side with financial options.

These recently introduced, and the contemplated instruments are a confirmation of the usefulness of the futures markets and of the increased sophistication of financial markets and of market participants.

Mechanics of Futures Trading

Trading in the futures markets is regulated by the Commodity Futures Trading Commission (CFTC), an independent five-member agency of the U.S. government.[5] The CFTC requires the registration of futures commission brokers and approves the exchanges

---

[5] As of June 1982, the halls of the U.S. Congress were filled with rumors that the CFTC would be abolished, or its duties sharply curtailed. The jurisdictions of the SEC, the competing agency, were expected to expand.

where futures contracts are traded, the type of contract traded, its terms, and any changes thereof.

All contracts on an underlying security are standardized as to size, maturity, type of deliverable security against the position, delivery time or period, minimum and maximum daily fluctuation, and the way the price is quoted.

For illustration purposes, we shall use T-bill contracts to explain the mechanics of futures trading. Covering every type of contract is far beyond the scope of this chapter.

An investor interested in purchasing a T-bill contract contacts a broker who is a member of the exchange on which the contract is traded (assume the IMM). The message is wired to the floor broker. The floor broker at the IMM enters the trading pit signals and shouts out the bid. Another broker with an order to sell does likewise, and if both can agree on a price, a transaction is consummated. Once the agreement is reached, the IMM clearinghouse (each major exchange has its own clearinghouse) steps in and assumes responsibility for the contract by interposing itself between the buyer and the seller. The buyer's and the seller's contracts are with the clearinghouse and not with each other. The clearinghouse guarantees delivery and demands receipt of T-bills. It is the "pay-and-collect" agency.

The contract delivery procedure for IMM-listed futures contracts (a typical procedure) is shown in Figure 14.5. In order to maintain its financial integrity, the clearinghouse requires member firms to post margin on each contract and marks them to the market at the end of each business day. Each clearing firm must pay (using cash, a letter of credit, or an approved security) the clearinghouse its previous day's debit balance or receive the previous day's profit based on that day's settling price.

Financial futures contracts are traded on an exchange. None are traded over the counter. Each contract has a buyer (long) and a seller (short). Futures contracts have a specific maturity date, or a settlement date determined by the seller. The delivery of securities against a futures contract is not frequent. Almost 95 percent[6] of all financial futures contracts are closed out by an offsetting transaction (long if short originally or short if long originally) prior to their last delivery date.

Short positions in the futures market (contrary to the cash market) always offset the long positions. Short positions, unlike their counterpart in the stock market, do not have to be preceded by an uptick. Furthermore, no securities will have to be borrowed against a short position in the futures market because delivery would not have to be effected until the expiration date of the contract, if at all. A futures contract is a future obligation and does not involve an exchange of title. The absence of the need to borrow securities obviously helps the investor to avoid interest costs as well as dividends (which are owed by the short seller to the individual or brokerage house that lent the securities for the short position in a stock). Additionally, while the short position in a stock has unlimited downside risk on any given day, the short position in the futures market can incur only a maximum loss set by the daily price-limit change allowed by the exchange (provided that covering the short position is possible at any time).

T-bill contracts are quoted using the difference between 100 and the actual T-bill yield. A T-bill yielding 8 percent would be quoted at 92 (100 − 8). This form of quoting prices allows prices on futures contracts to be quoted in a manner consistent with that

---

[6] The 5 percent delivery—a high percentage relative to agricultural commodities (3 percent)—is explained by the fact that delivery can be a good way for dealers to liquidate securities with a thin cash market and by the difficulty of closing out arbitrage positions in the cash market.

FIGURE 14.5   Delivery procedure for IMM-listed futures contracts.

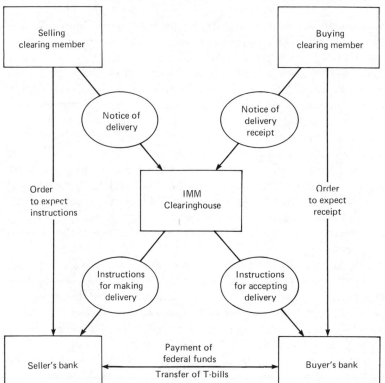

Source: Opportunities in Interest Rates Treasury Bills Futures. Chicago Mercantile Exchange, November 1977.

of other financial instruments listed on other exchanges—that is, with a bid price lower than the ask (offer) price. Had T-bills been quoted on a yield basis, the bid would be higher than the ask because the buyer wants the highest possible yield and the seller wants to give up the lowest possible yield.

Minimum price fluctuations on T-bill futures are quoted in multiples of 0.01 or one basis point (one hundredth of 1 percent). The dollar value of the minimum price fluctuation, given that the face value or the size of the T-bill contract is $1 million, is equal to

$$1,000,000 \times \left(\frac{1}{100}\right)[1\%] \times \frac{1}{4}\left[\frac{90\ (\text{days})}{360}\right] = \$25$$

The 90 days were used because the contracts are for 90-day T-bills.

The maximum daily price fluctuation is 100 basis points or 1 percent for NYFE and 60 basis points for IMM.

The leverage possibilities on the financial futures market are truly remarkable. On a $1 million par value of T-bills, the initial margin requirement is $2,000 on IMM. The maintenance margin for the same contract is $1,500. This means that if the market yields change in a direction unfavorable to the position of the investor by more than

$500, a margin call will be made by the brokerage house. If, on the other hand, market yields move in a favorable direction, the margin account of the trader will be credited by the full profit realized on that day. A margin call must be met in cash and a credit may be withdrawn in cash. This process is what we referred to as "mark to the market" and is done daily. The minimum margin requirements on futures contracts are set by the exchange (the Federal Reserve System in the cash market for stocks and bonds) and may be revised at the discretion of the exchange. Some brokerage firms require higher margins. Margins are considered a "good faith" deposit and not a down payment on the price of the contract because the remaining value of the contract is likely never to be paid. Margins are required for both long and short positions and are strongly related to the daily price limits in effect. We now further focus our discussion on T-bills.

An investor having to make a delivery against a 90-day T-bill contract can either deliver a three-month bill, a six-month T-bill with three months to run, or a one-year T-bill with three months to run. (The one-year T-bill is deliverable only against T-bill futures contracts traded on the New York Futures Exchange.)

The popularity of T-bill futures contracts as hedging, speculative, and arbitrage vehicles has been spectacular. On a typical day in 1981, $22 billion in face-value three-month T-bills (each contract having $1 million face value at maturity) was transacted on the IMM alone, with all indications pointing toward even higher volumes.

Corporations wishing to lock in borrowing costs prior to the actual financing date, investors interested in earning today's rate beginning at a certain time in the future, and other hedgers may not be able to sell a futures contract on the specific asset they are trying to protect. Then what is the usefulness to these economic agents of having T-bill futures contracts? To the extent that T-bill rates are highly correlated with those rates on the financial instruments for which protection is sought, T-bill futures can achieve the desired objective. The fact is that the correlation between T-bill rates and other rates are high and significant, as shown in Table 14.2.

T-bills have many other attractive if not peculiar features that make them prime candidates for trading in the futures markets. Among them are the following:

1. *Liquidity.* T-bills enjoy a very highly developed secondary market with considerable depth. The primary market (new issues) is equally strong, with approximate weekly offerings of $3 billion. These features are essential if the investor is to guard against a delivery squeeze.

TABLE 14.2
Relationship Between Yields on 90-Day T-Bills and Other Short-Term Instruments (Monthly 1968 through 1979)

Financial Instrument	Coefficient of Correlation with 90-Day T-Bills
Six-month T-bill rate	.994
One-year T-bill rate	.981
90-day CD rate	.961
Four- to six-month commercial paper rate	.963

Source: Calculated from Federal Reserve Board data.

2. *Security.* T-bills are backed by the full faith and credit of the U.S. government. They are considered riskless.

3. *Homogeneity.* All T-bills are alike in terms of quality, unlike other financial instruments issued by private parties or even by federal agencies. The only difference among T-bills is in their maturity.

4. *Familiarity and ease of delivery.* Investors of varied level of sophistication and nationality are usually familiar with T-bills. The Federal Reserve wire transfer system is used for the quick and efficient transfer of T-bills.

With all of these qualities, the marked success of T-bills as a prime vehicle for hedging in the futures market should not surprise any observer.

Another financial instrument issued by the U.S. government that has found considerable popularity in the futures markets is the T-bond. T-bills and T-bonds contracts are currently the most actively traded in the futures markets. We shall, therefore, concentrate on the features of these futures contracts, on the differences and similarities in the requirements and trading rules of the major exchanges on which the contracts are traded, and on the determinants of the contract prices.

Features of T-Bond and T-Bill Contracts

The main features of T-bill and T-bond futures contracts on the major futures exchanges are summarized in Tables 14.3 and 14.4.* A few entries in the tables warrant elaboration.

Since Nov. 1, 1979, one-year T-bills have been auctioned and issued the Thursday of every fourth week. Given the auction cycle, a one-year T-bill can be delivered against a 91-day T-bill futures contract on one or two Thursdays of the delivery month. Table 14.5 illustrates the uneven ("not uniform") time gaps between consecutive contracts on the NYFE calculated as of Aug. 11, 1980. The delivery day on an NYFE contract could thus be on the first, second, third, or fourth Thursday of the delivery month, while it is always on the third Thursday of the delivery month on IMM-listed futures T-bill contracts.

The two deliverable dates on the NYFE are intended to help prevent a "fail." A fail occurs when those investors with a long position in the cash-when-issued market fail to receive delivery on the specified day and are therefore unable to deliver on their short position in the futures market. The invoice price, it must be noted, is constant during the two days. This price fixity encourages the holder of the short position to deliver on the first day because he or she can deliver a cheaper bill (the bill still has a day to go) and produces a net advantage for the holder of a long futures position to take delivery on the second day. This is so because T-bills are not coupon bonds and are sold at a discount. The holder of the long futures position would want to pay for the futures contract on the last possible day—that is, to leave the funds to accumulate a one-day interest elsewhere.

The deliverable security on the NYFE can be a one-year T-bill with 91 days remaining to maturity. This obviously increases the liquidity of the market, since meeting the

---

* Trading in T-bill futures contracts on NYFE has been discontinued in 1982. Trading in T-bond futures contracts on NYFE is being discontinued (October, 1982). However, the analysis, as presented, should allow the reader to further understand the financial futures markets and the various feasible pricing mechanisms.

TABLE 14.3
Features of T-Bill Futures Contracts

	NYFE	IMM
Contract size	$1 million	$1 million
Time gap between contracts	Not uniform	Uniform: 91 days
Delivery month	January, April, July, and October	March, June, September, December
Delivery date	The Thursday and the following business day of the delivery month on which a T-bill initially auctioned as a "year bill" is deliverable (that is, it has 90 or 92 days to delivery).	On the Thursday of the third week of the delivery month.
Deliverable security	Current 3-month (90- to 92-day) bills. 3-month, 6-month (with 3 months to run) and one-year bill (with 3 months to run).	Current 3-month (90- to 92-day) bills. 3-month and 6-month (with 3 months to run).
Price fluctuations		
Minimum	1 basis point	1 basis point
Maximum	100 basis points	60 basis points (no limit on last day of trading).
Margin requirement		
Initial	$1,500	$2,000
Maintenance	$1,200	$1,500

obligations of the futures contract is made easier by the increased supply of securities deliverable against it.

On the T-bond side (Table 14.4), the most important issue deals with invoice pricing and the differing method of arriving at it on the NYFE and the CBT. The next section deals with this issue. Another important concern is the delivery date. Any day during the delivery month is a delivery date on the CBT. Trading in the futures contract ends on the eighth business day before the end of the month, however. The notice date[7] is two business days prior to the delivery date. The short must give notice by 8 P.M. (CST). However, if the delivery is to be made on the last business day of the delivery month, the short has until 2 P.M. (CST) of the day preceding the delivery day to notify the clearing corporation.

Mathematics of Treasury Futures Contracts

The pricing of futures contracts is both simple and confusing. Table 14.6 shows the price quotations on T-bond and T-bill futures contracts traded on the major exchanges. How these prices are determined, and what relationship they have to each other and to the cash market is the subject of this section.

---

[7] The notice date is the day on which notice of intent to deliver is made by the seller.

TABLE 14.4
Features of T-Bond Futures Contracts

New York Futures Exchange	Chicago Board of Trade
Contract size = $100,000	Contract size = $100,000
Deliverable security: a T-bond with a minimum of 20 years to maturity and a 15-year call protection.	Deliverable security: a T-bond with a minimum of 15 years to maturity and a 15-year call protection.
Invoice pricing mechanism: based on yield maintenance. The yield to maturity on the bond delivered is determined so that it equals the yield to maturity on a 9% 20-year bond traded at the contracted futures price. If the bond is callable and is selling at a premium, the invoice price is calculated using the yield to call.	Invoice pricing mechanism: based on price maintenance determined by *factors.*[a] Invoice price (IP) = settlement price SP × factor *F* $$IP = SP \times F$$
Price fluctuations: Minimum 1/32 of 1% Maximum 96/32 (3 points)	Price fluctuations: Minimum 1/32 of 1% Maximum 64/32 (2 points)
Margin requirements (set by the exchange and subject to change at any time) Initial $2,500 Maintenance $2,000	Margin requirements (set by the exchange and subject to change at any time)

	Initial	Maintenance
Hedgers	$1,500	$1,500
Speculators	$2,000	$1,500

New York Futures Exchange	Chicago Board of Trade
Delivery months: February, May, August, November	Delivery months: March, June, September, and December
Delivery day: 3 delivery days, each of which is 2 business days after a notice day.	Delivery can be made on any business day of the delivery month.
Notice day: 15th calendar day of the delivery month (or the following business day if the 15th is not a business day) and the next two business days.	

[a] A factor *F* is an invention of CBT. It is the price of a bond as if yielding 8 percent divided by 100. If the coupon rate on delivered bond is higher than 8 percent, the factor is greater than 1, otherwise $F \leqslant 1$. $0.5 \leq F \leq 1.5$.

Pricing of T-Bonds

A perfectly competitive economy precludes, through arbitrage, perfect substitutes from selling at different prices. It is the arbitrage mechanism that cements the relationship among the various futures contracts and between the futures and the cash markets.

A short position in the NYFE February '81 T-bonds futures established on Dec. 9, 1980 will require delivery of T-bonds by Feb. 23, 1981. Four options are available in fulfilling the delivery requirements:

TABLE 14.5
Time Gaps Between NYFE T-Bill Futures Contracts

First Delivery Day	Time Gaps Between Consecutive Contracts (in Days)
10/02/80	—
1/22/81	112
4/16/81	84
7/09/81	84
10/01/81	84
1/21/82	112
4/15/82	84
7/08/82	84

Source: Frank J. Jones, "Pricing Three NYFE T-Bill Futures Contracts." *The Money Manager,* vol. 9, no. 34 (Aug. 25, 1980).

1. Borrow money now, buy T-bonds, and deliver them on February 23.

2. Buy a December CBT contract (the last contract month available on any futures exchange before the February contract month) and take delivery of the bonds against the short position on the NYFE.

TABLE 14.6
T-Bond and T-Bill Price Quotations on the Major Futures Exchanges

Treasury Bonds

New York Futures Exchange

December 9, 1980 – FUTURES PRICES
20 YEAR 9% U.S. TREASURY BONDS – $100,000
pts 1/32 of 100%

	Open	High	Low	Stle	Chg	Yield Settle	Chg	Open Interest
Feb81	75-29	75-29	74-15	74-16	−1-21	12.496	+ .214	1,932
May	76-10	76-18	76-08	75-18	−1-16	12.312	+ .251	1,051
Aug	77-12	77-12	77-12	76-12	−1-13	12.175	+ .232	353
Nov	....	....	....	76-29	−1-12	12.086	+ .224	236
Feb82	77-19	77-19	77-19	77-08	−1-11	12.030	+ .218	726
May	77-29	77-29	77-29	77-18	−1-10	11.978	∓ .211	1,440
Aug	78-07	78-07	78-07	77-28	−1-09	11.927	+ .205	720
Nov	....	....	....	78-06	−1-08	11.877	+ .199	....

Vol 2,199; Vol Mon., 1,901; open int 6,458, +135.

Chicago Board of Trade

TREASURY BONDS (CBT) – $100,000; pts. 32nds of 100%

	Open	High	Low	Settle	Chg	Settle	Chg	Open Interest
Dec	67-05	67-09	65-28	65-27	−129	12.759	+ .365	9,676
Mar81	68-19	68-24	67-10	67-13	−124	12.458	+ .323	43,996
June	69-28	69-28	68-12	68-14	−124	12.266	+ .316	26,973
Sept	70-20	70-20	69-02	69-05	−123	12.135	+ .305	23,601
Dec	70-25	70-29	69-16	69-17	−122	12.067	+ .296	23,737
Mar82	71-08	71-10	69-26	69-27	−122	12.011	+ .294	20,417
June	71-14	71-16	70-02	70-03	−123	11.967	+ .298	25,053
Sept	71-22	71-22	70-19	70-11	−123	11.923	+ .297	25,109
Dec	71-30	71-30	70-18	70-19	−123	11.879	+ .295	22,448
Mar83	72-06	72-06	70-26	70-27	−123	11.835	+ .293	9,692
June	72-14	72-14	71-02	71-03	−122	11.792	+ .286	517

Est vol 50,000; vol Mon 53,007; open int 231,219, +1,066.

Treasury Bills

New York Futures Exchange

90-DAY U.S. TREASURY BILLS – $1 mil; pts of 100%

	Open	High	Low	Settle	Chg	Discount Settle	Chg	Open Interest
Jan81	84.35	84.42	84.03	84.10	− .47	15.90	+ .47	806
Apr	....	....	....	85.80	− .47	14.20	+ .47	174
July	....	....	....	86.99	− .23	13.01	+ .23	101
Oct	....	....	....	87.75	+ .07	12.25	− .07	2
Jan82	....	....	....	88.15	+ .16	11.85	− .16	2
Apr	....	....	....	88.30	+ .16	11.70	− .16	....
July	....	....	....	88.42	+ .24	11.58	− .24	....
Oct	....	....	....	88.55	+ .33	11.45	− .33	....

Vol 517; Vol Mon., 790; open int 1,085, +275.

International Monetary Market

TREASURY BILLS (IMM) – $1 mil.; pts. of 100%

	Open	High	Low	Settle	Chg	Discount Settle	Chg	Open Interest
Dec	83.82	83.92	83.45	83.61	− .72	16.39	+ .72	5,284
Mar81	85.80	85.90	85.42	85.52	− .50	14.48	+ .50	20,883
June	86.99	86.99	86.48	86.77	− .26	13.23	+ .26	8,832
Sept	87.60	87.72	87.22	87.57	− .09	12.43	+ .09	5,832
Dec	87.88	88.06	87.67	88.07	+ .13	11.93	− .13	1,962
Mar82	88.13	88.26	87.91	88.24	+ .14	11.76	− .14	1,745
June	88.14	88.40	88.00	88.35	+ .13	11.65	− .13	497
Sept	88.14	88.54	88.08	88.40	+ .34	11.60	− .34	215

Est vol 24,602; vol Mon 21,964; open int 45,250, −1,509.

Source: Wall Street Journal, Friday, Dec. 10, 1980.

3. Wait until February and buy T-bonds in the cash market for delivery against the short position.

4. Make no delivery; that is, close the position by buying an equivalent contract on NYFE.

The first option requires borrowing 90 percent of the value of T-bonds and committing the 10 percent margin requirement. The interest costs are offset (to some degree) by the interest income from the bonds owned. The net interest costs represent the cost of carrying the bonds. It is similar to the storage cost in the commodity's case (see Chapter 15).

The second option also involves a carry cost, but only from the end of December until Feb. 23, 1980. If the interest costs are higher than the interest revenue ("negative carry"), settlement of the NYFE contract would be made at the earliest possible date (Feb. 19, 1981). If, on the other hand, the interest costs are lower than the interest revenues ("positive carry"), settlement will be made on the last possible date in the delivery month. Let us now examine how the T-bond futures contract on the NYFE is priced off the nearest T-bond futures contract listed on the CBT. The steps are as follows:

1. Buy CBT T-bond contract.

2. Determined the cheapest deliverable bond against the long CBT position (this holds only at a given point in time).

The process is as follows:

   a. Determine the ask price (CP) on T-bonds deliverable against the long CBT position.

   b. Look up the factor F on the bond. The factor is a CBT invention and is equal to the price of the bond, as if yielding 8 percent divided by 100. $F > 1$ when the deliverable bond carries a coupon rate higher than 8 percent, $F = 1$ when the deliverable bond carries and 8 percent coupon, and $F < 1$ when the coupon rate on the deliverable bond is less than 8 percent.

   c. Calculate CP/F. The deliverable bond with the lowest CP/F value will be the cheapest deliverable bond. Corresponding to this CP/F is a bond with a given coupon rate having 15 years to call and 15 years to maturity. Table 14.7 shows that the cheapest deliverable bond is the 8⅜ percent T-bond maturing in 2003.

3. Determine the invoice price IP on a CBT contract maturing in December:

$$\text{IP} = \text{settlement price SP} \times \text{factor } F \qquad\qquad (14.1)$$

The settlement price is reported daily in *The Wall Street Journal* (Table 14.6). The factor is shown in Table 14.7 to equal 1.0389. Therefore,

$$\text{IP} = \text{SP} \times F = \frac{65.27}{32}\,(1.0389)$$
$$= 65.84375 \times 1.0389 = 68.405$$

This is the sum owed on each \$100 of bond value.

4. Determine the carry cost. The carry cost is best conceived when looked upon as the difference between the cash outflow (the interest costs) and the cash inflows (the interest revenue).

TABLE 14.7
Deliverable T-Bonds on CBT December Contracts

Coupon	Call Date	Factor[a]	Cash Price (Ask)	Cash Price/Factor $\left(\dfrac{CP}{F}\right)$
8%	1996	1	66.23/32	66.718
8¼%	2000	1.0241	67.30/32	66.338
7⅝%	2002	.9622	63.31/32	66.482
7⅞%	2002	.9870	66.28/32	67.756
8⅜%	2003	1.0389	68.24/32	66.176
8¾%	2003	1.0778	71.11/32	66.200
9⅛%	2004	1.1177	74.10/32	66.487
10⅜%	2004	1.2505	83.9/32	66.598
11¾%	2005	1.3974	93.12/32	66.820
10%	2005	1.2124	80.30/32	66.758
12¾%	2005	1.5082	100.24/32	66.801

[a] Tables titled *Treasury Bond Futures Conversion Factors,* published by the Financial Publishing Company of Boston, Mass., are used to find the appropriate factor.

Source: The Wall Street Journal, Dec. 10, 1980.

$$CC = \frac{T}{365}\left[\underbrace{\frac{RR}{100}(IP)}_{\text{outflows}} - \underbrace{\left(\frac{CR}{100}\right)100}_{\text{inflows}}\right] \tag{14.2}$$

where CC = carry cost

T = time period during which the loan is outstanding (from the maturity date of the CBT contract to the maturity date of the NYFE contract)

RR = repurchase rate to equal the borrowing rate

CR = coupon rate

$$CC = \frac{50}{365}\left[\left(\frac{16.75}{100}\right)68.405 - 8.375\right]$$
$$= 0.4223$$

5. Determine the theoretical price:

$$TP = \text{invoice price} + \text{financing costs} - \text{interest revenue} \tag{14.3}$$
$$= \text{invoice price (IP)} + CC$$
$$TP = 68.405 + 0.4223$$
$$= 68.8273$$

The theoretical price is based on the assumption that the cheapest deliverable bond on the CBT is also the cheapest deliverable bond on NYFE. The yield maintenance system on NYFE, however, biases the results in favor of high-coupon bonds. It is very unlikely, therefore, that the 8⅜ bond deliverable on the CBT would turn out to be the cheapest deliverable on the NYFE. Other problems leading to a difference between the actual market price and the theoretical price are:

1. The accuracy of the repo rate. An implied repo rate can be easily derived from the TP equation by setting it equal to the market price.
2. The delivery rate on the long futures bonds could be any business day in the delivery month. This could lengthen or shorten the time period by 1 to 22 business days.
3. Transactions costs and market inefficiencies (to the extent they exist).

The theoretical price of the NYFE contract (68.8273) was derived based on the delivery of an 8 percent coupon bond. The NYFE February contract listed in Table 14.6 (settlement price $= 74\frac{1}{32}$, settlement yield $= 12.496$) is based on a 9 percent bond. Hence the need to convert from one pricing system to another. That is, we must price the $8\frac{3}{8}$ deliverable bond so as to yield 12.496 percent, as does the NYFE contract. The conversion equation is too complex for a book of this level. Its application, however, yields a theoretical price of 64.66.

The difference between 64.66 and the theoretical price of an NYFE contract (68.8273) is accounted for primarily by the assumption (not a practical or an accurate one) that the cheapest deliverable on the CBT is also the cheapest deliverable on NYFE. The 64.66, therefore, should represent the lower bound on the price of a NYFE contract.

We therefore recommend, given the problems discussed above, that T-bond futures contracts be priced off the cash market. The literature on this issue distributed by NYFE is wrong and misleading. The simple procedure for pricing futures contracts off the cash market is as follows:

1. Determine the cheapest deliverable bond against the T-bond contract under consideration. That is, determine which of the deliverable bonds has the highest invoice price relative to the market value of the underlying cash instrument.
2. To the price of this bond add the carry cost CC. The financing cost is equal to the repo rate for the period or the yield on a T-bill plus 0.5. The carry cost is determined using Equation 14.2.

Pricing T-Bill Futures Contracts

The price of a T-bill futures contract can be determined, as in the T-bond case, on the basis of the arbitrage relationship between the spot market and the futures market. Our model is based on the work of W. Poole[8] as well as that of R. Rendleman and C. Carabini.[9] Poole determined the upper and lower price limits of the T-bill futures contract. Using essentially a similar approach, Rendleman and Carabini arrive at similar upper and lower bounds and at a formula for determining the IMM index value assuming no transactions costs. In both papers, the upper and lower limits are determined by transactions costs and the margin requirement on IMM contracts.

The term *arbitrage* will be used rather loosely in this section, without necessarily meaning pure arbitrage. A pure arbitrage opportunity results in a return on a riskless position requiring no commitment of funds. Pure arbitrage is not always possible in T-bill futures contracts because it is not always possible to match maturities, because

---

[8] **William Poole,** "Using T-Bill Futures to Gauge Interest Rate Expectations." *Federal Reserve Bank of San Francisco Economic Review,* Spring 1978, pp. 7–19.

[9] **Richard J. Rendleman** and **Christopher E. Carabini,** "The Efficiency of the Treasury Bill Futures Market." *Journal of Finance,* vol. 34, no. 4 (September 1979), pp. 895–914.

of the marking to the market requirements that generate opportunity losses to those on the wrong side of the market, and because the borrowing rate is not uniform for all borrowers. Therefore, the arbitrage we speak of is not necessarily risk-free and may require commitment of funds.[10]

The pricing of futures T-bill contracts is rather simple. Consider the case of an investor faced with the following choice: (1) invest in 182 day T-bill or (2) invest in a 91 day bill and buy a futures contract maturing 91 days hence.

In a perfect market, the investor should be indifferent between the two options, for both offer equivalent returns.

Let K_m = yield on a 91-day T-bill

K_n = yield on a 182-day T-bill

$K_{Ft,m}$ = yield on a futures contract maturing m days from now

$K_{FW,n-m}$ = implied forward rate on a T-bill with a life equal to $n - m$

Therefore, if the market is in equilibrium,

$$[(1 + K_m)(1 + K_{Ft,m})]^{1/n} = [(1 + K_m)(1 + K_{FW,n-m})]^{1/n} = (1 + K_n) \qquad (14.5)$$

Arbitrage presents itself when

$$K_{Ft,m} \gtreqless K_{FW,n-m}$$

(i) $K_{Ft,m} > K_{FW,n-m}$

Assume that the six-month T-bill rate is 14 percent and the three-month T-bill rate is 15 percent. The implied three-month forward rate is, therefore equal to

$$K_{FW,3} = \frac{(1 + 0.14)^2}{(1 + 0.15)} - 1 = 13 \text{ percent}$$

An arbitrageur observing that the futures rate is above the 13 percent forward rate would employ the following strategy:

1. Borrow money long term at 14 percent. This assumes that the borrowing and the lending rates are equal.
2. Buy a three-month T-bill.
3. Simultaneously, go long (buy) one T-bill futures contract with a three-month maturity.

The spot and futures T-bill positions have the effect of creating a synthetic six-month T-bill with a yield exceeding that realized on the six-month T-bill. If the future rate is equal to 14 percent, the six-month annualized rate on the "synthetic" position is

$$\sqrt{(1 + 0.15)(1 + 0.14)} - 1 = 14.45\%$$

---

[10] See **Douglas T. Breeden**, "Comments on Selected Articles Concerning T-Bill Futures Market Efficiency" and "The Effect of Interest Rate Futures on the Variations In Spot Rates." Center for the Study of Futures Markets, Columbia Business School, p. 198.

The 14.45 percent is larger than the 14 percent that could be realized on a six-month T-bill bought in the spot market.

(ii) $K_{\text{Ft},m} < K_{\text{FW},n-m}$

Assume that the rates in the preceding example were reversed; the forward rate would then be equal to

$$K_{\text{FW},3} = \frac{(1+0.15)^2}{(1+0.14)} - 1 = 16\%$$

An arbitrageur observing this forward rate and judging the difference between it on the futures rate to be too high would undertake the following:

Borrow money for three months.
Buy longer-term (six-month) T-bills.
Simultaneously go short (sell) one (or more) T-bill futures contract with a three-month maturity.

The long bill will be delivered against the short contract upon maturity of the futures contract. The debt will be repaid from the proceeds on the short position. The arbitrage profit would equal the profit on the short futures position less net borrowing costs.

From Equation 14.5 we can derive the theoretical price of the T-bill futures contract. Taking the inverse, or equation 14.5 we get

$$\frac{1}{(1+K_m)} \cdot \frac{1}{(1+K_{\text{Ft},m})} = \frac{1}{(1+K_n)^n}$$

or

$$P_m \cdot P_F = P_n = \text{price of a T-bill that pays \$1 at maturity}$$

Therefore $P_F = \dfrac{P_n}{P_m}$ (14.6)

where P_F = price of a futures contract using the bankers' discount method of pricing T-bills—price equals the difference between \$100 and the annualized discount from par assuming 360 days in a year

P_n = spot price of an n-day T-bill

P_m = spot price of an m-day T-bill

Equation 14.6 assumes no commission costs and zero bid-ask dealer spread. If these transactions costs are accounted for, the price of the forward contract will have to fall in the following range—assuming \$6 or \$0.006 per \$100 of par round-trip commission costs:

$$100\,\frac{P_n^A}{P_m^B} - 0.006 \le P_F \le 100\,\frac{P_n^A}{P_m^B} + 0.006 \tag{14.7}$$

where P_n^A = asking price

P_m^B = bid price

0.006 = $60 round commission on a $1 million contract

Subtracting both sides of Equation 14.7 from 100, then multiplying by 360/91 days to arrive at the annualized discount from par and subtracting from $100 to arrive at the IMM index value, we get the following range:[11]

$$100 - 395.6\left(1 - \frac{P_n^B}{P_m^A}\right) - 0.0237 \leq P_F \leq 100 - 395.6\left(1 - \frac{P_n^A}{P_m^B}\right) + 0.0237 \qquad (14.8)$$

Example

What should be the theoretical price of an IMM March 81 contract as of Dec. 9, 1980, if the deliverable bill against the futures contract is the June 18, 1981 bid price, equal to 15.35, and asked price, equal to 15.17, or an average price of 15.26.

Answer

1. Determine the T-bill rate applicable to the m period—the period between Dec. 9, 1980, and the third Thursday of March when the T-bill is deliverable. This period is equal to 100 days.

2. Find the price on a T-bill maturing 100 days hence (March 19, 1981). From *The Wall Street Journal* Dec. 10, 1980 issue, we read that the bid price is 16.71 and the ask is 16.51, giving an average price of 16.61.

3. Calculate $P_F = \dfrac{100 - [15.26 \times (191/360)]}{100 - [16.61 \times (100/360)]} =$

$$= \frac{100 - 8.096}{100 - 4.613} = \frac{91.904}{95.387} = 0.96348$$

Therefore $100 - 96.348 = 3.652$

the annualized yield $= 3.652 \times \dfrac{360}{91} = 14.447$

$P_F = 100 - 14.447 = \mathbf{85.553}$

This price should be compared with the actual price of a March contract on the IMM. From Table 14.6, we find that the price is 85.52. The 3.3 basis points difference must be the transactions costs mentioned by Rendleman and Carabini.

Table 14.8 shows relevant T-bill data available from the IMM. It allows for easy translation of an IMM index into the actual value (price) of a contract.

Uses of T-Bills and T-Bond Futures

The investment strategies that T-bill futures afford can be devised, the reader should be reminded, using other vehicles (forward contracts,[12] repurchase agreements, the cash markets, etc.) as was discussed earlier in this chapter. The futures markets, however,

---

[11] **Rendleman** and **Carabini,** pp. 898–899.

[12] A forward contract is a cash contract with a deferred delivery.

TABLE 14.8
Translating an IMM Index

91-Day Bills					91-Day Bills				
IMM Index	Disc. Rate	Coupon Equiv.	Disc. on $1,000,000	Price	IMM Index	Disc. Rate	Coupon Equiv.	Disc. on $1,000,000	Price
91.61	8.39	8.691	21,208.06	978,791.94	92.12	7.88	8.152	19,918.89	980,081.11
91.62	8.38	8.680	21,182.78	978,817.22	92.13	7.87	8.141	19,893.61	980,106.39
91.63	8.37	8.670	21,157.50	978,842.50	92.14	7.86	8.131	19,868.33	980,131.67
91.64	8.36	8.659	21,132.22	978,867.78	92.15	7.85	8.120	19,843.06	980,156.94
91.65	8.35	8.648	21,106.94	978,893.06	92.16	7.84	8.110	19,817.78	980,182.22
91.66	8.34	8.638	21,081.67	978,918.33	92.17	7.83	8.099	19,792.50	980,207.50
91.67	8.33	8.627	21,056.39	978,943.61	92.18	7.82	8.088	19,767.22	980,232.78
91.68	8.32	8.617	21,031.11	978,968.89	92.19	7.81	8.078	19,741.94	980,258.06
91.69	8.31	8.606	21,005.83	978,994.17	92.20	7.80	8.067	19,716.67	980,283.33
91.70	8.30	8.596	20,980.56	979,019.44	92.21	7.79	8.057	19,691.39	980,308.61
91.71	8.29	8.585	20,955.28	979,044.72	92.22	7.78	8.046	19,666.11	980,333.89
91.72	8.28	8.574	20,930.00	979,070.00	92.23	7.77	8.036	19,640.83	980,359.17
91.73	8.27	8.564	20,904.72	979,095.28	92.24	7.76	8.025	19,615.56	980,384.44
91.74	8.26	8.553	20,879.44	979,120.56	92.25	7.75	8.015	19,590.28	980,409.72
91.75	8.25	8.543	20,854.17	979,145.83	92.26	7.74	8.004	19,565.00	980,435.00
91.76	8.24	8.532	20,828.89	979,171.11	92.27	7.73	7.994	19,539.72	980,460.28
91.77	8.23	8.522	20,803.61	979,196.39	92.28	7.72	7.983	19,514.44	980,485.56
91.78	8.22	8.511	20,778.33	979,221.67	92.29	7.71	7.972	19,489.17	980,510.83
91.79	8.21	8.500	20,753.06	979,246.94	92.30	7.70	7.962	19,463.89	980,536.11
91.80	8.20	8.490	20,727.78	979,272.22	92.31	7.69	7.951	19,438.61	980,561.39
91.81	8.19	8.479	20,702.50	979,297.50	92.32	7.68	7.941	19,413.33	980,586.67
91.82	8.18	8.469	20,677.22	979,322.78	92.33	7.67	7.930	19,388.06	980,611.94
91.83	8.17	8.458	20,651.94	979,348.06	92.34	7.66	7.920	19,362.78	980,637.22
91.84	8.16	8.448	20,626.67	979,373.33	92.35	7.65	7.909	19,337.50	980,662.50
91.85	8.15	8.437	20,601.39	979,398.61	92.36	7.64	7.899	19,312.22	980,687.78
91.86	8.14	8.426	20,576.11	979,423.89	92.37	7.63	7.888	19,286.94	980,713.06
91.87	8.13	8.416	20,550.83	979,449.17	92.38	7.62	7.878	19,261.67	980,738.33
91.88	8.12	8.405	20,525.56	979,474.44	92.39	7.61	7.867	19,236.39	980,763.61
91.89	8.11	8.395	20,500.28	979,499.72	92.40	7.60	7.856	19,211.11	980,788.89
91.90	8.10	8.384	20,475.00	979,525.00	92.41	7.59	7.846	19,185.83	980,814.17
91.91	8.09	8.374	20,449.72	979,550.28	92.42	7.58	7.835	19,160.56	980,839.44
91.92	8.08	8.363	20,424.44	979,575.56	92.43	7.57	7.825	19,135.28	980,864.72
91.93	8.07	8.352	20,399.17	979,600.83	92.44	7.56	7.814	19,110.00	980,890.00
91.94	8.06	8.342	20,373.89	979,626.11	92.45	7.55	7.804	19,084.72	980,915.3
91.95	8.05	8.331	20,348.61	979,651.39	92.46	7.54	7.793	19,059.44	980,940.6
91.96	8.04	8.321	20,323.33	979,676.67	92.47	7.53	7.783	19,034.17	980,965.83
91.97	8.03	8.310	20,298.06	979,701.94	92.48	7.52	7.772	19,008.89	980,991.11
91.98	8.02	8.300	20,272.78	979,727.22	92.49	7.51	7.762	18,983.61	981,016.39
91.99	8.01	8.289	20,247.50	979,752.50	92.50	7.50	7.751	18,958.33	981,041.67
92.00	8.00	8.278	20,222.22	979,777.78	92.51	7.49	7.741	18,933.06	981,066.94
92.01	7.99	8.268	20,196.94	979,803.06	92.52	7.48	7.730	18,907.78	981,092.22
92.02	7.98	8.257	20,171.67	979,828.33	92.53	7.47	7.720	18,882.50	981,117.50
92.03	7.97	8.247	20,146.39	979,853.61	92.54	7.46	7.709	18,857.22	981,142.78
92.04	7.96	8.236	20,121.11	979,878.89	92.55	7.45	7.698	18,831.94	981,168.06
92.05	7.95	8.226	20,095.83	979,904.17	92.56	7.44	7.688	18,806.67	981,193.33
92.06	7.94	8.215	20,070.56	979,929.44	92.57	7.43	7.677	18,781.39	981,218.61
92.07	7.93	8.205	20,045.28	979,954.72	92.58	7.42	7.667	18,756.11	981,243.89
92.08	7.92	8.194	20,020.00	979,980.00	92.59	7.41	7.656	18,730.83	981,269.17
92.09	7.91	8.183	19,994.72	980,005.28	92.60	7.40	7.646	18,705.56	981,294.44
92.10	7.90	8.173	19,969.44	980,030.56	92.61	7.39	7.635	18,680.28	981,319.72
92.11	7.89	8.162	19,944.17	980,055.83	92.62	7.38	7.625	18,655.00	981,345.00

Source: 91-Day U.S. Treasury Bills, International Monetary Market, Chicago Mercantile Exchange.

allow for greater convenience, greater flexibility, greater liquidity, and lower transactions costs in implementing the strategies.

Futures contracts are generally used to hedge risk and to speculate. The speculation is either on the level of the interest rate or on the relationship among rates. Thomas A. Hieronymus makes clear in his book that the distinction between hedging and speculating is misleading:

> *It is sometimes said that hedging is the opposite of speculation. This is not so. They are different kinds of the same thing. The thing that is usually identified as speculation, that is, long or short positions in futures contracts, is speculation in changes in price level. The thing that we identify as hedging, that is, long cash and short futures or vice versa, is speculation in price relationships.* [13]

---

[13] **Thomas A. Hieronymus,** *Economics of Futures Trading For Commercial and Personal Profit.* Commodity Research Bureau, Inc., New York, p. 150.

With this qualifier, we proceed in the analysis of various hedging and speculative strategies.

Hedging

In futures, hedging is "The assumption of a position in futures . . . opposite to an already existing or immediately anticipated cash position . . . to hedge is to insulate one's business activities from price level speculation while retaining the opportunity to speculate in basis variation."[14] In effect, hedging exchanges absolute market risk for basis risk. The difference and similarities between the two definitions should become obvious from the examples to follow.

The particular situation of an investor could dictate one of two possible hedging strategies: a short hedge (referred to at times as "long the basis"), or a long hedge (referred to at times as "short the basis"). The short hedge involves the sale (a short position) of a futures contract, and the long hedge involves the purchase (a long position) of a futures contract.

Short Hedge. The purpose of a short hedge is to offset risk in a cash position. Consider the case of a bank with a $5 million holding of government securities. The bank investment committee expects a rise in the yield on government bonds within the next two months and a leveling off thereafter. That is, the investment committee expects a capital loss on the bank holdings of government bonds. The futures market, it was decided, should be used to hedge against the expected depreciation. The process involves the following:

Date	*Cash Market*	*Futures Market*

Jan. 5, 1981 (today's date)	No transaction. Average price of bonds is equal to: $5,000,000 × 92.2% = $4,610,000	Sell 50($100,000 each)[15] March 81 T-bonds contracts on the CBT. Invoice price IP = settlement price SP × conversion factor CF
		
		The CF for a 10¾ bond (assumed deliverable bond) is 1.2922.
		Therefore
		    IP = 0.71875 × 1.2922
		       = 0.92876 per $1 of contract.
		Total value = IP × contract size × no. of contracts.
		Total value = 0.92876 × $100,000 × 50 = $4,643,800.
		
		(This sum is not received in cash, only the appreciation on the short position is credited daily to the bank's account.)

---

[14] Ibid., 149. A "basis" is the difference between the yield on the futures contract and on a cash contract.

[15] The sale of futures contracts is not necessarily done on a one-to-one basis, as we discuss later in this chapter. This form of hedging is referred to as a naive hedge.

Date	Cash Market	Futures Market
March 1, 1981	No transaction; average price of bond is equal to: $5,000,000 × 90.2 = $4,510,000.	Cover short position (buy 50 March contracts). Invoice price = 0.90876.

<table>
<tr><td></td><td>Book loss =</td><td>Total value = 0.90876 × 100,000 × 50 =</td></tr>
</table>

Cash Market:

Book loss =
$4,610,000
−4,510,000
($ 100,000)

Futures Market:

Total value =
0.90876 × 100,000 × 50 =
$4,543,800

gain: $\left\{\begin{array}{l} 4,643,000 \\ 4,543,800 \end{array}\right.$

$ 100,000

In this example, the book loss is offset exactly by the gain in the futures market. This is an example of a perfect hedge.[16] The net gains (losses) are zero. The bond holdings have been fully protected against rising interest rates. The example ignores, however, transactions costs, which are not very significant (about $60 round-trip costs per contract).

The full protection results from an equal movement in price in the cash and the futures market. That is, the basis—the differential between the yield on the futures contract and the yield on a cash contract—has remained constant between January 5 and March 1, 1981 (assuming a flat yield curve). Such occurrences are rare, however, in the real world. The basis may shrink or expand with advantageous or harmful results to the bank. If the yield on futures contracts rises faster than its cash counterpart, the bank stands to realize a profit from the hedge. If, on the other hand, the yield on futures contracts rises more slowly than its cash counterpart, the bank will not realize a gain in the futures market sufficiently large to offset the losses in the cash market. The bank, under these circumstances, is not fully hedged. The implications of the changes in the basis will become more obvious as more examples are given below. Three additional considerations must be noted:

1. The $100,000 gain in the futures market is not realized all at once, as may be deduced from the example above. Brokers are required to mark their clients to the market on a daily basis. If a profit in the short position accrues, the client's account is credited the full amount on a daily basis. This credit can be withdrawn and invested elsewhere; a possibility that is ignored here.

2. The hedge in this case, basis concerns aside, works well because there exists a futures contract on the exact bond that the bank is trying to protect. Were the bank the owner of corporate bonds instead of government bonds, for example, the extent of the protection provided by the futures market would depend on the degree of correlation between the yields on corporate bonds and that on futures T-bonds contracts. Shorting the T-bond futures contract in this case is referred to as a "cross hedge," which offers less protection than the exact hedge.

3. In the event that the expectations of the investment committee do not materialize, a real loss would be incurred on the short position, offset (partially or totally) by paper

---

[16] Lest the reader be misled, the T-bond futures contract used here is a good hedge *only* against 8 percent 20-year government bonds. Any other coupon or maturity requires the application of a factor to improve the basis; this is conveniently ignored in this example.

gains in the cash position. Thus the aversion of some portfolio managers to interest rate futures.

The inevitable conclusion to be drawn from the above observations is that the strategy of always hedging is not always optimum. Additionally, the strategy of hedging 100 percent of the exposed assets is also not always optimum.

A short hedge can also be used to manage the liability side of the balance sheet. A bank expecting to issue $1 million in one-year certificates of deposits (CDs) three months from now is obviously concerned with rising interest rates. In order to "lock-in" today's CD rate, the bank could enter the following transactions:*

Date	Cash Market	Futures Market
Jan. 5, 1981	No transaction.	Sell one 90-day April U.S. T-bill on NYFE (current settlement price = 87.70). Proceeds = $1,000,000 - (91/360 \times 12.30/100 \times 1,000,000) = \$968,908.33$
April 5, 1980	Issue $1 million of CDs at 13 percent. Additional annual interest costs = $1/100 \times 1,000,000$ = **$10,000**	Cover the short position (April contract quoted at 87.00). Costs = $1,000,000 - (91/360 \times 13/100 \times 1,000,000) = \$967,138.89$ Profit on short position = $\$968,908.33 - \$967,138.89 = $ **$1,769.44**

The profits realized in the futures market were clearly insufficient to offset the losses (the increased costs) in the cash market. The bank could have elected to short six futures contracts instead of one had it correctly anticipated the narrowing in the basis.

A short hedge is sometimes referred to by practitioners as "long the basis": a long position in the cash market and a short position in the futures market. The cash market will be selling at a discount from the futures market. For profits to accrue, the cash price must appreciate more or depreciate less than the futures price by the maturity date of the futures contract. Upon maturity, the futures contract is equivalent to a cash contract.

The opposite of a short hedge is a long hedge, referred to sometimes as "short the basis."

Long Hedge. The long hedge is the opposite of a short hedge. The intent is the same; however, the long hedge is established in order to offset risk in an actual or prospective cash position. A pension fund manager expecting to receive $5 million in three months is concerned about falling yields requiring him to invest at a much lower rate in the future than he presently could. In order to lock in today's rate, the manager decides to go long 50 futures T-bond contracts. The process is as follows:

---

* By June 29, 1981, banks were able to buy or sell CD futures contracts on the IMM. Such contracts allow for a more effective hedge than T-bill futures contracts would, unless the correlation between their price movements and those of T-bill futures is perfect.

Our example illustrates the cross-hedge case. A cross hedge occurs when the hedged and hedging instrument differ in terms of coupon, risk level, maturity, or the life of the hedged instrument and that of the instrument deliverable against the futures contract. The banker may well opt for hedging in the T-bill futures market instead of the CD futures market for liquidity reasons.

Date	*Cash Market*	*Futures Market*
Jan. 5, 1981	No transaction. Average yield on long-term bonds is 12.25 percent.	Buy 50 May T-bond futures contracts on NYFE. Settlement price = $79^{21}/_{32}$. This price is based on the delivery of a 9 percent coupon bond. Assuming that such a bond is available and deliverable, the cost of 50 contracts is: $50 \times 0.7965625 \times 100,000 = \$3,982,812.50$
		(The pension fund manager is only obligated to pay the margin requirement per contract and is expected to be ready to meet the margin calls.) The cost is the financial commitment required if the manager takes delivery of the bonds when the futures contract matures.
April 5, 1981	Invest the $5 million at 11.50 percent opportunity loss = 0.75 percent per year or $0.0075 \times 5,000,000 = $ **$37,500**	Sell 50 May T-bonds futures contracts at 82. The proceeds are = $50 \times 100,000 \times 0.82 = \$4,100,000$
	This opportunity loss will be incurred over the life of the investment, which can well exceed a year in the case of a pension fund.[17]	Profits = $\begin{array}{r} \$4,100,000.00 \\ -3,982,812.50 \\ \hline \mathbf{\$\ \ 117,187.50} \end{array}$ This is a one-time gain.

The long hedge demonstrates once again the dependence of the hedge strategy on the basis. This turns the hedge into a speculation on the size of the basis. Understanding the basis behavior is paramount to establishing a successful hedging strategy. Once again, fundamentalists look for an economic rationale for basis behavior and chartists look at past trends, hoping to cash in on their recurrence. The fundamentalists argue that the basis is determined primarily by market expectations concerning interest rates and by dealer behavior.

---

[17] The actual value of the loss due to a one-time drop in interest rates is equal to the present value of the annual losses. This value is equal to:

$$PV = \sum_{t=1}^{n} \frac{L_t}{(1+0.1225)^t} = \$37,500 \times PVDF_a$$

where L_t = loss at time t

Assuming a 20-year time horizon:

$$PV = \$37,500 \times 7.320 = \$274,500$$

Assuming a constant basis, the bank would have had to sell $274,500/117,187.50 \approx 2.35$ times the value of the investment in the cash market.

FIGURE 14.6 **Yield curves showing interest rate expectations.**

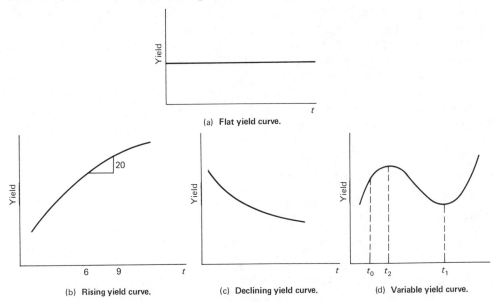

Interest rate expectations are embodied in the yield curve. A flat yield curve (Fig. 14.6a) implies a constant basis. Figure 14.6b shows a rising yield curve, although at a diminishing rate. The farther we move along the t axis, the smaller the basis. The problem lies in correctly defining the basis. The optimum way is to think of the basis as the difference between the futures yield and the yield on a six-month T-bill to be delivered three months from now against the futures contract. Therefore, as we move through time and each future contract turns into a cash contract as its life shrinks to zero, the basis shrinks. The size of the shrinkage depends on the size of the rate of change in the yield.

Figure 14.6c shows the declining yield curve. Again, the changes in the basis will depend on the size of the change in the slope of the curve.

Figure 14.6d is most interesting in that it describes the conditions under which basis trading could bring sizable gains or losses depending on the starting point and the established hedge strategy. A hedger at time t_0, expecting a reversal in the yield curve and judging its size correctly, is obviously at an advantage when compared with a hedger anticipating an upward sloping yield curve. A correctly anticipated yield-curve slope is most helpful in timing a hedge. The maximum basis size is between t_2 and t_1, suggesting to the hedger standing a time t_0 to wait until time t_2 to establish a hedge provided that the particular situation allows.

The maximum swings in the basis are more likely to occur with yield curves changing slopes. The factors influencing the behavior of bond dealers also affect the basis. The influence emanates from the cost of financing the inventory of corporate and government bonds—a cost determined by the relationship between short and long rates. The higher short rates are in relation to long rates, the higher the inventory carrying costs and the higher the price quotations on deferred contracts. The lower the short rates are in relation to long rates, the larger the profits from carrying bond inventory and the lower the price on deferred contracts.

No matter how well conceived a hedging strategy is, it is not always superior to a no-hedge position. Real losses in a futures position established to hedge against interest-rate risks in the cash market are offset (partially or totally) by gains in the cash market, but a no-hedge position would have produced only gains in the cash market and zero losses in the futures market. Furthermore, as the reader must have noted by now, hedging, depending on expectations, may require a long or a short position in the futures market equal to a fraction of that in the cash market. Once again, the ability to predict the behavior of the basis should dictate the hedge ratio. The operating constraint, however, is that futures contracts are not divisible. Only multiples of the standard contract size on the particular exchange are achievable.

Determination of the Hedge Ratio

The ideal hedge is the one that produces gains which exactly offset losses. Stated mathematically, a perfect hedge is as follows:

$$\Delta P_i + \Delta P_J(N) = 0 \tag{14.9}$$

where ΔP_i = change per unit in the value of bond i to be hedged

ΔP_J = change per unit in the value of a futures contract J

N = number of units of a futures contract

If Equation 14.9 holds, the wealth of the hedger will be unaffected by changes in the interest rate.

Studies on the hedge ratio have traditionally emphasized that a way to arrive at a perfect hedge (or an approximation thereof) is to equate the face value of the securities to be hedged with those used to hedge.[18] This, unfortunately, works only under very limited assumptions such as the equality of coupons and maturity between the hedged and hedging instrument.

A new method divised by Kolb and Chiang offers greater but limited promise. The new method "takes account of differences between the maturity and coupon structures of the hedged and hedging instrument."[19]

The new method was dubbed by Kolb and Chiang as the price-sensitivity (PS) strategy.

Using PS, the number of futures contracts necessary to hedge a cash position is arrived at as follows:

$$N = -\frac{\overline{R}_J P_i D_i}{\overline{R}_i \mathrm{FP}_J D_J} \cdot \frac{(d\overline{R}_i/dR_F)}{(d\overline{R}_J/dR_F)} \tag{14.10}$$

where $R_F = 1 +$ the risk-free rate

$\overline{R}_J = 1 +$ expected yield to maturity on the asset underlying futures contract J

$\overline{R}_i = 1 +$ expected yield to maturity on asset i

---

[18] See for example **P. Bacon** and **R. Williams,** "Interest Rate Futures: New Tools for the Financial Manager." *Financial Management,* Spring 1976, pp. 32–38.

[19] **Robert W. Kolb** and **Raymond Chiang,** "Improving Hedging Performance Using Interest Rate Futures." *Financial Management,* Autumn 1981, p. 77.

FP_J = Agreed upon price to the bond underlying J

P_i = The expected price of asset i when the hedge is terminated

D_i = The duration of asset i expected at the end of the hedge period

D_J = The duration of the asset underlying contract J expected at the end of the hedge period

While Kolb and Chiang took a major step forward, their model has very limited applications. It produces a perfect hedge only when the yield curve is flat and changes in interest rates are "infinitesimal."

Another method for computing the hedge ratio is extensively used by Salomon Brothers, Inc. It is quite effective and involves three simple steps:

1. Determine the yield volatility of the asset to be hedged relative to that of the futures contract. This is done using regression analysis. If a 12 basis-point change in B, the security to be hedged, is associated with a 10 basis-point in the appropriate futures contract (A), the relative yield volatility is then 1.2 to 1.

2. Determine the price value change per basis-point, that is, the change in dollar price of the asset to be hedged and the hedging instrument corresponding to a change of one basis-point in yield. Assume that:

Price value change per basis-point for A = 0.055

Price value change per basis-point for B = 0.061

Therefore, a one basis-point change in A's yield produces a dollar price change of 0.055. The dollar price change in B is, therefore, equal to $1.2 \times 0.061 = 0.0732$.

3. Determine the hedge ratio.

$$\text{Hedge ratio} = \frac{\text{volatility of security to be hedged}}{\text{volatility of futures contract}}$$

$$= \frac{0.0732}{0.055} = \mathbf{1.33}$$

Thus, one futures contract unit, in this example, is needed to hedge 1.33 units of A.

The problem of determining the hedge ratio that produces a perfect hedge under varying states of the world has yet to be completely resolved. Meanwhile, every hedge remains a speculation on the basis.

Speculation[20]

The financial futures markets offer interesting opportunities for speculators. They are characterized by high leverage possibilities, very high liquidity, low transactions costs, a large body of information on the behavior (past, actual, and expected) of the underlying security, and a special tax treatment of the results of speculative strategies. Long-term capital gains (if any) on financial futures contracts are established only after a six-month

---

[20] The coverage of speculation is intended to give the reader an idea (general) on how to capitalize on certain opportunities using futures contracts. It is not a comprehensive analysis.

holding period, compared with a one-year holding period for the underlying financial asset. Market participants may speculate on the level of the rate or on the relationship among rates.

Rate-Level Speculation.   Speculators are hedgers without offsetting positions in the cash market. They simply bet on the direction of the yield curve and the size of the change by holding an open futures position. If a drop in yields is expected (a rise in the price of bonds), a long position is established. If a rise in yields is expected, on the other hand, a short position is established.

These rate-level speculations are less widespread than those on rate relationships, which we examine next.

Rate-Relationship Speculation.   Rate-relationship speculations are known as spreads. They are varied in kind and in level of sophistication.

A spread involves the concurrent sale of one contract and the purchase of another. The most frequently used spreads are the intermonth and interinstrument spreads. The intermonth spread involves the sale (a short position) of one contract delivery month and simultaneously the purchase (a long position) of another contract delivery month on the same financial instrument. The interinstrument spread involves the sale of one contract month on one instrument (say March '81, GNMA) and the purchase of the same contract month on another (say March '81 T-bonds). If the contract month is different, then the spread becomes both an intermonth as well as an interinstrument spread.

The purpose of spreads is to capitalize on aberrations in relationships among futures contracts traded in the financial futures markets.

Intermonth Spreads.   The intermonth spread, as stated in the stock option case, involves the purchase of one contract month and the sale of another on the same underlying instrument. The speculator is betting that the yield on the contract bought will fall by more than (or rise by less than) the yield on the contract sold.

The empirical evidence on the price behavior of financial futures contracts suggests that near contracts (contracts with shorter maturities) are generally affected to a larger degree by a set of events than are distant contracts (contracts with longer maturities). A bullish spreader would, therefore, buy the near contract and sell the distant contract. The bearish spreader would do precisely the opposite. Profits will accrue depending on whether the market is inverted (price of near contract P_N > price of distant contract P_D) or is noninverted ($P_N < P_D$) and on whether the spread strengthens or weakens.

1. $P_D > P_N$ (noninverted market) with $P_D - P_N > 0$
    a. If $P_D - P_N$ approaches zero, the spread is strengthening (narrowing).
    b. If $P_D - P_N \gg 0$, the spread is weakening (widening).
2. $P_D < P_N$ (inverted market) with $P_D - P_N < 0$.
    a. If $P_D - P_N \ll 0$, the spread is strengthening.
    b. If $P_D - P_N$ approaches zero, the spread is weakening.

The price differentials reported on spreads are not absolute values. Practitioners prefer absolute values, however. We believe that our method is easier and can be consistently used across futures contracts regardless of the underlying commodity, as demonstrated in this and the following chapter.

To illustrate the various intermonth strategies and their consequences, we begin with the bull spread in the noninverted market case.

Noninverted Market

		Yield	Price
Assume	Distant contract (D, six-month)	11.60	88.40
	Near contract (N, three-month)	11.80	88.20

Bull spread strategy	Buy near	88.20	$P_D - P_N = 0.20$
	Sell distant	88.40	

The near contract is expected to appreciate by more than the distant contract. Otherwise, no profit will accrue from the position. Thus, a profitable bull spread.

After (with greater appreciation)

	Sell near	88.30	$P_D - P_N = 0.15$
	Buy distant	88.45	

Profit on near $= 88.30 - 88.2 = 0.10$,
Loss on distant $= 88.40 - 88.45 = (0.05)$
Net profit $= 0.10 - 0.05 = $ **0.05**

Profits can also accrue if the near contract, for whatever reason, depreciates by less.
(with less depreciation)

Near	88.15	$P_D - P_N = 0.15$
Distant	88.30	

Loss on near $= (0.05)$, profit on distant $= 0.10$,
Net profit $= 0.10 - 0.05 = $ **0.05.**
The spread has strengthened: $0.20 > 0.15$.

Bear spread

		Yield	Price
Assume	Distant	11.60	88.40	$P_D - P_N = 0.20$
	Near	11.80	88.20

Bear spread strategy	Sell near	88.20	$P_D - P_N = 0.20$
	Buy distant	88.40	

The near contract is expected to depreciate by more.

After

	Buy near	88.10	$P_D - P_N = 0.25$
	Sell distant	88.35	

The spread has weakened (widened), thus the profitability of the bear spread.

Profit on near $= 88.20 - 88.10 = 0.10$
Loss on distant $= 88.40 - 88.35 = 0.05$
Net profit $= 0.10 - 0.05 = $ **0.05**

We now discuss the bull and bear spreads under inverted market conditions.

Inverted Market

An inverted market is quite normal for financial futures.

		Yield	Price
Assume	Distant (six month)	11.80	88.20
	Near (three-month)	11.60	88.40

Bull spread strategy Buy near $\quad$ 88.40
Sell distant $\quad$ 88.20 $\quad$ $P_D - P_N = -0.20$

Expect the near contract to appreciate more

After $\quad$ Sell near $\quad$ 88.55
Buy distant $\quad$ 88.25 $\quad$ $P_D - P_N = -0.30$

The spread has strengthened $-0.30 < -0.20$, thus the profitability of a bull spread in an inverted market.

Profit near $= 88.55 - 88.40 = 0.15$
Loss on distant $= 88.20 - 88.25 = (0.05)$
Net profit $= 0.15 - 0.05 =$ **0.10**

Bear spread strategy Sell near $\quad$ 88.40
Buy distant $\quad$ 88.20 $\quad$ $P_D - P_N = -0.20$

After $\quad$ Buy near $\quad$ 88.30
Sell distant $\quad$ 88.15 $\quad$ $P_D - P_N = -0.15$

The basis has weakened $-0.15 > -0.20$, which explains the profitability of the bear spread in an inverted market.

Profit on near $= 88.40 - 88.30 = 0.10$
Loss on distant $= 88.20 - 88.15 = (0.05)$
Net profit $= 0.10 - 0.05 =$ **0.05**

We now use an example to further illustrate the intermonth spreads.

Example 1

The current (Jan. 8, 1981) spread between the June '81 T-bill contract listed on the IMM and the December '81 contract is $+0.60(88.86 - 88.26)$ defining a downward sloping yield curve. The yield on the near contract $(100 - 88.26 = 11.74)$ is higher than the yield on the distant contract $(100 - 88.86 = 11.14)$. If, as a result of the budget cuts by the Reagan Administration, inflationary expectations are dampened considerably, and if, in addition, the Federal Reserve System pursues a less stringent monetary policy, the speculator may anticipate a change in the slope of the yield curve. If the expected price differential (the spread) is -0.20 $(P_D - P_N)$, the yield on the near contract would have to fall faster than that on the distant contracts (prices on nearby contracts rising faster than those on distant contracts.) The speculator would, therefore, set up a bull spread, for he expects the spread to strengthen.

1. Buy the June '81 contract.
2. Simultaneously, sell the December '81 contract.

If expectations materialize, large profits would accrue. Margin requirement on the spread $= \$1,000$ (less than one-third the margin requirement on either the long or the short position separately).

Returns = 80 basis points × 1,000,000 = **$8,000**
  (60 + 20)

Interinstrument Spreads.   From the diary of a financial futures trader,[21] we quote the following scenario and associated trading strategy. We think this is the easiest way to understand interinstrument spreads. The date is Sept. 26, 1979.

> *Currently, the GNMA market has been in a state of disarray. Demand has completely dried up and of course as a result an excess of supply has developed. This weak demand can be explained by several conditions.*
>
> *1. The current coupon is 9½% and the market is anticipating an increase to 10% coupon rate.*
> *2. When GNMAs are selling at a discount they become attractive to investors, because of the monthly paydown characteristic. Since all paydowns occur at par the purchaser of a discounted GNMA hopes for as much paydown results in a capital gain which increases the overall yield on the GNMA investment. The current situation is that housing turnover has slowed because of a slowing economy and higher interest rates which make home owners reluctant to give up their low-interest mortgages and assume new mortgages at today's rates.*
> *3. The spike in interest rates since Volcker took office as Chairman of the Federal Reserve and his announced intention to continue any necessary tightening has created a cautious atmosphere in the debt market. This skepticism leads to less institutional buying of long-term securities and what buying is done tends to occur in the safest issues. As a result, Treasury bonds experience strength relative to GNMAs.*
> *4. Technical factors have created a shortage of collateral in some of the Treasury bond issues. This also has resulted in strength in the T-bond market relative to the GNMA market.*
>
> *As a result of this market activity since early August, the spread relationship between Treasury bonds and GNMA futures has widened from its normal 2–4 point range (6.4/32–12.8/32) to a record 5½ points (17.6/32). While there is little reason to suggest that this spread will return to its normal range within the next 30 days, I feel that the risk reward level on the trade is rapidly becoming attractive. If the conditions which have created this aberration normalize, one would expect the spread relationship to come into 3 points (96/32) by June 1980.*
> *Specifically one might:*
>
> *Buy June 80 GNMAs*
> *Sell June 80 Treasury bonds*
> *Price difference—5½ pts.*
>
> *Because I see nothing to create an improvement in this technical situation before the November refunding, I would commit only half of available funds now and the other half in late October. I view the profit potential by June of 80 as being $2500/ct (read 25.00 per contract). I view the risk as $1000/ct. The margin requirement for this trade is $500/ct. The round trip commission cost is $140/ct. This trade should be profitable not as a function of any change in direction of interest rates, but as a function of a correction in technical factors.*

---

[21] From **Frank Mickel,** Vice President, E. F. Hutton, New York.

14.6 EFFICIENCY OF FINANCIAL FUTURES MARKETS

The futures markets play a dual role. They allow investors to hedge and they provide a mechanism for price discovery—information on the expected pattern of future spot prices on financial instruments. The efficiency question deals with how well futures predict spot rates to prevail in the future; that is, are futures prices unbiased predictors of future interest rates?

In an efficient market (even weakly efficient), perfect substitutes should sell at the same price; that is, no arbitrage opportunities exist. Donald J. Puglisi[22] tested this hypothesis for T-bill futures. His investor is presented with two options:

1. Buy nearby T-bill.
2. Buy distant T-bill and short futures contract.

In an efficient market, the investor should be indifferent between 1 and 2 and between:

3. Buy distant T-bill.
4. Buy nearby T-bill and go long the futures contract.

Puglisi tested whether the difference between alternatives 4 and 2 and alternatives 3 and 1 is substantially different from zero, using returns on futures contracts with nine months or less to maturity. His results led him to conclude that "the T-bill futures market is inefficient. While the major inefficiencies occurred early in the life of the new commodity future and have ebbed as the market has continued to mature. The systematic mispricing of T-bill futures has not been corrected over time."[23]

To arrive at this conclusion, Puglisi relied on the sign test to measure whether the mean difference between the investment strategies was significantly different from zero. He found that it was significantly different in six of the seven futures contracts examined. The sign test, however, does not take into account the economic significance of the signs, that is, the size of the deviations. The use of autocorrelation would have been far superior, for they would have measured reversals in the mean difference of returns on the two strategies—reversals that could be significant enough to negate earlier returns.

Anthony J. Vignola and Charles J. Dale used tests different from those of Puglisi, as well as different data sources to measure the efficiency of the T-bill futures market. Based on the values of the t statistics, they concluded that the T-bill futures market is inefficient and that "inefficiency has not diminished with the maturation of the market."[24]

William Poole tested the efficiency of the T-bill futures market by assuming that the arbitrageur holds a long-term T-bill, and that no interest is earned on margin deposited (an incorrect assumption for those investors who use T-bill to meet margin requirements). After developing an upper and a lower limit on the price of a T-bill futures contract trading on the IMM, he wanted to test whether futures rates fell within this quasi-arbitrage band. His conclusion was that "Quotes on the nearest maturity in the bill

[22] **Donald J. Puglisi,** "Is the Futures Market for Treasury?" *Journal of Portfolio Management,* Winter 1978.

[23] Ibid., p. 57.

[24] **Anthony J. Vignola** and **Charles J. Dale,** "Is the Futures Market for Treasury Bills Efficient?" *Journal of Portfolio Management,* Winter 1979, p. 62.

futures market can, therefore, be interpreted for all practical purposes as the market's unbiased estimates of the future spot rates on 13-week bills."[25]

Poole's analysis implied that the conclusion above applied to all maturities. Richard W. Lang and Robert Rasche set out to disprove this. Their results "do not support these conclusions about the relationship between futures rates and forward rates for futures contracts, except for the ones closest to delivery, which were the ones investigated by Poole."[26] Their null hypothesis (that the futures rate is equal to the associated forward rate) was tested by measuring if the mean absolute difference is significantly different from zero for each category. The categories used were determined by the time period between the spot market and the maturity date of the futures contract. Their tests led them to the following statement: "On the basis of this evidence, we cannot conclude that the differences between the futures and forward rates have been narrowing consistently over time as the futures market for Treasury bills has become more developed."[27]

Starting with an excellent data base and using a superior t-statistic, which takes autocorrelation into account, Richard Rendelman and Christopher Carabini tested if the observed IMM index values fall within their price range—a range equivalent to that derived by Poole. Their conclusion was as follows:

> *To the extent that quasi-arbitrage [arbitrage involving transactions costs and commitment of funds] opportunities have existed in the market, there appears to have been a tendency for the market to become less efficient over time. The pricing of the near term contract has become less efficient while the pricing of the third contract has become more efficient. However, it is doubtful that these inefficiencies have been large enough to induce portfolio managers to alter their investment policies.*[28]

14.7 EFFECTS OF THE T-BILL FUTURES MARKET ON THE CASH T-BILL MARKET

The effects of T-bill futures market on the cash T-bill market is of great concern to policymakers. If futures markets increase the volatility of the cash markets, investors would demand a larger risk premium on cash T-bills and consequently the cost to the borrower, the government of the United States, increases. Observers of the government securities market report a rising demand for T-bills in months in which futures conracts mature.[29]

Richard Gardner ran various regression tests to measure the impact of T-bill futures on the stability of cash T-bill rates. His conclusion is that "The regression results strongly indicate that Treasury bill futures have not destabilized the Treasury bill cash market. In addition, the systematic and random variability of cash T-bill rates were reduced in

---

[25] **Poole, William,** "Using T-Bill Futures to Gauge Interest Rate Expectations." *Federal Reserve Bank of San Francisco & Economic Review,* Spring, 1978.

[26] **Richard W. Lang** and **Robert H. Rasche,** "A Comparison of Yields on Futures Contracts and Implied Forward Rates." *Review, Federal Reserve Bank of St. Louis,* December 1978, p. 21.

[27] Ibid., p. 25.

[28] **Richard J. Rendelman** and **Christopher E. Carabini,** "The Efficiency of the Treasury Bill Futures Market." *Journal of Finance,* vol. 34, no. 4 (September 1979), p. 913.

[29] See *Financial Times,* Aug. 7, 1980.

the period after futures trading and cash T-bill rates became more efficient in a capital market theory sense."[30]

The problem with Gardner's conclusion lies in the nature of the statistical technique he employs. Regression analysis, while it measures the relationship among variables, says nothing about causation. It is not possible to isolate the impact of the introduction of futures contracts on the financial markets. The reduction in "random variability" could be due to factors other than futures contracts. Gardner's conclusion about the impact of futures markets on stability must be considered tentative. Further research in the area is required.

14.8 TAX CONSIDERATIONS

In November 1978, the IRS ruled that T-bill futures are capital assets.[31] As capital assets, they enjoy a very peculiar feature. Gains or losses on T-bill futures contracts are considered long-term only after a six-month holding period.[32] The ruling by the IRS also disallowed the deductibility of losses from spread unless a real economic loss is incurred. Prior to the ruling, investors set up spreads in order to reduce tax liability. Before the end of the tax year (1980), investors would, for example:

1. Buy March 81 contracts.
2. Simultaneously, sell September 81 contracts.

Assuming the yields on both contracts are highly correlated, and they usually are, the loss (gain) on one contract should offset the gain (loss) on the other.

When the end of 1980 arrives, the spreader would close the position that produced a loss. The other half of the spread will be closed in 1981. Spreads of this kind, intended to reduce the tax liability, would not produce tax-deductible losses under the 1978 rule.

Investors are advised to seek competent legal advice before establishing positions in the futures markets, particularly for the complex ones.

CONCLUSIONS

The interest of hedgers and speculators in financial futures continues to increase steadily. While mindful of the advantages of the financial futures market, a trader should be careful of the pitfalls. What this chapter attempts to do is to provide the basic framework for analyzing relationships in the marketplace and to show a few of the many ways to capitalize on them. Chapter 15 delves further into futures contracts: commodities futures.

---

[30] **Richard M. Gardner,** "The Effects of the T-Bill Futures Market on the Cash T-Bill Market." Working Paper, *Chicago Mercantile Exchange,* April 1979.

[31] Rev. Rul. 78–414, 1978–42 CB 213.

[32] Only long positions qualify, however. All gains and losses on short positions are short-term, regardless of the holding period.

QUESTIONS

1. "The presence of more than one commodity exchange is socially undesirable, for it contributes to the decentralization of the market." Comment.

2. How does interest rate volatility affect the investor? What opportunities do current wide gyrations offer that were not available in past stable conditions?

3. There are several alternatives to the financial futures market. What are they? Why have they not been very successful as a hedging or a speculative tool?

4. The profitability of an intermonth financial futures spread depends on the behavior of the basis. What must the basis do for a bull spread to realize a profit in a noninverted market?

5. Spreading is quite popular among speculators. What are the special characteristics that will make spreads more attractive than other strategies?

6. What is the difference between yield maintenance and price maintenance?

7. The pricing of futures contracts traded on the CBT off NYFE is a very treacherous if not a misguided endeavor. Why? Be specific.

8. The liquidity of a futures contract is critical to its success. Do you believe that the lack of success of NYFE is attributable to the limited liquidity of their contract? Explain.

9. Show the easiest and most correct way for pricing a financial futures contract.

10. What opportunities will stock market index futures offer investors? What effects should they have on the stock market itself?

11. A strategy known as "cash and carry" is gaining popularity among bond traders. It involves a short position in a financial futures contract and owning a U.S. government bond that is deliverable against the contract. What requirements concerning a bond's deliverability make the strategy possible? Might this strategy explain a flat yield curve beyond 15 years?

12. What properties do T-bills have that make them an ideal instrument upon which to write futures contracts?

13. To what factors would you attribute the growth of futures markets?

14. What options does an investor have to close out a short position in the futures market?

15. An investor feels she may have made an unwise purchase of a T-bill. How might she use the futures market?

16. Define the "basis." What are its implications to futures strategies?

17. How might speculators use futures markets? What opportunities, otherwise unavailable, do they offer?

18. How does the relationship between the basis and carrying costs offer a profit potential to speculators?

19. Based on the evidence presented in this chapter, what can you conclude about the efficiency of the futures market? What would be the implications of proof that futures markets affect the cash markets?

PROBLEMS

1. What is the maximum daily price fluctuation for a $1 million T-bill future selling on the NYFE? The CBT? What implications do these restrictions have?

2. An arbitrageur observes that a 91-day T-bill yields 9.20 percent, a 182-day bill yields 9.80 percent, and a futures contract requiring delivery of a 91-month T-bill three months hence is priced so as to yield 10.2 percent. What action would he take?

3. Calculate the theoretical price (on April 1) of a futures contract to deliver a six-month T-bill on October 1. A one-year bill maturing in six months (on October 1) yields 10.3 percent and a newly issued one-year T-bill currently yields 10.8 percent.

4. On Jan. 12, 1982, a banker intends to roll over $10 million in CDs (liability) maturing in three months. He is obviously concerned with changes in interest rates and decides to protect his position. The current quotation on the closest contract to his time horizon (the June 1982 contract) is 86.67 (settlement price).
    a. Would he establish a long or a short position?
    b. How many contracts? Justify.
    c. Calculate his profits or losses on April 12, 1982, if the spot T-bill rate is now 86.0 and if the basis weakens by 10 basis points. Recalculate if the basis strengthens by 10 points.

CHAPTER

15

Nonfinancial Commodities Futures

15.1 AN OVERVIEW

The preceding chapter dealt with financial futures and their use for hedging bond portfolios and for speculation. This chapter looks at some of the remaining commodities futures, leaving currency futures contracts for Chapter 16.

15.2 FUTURES CONTRACT REDEFINED

A futures contract is evidence of a commitment to deliver or accept delivery, at a designated time in the future, of a specified quantity and quality of a commodity at an auction price determined at the time the contract is entered into.

Definitions of terms related to futures contracts appear in the appendix of this chapter.

15.3 THE ORIGIN OF COMMODITY FUTURES CONTRACTS

Futures contracts began as forward contracts where buyers and sellers agreed to sell or take delivery of a specified quality and quantity of a commodity at a specified future date.

The use of forward contracts became a necessity once spot markets proved their inability to handle excess supply or excess demand for commodities. For example, the dumping of excess grain in the Chicago River[1] became a common practice among wheat producers who were unable to sell their harvest in the spot market because of excessively low prices and the absence of adequate storage facilities.

The forward contract was only a partial answer to the problem. While it matched buyers with sellers, so that farmers were assured a sale at a certain price and users were assured an adequate supply of commodities at a known price, the forward contract was unable to provide a mechanism for hedging price risks due to sudden price changes and was not sufficiently liquid. The forward contract was merely a mechanism for making

---

[1] See the *Commodity Trading Manual* of the Chicago Board of Trade, 1980.

or assuring delivery of the actual commodity. It is simply a cash market with a deferred delivery. The first centralized market in futures contracts began with the establishment of the Chicago Board of Trade in 1848. The first futures contract was traded in the mid 1870s.

15.4 ORGANIZATION OF FUTURES MARKETS

Today there are 11 commodity changes: the Chicago Board of Trade; the Chicago Mercantile Exchange with its important division, the International Monetary Market; the Coffee, Sugar and Cocoa Exchange (New York); the Commodity Exchange, Inc. (New York); the Board of Trade of Kansas City, Missouri, Inc.; the Mid-American Commodity Exchange (Chicago); the Minneapolis Grain Exchange; the New York Cotton Exchange; the Citrus Associates of the New York Cotton Exchange, Inc.; the Petroleum Associates of the New York Cotton Exchange, Inc.; and the New York Mercantile Exchange. The most significant commodity exchange and one of the most innovative is the Chicago Board of Trade.

Most of these exchanges are not-for-profit associations with limited memberships. A member can be an individual, a partnership, a cooperative, or a corporation. A membership may be purchased as an investment, may be leased, or may be used by the holder to transact business on the floor of the exchange.

Settlements of day-to-day transactions on the exchanges are handled by the clearinghouses, which are either independent organizations or subsidiaries of the exchanges. The clearing corporation, as explained in Chapter 14, interposes itself between the buyer and the seller in each contract. The sale of a futures contract is effectively a sale to the clearing corporation, and a purchase of a futures contract is a purchase from the clearing corporation.

Additionally, and in order to preserve the liquidity and the integrity of the futures market, the clearing corporation clears margins. The margin requirements (a "performance bond" of sorts) on each futures contract are set by the exchanges on which the contracts are traded. Exchange members must post the required margin on their net short or long position on a daily basis. That is, if the net short (sell) position of a member is five contracts, that member would be required to deposit five times the margin requirements of one contract. Some exchanges do not allow for the netting of short positions against long positions and thus require separate margins on both the long and the short positions.

The settlement of the clearing margins is made daily, prior to the opening of trading the following day. The clearing member can use cash, government securities, stock in the clearing corporation, and letters of credit issued by an approved bank in meeting the margin call.

Under certain circumstances, the clearing corporation will vary the margin requirement. This is referred to as a *variation margin call,* which must be paid within an hour using a certified check. Such calls are made when market conditions are very volatile.

Members with losses in their open positions are required to put up additional margin (maintenance margin), and those with gains will be able to withdraw the full amount of the profit.

The clearing corporation provides several additional services. Among them are market

FIGURE 15.1 Futures trading on the U.S. exchanges—volume of trading FY 1956–1980. (Figures include volume of trading of nonregulated commodities for the years 1956–1974.)

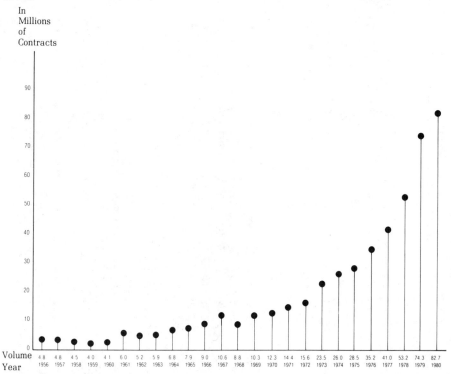

In Millions of Contracts

| Volume | 4.8 | 4.8 | 4.5 | 4.0 | 4.1 | 6.0 | 5.2 | 5.9 | 6.8 | 7.9 | 9.0 | 10.6 | 8.8 | 10.3 | 12.3 | 14.4 | 15.6 | 23.5 | 26.0 | 28.5 | 35.2 | 41.0 | 53.2 | 74.3 | 82.7 |
| Year | 1956 | 1957 | 1958 | 1959 | 1960 | 1961 | 1962 | 1963 | 1964 | 1965 | 1966 | 1967 | 1968 | 1969 | 1970 | 1971 | 1972 | 1973 | 1974 | 1975 | 1976 | 1977 | 1978 | 1979 | 1980 |

Source: Commodity Futures Trading Commission: Annual Report 1980. Washington, D.C., p. 88.

information and a systematic procedure for deliveries against the contracts. Less than 3 percent of commodity contracts are delivered against, yet detailed prescriptions for deliveries have been instituted by all the exchanges.

15.5 THE NATURE OF THE COMMODITIES FUTURES MARKET

The success of the futures markets is evidenced by the explosive growth in the volume of trades and the frequent addition of new contracts.

The growth of futures contract trading is illustrated in Figure 15.1. From 4.8 million contracts in 1956, trading grew to 82.7 million contracts in 1980. The distribution of these trades among the various commodities is shown in Table 15.1. Grain, oilseed products, metals, and financial futures contracts lead respectively in terms of trading activity. Only a slim percentage of contracts traded is ever delivered against, as shown in the bottom of Table 15.1.

The characteristics of the various nonfinancial futures contracts by category are shown in Table 15.2. Several entries in this table merit some discussion.

The trading months are select months of the year, occasionally every month, which best correspond to the nature of the demand by hedgers of a given commodity.

TABLE 15.1

Average Month-End Open Interest, Estimated Number of Contracts Traded, and Number of Contracts Settled by Delivery, by Major Groups, All Markets Combined

Fiscal Year	Total	Grain	Oilseeds/ Products	Livestock/ Products	Foodstuffs	Industrial Materials	Metals	Financial Instruments	Currencies
Average Monthend Open Interest (in Contracts)									
1960	149,356	41,781[a]	39,906	—	50,592	7,088	9,989	—	—
1970	348,630	72,745[a]	86,809	47,457	59,784	4,455	77,380	—	6,278
TQ	888,080	189,604	172,809	52,329	73,873	37,148	350,556	5,483	10,204
1977	1,121,570	176,270	196,513	76,027	88,662	38,728	517,257	17,909	22,578
1978	1,385,112	209,751	203,352	121.126	77,133	44,146	649,805	57,221	34,257
1979	1,710,727	247,756	244,532	143,776	74,270	50,578	729,148	186,410	34,257
1980	1,488,306	289,159	249,306	126,881	117,765	61,538	400,483	190,966	52,262
Number of Contracts Traded[b]									
1960	3,656,381	1,117,827[a]	1,434,368	—	875,592	129,601	98,993	—	—
1970	12,398,188	2,162,179[a]	3,676,702	3,431,947	1,960,894	56,057	1,110,409	—	—
TQ	9,546,331	2,749,329	2,696,595	1,204,492	535,198	382,151	1,875,335	63,602	39,629
1977	41,022,825	7,928,127	13,474,905	5,632,917	2,447,436	1,677,355	8,864,229	604,622	393,234
1978	53,222,321	10,227,983	14,037,111	8,501,774	2,335,210	1,785,649	13,393,704	1,595,363	1,345,527
1979	74,309,239	13,023,423	16,569,675	11,529,178	2,359,884	2,374,090	21,878,549	4,570,694	2,003,746
1980	82,727,169	18,323,003	15,691,770	11,807,659	5,314,210	3,559,799	14,099,125	10,212,968	3,718,635
Number of Contracts Settled by Delivery									
1960	48,495	21,416	14,289	—	8,595	2,030	2,165	—	—
1970	76,908	15,948	14,774	7,516	9,404	1,862	27,404	—	—
TQ	98,565	21,317	32,789	1,561	3,725	4,316	33,763	372	722
1977	318,562	66,089	92,645	6,025	21,424	11,463	114,589	2,267	4,060
1978	314,315	56,974	52,219	5,931	15,966	8,164	160,916	5,315	8,830
1979	410,606	65,093	93,217	14,171	25,194	5,588	179,132	21,350	6,861
1980	598,898	65,998	170,748	15,088	29,798	7,189	254,679	32,854	22,544

Source: Commodity Futures Trading Commission: Annual Report 1980. Washington, D.C., p. 89.

[a] Based on a standard 5,000-bushel contract.

[b] Figures from Futures Industry Association.

TABLE 15.2a
Trading Facts and Figures

Exchange	Commodity	Trading Months	Trading Hours (Central Time)	Contract Size	Price Quoted In	Minimum Price Fluctuation	Daily Limit
Chicago Board of Trade	Iced Broilers	Jan/Feb/Mar/Apr/ Sept/Oct/Nov	9:15-1:05	30,000 lbs	¢/lb	2.5/100¢/lb = $7.50	2¢ = $600
	Commercial Paper 90-Day	Mar/June/Sept/Dec	8:30-1:35	Face Value at maturity of $1,000,000	as an annualized discount	1/100 of 1% of $1,000,000 (1 basis point) = $50.00	50 pt = $1250 Points = $625
	Commercial Paper 30-Day	Mar/Jun/Sept/Dec	8:30-1:45	Face Value at maturity of $3,000,000	as an annualized discount	1 pt. = $50.00	25 pt. = $1,250
	Corn	Mar/May/July/Sept/ Dec	9:30-1:15	5,000 bu	¢/bu	¼¢/bu = $12.50	10¢ = $500
	GNMA	Mar/May/Jun/Sept/ Oct/Nov/Dec	8:00-2:00	$100,000 principal	32nds/per point	1/32 point = $31.25	64/32 = $2,000
	Gold	All months	8:25-1:35	100 Troy Oz.	$/oz	10¢/oz = $10.00	$25 = $2,500
	Oats	Mar/May/July/ Sept/Dec	9:30-1:15	5,000 bu	¢/bu	1/4¢/bu = $12.50	6¢ = $300
	Plywood	Jan/Mar/May/July/ Sept/Nov	9:00-1:00	76,032 sq ft	$/thousand square feet	10¢/1000 sq ft. = $7.60 (1 pt = 76¢)	$7 = $532 (700 pts)
	Silver	Feb/Apr/June/Aug/ Oct/Dec	8:40-1:25	5,000 troy oz	¢/oz	1/10¢/oz = $5	40¢ = $2000
	Soybeans	Jan/Mar/May/July/ Aug/Sept/Nov	9:30-1:15	5,000 bu	¢/bu	1/4¢/bu = $12.50	30¢ = $1,500
	Soybean Meal	Jan/Mar/May/July/ Aug/Sept/Oct/Dec	9:30-1:15	100 tons (200,000 lbs)	$/ton	10¢/ton = $10	$10 = $1,000
	Soybean Oil	Jan/Mar/May/July/ Aug/Sept/Oct/Dec	9:30-1:15	60,000 lbs	¢/lb	1/100¢/lb = $6	1¢ = $600 (100 pts)
	Long-Term U.S. Treasury Bonds	Mar/June/Sept/Dec	8:00-2:00	Bonds with face value at maturity of $100,000 and coupon rate of 8%	32nds per point	1/32nd of a point = $31.25	64/32 = $2,000
	Wheat	Mar/May/July/Sept/ Dec	9:30-1:15	5,000 bu	¢/bu	1/4¢/bu = $12.50	20¢ = $1,000
MidAmerica Commodity Exchange	Silver	Feb/Apr/June/Aug/ Oct/Dec/	8:40-1:25	1,000 troy oz	¢/oz	1/10¢/oz = $1	40¢ = $400
	Corn	Mar/May/July/Sept/ Dec	9:30-1:30	1,000 bu	¢/bu	1/8¢/bu = $1.25	10¢ = $100
	Gold	Mar/Jun/Sept/Dec	8:25-1:40	33.2 (troy oz)	$/oz	2.5¢/troyoz = .83	$50 = $1,660
	Hogs	Feb/Apr/June/July/ Aug/Oct/Dec	9:15-1:05	15.000 lbs	¢/lbs	2.5/100¢/lb = $3.75 (1 pt = $1.50)	1.5¢ = $225 (150 pts)
	Oats	Mar/May/July/Sept/ Dec	9:30-1:30	5,000 bu	¢/bu	1/8¢/bu = $6.25	6¢ = $300
	Silver	Feb/Apr/June/Aug/ Oct/Dec/Spot	8:40-1:40	1,000 troy oz	¢/oz	5/100¢/oz = $.50	40¢ = $400
	Cattle	Jan/Feb/Apr/June/ Aug/Oct/Dec	9:05-1:00	20,000lbs	¢/lb	2.5/100¢/lb = $5 (1 pt = $2)	1.5¢ = $300 (150 pts)
	Soybeans	Jan/Mar/May/July/ Aug/Sept/Nov	9:30-1:30	1,000 bu	¢/bu	1/8¢/bu = $1.25	30¢ = $300
	Wheat	Mar/May/July/Sept/ Dec	9:30-1:30	1,000 bu	¢/bu	1/8¢/bu = $1.25	20¢ = $200
Chicago Mercantile Exchange	Boneless Beef	Feb/Apr/June/Aug/ Oct/Dec	9:05-12:45	38,000 lbs	$/cwt	2.5/100¢/lb = $9.50 (1 pt = $3.80)	1.5¢ = $570 (150 pts)
	Broilers, Fresh	Feb/Apr/Jun/ Jul/Aug/Oct/Dec	9:10-1:00	30,000 lbs	¢/lb	2.5/100¢/lb = $7.50 (1 pt = $3.00)	2¢ = $600 (200 pts)
	Butter	Mar/May/Oct/Nov/Dec	9:25-12:35	38,000 lbs	¢/lb	2.5/100¢/lb = $9.50 (1 pt = $3.80)	1.5¢ = $570 (150 pts)
	Cattle, Feeder	Jan/Mar/Apr/May/ Aug/Sept/Oct/Nov	9:05-12:45	42,000 lbs	¢/lb	2.5/100¢/lb = $10.50 (1 pt = $4.20)	1.5¢ = $630 (150 pts)
	Cattle, Live	Jan/Feb/Apr/June/ Aug/Oct/Dec	9:05-12:45	40,000 lbs	¢/lb	2.5/100¢/lb = $10 (1 pt = $4)	1.5¢ = $600 (150 pts)
	Eggs, Shell (Fresh)	All Months except Aug	9:20-1:00	22,500 doz	¢/doz	5/100¢/doz = $11.25 (1 pt = $2.25)	2¢ = $450 (200 pts)
	Eggs, Frozen	Jan/Sept/Oct/Nov/ Dec	9:20-1:00	36,000 lbs	¢/lb	2.5/100¢/lb = $9 (1 pt = $3.60)	1.5¢ = $540 (150 pts)
	Eggs, Nest Run	All Months	9:20-1:00	22.500 doz	¢/doz	5/100¢/doz = $11.25 (1 pt = $2.25)	2¢ = $450 (200 pts)
	Hams, Skinned	Mar/July/Nov	9:10-1:00	36,000 lbs	¢/lb	2.5/100¢/lb = $9 (1 pt = $3.60)	1.5¢ = $540 (150 pts)
	Hogs	Feb/Apr/June/July/ Aug/Oct/Dec	9:10-1:00	30,000 lbs	¢/lb	2.5/100¢/lb = $7.50 (1 pt = $3)	1.5¢ = $450 (150 pts)

TABLE 15.2a (*Continued*)
Trading Facts and Figures

Exchange	Commodity	Trading Months	Trading Hours (Central Time)	Contract Size	Price Quoted In	Minimum Price Fluctuation	Daily Limit
	Lumber	Jan/Mar/May/July/Sept/Nov	9:00-1:05	100,000 board feet	$/thousand board ft	10¢/1,000 bd ft = $10 (1 pt = $1)	$5 = $500 (500 pts)
	Stud Lumber	Jan/Mar/May/July/Sept/Nov	9:00-1:05	100,000 board feet	$/thousand board feet	10¢/1,000 bd ft = $10 (1 pt = $1)	$5 = $500 (500 pts)
	Milo	Mar/May/July/Sept/Oct/Dec	9:30-1:15	400,000 lbs	$/cwt	2.5/100¢/cwt = $10 (1 pt. = $4.00)	15¢ = $600 (15 pts)
	Pork Bellies	Feb/Mar/May/July/Aug	9:10-1:00	38,000 lbs	¢/lb	2.5/100¢/lb = $9.50 (1 pt = $3.80)	2¢ = $760 (200 pts)
	Potatoes, Russet Burbank	Jan/Mar/May/Nov	9:00-1:00	80,000 lbs	¢/cwt	1¢/cwt = $8 (1 pt. = $8.00)	50¢ = $400** (50 pts)
	Turkeys	Jan/Mar/May/Aug/Oct	9:10-12:45	36,000 lbs	¢/lb	2.5/100¢/lb = $9 (1 pt = $3.60)	1.5¢ = $540 (150 pts)
International Monetary Market of the Chicago Mercantile Exchange	Copper	Jan/Mar/May/July/Sept/Nov	8:45-1:15	12,500 lbs	¢/lb	10/100¢/lb = $12.50 (1 pt = $1.25)	5¢ = $625 (500 pts)
	Currencies: British Pound	Jan/Mar/Apr/Jun/Jul/Sept/Oct/Dec & Spot	7:30-1:24	25,000 BP	¢/BP	.0005/lb = $12.50 (1 pt = $2.50)	5¢ = $1,250 (500 pts)
	Canadian Dollar	Jan/Mar/Apr/Jun/Jul/Sept/Oct/Dec & Spot	7:30-1:22	100,000 CD	¢/CD	.0001/CD = $10 (1 pt = $10)	3/4¢ = $750 (75 pts)
	Dutch Guilder	Jan/Mar/Apr/Jun/Jul/Sept/Oct/Dec & Spot	7:30-1:30	125,000 DG	¢/DG	.0001/DG = $12.50 (1 pt = $12.50)	.0100 = $1250 (100 pts)
	French Franc	Jan/Mar/Apr/Jun/Jul/Sept/Oct/Dec & Spot	7:30-1:28	250,000 FF	¢/FF	5/1000¢/FF = $12.50 (1 pt = $2.50)	1/2¢ = $1,250 (500 pts)
	Deutschemark	Jan/Mar/Apr/Jun/Jul/Sept/Oct/Dec & Spot	7:30-1:20	125,000 DM	¢/DM	.0001/DM = $12.50 (1 pt = $12.50)	.0100 = $1,250 (100 pts)
	Japanese Yen	Jan/Mar/Apr/Jun/Jul/Sept/Oct/Dec & Spot	7:30-1:26	12,500,000 Yen	¢/Yen	.000001/Y = $12.50 (1 pt = $12.50)	.0001 = $1,250 (100 pts)
	Mexican Peso	Jan/Mar/Apr/Jun/Jul/Sept/Oct/Dec & Spot	7:30-1:18	1,000,000 Peso	¢/Peso	.00001/P = $10 (1 pt = $10)	3/20¢ = $1,500 (150 pts)
	Swiss Franc	Jan/Mar/Apr/Jun/Jul/Sept/Oct/Dec & Spot	8:45-1:13	125,000 SF	¢/SF	1/100¢/SF = $12.50 (1 pt = $12.50)	3/5¢ = $1,875 (150 pts)
	Gold	Jan/Mar/Apr/Jun/Jul/Sept/Oct/Dec/ & Spot	8:25-1:30	100 troy oz	$/oz	10¢/oz = $10 1 pt = $1	$50 = $5,000 (5000 pts)
	U.S. Silver Coins	Mar/June/Sept/Dec	8:50-1:25	$5,000 (5 bags @ $1,000)	$/bag	$2/bag = $10 1 pt = $1	$150 = $750 (150 pts)
International Monetary Market of the Chicago Mercantile Exchange (cont'd.)	Treasury Bills 13 Weeks	Jan/Mar/Apr/Jun/Jul/Sep/Oct/Dec	8:00-1:40	$1,000,000	Basis Point(IMM Index)	.01 1 basis point = $25	60 pts = $1,250 (60 pts)
	Treasury Bills 1 Year	Mar/June/Sept/Dec	8:15-1:35	250,000	Basis Point (1MM Index)	1 basis point = $25	50 pts = $1,250
	U.S. Treasury Notes Four Year	Feb/May/Aug/Nov	8:20-1:55	$100,000		.01 (in 64ths of 1%) 1 pt. = $15.62	48 = $750
Commodity Exchange (Comex)	Copper	Jan/Feb/Mar/May/July/Sept/Dec	8:50-1:00	25,000 lbs	¢/lb	5/100¢/lb = $12.50 (1 pt = $2.50)	5¢ = $1250 (500 pts)
	GNMA	Jan/Feb/Apr/July/Oct/Dec	8:00-2:30	$100,000	$/¹⁄₆₄	¹⁄₆₄ = $15.62	⁶⁴⁄₆₄ = $1.000
	Gold	Jan/Feb/Apr/June/Aug/Oct/Dec	8:25-1:30	3 Kilo (100 troy oz)	$/oz	.10¢/oz = $10	$25 = $2500
	Silver	Jan/Feb/Mar/May/July/Sept/Dec	8:40-1:15	5,000 troy oz	¢/oz	10/100¢/oz = $25.00	50¢ = $2500
	Treasury Bills	Feb/May/Aug/Nov	8:00-2:30	$1,000,000	Basis Point (Comex Index)	.01 = $25	60 pts. = $1500
	Treasury Notes Two-Year	Mar/June/Sept/Dec	8:00-2:30	$100,000	$/¹⁄₆₄	¹⁄₆₄ = $15.62	⁶⁴⁄₆₄ = 1.000
	Zinc	Jan/Feb/Mar/May/July/Sept/Dec	9:15-11:45	60,000 lbs	¢/lb	5/100¢/lb = $30 (1 pt = $6.00)	.3¢ = $1800 (300 pts)
New York Coffee Sugar & Cocoa Exchange	Cocoa	Mar/May/July/Sept/Dec	8:30-2:00	10 metric tons	¢/ton	$1.00/ton = $10.00 (1 pt. = $10.00)	$88 = $880 (88 pts)
	Coffee "C"	Mar/May/July/Sept/Dec	8:45-1:30	37,500 lbs	¢/lb	1/100¢/lbs = $3.75 (1 pt = $3.75)	4¢ = $1,500 (400 pts)
	Coffee "B"	Mar/May/July/Sept/Dec	8:45-1:30	32,500 lbs	¢/lb	1/100¢/lb = $3.25 (1 pt = $3.25)	4¢ = $1,300 (400 pts)

Exchange	Commodity	Trading Months	Trading Hours (Central Time)	Contract Size	Price Quoted In	Minimum Price Fluctuation	Daily Limit
	Sugar No. 11 (World)	Jan/Mar/May/July/ Sept/Oct	9:00-1:45	112,000 lbs	¢/lbs (1 pt = $11.20)	1/100¢/lb = $11.20 (100 pts)	½¢ = $560 (50 pts)
	Sugar No. 12 (Domestic)	Jan/Mar/May/July/ Sept/Nov	9:00-1:45	112,000 lbs	¢/lb	1/100¢/lb = 11.20 (1 pt = $11.20)	½¢ = $560 (50 pts)
New York Cotton Exchange	Cotton No. 2	All months	9:30-2:00	50,000 lbs	¢/lb	1/100¢/lb = $5 (1 pt = $5)	2¢ = $1,000 (200 pts)
	Crude Oil	Mar/June/Sept/Dec	8:50-1:20	5,000 barrels	¢/barrels	1/10¢/barrel = $5	25¢ = $1,250 (250 pts)
	Orange Juice	Jan/Mar/May/July/ Sept/Nov	9:15-1:45	15,000 lbs	¢/lb	5/100¢/lb = $7.50 (1 pt = $1.50)	5¢ = $750 (500 pts)
	Propane, Liquified	Jan/Mar/May/July/ Sept//Dec	8:45-1:35	100,000 gals	¢/gal	1/100¢/gal = $10 (1 pt = $10)	1¢ = $1,000 (100 pts)
New York Mercantile Exchange	Gold	Jan/Mar/May/ July/Sep/Dec	8:25-1:30	1 kilo (32 troy oz)	$/oz	20¢/oz = $6.40	$24 = $768
	Gold, 400 oz	Mar/June/Sept/Dec	8:25-1:30	400 oz bar (Four 100 oz bars) (12 or 13 kilo bars)	$/oz	5¢/oz = $20	$25 = $10,000
	Imported Boneless Beef	Jan/Mar/May/July/ Sept/Nov	9:15-12:45	36,000 lbs	$/100 lbs (or ¢/lb)	2¢/100 lbs = $7.20 (1 pt = $3.60)	$1.50 = $540 (150 pts)
	Oil, Heating No. 2	Jan/Feb/Mar/May/ July/Aug/Sept/ Nov/Dec	9:30-1:45	42,000 gal	¢/gal	$.0001/gal = $4.20	.02/gal = $840
	Oil Industrial No. 6	Jan/Feb/Mar/May/ July/Sept/Nov/Dec	9:35-1:43	42,000 gal	¢/gal	$.0001/gal = $4.20	.02/gal = $840
	Palladium	Jan/Apr/July/Oct	8:35-1:20	100 troy oz	$/oz	5¢/oz = $5	$6 = $360 (600 pts)
	Platinum	Jan/Apr/July/Oct	8:30-1:30	50 troy oz	$/oz	10¢/oz = $5	$20 = $1,000
	Potatoes, Maine and Round White	Mar/Apr/May/Nov	9:00-1:00	50,000 lbs	$/100 lbs (or ¢/lb)	1¢/100 lbs = $5 (1 pt = $5)	50¢ = $250 (50 pts)
	U.S. Silver Coins	Jan/Apr/July/Oct	8:40-1:15	$10,000 (10 bags @ $1,000)	$/bag	$1/bag = $10	$150 = $3,000 ($300 per bag)
New York Futures Exchange NYFE	U.S. Treasury Bond, 20 Year	Feb/May/Aug/Nov	8:00-2:00	$100,000	32nds per pt	1/32 of a point $31.25	96/32 (3 pts) = $3000
	Treasury Bills 90-Day	Jan/Apr/July/Oct	8:00-2:00	$1,000,000	.01 (1 Basis Point)	.01 = $25	1.00 (100 Basis Points)
	British Pound	Feb/May/Aug/Nov	7:30-1:30	25,000 BP	¢/Pound	.0005 (5 pts) = $12.50	No Limit
	Canadian Dollar	Feb/May/Aug/Nov	7:30-1:30	100,000 CD	¢/CD	.0001/CD = $10 (1 pt = $10)	No Limit
	Deutsche Mark	Feb/May/Aug/Nov	7:30-1:30	125,000 DM	¢/DM	.0001/DM = $10 (1 pt = $10)	No Limit
	Japanese Yen	Feb/May/Aug/Nov	7:30-1:30	12,500,000	¢/Yen	.000001 (1 pt = $12.50)	No Limit
	Swiss Franc	Feb/May/Aug/Nov	7:30-1:30	125,000	¢/SF	.0001 = $10, (1 pt = $12.50)	No Limit
Minneapolis Grain Exchange	Spring Wheat	Mar/May/July/Sept/ Dec	9:30-1:15	5,000 bu	¢/bu	1/8¢/bu = $6.25	20¢ = $1,000
	Sunflower seed	Jan/Mar/May/July/ Nov	9:30-2:15	100,000 lbs.	¢/lb.	1¢/lb. = $10	50¢ = $500
Kansas City Board of Trade	Milo	Mar/May/July/Sept/ Dec	9:30-1:15	5,000 bu	¢/bu	1/4¢/bu = $12.50	10¢ = $500
	Wheat (Hard Red Winter)	Mar/May/July/Sept/ Dec	9:30-1:15	5,000 bu	¢/bu	1/4¢/bu = $12.50	25¢ = $1,250
Winnipeg Commodity Exchange	Barley	May/July/Oct/Dec	9:30-1:15	20 metric tons	$/ton	10¢/ton = $10	$5 = $1,000
	Flaxseed	May/July/Oct/Nov/ Dec	9:30-1:15	20 metric tons	$/ton	10¢/ton = $10	$10 = $2,000
	Gold, Centum	Feb/May/Aug/Nov	8:15-1:30	100 oz	$/oz	5¢/oz = $5	$10 = $1,000
	Gold, Standard	Jan/Apr/July/Oct	8:15-1:30	400 oz	$/oz	5¢/oz = $20	$10 = $4,000
	Oats	May/July/Oct/Dec	9:30-1:15	20 metric tons	$/ton	10¢/ton = $10	$5 = $1,000
	Rapeseed (Vancouver)	Jan/Mar/June/Sept/ Nov	9:30-1:15	20 metric tons	$/ton	10¢/ton = $10	$10 = $2,000
	Rye	May/July/Oct/Nov/ Dec	9:30-1:15	20 metric tons	$/ton	10¢/ton = $10	$5 = $1,000
	Wheat	May/July/Oct/Dec	9:30-1:15	20 metric tons	$/ton	10¢/ton = $10	$5 = $1,000

TABLE 15.2a (*Continued*)
Trading Facts and Figures

Exchange	Commodity	Trading Months	Trading Hours (Central Time)	Contract Size	Price Quoted In	Minimum Price Fluctuation	Daily Limit
New Orleans Commodity Exchange	Rough Rice	Jan/Mar/May July/Sep/Nov	9:45-1:45	2000 100wt 200,000 lbs	¢/cwt	.005/cwt ($10.00)	.30/cwt ($600)
	Milled Rice	Jan/Mar/May Sep/Nov	9:45-1:45	1200 100wt 120,000 lbs	¢/cwt	.005/cwt	.50/cwt ($600)
	Soybeans	Jan/Mar/May July/Oct/Nov	9:30-1:15	5,000 Bu	¢/Bu	.0025/Bu $12.50	.30/Bu ($1500)
	Cotton	Mar/May/July Oct/Dec	9:15-2:00	50,000 lbs 100 Bales	¢/lb	.0001/lb ($5.00)	.02/lb ($1000)

TABLE 15.2b
Overseas Exchanges

Exchange	Commodity	Trading Positions (Months)	Contract Size	Minimum Price Fluctuation	Trading Hours	Local times shown. London time = U.S. Eastern time plus 5 hours. Sydney, Australia time = U.S Eastern time plus 15 hours; i.e. noon Eastern time = 3 a.m. the next day in Sydney
Coffee Terminal Market Association of London	Coffee, Arabica	Feb/Apr/June/Aug/ Oct/Dec	3,450 kilos	1 lb/metric ton	10:15-4:15, Kerb calls 10:15, 5:05	
	Coffee, Robusta	Jan/Mar/May/July/ Sept/Nov	5 metric tons	1 lb/ton	10:30-5:00, Kerb calls 10:30, 12:20, 2:30, 4:50	
Grain & Feed Trade Association (GAFTA) (London)	EEC Grains (Wheat, Barley)	Jan/Mar/May/Sept/ Nov	100 tons	5 pence/ton	11:00-4:00	
	Soybean Meal	Feb/Apr/June/Aug/ Oct/Dec	100 tons	10 pence/ton	10:30-5:10 (Kerb and option trading are permitted)	
London Bullion Market	Gold Bullion	Spot and forward positions dated	400 troy oz	none	Twice daily with official fixings at 10:30 and 3:00, Kerb calls 1:05 and 4:35	
	Silver Bullion	Spot, 3-, 6- and 12-months forward dated	5,000 fine oz	1/10 pence/oz	Once daily with official fixing at 12:15, Kerb calls 1:05 and 4:35	
London Cocoa Terminal Market Association	Cocoa	Mar/May/July/ Sept/Dec	10 metric tons	50 pence/ton	10:00-4:00, Kerb calls 10:00, 12:58, 2:30, 3:30, 4:45	
London Rubber Terminal Market Association	Rubber No. 1	3-month contracts: Jan/Feb/Mar Apr/May/June July/Aug/Sept Oct/Nov/Dec	15 metric tons	5 pence/kilo	24 hours, Kerb call 9:45, 12:30, 2:30, 3:15, 4:45	
United Terminal Sugar Association (London)	Sugar No. 2	Mar/May/Aug/Oct/ Dec	50 metric tons	5 pence/ton	10:00-3:00, Kerb calls 10:40, 11:30, 1:30, 2:30, 3:45	
London Metal Exchange	Copper, Cathodes	****	25 metric tons	50 pence/ton	12:00-12:05, 12:40-12:45, 4:20-4:25, 3:45-3:50, Kerb calls 12:45-1:05, 4:25-4:45	
	Copper, Wirebars	****	25 metric tons	50 pence/ton	12:00-12:05, 12:35-12:40, 3:45-3:50, 4:15-4:20, Kerb calls 12:45-1:05, 4:25-4:45	
	Lead	****	25 metric tons	50 pence/ton	12:15-12:20, 12:50-12:55, 3:35 3:40, 4:06-4:10, Kerb calls 12:55-1:15, 4:10-4:30	
	Silver	****	10,000 troy oz	1/10 pence/ton	12:05-12:10, 1:00-1:05, 3:55-4:00 4:30-4:35, Kerb calls 4:30-4:35, Kerb calls 1:05-1:25 4:35-5:55	
	Tin	****	5 metric tons	1/ton	12:10-12:15, 12:45-12:50, 3:50-3:55 4:25-4:30, Kerb calls 12:50-1:10 4:30-4:50	
	Zinc	****	25 metric tons	25 pence/ton	12:20-12:25, 12:55-1:00, 3:40-3:45, 4:10-4:15, Kerb calls 1:00-1:20 4:15-4:35	

*****Any single market day between current day (spot) and three months forward is traded on the London Metal Exchange.

Note > there are no daily limits on London or Sydney exchanges

Source: Archer Commodities, Inc., Chicago.

The contract size is standard for each commodity. This guarantees uniformity and increases the liquidity of the contract.

The daily limit on each contract is not permanent and can change rather frequently depending on market conditions. The daily limit is the maximum permitted price movement below or above the previous day's settlement price. It differs from one contract to another and sometimes from one exchange to another. Another limit is on the "range." The "daily range" is frequently the same as the daily limit. If the limit is 1 cent and the range is 2 cents, a contract can trade up 1 cent and then fall by the 2 cents allowed by the daily range.

Missing from Table 15.2 is the margin requirement. For a wheat contract, for example, the margin requirement is 20 cents per bushel or $1,000 per contract. This represents not a deposit on the contract but a performance bond. It is intended to at least cover the maximum allowable daily price fluctuation in the contract. A fall in the price of the contract calls for an additional commitment by the trader, and a rise (assuming a long position) releases cash to the trader. The settlement must be done daily. This should explain why commodities traders must have considerable liquidity in order to meet their margin calls.

Occasionally, the behavior of the price of a commodity may warrant revision of the margin requirements. The clearing corporation may call on its member firms to deposit additional margin under these circumstances. This is known as a variation margin call, which must be met by the member within one hour using a certified check. The member firm, in turn, would require its customer to increase his or her margin.

15.6 TYPES OF ORDERS

The various types of orders available to commodity hedgers and speculators are as follows:

Market Order

A market order is an order to buy or sell at the best available price—the market-determined price. A buy order is filled at the ask and a sell order is filled at the bid.

Limit Order

A limit order to buy is an order to buy at no more than a specific price. A limit order to sell is an order to sell at a price no lower than the specified price.

There is no guarantee with this type order that the order will be filled, particularly in a fast moving market.

Stop Order

A stop order can be placed on the buy as well as on the sell side of the market.

A buy stop order instructs the broker to buy when the market reaches the stop-order price. This type order is placed above the current market price and is executed as soon as the stop price is touched. The execution price may be equal to, less than, or greater than the stop-order price.

A stop order may also be a stop-limit order. Here both the stop price and the limit price must be specified. For example the buyer may instruct the broker to "buy stop at $2.67 but don't give more than $2.69."

A sell stop order is placed below prevailing market price, usually to protect a profit in a long position or to limit loss. A seller may instruct a broker to sell at $2.65 (purchase price equal to $2.75) in order to limit the loss to ten cents.

A stop order may also be of the "trailing" variety. A trailing stop order moves with the market. A holder of a long position in corn, for example, may instruct the broker every day to place a sell order at a price below that day's closing price.

Scale Order

With this type order the seller of a commodity can, for example, instruct his or her broker to sell x bushels of, say, corn at $2.60, sell y bushels at $2.70, and z bushels at $2.80, based on the belief that the corn market is in an uptrend.

Market-if-Touched Order

The market-if-touched (MIT) order is like a limit order. It allows substantially more leeway in the execution of the order. The order must be executed at the limit price or at a price more beneficial to the client.

Take-Your-Time (TYT) Order

Here the trader wishes to give the floor broker the opportunity to use judgement in filling an order. However, the floor broker, unless negligent, could not be held responsible if a good opportunity in the market were missed.

In addition, a trader may specify the time when an order is to be filled: "on close," "on opening," or at any other specified time during the trading hours.

15.7 THE FILLING OF AN ORDER

The order begins with a telephone call from the trader to the broker. The brokerage firm, using its teletype machine, wires the order in to the telephone center on the floor of the exchange. The order is then relayed to the appropriate commodity. The pit broker looks for another broker on the opposite side of the transaction. Using "open outcry" and hand signals, the pit broker flashes the bid (if buying), hoping to receive a "sold" signal from a seller. Upon the receipt of such a signal, the order is completed. The broker then writes the agreed-upon price and the seller's initials on the order blank, endorses it, and throws it back for a messenger to pick up and return to the brokerage firm's floor phone network operator. The phone operator verifies the order and wires the information to the office where the order was initially placed. Upon receipt of the information that the order has been filled, the broker informs the client of the details of the transaction.

15.8 PRICE QUOTATIONS

Using sophisticated communications networks, the commodity exchanges report futures prices promptly and accurately. The Chicago Board of Trade has in place an advanced system called the Commodity Price Reporting System.

As soon as a transaction is consummated in the pit, a "market reporter," employed by the exchange, records the time and price of the transaction and enters the price quotation in a computer terminal. The trade is validated automatically and is then flashed on screens throughout the country and transmitted to more than eighty foreign countries.

It must be noted that reported prices are not necessarily prices resulting from actual transactions. Prices may merely be indicators of bids and offers for which there were no takers.

The formats used by newspapers in reporting futures prices are not uniform. Table 15.3 is quoted from *The Wall Street Journal.* The first column under the corn futures, for example, indicates the various maturity months followed by the opening prices in cents per bushel ($2.72), the high price for the day ($2.72¾), the low price for the day ($2.65¾), and the closing (settlement) price of the day. "Change" represents the net change from the previous day's closing price. "Open Interest" indicates the number of unliquidated contracts (open buy and sell contracts) for a given contract month. The headline for each commodity: "Corn (CBT)—5,000 bu.; cents per bu.," indicates the commodity (corn), the exchange on which it is traded (the Chicago Board of Trade), the contract size (5,000 bushels), and the basis of the price quotation (cents per bushel).

15.9 THE MAJOR OPERATORS IN THE FUTURES MARKETS

The operations of the exchange depend on the activities of hundreds of persons each filling an assigned role or assuming a role. The manner in which these responsibilities are discharged has significant implications for market efficiency and liquidity.

The activities of speculators who are members of the exchanges have a pronounced effect on the efficiency and the liquidity of the markets. Speculators are professional risk takers trying to capitalize on their supposedly greater foresight into future price movements. Without the speculators the futures market would not function. Three types of speculators play important roles on the various exchanges: the position trader, the scalper, and the spreader.

The position trader, using his or her own or borrowed capital, establishes a position in the futures market in the hope of capitalizing on advantageous price movements. The position is held for only a day by the day traders and usually for short periods of time by other position traders.

Scalpers trade for their own accounts in the pits of the exchanges and rarely hold positions for more than one day. They buy at the ask and sell at the bid, hoping to capitalize on small movements in commodity prices and on the volume of their activity. Their willingness to take positions at prevailing bids and asks contributes enormously to the liquidity of the market.

Spreaders are speculators attempting to capitalize on "unnatural" or "unjustifiable"

TABLE 15.3
Daily Commodity Futures Quotations

–GRAINS AND OILSEEDS–

CORN (CBT)–5,000 bu.; cents per bu.

	Open	High	Low	Settle	Change	Lifetime High	Lifetime Low	Open Interest
Dec	272	272¾	265¾	266	-6½	396¼	265¾	42,789
Mar82	289	289½	283¼	283¼	-5¾	406½	283¼	63,200
May	300½	300½	294¼	294¼	-5½	410¾	294¼	18,817
July	307½	308	302¼	302¼	-5¼	399	302¼	12,373
Sept	313	313½	307	307	-6	388½	307	2,194
Dec	317½	318½	312¼	312¼	-6	345½	312¼	5,090

Est vol 47,222; vol Mon 52,142; open int 144,463, -1,969.

OATS (CBT)–5,000 bu.; cents per bu.

	Open	High	Low	Settle	Change	Lifetime High	Lifetime Low	Open Interest
Dec	226½	227	220½	221¼	-5	237	186	2,836
Mar82	217½	217¾	210½	210½	-5¾	239	183½	2,896
May	209¾	210	203½	204¼	-5¼	231½	180½	1,507
July	195	915	188	190½	-3	207	178½	731
Sept	192	192	185½	187¼	-4¼	204¾	178½	277

Est vol 2,510; vol Mon 3,721; open int 8,247, +383.

SOYBEANS (CBT)–5,000 bu.; cents per bu.

	Open	High	Low	Settle	Change	Lifetime High	Lifetime Low	Open Interest
Nov	....	....	....	....	....	....	....	2
Jan82	642½	643	636½	637	-3½	916½	636½	39,716
Mar	658	659½	653	654	-3	908	653	27,067
May	677	677	670	670¼	-4½	922	670	11,117
July	691	691	684	684¾	-3¾	866	684	9,318
Aug	693	694	686	686	-5	847	686	1,836
Sept	693	694½	688	688	-5	777	688	1,120
Nov	701	701½	695	695	-5	786	695	4,288
Jan83	715½	716	711	711	-6	783½	711	36
Mar	733	733	730	730	-5	744	730	2

Est vol 25,696; vol Mon 42,538; open int 94,502, +745.

SOYBEAN MEAL (CBT)–100 tons; $ per ton.

	Open	High	Low	Settle	Change	Lifetime High	Lifetime Low	Open Interest
Dec	184.50	184.80	182.70	182.90	-1.20	259.00	182.70	14,431
Jan82	187.50	187.50	185.80	186.10	-1.00	259.00	185.80	15,478
Mar	191.50	191.80	190.00	190.10	-1.60	259.00	190.00	9,507
May	196.00	196.00	194.10	194.50	-1.50	260.50	194.10	4,203
July	200.50	200.50	198.00	198.80	-1.70	242.20	198.00	2,741
Aug	201.50	201.50	199.50	199.80	-.90	244.00	199.50	678
Sept	200.50	200.50	200.50	200.50	-1.40	220.50	200.50	128
Oct	200.00	201.00	199.50	200.50	-2.50	226.00	199.50	717
Dec	203.00	203.50	203.00	203.50	-3.50	224.00	203.00	496

Est vol 7,356; vol Mon 9,684; open int 48,459, -185.

SOYBEAN OIL (CBT)–60,000 lbs.; cents per lb.

	Open	High	Low	Settle	Change	Lifetime High	Lifetime Low	Open Interest
Dec	20.22	20.22	19.93	19.94	-.17	29.73	19.93	15,046
Jan82	20.54	20.55	20.28	20.29	-.17	29.65	20.28	16,844
Mar	21.05	21.07	20.70	20.78	-.23	28.77	20.70	9,777
May	21.50	21.55	21.20	21.22	-.25	28.50	21.20	3,564
July	22.00	22.05	21.60	21.68	-.33	29.50	21.60	2,896
Aug	22.10	22.10	21.70	21.70	-.41	27.70	21.70	538
Sept	22.20	22.20	22.00	22.00	-.21	25.38	22.00	206
Oct	22.00	22.00	22.00	22.00	-.32	25.10	22.00	533
Dec	22.60	22.60	22.25	22.25	-.40	25.30	22.25	496

Est vol 13,199; vol Mon 13,694; open int 49,900, +181.

WHEAT (CBT)–5,000 bu.; cents per bu.

	Open	High	Low	Settle	Change	Lifetime High	Lifetime Low	Open Interest
Dec	414½	415½	408	408¼	-4¼	569	408	15,934
Mar82	439½	440¾	433½	434	-5	538	433½	35,588
May	448½	451	444½	444½	-4	526	444½	8,712
July	446	447¾	442	442¼	-3½	497½	442	12,266
Sept	456½	457	452½	452½	-4	502	452½	932
Dec	470	471	466½	467½	-1½	501	466	1,285

Est vol 76,277; vol Mon 32,023; open int 74,697, -2,942.

WHEAT (KC)–5,000 bu.; cents per bu.

	Open	High	Low	Settle	Change	Lifetime High	Lifetime Low	Open Interest
Dec	438½	440	436	436¼	-1½	525	421¼	10,952
Mar82	451	453¾	450	450	-¼	505	436½	21,322
May	456	456½	452½	452½	-2	495	445¼	3,184
July	445½	446¼	443½	443½	-2	496	443½	2,053
Sept	455½	456	454	454	-2	502	452	32
Dec	....	....	....	470	....	475	473	1

Est vol 8,268; vol Mon 6,763; open int 37,544, -177.

WHEAT (MPLS)–5,000 bu.; cents per bu.

	Open	High	Low	Settle	Change	Lifetime High	Lifetime Low	Open Interest
Dec	418½	419½	411	411¼	-6¾	500	400	3,765
Mar82	429	429½	423	423¼	-5½	478¾	423	2,987
May	441	441	434	425	-5	485	434	564
July	444½	445	436	436	-8½	457	436	82
Sept	450	452	448	448	-6	464	448	10

Est vol 3,820; vol Mon 1,188; open int 7,408, +55.

BARLEY (WPG)–20 metric tons; Can$ per ton

	Open	High	Low	Settle	Change	Lifetime High	Lifetime Low	Open Interest
Dec	117.70	117.80	117.30	117.60	+.30	165.20	116.80	3,293
Mr82	125.20	125.20	124.30	124.60	....	152.50	123.50	3,119
May	128.30	128.30	127.60	127.60	-.20	144.20	127.30	3,725
July	129.10	129.10	129.10	129.10	-.10	135.80	129.10	603

Est vol 1,300; vol Mon 965; open int 10,740, -47.

FLAXSEED (WPG)–20 metric tons; Can$ per ton

	Open	High	Low	Settle	Change	Lifetime High	Lifetime Low	Open Interest
Dec	381.40	383.50	379.80	382.50	+1.10	415.00	345.00	1,667
My82	411.30	413.00	409.50	411.70	+.40	426.20	376.70	3,745
July	419.00	419.50	419.00	419.50	+.10	436.00	393.50	372
Oct	....	....	....	423.00	-1.00	431.00	422.00	32

Est vol 1,410; vol Mon 1,867; open int 5,816, +347.

RAPESEED (WPG)–20 metric tons; Can$ per ton

	Open	High	Low	Settle	Change	Lifetime High	Lifetime Low	Open Interest
Jan82	327.00	327.00	324.90	324.90	-1.40	387.80	324.90	9,624
Mar	336.00	336.00	334.00	334.20	-1.30	384.30	334.00	4,791
June	346.60	346.60	345.30	345.60	-1.00	391.00	345.30	2,422
Sept	....	....	....	358.00	-2.00	367.00	360.00	16

Est vol 1,250; vol Mon 1,604; open int 16,853, -112.

RYE (WPG)–20 metric tons; Can. $ per ton

	Open	High	Low	Settle	Change	Lifetime High	Lifetime Low	Open Interest
Dec	167.20	168.10	167.20	167.60	+.70	219.00	141.50	1,168
My82	183.30	184.00	183.30	183.60	+.60	232.50	160.00	3,472
July	....	....	....	188.00	....	196.70	193.60	32
Oct	....	....	....	169.60	+.60	168.50	168.50	5

Est vol 450; vol Mon 418; open int 4,677, -40.

–LIVESTOCK & MEAT–

CATTLE–FEEDER (CME)–42,000 lbs.; cents per lb.

	Open	High	Low	Settle	Change	Lifetime High	Lifetime Low	Open Interest
Jan82	65.60	66.50	65.60	66.35	+1.17	75.57	63.60	1,637
Mar	64.20	65.35	64.20	65.20	+1.35	74.25	63.75	3,694
Apr	64.65	65.70	64.60	65.37	+1.17	70.80	64.00	1,232
May	64.40	65.65	64.40	65.25	+1.10	72.00	63.95	941
Aug	64.50	65.00	64.50	65.00	+1.50	70.00	63.50	114
Sept	....	....	....	64.50	+1.10	69.00	63.40	133
Oct	64.00	64.00	64.00	64.00	no comp	64.00	64.00	0

Est vol 1,883; vol Mon 2,327; open int 7,791, +253.

CATTLE–LIVE (CME)–40,000 lbs.; cents per lb.

	Open	High	Low	Settle	Change	Lifetime High	Lifetime Low	Open Interest
Dec	61.95	63.10	61.95	62.67	+.95	75.85	61.65	15,389
Feb82	61.65	62.55	61.50	61.97	+.72	72.55	61.05	25,991
Apr	61.45	62.60	61.45	62.05	+.80	72.40	61.10	14,715
June	62.50	63.50	62.40	62.92	+.75	72.30	62.10	6,092
Aug	62.15	63.20	62.15	62.75	+.70	66.85	61.90	2,041
Oct	61.27	62.00	61.27	61.50	+.60	65.90	60.77	505
Dec	62.00	63.00	62.00	62.80	+.97	64.65	61.80	59

Est vol 17,978; vol Mon 24,857; open int 64,792, +414.

HOGS–LIVE (CME)–30,000 lbs.; cents per lb.

	Open	High	Low	Settle	Change	Lifetime High	Lifetime Low	Open Interest
Dec	43.75	44.40	43.20	43.37	-.30	61.75	43.20	6,584
Feb82	44.90	45.70	44.60	44.65	-.15	61.85	44.60	10,534
Apr	43.10	43.75	42.92	43.00	+.27	61.50	42.72	4,389
June	45.50	46.25	45.45	45.82	+.47	59.90	45.30	1,025
July	46.75	47.47	46.40	46.75	+.10	59.97	46.20	678
Aug	45.50	46.70	45.40	45.40	-.07	59.50	45.40	247
Oct	44.30	44.90	44.05	44.70	+.45	55.20	44.05	70
Dec	45.00	45.75	45.00	45.75	+.10	54.20	45.00	24
Feb83	....	....	....	47.85	+.35	49.30	47.80	3

Est vol 7,750; vol Mon 10,028; open int 23,554, -42.

PORK BELLIES (CME)–38,000 lbs.; cents per lb.

	Open	High	Low	Settle	Change	Lifetime High	Lifetime Low	Open Interest
Feb	63.00	63.60	61.20	61.35	-.85	74.45	54.80	10,174
Mar	62.50	63.55	61.20	61.35	-.72	74.80	56.00	2,583
May	63.45	64.60	62.40	62.67	-.37	75.90	61.75	1,426
July	64.60	65.05	63.10	63.35	-.07	77.40	63.10	835
Aug	63.07	63.95	62.40	62.42	-.97	75.00	62.40	354

Est vol 9,626; vol Mon 10,572; open int 15,372, -318.

CBT–Chicago Board of Trade; CME–Chicago Mercantile Exchange; CMX–Commodity Exchange, New York; CSCE–Coffee, Sugar & Cocoa Exchange, New York; CTN–New York Cotton Exchange; IMM–International Monetary Market at CME, Chicago; KC–Kansas City Board of Trade; MPLS–Minneapolis Grain Exchange; NOCE–New Orleans Commodity Exchange; NYFE–New York Futures Exchange, unit of New York Stock Exchange. NYM–New York Mercantile Exchange; WPG–Winnipeg Commodity Exchange.

–FOOD & FIBER–

COCOA (CSCE)–10 metric tons; $ per ton.

	Open	High	Low	Settle	Change	Lifetime High	Lifetime Low	Open Interest
Dec	1,871	1,895	1,838	1,889	+57	2,595	1,538	1,055
Mar82	1,902	1,925	1,882	1,920	+47	2,360	1,625	8,340
May	1,955	1,966	1,935	1,963	+41	2,394	1,690	2,051
July	1,980	1,981	1,980	2,010	+43	2,406	1,740	1,903
Sept	2,020	2,045	2,010	2,045	+54	2,436	1,790	1,005
Dec	....	....	....	2,082	+61	2,455	2,000	1,015
Mar83	....	....	....	2,119	+68	2,295	2,295	1

Est vol 2,325; vol Mon 2,078; open int 15,370, -60.

COFFEE (CSCE)–37,500 lbs.; cents per lb.

	Open	High	Low	Settle	Change	Lifetime High	Lifetime Low	Open Interest
Dec	143.00	143.00	138.60	139.66	-3.59	165.50	82.00	723
Mr82	134.75	134.75	132.50	132.75	-2.69	144.25	81.00	4,994
May	129.00	129.99	127.45	128.03	-1.79	138.00	80.50	1,996
July	127.25	128.00	126.00	126.75	-1.35	135.00	81.00	698
Sept	127.50	127.50	125.25	125.25	-2.75	133.50	81.00	698
Dec	125.50	125.50	124.00	124.00	-1.75	130.75	81.25	172
Mr83	123.25	123.25	123.25	123.25	-2.00	130.00	119.00	24

Est vol 3,560; vol Mon 2,596; open int 9,305, -164.

COTTON (CTN)–50,000 lbs.; cents per lb.

	Open	High	Low	Settle	Change	Lifetime High	Lifetime Low	Open Interest
Dec	61.45	61.45	60.30	60.35	-.72	86.10	60.30	2,636
Mr82	63.60	63.90	63.06	63.28	-.51	86.80	63.06	14,424
May	65.31	65.45	64.75	64.82	-.68	87.00	64.75	3,815
July	67.05	67.10	66.50	66.57	-.58	86.10	66.50	4,202
Oct	69.00	69.00	68.50	68.45	-.65	85.00	68.50	531
Dec	70.10	70.10	69.41	69.45	-.77	80.85	69.41	4,007
Mr83	71.00	71.00	71.00	70.70	-.80	75.70	71.00	61

Est vol 6,100; vol Mon 5,001; open int 29,676, -257.

ORANGE JUICE (CTN)–15,000 lbs.; cents per lb.

	Open	High	Low	Settle	Change	Lifetime High	Lifetime Low	Open Interest
Nov	....	....	....	....	....	....	....	173
Jan82	122.80	124.00	123.10	123.65	+.25	154.50	91.50	3,828
Mar	124.70	125.00	124.10	124.65	+.45	155.00	92.75	1,719
May	125.60	126.00	125.60	125.80	+.50	155.75	99.25	864
July	126.60	127.00	126.60	126.80	+.50	152.50	122.25	684
Sept	....	....	....	128.20	+.50	152.00	123.40	179
Nov	....	....	....	129.30	+.50	151.25	124.30	274
Jan83	130.00	130.00	130.00	130.40	+.50	150.00	125.50	170
Mar	....	....	....	131.60	+.50	140.50	126.50	63

Est vol 500; vol Mon 581; open int 7,954, -14.

POTATOES (NYM)–50,000 lbs.; cents per lb.

	Open	High	Low	Settle	Change	Lifetime High	Lifetime Low	Open Interest
Nov	....	....	....	....	....	....	....	1
Fb82	....	....	....	7.05	-.02	10.00	6.95	32
Mar	7.44	7.47	7.44	7.46	....	11.50	7.21	370
Apr	8.29	8.43	8.28	8.37	+.06	12.44	8.14	3,243
Nov	....	....	....	7.64	....	7.80	7.52	16

Est vol 463; vol Mon 417; open int 3,662, -75.

SUGAR–WORLD (CSCE)–112,000 lbs.; cents per lb.

	Open	High	Low	Settle	Change	Lifetime High	Lifetime Low	Open Interest
Jan82	....	....	....	11.85	+.24	37.80	11.00	703
Mar	11.95	12.28	11.93	12.15	+.17	36.60	11.50	34,525
May	12.23	12.54	12.22	12.45	+.18	26.50	11.85	10,945
July	12.47	12.75	12.44	12.65	+.16	23.75	12.16	5,917
Sept	12.87	13.00	12.85	12.92	+.14	19.15	12.42	3,050
Oct	12.93	13.20	12.93	13.06	+.07	19.17	12.68	8,284
Jan83	....	....	....	13.15	+.07	13.95	13.95	1
Mar	13.60	13.75	13.60	13.72	+.07	15.00	13.26	783

Est vol 7,150; vol Mon 4,767; open int 64,208, -125.

–METALS AND PETROLEUM–

COPPER (CMX)–25,000 lbs.; cents per lb.

	Open	High	Low	Settle	Change	Lifetime High	Lifetime Low	Open Interest
Nov	....	....	....	71.40	+.60	76.05	71.80	0
Dec	71.50	71.60	71.05	71.40	+.55	154.50	70.80	12,776
Jan82	72.20	72.20	72.10	72.25	+.55	120.50	71.95	1,124
Mar	73.90	74.10	73.50	74.00	+.65	113.50	73.30	25,953
May	75.55	75.70	75.15	75.60	+.65	114.55	74.85	6,199
July	77.10	77.35	76.80	77.25	+.70	117.00	76.40	4,485
Sept	78.60	78.80	78.20	78.90	+.75	106.00	78.20	1,467
Dec	81.10	81.60	81.00	81.50	+.85	107.00	80.65	2,143
Jan83	81.80	82.00	81.80	82.35	+.85	109.20	82.10	388
Mar	83.30	83.60	83.30	84.05	+.85	107.00	83.30	474
May	....	....	....	85.75	+.85	108.30	84.90	215
July	87.20	87.20	87.20	87.45	+.85	103.00	87.20	121
Sept	88.50	88.50	88.50	89.15	+.85	93.60	88.50	40

Est vol 15,000; vol Mon 8,341; open int 55,385, -244.

GOLD (CMX)–100 troy oz.; $ per troy oz.

	Open	High	Low	Settle	Change	Lifetime High	Lifetime Low	Open Interest
Nov	399.50	399.50	397.00	401.80	+8.00	455.00	394.00	5
Dec	398.00	402.50	397.00	401.80	+7.80	981.00	392.50	28,810
Jan82	....	....	....	404.90	+8.00	435.00	400.00	4
Feb	402.50	409.00	401.50	408.00	+8.10	887.30	398.00	30,631
Apr	409.00	417.00	409.00	415.30	+8.20	898.00	405.50	21,988
June	417.00	424.50	417.00	423.40	+8.20	925.00	413.00	24,577
Aug	426.50	430.00	426.50	431.70	+8.30	887.00	421.50	18,930
Oct	434.50	438.00	434.50	440.30	+8.40	842.00	431.80	20,626
Dec	445.50	451.00	444.00	448.90	+8.50	666.50	437.00	14,189
Fb83	453.50	453.50	453.50	457.70	+8.70	642.00	445.00	22,530
Apr	460.00	460.00	460.00	466.80	+8.80	604.00	455.50	11,104
June	....	....	....	476.10	+8.90	596.00	487.50	603
Aug	....	....	....	485.40	+9.00	515.50	483.50	240

Est vol 60,000; vol Mon 51,365; open int 194,247, -2,559.

GOLD (IMM)–100 troy oz.; $ per troy oz.

	Open	High	Low	Settle	Change	Lifetime High	Lifetime Low	Open Interest
Dec	398.00	402.00	396.80	401.70	+7.8	1031.9	392.00	5,806
Mr82	406.50	413.00	406.40	412.20	+8.8	895.00	401.80	7,090
June	418.00	425.90	417.50	424.70	+9.8	920.00	413.50	7,306
Sept	431.00	433.10	431.00	437.40	+10.8	948.00	426.00	4,591
Dec	442.70	450.30	442.70	450.30	+11.9	974.00	438.40	5,961
Mr83	454.00	463.40	454.00	463.40	+13.0	887.20	450.40	5,630
June	469.50	476.70	467.00	476.70	+14.1	674.50	462.60	3,004
Sept	....	....	....	490.20	+15.2	626.20	480.50	427

Est vol 6,745; vol Mon 7,757; open int 39,815, +473.

HEATING OIL NO. 2 (NYM)–42,000 gal.; $ per gal.

	Open	High	Low	Settle	Change	Lifetime High	Lifetime Low	Open Interest
Dec	1.0140	1.0150	1.0135	1.0149	+.0004	1.1025	.9560	4,899
Jan82	1.0243	1.0248	1.0235	1.0245	+.0003	1.1200	.9670	10,521
Feb	1.0295	1.0308	1.0290	1.0304	+.0002	1.1380	.9800	12,075
Mar	1.0199	1.0200	1.0185	1.0197	-.0007	1.1385	.9890	4,894
Apr	1.0050	1.0055	1.0040	1.0045	-.0014	1.1276	.9940	1,404
May	1.0000	1.0015	1.0000	1.0015	-.0005	1.1300	.9950	443
June	1.0050	1.0050	1.0045	1.0045	-.0015	1.0800	1.0000	88
July	1.0060	1.0060	1.0060	1.0060	-.0015	1.0800	.9925	57
Aug	1.0110	1.0110	1.0110	1.0080	-.0040	1.0850	1.0110	6
Sept	....	....	....	1.0220	-.0055	1.0850	1.0450	2
Oct	....	....	....	1.0320	-.0055	1.0950	1.0425	6
Dec	....	....	....	....	....	1.0750	1.0700	0

Est vol 2,483; vol Mon 3,813; open int 34,395, -90.

PLATINUM (NYM)–50 troy oz.; $ per troy oz.

	Open	High	Low	Settle	Change	Lifetime High	Lifetime Low	Open Interest
Nov	....	....	....	378.00	+4.30	412.00	371.00	4
Dec	....	....	....	379.00	+5.30	380.00	379.00	1
Jan82	376.00	380.00	376.00	379.80	+6.10	770.00	371.00	4,812
Apr	385.50	388.50	385.10	388.80	+5.80	624.70	381.00	3,113
July	395.00	397.50	395.00	399.30	+5.50	535.50	392.50	453
Oct	409.00	409.50	409.00	411.00	+5.20	523.00	408.50	163

Est vol 1,180; vol Mon 1,451; open int 8,546, -15.

SILVER (CMX)–5,000 troy oz.; cents per troy oz.

	Open	High	Low	Settle	Change	Lifetime High	Lifetime Low	Open Interest
Nov	808.0	808.0	807.0	807.0	+7.0	926.0	797.0	24
Dec	811.0	814.0	802.0	807.0	+6.0	4140.0	797.0	7,187
Jan82	820.0	820.0	820.0	815.1	+6.4	4165.0	808.0	1,754
Mar	840.0	840.0	825.0	831.5	+6.5	2830.0	822.0	11,641
May	858.0	858.0	845.0	850.0	+6.8	2895.0	840.0	3,189
July	875.0	878.0	870.0	868.5	+7.1	2617.0	860.0	2,701
Sept	891.0	894.0	875.0	887.0	+7.4	2550.0	875.0	2,028
Dec	918.0	923.0	913.0	914.8	+7.7	1715.0	911.0	1,038
Jan83	....	....	....	924.0	+7.8	1163.0	927.0	39
Mar	950.0	950.0	950.0	942.5	+8.1	1555.0	950.0	178
May	....	....	....	961.0	+8.4	1449.0	962.0	29
July	....	....	....	979.5	+8.7	1350.0	885.0	16
Sept	....	....	....	998.0	+9.0	1183.0	1130.0	2

Est vol 8,000; vol Mon 8,539; open int 29,826, -38.

Source: The Wall Street Journal, Nov. 25, 1981.

relationships between commodity prices. They may find opportunities in the differences in contract prices between maturity months for a given commodity, between the same maturity month of two different commodities, and between the same (or different) maturity months of a commodity futures contract and that of a derivative product (for example, between November soybeans and October soybean oil). The activities of spreaders allow for realignment of commodities futures prices and thus contribute to the efficiency of the market as long as their activities produce profits in the long run. Spread positions are discussed in greater detail later in this chapter.

Other individuals playing a critical role in the operations of the exchange are the floor brokers who fill the orders of various clients, ranging from farmers to manufacturers to food exporters or importers and to speculators.

15.10 THE ANALYTICAL APPROACHES TO COMMODITIES

Two schools of thought dominate commodities analysis as they do stock analysis. They are the fundamentalist school and the technical school.

The technical school believes in the same principles and uses the same techniques discussed in Chapter 4. Most commodities technicians pay considerable attention to moving averages and related forecasting tools, and frequently to the changes in the fundamentals of a commodity.

The fundamental school, on the other hand, concentrates its efforts on the factors influencing supply and demand and on the resulting impact on commodities prices. The interaction between supply and demand produces equilibrium prices. It is the departure from equilibrium prices that offers opportunities in the marketplace on which traders may capitalize.

To cover the supply and demand factors for every commodity is beyond the scope of this book. Instead, we shall undertake a brief analysis of the case of wheat.

Wheat

The supply of and demand for wheat are influenced by a variety of factors, some of which are predictable and quantifiable and others that are not. The major relationships in the wheat economy are shown in Figure 15.2.

The identification of the supply and demand factors and the evaluation of their relative importance is at the heart of fundamental analysis.

The sources of wheat supplies in the United States are current production, imports, old-crop carry-over, and government supply from accumulated inventory under various subsidy schemes administered by the U.S. Department of Agriculture. The most important source of supply is current production.

The wheat crop year runs from July 1 to June 30. During this period, seven grades of wheat are harvested: hard red winter, soft red winter, hard red spring, durum, red durum, white, and mixed wheat. About 75 percent of U.S. wheat production is in the form of hard red winter wheat. Hard wheat is used for bread; soft wheat for pastry.

In terms of yield per acre, the winter wheat is most productive. Winter wheat produces about 31 bushels per acre, spring wheat about 28 bushels, and durum wheat about 26

FIGURE 15.2 Major relationships in the wheat economy.

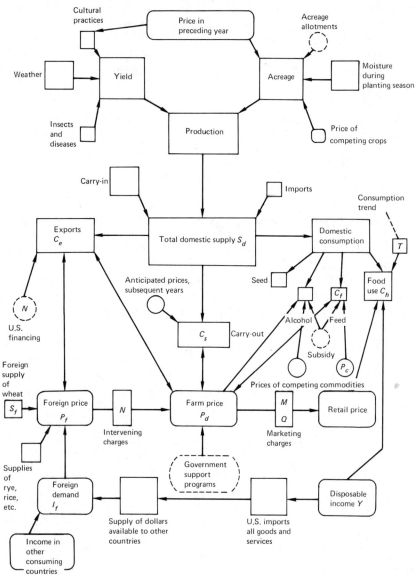

Source: The Demand and Price Structure for Wheat. Technical Bulletin 1136, U.S. Department of Agriculture, 1955, p. 12.

bushels. The average expected production of wheat, assuming no weather or other disasters, should equal the yield per acre (average of 28 bushels) multiplied by the number of acres expected to be planted (taking the federal acreage diversion program and other limiting programs into consideration).

Since the wheat market is a world market, the supplies of other countries should also be estimated. The estimates by Merrill Lynch for the 1980–81 crop year per country is shown in Table 15.4. The U.S.S.R. leads all countries not only in wheat production but also in wheat imports. Of all the wheat produced in the United States, about 60

TABLE 15.4
Total World Wheat Production, Export and Import by Countries
(in Million Metric Tons)

	1976–77	1977–78	1978–79	1979–80	ML Estimates[a] 1980–81
Production					
U.S.	58.3	55.4	48.9	58.3	64.3
Canada	23.6	19.9	21.1	17.2	18.7
Australia	11.7	9.4	18.1	16.1	10.0
Argentina	11.0	5.7	8.1	8.0	7.5
EC-9[b]	39.1	38.4	47.6	46.1	51.3
U.S.S.R.	96.9	92.2	120.8	90.1	90.0
China	45.0	41.0	54.0	60.5	55.0
India	28.8	29.0	31.7	35.0	30.5
World	**415.5**	**383.9**	**447.6**	**419.8**	**428.0**
Export					
U.S.	26.1	31.5	32.3	37.2	41.5
Canada	12.9	15.9	13.5	15.0	15.0
Australia	8.5	11.1	6.7	15.0	10.5
Argentina	5.6	2.6	3.3	4.7	4.3
EC-9[b]	4.9	5.0	8.0	9.8	12.0
World	**63.1**	**73.1**	**71.9**	**85.4**	**90.0**
Import					
Japan	5.5	5.8	5.7	5.6	5.5
U.S.S.R.	4.6	6.6	5.1	12.0	14.0
China	3.2	8.6	8.0	8.8	13.0
EC-9[b]	4.4	5.5	4.6	4.5	4.5
East Europe	6.3	5.0	4.2	5.9	5.8
World	**63.1**	**73.1**	**71.9**	**85.4**	**90.0**

Source: Merrill Lynch Pierce Fenner & Smith, Inc., Commodity Division.

[a] ML = Merrill Lynch.

[b] EC = European Economic Community.

percent is exported annually, 30 percent is milled into flour, and the remaining 10 percent is used for seeding and for animal feed.

The demand for U.S. wheat is predominantly a world demand for U.S. wheat exports. The United States is and has been the leading exporter of wheat in the world. The factors influencing this demand are as follows:

1. Wheat prices and the prices of substitutable commodities.

2. Income levels overseas and availability of dollars in the importing countries, or the availability of credit.

3. The income and price elasticity of demand for wheat. A demand function is price elastic if for a small decrease in price, the quantity demanded increases sufficiently to increase the total revenue of the selling firm. Mathematically:

$\xi = \Delta Q / \Delta P \cdot P/Q$

where ξ = price elasticity

Q = quantity

P = price

if $\xi > 1$, the demand function is said to be elastic.

4. The nature of government programs.

5. A host of other factors such as taste, customs, tariffs, etc., which may not be possible to incorporate in an equilibrium model.

The problem to the fundamentalist is not only to isolate the relevant factors that bear on supply and demand but also to determine their relative importance and the extent to which they are already reflected in observable spot prices.

It is this complexity of fundamental analysis, and its susceptibility to error in fact or in judgment, that drives many traders into technical analysis. Some traders have derived larger payoffs from studying the market itself (technical analysis) than from the elaborate and often imperfect study of supply and demand factors and the resulting "equilibrium prices." Having briefly looked at the determinants of spot prices, we now examine futures commodities prices.

15.11 THE DETERMINANTS OF COMMODITY FUTURES PRICES

The inability of those who produce, handle, and process commodities to purchase insurance for protection against value risks provided the impetus for the futures markets, where hedgers can shift risk onto speculators.

The activities of three agents in the futures market must be understood in order to arrive at a method for rationalizing the process of determining future prices. These agents are the hedger, the speculator, and the arbitrageur.

The hedger is primarily motivated by the security and not the profit derived from a futures transaction. A hedger protects a cash position against price declines through the sale of a futures contract and gains protection against the possibility of increased costs of anticipated future purchases through the purchase of a futures contract. Examples of precisely how a hedge is achieved are provided later in this chapter.

A speculator, on the other hand, is motivated by the profits, achieved through the successful prediction of price movements, in a futures transaction. As compensation for the uncertainty of price expectations, the speculator charges a risk premium. Speculators expecting a price rise exceeding that suggested by a futures price would buy futures contracts. They would sell these contracts if their expectations were the opposite.

An arbitrageur capitalizes on unjustifiable price differences over space (for example, between one market and another) or over time (between one maturity month and another). Pure arbitrage involves zero risk and no commitment of capital.

In addition to understanding the function of these three operators, we must understand the "basis."

The basis is the differential at a point in time between the future price of a commodity and the cash or spot price of the same commodity. For example, if the July corn futures contract is trading at \$2.70 and the spot price is \$2.40, the basis is "30 under." Futures prices often exceed spot prices, but *not* always. The closer the spot price is to the higher futures price, the *stronger* the basis is said to be. The wider the difference, the *weaker* the basis. A strong basis (spot price close to or exceeding the futures price) reflects excess demand for the commodity. In this case, the cash market is indicating its willingness to pay for spot delivery earlier than normal. A weak basis indicates that the market has a sufficient supply cash crop and is unwilling to make early storage payments. This (weak basis) usually occurs at harvest time when supplies are plentiful.

An understanding of the basis—that is, the relationship between futures prices and spot prices—therefore requires an understanding of net carrying (storage) costs.

$$\text{Let} \quad SP = \text{spot price}$$
$$FP = \text{future price}$$
$$c = \text{net carrying charges}$$
$$c = C - CY$$

where C = carrying (storage) charges = interest costs + insurance costs + storage costs + loading and unloading charges associated with carrying a commodity inventory

CY equals the convenience yield[2] or the benefits accruing from holding stock of a commodity today instead of the cash for purchasing that commodity tomorrow. The benefits manifest themselves in the form of lower costs of maintaining an output or sales level and in lower cost for varying the level of output by relying on existing stock as opposed to the purchase of stock as needed. The more specialized the commodity is, the greater the benefits will be.[3]

The value of c could, therefore, be positive or negative depending on the relationship between C and CY. The concept of convenience yield can thus explain why deferred deliveries can be priced below or above near deliveries or spot deliveries (the nearest delivery of all). Storage of commodities in this case will not be done exclusively on the basis of expected price appreciation, which implies that the price of a deferred delivery will always exceed that of nearer deliveries.

Therefore

$$FP - SP \gtrless 0$$

If $FP - SP > 0 \rightarrow$ contango[4]
$\quad FP - SP < 0 \rightarrow$ backwardation[4] or an *inverted market*

Which of the signs prevail in the equation above obviously depends on the value of c.

Under conditions of certainty,

$$FP = SP + c$$

---

[2] See **Nicholas Kaldor,** "Speculation and Economic Stability." *Review of Economic Studies,* vol. 7, (1939–1940).

[3] See the excellent work of **Gerda Blau,** "Some Aspects of the Theory of Futures Trading." *Review of Economic Studies,* vol. 12, no. 1 (1944–1945), pp. 1–30.

[4] These two terms were used by **Keynes** in an essay in the *Manchester Guardian Commercial* in 1923.

for if FP < SP + c, hedgers would be better off carrying their stock and selling it at the date coinciding with the maturity of the future contract instead of selling their commodities forward for future delivery. The reverse strategy would be more profitable if FP > SP + c.

Under conditions of uncertainty, speculators would buy or sell futures contracts depending on their expectations about future prices EP coinciding with the maturity of the futures contract. If EP > FP, speculators would be long the futures contract, that is, they would buy for future delivery and close (sell) the contract at a higher price in the future or take delivery (the unlikely course) of the commodity and sell it at the higher spot rate. A short position would be established by speculators if EP < FP. They sell at FP and close the position by buying at EP. Assuming their expectations materialize, profits will accrue to the speculators.

The hedgers would enter futures contracts to offset their current or expected cash position independent of what the EP is going to be. Hedgers do not forecast EP and are only interested in shifting the risk resulting from price fluctuations onto the speculators.

Those who make sure that the relationship between future prices and spot prices is in equilibrium are the arbitrageurs. They capitalize on any deviation between FP and SP + c.

If FP − SP > c, arbitrageurs would profit by selling futures, buying spot, and holding stock until delivery. If, on the other hand, FP − SP < c, arbitrageurs would pursue the opposite strategy: they would sell spot and buy futures. The arbitrage profit would equal to FP − SP − c. If arbitrage is working perfectly, it would ensure that, at least for a while, equilibrium prices prevail; that is, FP = SP + c.

The above discussion on the determinants of futures prices is referred to as the *price-of-storage theory*. This theory explains all the cases where $FP \gtrless SP + c$:

> *the negative prices occur when supplies are relatively scarce. They then impose pressure on hedging merchandisers and processors to avoid holding unnecessarily large quantities out of consumption in the form of stocks which they can do without. Thus a negative price of storage makes available for consumption in a year of shortage, supplies which would otherwise be tied up in "convenience stocks."* [5]

If supplies are plentiful—and this is usually the case around harvest time—the calculation of future prices using wheat is made as follows (CBT):

1. Find the cash price (quoted daily in *The Wall Street Journal* and other sources) for a given type wheat deliverable against the contract).
2. Determine the storage and insurance rate per month per bushel.
3. Determine the interest-rate charge per bushel per month using the prime interest rate.
4. Add 2 and 3 to arrive at total carrying charge.
5. Add 4 and 1 to arrive at the appropriate future price of a bushel.

---

[5] **Holbrook Working**, "The Theory of Price of Storage." *American Economic Review*, December 1949, p. 1262.

In the wheat case, the spot price of a bushel of no. 2 soft red wheat deliverable against a CBT futures contract was $3.98¾ on Nov. 24, 1981.

Storage and insurance costs per month per bushel = 4.2 cents

Interest costs per month per bushel at a 16 percent prime rate =

$$0.16\left(\frac{1}{12}\right) \times 3.98\tfrac{3}{4} = 0.0530$$

Total carrying charges = 0.0530 + 0.042 = 0.0950

Total carrying charges per bushel until the maturity of the futures contract = 0.0952 × number of months until delivery.

To determine the exact time period until delivery is very hard, for the delivery is at the option of the seller. The rules of the exchanges require that the last notice day for delivery be the next to the last business day of the delivery month, with the oldest contract receiving delivery first, and that no trading in the maturing contract take place in the last seven business days.[6]

Since 97 percent of the contracts are not delivered against, it makes sense to price a contract up to the last business day on which it can be traded, which is Dec. 22 in our case.

Thus, the time period left in the life of the contract is that period falling between Nov. 24, 1981, and Dec. 22, which is equal to 29 days.

Thus, the adjusted carrying costs are equal to

$$0.0950 \times 29/30 = 0.092$$

The future price = spot + carrying costs

$$= \$3.98\tfrac{3}{4} + 0.092 = \textbf{\$4.08}$$

which approximates the settlement price on the December CBT futures contract shown in Table 15.3.

We now discuss the theory of "normal backwardation" advanced by J. M. Keynes and by J. R. Hicks.[7]

Normal Backwardation

J. M. Keynes and J. R. Hicks argued that it is in the nature of the market to have the future price lie below the expected spot price, whether the market is inverted (SP > FP) or is a carry market (SP < FP). The future price is a downward-biased estimate of the expected price, and the future price rises as the futures contract approaches maturity date.

In this world the speculator is seen as providing a valuable service to the hedger, a

---

[6] Speculators, who should avoid the possibility of a delivery, should avoid long speculative positions in the nearby months after the first notice day. The first notice day is specified by the exchange and the notice is made by the seller.

[7] See **J. R. Hicks,** *Value and Capital,* ed. 2. Clarendon Press, Oxford, 1950, chap. 10, pp. 130–152.

service that warrants a positive price. The hedger wishing to shift the price (value) risk onto the speculator would be willing to pay a price, a risk premium. The implication is that the net cost of hedging is always positive. It is possible, however, as we shall demonstrate later, that the gains (losses) in the futures market will more than offset the losses (gains) in the cash market. That is, hedgers can conceivably, and often do, realize a profit from the hedging transaction itself.

Stated differently, the normal backwardation theory looks at speculators as sellers of insurance to hedgers. Since hedgers, on the average, are net sellers of futures contracts (net short position), speculators must be net buyers of futures contracts.[8] In order to maintain a net long position, speculators charge a positive premium which is equal to the difference between EP and FP. The speculator buys at FP and sells at EP. This premium should be the necessary inducement to the speculator to bear price risk. The determinants of this premium are summarized in Figure 15.3.

Would the theory of backwardation hold if we observe that the future price exceeds the spot price? Keynes answers in the affirmative. Keynes "maintained that there is still backwardation because the expected spot price exceeds both the current spot price and the futures price."[9]

The normal backwardation theory relies on the following assumptions:

1. Speculators have net long positions in the commodity.
2. Speculators are not capable of forecasting expected spot prices.
3. Speculators are risk-averse.

The speculator (or anyone), the theory argues, could earn a profit simply by having a net long position in futures. He or she simply capitalizes on the upward trend in commodity prices, although unable to forecast expected spot prices. The larger the speculator's position is, the larger the profit. Even if markets were efficient, this trend would exist because of the required risk premium, which is a decreasing function of the life of the contract.

The acceptance or the rejection of the theory depends, according to Telser, on testing two implications of the theory:

> *The first is that, on the average, long speculators should receive profits and short hedgers should suffer losses on their futures transactions. The long speculators' profits must be net of transactions costs.*

> *A second implication, the one explored here, is that there is an upward trend in futures prices as the contract approaches maturity. In their (Keynes and Hicks) theory, the futures price is below the expected spot price by the amount of the insurance premium paid the long speculators by the short hedgers. This insurance premium is the remuneration for the risk of price changes. The risk of an unanticipated price change increases the farther away the maturity date of the futures contract is from the current date, assuming that it is more difficult to foresee the distant future. Since the risk premium is the excess of the expected spot prices over the futures price, this excess decreases as the futures contract approaches maturity. Under normal conditions, when the ex-*

---

[8] See **Lester G. Telser,** "Reply." *Journal of Political Economy,* vol. 68, no. 4 (August 1960).

[9] **Lester Telser,** "Futures Trading and the Storage of Cotton and Wheat." *Journal of Political Economy,* vol. 66, no. 3 (June 1958), pp. 233–255.

FIGURE 15.3 **Summary of factors influencing the marginal risk premiums of hedgers and speculators.**

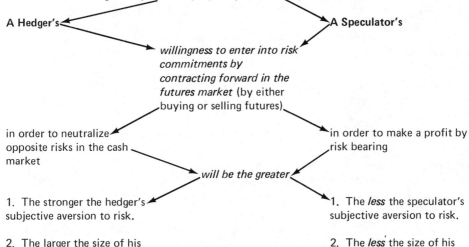

Given: the degree of uncertainty of expectations and the degree of perfection, liquidity and security in the market.

A Hedger's ⟵ ⟶ A Speculator's

willingness to enter into risk commitments by contracting forward in the futures market (by either buying or selling futures)

in order to neutralize opposite risks in the cash market

in order to make a profit by risk bearing

will be the greater

1. The stronger the hedger's subjective aversion to risk.

2. The larger the size of his risk commitments *in the cash market* (i.e. the possible loss relatively to total assets);

3. The *less* definite his opinion on the expected price EP; (the more definite the hedger's opinion on EP, the greater his inducement to turn into a speculator by leaving his cash commitments unhedged;

4. The higher the expected degree of price variability in general for the standard grade as compared with the variability of the index of *all* other prices relevant to the trader;

5. The higher the proportion of hedgeable risks to nonhedgeable risks.

1. The *less* the speculator's subjective aversion to risk.

2. The *less* the size of his *total risk* commitments; (i.e., the possible loss relatively to total assets).

3. The *more* definite his opinion of the expected price (EP);

4. The greater the difference between the forward price (FP) and the expected price (EP).

Source: Gerda Blau, "Some Aspects of the Theory of Futures Trading." *Review of Economic Studies,* vol. 12, no. 1 (1944–1945), pp. 18–19.

pected spot price is not expected to change, this implies that futures price rises as it approaches maturity. Although we cannot directly observe the expected spot price, the theory that the futures price is a biased estimate of the expected spot price *can be tested by observing whether there is an upward trend in the futures price as it approaches maturity* [emphasis added].[10]

Telser tested the hypothesis that futures prices are unbiased predictors of expected spot prices and was unable to reject the null hypothesis. Futures prices did not display a trend.

Stone,[11] in an earlier study (1901), also found no evidence of biasedness.

A study by the Federal Trade Commission showed a downward bias in futures prices of wheat and corn but not of oats.[12]

Paul Cootner[13] presented evidence confirming the presence of risk premiums in several commodity futures contracts.

Charles Rockwell,[14] in a very extensive study covering the 1947–1965 period, found evidence of consistent price rises when speculators held *net short* positions, and that the tendency toward normal backwardation when speculators held a net long position was insignificant.

These and other studies do not allow the researcher convincingly to confirm or deny the validity of the normal backwardation theory. This must await further evidence.

15.12 THE USES OF COMMODITIES FUTURES CONTRACTS

Commodities futures contracts have proved and continue to prove their utility to various economic agents and to the economy as a whole. The dramatic increase in commodities futures contracts traded on the various exchanges (Table 15.1) is a strong indicator of the merits of futures trading.

Commodities futures are used by hedgers, speculators, and arbitrageurs.

Hedging with Commodities Futures

Producers, processors, and marketers of actual physical commodities have found a refuge from price risk in the futures market. This market has permitted them to shift risk onto the speculators.

The essence of hedging is to take a position in the futures market opposite that in the cash market. If a farmer is long (actually or prospectively) a million bushels of wheat, he would sell (short)[15] 200 contracts (each wheat futures contract covers 5,000

---

[10] Ibid., **Telser,** p. 243.

[11] U.S. 56th Congress, 2nd session, U.S. Industrial Commission Report (1900–1901), House Document 94.

[12] U.S. Federal Trade Commission, Report on Grain Trade, Washington, D.C., 1920–1926.

[13] **Paul Cootner,** "Speculation and Hedging." Food Research Institute Studies, Supplement 7 (1967), pp. 84–103.

[14] **Charles Rockwell,** "Normal Backwardation, Forecasting and the Returns to Commodity Futures Traders." *Food Research Institute Studies,* Supplement 7 (1967), pp. 107–130.

[15] A short position in the futures market, unlike its counterpart in the stock market, does not require the borrowing of a commodity for delivery to the buyer. The reasons are that the contract does not require delivery until maturity date and that almost all buyers never intend to take delivery of the commodity. There is no "equity" in a futures margin position as there is in a stock margin.

bushels) in the wheat futures markets. Since cash and future prices tend to move in tandem, for they are influenced by the same supply/demand factors, whatever gains (losses) are realized in the futures market will offset the losses (gains) in the cash market and the farmer would have locked in a price for his wheat. This obviously assumes that the farmer holds the futures contract until maturity. Otherwise, the gains (losses) on the futures market may be larger or smaller than the losses (gains) in the cash market, depending on how future prices move in relation to cash prices (that is, depending on the change in the basis).

The basis, as discussed earlier, is the difference between the futures price and the cash price. As the maturity date of a futures contract approaches, the futures contract would approximate more and more the cash contract. That is why a cash contract is a special case of a futures contract where the delivery period shrinks to one day. Therefore, the farther away from maturity one is, the larger, ceteris paribus, the size of the basis will be and the greater the instability in the basis given changes in supply and/or demand. The stability of the basis is of considerable significance to the hedger if the futures contract is not going to be carried to maturity—that is, if the futures contract is not going to be delivered against or the hedger accepts delivery on it.

Since 97 percent or more of futures contracts are never delivered against, the behavior of the basis becomes of paramount importance. We now look at the impact of changes in the basis on a long hedge and on a short hedge. Before doing so, let us quote from the *Commodity Trading Manual* of the Chicago Board of Trade:

> *By counterbalancing his cash position with an opposite and equivalent position in the futures market, a hedger replaces the risk of price fluctuation with risks of a change in the relationship between the cash price and the futures price of a commodity, thus the importance of the basis.*

Long Hedge

A long hedge is used by the processor, seller, exporter, or user of a commodity. The objective is to "fix" the purchase price of a commodity between the consideration date and the actual purchase date.

A cereal manufacturer anticipating a need for 40,000 bushels of wheat in April 1982 could buy them today and store them until April; the alternative would be to wait until April to buy them in the spot (cash) market. The latter option would leave the manufacturer exposed to price risk. By April the price of wheat could be higher. To gain protection against a price increase, the manufacturer would hedge in the futures market. The process is as follows:

Cash Market

Nov. 24, 1981

Expect 40,000 bushels of wheat in April 1982. Current price per bushel is equal to $3.9875.

April 15, 1982

Buy 40,000 bushels, spot market price (assumed) $4.1000.

Futures Market

Nov. 24, 1981

Buy eight May futures contracts (CBT) at per bushel $4.0825.

April 15, 1982

Sell (to offset) eight May futures contracts at $4.250.

Results

Opportunity loss = $4.1000 − 3.9875   Actual gain = $4.250 − $4.0825
           = $0.1125   = 0.1675

Net gain per bushel = 0.1675 − 0.1125 = **$0.055**

Had the opportunity loss equaled the actual gain, the hedge would be a "perfect" hedge.

The net gain on the hedge results from the fact that the basis has weakened; that is, the difference between the futures price and the cash price has widened, FP $\gg$ SP. Had the basis remained the same, the net gain would be zero. Had the basis strengthened, the net gain could have become negative and the hedge would not have been as effective as the manufacturer would have wished. We now look at the effects of a stronger basis.

Cash Market	**Futures Market**
April 15, 1982	**April 15, 1982**
Cash price = $4.15	Futures price = $4.20

Results

Opportunity loss = $4.15 − 3.9875   Actual gain = $4.20 − $4.0825
           = $0.1625   = $0.1175

Net gain = 0.1175 − 0.1625 = **$−0.045**

Thus, in this case, the strengthening of the basis has produced a net loss. The hedge is not a very effective one.

The Short (Selling) Hedge.   A farmer expecting to harvest and sell his wheat in July 1982 is obviously concerned with the price of wheat falling from its current levels. If satisfied with the current price levels and wishing to at least lock them in, the wheat farmer would hedge in the futures market by selling futures contracts to offset the long expected cash position. The process is as follows:

Cash Market	**Futures Market**
Nov. 24, 1981	**Nov. 24, 1981**
Expect to harvest and sell 10,000 bushels of wheat. No actual position in the cash market. Current cash price for wheat = 3.9875.	Sell two July futures contracts (CBT) at $4.4225 per bushel (Table 15.3).
July 1982	
Sell 10,000 bushels at $3.90*	Buy (to offset) two July futures contracts at $4.20.

---

* It must be noted that the difference between the futures price and the spot price represents the cost of delivering wheat against the futures contract. If the farmer had the wheat that is acceptable for delivery against the futures contracts, and if that wheat was in the location designated by the exchange, he would have simply chosen to deliver the harvested wheat against the futures contract and would have effectively locked in the futures price back on Nov. 24, 1981.

Results

Opportunity loss = 0.0875	Actual gain = $0.2225

$$\text{Net gain} = 0.2225 - 0.0875 = \textbf{0.135}$$

The net gain in this short hedge results from the strengthening of the basis. This is precisely the opposite result obtained in a long hedge with a strenghtening basis. Similarly, a weakening basis will diminish, if not eliminate, the effectiveness of a short hedge.

Had the basis weakened, the farmer might have decided to roll the hedge forward, that is, close out the hedge in the July contract and establish a new short position in another contract month where the basis is expected to strengthen. Meanwhile, he holds on to his wheat longer, with the attendant storage costs.

Thus far we have concentrated on hedging in the wheat market. Hedges in other markets work in essentially the same way. To cover hedging for each commodity is beyond the scope of this book.

Before we move to a discussion on spreads, we shall list the other advantages of hedging to, for example, a farmer.[16] They are, in addition to reducing price risk and locking in the basis, as follows:

1. Improve the chances for a bank loan if not for lower interest rates. A hedged crop is a "safer" crop from a banker's perspective.

2. Set a ceiling on production costs. An example of this is the cost of feed to a hog farmer.

3. Allow for better production plans as prices fluctuate and as the demand for the crop fluctuates.

4. Stabilize profit margins through hedging production costs and the sale price of the final product.

5. Since the futures market is a costless tool for price discovery of expected spot prices, help the farmer plan his sales (sell now vs. sell tomorrow).

6. Extend the selling season through the sale of a crop yet to be harvested in the futures market.

7. Reduce inventory levels. Futures contracts are an excellent vehicle for farmers with insufficient storage capacity and with a desire to minimize the holding of an inventory stock while maintaining an access (a commitment) to the commodity.

We now look at an increasingly popular investment/speculative strategy.

Spreads

A spread represents a simultaneous long position in one futures contract and a short position in another.

A spread is established in order to take advantage of expected changes in the relationships between different futures prices.

The popularity of spreads stems from two basic features:

1. Spreads have a lower price risk than an outright position in a futures contract, for the same market factors influence the short position as the long position.

---

[16] Based on *Professional Hedging Handbook.* MidAmerican Commodity Exchange, Chicago, pp. 6–7.

2. The margin requirements on spreads are lower than those on an equivalent but separate position in the futures market.

There are four basic types of spreads, the intermonth spread, the intermarket spread, the intercommodity spread, and the commodity product spread.

Intermonth Spreads.   Experience with commodities indicates that near-month contracts gradually appreciate in price, for a given set of events, more than do distant ones. This is so for most commodities except precious metals and currencies.[17] Thus, a bull spread calls for a long position in the near month and a short position in the distant month. The bear spread, on the other hand, calls for a short position in the near month and a long position in the distant month.

The results of the spread, as in the financial futures case, would depend on whether the market were inverted—price of near contract P_N > price of distant contract P_D—or noninverted—P_N < P_D—and on whether the spread strengthened or weakened. We now discuss spread strategies when markets are noninverted and when they are inverted.

P_D > P_N or Noninverted Market.   Figure 15.4 shows the behavior of the spread between July 82 soybean and November 82 soybean during November 1981. An astute trader could have capitalized on at least the major swings in the spread. With the expectation that the spread will weaken further from its level at the end of November 1981, the trader may wish to:

Dec. 1, 1981

Sell one (or more) July soybean at   685
Buy one (or more) November soybean at   695 $\}$ $P_D - P_N = 10$

If the trader's expectations materialize, in, say, two months, he would reverse the positions and realize profit on this bear spread.

Jan. 29, 1982

Buy one July soybean at   670
Sell one November soybean at   690 $\}$ $P_D - P_N = 20$

Profits/Losses

Profit on short position = 685 − 670 = $0.15
Loss on long position   = 695 − 690 = 0.05
Net profit   **$0.10**

---

[17] **Paul A Samuelson,** in a classic article titled "Proof That Properly Anticipated Prices Fluctuate Randomly" (*Industrial Management Review* 6 (1965):120–123), advanced a theory stating that the volatility of futures price changes per unit of time increases as the time to maturity decreases. The empirical evidence provides weak support for this theory. The latest study by Ronald W. Anderson, "The Determinants of the Volatility of Futures Prices" (Columbia University Working Papers Series, Dec. 1981), showed that Samuelson's theory applies only to few commodities.

FIGURE 15.4 **Behavior of the spread between July 1982 soybean and November 1982 soybean.**

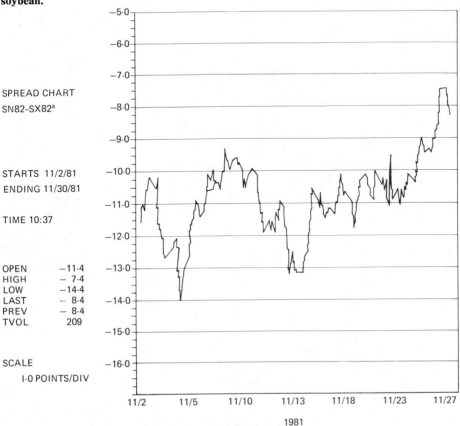

SPREAD CHART
SN82-SX82[a]

STARTS 11/2/81

ENDING 11/30/81

TIME 10:37

OPEN	−11-4
HIGH	− 7-4
LOW	−14-4
LAST	−· 8-4
PREV	− 8-4
TVOL	209

SCALE

    1-0 POINTS/DIV

1981

The profits result from the weakening in the spread from 10 to 20. The spread strengthens as it approaches zero in a noninverted market.

Bull Spread

A bull spread would be established if the spreader expected the spread to strengthen. It requires a long position in the near contract and a short position in the distant.

Dec. 1, 1981

Buy July soybean   685
Sell November soybean   695 $P_D - P_N = 10$

Jan. 29, 1982

Sell July soybean   700
Buy November soybean   700 $P_D - P_N = 0$

Profits/Losses

Profit on long position	$0.15
Loss on short position	0.05
Net profit	**$0.10**

These profits accrued as a result of a strengthening spread from 10 to zero. The above assumes that the soybean contracts are for the same crop year.

The interesting thing about spreads is the protection they provide in the event that expectations do not materialize. The protection comes from the fact that contracts of different maturities tend to move in the same direction pricewise, although not necessarily with equal vigor. Thus what may be lost on the short position will be made up for (partially or totally) on the long position, and vice versa.

To further drive the point home, contrast a spread with an open position in the commodity. Assume, for example, that the expectations of the bear spreader in the above example did not materialize on Jan. 30, 1982 and that he closed his position at the following prices:

Jan. 29, 1982

Buy one July soybean at	705
Sell one November soybean at	700

Profits/Losses

Losses on short position	$= 705 - 685 = $0.20
Profit on long position	$= 700 - 695 =$ 0.05
Net loss per bushel of soybeans	**$0.15**

Had the trader established a short position in July soybean without a long position in November soybean, his loss would have amounted to 20 cents. One can argue, however, that a long position in November soybean would have been the best of all alternatives. This is so under perfect hindsight.

$P_D < P_N$ **or Inverted Market.** In an inverted market, a bull spread would still require a long position in the near contract and a short position in the distant and would produce profits if the spread strengthened.

Bull Spread

Strategy Buy near wheat   3.70
⟍
Sell distant wheat 3.50 ⟋ $P_D - P_N = -0.20$

After Sell near wheat   3.80
⟍
Buy distant wheat   3.55 ⟋ $P_D - P_N = -0.25$

Profits in long position	$= 3.80 - 3.70 =$ $0.10
Losses in short position	$= 3.50 - 3.55 =$ $0.05
Net profits	**$0.05**

The profits result from the strengthening of the spread $-0.25 < -0.20$.

Bear Spread

Once again, a bear spread calls for a short position in the near contract and a long position in the distant. Profits will accrue as the spread weakens.

Strategy Sell near   3.70
          Buy distant 3.50 $\searrow\nearrow P_D - P_N = -0.20$

After   Buy near   3.60
          Sell distant 3.45 $\searrow\nearrow P_D - P_N = -0.15$

Profits in short position $= 3.70 - 3.60 = \$0.10$
Losses in short position $= 3.50 - 3.55 = \underline{0.05}$
Net profits   **$0.05**

The profits result from the weakening of the spread, $-0.20 < -0.15$.

Intermarket Spreads.   Intermarket spreads attempt to capitalize on "unwarranted" price disparities between two contracts on the same commodity with the same maturity month but traded on two different exchanges.

From Table 15.3 we see that the March 82 wheat contract on the Chicago Board of Trade (CBT) was trading at 434 cents per bushel and the same contract was trading at 450 cents per bushel on the Kansas City Board of Trade (KC). This difference in prices can be explained, partially or totally, by the difference in the quality of deliverable wheat against each of the contracts and by transportation and other costs.

Assume, however, that a trader observing this spread concludes that it is too wide and is likely to narrow. The spread strategy would, therefore, call for the following:

Nov. 25, 1981

Buy March 82 CBT wheat at	424 cents
Sell March 82 KC wheat at	450 cents

If profits are to be realized, the CBT contract should appreciate in price and the KC contract should depreciate in price. By, say, Jan. 5, 1982, if the expected had materialized, the following would be executed:

Jan. 5, 1982

Buy March 82 CBT wheat at	440 cents
Sell March 82 KC wheat at	445 cents

Net
profit $= (440 - 434) + (450 - 445)$
$= 11$ (cents per bushel)

Intercommodity Spreads.   Intercommodity spreads are intended to capitalize on "unwarranted" price differentials between futures contracts with similar maturities on two commodities considered to be close substitutes. For example, intercommodity spreads can be used on oats and corn contracts, for both commodities are used as feed grain.

Table 15.3 shows that on Nov. 24, 1981, a March 82 corn contract traded at 283.25 cents per bushel while a March 82 oats contract traded at 210.5 cents per bushel. After close study and much deliberation, a trader decides that the gap (spread) is too wide and is bound to narrow. Thus, the following spread is established:

Nov. 25, 1981

    Sell March 82 CBT oats at   210.50 cents
    Buy March 82 CBT oats at   210.50 cents

If the traders' expectations materialize, the above transaction is reversed.

Jan. 11, 1981

    Buy March 82 CBT corn at   265.00 cents
    Sell March 82 CBT oats at   230.00 cents

Net profits = (283.25 − 265) + (230.00 − 210.50)
            = **37.75** cents per bushel

We now move to the discussion of a commodity-product spread.

Commodity-Product Spread.   This type spread attempts to capitalize on the changes in the price differential between a commodity futures contract of a certain maturity (or a different maturity) and that on a product or products derived from it. For example, a commodity-product spread could involve a long position in November soybean and a short position in October soybean oil.

In order to achieve approximate weight equivalency between contracts, the nature and results of the conversion process from commodity to product must be kept in mind. The crushing of a 60-pound bushel of soybeans produces 11 pounds of soybean oil and 48 pounds of soybean meal, with 1 pound wasted. The achievement of weight equivalency in contracts would require 50,000 bushels of soybeans (10 contracts), 9 contracts of soybean oil, and 12 contracts of soybean meal.

The nature of the commodity-product spread depends to a large degree on the profit margins realized from processing the commodity. The difference between the contracts, say soybean and soybean oil, should approximate the cost of processing soybeans into soybean oil. This cost should include a reasonable rate of return on the processing activity.

If the price differential is considered by the trader to be a bit low and the expectation is that soybean futures prices will fall while soybean oil prices would appreciate, a spreader may enter the following order:

        Buy 9 March 82 soybean oil at   20.78 cents
        Sell 50 March 82 soybeans at   654.00 cents

A nonprocessor spreader may not be concerned with weight equivalence and may well establish the above spread independent of the processing margins. The spread would yield profits if the price of soybean oil rose and that of soybeans rose by less (in percentage terms) than that of soybean oil, stayed the same, or—better yet—fell.

A more complex commodity spread is used by commodities processors. It involves a short (long) position in the commodity (soybeans, for example) and a long (short) position in the finished products derived from that commodity (oil and meal in the case of soybeans). A soybean-based spread of this type is referred to as a BOM (beans-oil-meal) spread.

To understand BOM spreads, one must understand "board" or gross processor margin.

To arrive at a gross processor margin, begin with the prices from Table 15.3 for soybeans, soybean oil, and soybean meal March 82 contracts. We find the following prices:

March 82 soybeans/bushel	$ 6.54
March 82 soybean oil/pound	$ 0.2078
March 82 soybean meal/ton	$190.10

We now convert oil and meal prices into prices per bushel, using the weight equivalence factors cited earlier as a benchmark:

1. Multiply oil prices by 11: $0.2078 \times 11 = \$2.28$ per bushel
2. Find price of soybean meal per pound (a short ton of meal is 2,000 pounds):

$$\frac{190.10}{2,000} = 0.09505$$

3. Convert the price of soybean meal to a price per bushel:

$0.09505 \times 48 = \$4.5624$

4. Calculate the gross processor margin:

oil price + meal price − soybean price = $\$2.28 + 4.5624 - 6.54 = \textbf{\$0.30}$

Therefore, the products are at a premium in relation to the commodity and that premium is equal to $0.30. Figure 15.5 shows the history of this premium for the various harvest seasons. The $0.30 represents a positive "crush." Had the margin been negative, we would have a "reverse crush" and processors would have no incentive to produce oils or meals.

A speculator may find the $0.30 margin too high (average margins equal to $0.15) and may wish to enter the following order:

Buy 50 March 82 soybean
Sell 9 March 82 soybean oil
Sell 12 March 82 soybean meal

Again, the distribution of the number of contracts may be different. Profits will accrue if soybean prices rise and those of soybean products fall or do not rise as much in percentage terms.

A soybean processor, on the other hand, would—having observed a reasonable premium between, say, March and May contracts—enter the following order:

FIGURE 15.5   Processor type futures spreads—margin products futures over/under margin soybean futures.

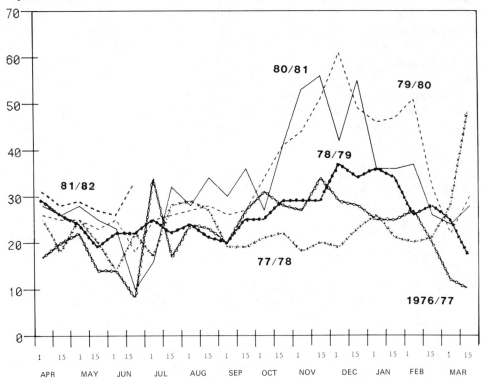

Source: Merrill Lynch Commodities, Inc., Commodity Research, New York, 1981.

> Buy 50 March 1982 soybeans
> Sell   9 May 1982 soybean oil
> Sell 12 May 1982 soybean meal

With this order, the processor would have hedged the position by locking in the cost of the soybean and the selling price of the derivative products if the plan was to sell them in May.

Other spread strategies are used. To cover them is beyond the scope of this book.

15.13 PORTFOLIO AND OTHER CONSIDERATIONS

The size of the commitment to commodities in any given portfolio depends to a large extent on the risk profile of the portfolio owner and on the expected return and riskiness of the commodities. The long-term trends as well as the shorter-term trends in commodity prices are shown in Figure 15.6. The price performance of commodities does not appear to surpass that of stocks but appears to have provided an adequate hedge against inflation. The inflation hedge is normal, for during inflationary periods investors shift from fiat money to commodities, that is, from a depreciating to an appreciating asset.

The extent to which commodities allow for portfolio risk diversification depends largely on the correlation coefficient ρ between the rate of return on commodities and that on

FIGURE 15.6 Commodity prices, stock prices, wholesale and consumer prices.

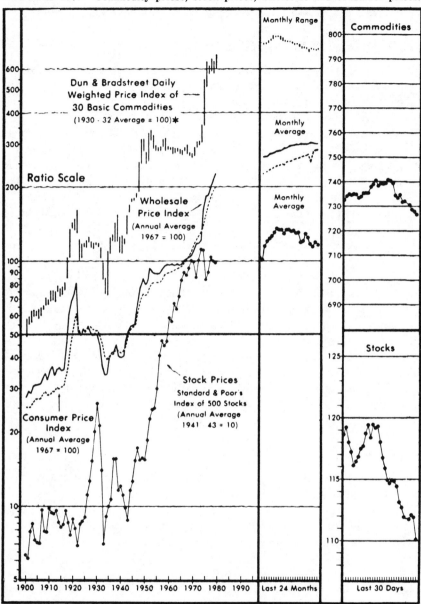

Source: The Media General Financial Weekly, Nov. 16, 1981.

the remainder of the portfolio. The closer the value of ρ is to +1, the lower the risk-diversification potential. When ρ = 1, there is no diversification possibility, as was extensively discussed in Chapter 5.

Portfolio managers generally recommend that 10 percent of the portfolio be invested in commodities. The less risk-averse the investor is, the greater this percentage should be.

Thus far, our discussion has centered on commodities futures in agricultural commodities. Another active and interesting market is that of metals futures. The balance of this chapter examines the spot and the futures market for a precious metal: gold.

15.14 GOLD AND GOLD FUTURES

The fascination with gold dates back 6,000 years. Stories about the gold rush into California and similar adventures have filled pages in history books. Pioneering men and women have risked their lives and in many cases broken the law in pursuit of gold. During the middle ages, nations undertook vast expeditions in search of gold.

The fascination with gold results from the special qualities of the metal: brilliance, unusual flexibility and workability, durability, and scarcity. Gold is indestructible.

The role played by gold in the last two hundred years deserves a brief discussion. The first step was taken by England in 1816, when the British government circulated the gold sovereign as its primary monetary unit. The United States was later, in 1873, to pass the U.S. Coinage Act, which tied the dollar to gold. The age of the gold standard had begun. By 1879, the price of gold was fixed at $20.67 an ounce. Between 1879 and 1933, the price of gold was set at $20 an ounce; it was at $35 an ounce between 1933 and 1971.

The role of gold as an official international currency effectively ended in 1971, when President Richard Nixon suspended the dollar's convertibility into gold. If dollars were not acceptable, Special Drawing Rights (SDRs) were the alternative currency. SDRs, referred to as "paper gold," are a synthetic currency created by the International Monetary Fund (IMF) in 1968 and consisting of entries on its books. The value of an SDR is currently determined in relation to five currencies: the dollar (42 percent), the German mark (19 percent), the Japanese yen (13 percent), the French franc (13 percent), and the British pound (13 percent). SDRs are allocated to IMF member countries in accordance with each country's quota with the IMF. The United States has the lion's share.

We now look at the supply of and demand for gold.

The Supply of Gold

The supply of gold is almost totally cumulative. Once mined, gold is not destroyed. The sources of supply are

1. Newly mined gold from noncommunist and communist countries
2. Sales by official bodies or agencies
3. Hoarders

The supply by hoarders is normally insignificant, although a decision by a group of, for example, wealthy Arabs to sell gold could have a significantly destabilizing effect on the market considering its thinness (witness the events of 1981–1982 where soft oil prices led to the sale of gold by many Arab individuals and nations). We shall, therefore, concentrate on the first two sources of supply.

Newly Mined Gold

The total gold output in the world is approximately equal to 40 million troy ounces a year. Over 50 percent of this total and occasionally as much as 70 percent comes from South Africa. During the 1968–1980 period, South Africa supplied 65 percent of the total world output.

TABLE 15.5
World Gold Production (Thousands of Fine Troy Ounces)

	1971	1973	1975	1977	1979
South Africa	31,389	27,495	22,938	22,600	22,617
Canada	2,243	1,954	1,654	1,740	1,581
U.S.	1,495	1,176	1,052	1,030	920
U.S.S.R.*a*	6,700	7,100	7,500	7,900	8,000
Others					
World total	46,495	42,997	38,675	40,000	39,238

Source: U.S. Bureau of Mines.
a Estimated

The second largest supplier of gold is the Soviet Union, followed by Canada and the United States (Table 15.5). No published figures on gold production in the Soviet Union are available, hence the reliance on estimated figures. The Nov. 9, 1981, issue of *Business Week* reports estimates by London metal traders of Soviet sales of gold. The Soviets sold approximately 200 tons of gold in 1981, compared with 90 tons in 1980, mostly to finance trade deficits and to support military and political objectives.

Considering the limited availability of gold, total known resources are of utmost importance. About 1 billion troy ounces of gold are known to exist in discovered gold mines, 60 percent being in the Republic of South Africa. Supply is not expected to change radically over the foreseeable future. As gold is exhausted, however, the remaining deposits become even harder to extract. Considering the labor intensity of gold mining, one should expect increased costs and higher prices to the extent that costs and prices are correlated.

Official Supply

The IMF, which held sizable gold reserves, has sold them in the open market at prevailing market prices. The sale program by the IMF terminated in May 1980. The U.S. Treasury continues to bring gold to the market in the form of gold coins: the 1-ounce Grant Wood and ½-ounce Marian Anderson commemoratives. The U.S. Treasury, with about 250 million fine troy ounces (down from 652 million in 1950) left in its vaults at the end of 1981, cannot continue selling gold indefinitely. There is something to be said for holding on to the nation's dowry. This source of supply is likely to dry up in the future. The U.S. Treasury has already slowed down its sales program considerably.

In summary, it can be said that the supply of gold is rather steady and quite predictable.

The Demand for Gold

The demand for gold comes from the following sources: governments, industrial users, dental clinics, hoarders, and speculators. Approximately 78 percent of total annual world demand comes from the industrial and the health-related sector. Electronic firms value gold for its exceptional ability to conduct electric current, and dentists use it to fill teeth. The other major industrial users of gold are jewelry manufacturers who account for 62 percent of total demand for gold worldwide. Gold used in the creation of medals accounts for less than 3 percent of total demand. The demand for gold coins minted by official institutions accounts for 10 percent of total demand for gold. The demand for gold among American investors and speculators has steadily increased since the ban on ownership of gold by U.S. citizens was lifted on Dec. 31, 1974.

The most recent entrants into the gold market are the Arabs. Using their massive oil wealth, they have contributed to the large increases and fluctuations in gold prices. Some experts estimate that about 40 percent of newly mined gold is sold in the Middle East. The Arab entry into the gold market makes the estimation of the demand function for gold a bit harder but not impossible.

The Price of Gold

Barbara Young and the author have conducted a study and summarized the determinant of the price of gold in the following equation:

$$Y = -751.373 - 2.889\,X_1 - 0.31\,X_2 + 0.3253\,X_3$$
$$(-4.47)\quad (-1.97)\quad (-1.95)\quad (1.965)$$
$$+ 0.00592\,X_4 + 679.798\,X_5$$
$$(2.23)\qquad (8.47) \tag{15.1}$$

$$R^2 = 0.94,\ \bar{R}^2 = 0.935,\ \mathrm{DW} = 1.91$$

Values in parentheses are t statistics. The variables are as follows:

Y = price of a troy ounce of gold

X_1 = "real" interest rate = T-bill rate minus the rate of inflation lagged by one period to reflect expectations

X_2 = rate of return on the S&P 500 Composite Index—used here as a proxy for return on alternative investments

X_3 = real income in the United States—used as a measure of investable funds

X_4 = average monthly foreign exchange holdings of major official participants in the gold market

X_5 = monthly U.S. consumer price index—used to test the hypothesis that gold is a hedge vehicle against inflation

All the regression coefficients were significant at the 95 percent confidence interval and had the theoretically correct sign. The data are monthly, covering the January 1975–December 1978 period.

The price of gold is, therefore, largely dependent on income levels, on the inflation rate, and on rates of return on alternative investment opportunities.

Investing in Gold

There are a number of alternatives for investing in gold. The direct method involves the purchase of gold coins and gold bullion. The indirect method involves the purchase of gold certificates, shares of mining companies, and gold futures contracts.

Gold Coins

Gold coins are of two types: numismatic or intrinsic. Numismatic coins are collectors' items and part of their value lies in their relative scarcity. The market price of these coins does not necessarily equal the worth of their gold content. Intrinsic coins can be purchased at a price just above the value of their content. The difference represents the commission cost. Examples of intrinsic coins are the South African Krugerrand, the U.S. double eagle, and the British sovereign.

The advantages of owning gold coins lie in the physical possession of the gold and the psychic gains derived therefrom, in the ease of portability and concealment, and in the fact that gold is the most acceptable "currency" in the world. Citizens of countries with unstable political and social institutions have a great affinity for gold because of the aforementioned advantages. The disadvantages of gold ownership are as follows:

1. Outright ownership does not produce periodic income. The return (if any) takes the form of capital appreciation.
2. The risk of theft or loss and the associated cost of protection through various insurance plans may be substantial.
3. There are relatively high transactions costs. Coins are considerably less liquid than, for example, corporate securities, and commission costs are high on both the buy and sell sides.
4. Some level of sophistication is required in buying and selling coins, and it takes some time to develop the needed level of expertise.

The American Numismatic Association (ANA), a nonprofit educational association, offers considerable assistance in the education of investors and in improving the operations of the market. The ANA provides a coin-authentication service and publishes the *Blackbook Price Guide of the United States Coins,* which reports average bid and ask prices on various grades of coins.

Another publication assisting coin buyers and sellers is *R. S. Yeoman's Guide Book of United States Coins* and the *Handbook of United States Coins.* The former publication provides retail price information; the latter gives dealer prices.

None of the publications cited guarantees price accuracy, nor does any provide information on the timeliness of prices. A more timely source of information on coin prices is the *Coin Dealer Newsletter,* which publishes dealer-to-dealer prices on a weekly basis.

Investors interested in purchasing gold coins may buy them from jewelry stores, from coin shops, or through a broker. The reasonableness of the purchase price can be ascertained by dividing the number of ounces in a coin by the total purchase price and then comparing the result with the daily price quotation on gold prices in the various financial publications. This may not be adequate, however, for numismatic coins.

The price appreciation of collector-quality coins over the last 12 years has kept ahead of inflation and well ahead of the rate of return on financial instruments. *Business Week* reported in its June 11, 1979, issue that collector-quality coins appreciated on the average between 200 and 400 percent during the 1969–1979 period.

The value of a coin is influenced by whether it is minted by the government or privately. The Philadelphia Mint is currently the largest supplier of minted coins. Privately minted coins are the most valuable. The highest price ever paid for a coin was $725,000, which purchased a Brasher doubloon (minted in New York in 1789) in Novem-

TABLE 15.6
Popular Gold Coins

Krugerrand South Africa 1 troy ounce fine gold 33.1903 grams, 916 2/3/1,000 31mm diameter	100 Schillings Austria 23.5240 grams, 900/1,000 fine gold 33mm diameter
Sovereign Great Britain 7.9881 grams, 916 2/3/1,000 fine gold 22mm diameter	10 soles Peru 4.68 grams, 900/1,000 fine gold 18mm diameter
Half sovereign Great Britain 3.9940 grams, 916 2/3/1,000 fine gold 19mm diameter	Vreneli (or 20 francs) Switzerland 6.4516 grams, 900/1,000 fine gold 21mm diameter
Double eagle United States 20-dollar gold piece 33.4370 grams, 900/1,000 fine gold 34mm diameter	10 francs Switzerland 3.2258 grams, 900/1,000 fine gold 19mm diameter
Eagle United States 10-dollar gold piece 16.7185 grams, 900/1,000 fine gold 27mm diameter	Chervonetz Soviet Union 8.6026 grams, 900/1,000 fine gold 22.5mm diameter
Ducat Austria 3.4909 grams, 986 2/3/1,000 fine gold 20mm diameter	20 francs France Known as Napoleon 6.4516 grams, 900/1,000 fine gold 21mm diameter
Sovrano Austria 11.060 grams, 919/1,000 fine gold 28.5mm diameter	20 dollars Canada 18.2733 grams, 900/1,000 fine gold 27mm diameter
50 peso piece Mexico 41.6666 grams, 900/1,000 fine gold 37mm diameter	20 francs Belgium Known as Lator 6.4516 grams, 900/1,000 fine gold 21mm diameter
20 peso piece Mexico 16.6666 grams, 900/1,000 fine gold 27mm diameter	20 lira Italy Also known as Lator 6.4516 grams, 900/1,000 fine gold 21mm diameter
10 peso piece Mexico 8.3333 grams, 900/1,000 fine gold 22mm diameter	

Source: Guide to Precious Metals and Their Markets, by Peter Robbins and Douglas Lee. Copyright © 1979 by Peter Robbins and Douglas Lee. Reprinted by permission of Van Nostrand Reinhold Company.

ber 1979. Other factors influencing the price of coins are gold content, rarity, brilliance, and beauty. A list of popular gold coins appears in Table 15.6.

The purchase of gold bullion is subject to essentially similar but simpler considerations. The prices of gold bars are determined by the intrinsic value of the gold content. The market price of an ounce of gold is determined by supply and demand factors and is reported regularly in daily financial publications.

Gold Certificates

Cautious investors wishing to own gold without taking physical possession of the metal may purchase gold certificates. These certificates are the equivalent of warehouse receipts. The metal represented by the receipts can be sold at any time. Gold certificates are traded in much the same way as gold coins and gold bullion. Gold certificates are usually issued by major banks like the Bank of Nova Scotia, Canadian Imperial Bank of Commerce, and Citicorp.

Citicorp offers a $1,000 minimum certificate with additional increments of $100 available. A commission of approximately 3 percent is charged, but this declines with the size of the sale. This commission is deducted before the certificate is issued to the purchaser. If the customer wishes to redeem a certificate and take possession of the gold, a 1 percent redemption fee is charged. Also, for each year after the initial year of purchase for which Citicorp has possession of the gold, a nonrefundable administrative fee of 0.5 percent of the U.S. dollar value of the client's gold is charged. Additional costs to keep in mind when taking possession of the gold include insurance, state sales taxes, transportation, and assaying charges. Speculators are particularly interested in gold certificates, for they can be purchased on margin. Banks are averse to lending money to investors or speculators to be used for purchasing gold coins and gold buillion.

Stocks in Mining Companies

Publicly traded stocks of companies with interests in gold mines are a viable alternative to physical ownership of gold. These companies are unique in the sense that their main asset (gold) is constantly being depleted, which has a significant impact on stock prices. The lower the size of gold holdings, the less the earning potential of the company—unless its share in world reserves remains constant and the depletion rate is not very high. This concern is based on the fact that future cash flows are the determinants of stock prices and that a depleted asset is not going to generate much cash flow.

Buying gold stocks, like any other stock, is done through a stockbroker. Commission costs are approximately 2 percent of the value of a round lot (100 shares or multiple thereof). Brokers usually have a minimum commission of about $30. Most gold stocks, like any other approved stock, are marginable; that is, a portion (50 percent currently) of the stock value may be purchased on credit provided the minimum required deposit is on hand.

Investors interested in gold stocks must be aware, in addition, of the factors that must be taken into consideration in the purchase of any stock:

1. The price/earnings (P/E) ratio of the company relative to the industry and to other companies in similar risk classes. An excessively high P/E ratio is not a good indication. Gold stocks tend to have particularly volatile P/E ratios.
2. The age of the gold mine and the size of the remaining deposits in relation to annual production.
3. The method of production used by the company and its costliness relative to the industry.
4. The accessibility of the gold deposits and their quality.
5. The location (geographic) of the gold deposits and of the company under consideration, the impact of the sociopolitical environment on the company's operations, and the returns on investment.

6. The significance of the gold operations in the totality of corporate activity.
7. The size of the dividend payout ratio in relation to the expectations and the needs of the investor.

Gold mining companies most widely considered for investment portfolios are those located in South Africa and North America. South African gold shares are referred to as "Kaffirs." Over one hundred different Kaffirs are traded in the U.S. over-the-counter market or in the London market. These shares represent an ownership interest in companies that are exclusively involved in gold-mining operations. *The Wall Street Journal* reports regularly on selected gold mine stocks under "African Mines."

In North America the choice of gold stocks is much more limited. Only five U.S. corporations with gold interests are publicly owned. The corporation with the largest gold deposits is Homestake Mining Co. (Table 15.7). American investors can also buy shares of Canadian companies involved in gold-mining operations, such as Giant Yellow Knife, Inc., Dome Mines, and Campbell Red Lake Mines.

The appreciation potential of gold shares, we must emphasize, is not perfectly correlated with that of gold prices. The special characteristics of the company under consideration can influence the degree of correlation, however. The Feb. 16, 1981, issue of *Business Week* reports that between Dec. 31, 1980, and Feb. 3, 1981, the price of an ounce of gold fell 25 percent while the price of major gold stocks fell by varied percentages. ASA, a South African company that owns several mines, fell from $64¼ to $53 during the same period. Campbell Red Lake Mines fell from $57 to $49½, Dome Mines fell from $86 to $77¾, and Homestake Mining from $65½ to $53¼. Investors interested in gold shares must take their volatility into consideration and must consider the options market (if an option on the particular stock exists) before making the final portfolio decision.

Gold Futures

The lifting of the ban prohibiting Americans from owning gold in 1974 brought about a greater interest in gold and the development of the gold futures market. Many of the Chicago and New York commodity exchanges were already tooled to quickly introduce a new contract in gold to accommodate the needs of hedgers, speculators, and arbitrageurs.

Definition. A gold futures contract, like other futures contracts, is a commitment to deliver a specified quantity (100 troy ounces) and grade (not less than 0.995 fineness) of refined gold during a designated month in the future at a price determined today by the auction system on the floor of the exchange.

Gold Futures Exchanges. The leading gold futures exchanges are the International Monetary Market, a division of the Chicago Mercantile Exchange, and the Commodity Exchange Inc. of New York. Both exchanges perform the same function. They provide facilities for trading futures contracts in gold within established rules and regulations. Neither of the exchanges buys or sells gold for its own account. Their clearing corporations interpose themselves, as in the other futures contracts case, between buyers and sellers and assume responsibility for the performance of the contract. Thus, the buyer of gold futures contracts looks to the clearing corporation to deliver the gold; the seller looks

TABLE 15.7
Gold Ores[a]

Callahan Mining Corp	Day Mines Inc
6245 N 24th St	Day Bldg
Phoenix, AZ 85016	Wallace ID 83873
Gold Field Deep Mines Co NV*	McCravey David L
2695 Del Rosa	816 Sunset
San Bernardino, CA 92404	Williamsburg, NM 87942
Homestake Mining Co*	Carlin Gold Mining Co*
650 California St 9th Fl	300 Park Ave
San Francisco, CA 94108	New York, NY 10022
Placer Amex Inc	Neptune Mining Co*
1 California St	120 Broadway
San Francisco, CA 94111	New York, NY 10005
Golden Cycle Corp	Standard Metals Corp
228 N Cascade Ave	645 5th Ave
Colorado Spgs, CO 80901	New York, NY 10022
Minerals Engineering Co*	Chesapeake International Corp
950 17th St	Hwy #70 E
Denver, CO 80202	Durham, NC 27701
Bobcat Properties Inc	Glasgow Kent
1015 NE 38th St	3532 NW 23rd
Ft Lauderdale, FL 33334	Oklahoma City, OK 73107
Goldfield Corp De	Duval Corp
65 E Nasa Blvd	Pennzoil Place Bldg
Melbourne, FL 32901	Houston, TX 77001
Golden Eagle Mines	Pennzoil Co*
Rt #2 Box 55 C-Z	Pennzoil Place Bldg
Grangeville, ID 83530	Houston, TX 77001
United Silver Mines Inc	Campbird Colo Inc
208 S Wilson Ave	350 W 300 S
Oakley, ID 83346	Salt Lake Cy, UT 84101

[a] An asterisk indicates that the firm is a corporation.
Source: Dun & Bradstreet Million Dollar Directory, Volume I, 1982.

to the clearing corporation to buy the gold. This effectively substitutes the credit riskiness of the transaction from the buyer or the seller to the clearing corporation. The focus is now on the exchange, and neither party to the contract knows or even cares about the identity of the buyer (if contract is sold) or the seller (if contract is bought).

Trading on the exchanges is not done through a specialist, as is the case, for example, on the New York Stock Exchange. Members of the exchange, like their counterparts

TABLE 15.8
Gold Futures Transactions on the
IMM and on COMEX

Open Interest Reflects Previous Trading Day.

	Open	High	Low	Settle	Change	Lifetime High	Low	Open Interest
GOLD (CMX) — 100 troy oz.; $ per troy oz.								
May	485.00	485.00	485.00	478.40	− 9.10	498.00	475.20	669
June	490.00	490.00	481.00	482.00	− 9.50	999.80	324.00	28,223
July	499.00	499.00	499.00	489.50	− 9.50	494.00	486.00	2
Aug	504.50	505.00	495.00	496.90	− 9.50	963.10	495.00	17,150
Oct	520.50	520.50	512.00	511.80	− 9.5	1026.4	485.20	9,696
Dec	533.00	535.00	525.00	526.80	− 9.50	981.00	497.20	18,667
Fb82	547.50	549.50	544.00	541.80	− 9.50	887.30	509.10	20,540
Apr	564.50	564.50	554.50	556.80	− 9.50	898.00	523.50	18,440
June	574.50	574.50	570.00	571.80	− 9.50	925.00	533.40	19,787
Aug	....	....	....	586.80	− 9.50	887.00	560.00	24,100
Oct	603.00	603.00	603.00	601.80	− 9.50	842.00	577.60	22,094
Dec	623.50	623.50	623.50	617.00	− 9.50	666.50	580.80	17,445
Fb83	640.30	640.30	640.30	632.30	− 9.50	642.00	613.30	3,637
Est vol 40,000; vol Tue 50,410; open int 200,450, +531.								
GOLD (IMM) — 100 troy oz.; $ per troy oz.								
June	489.30	490.20	482.00	482.50	− 9.50	993.90	351.70	7,581
Sept	512.00	512.00	503.50	504.40	− 9.7	1011.0	455.90	4,516
Dec	534.00	534.00	525.70	526.50	−10.0	1031.9	498.10	4,897
Mr82	554.00	555.00	548.00	548.70	−10.30	895.00	516.00	8,176
June	576.50	576.50	571.00	571.00	−10.70	920.00	531.50	15,702
Sept	597.50	598.00	593.40	593.40	−11.20	948.00	548.50	11,162
Dec	622.10	622.20	615.90	615.90	−11.80	974.00	570.00	7,779
Mr83	644.70	644.70	638.50	638.50	−12.50	887.20	591.00	5,361
June	....	....	....	661.20	−13.30	674.50	642.20	1,744
Est vol 10,393; vol Tue 15,239; open int 66,918, +296.								

Source: Wall Street Journal, May 14, 1981.

trading other commodities futures, step into a designated "pit," shout out, and signal their bid or offer. The highest bid and the lowest offer determine the market price of a contract for a given maturity month.

Contracts on both exchanges are standardized. They call for delivery of 100 fine troy ounces of gold with no less than 0.995 fineness. The minimum price fluctuation per contract on the IMM and COMEX is equal to $10. The delivery month on the IMM is the current month and any subsequent months; on COMEX it is the current calendar month, the next two calendar months, and "any February, April, June, August, October and December falling within a 23-month period beginning with the current month."[18]

The delivery of gold bullion on either of the exchanges is done on any business day of the delivery month and to the vaults of exchange-licensed depositories.

Traders on either of the exchanges should expect a margin requirement of 10 percent of the value of the contract and should have sufficient liquidity to meet the unfavorable margin calls. A profitable position provides a withdrawable credit balance in the trader's account; a losing position produces daily margin calls.

In terms of open interest, COMEX leads the activity in gold futures contracts. Founded in 1933, COMEX is the world's largest metals futures exchange.

The Wall Street Journal reports regularly the gold futures transactions on the IMM and on COMEX. A sample is shown in Table 15.8. The $475.20 × 100 of the COMEX (CMX) May contract is the price per troy ounce. The value of the May contract, therefore, is equal to $475.20 × 100 as of May 14, 1981. Successively higher future prices for different delivery months are referred to as "contango." Successively *lower* prices on future delivery months are referred to as "backwardation."

---

[18] *Gold Futures.* Commodity Exchange Inc., 1980, p. 7.

Advantages of the Gold Futures Markets. The advantages of gold futures contracts are similar to those of other commodities futures contracts. They are as follows:

1. *Standardization.* Standardized contracts guaranteed by the Exchange's Clearing Corporation and indirectly by every member of the exchange.

2. *Liquidity.* As opposed to high transactions costs in the markets for physical gold, the futures market is characterized by low transactions costs and substantial depth for every contract month.

3. *Leverage.* The low margin requirements for gold futures contracts allow for considerable leverage, with all its promises and pitfalls. Margin requirements, depending on the brokerage firm, are in the 5 to 15 percent range.

4. *Information.* The prices and volume of transactions on the gold futures markets are reported instantly. Both buyers and sellers are continuously appraised of the activity in the markets.

5. *Flexibility.* Activity on the gold futures markets does not result (in 99 percent of the cases) in a transfer of the metal between a buyer and a seller. Contracts are closed out by entering offsetting transactions, a buy if a sale (short position) was made and a sell if a purchase (a long position) was established.

In the futures market, the trader can capitalize on upward or downward movement in prices. It is very difficult, and certainly impossible for smaller investors, to go short in the cash market. A short position in the futures market is as easy to establish as a long position.

Uses of Gold Futures

Gold futures contracts are used for three different purposes: hedging, speculating, and buying or selling physicals. All three are best understood through examples.

Hedging

Hedging is intended to reduce if not eliminate the risk of financial loss resulting from an existing or a prospective position in the cash market.

Hedging requires a position in the futures market (e.g., short) opposite that of the cash market (long). The gain in the futures position should offset the loss in the cash position if futures price movements are highly positively correlated with price movements in the cash market. Hedging can take two forms: a long (buy) hedge and a short (sell) hedge.

Long Hedge

The long hedge in gold futures works in exactly the same way as that for other commodities discussed earlier in this chapter.

A small jewelry manufacturer who contracted to deliver jewelry in October 1981, the beginning of the holiday season, must buy gold now or at the latest in August 1981 to have sufficient time to manufacture the jewelry. Unwilling to commit the large sum required for buying gold now and worried about increases in the price of gold (spot—immediate delivery) in August, the jewelry manufacturer decides to hedge. Needing 400 ounces of gold in August 1981, she would buy (go long) four August COMEX gold futures contracts at $58,680 each (Table 15.8). For this her total downpayment would be approximately equal to (58,680 × 4) × 10% = $23,472. During the life of the contract, the manufacturer has three options:

> *Take delivery.* In August, the hedger would accept physical delivery of 400 ounces of gold against the four COMEX contracts she holds.
>
> *Exchange for physical (EFP).* This involves a simultaneous transaction between two traders. The manufacturer buys physical gold and sells futures contracts and the other trader (a supplier of physical gold) sells physical gold and buys futures contracts.
>
> *Lift a hedge.* Any time before August 1981, the manufacturer can purchase gold for spot or August delivery and sell (close out—enter a closing transaction) the August COMEX contract.

In any case, the futures contract has allowed the hedger to lock in the price at which gold is bought in August.

Locking in the price, however, does not eliminate the risk of a financial loss unless the futures contract expires at the exact date on which production is scheduled to begin or, if earlier or later, the future price moves by the exact month as the cash (spot) price.

The delivery of gold during the delivery month is at the option of the seller. If the manufacturer has to close out her contract prior to the actual contract delivery date, she will collect the market price of the futures contract at that time. If the price is $600, the gross profit per contract would equal $60,000 − $58,680 or $1,320. The $1,320 would be used to compensate for the price increase in the cash market. If this gain does not offset the spot price increase, the hedge would not be a "perfect hedge."

If the spot price has increased to $610 per ounce, the manufacturer would have achieved only a partial hedge, thus not completely eliminating the financial risk resulting from changes in gold prices. The relationship between the future price and the spot price is referred to as the "basis" as was explained in detail early in this chapter. The behavior of the basis is of paramount importance in determining the extent to which the hedge is effective.

A Short Hedge

A gold refining firm intending to bring 1,000 troy ounces of gold to the market in October 1981 would be concerned with a drop in gold prices. To hedge against this possibility, the firm would sell (short) ten October gold futures contracts on COMEX. If prices fall, the short position would realize a profit that can be used to offset the loss resulting from having to sell the firm's gold output at lower spot prices. Once again, the degree to which the hedge is effective depends on the behavior of the basis.

If futures prices rise instead, the loss on the futures contracts will be offset (partially or totally) by the gains resulting from selling the gold output at higher spot prices.

Speculation

Speculators are concerned only with gold price fluctuations. If the price of gold is expected to go up, a speculator may purchase gold in the spot market to be sold later, with luck, at a higher price, or a gold futures contract with the appropriate maturity may be purchased.

The advantages futures contracts hold over spot contracts, the aversion of speculators to dealing in the physical metal (thus avoiding all types of risks and transactions costs), and the leverage the futures market offers are an inducement for speculators to deal in the futures market instead of the cash market.

If, on the other hand, the speculator expected gold prices to fall, he or she would sell (short) a gold futures contract (or a number of them) and realize a profit if expectations materialized.

The more sophisticated speculators do not speculate in the manner indicated above but rather on the basis.

As mentioned earlier in this chapter, the basis is the difference between the spot price and the gold futures price. This relationship is best understood if we resurrect the example of the jewelry manufacturer. The manufacturer could have, as an alternative to buying a futures contract, bought the gold in the spot market and held it until she needed it for production. Had this avenue been followed, the manufacturer would have had to borrow money (or forego interest income) to buy the gold, to pay storage costs on the metal, and to pay the transport cost from London to the United States. The inclusion of the transport costs stems from the fact that the basis is usually calculated as the difference between the futures price and the London spot gold price.

The formula for basis calculation is therefore equal to:[19,20]

$$\text{Basis} = \left[(\text{borrowing cost}) \left(\frac{\text{days to maturity}}{360} \right) (\text{spot price}) \right]$$
$$+ \text{ storage charges} \pm \text{ transport costs}$$

Example:

An October contract (delivery on Oct. 15, 1981) being considered on May 15, 1981—when the prime rate is 20 percent, the storage costs equal to $0.03 per ounce per month, the shipping costs from London to New York equal to $0.4 per ounce—would have the following basis if the current spot price were $475:

$$\text{Basis} = \left[\left(\frac{20}{100} \right) \times \left(\frac{150}{360} \right) \times (475) \right] + 0.03 \, (5) + 0.40 = \$40.13$$

This means that the October contract should sell for $475 + $40.13 = $515.13 if the interest charges, the time period, and other charges were correctly calculated.

Similar calculations can be made for bases for various futures contracts, for example, the basis for the December contract vs. the October contract on COMEX.

Any deviation in the market between the theoretical price (spot price plus basis) of a futures contract and its current market price offers an opportunity for arbitrage by trading the basis. Assuming that on May 15 the October COMEX contract was selling for $505, a gold dealer could do the following:

Sell gold in the spot market at $475
Buy October futures at $505

---

[19] See *Gold Futures Trading for Bullion Dealers.* International Monetary Market, Chicago, 1980.

[20] Storage costs include insurance and other carrying costs.

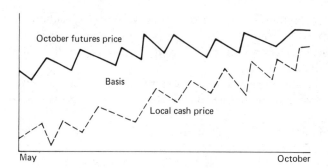

FIGURE 15.7 Convergence of futures prices with cash prices.

As soon as market prices are realigned and the futures contract is trading at $515, the theoretical price, the transaction above is reversed:

Buy spot at $475
Sell October contract at $515

The profit per ounce is equal to $515 − $505 or $10. The profit per contract is thus equal to: $10 \times 100 = \$1,000$.

Several other basis trading strategies have been devised. The reader is urged to read the literature published by the IMM and COMEX on this subject.

Before we leave the discussion of the basis, we must point out a few of its properties. It is influenced by a number of factors, including the following:

1. Supply and demand conditions in the cash and futures markets. An excessively high demand for gold in the cash market will increase its price and, ceteris paribus, decrease the basis.

2. The location of the gold to be delivered. The transportation costs will change depending on the location.

3. Time. As time passes, the futures contract approaches a spot contract. At expiration, the futures contract becomes a spot contract. The closer to expiration the contract is, the narrower the basis because of lower interest and storage costs. The convergence of futures prices with cash prices is not necessarily smooth as in Figure 15.7.

Understanding the basis is of critical importance for gold traders, for it is of considerable help in determining whether to accept or reject a given price; whether or when to store gold; whether, when, and in what delivery month to hedge; when to close a hedge; and how to spot a profitable arbitrage or speculative situations.

Conclusions

Sophisticated strategies such as the spreads discussed earlier in this chapter are also used with gold contracts. The reader is encouraged to retrace that discussion.

Commodities futures contracts are an excellent vehicle for preserving wealth, for accumulating wealth, and also for losing it. Any trader who is not willing to spend the needed time to study, understand, and follow the markets should avoid commodities unless he or she is willing to rely on the advice of a thoroughly investigated (in terms of performance record and attention to customer needs) broker.

The same degree of caution should also be expressed when buying spot gold and gold futures contracts. The volatility of both markets is very high, and the choices are not always very clear.

The material presented in this chapter summarizes the major issues but does not exhaust all the concerns and considerations. The interested reader should investigate these investment/speculative vehicles further.

Questions

1. Discuss the differences and the similarities between the normal backwardation theory and the storage theory.

2. Few commodities futures contracts are ever delivered against. What does this reveal about the nature of the market?

3. What roles do commodities futures contracts play in the U.S. and the world economy? Justify your answer.

4. "Hedging in the futures market is always a speculation." Comment.

5. What are the differences and similarities between a futures and a forward contract?

6. What role does the CFTC play in the futures market? What are the implications of this for market efficiency?

7. Do you think the daily price limits on futures contracts retard or enhance speculation? What are the implications of this for market efficiency?

8. Outline the mechanics of a BOM spread. Who could use it? Establish a bull BOM spread. When does such a strategy pay off?

9. Compare and contrast the advantages and disadvantages of direct investment in gold vs. the purchase of gold certificates.

10. Explain the advantages of investing in the gold futures market instead of investing directly in gold bullion.

11. Discuss how the leading gold futures exchanges reduce the risks for a buyer or a seller in the gold futures market.

12. You are a gold buyer for a small private mint that produces coins. You anticipate a need for 5,000 ounces of gold in three months to meet production requirements. You expect a price appreciation in gold over the next three months. Due to high interest rates, you do not want to tie up large amounts of cash. What would be your investment strategy?

13. "The greatest danger in gold investments lies in the thinness of the market." Do you agree? Explain.

14. "Fundamental analysis in commodities futures is helpful and desirable, but it cannot be used as a basis for active trading or even as a timing device." Do you agree?

15. The profitability of intermonth commodity spreads depends on the behavior of the spread. What must the spread do for a bear spread to realize a profit in an inverted market? In a noninverted market?

16. An inverted market is not a common occurrence. Outline the conditions under which an inverted market may prevail.

17. "A stop order on a commodities futures contract works in exactly the same way as a stop order on a common stock." Do you agree?

18. "Commodities markets are too speculative, stay out of them." Comment.

19. How important a role do speculators play in the commodities markets?

20. The commodities exchanges are quite concerned about "excessive speculation." Discuss some of the tools used by the exchanges to limit speculative fevers.

PROBLEMS

1. You are a gold dealer in New York. On April 15, the spot rate of gold is $525, the prime rate is 19½ percent, the storage cost per ounce of gold is $0.04/month, and the shipping cost from London to New York is $0.05 per ounce.
   a. Calculate the theoretical price of an August futures contract (delivery on Aug. 15).
   b. What strategy would you follow if the actual August contract's price is $548?
   c. Why should the market adjust to this price?

2. On January 7, 1982, Hillsman's Coffee, Inc., a Chicago-based company, forecasts a need for coffee beans of 187,500 lb. by December 1982. Concerned with possible increases in the price of coffee, Hillsman's Coffee decides to hedge in the futures market.
   a. What type of hedge would it establish?
   b. What are the consequences of a weakening of 10 percent in the basis?
   c. What are the consequences of a strengthening of 10 percent in the basis?
   d. Comment on the results above.

3. R. B. O'Neill, head of an Iowa corn farming family, fears a fall in the price of corn by harvest time (September). R. B. expects 100,000 bushels. On Jan. 7, 1982, the spot price for corn is $2.63¼/bu.; the September futures price is $2.94¼/bu. R. B. decides to hedge in the futures market.
   a. What type of hedge would he establish?
   b. What are the consequences of a 15 percent weakening in the basis?
   c. What are the consequences of a 15 percent strengthening in the basis?
   d. Comment on the results of the strategy.

4. The March 15 spot rate for gold is $485, the prime rate is 18 percent, the storage cost per ounce of gold is $0.05/month, and the shipping cost from London to New York is $0.40/ounce. What action would a speculator undertake if the March 15 price of a June gold futures contract is $525?

5. A jeweler needs 100 ounces of gold on Aug. 20. The spot price for gold on Feb. 24 is $363.80. The jeweler is worried about an increase in the price of gold. The price of an August gold futures contract is $384.10. How could the jeweler hedge against the anticipated price increase? What would be his commitment? (Assume 10 percent margin requirement.) Under what circumstances would he undertake such a hedge?

6. You are an investor with 500 ounces of gold in your portfolio on Feb. 23; you wish to dispose of this gold but cannot sell it until June 15. You anticipate that the price of gold will fall over the next four months. What strategy would you undertake to hedge in the futures market?

APPENDIX

Glossary

arbitrage: The simultaneous purchase and sale of similar financial instruments or commodity futures in order to benefit from an anticipated change in their price relationship.

bear: One who believes prices will move lower (See *bull.*)

bear market: A market in which prices are declining.

bid: An offer to purchase at a specified price (See *offer.*)

break: A rapid and sharp price decline.

bull: One who expects prices to rise (See *bear.*)

bull market: A market in which prices are rising.

buy in: To cover, offset or close out a short position. (See *evening up, liquidation, offset.*)

buy on close: To buy at the end of the trading session at a price within the closing range.

buy on opening: To buy at the beginning of a trading session at a price within the opening range.

car: A loose quantity term sometimes used to describe a contract, e.g., "a car of bellies." Derived from the fact that quantities of the product specified in a contract used to correspond closely to the capacity of a railroad car.

cash commodity: The actual physical commodity as distinguished from a futures commodity.

CFTC: The Commodity Futures Trading Commission is the independent federal agency created by Congress to regulate futures trading. The CFTC Act of 1974 became effective April 21, 1975. Previously, futures trading had been regulated by the Commodity Exchange Authority of the USDA.

clearinghouse: An adjunct to a futures exchange through which transactions executed on the floor of the exchange are settled using a process of matching purchases and sales. A clearing organization is also charged with the proper conduct of delivery procedures and the adequate financing of the entire operation.

clearing member: A member firm of the clearinghouse or organization. Each clearing member must also be a member of the exchange. Not all members of the exchange, however, are members of the clearing organization. All trades of a non-

---

Note: This glossary was compiled by the Chicago Mercantile Exchange from a number of sources. The definitions are not intended to state or suggest the correct legal significance or meaning of any word or phrase. The sole purpose of this compilation is to foster a better understanding of futures.

clearing member must be registered with, and eventually settled through, a clearing member.

close, the: The period at the end of the trading session. Sometimes used to refer to the closing price. (See *opening, the.*)

closing range (or range): The high and low prices, or bids and offers, recorded during the period designated as the official close. (See *settlement price.*)

commission (or round-turn): The one-time fee charged by a broker to a customer when a position is liquidated either by offset or delivery.

commission house: (See *futures commission merchant, omnibus account.*)

commitment: A trader is said to have a commitment, when he assumes the obligation to accept or make delivery on a futures contract. (See *open interest.*)

contract: A term of reference describing a unit of trading for a financial commodity future. Also, actual bilateral agreement between the buyer and seller of a futures transaction as defined by an exchange.

contract month: The month in which futures contracts may be satisfied by making or accepting a delivery. (See *delivery month.*)

cover: The purchase of futures to offset a previously established short position.

day order: An order that is placed for execution, if possible, during only one trading session. If the order cannot be executed that day, it is automatically canceled.

day trading: Refers to establishing and liquidating the same position or positions within one day's trading.

deferred futures: The most distant months of a futures contract. (See *nearby.*)

delivery: The tender and receipt of an actual commodity or financial instrument or cash in settlement of a futures contract.

delivery month: (See *contract month.*)

delivery notice: The written notice given by the seller of his intention to make delivery against an open, short futures position on a particular date. (See *notice day.*)

delivery points: Those points designated by futures exchanges at which the financial instrument or commodity covered by a futures contract may be delivered in fulfillment of such contract.

delivery price: The price fixed by the clearinghouse at which deliveries on futures are invoiced, also the price at which the futures contract is settled when deliveries are made.

discretionary account: An account over which any individual or organization other than the person in whose name the account is carried, exercises trading authority or control.

equity: The residual dollar value of a futures trading account, assuming its liquidation at the going market price.

evening up: Buying or selling to offset an existing market position. (See *buy in liquidation offset.*)

first notice day: The first date, varying by contracts and exchanges, on which notices of intention to deliver actual financial instruments or physical commodities against futures are authorized.

floor broker: A member who is paid a fee for executing orders for clearing members or their customers. A floor broker executing customer orders must be licensed by the CFTC.

floor trader: A member who generally trades only for his own account, for an account controlled by him or who has such a trade made for him. Also referred to as a "local."

futures: A term used to designate all contracts covering the sale of financial instruments or physical commodities for future delivery on a commodity exchange.

futures commission merchant: A firm or person engaged in soliciting or accepting and handling orders for the purchase or sale of futures contracts, subject to the rules of a futures exchange and, who, in connection with such solicitation or acceptance of orders, accepts any money or securities to margin any resulting trades or contracts. The FCM must be licensed by the CFTC. (See *commission house, omnibus account.*)

give up: At the request of the customer, a brokerage house which has not performed the service is credited with the execution of an order.

hedge: The purchase or sale of a futures contract as a temporary substitute for a transaction to be made at a later date. Usually it involves opposite positions in the cash market and the futures market at the same time. (See *long hedge, short hedge.*)

hedger: One who hedges.

initial margin: (See *security deposit—initial.*)

inverted market: A futures market in which the nearer months are selling at premiums to the more distant months. (See *premium.*)

last trading day: The final day under an exchange's rules during which trading may take place in a particular delivery futures month. Futures contracts outstanding at the end of the last trading day must be settled by delivery of underlying physical commodities or financial instruments, or by agreement for monetary settlement if the former is impossible.

limit price: (See *maximum price fluctuation.*)

limit order: An order given to a broker by a customer which has restrictions upon its execution. The customer specifies a price and the order can be executed only if the market reaches or betters that price.

liquidation: Same as evening up or offset. Any transaction that offsets or closes out a long or short position. (See *buy in, evening up, offset.*)

long: One who has bought a futures contract(s) to establish a market position and who has not yet closed out this position through an offsetting sale; the opposite of *short.*

long hedge: The purchase of a futures contract(s) in anticipation of actual purchases in the cash market. Used by processors or exporters as protection against an advance in the cash price. (See *hedge, short hedge.*)

margin: A cash amount of funds that must be deposited with the broker for each futures contract as a guarantee of fulfillment of the contract. Also called *security deposit.*

maintenance margin: A sum, usually smaller than—but part of—the original margin, which must be maintained on deposit at all times if a customer's equity in any futures position drops to, or under, the maintenance margin level, the broker must issue a "margin call" for the amount of money required to restore the custom-

er's equity in the account to the original margin level. (See *margin call, security deposit—maintenance.*)

margin call: A demand for additional cash funds because of adverse price movement. (See *maintenance margin; security deposit—maintenance.*)

mark to market: The daily adjustment of an account to reflect profits and losses.

market order: An order for immediate execution given to a broker to buy or sell at the best obtainable price.

maximum price fluctuation: The maximum amount the contract price can change, up or down, during one trading session, as fixed by exchange rules. (See *limit price.*)

minimum price fluctuation: Smallest increment of price movement possible in trading a given contract. (See *point.*)

M.I.T.: Market if touched. A price order that automatically becomes a market order if the price is reached.

nearby: The nearest active trading month of a financial or commodity futures market. (See *deferred futures.*)

nominal price: Price quotations on futures for a period in which no actual trading took place.

notice day: A day on which notices of intent to deliver pertaining to a specified delivery month may be issued. (See *delivery notice.*)

offer: Indicates a willingness to sell a futures contract at a given price. (See *bid.*)

offset: (See *buy in, evening up, liquidation.*)

omnibus account: An account carried by one futures commission merchant with another futures commission merchant in which the transactions of two or more persons are combined and carried in the name of the originating broker, rather than designated separately. (See *commission house, futures commission merchant.*)

open contracts: Contracts which have been bought or sold without the transaction having been completed by subsequent sale or purchase, or by making or taking actual delivery of the financial instrument or physical commodity. (See *position.*)

open interest: Number of open futures contracts. Refers to unliquidated purchases or sales.

open order: An order to a broker that is good until it is canceled or executed.

opening, the: The period at the beginning of the trading session officially designated by the exchange during which all transactions are considered made "at the opening." (See *close, the.*)

opening price (or range): The range of prices at which the first bids and offers were made or first transactions were completed.

original margin: The margin needed to cover a specific new position. (See *security deposit—initial.*)

P&S: Purchase and sale statement. A statement provided by the broker showing change in the customer's net ledger balance after the offset of a previously established position(s).

point: (See *minimum price fluctuation.*)

position: An interest in the market, either long or short, in the form of open contracts. (See *open contracts.*)

premium: The excess of one futures contract price over that of another, or over the cash market price. (See *inverted market.*)

primary market: The principal underlying market for a financial instrument or physical commodity.

rally: An upward movement of prices following a decline, the opposite of a *reaction.* (See *recovery.*)

range: The high and low prices or high and low bids and offers, recorded during a specified time.

reaction: A decline in prices following an advance; the opposite of *rally.*

recovery: Usually describes a price advance following a decline. (See *rally.*)

registered representative: A person employed by, and soliciting business for, a commission house or futures commission merchant.

round-turn: Procedure by which the long or short position of an individual is offset by an opposite transaction or by accepting or making delivery of the actual financial instrument or physical commodity.

scalp: To trade for small gains. It normally involves establishing and liquidating a position quickly, usually within the same day.

security deposit: (See *margin.*)

security deposit (initial): Synonymous with the term *margin,* a cash amount of funds that must be deposited with the broker for each contract as a guarantee of fulfillment of the futures contract. It is not considered as part payment or purchase. (See *initial margin, original margin.*)

security deposit (maintenance): A sum usually smaller than, but part of, the original deposit or margin that must be maintained on deposit at all times. If a customer's equity in any futures position drops to or below the maintenance level, the broker must issue a call for the amount of money required to restore the customer's equity in the account to the original margin level. (See *maintenance margin, margin call.*)

settlement price: A figure determined by the closing range which is used to calculate gains and losses in futures market accounts. Settlement prices are used to determine gains, losses, margin calls, and invoice prices for deliveries. (See *closing range.*)

short: One who has sold a futures contract to establish a market position and who has not yet closed out this position through an offsetting purchase; the opposite of a *long.*

short hedge: The sale of a futures contract(s) to eliminate or lessen the possible decline in value of ownership of an approximately equal amount of the actual financial instrument or physical commodity. (See *hedge, long hedge.*)

short selling: Establishing a market position by selling a futures contract.

short squeeze: A situation in which a lack of supply tends to force prices upward.

speculator: One who attempts to anticipate price changes and, through buying and selling futures contracts, aims to make profits; does not use the futures market in connection with the production, processing, marketing or handling of a product.

spread: Refers to simultaneous purchase and sale of futures contracts for the same commodity or instrument for delivery in different months, or in different but related markets.

stop order (or stop): An order to buy or sell at the market when a definite price is reached, either above or below the price that prevailed when the order was given.

switching: Liquidating an existing position and simultaneously reinstating a position in another futures contract of the same type.

tender: To offer for delivery against futures.

tick: Refers to a change in price, either up or down.

trend: The general direction of the market.

volume: The number of transactions in a futures contract made during a specified period of time.

wire house: A firm operating a private wire to its own branch offices, or to other firms, commission houses and brokerage houses.

16 | The Foreign Exchange Markets

16.1 AN OVERVIEW

The international monetary system has evolved through the years into its present form. The gold standard prevailed between 1870 and 1914. International settlements were made in gold. Countries with balance-of-payments deficits lost gold, which led to lower incomes and prices. Countries with balance-of-payments surpluses increased their gold reserves, with resulting increases in incomes and prices. International disequilibrium was thus eliminated through the price system, leaving the exchange rates (value of currency in terms of gold) intact.

The second international economic system was agreed to by the participants at the Bretton Woods Conference in 1944. Under this agreement, all currencies were pegged to gold, but only the dollar was convertible into gold. Exchange rates were allowed to fluctuate within ±1 percent of par value (value in terms of U.S. dollars). The system worked well until the 1960s, when it showed major signs of weakness. Confidence in the dollar was waning at a time when world trade was expanding, necessitating a larger supply of a common denominator for international payments. This would have required continued and increasing U.S. balance-of-payments deficits.

Despite various attempts at patching up the system, the central bankers of the world finally rediscovered the free market system. Today, major currency prices are determined by the forces of supply and demand. International adjustments thus take place in the foreign exchange market, not through the domestic price system, despite occasional interventions by the government intended to "stabilize the market."

16.2 DEFINITIONS

Foreign Exchange

Foreign exchange is the price of one currency in terms of another. A foreign exchange contract is like any commodity contract specifying the delivery of one good (currency) for another. However, commodity contracts in developed economies do not specify the price of one commodity in terms of another but rather in terms of a common denominator (a currency). A foreign exchange contract consists of an entry on the books of a market maker (almost always a bank) reflecting a transaction in the spot (immediate delivery) market or in the forward or futures (future delivery) markets.

The Demand and Supply of Foreign Exchange

The demand for foreign exchange is a derived demand. Economic agents demand foreign currencies not for the sake of having them but rather to purchase goods and services and/or to make portfolio investments abroad. Holding foreign currency for speculative purposes is not, as we shall demonstrate, the optimum method for speculation. There exist several more attractive methods for speculation. Table 16.1 summarizes the supply and demand factors for foreign exchange, the dollar in particular.

The demand and supply of goods and services are functions of price differentials between the United States and the rest of the world, income levels, and consumer taste. The demand for and supply of financial assets are functions of interest-rate differentials between the United States and the rest of the world and the perceived risk of the investment. Much will be said in this chapter about the supply and demand for financial assets and about the relationship between interest rates and exchange rates.

The linkages between the product and the financial markets and between both of these markets and the foreign exchange market are summarized in Figure 16.1.

The first linkage (1) is internal to the economy (U.S. or foreign). It represents the relationship between the product market and the money and capital markets resulting from firms financing their inventories, capital equipment, physical facilities, etc. The second linkage (2) represents international trade between the United States and other countries. Which goods and services are bought or sold by one country depend on the factors listed in Table 16.1. The third linkage (3) represents the role played by the foreign exchange markets in bridging the financial markets of the world as investors seek to maximize returns and minimize risk on their portfolios in an international setting.

TABLE 16.1
Supply of and Demand for Dollars

Supply Factors	Demand Factors
1. Demand for foreign goods and services, which, in turn, is determined by: a. Foreign prices *relative* to U.S. prices b. U.S. income levels c. Preferences for things foreign, e.g., foreign cars	1. Demand for U.S. goods and services, which, in turn, is determined by: a. U.S. prices *relative* to foreign prices b. Foreign income levels c. Preferences for things American, e.g., Levi's jeans
2. Demand for foreign financial assets, which, in turn, is determined by: a. Foreign interest rates *relative* to U.S. rates	2. Demand for U.S. financial assets which, in turn, is determined by: a. U.S. interest rates *relative* to foreign rates
b. Perceived risk of foreign investment	b. Perceived risk of U.S. investment

Source: Monthly Economic Report. First Pennsylvania Corporation, Philadelphia, June 1980.

FIGURE 16.1   The market linkages.

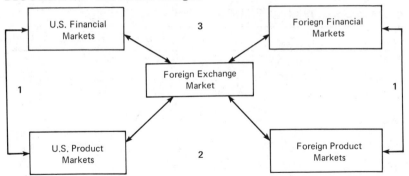

Source: *Monthly Economic Report.* First Pennsylvania Corporation, Philadelphia, June 1980.

The second and third linkages result in international transactions which are summarized and periodically reported as balance-of-payments statistics, which show the results of transactions between domestic and foreign residents.

As Table 16.2 makes clear, there is a multitude of ways to measure whether the international transactions of the United States are in balance or not. Each "balance" has a different meaning and different implications. None of the balances is perfect, and none gives the complete picture by itself.

The merchandise trade balance is the difference between exports and imports of goods.

The balance on goods and services is the export of goods and services minus import of goods and services excluding unilateral transfers. All government grants and transfers, private transfers, and capital transactions are placed below the line (the double line in Table 16.2); that is, they are not included in the calculation of the balance.

The balance on current account places U.S. government grants, U.S. government pension and other transfers, and private remittances and other transfers above the line. Capital transactions, whether short- or long-term, private or government, are placed below the line; that is, they are not included in the calculations.

In terms of usefulness, the merchandise trade balance figures, published on a monthly basis and therefore quickly available, are useful indicators as to the international competitiveness of U.S. products.

In a time horizon exceeding five years, fundamental equilibrium requires that the balance on current account be equal to zero, because foreign capital inflows which may have been offsetting a current account deficit generally begin to generate outflows in the form of profits and interest payments, which can worsen the external position of the country.

Before concluding this discussion, a word on the errors and omissions (statistical discrepancy) account is warranted. Data on credits do not necessarily come from the same source as debits. Trade or real flows may be recorded on a different date from financial flows. Trade flows are ordinarily recorded at the time the merchandise crosses the border, while financial flows are recorded on the payment date. The two dates are not usually the same. Furthermore, the figures used in the accounting entries are frequently estimated, such as the amount of money spent by tourists; and some transactions (illegal ones, usually) are just not reported.

TABLE 16.2
U.S. Balance of Payments, 1980 (in Billions of Dollars)

	Receipts	Payments
Merchandise exports (other than military)	224.00	
Merchandise imports (other than military)		249.3
Merchandise Trade Balance		**25.3**
Military transactions	8.2	10.7
Travel	10.1	10.4
Passenger fares	2.6	3.6
Other transportation	11.4	10.9
Fees and royalties	6.9	.8
Income from foreign assets	75.9	43.1
Other services	5.6	5.0
Balance on Goods and Services	**10.8**	
Net unilateral transfers		7.1
Balance on Current Account	**3.7**	
Private capital payments		
U.S. direct investments overseas		18.6
Other private investment overseas		52.9
Private capital receipts		
Foreign direct investment in the United States	10.9	
Other foreign investment in the United States	23.9	
Change in U.S. government assets abroad		5.1
Change in foreign official assets in the United States		15.5
Change in official reserve assets		8.2
New allocation of SDRs	1.2	
Statistical discrepancy	29.6	
Accounting balance = 0		

Source: Survey of Current Business, June 1981.

Foreign Exchange Market

The foreign exchange market is where currencies are traded. It is not a centralized market in the sense of a trading floor where all buyers and sellers meet to transact business. Transactions are effected over the Telex wire or by telephone. Face-to-face contact is hardly ever necessary. London, Frankfurt, Amsterdam, Zurich, Paris, Brussels, New York, and Toronto are the financial centers through which most of the transactions flow. These centers are connected by sophisticated communications networks (SWIFT[1] and CHIPS[2]). The market is a continuous one with no opening or closing hours, particularly with Hong Kong and Singapore becoming important centers for currency trading. It is a very competitive market.

---

[1] SWIFT = Society for Worldwide Interbank Financial Telecommunication.

[2] CHIPS = The Clearing House Interbank Payments System.

FIGURE 16.2 Total foreign exchange activity.

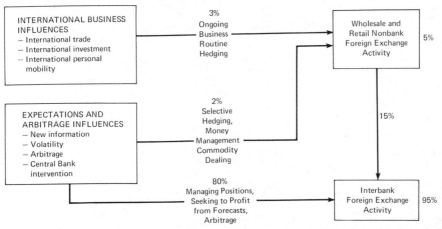

Source: Ian H. Giddy, "Measuring the World Foreign Exchange Market." *Columbia Journal of World Business,* Winter 1979, p. 42.

16.3 SIZE OF MARKET

No one really knows how large the market is, although many studies have attempted to estimate its size. The range of estimates is very wide indeed. An official of the Federal Reserve Bank of New York estimates the size of the market to be $30 trillion (yes, trillion) for 1977.[3] Citibank's estimate is $50 trillion[4] for the same period. The latest estimate is provided by Ian Giddy, who puts the size of the market at $29 trillion per annum.[5] The estimating procedure used by Giddy is worth summarizing. Using the transactions flowing through CHIPS, the dominant channel for international transactions calling for fund transfer, and adjusting for "non-foreign exchange transfers through CHIPS for forward and book transfer transactions that do not go through CHIPS, and for foreign exchange transactions not involving the U.S. dollar." Giddy arrived at $29 trillion for the year 1977, or an average daily volume of $118 billion.

The growth of the foreign exchange market, while impressive, was certainly not very smooth. The market was severely jolted by the failures of the Herstatt Bank and the Franklin National Bank in 1974. Much of the speculation was curtailed as banks attempted to keep their foreign exchange exposure to a minimum. Early in 1975 volume began to pick up once again and continued a steep rise, reaching new highs by the end of 1978.

16.4 MARKET PARTICIPANTS

The major participants in the foreign exchange market are commercial banks, central banks, and nonbanking institutions. The distribution of the foreign exchange activity among the participants is depicted in Figure 16.2. As this figure makes clear, 82 percent

---

[3] *The Wall Street Journal,* Jan. 15, 1979.

[4] See **James H. Wooden,** *U.S. Multinational Banks–Foreign Exchange Operations.* Merrill Lynch Institutional Report, New York, July 1979.

[5] **Ian H. Giddy,** "Measuring the World Foreign Exchange Market." *Columbia Journal of World Business,* Winter 1979, pp. 36–48.

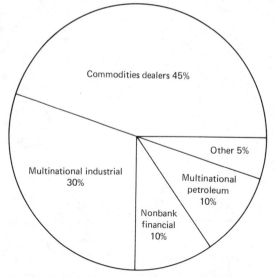

Commodities dealers 45%

Other 5%

Multinational industrial
30%

Multinational
petroleum
10%

Nonbank
financial
10%

FIGURE 16.3 Nonbank participants
in foreign exchange trading.

Source: Ian H. Giddy, "Measuring the World Foreign Exchange Market." *Columbia Journal of World Business,* Winter 1979, p. 43.

of the activities are motivated by speculation and arbitrage opportunities. Only 3 percent
of total volume is motivated by commercial transactions. The distribution of nonbank
activities is shown in Figure 16.3. The largest activity is that of commodity dealers,
particularly those in the metals markets. These activities are predominantly speculative
in nature.

While interbank trading dominates the foreign exchange market, it must be remem-
bered that the motivating force behind the market is those transactions associated with
the movement of goods and capital. It is these transactions which create the legitimate
need for foreign exchange and to which the banking system must ultimately answer.
The speculative and arbitrage activities of commercial banks are the result of attempts
by banks to protect and to maximize the rate of return on positions held to accommodate
trade and capital transactions. Note further that speculative and acommodating transactions are not always undertaken by banks for their own account.

16.5 CURRENCY COMPOSITION

The currencies playing major roles in the foreign exchange markets are those of countries
with well-developed markets characterized by minimal interference by the indigenous
government in the market mechanism and by liberal policies regarding conversion and
flow of capital across national borders. The strength of these markets is not always
derived from the strength of the indigenous economy or from the country's position
in international trade. The role of the United States in the world economy and the
strength of the ties between many European countries and developing nations began
during the industrial revolution and solidified during periods of colonialism. These factors
have contributed to the role played by the dollar and other European currencies, such
as the Dutch guilder and the British pound. The Swiss case is most peculiar; the position

TABLE 16.3
Estimated Currency Composition of
Foreign Exchange Trading

Currency	Percentage of Total Transactions
U.S. dollar	99%
German mark	40
British pound	15
Swiss franc	18
Canadian dollar	5
Japanese yen	5
French franc	6
Dutch guilder	5
Belgian franc	2
Italian lira	1
Swedish krona	1
Other	3
Total	200%

Source: Ian H. Giddy, "Measuring the World Foreign Exchange Market." *Columbia Journal of World Business,* Winter 1979, p. 41.

Note: Total adds to 200% because two currencies are involved in every foreign exchange transaction.

of the Swiss franc in the world market stems from the strength of the Swiss economic and political system and from the position Switzerland enjoys in world politics.

Currencies that are allowed to float freely or jointly as opposed to being pegged account for approximately 70 percent of the denominations of world trade. So, while history is important, economics plays an overriding role. This view is supported by the relatively weak role played by the Japanese yen because of the interference of the Japanese government in the foreign exchange market.

The relative importance of each currency in the foreign exchange market is summarized in Table 16.3. The roles played by the dollar, the German mark, the British pound, and the Swiss franc far exceed those played in international trade by their respective countries.

16.6 TRADING MECHANICS

Trading in the foreign exchange market almost invariably involves the U.S. dollar. Giddy's work indicates that it is involved in 99 percent of the value of foreign exchange transactions.[6] Transactions between two European currencies, for example, are almost never direct. They are indirect transactions involving the U.S. dollar because of the depth of the dollar–foreign-currency market and the associated lower transaction costs. (A British importer wishing to buy German marks to pay a German exporter would sell pounds for dollars and then buy German marks with the proceeds.) What the bank would do in a foreign exchange transaction is illustrated in Figure 16.4. Intricate as

[6] Ibid, p. 39.

FIGURE 16.4   **The international dollar payments system.**

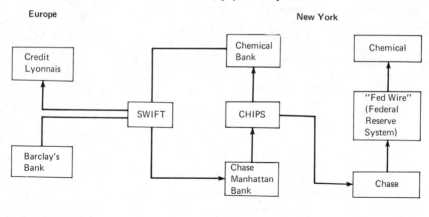

Steps in the transfer of funds resulting from a foreign exchange transaction:

1. Barclay's Bank buys German marks from Credit Lyonnais; to consummate this it must transfer funds in the U.S. to Credit Lyonnais' account in Chemical Bank, New York.
2. Barclay's uses SWIFT, a worldwide financial communications network, to instruct Chase to transfer funds out of the Barclay's account.
3. Chase debits Barclay's account and transfers the funds through SHIPS, the payments clearing system for international transactions; in effect it sends an electronic check to CHIPS; those "clearing house funds" get credited to Chemical on the same day. Night falls.
4. Next day, the net amount is settled between Federal Reserve member banks by transfers in "Fed funds" —deposits held at the various Federal Reserve banks. This is done through the domestic interbank clearing system the "Fed wire".
5. Chemical credits Credit Lyonnais' account and notifies Credit Lyonnais, again through the SWIFT network.

Source: Ian H. Giddy, "Measuring the World Foreign Exchange Market." *Columbia Journal of World Business,* Winter 1979, p. 40.

this figure may appear, transactions are executed effectively and quickly. Electronic communications have facilitated considerably the movement of funds. We must note, however, that no currency of whatever nationality has changed hands here. The foreign exchange contract is simply a bookkeeping entry. The correspondent banks in the United States that are called upon to execute foreign exchange transactions are usually New York banks. The twelve largest U.S. banks, anchored in New York, constitute the totality of the U.S. market. These banks, by arbitraging their own foreign exchange position and that of their clients, in a currency or across currencies, provide a continuous marketplace for currencies. Banks trading in New York deal through a broker in order to preserve anonymity and to centralize the communication network.

The role of the central bank is not always a passive one (a transfer agent) in foreign exchange transactions (Figure 16.2). Central banks continue to intervene in order to maintain an "orderly market." They do so by trading with commercial banks or with each other. The greater the role of the central bank, the less freedom commercial banks enjoy and the less the foreign exchange rate is market determined.

16.7 NECESSARY DEFINITIONS

Forward Exchange

A forward exchange contract is an agreement to buy (sell) a certain amount of foreign currency at a specified price at a specified date in the future (one, two, three, six, or twelve months, usually).

Spot Exchange

A spot exchange contract is a special case of a forward contract where the time period shrinks to a few days (two days or less, usually).

Swap Transaction

A swap is the simultaneous purchase and sale of spot and forward exchange or two forward transactions of different maturities.

16.8 TYPES OF SPOT RATES

Freely Fluctuating Rates

These rates are determined by the forces of supply and demand without government intervention.

Two-Tier Exchange Rate

This rate system segments the foreign exchange market into two tiers: one for current account transactions (involving mostly the export and import of goods and services) and the other for capital transactions (involving mostly funds) flows across national borders.

Multiple Exchange Rates

A complex system of exchange rate determination is tuned by government bureaucrats, with differing exchange rates applying to various classes of imports depending on their degree of essentiality. This practice is widespread in Latin America but not elsewhere.

   The Wall Street Journal reports daily quotations on 23 different currencies (Table 16.4). The activity in the spot market centers around a handful of currencies, as indicated earlier. Few currencies—seven, to be precise—are widely traded in the forward market. The other currencies have either very thin forward markets or none at all. In this market the life of the contract is standardized. Tailored contracts are not common and are usually more expensive.

16.9 EXCHANGE QUOTATIONS

Spot rates are quoted in either of two ways: direct or indirect. The direct quote gives the price of a unit of the foreign currency in terms of domestic currency, that is, how many dollars it takes to buy, say, a Lebanese pound; it takes 0.2908 according to the first column of numbers in Table 16.4. The indirect quote gives the price of a unit of domestic currency in terms of foreign currencies; that is, how many Lebanese pounds it takes to purchase a dollar; the answer, according to Table 16.4, is 3.4390 on Wednesday, Oct. 1, 1980. The direct quote is referred to as the U.S. basis and the indirect quote as the European basis. The reader may have noted that the indirect quote is the inverse

TABLE 16.4
Foreign Exchange Rates

Wednesday, October 1, 1980

The New York foreign exchange selling rates below apply to trading among banks in amounts of $1 million and more, as quoted at 3 p.m. Eastern time by Bankers Trust Co. Retail transactions provide fewer units of foreign currency per dollar.

Country	U.S. $ equiv. Wed.	U.S. $ equiv. Tues.	Currency per U.S. $ Wed.	Currency per U.S. $ Tues.
Argentina (Peso)				
Financial	.00052	.00052	1933.00	1932.00
Australia (Dollar)	1.1765	1.1715	.8500	.8536
Austria (Schilling)	.07831	.07813	12.77	12.80
Belgium (Franc)				
Commercial rate	.03457	.034483	28.93	29.00
Financial rate	.03439	.034376	29.08	29.09
Brazil (Cruzeiro)	.01802	.01802	55.48	55.49
Britain (Pound)	2.3930	2.3860	.4179	.4191
30-Day Futures	2.3860	2.3807	.4191	.4200
90-Day Futures	2.3803	2.3761	.4201	.4209
180-Day Futures	2.3807	2.3754	.4200	.4210
Canada (Dollar)	.8540	.8543	1.1710	1.1706
30-Day Futures	.8557	.8561	1.1686	1.1681
90-Day Futures	.8581	.8586	1.1654	1.1647
180-Day Futures	.8593	.8601	1.1638	1.1626
China (Yuan)	.6767	.6770	1.4777	1.4777
Colombia (Peso)	.0216	.0216	46.25	46.25
Denmark (Krone)	.1796	.1791	5.5670	5.5840
Ecuador (Sucre)	.0375	.0375	26.75	26.75
Finland (Markka)	.2734	.2727	3.6575	3.6665
France (Franc)	.2385	.2380	4.1920	4.2010
30-Day Futures	.2387	.2384	4.1900	4.1955
90-Day Futures	.2390	.2390	4.1840	4.1835
180-Day Futures	.2393	.2392	4.1790	4.1810
Greece (Drachma)	.0233	.0233	42.80	42.80
Hong Kong (Dollar)	.2004	.2004	4.9900	4.9900
India (Rupee)	.1290	.1290	7.751	7.751
Indonesia (Rupiah)	.0016	.0016	625.00	625.00
Ireland (Pound)	2.0790	2.0745	.4810	.4820
Israel (Shekel)	.1702	.17021	5.875	5.875
Italy (Lira)	.001163	.001160	860.00	862.00
Japan (Yen)	.004806	.004752	208.05	210.45
30-Day Futures	.004812	.004759	207.80	210.15
90-Day Futures	.004826	.004772	207.20	209.55
180-Day Futures	.004864	.004808	205.60	208.00
Lebanon (Pound)	.2908	.2905	3.4390	3.4420
Malaysia (Ringgit)	.4700	.4700	2.1275	2.1275
Mexico (Peso)	.04342	.04355	23.03	22.96
Netherlands (Guilder)	.5096	.5084	1.9625	1.9670
New Zealand (Dollar)	.9840	.9810	1.0163	1.0194
Norway (Krone)	.2055	.2055	4.8670	4.8658
Pakistan (Rupee)	.1015	.1015	9.852	9.852
Peru (Sol)	.0037	.0037	270.00	270.00
Philippines (Peso)	.1360	.1360	7.353	7.353
Portugal (Escudo)	.01996	.01996	50.10	50.10
Saudi Arabia (Riyal)	.3014	.3013	3.3180	3.3193
Singapore (Dollar)	.4760	.4760	2.1010	2.1010
South Africa (Rand)	1.3290	1.3280	.7524	.7530
South Korea (Won)	.00168	.00168	595.24	595.24
Spain (Peseta)	.01365	.01353	73.25	73.90
Sweden (Krona)	.2407	.2404	4.1550	4.1600
Switzerland (Franc)	.6094	.6053	1.6410	1.6520
30-Day Futures	.6135	.6099	1.6300	1.6397
90-Day Futures	.6212	.6177	1.6098	1.6188
180-Day Futures	.6331	.6291	1.5795	1.5895
Taiwan (Dollar)	.0278	.0278	36.00	36.00
Thailand (Baht)	.05	.05	20.00	20.00
Uruguay (New Peso)				
Financial	.1147	.1147	8.72	8.72
Venezuela (Bolivar)	.2329	.2329	4.2930	4.2940
West-Germany (Mark)	.5531	.5516	1.8080	1.8128
30-Day Futures	.5550	.5539	1.8019	1.8054
90-Day Futures	.5595	.5587	1.7874	1.7898
180-Day Futures	.5661	.5652	1.7662	1.7692

Source: The Wall Street Journal, Oct. 10, 1980.

of the direct quote (3.4390 is the inverse of 0.2908). Each quote must reflect both sides of the market: the sell side (ask) and the buy side (bid).

Forward rates are also quoted the direct and indirect way with an interesting and sometimes confusing twist. A trader in New York may quote the German mark (Deutsche Mark or DM) spot—one-month, three-month, and six-month—as follows (Oct. 1, 1980):

0.5528–0.5531   12–19 (or 12/19, or 12 to 19), 45–64, 95–130

The bid/ask spread on the forward rates is referred to in terms of points. A point is the third and fourth digits to the right of the decimal (e.g., 12 points is equivalent to 0.0012).

These quotes correspond to the following rates:

Maturity	Buy	Sell	Wire Quote
Spot	0.5528	0.5531	
1-month	0.5540	0.5550	12–19 or 12/19
3-month	0.5573	0.5595	45–64
6-month	0.5623	0.5661	95–130

Since the forward rate is higher than the spot rate, we can say that the DM is selling at a premium. The size of the premium for one month is 0.0019 on the sell side, or 0.0019/[0.5531 (the spot rate)] = 0.003435, or 0.343 percent or an annual rate of 4.12 percent (0.343 × 12). A possible reason for this premium is that the market expects the spot rate one month from now to be higher than the current spot rate. This point will be discussed further in the next chapter.

Whenever the currency is selling at a premium, the quote from the trader will have a smaller number (12, bid) followed by a larger number (19, ask). These numbers must be added to the spot rate quotation to arrive at the outright forward rate. When a currency is selling at a discount, the trader's quote will be flashed in reverse order, with the larger number (the bid) preceding the smaller number (the ask). These numbers will have to be *subtracted* from the spot quotation to arrive at the outright forward rate.

The preceding is based on the direct quotation system (the U.S. point of view). Using the European indirect quotation, we arrive at an opposite and important conclusion: the U.S. dollar is selling at a discount. The size of the discount (in percentage terms) would not equal that of the premium on the opposing currency simply because of the nature of the arithmetic. For the DM case, the European quotations on the ask side are 1.8080 and 1.8018 respectively for the spot and the 30-day forward rate. This yields a discount on the dollar equal to (1.8018 − 1.8080)/1.8080 = −0.0062/1.8080 = −0.00343 or −0.343 percent. This is equivalent to an annual discount rate of 4.115 percent (0.343 × 12). If the quotations were reversed—that is, if the forward rate equaled 1.8080 and the spot equaled 1.8018—the monthly premium would equal 0.344 percent or an annual premium of 4.13 percent.

Forward rates in London are quoted with the offer price first. The 12–19 forward rate quote on the DM in New York will come over the wire from London as 19–12 to be used as 0.0019–0.0012.

16.10 BUYING FOREIGN EXCHANGE

Corporate executives wishing to purchase or sell foreign exchange do so directly with their banks. No broker is needed. The bank acts as a dealer, realizing its profits from the spread (the difference between the bid and the ask). It is advisable to check with several banks before deciding to enter into a transaction. The bank selling a forward contract does not have to keep an open position, with its attending risks. The bank can turn around and buy a forward contract to match the one sold. If Citibank sells a DM forward contract to an American corporation, it buys, to cover itself, a forward contract, say, from a German bank which, in turn, finds a German customer buying U.S. goods and needing to buy dollars forward (sell German DM forward) to sell the contract to. Citibank can also engage in a swap transaction in order to avoid exchange risk. This could involve the simultaneous purchase and sale of forward contracts with differing maturities or on different currencies.

It is instructive to remember that the spread earned by the bank is not the equivalent of an insurance premium. The bank is not insuring the foreign exchange contract buyer against foreign exchange risk. By matching its buy and sell positions, the bank assumes no risk. The example above points out how risk is dissipated through the foreign exchange system as a whole.

16.11 USES OF FORWARD EXCHANGE

The forward exchange market is used for several purposes:

Covering Commercial Transactions/Hedging

U.S. exporters expecting to receive foreign currency sell the currency forward in order to lock in a certain exchange rate. Alternatively, they may insist that they be paid in dollars, thereby eliminating risk altogether. However, in that case the buyers may offer a lower price.

A U.S. importer expecting to make payments in DM for imports from Germany may buy DM forward, to avoid higher costs resulting from the appreciation in the value of DM.

The forward market is also used to hedge against reduction of value of assets and/or earnings subject to foreign exchange risk.

Arbitrage

Arbitrageurs, using the foreign exchange market, attempt to capitalize on differences in interest rates across national boundaries by simultaneously buying and selling currency in two different markets to lock in a profit. An extensive discussion of this topic follows later.

Speculation

Speculators try to outguess the market. They are actually betting that the expected spot rate implied by the forward rate will be different from the spot rate that will prevail at the end of the period covered in the forward contract.

The speculator has a preference for the forward market because little or no capital is required (the transaction is consummated in a margin account with a very low margin requirement). Speculation in the spot market could require commitment of 100 percent of the value of the contract. Speculators can buy foreign currency in hopes of selling it later at a profit. If they expect the spot rate to drop, they borrow the depreciating currency, sell it immediately, and buy back the currency in the market to repay their loans when these loans mature or when they deem the time is right. The speculators, in this case, profit if the currency depreciates and lose if it appreciates.

Speculators may also speculate in the futures market, as we shall show later in this chapter.

16.12 CONSISTENCY IN THE FOREIGN EXCHANGE MARKET

Two consistencies are required of the foreign exchange market: one across markets for a given currency and the other across currencies.

Consistency Across Market

This consistency requires that the price of the dollar in New York should be the same as that in, say, London. If not, an arbitrage opportunity would present itself, leading to a flow of funds across borders. If the value of the pound were $1.90 in New York and $1.80 in London, the arbitrageur would sell pounds in New York, where the value is high, and receive $190 (assuming 100 pounds is held). In London the $190 is sold for sterling, fetching £105.55. The gross gain from this arbitrage transaction is £5.55. The gain will be less if transactions costs are accounted for. With minimal transactions costs and no impediments to the flow of funds, the price of one currency in terms of another should be the same.

Consistency Across Currencies (Consistent Cross Rate)

If the equilibrium rate between the U.S. dollar and the British pound were $2 to £1 and that between the dollar and the franc $0.25 to Fr 1, the equilibrium rate between the franc and the British pound would then have to be £1 = Fr 8. Restated, the equilibrium rates are:

$$\$1 = £0.5 \quad £1 = Fr\ 8 \quad Fr\ 1 = \$0.25$$

The product of the right-hand side of the equalities is $(0.5 \times 8 \times 0.25) = 1$, as it must be. Otherwise, arbitrage opportunities would present themselves. Had the pound sold for Fr 10, an arbitrageur would, observing that the pound is overvalued, sell dollars for pounds and pounds for francs. Starting, say, with $100 we buy £50, sell the pounds for francs, and get Fr 500. We then cash the francs for $125 for a net profit of $25. As this process continues, the price of the pound will fall until consistency across exchange rates is established.

16.13 TYPES OF FOREIGN EXCHANGE RISK

Citibank, in a 1979 study, classifies foreign exchange risk into three categories:

1. *Rate risk:* Risk resulting from an exchange rate movement opposite that expected.
2. *Credit risk:* Risk resulting from the party issuing the foreign exchange contract going out of business before the contract matures.
3. *Liquidity risk:* Risk resulting from deviation of the realized future price from the actual price. High transaction costs and/or high discount on the contract may have to be accepted because of the thinness of the market at the time of liquidation.

16.14 RELATIONSHIP BETWEEN SPOT AND FORWARD RATE

Suppose we have the following prices:

$P\$$ ⎫ Current prices of $ and £ for current (P) or
$F\$$ ⎪ future delivery (F). Prices are defined in terms
$P£$ ⎬ of some standard tradeable commodity that can be
$F£$ ⎭ purchased in either country.

Given these four prices, three independent prices must exist. The obvious two are

$$S = \frac{P\$}{P£} = \text{spot rate}$$

$$F = \frac{F\$}{F\pounds} = \text{forward rate}$$

The third price is

$$\frac{F\$}{P\$} = 1 + i_{\text{U.S.}}$$

or

$$\frac{F\pounds}{P\pounds} = 1 + i_{\text{U.K.}}$$

The equality of the ratio of the forward price of the dollar $F\$$ to the spot price of the dollar $P\$$ to the interest rate in the United States $i_{\text{U.S.}}$ covering the same period as the forward contract may not be intuitive. The $F\$/P\$$ ratio represents the future value of a unit of currency in relation to its current value in terms of the standard tradeable commodity. The sum $1 + i_{\text{U.S.}}$ represents equally the future value of \$1 in relation to the current value (\$1). If markets are efficient, the two returns must be equal to each other; otherwise, arbitrage opportunities will present themselves.

We can rewrite the preceding relationships as follows:

$$\frac{1 + i_{\text{U.S.}}}{1 + i_{\text{U.K.}}} = \frac{(F\$/P\$)}{(F\pounds/P\pounds)} = \frac{F\$}{P\$} \cdot \frac{P\pounds}{F\pounds} = \frac{(F\$)\,(P\pounds)}{(F\pounds)\,(P\$)}$$

$$= \frac{(F\$/F\pounds)}{(P\$/P\pounds)}$$

$$\frac{1 + i_{\text{U.S.}}}{1 + i_{\text{U.K.}}} = \frac{F_{\$,\pounds}}{S_{\$,\pounds}} = \frac{\text{annualized forward rate of the British sterling in terms of the U.S. dollar}}{\text{spot rate of the British sterling in terms of the U.S. dollar}} \qquad (16.1)$$

In general:

$$\frac{1 + i_d}{1 + i_f} = \frac{F}{S} \qquad (16.2)$$

where i_d = domestic rate of interest
i_f = foreign rate of interest
F = forward rate (direct quote)
S = spot rate (direct quote)

Equation 16.2 is referred to as the *interest-rate parity theory* (IRPT).

16.15 INTEREST-RATE PARITY THEORY

The equilibrium shown in Equation 16.2 among the current exchange rate, the forward exchange rate, the domestic interest rate, and the foreign rate of interest is realized through the process of arbitrage according to IRPT. This arbitrage is referred to as *investor arbitrage* or *borrower arbitrage*.

Investor Arbitrage

Consider a world made up of the United States and Britain and assume:

1. No government intervention in the flow of funds across national borders
2. Tax treatment of arbitrage profits the same in both countries
3. Flexible exchange rates without limit

A disequilibrium in Equation 16.2 brings about arbitrage opportunities. To see how, let us rewrite Equation 16.2. Subtracting 1 from both sides of the equation, we get:

$$\frac{F_{\$,£}}{S_{\$,£}} - 1 = \frac{1 + i_{U.S.}}{1 + i_{U.K.}} - 1$$

$$\frac{F_{\$,£} - S_{\$£}}{S_{\$,£}} = \frac{1 + i_{U.S.} - 1 - i_{U.K.}}{1 + i_{U.K.}}$$

or

$$\frac{F_{\$,£} - S_{\$,£}}{S_{\$,£}} = \frac{i_{U.S.} - i_{U.K.}}{1 + i_{U.K.}} \tag{16.3}$$

Equation 16.3 represents the no-arbitrage case. The left-hand side of the equation is referred to as the *implicit rate,* the right hand side as the *interest-rate differential.*

$$\frac{F_{\$,£} - S_{\$,£}}{S_{\$,£}} - \frac{i_{U.S.} - i_{U.K.}}{1 + i_{U.K.}} = \text{AM (arbitrage margin)}$$

Note that the arbitrage margin can exist although the interest-rate differential is equal to zero.

Example

From Table 16.4 we find the spot DM at 0.5531 and the 90-day DM forward rate at 0.5595. The U.S. three-month T-bill rate is 11.50 percent and the German three-month T-bill rate is, say, 8 percent. Is there an arbitrage opportunity? In what direction would money flow?

Arbitrage Opportunity?

$$\frac{F_{\$,DM} - S_{\$,DM}}{S_{\$,DM}} - \frac{i_{U.S.} - i_{Ger}}{1 + i_{Ger}} = \text{AM}$$

$$\frac{0.5595 - 0.5531}{0.5531} - \frac{0.02875 - 0.02}{1.02} =$$

$$0.01157 \quad - \quad 0.00858 \quad =$$

$$1.157\% \quad - \quad 0.858\% \quad = \mathbf{0.2923\%}$$

The implicit rate is positive and equal to 1.157 percent, or 4.628 percent annually. The interest-rate differential favors the United States. The DM is selling at a forward premium, that is, the U.S. dollar is selling at a forward discount. This condition in the foreign exchange market is favorable to Germany, as will be shown in detail below. The numbers thus far indicate that an arbitrage opportunity exists and funds must flow out of the United States (a negative AM would have required a flow of funds in the direction of the United States).

A U.S. investor observing this would decide to invest in Germany. Owning German securities, however, is owning DM-denominated assets with attending foreign exchange risk. This risk is eliminated through the forward market. The process is as follows.

The Mechanics

Assume the U.S. investor has $10,000 invested in U.S. T-bills (or may be willing to borrow funds in the United States at $i_{U.S.}$). Considering the arbitrage opportunity that exists between the United States and Germany, the investor would do the following:

1. Sell the U.S. T-bills.
2. Buy DM in the spot market.

   Proceeds $= 10,000/0.5531 =$ DM 18,080

3. Buy German T-bills for DM 18,080
4. Calculate the total exposure in DM at the end of the 90-day period.

   Total exposure $= 18,080 (1 + 0.02) =$ DM 18,441.6

5. Sell DM 18,441.6 forward to eliminate foreign exchange exposure. (Note that this high DM forward rate translates itself into a higher transaction cost—a reduced incentive—for buying German securities.)

Expected proceeds in 90 days are

$(18,441.6) (0.5595) = \$10,318.075$

The U.S. investor has just realized $318 on a three-month investment in risk-free German securities. Had U.S. T-bills been purchased, the total return would have been $10,000 (0.02875) = \$287.50$. Gross profit from looking at world opportunities as opposed to just domestic (U.S.) opportunities is $\$318 - \$287.50 = \$30.50$.

In order to generalize the results of the preceding example, we state the general version of Equation 16.2.

$$a[1 + i_{U.S.} (90)] = \frac{a}{S_{\$,DM}} [1 + i_{Ger}(90)] \cdot F_{\$,DM}(90) \tag{16.4}$$

$a[1 + i_{U.S.} (90)] =$ dollar return on U.S. investment of a for 90 days.

$\dfrac{a}{S_{\$,DM}} =$ DM the U.S. arbitrageur gets upon converting dollars

$\dfrac{a}{S_{\$,DM}} [1 + i_{Ger} (90)] \cdot F_{\$,DM}(90) =$ dollar return on covered investment in Germany

From Equation 16.2 or Equation 16.4, one can easily derive the equilibrium (or no-arbitrage) forward rate.

$$F_{\$,DM}^*(t) = \frac{1 + i_{U.S.}(t)}{1 + i_{Ger}(t)} \cdot S_{\$,DM} \tag{16.5}$$

If Equation 16.5 holds, no funds will move from either country to the other. Knowing the values of the exogenous variables $i_{U.S.}$, i_{Ger}, and $S_{\$,DM}$, we can easily calculate $F_{\$,DM}^*(t)$. If $F_{\$,DM}(t)$ is different from $F_{\$,DM}^*(t)$, funds will flow from one country to another.

Impact Analysis

Let us briefly examine the consequences of the flow of funds from the United States to Germany.

Effects on Interest Rate

The U.S. rate of interest will rise as investors sell their U.S. securities and substitute them for German securities. The German rate of interest will decline as U.S. investors increase the demand for German securities and, in the process, raise their price. This will increase the interest-rate differential between the two countries.

Effects on Spot Rates

As the dollar is sold in the spot market, that is, as the German DM is bought, the spot rate will move against the dollar in favor of the German mark.

Effects on the Forward Rate

The forward rate on the dollar rises as arbitrageurs buy dollars forward. The opposite is true for the forward rate on DM.

With the spot DM rising and the forward DM falling, the implicit rate is shrinking. The process continues until the implicit rate is equal to the interest-rate differential between the two countries and the no-arbitrage position is reached.

Considering that both the money markets and the foreign exchange market do not have the same degree of depth, most of the adjustment would take place in the forward exchange market. Therefore, the interest parity relationship determines the forward exchange rate.

Interest-Rate Parity Theory—A Graphic Illustration

Referring again to Equation 16.2,

$$\frac{F_{\$,DM} - S_{\$,DM}}{S_{\$,DM}} = \frac{i_{U.S.} - i_{Ger}}{1 + i_{Ger}}$$

If $i_{U.S.} > i_{Ger}$, then $F_{\$,DM}$ must be greater than $S_{\$,DM}$ by an offsetting amount for equilibrium to prevail. The reverse must also be true.

FIGURE 16.5

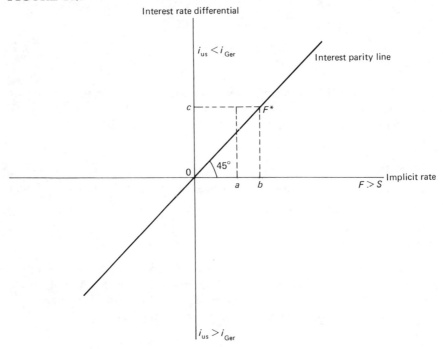

Anywhere along the interest parity line $F = F^*$, no funds will flow from one country to the other. If the interest-rate differential were at c and the implicit rate at a (Fig. 16.5), $Oc > Oa$ and the investor will clearly be interested in shifting funds from Germany to the United States. The process will continue until a new equilibrium is reached where $F = F^*$ and we are once again back on the interest-parity line. The adjustments in the money and foreign exchange markets will be along the lines described earlier. We can, therefore, conclude that forward rates lying above the interest-parity line cause a flow of capital into the United States and those below the line cause flows in the opposite direction.

Problems with the Interest-Rate Parity Theory

The interest-rate parity theory is limited in many ways by its own assumptions and by market considerations. Its weaknesses are as follows:

1. IRPT considers only the behavior of arbitrageurs and looks at the adjustment process as one determined by their behavior in the marketplace (i.e., a consequence of the covered interest arbitrage activity). In so doing, IRPT ignores the activities of speculators, hedgers, and traders. Speculators' activities could have a dramatic impact on exchange rates both in the spot and in the forward markets. If the speculators' demand schedule intersects the supply schedule of arbitrageurs in its inelastic portion, as we shall later demonstrate, speculators would dominate the market.

2. Borrowers and lenders may face different interest-rate schedules. The borrowing rate is not always equal to the lending rate.

3. IRPT looks only at the level of the rate but not at the risk associated with that rate. Holding investment vehicles in more than one country is desirable from a risk-diversification point of view.

4. While the comparison of short-term rates among countries such as the United States and England and Germany is quite possible because of the similarity of instruments in terms of maturity and risk profile, this is not the case across all countries because of the difficulty of specifying short-term interest rates.

5. The incorporation of default risk on currency contracts may well explain, according to Adler and Dumas,[7] the deviation between the observed forward rate and the equilibrium forward rate.

6. IRPT ignores transactions costs associated with covered-interest arbitrage. These costs can be significant and are incurred (following an example earlier in this section) when the U.S. securities are liquidated, when the swap transaction in the foreign exchange market is affected, and when securities denominated in the foreign currency are purchased. Direct measures of these transactions costs are not always possible. A worthwhile attempt was made by T. Holley, C. Beidleman, and T. Greenleaf.[8] They divided transactions costs into two categories: those related to the spread in foreign exchange transactions (bid-ask) and non-spread costs. The U.S. investor in our example would, therefore, buy DM at the ask and sell them forward at the bid. This will take care of the spread costs. The non-spread costs are summarized in the following equation:

$$K = (1 - t)(1 - t^*)(1 - t_s)(1 - t_f)$$

where t = percent transaction cost arising from brokerage fees and costs of information involved in selling a dollar-denominated asset

t^* = percent transaction cost of buying a DM-denominated asset.

t_s = percent transaction cost of purchasing spot DM

t_f = percent transaction of selling DM forward

Accounting for both K costs and the spread costs, the IRPT equilibrium condition would look as follows:

$$\frac{F_b - S_a}{S_a} = \frac{(1 + i_{\text{U.S.}}) - K(1 + i_{\text{Ger}})}{K(1 + i_{\text{Ger}})} \tag{16.6}$$

where F_b = forward exchange rate (bid)

S_a = spot exchange rate (ask)

Empirical tests run on Equation 16.6 showed, consistent with other empirical studies, that the K factor is significant and that "covered interest arbitrage dominates in the foreign exchange markets."[9]

---

[7] **M. Adler** and **B. Dumas,** "Portfolio Choice and the Demand for Forward Exchange." *American Economic Review,* May 1976, pp. 332–339.

[8] **John L. Holley, Carl Beidleman,** and **James Greenleaf,** "Does Covered Interest Arbitrage Dominate in Foreign Exchange Markets." *Columbia Journal of World Business,* Winter 1979, pp. 99–107.

[9] Ibid, p. 103.

16.16 THE MODERN THEORY OF FORWARD EXCHANGE RATE

The modern theory of forward exchange rate (MT) states that the behavior of arbitrageurs as determined by the IRPT and that of speculators as determined by their expectations with regard to the spot rate determines the foreign exchange rate. In other words, MT states that the forward rate is a weighted average of two rates: one resulting from the behavior of arbitrageurs alone the other from the behavior of speculators alone.

The Arbitrageur's Schedule

Our objective here is to determine conditions under which the arbitrageur would supply forward contracts or demand forward contracts and the impact this has on the forward rate. Consider a world made up of two countries, Germany and the United States, and assume that the exchange rate is quoted the direct way and that the interest rate differential is given.

At $F^*_{\$,DM}$ no funds will flow in either direction (Fig. 16.6). Hence there is no supply of or demand for forward contracts by arbitrageurs. For equilibrium to prevail, the interest rate in the United States must be higher than that of Germany, because $F^*_{\$,DM} > S_{\$,DM}$. If the forward rate is quoted at $F'_{\$,DM}$, then the forward premium on DM—that is, the forward discount on the dollar—is higher than the interest-rate differential and funds will flow from the United States to Germany. This will require a swap transaction involving the spot sale of a dollar for DM and simultaneously the sale of DM forward. That is, arbitrageurs will be selling forward contracts (OK's worth—Fig. 16.6). If, on the other hand, the forward rate is quoted at $F''_{\$,DM}$, the forward discount on the dollar is lower than the interest-rate differential and funds will flow into the United States. This will require the forward sale of dollars, that is, the forward purchase of DM (OJ's worth—Fig. 16.6).

The Speculator's Schedule

Speculators are investors who, expecting a certain rate of return, expose themselves to foreign exchange risk. Speculation is made in the spot or in the forward market. Expecting the spot rate to rise, speculators would purchase foreign currency and wait until its

FIGURE 16.6

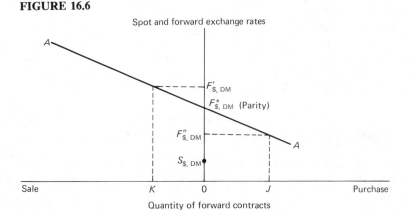

FIGURE 16.7

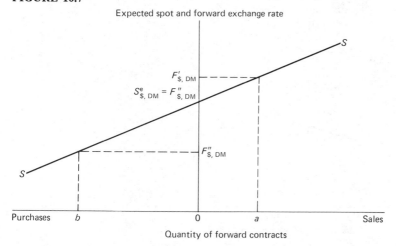

price appreciated. When it did, they would sell and realize a profit. If the speculators expected the DM to drop in price, they would borrow DM and convert them into dollars. When the DM depreciated in value, they would close the loan transaction. Their profit is the change in value of the DM net of interest cost and transaction costs. Both the long and the short positions require a commitment of funds (own or borrowed). Less costly and more profitable opportunities present themselves in the forward market because the margin requirement on a forward contract is about 10 percent of the face value of the contract and can be as low as 2.5 percent.

Speculators operating in the forward market expect to cash in on the probability that they are wiser than the market. Their concern is not with the current spot rate but rather with the forward rate as compared with the spot rate expected to prevail concurrently with the expiration of the forward contract.

The decision by the speculator to be on the supply or the demand side of forward contracts is, therefore, a function of the differential between the prevailing forward rate on DM and the expected spot rate at the end of the period covered by the forward contract. Let $K_s(t)$ equal the supply of forward DM contracts by speculators.

$$K_S(t) = f[F_{\$,DM}(t) - S^e_{\$,DM}(t)]^* \tag{16.7}$$

If $K_s(t) > 0$, the speculator would sell DM forward. The reason is simple. The speculator would sell when the rate $F_{\$,DM}(t)$ is high and buy at $S^e_{\$,DM}(t)$, a lower price (if expectations prove to be correct), to deliver against the forward contract.

If $K_s(t) < 0$, the speculator would buy DM forward. If expectations proved right, that is, if the spot rate forecasted by the forward rate proved incorrect, the speculator would take delivery of the DM and sell the proceeds in the spot market at a higher price than that specified in the forward contract.

Figure 16.7 depicts the speculators' schedule. At $F'_{\$,DM}$, $F'_{\$,DM} > S^e_{\$,DM}$, and the specula-

---

* This equation assumes a linear relationship among the variables. The shape of the curve may well be curvilinear because of transactions costs, measurement errors, risk of exchange controls, and the risk profile of the speculator.

FIGURE 16.8   Equilibrium forward rate.

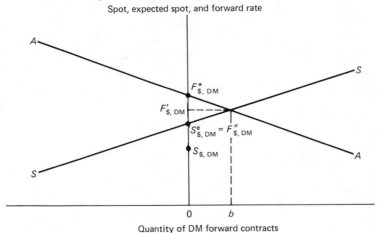

tor would sell forward contracts Oa hoping to deliver against those contracts by buying in the future at the lower expected spot rate. At $F''_{\$,DM}$, $S^e_{\$,DM} > F''_{\$,DM}$ and the speculator would purchase forward DM Ob with the hope of selling them at a higher price. The larger the difference between $F_{\$,DM}$ and $S_{\$,DM}$, the larger the sale or purchase commitment by the speculator.

Determination of the Equilibrium Rate

If we superimpose Figure 16.6 on Figure 16.7, we can easily arrive at the equilibrium forward rate. This is depicted in Figure 16.8. At $F'_{\$,DM}$ we have an equilibrium forward rate. Arbitrageurs would buy Ob of DM forward contracts, and speculators would sell the exact amount. Arbitrageurs are net buyers because the forward rate $F^*_{\$,DM}$ is above the spot rate and the forward premium is less than the interest-rate differential, that is, the forward rate is below the parity level. Therefore, funds flow into the United States. To cover this flow against exchange rate losses requires the sale of forward dollars or the purchase of DM forward contracts. The speculators, noting that the market forward rate $F'_{\$,DM}$ is higher than $S^e_{\$,DM}$, would be net sellers of forward contracts. The reader must note that $F'_{\$,DM}$ is lower than $F^*_{\$,DM}$ because of the role of the speculator. Equilibrium was possible only at F^* under IRPT.

Who Dominates the Marketplace?

The identification of which of the market participants ultimately dominates the market, that is, determines the forward rate, depends on the elasticity (sensitivity) of the AA and SS schedules. We examime three cases shown in Figure 16.9.[10]

Figure 16.9a shows two schedules with approximately equal elasticity. Both speculators and arbitrageurs determine the forward rate. In Figure 16.9b, arbitrageurs dominate

---

[10] Based on **Houston H. Stokes** and **Hugh Neuberger**, "Interest Arbitrage, Forward Speculation and the Determination of the Forward Exchange Rate." *Columbia Journal of World Business*, Winter 1979, pp. 86–98.

FIGURE 16.9   Three market situations.

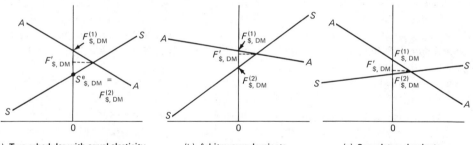

(a) Two schedules with equal elasticity.   (b) Arbitrageurs dominate.   (c) Speculators dominate.

the market. Their supply/demand schedule is much more elastic than that of the speculators. If arbitrageurs were the only market participants, the forward rate would be at $F_{\$,DM}^{(1)}$ (Fig. 16.9b), which is much closer to $F_{\$,DM}'$ than $F_{\$,DM}^{(2)}$. Figure 16.9c depicts the opposite case of Figure 16.9b. The size of the elasticity is the measure of responsiveness to price changes. For very small changes in price, the speculator will be willing to supply (demand) much more than the arbitrageur in Figure 16.9c, hence the control over the market. Were the speculators the only market participants, the equilibrium rate would be at $F_{\$,DM}^{(2)}$, which is much closer to $F_{\$,DM}'$ than $F_{\$,DM}^{(1)}$ is in Figure 16.9c.

Empirical evidence referred to earlier (H. Holley, C. Beidleman, and James Greenleaf) and additional evidence provided by H. Stokes and H. Neuburger, show, in support of many previous studies, that Figure 16.9b correctly depicts the foreign exchange market; that is, the arbitrageur dominates.

It may be worthwhile at this juncture to mention reasons for speculators being on the opposite side of the market than arbitrageurs. When arbitrage funds are flowing into the United States, for example, the dollar is being sold forward, forecasting a lower spot rate in the future. If speculators agreed with the market, they would have nothing to speculate on and might well become arbitrageurs themselves. It is only when speculators consider market expectations to be erroneous that they begin speculating. Gamblers betting on a roulette wheel are aware that the odds of winning are 1/36. When the wheel is spun, the gamblers' attitude is that the chance of winning is a lot higher than 1/36. In fact they believe that they have picked the winning number. That is, the gambler banks on outsmarting the house. Speculators similarly feel that they are outguessing the market as it forecasts the future spot rate through the forward rate.

Causes for Shifts in the AA, SS Schedules

Shifts in the arbitrageurs' schedule (AA) or the speculators' schedule are caused by market forces and/or government intervention. Changes in the spot rate and the interest-rate differential between the United States and Germany can shift the AA schedule up or down because they change the value of F^*, the no-arbitrage forward rate. Changes in the forward rate or some economic or political developments may cause speculators to revise their expectations about the expected spot rate at time t. Such revision will obviously affect the size of the speculators' forward commitments, long or short. If the expected spot rate is revised upward, the difference between it and the forward rate will shrink (expand) and the speculators would supply (demand) less (more) forward contracts.

The reader should take notice of the fact that a movement in one variable is not independent of the movement in another. A rise in the interest rate in the United States $i_{U.S.}$ will cause larger flows of funds into the United States assuming the starting point is F^*. Associated with these flows are the spot sales of the foreign currency and the forward sales of the dollar. The value of the dollar will appreciate in the spot market, and will fall in the forward market.

The analysis above also assumes an unlimited ability on the part of the arbitrageur to raise funds and willingness to shift from, say, a U.S. asset to a foreign asset or vice versa. A sudden shift in the arbitrage equation indicating the need to shift funds to Germany may go unheeded depending on whether the arbitrageur has a capital gain or loss in the U.S. securities held or whether he or she has sufficient investment funds and/or ability to borrow at an advantageous rate. The liquidation of existing holdings may further be complicated by the size of transactions costs.

The Relationship Between Interest Rates and Exchange Rates—Some Sobering Comments

One conclusion the reader may draw from the preceding discussions is that exchange rates move in tandem with interest rates. As the interest rates in the United States fall in relation to foreign interest rates, the United States will experience a capital outflow; this, in turn, will result in a lower value of the dollar in the foreign exchange markets as investors sell dollars to acquire foreign currencies, which will be used to acquire foreign financial instruments.

This is an oversimplification of what happens in the real world if not an occasionally misleading hypothesis, as shown in Figure 16.10.[11]

Figure 16.10 dispels the simple, direct, and positive relationship between interest-rate differentials and the exchange rate. It shows the dollar declining in value against the DM, although the interest-rate differential favors the United States. The reader should observe that the conventional relationship between interest rates and exchange rates reemerged in early 1980. Then why the serious aberrations between 1976 and 1980?

As we made clear earlier, the demand and supply for dollars emanate from the goods and services markets as well as in response to changes in the financial markets. A shift in U.S. consumers' tastes in favor of foreign goods increases the demand for foreign currency; that is, the increasing supply of dollars leads to a drop in the value of the dollar in relation to foreign currencies. In addition, the conventional relationship ignores the dynamic relationships between the foreign exchange markets and the financial and goods markets. A weakness in the U.S. economy relative to other industrial powers leads to lower interest rates in the United States in relation to the other markets, and this leads U.S. investors to invest overseas. As this is done, upward pressures are put on U.S. interest rates as U.S. investors sell U.S. securities to purchase foreign securities. Furthermore, a weakness in the U.S. dollar could result from the transactions having no relationship to U.S. interest rates. Arab sheikhs may decide to dump dollars in the

---

[11] See **Douglas R. Mudd,** "Do Rising Interest Rates Imply a Stronger Dollar." *Review,* Federal Reserve Bank of St. Louis, June 1979; also **G. J. Santoni** and **Courtenay C. Stone,** "Navigating Through the Inter-Rate Morass: Some Basic Principles." *Review,* Federal Reserve Bank of St. Louis, March 1981.

FIGURE 16.10   **Fluctuations in U.S./German currency exchange and interest rates.**

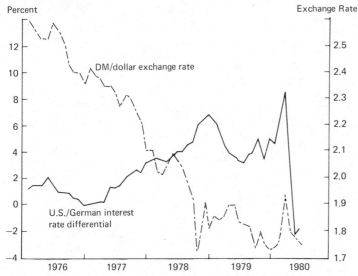

Source: Weekly Letter. Federal Reserve Bank of San Francisco, Sept. 12 and 19, 1980.

foreign exchange markets in order to acquire gold, and banks may decide to sell or buy a given currency or currencies as they adjust their portfolios. All these events produce weaknesses or strengths in the U.S. Dollar, and these will ultimately influence the U.S. financial markets.

Additional insightful reasons for the weaknesses in the conventional theory are provided in the *Weekly Letter* of the Federal Reserve Bank of San Francisco. One of their most interesting observations is that, while the conventional relationship has broken down, the interest-rate differential was closely reflected in the future value of the dollar as measured by the forward discount (Fig. 16.11).

This paradox was explained by looking at the components of interest rates. The nominal rate of interest is always made up of at least two components.

$$R = r + E\left(\frac{DP}{P}\right)$$

where R = nominal rate of interest

$$r = \text{real rate of interest} = R - E\left(\frac{DP}{P}\right)$$

$$E\left(\frac{DP}{P}\right) = \text{expected rate of inflation}$$

Investors in the world markets are sufficiently sophisticated not to be fooled by the level of the rates, and they are persistent in their pursuit of a real increment to their wealth—that is, in realizing a positive real rate of interest that reflects in the long run "the productivity of the nation's economy." This real rate represents the tradeoff in

FIGURE 16.11   Fluctuations in U.S./German forward discount and interest rates.

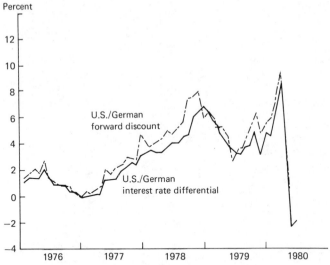

Percent

Source: Weekly Letter. Federal Reserve Bank of San Francisco, Sept. 12 and 19, 1980.

the consumption/investment decision process. Consider a one-period model where an individual has a choice between consumption now C_0 and consumption tomorrow C_1. This person can either consume all of his or her wealth today, consume all of it tomorrow, or find a convenient distribution between today's famine (opulence) and tomorrow's opulence (famine). Graphically, the tradeoff between C_0 and C_1 is represented by Figure 16.12.

Where the investor would choose to be along the market opportunities line *AB* depends on his or her utility curve (Fig. 16.13).

At *K* the investor is at the optimal point in the consumption/investment decision process, consuming OC_0^1 now and investing $C_0^1 B$ in order to be able to consume OC_1^1 next period. The value of *r*, therefore, given one's preference map, determines the allocation of resources between one time period and another or similarly between one country and another. The slope of *AB* is influenced by cyclical factors (changes in real income can lead to changes in the real rate of interest through changes in the real demand

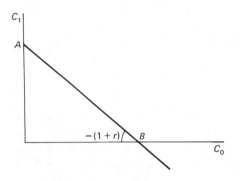

FIGURE 16.12   Tradeoff between consumption now and consumption tomorrow.

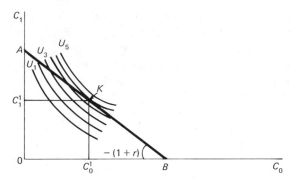

FIGURE 16.13 Market opportunities line and utility curves.

for money), which could shift investors' liquidity preference either as a result of changes in economic conditions or because of changes in government policy, such as tax policy. These policies may penalize or encourage investment.

With the real rate as the target rate, an investor can achieve it by arbitraging between two different markets using covered transactions. The interest rate differential is locked in by the investor through the forward exchange market, which effectively insulates the financial markets from the vagaries of the foreign exchange market. A rise in the real rate is, therefore, beneficial to the spot dollar, and a rise in $E(DP/P)$ is detrimental to the forward rate. A rise in $r_{U.S.}$ (an upward rotation in AA; Fig. 16.8) with $E(DP/P)$ constant would cause a rise in the spot rate of the dollar; thus the interest rate differential will be moving with the exchange rate. If R rises due to a rise in $E(DP/P)$, investors would have no incentive to move capital into the United States because the increase in R merely compensates for the expected depreciation in wealth. A higher $E(DP/P)$, however, spells a weaker dollar in the future, leading to a lower forward rate (a higher forward discount on the dollar). These observations should explain the phenomenon shown in Figure 16.10. As U.S. interest rates increased relative to those of Germany, the forward discount on the U.S. dollar also increased because inflationary expectations were running higher in the United States than they were in Germany.

All of the above is based on two assumptions: (1) that there are no exchange controls and (2) that both the United States and the German markets are equally efficient in reflecting the real underlying inflationary pressures in their economies and that investors are equally discriminating in their analyses of the components of interest rates.

Government Intervention

Governments have rarely allowed foreign exchange markets to function free of intimidation or outright intervention. As we have discussed in the earlier section, government can intervene indirectly in the foreign exchange market by influencing the real rate of interest or the rate of inflation using fiscal and/or monetary policy. Government can also influence the income levels of citizens and consequently trade flows and the foreign exchange rate.

Direct intervention by government in the foreign exchange markets is achieved either by exchange controls or by buy or sell transactions in these markets. Those transactions can be entered into in either the spot market (the most common case) or the forward market or both.

Spot Market Intervention. The U.S. government, if faced by downward pressures on the spot value of the U.S. dollar, would attempt through its agent, the Federal Reserve Bank of New York, to buy dollars in the foreign exchange markets using its own reserves of convertible foreign currencies or borrowed reserves. These borrowed reserves are usually in the form of swap agreements[12] entered into with foreign central bankers whereby the United States exchanges dollars for foreign currencies. The exchange will be reversed at a later date. Countries can also borrow from the International Monetary Fund (IMF) against their reserve position or credit line and from the Bank of International Settlement in Basel, Switzerland.

16.17 FOREIGN EXCHANGE FUTURES

The forward market lost its monopoly on foreign exchange contracts for future delivery on May 16, 1972, when the International Monetary Market (IMM), a subsidiary of the Chicago Mercantile Exchange, began trading futures contracts in seven currencies. Two currencies were later added (the French franc and the Dutch guilder) and one was dropped (the Italian lira).

A futures contract is an obligation to the buyer (the seller) to buy (sell) a set amount of foreign exchange at a specified price (agreed upon today) at some future date. The contract, as in the case of T-bills futures, is not between the buyer and the seller but between the buyer and the Clearing Corporation (CC) and the seller and the CC of the IMM. It is the CC which guarantees payments (delivery) on foreign exchange futures contracts traded on its exchange.

On Aug. 7, 1980, The New York Futures Exchange (NYFE), a wholly owned subsidiary of the New York Stock Exchange, began trading futures contracts in five currencies: British pounds, Canadian dollars, German marks, Japanese yen, and Swiss francs. The success of the NYFE was very limited, however. NYFE found it very hard to compete with the well-established IMM. The volume on the NYFE was so low that the exchange had to purchase advertising space in *The Wall Street Journal* to report transaction prices and volume. Of the five currency contracts traded on the NYFE, the Japanese yen had an activity of only three contracts on Dec. 18, 1980. The remaining contracts did not trade. By contrast, comparable contracts traded on the IMM had the following volumes: British pound, 1,877; Canadian dollar, 3,575; Japanese yen, 1,855; Swiss franc, 2,989; and West German mark, 4,469 (Table 16.5). By mid-1981, no trading of currency futures on NYFE was taking place, although the contracts remain "active" as of June 1982. Overall, however, currency futures contracts have been very successful. A total of 3,718,635 currencies futures contracts were traded on all the exchanges in 1980.

The contract specifications and trading rules for the actively traded contracts on the IMM are summarized in Table 16.6.

Considering the dominance of the IMM, we shall, henceforth, concentrate on contracts traded on it.

---

[12] **Richard Abrams,** in an article published in *Economic Review* (March 1979), describes a swap contract as one "written at the end of each day that Federal Reserve swap intervention takes place. To write a contract the Federal Reserve calculates the dollar amount of the intervention and receives sufficient foreign exchange to cover its dollar purchases. The foreign bank's dollars are then invested in a nonnegotiable U.S. Treasury Certificate of indebtedness until the swap is retired. Swaps mature in 90 days. They are retired by purchasing the foreign bank's dollars at the original exchange rate" (p. 16).

TABLE 16.5
Foreign Exchange Quotations

Spot and Forward Exchange Rates

Thursday, December 18, 1980

The New York foreign exchange selling rates below apply to trading among banks in amounts of $1 million and more, as quoted at 3 p.m. Eastern time by Bankers Trust Co. Retail transactions provide fewer units of foreign currency per dollar.

Country	U.S. $ equiv. Thurs.	U.S. $ equiv. Wed.	Currency per U.S. $ Thurs.	Currency per U.S. $ Wed.
Argentina (Peso)				
Financial	.000506	.000506	1977.00	1977.00
Australia (Dollar)	1.1655	1.1670	.8580	.8569
Austria (Schilling)	.0709	.0710	14.10	14.09
Belgium (Franc)				
Commercial rate	.03130	.031546	31.95	31.70
Financial rate	.03111	.030922	32.14	32.34
Brazil (Cruzeiro)	.01565	.01565	63.89	63.89
Britain (Pound)	2.3270	2.3310	.4297	.4290
30-Day Futures	2.3433	2.3462	.4267	.4262
90-Day Futures	2.3643	2.3690	.4229	.4221
180-Day Futures	2.3730	2.3800	.4214	.4202
Canada (Dollar)	.8316	.8289	1.2025	1.2064
30-Day Futures	.8337	.8316	1.1994	1.2025
90-Day Futures	.8373	.8354	1.1942	1.1971
180-Day Futures	.84104	.8393	1.1890	1.1915
China (Yuan)	.6473	.6414	1.5449	1.5590
Colombia (Peso)	.0198	.0198	50.45	50.45
Denmark (Krone)	.1641	.1653	6.092	6.05
Ecuador (Sucre)	.0398	.0398	25.10	25.10
Finland (Markka)	.2566	.2574	3.8970	3.8850
France (Franc)	.2174	.2186	4.60	4.5750
30-Day Futures	.2196	.2207	4.5530	4.5305
90-Day Futures	.2227	.2240	4.4900	4.4650
180-Day Futures	.2244	.2260	4.4570	4.4250
Greece (Drachma)	.0211	.0210	47.35	47.50
Hong Kong (Dollar)	.1947	.1942	5.1350	5.15
India (Rupee)	.1260	.1260	7.94	7.94
Indonesia (Rupiah)	.0016	.0016	625.00	625.00
Ireland (Pound)	1.8700	1.8580	.5347	.5382
Israel (Shekel)	.1336	.1336	7.4854	7.4854
Italy (Lira)	.001058	.001065	945.00	939.00
Japan (Yen)	.004769	.004795	209.70	208.55
30-Day Futures	.004822	.004844	207.40	206.45
90-Day Futures	.004896	.004925	204.25	203.05
180-Day Futures	.004967	.004999	201.35	200.05
Lebanon (Pound)	.2717	z	3.68	z
Malaysia (Ringgit)	.4540	.4525	2.2025	2.21
Mexico (Peso)	.0432	.0432	23.15	23.15
Netherlands (Guilder)	.4633	.4649	2.1585	2.1510
New Zealand (Dollar)	.9497	.9505	1.0530	1.0521
Norway (Krone)	.1928	.1949	5.1875	5.13
Pakistan (Rupee)	.1011	.1011	9.884	9.884
Peru (Sol)	.003436	.003436	291.04	291.04
Philippines (Peso)	.1324	.1324	7.5529	7.5529
Portugal (Escudo)	.01867	.01855	53.55	53.90
Saudi Arabia (Riyal)	.3003	.3002	3.3298	3.3308
Singapore (Dollar)	.4734	.4728	2.1125	2.1150
South Africa (Rand)	1.3250	1.3250	.7547	.7547
South Korea (Won)	.00151	.00151	660.90	660.90
Spain (Peseta)	.01251	.01255	79.95	79.70
Sweden (Krona)	.2257	.2273	4.4300	4.40
Switzerland (Franc)	.5543	.5573	1.8040	1.7945
30-Day Futures	.5618	.5647	1.7801	1.7709
90-Day Futures	.5742	.5774	1.7415	1.7319
180-Day Futures	.5860	.5922	1.7040	1.6885
Taiwan (Dollar)	.0279	.0279	35.84	35.84
Thailand (Baht)	.05	.05	20.00	20.00
Uruguay (New Peso)				
Financial	.1029	.1029	9.72	9.72
Venezuela (Bolivar)	.2330	.2330	4.2915	4.2915
West Germany (Mark)	.5033	.5062	1.9970	1.9755
30-Day Futures	.5089	.5112	1.9652	1.9550
90-Day Futures	.5176	.5202	1.9320	1.9225
180-Day Futures	.5255	.5284	1.9030	1.8925

International Monetary Market
Foreign Futures Quotations.

	Open	High	Low	Settle	Change	Lifetime High	Lifetime Low	Open Interest
BRITISH POUND (IMM) – 25,000 pounds; $ per pound								
Mar81	2.3630	2.3650	2.3600	2.3605	−.0060	2.4455	2.2159	9,282
June	2.3750	2.3760	2.3695	2.3705	−.0080	2.4440	2.2970	1,285
Sept	2.3740	2.3750	2.3720	2.3725	−.0025	2.4440	2.3380	216
Est vol 1,877; vol Wed 4,279; open int 10,863, −872.								
CANADIAN DOLLAR (IMM) – 100,000 dlrs.; $ per Can$								
Mar81	.8360	.8398	.8357	.8374	−.0021	.8950	.8290	6,093
June	.8402	.8435	.8400	.8402	+.0015	.9000	.8290	825
Sept	.8423	.8460	.8415	.8420	+.0014	.8730	.8389	175
Dec	....	....	....	.8420	....	.8570	.8361	19
Est vol 3,575; vol Wed 3,475; open int 7,112, −446.								
JAPANESE YEN (IMM) 12.5 million yen; cents per yen								
Mar81	.4902	.4912	.4864	.4883	−.0025	.4964	.4290	5,677
June	.4985	.4985	.4938	.4959	−.0021	.5048	.4445	280
Sept	....	....	....	.5005	−.0025	.5065	.4760	119
Est vol 1,855; vol Wed 1,675; open int 6,076, −68.								
SWISS FRANC (IMM) – 125,000 francs-$ per franc								
Mar81	.5707	.5741	.5693	.5727	−.0018	.6700	.5637	6,103
June	.5832	.5862	.5826	.5853	−.0034	.6581	.5542	1,157
Sept	.6000	.6000	.5960	.6000	−.0010	.6580	.5920	128
Dec	....	....	....	.6100	−.0015	.6350	.6015	17
Est vol 2,989; vol Wed 4,023; open int 7,405, −458.								
W.GERMAN MARK(IMM) – 125,000 marks; $ per mark								
Mar81	.5160	.5172	.5140	.5160	−.0034	.5816	.5069	8,160
June	.5250	.5253	.5228	.5240	−.0041	.5828	.5164	1,444
Sept	.5328	.5328	.5310	.5310	−.0052	.5790	.5254	154
Dec	....	....	....	.5350	....	.5480	.5250	2
Est vol 4,469; vol Wed 5,114; open int 9,760, −194.								

Source: The Wall Street Journal, Dec. 19, 1980.

TABLE 16.6
IMM Contract Specifications

Currency	Units/ Contract	Decimal Equivalent of One Point	Dollar Value
BP (British pound)	25,000	.0001	$ 2.50
DM (German mark)	125,000	.0001	$12.50
SF(Swiss franc)	125,000	.0001	$12.50
CD (Canadian dollar)	100,000	.0001	$10.00
JY (Japanese yen)	12,500,000	.000001	$12.50
DG (Dutch guilder)	125,000	.0001	$12.50
FR (French franc)	250,000	.00001	$ 3.50

Source: International Monetary Market, Chicago, 1979.

The IMM Foreign Exchange Contract

The IMM uses the direct quotation system: the price of a unit of foreign currency in terms of domestic currency. All foreign exchange rates are quoted with four digits to the right of the decimal except for the Mexican peso, the Japanese yen, and the French franc. Table 16.6 illustrates the point system and the equivalent dollar value per contract. Contracts have a standard size, minimum and maximum daily price fluctuations, and delivery date. All contracts have a high degree of liquidity and allow for a very high leverage possibility (Table 16.7). Contracts are guaranteed by the CC which is, in turn, guaranteed by the capital of the defaulting firm and as a last resort by the collective capital of the members of the exchange, who encompass most major securities and commodities firms. It is this very high level of safety, the standard size of the contracts, the centralized nature of the market, and depth and breadth (all major currencies with several maturity months are covered) that account for the high level of liquidity the contracts enjoy.

While futures contracts accomplish the same economic ends as forward contracts, there are several distinguishing elements in the two vehicles that give futures contracts the competitive advantage. Prices in both markets should not differ significantly, however; otherwise arbitrageurs would step in and bring the prices into equality. The differences and the similarities between the two vehicles are summarized in Table 16.8. Substantial evidence on the superiority of futures contracts in terms of liquidity and transactions costs have been provided by Janis Petersen[13] in her doctoral dissertation on the subject. Using transactions costs required on forward market contracts in British pounds, Canadian dollars, Swiss francs, and German marks and comparing them with transactions costs on futures contracts in the same currencies, Petersen concluded that the futures market is more efficient. She reasoned as follows:

> One reason why transactions costs are lower in the futures market may be because the futures market is the more perfect market, that is, it more closely resembles a perfectly competitive market. Costs (commissions) are determined by the forces of competition. Customers can "shop around" among brokerage firms to find the lowest price. This tends to keep transactions costs down.

---

[13] **Janis Petersen,** *A Study of Transactions Costs in the Forward and Futures Exchange Markets During the Years of Floating Exchange Rates.* Unpublished doctoral dissertation, Department of Economics, University of Notre Dame, South Bend, Ind., May 1980.

TABLE 16.7
Foreign Currencies Futures Contracts

Contract	British Pound	Canadian Dollar	German Mark	Dutch Guilder	Swiss Franc	Japanese Yen
Exchange	IMM	IMM	IMM	IMM	IMM	IMM
Contract size	25,000 British pounds sterling	100,000 Canadian dollars	125,000 German marks	125,000 Dutch guilders	125,000 Swiss francs	12,500,000 Japanese yen
Contract months	Jan., Mar., Apr., June, July, Sept., Oct., Dec.	Jan., Mar., Apr., June, July, Sept., Oct, Dec.,	Jan., Mar., Apr., June, July, Sept., Oct., Nov.	Same	Jan., Mar., Apr., June, July, Sept., Oct., Nov.	Jan., Mar., Apr., June, July, Sept., Oct., Nov.
Minimum price fluctuations	.0005 (5 pts.)	.0001 (1 pt.)	.0001 (1 pt.)	.0001 (1 pt.)	.0001 (1 pt.)	.000001 (1 pt.)
Minimum price fluctuations in dollars (per point)	$12.50	$10.00	$12.50	$12.50	$12.50	$12.50
Maximum price fluctuation	.05 (500 pts.)	.0075 (75 pts.)	.0100 (100 pts.)	.0100 (100 pts.)	.0150 (150 pts.)	.000100 (100 pts.)
Maximum price fluctuations in dollars	$1,250	$750	$1,250	$1,250	$1,875	$1,250
Margin: Initial / Maintenance	1,500 / 1,000	900 / 700	1,500 / 1,000	1,200 / 900	2,000 / 1,500	1,500 / 1,000
Last day of trading	2nd business-day before 3rd Wednesday of delivery month	2nd business day before …	Same	Same	Same	Same
Delivery date	3rd Wednesday of delivery month	Same	Same	Same	Same	Same

TABLE 16.8
Comparison of Futures Market and Forward Market

	Forward	Futures
Size of contract	Tailored to individual needs.	Standardized.
Delivery date	Tailored to individual needs.	Standardized.
Method of transaction	Established by the bank or broker via telephone contact with limited number of buyers and sellers.	Determined by open auction among many buyers and sellers on the exchange floor.
Participants	Banks, brokers, and multinational companies. Public speculation not encouraged.	Banks, brokers, and multinational companies. Qualified public speculation encouraged.
Commissions	Set by "spread" between bank's buy and sell price. Not easily determined by the customer.	Published small brokerage fee and negotiated rates on block trades.
Security deposit	None as such, but compensating bank balances required.	Published small security deposit required.
Clearing operation (financial)	Handling contingent on individual banks and brokers. No separate clearinghouse function.	Handled by exchange clearinghouse. Daily settlements to the market.
Marketplace	Over the telephone worldwide.	Central exchange floor with worldwide communications.
Economic justification	Facilitate world trade by providing hedge mechanism.	Same as forward market. In addition, it provides a broader market and an alternative hedging mechanism.
Accessibility	Limited to very large customers who deal in foreign trade.	Open to anyone who needs hedge facilities or has risk capital with which to speculate.
Regulation	Self-regulating.	April 1975—regulated under the Commodity Futures Trading Commission.
Frequency of delivery	More than 90% settled by actual delivery.	Theoretically, no deliveries in a perfect market. In reality, less than 1%.
Price fluctuations	No daily limit.	Daily limit imposed by exchange with a rule provision for expanded daily price limits.
Market liquidity	Offsetting with other banks.	Public offset. Arbitrage offset.

Source: Understanding Futures in Foreign Exchange. International Monetary Market, Chicago, August 1979.

> *In the forward market, banks deal with other banks using a foreign exchange broker as a middleman. The fee for using the services of a foreign exchange broker is the bid-ask spread in the interbank market. The bank, when dealing with its customers, widens the spread, resulting in a higher price to the customer. Thus, the elements of monopolistic competition results in slightly higher costs in the forward market.* [14]

Uses of the Futures Markets

Hedgers and speculators can use the futures market in a manner similar to the way in which they use the forward market. The hedger enters the futures market to offset a cash position (actual or prospective), expecting that the profits in the futures market will offset those in the cash market. As in the interest-rate futures case, the success of the hedger is determined by the basis—the difference between the futures exchange rate and the cash (spot) rate.

The relationship between the futures market and the cash market is complex and not very easy to predict. The basis is influenced by interest-rate differentials among countries (and, consequently, by the arbitrage opportunities they create), by investors' expectations, and by a host of government actions ranging from exchange controls to interest-rate manipulations to promote domestic or international equilibrium. Expectations can have most dramatic effects on the exchange rate. If speculators anticipate a weakness in the dollar, as they did in 1971, they will shift funds out of dollars into a stronger currency like the German mark. The results are a cheaper dollar and a dearer DM. As discussed earlier in this chapter, speculators can manifest their expectations in the spot or in the forward market. Speculators prefer the forward or futures markets, however, because of the very low margin requirements and lower transactions costs. Their transactions affect the basis and consequently the effectiveness of the hedged position.

We now offer examples of a long and a short hedge.

Short Hedge

A short hedge involves a long position in the spot market and simultaneously a short position in the futures market. The easiest way to illustrate the short hedge is to resurrect the examples of interest arbitrage presented earlier in this chapter. The arbitrage margin was positive and favored Germany, thus creating an arbitrage opportunity requiring investment in German securities. The arbitrageur, in order to invest in Germany, would have to sell dollars for DM and simultaneously sell DM forward (or sell a futures contract—short a contract—on DM maturing in the contract month equal to or nearest his or her time horizon).

Consider now the case of an American tool maker with a German subsidiary in need of cash to meet operating expenses. The cash infusion into the subsidiary requires the sale of dollars for DM and simultaneously the sale of a DM futures contract with a maturity coinciding with the debt repayment date (to the extent possible). The objective is to lock in today's exchange rate, no matter how the exchange rates move in the future.

---

[14] Ibid, p. 176.

The transactions will be as follows:

Cash (Spot) Market	**Futures Market**

Dec. 19, 1980

Buy 1 million DM at 0.5035
  Cost $503,500

Futures Market — Dec. 19, 1980

Sold 8 June DM contracts at 0.5240
  Proceeds $524,000

May 30, 1981

Case 1 $/DM = 0.5221

Sell 1 million DM
Proceeds $522,100
Profit (522,100 − 503,500) = $ 18,600

Case 1 $/DM = 0.5221* (May 30 price of the June contract)
Buy the 8 June contracts back
Cost $522,100
Profit (524,000 − 522,100) = $ 1,900

Net gain = $18,600 + $1,900 = **$20,500**

Case 2 $/DM = 0.495
Sell 1 million DM
Proceeds $495,000
Loss (495,000 − 503,500) = ($ 8,500)

Case 2 $/DM = 0.5200
Buy 8 June contracts
Cost $520,000
Profit (524,000 − 520,000) = $ 4,000

Net gain = ($8,500) + $4,000 = **($4,500)**

Case 3 $/DM = 0.5000
Sell 1 million DM
Proceeds $500,000
Loss (500,000 − 503,500) = ($ 3,500)

Case 3 $/DM = 0.5010
Buy 8 June contracts
Cost $500,000
Profit (524,000 − 501,000) = $ 23,000

Net gain = ($3,500) + $23,000 = **$19,500**

* As we move closer to the maturity date (June 17), the basis shrinks. On Dec. 19 the hedger can calculate the implied futures rate for a contract maturing on May 30, 1981, instead of June 17, 1981. This rate = 0.5035 + (0.5240 − 0.5035) 162/178 = 0.5221 where 162 = 162 days, the time period between Dec. 19, 1980, and May 30, 1981; and 178 = 178 days, the time period between Dec. 19, 1980, and June 17, 1981.

Before we comment on the preceding transactions and their consequences, let us review the alternative strategy of hedging in the forward market.

Cash (Spot) Market	**Forward Market**

Dec. 19, 1980

Buy 1 million DM
Cost $503,500

Forward Market — Dec. 19, 1980

Sell 1 million DM forward for delivery on May 30, 1981, at 0.5221*

* The forward rate of 0.5221 corresponds to the futures rate for the same period. Any deviation between the forward rate and the futures rate will be eliminated by arbitrage, assuming no significant market imperfection.

Case 1. Spot rate (May 30, 1981) = 0.5221. The hedger will simply deliver 1 million DM at 0.5221. The profits from foreign exchange transactions are equal to $522,100 − 503,500 = **$18,600.** Profits result from the fact that the DM was selling at a forward premium.

Case 2. Spot rate (May 30, 1981) = 0.5500. (set intentionally to be different from case 2 in the futures case). The hedger cannot take advantage of a current spot rate that is higher than the forward rate and must deliver DM at 0.5221. The loss is only an opportunity loss equal to **$27,900.** This loss would have been a real loss in the futures market (offset partially or totally by gains in the spot market).

Case 3. Spot rate (May 30, 1981) = 0.5000. No matter how low the spot rate turns out to be, the hedger will sell DM at 0.5221. Gains are once again equal to $18,600. The gains in the futures market would have been $23,000 − $3,500 = **$19,500.**

The conclusion is that the forward market represents a true hedge by locking in $18,600 in profits regardless of the direction of the spot rate. There are no such guarantees in the futures case, although there is a probability that the profits resulting from a spot futures hedge would equal $18,600. The speculative nature of a futures market hedge must once again be emphasized.

As the short futures hedge transactions make obvious, the profits (losses) in the cash market may more than offset the losses (profits) in the futures market. Cases 2 and 3 illustrate that the net profit from a selling hedge is very much dependent on the size of the basis, that is, the differential between the spot rate and the futures rate on May 30, 1981. A "perfect" hedge would have resulted in zero net loss or gain (long − short position profits or losses) no matter the direction of the exchange rates. Given the hedger's expectations about the basis, it may not be necessary, therefore, to offset the cash position on a one-to-one basis by a futures position. Only one future DM contract would have produced profits large enough to almost cover the loss in the spot market (Case 3). A way to arrive at the approximate hedge ratio was shown in Chapter 14.

We can, therefore, conclude that profits (losses) from a short hedge depend to a great degree on the basis, and that it may be best not to hedge at all—the case of the spot rate moving above 0.5240. The reader must have observed that it is quite possible to use a certain foreign exchange rate so that the hedge using seven futures DM contracts produces zero net profits and that the calculations in the preceding example do not account for the very small transactions costs. Also, the reader must observe that the smaller the basis (a strengthening basis), the larger the net profits in a short hedge. The opposite is true in a long hedge. Since perfect hedges are not always possible (given indivisibilities in the market and noncoinciding maturities), the hedger is a speculator on part or all of his or her assets. Net exposure is positive with the attending rewards and penalties.

Long Hedge

A long hedge consists of a short position in the cash market and a long position in the futures market—the opposite of the short hedge.

Using the preceding example with the German subsidiary having the excess cash and its U.S. parent in need of it, the transactions will be as follows:

Cash (Spot) Market	Futures Market
Dec. 19, 1980	**Dec. 19, 1980**
Sell 1 million DM	Buy 8 June DM contracts
May 30, 1981	**May 30, 1981**
Buy 1 million DM	Sell (offset) 8 June DM contracts

The gains (losses) in the futures position should offset (partially or totally) the losses (gains) in the cash position in a manner similar to that described in the preceding section.

Speculation in the Futures Market

Futures markets have many features that are attractive to speculators: low commissions, low margin requirements, and very high liquidity.

Speculators who expected the DM to fall in value in relation to the dollar would sell a futures DM contract and buy it back at a lower price once their expectations had been realized. If, on the other hand, speculators expected the DM to strengthen against the dollar, they would purchase a DM futures contract and sell it at a higher price once the currencies were realigned in the expected direction. In either case, speculators have the option of closing out their position in the futures market if their expectations do not materialize.

Speculators can also speculate in currency futures in ways similar to those discussed in detail in the chapters on commodities futures. Three types of spread positions can be utilized: intermonth, intermarket, and intercurrency. The intermonth spread involves a short position in one contract month and simultaneously a long position in another contract month on the same currency.

The intermarket spread involves a long position in a currency contract on one exchange and a short position on another exchange involving the same currency. The intercurrency spread involves a short position in one currency and a long position in another in the same market and on the same exchange.

While the rewards may be great, the risks are commensurate. Speculation in foreign currencies is not for amateurs. Even "professionals" get burned and bring down organizations with them. Witness what happened to the Franklin National Bank. Its failure as a banking institution was primarily the result of excessive speculation in the foreign exchange market.

16.18 FORECASTING FOREIGN EXCHANGE RATES

An art or a science? No matter! Many services are selling foreign exchange forecasts to banks, corporations, investors, and speculators and are making a profit. In fact, as of May 1979 there were at least 23 forecasting services[15] in the world, making their

---

[15] Stephen H. Goodman, "Foreign Exchange Forecasting Techniques: Implications for Business and Policy." *Journal of Finance,* May 1979, p. 415.

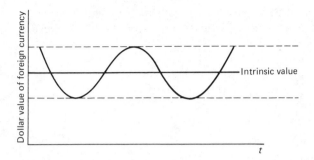

FIGURE 16.14 Fluctuation of foreign exchange rates around intrinsic value.

predictions available at rates ranging from zero (for corporate clients) to as high as $40,000 in minimum basic subscription fees.[16]

The presence of these services and their profitability have interesting implications on the efficiency of the foreign exchange market. A strongly efficient market requires that all information, publicly available or not, be reflected in the price of the security. The weakly efficient market, on the other hand, is an assertion that technical analysis has no usefulness to portfolio managers. It asserts that historical records of foreign exchange rates cannot be relied on in forecasting future spot rates, implying that no one can devise a strategy that can consistently outperform a naive buy-and-hold strategy. With this assertion, the market is signaling foreign exchange managers that regardless of the technique employed—sophisticated econometric models, simple forecasting tools, or chart reading—the market cannot be beaten. It is thus indicating, contrary to the observed reality, that there is no market for forecasting services.

Efficiency requires that the currency trade at its intrinsic value—that it be equal to the discounted value of all information. The size and power of the information-gathering machinery in a given organization, the level of the responsiveness of the organization to market opportunities, dealer behavior, unforeseen events, inside information on the status of certain countries yielding very short-lived information monopolies, and so on may cause the exchange rate to fluctuate around the intrinsic value, as shown in Figure 16.14.

The value of the forecasting service thus lies in its ability to identify the peak of a currency value (give a sell or short signal) and the bottom of a currency value (give a cover or buy signal). The intrinsic value thus represents the long-run value of the currency.

The techniques used in forecasting exchange rates fall into two major categories: fundamental analysis and technical analysis.

Fundamental Analysis

The techniques used by fundamentalists are varied and range from simple to very complex. They all assume freely fluctuating exchange rates.

Purchasing Power Parity (PPP)

This is the oldest and simplest technique used in forecasting foreign exchange rates. Two versions are utilized: the absolute PPP and the relative PPP.

---

[16] Euromoney Publications, *The Management of Foreign Exchange Risk.* September 1978, pp. 191–199.

The Absolute PPP.   The absolute PPP theory argues that the equilibrium exchange rate between any two currencies should be equal to the ratio of the price levels in their respective countries.

$$S_{B,A} = \frac{P_B}{P_A} \quad \text{or} \quad P_A S_{B,A} = P_B$$

where $S_{B,A}$ = spot rate

P_B = price level in country B

P_A = price level in country A

If $P_B/P_A > S_{B,A}$ the rate of inflation in country B is higher than in country A. Goods produced in country B become less competitive, resulting in a balance-of-payment (BOP) deficit and consequently, unless offset by reciprocal changes in the capital account, to a fall in the value of its currency. $S_{B,A}$ would rise.

The Relative PPP.   The relative PPP theory asserts that relative to a period when equilibrium rates prevailed, changes in relative prices indicate the size of the adjustment in the exchange rate:

$$\frac{\Delta S_{B,A}}{S_{B,A}} = \frac{(P_{A(t)}/P_{B(t)}) - (P_{A(0)}/P_{B(0)})}{P_{A(0)}/P_{B(0)}} = \frac{\Delta P_A/P_B}{P_{A(0)}/P_{B(0)}}$$

Both versions of PPP have several drawbacks:

1. Both involve an exclusive emphasis on monetary theory—a higher money supply leading to a higher rate of inflation and lower value for the currency. This logic ignores the effect of income levels and income elasticities for demand for imports and the impact of the business cycle. Additionally, structural considerations are also ignored. The sudden discovery of oil in the North Sea helped England's BOP and thus the stability of its currency, despite a higher rate of inflation in England relative to its trading partners. Changes in consumers' tastes also impact the value of a currency. The change in the perceived quality of Japanese goods in the mid-1960s brought an avalanche of Japanese products into the United States and Europe.

2. The PPP model is based on the assumption of free trade. One should never underestimate the mischief of government.

3. The indexes used as proxies for PPP, the wholesale price index (WPI) or the consumer price index (CPI), are not free of deficiencies. The WPI measures goods that are and could be traded. It is not very adequate if heavily weighted with traded goods, the prices of which may reflect changes in the world markets rather than domestic inflationary pressures. The CPI suffers from the mix between goods and services consumed by the citizens of a given country. Consumption in developed countries is skewed in favor of services, while that in developing countries is skewed in favor of goods. Some researchers have experimented with the export price index (XPI). The weakness of the

XPI stems from the fact that it includes only traded goods and not potentially tradeable goods. Despite its weaknesses the WPI is the best measure to use in testing the PPP theory.

Henry Gailliot[17] used the WPI to test the validity of the PPP theory. His results showed support for the PPP. In the *long run* (five or more years), relative price levels do determine the level of exchange rates. Other studies showed PPP to have explanatory power when used as a single dependent variable or as one of several independent variables.[18] Pigott, Sweeney, and Willett showed that the variability in the dollar exchange rate of several currencies is only partially explained by price-level differentials.[19]

The International Fisher Effect

Again emphasizing the monetarist point of view, the international Fisher effect holds that exchange rates are determined by interest-rate differentials among countries. A higher interest rate in Germany relative to the United States (say, 2 percent) foretells a depreciation in the value of the DM by 2 percent. The higher interest rate is required in order to compensate U.S. investors in German securities for the expected depreciation in the value of DM-denominated assets resulting from a higher inflation rate in Germany relative to the United States.

Empirical tests[20] support the validity of interest-rate differentials as an explanatory variable for long-run exchange-rate changes or as one of several explanatory variables.

Interest-Rate Parity

The interest-rate parity theory states, as was detailed earlier in this chapter, that the implicit rate should equal the interest-rate differential; that is, the arbitage margin should be equal to zero, as shown in Equation 16.3. A higher interest rate in the United States relative to England should reflect itself in an equal forward discount on the dollar. If not, covered-interest arbitrage would exist and capital will flow across national borders.

The interest-rate parity theory advanced two important hypotheses dealing with the relationship between short-term interest rates and the forward rate and between the forward rate and the expected spot rate.

The Forward Rate

Several studies have attempted to determine whether the forward rate is an unbiased predictor of the future spot rate. The meaning of unbiased predictor is that the average difference between the forward rate and the future spot rate will be a small number

---

[17] **Henry J. Gailliot,** "Purchasing Power Parity as an Explanation of Long-Term Changes in Exchange Rates." *Journal of Money, Credit, and Banking,* August 1970, pp. 348–357.

[18] **Richard J. Rogalski,** and **Joseph D. Vinso,** "Empirical Properties of Foreign Exchange Rates." *Journal of International Business Studies,* Fall 1978, pp. 69–79.

[19] **Charles Pigott, Richard James Sweeney,** and **Thomas D. Willett,** "The Uncertainty Effects of Exchange Rate Fluctuations Under the Current F Cost." Unpublished, 1975.

[20] See, for example, **Ian Giddy,** "Exchange Risk: Whose Views?" *Financial Management,* Summer 1977, pp. 23–33; also **Robert T. Aliber,** *Exchange Risk and Corporate International Finance,* Wiley, New York, 1978, p. 76.

close to zero over long periods of time. Also, there should be no systematic positive or negative error—that is, predictable patterns of positive or negative differences between the forward and the future spot rate. An acceptance of this hypothesis has serious implications in terms of the market for foreign exchange forecasting services. The forward rate, a costless forecasting tool, is available for everyone to use as a predictor for future spot rates.

Efficient foreign exchange markets should lead to a result consistent with the hypothesis that the forward rate is an unbiased predictor of the future spot rate. Giddy and Dufey[21] and Kohlhagen[22] found evidence that the foreign exchange markets were efficient. A conclusion drawn by Giddy and Dufey is intriguing, however: "For short periods, one is able to detect a low degree of market inefficiency in the foreign exchange market. But the longer the forecasting horizon, the more evident is the inaccuracy of the time series forecasting of exchange rate changes."[23] These results have been duplicated recently in a paper entitled "A Test of the Rationality of Forward Exchange Rates." The author concludes that "the forward exchange rate is rational over the long run—in the short run the forward exchange market is not random walk efficient and, therefore, not rational."[24]

The significance of this conclusion is dependent upon the time horizon of speculators. Short-term market inefficiencies are precisely what speculators and arbitrageurs are looking at. Currency traders, in fact, look at minute-by-minute fluctuations in the value of currencies and establish positions based on the slightest of perceived disequilibriums in the market. The issue of long-term efficiency is suspect, if not irrelevant.

Bradford Cornell[25] and Richard Levich[26] also found evidence indicating that the forward market is an unbiased predictor of the future spot. The problem in this study, as in every other study of the same type, is the confusion of unbiasedness with efficiency. Unbiasedness simply implies that the foreign exchange market is fair game.

Using the mean forecast error as a measure of liquidity premium, Cornell found that the average liquidity premium for the seven currencies tested was equal to zero. He concluded, based on this and other tests, that the forward rate is an unbiased predictor of the future spot rate and that "the systematic risk of open exchange positions is insignificant."[27] The implication of this conclusion is that a portfolio manager should not be concerned with open (uncovered) exchange positions.

While an unbiased predictor, the forward rate was found by Cornell not to be the best predictor, confirming the findings of Giddy and Dufey. Cornell found that simple autoregressive models generally were superior predictors to the forward rate.

Levich studied nine currencies, using observations from 1973 to 1979 on seven of these. He studied the relationship between the 90-day forward rate at time t and the

[21] **Ian H. Giddy** and **Gunter Dufey,** "The Random Behavior of Flexible Exchange Rates." *Journal of International Business Studies,* Spring 1975, pp. 1–32.

[22] **Steven Kohlhagen,** "The Performance of the Foreign Exchange Markets: 1971–1974." *Journal of International Business Studies,* Fall 1975, pp. 33–39.

[23] **Giddy** and **Dufey,** p. 27.

[24] Paper submitted for publication to *Financial Management.*

[25] **Bradford Cornell,** "Spot Rates, Forward Rates and Exchange Market Efficiency." *Journal of Financial Economics,* 1977, pp. 55–65.

[26] **Richard M. Levich,** "Are Forward Exchange Rates Unbiased Predictors of Future Spot Rates?" *Columbia Journal of World Business,* Winter 1979, pp. 49–58.

[27] **Cornell,** p. 64.

spot rate at time $t + 90$. His results did not permit him to reject the hypothesis that the forward rate is an unbiased predictor of the future spot rate. The R^2 of the test was very low and in most cases insignificant. While unbiased, the forward rate was found by Levich to be a very poor predictor of the level and direction of the foreign exchange rate. The portfolio managers could have done just as well flipping a coin to determine the direction of the spot rate as they would have watching the forward rate. The results of the test led Levich to a conclusion opposite to that of Cornell, mainly that a firm subjects itself to sizable exchange gains or losses if it bases its investment and financing decisions on the forward rate.[28]

The Futures Rate

Another costless forecasting tool has become available since the early 1970s: the futures rate. The forecasting effectiveness of foreign currency futures has been examined by several researchers. The most recent study is by Joanne Hill and Thomas Schneeweis.[29] It attempts to duplicate earlier studies on the forward rate and to improve on the work of Panton and Joy.[30]

Using closing contract prices on the IMM for five currencies (British pound, German mark, Swiss franc, Canadian dollar, and Japanese yen) covering the period September 1972 through December 1978, Hill and Schneeweis tested the hypothesis that the futures rate is an unbiased predictor of the spot rate. Their conclusion was that "results from currency futures markets indicate prices set there are unbiased forecasts of spot rates as has been found for forward rates in other studies."[31]

The studies by the author referred to earlier do not confirm the findings of Hill and Schneeweis. They show, in fact, that neither the forward nor the futures rate is a good predictor of the spot rate. And that there exists no statistically significant difference between the futures and the forward rate. The latter result was supported by B. Cornell and M. Reinganum in their paper titled "Forward and Futures Prices: Evidence from the Foreign Exchange Markets" (*Journal of Finance* vol. 36, no. 12, Dec. 1981, 1035–1045).

Econometric Models

The econometric models used in forecasting exchange rates suffer from two major drawbacks:[32]

---

[28] **Levich's** results were recently supported by two separate studies conducted by the author. In both studies, the forward rate was found to be a poor predictor of the direction and the level of spot rates. (a) **Sarkis J. Khoury,** "Stability of Predictors and the Forecasting of Foreign Exchange Rates," working paper, University of Notre Dame, Dec. 1981. (b) **Sarkis J. Khoury,** "Foreign Exchange Rates: A Test of Two Naive Forecasting Tools," working paper, University of Notre Dame, June 1982.

[29] **Joanne Hill** and **Thomas Schneeweis,** "Forecasting Effectiveness of Foreign Currency Futures." *Business Economics,* May 1981, pp. 42–46.

[30] **D. P. Panton,** and **D. J. Joy,** "Empirical Evidence in International Monetary Currency Futures," in **R. M. Leuthold,** ed., *Commodity Markets and Futures Prices.* Chicago Mercantile Exchange, 1979.

[31] **Hill** and **Schneeweis,** p. 46.

[32] See **Laurent L. Jacque,** *Management of Foreign Exchange Risk.* Lexington Books, Lexington, Mass., 1978, chap. 3.

1. The use of historic time series data which do not take into account changes in the structural relationship among the variables.

2. The assumption that the independent variable (the exchange rate) is normally distributed. Studies by Janice Westerfield[33] and by R. Rogalski and J. Vinso[34] offer conclusive evidence that foreign exchange rates are not normally distributed.

To these drawbacks must be added one additional reservation about the wisdom of the whole process. To the extent that foreign exchange markets are efficient, the whole exercise is fruitless. That is, no additional price information useful for profitable trading can be gained by the most sophisticated of econometric models.

These drawbacks did not stop academicians and practitioners from trying. A frequently used approach is that of multiple discriminant analysis (MDA). MDA has been used extensively,[35] most recently by Animesh Ghoshal.[36] MDA is a regression technique that allows the researcher to classify an observation (a certain currency in this case) into an a priori determined grouping (appreciating or depreciating currency). The discriminant function is of the form

$$Z = B_1 X_1 + B_2 X_2 + \cdots + B_n X_n \tag{16.8}$$

where the B's represent the relative discriminant power of the variable.

Ghoshal, using data collected between 1972 and 1979 on 20 countries belonging to the Organization for Economic Cooperation and Development, arrived at a discriminant function of the following form (using a stepwise regression method):

$$Z = 0.71407R - 0.42282M2 - 0.37080P \tag{16.9}$$

where R = country's reserves evaluated at current market value (gold plus foreign
    exchange holdings)

  $M2$ = money supply relative to other countries

  P = wholesale prices

The classification accuracy of the discriminant function is 69 percent, well above the proportional chance criteria. Ghoshal does not report, however, the correlation among the independent variables. One should expect a high correlation between P and $M2$, which casts doubt on the results.

Technical Analysis

All the preceding analyses are of no value, technical analysts argue. It is better to spend the time identifying past price patterns, because they are likely to be repeated. Exchange rates are determined by the interaction of supply and demand, which are

---

[33] **Janice Westerfield,** "An Examination of Foreign Exchange Risk Under Fixed and Floating Exchange Rate Regimes." *Journal of International Economics,* vol. 7, no. 2 (1977), pp. 181–200.

[34] **Rogalski** and **Vinso.**

[35] See, for example, **Martin Murenbeeld,** "Economic Factors for Forecasting Foreign Exchange Rates." *Columbia Journal of World Business,* Summer 1975; **William R. Folks, Jr.,** and **Stanley R. Stansell,** "The Use of Discriminant Analysis in Forecasting Exchange Rate Movements." *Journal of International Business Studies,* Spring 1975.

[36] **Animesh Ghoshal,** "A Forecasting Model for Exchange Rate Changes." Working paper, DePaul University, Chicago, April 1981.

influenced by both rational and irrational factors. Understanding those factors requires understanding the "psychology" of the market participants.

The techniques employed by technicians are varied—simplistic in some cases and very complex in others. They are very similar to those used in determining stock price movements, as discussed in Chapter 4. We shall be content to have the reader review the contents of Chapter 4.

The Evidence

A comprehensive review of forecasting techniques was undertaken by Stephen Goodman, assistant treasurer of the Singer Company.[37] As in the case of all studies in this area, the research has a dual purpose: the examination of the merits of a given technique and simultaneously the testing of the hypothesis on market efficiency.

Goodman evaluated six economics-oriented and four technically oriented services on the basis of their predictive accuracy with regard to six currencies against the dollar. The economics-oriented services were evaluated using three criteria: "accuracy in predicting trends, accuracy of their point estimates, and speculative return on capital at risk."[38] The technically oriented services were evaluated using only the speculative return on capital at risk, calculated in a manner similar to that for economics-oriented services. The results were startling in light of the accumulating literature indicating market efficiency:

> Both the absolute performance of the services [economically oriented] and their performance relative to the forward rate, both in predicting the direction of trend and providing point estimates of future spot exchange rates, improves as the forecast horizon lengthens from three to six months.
>
> Blindly following the economics-oriented services' forecasts is profitable, but only marginally so. It is generally less profitable than a buy and hold strategy.
>
> All the technically oriented services do remarkably well. The speculative return on capital at risk for each of the services averages between 7.28% and 10.46% annually before transactions costs, compared with a 2.86% return on a buy and hold strategy. The average performance of the poorest technically oriented services is far better than the average performance of the best economics-oriented service.[39]

The clear implications of the Goodman study are that foreign exchange markets are not efficient. It is clear that the forecasting services have justified their existence and their charges. A contrary finding would indicate that corporations buying the services of forecasting firms are inefficient in the allocation of their resources and/or that corporate treasurers are fools. No forecasting service firm can permanently survive the onslaught of a market offering evidence contrary to the values forecasted.

A Few Guidelines

The mixed evidence on the efficiency of the foreign exchange market leaves many readers quite perplexed. Many variables have proven, time and again, their value as indicators of the direction in the value of a currency. They are as follows:

---

[37] **Stephen H. Goodman,** "Foreign Exchange Rate Forecasting Techniques: Duplications for Business and Policy." *Journal of Finance,* vol. 34, no. 2 (May 1979), pp. 415–427.

[38] Ibid., p. 419.

[39] Ibid., pp. 422–423.

1. Balance of payments data—the current balance in particular. A positive balance is an indication of a stable if not appreciating currency.

2. Relative price levels—prices in the home country vs. those of its trading partners. The wholesale price index is the most adequate measure.

3. Relative rates of interest between countries on instruments of comparable risk and maturity.

4. Country reserves—gold plus foreign currency holdings. Larger reserves indicate greater liquidity, greater ability to meet unfavorable balances in the international account, and greater ability to support a currency level.

5. Unemployment data and economic growth data. These statistics indicate the extent of domestic pressure and the direction of monetary and fiscal policies to deal with them. These policies could have serious repercussions on the value of the home currency.

6. Trends in international investments flows into or out of certain countries.

7. Political stability of a country and the quality of its leadership.

CONCLUSIONS

The trend in the investment community clearly favors a geocentric approach to portfolio management. The more this intensifies, the more important the issues discussed in this chapter become. While we have discussed all the basics of international finance, we cannot but urge readers to further familiarize themselves with other aspects of international portfolio management. Chapter 17 offers additional insight in this area.

QUESTIONS

1. Discuss in detail the effects of interest arbitrage on interest rates and exchange rates.

2. Explain how a BOP surplus or deficit was eliminated under the gold standard.

3. Compare and contrast the forward and the futures foreign exchange market. Be specific.

4. What is a foreign exchange contract?

5. What are the primary motivating forces behind the foreign exchange market?

6. What are the reasons for the dominant role played by the U.S. dollar in the foreign exchange market?

7. Suggest reasons for the arbitrageur schedule's negative slope.

8. Describe the process that would have to occur for a French bank to buy German marks from a Brazilian bank.

9. Who appears to dominate the foreign exchange market: arbitrageurs or speculators? What is the deciding factor?

10. Why might an exporter being paid in a foreign currency at some time in the future use forward contracts to hedge against foreign exchange risk? How would he or she do this?

11. Outline the limitations of the IRPT. How serious are they? Explain.

12. The following exchange rates are given: $1 = 200 yen, £1 = $2, 1 yen = £0.0025. Is there consistency across currencies? How do you know?

13. An arbitrageur in the United States calculates the interest differential between the United States and England to be 0.9 percent and the implicit rate between the three-month forward pound to be 1.15 percent.
   a. Explain the course of action that the arbitrageur would take given this data.
   b. According to the interest rate parity theory, what effect would this have on U.S. and English financial markets and exchange rates?

14. Discuss the reasons why the interest differential and the implicit rate between two countries usually are not equal, as predicted by the interest rate parity theory.

15. Differentiate between arbitrage and speculation.

16. How does the modern theory of foreign exchange rates differ from the interest rate parity theory?

17. Distinguish between a real rate of interest and a nominal rate of interest; does this distinction explain the discount (1976–1980) on the U.S. dollar relative to the DM, despite higher interest rates in the United States?

18. "The best way to forecast exchange rates is to flip a coin." Comment.

19. Under what market conditions is the forward rate the ultimate forecasting tool? Why?

20. Explain the major considerations of foreign exchange investors when deciding between buying a forward contract or a futures contract.

PROBLEMS

1. Given that £1 = $2.50, state the New York direct quote and indirect quote.

2. The following New York ticker quotes for the French franc are given:
   0.2376–0.2378   19–14, 57–46, 78–63
   a. State the bid and ask quotes for the spot and forward rates.
   b. Are the forward French francs selling at a premium or a discount? How can you tell?
   a. What is the annualized premium/discount on the buy side of the three-month forward franc?

3. The following exchange rates are given: $1 = DM 2, DM1 = £0.25, £1 = $1.60.
   a. What transactions would an arbitrageur with $100 undertake? What would his profit be?
   b. What would happen to the exchange rates as this process continued?

4. Given the spot pound at 2.3800 and the 30-day forward pound at 2.3830, the U.S. one-month T-bill rate is 12.30 percent and the British T-bill rate is 8.4 percent.
   a. Calculate the arbitrage margin.
   b. What are the implications of this margin?

c. Assuming an investor had £1,000 invested in British T-bills, what steps would she take to capitalize on this arbitrage opportunity?

d. What would be the consequences of similar actions taken by a number of people, assuming that interest rates did not change?

5. A DM spot rate of 0.52, a German 90-day T-bill rate of 12 percent, and a U.S. 90-day T-bill rate of 10.5 percent are given.
   a. What is the equilibrium forward rate?
   b. Would the 90-day DM sell at a discount or premium?

6. The following are given: an ask on the spot French franc of 0.2250, a 90-day U.S. T-bill rate of 8 percent, a 90-day French T-bill rate of 8.8 percent, and these transactions costs:

   1 percent on sale of dollars
   1 percent on purchase of spot francs
   1 percent on purchase of franc-denominated assets
   1 percent on sale of 90-day forward francs

   Find the price of the 90-day French franc at which arbitrageurs would no longer find it profitable to move funds from the United States to France.

7. The spot British pound is selling for $2.20 and the one-year forward pound is selling for $2.35. The annual interest rate in the United States is 20 percent, 10 percent in England. Speculators expect the spot rate for the British pound to be $2.25 in one year.
   a. Outline the steps that an English arbitrageur with £10,000 would undertake.
   b. What actions would a speculator in the forward market undertake and what would be his possible profit if his expectations were met?
   c. What are the implications of the actions of the arbitrageur and the speculator for the price of the forward contract?

8. A U.S. multinational owns a subsidiary in France which requires 1 million French francs from June 18 to Oct. 14. The June 18 spot rate for the French franc is 0.2198 and the October futures contract is 0.2234. Assume that the delivery date for the futures contract is Oct. 21.
   a. Calculate the implied futures contract rate on Oct. 14. Why can it be assumed that a forward contract for Oct. 14 will have the same rate?
   b. If the spot rate on Oct. 14 is 0.2230, calculate the profit/loss for hedging in both the futures market and the forward market, assuming the implied October 14 futures rate holds.
   c. Calculate the profit/loss for hedging in the futures market and for hedging in the forward market if the implied rate does not hold and if on Oct. 14 the spot rate is 0.2233 and the futures rate is 0.2225.
   d. Calculate the profit/loss for hedging in the futures market and for hedging in the forward market if the implied rate does not hold and if on Oct. 14 the spot rate is 0.2220 and the futures rate is 0.2229.
   e. What are the implications of these findings?

CHAPTER 17

Investing in the World Economy

17.1 INTRODUCTION

Evidence of an increasingly interdependent world abounds. American firms and investors continue to look overseas for investment opportunities, and foreign firms and investors are increasing their commitments in the United States at a phenomenal (alarming, some argue) rate.

Our concern in this chapter is with *portfolio investment,* that is, investment in corporate and government securities which does not result in control over the operations of the entity whose securities are being acquired. The other form of investment is referred to as *direct investment,* where the buying firm acquires control over the operations of the firm whose securities or assets are acquired. The only difference between these types of investment is in the degree of control. In portfolio investment, the investing firm neither seeks nor exercises control, although the implications for the securities markets are essentially the same. It must be noted, however, that portfolio investment is occasionally a prelude to direct investment, and that direct investment and portfolio investment generally exhibit a high level of interdependence. Foreign firms operating in the United States may invest some of their assets or their temporary excess cash in U.S. securities and/or issue securities in the U.S. market; some foreign portfolio investment may turn into direct investment.

Direct investment in the United States reached $65.5 billion[1] by the end of 1980, up 20 percent from $54.5 billion in 1979. Dutch firms lead all foreign firms in terms of foreign ownership of U.S. assets, followed by British, Canadian, West German, and Japanese firms. The income realized on these investments equaled $7.61 billion for 1980. Foreign direct investment by U.S. firms is still far ahead of foreign direct investment in the United States. At the end of 1980, U.S. foreign direct investment reached $213.5 billion and earned $28.8 billion. Foreign direct investment in the United States and by U.S. firms grew in all its forms: de novo expansion, mergers, and acquisitions. The growth in foreign acquisition of U.S. firms has been very dramatic, as was documented

---

[1] U.S. Department of Commerce, privately released data, Aug. 7, 1981.

by the author.[2] The major motives for acquisitions are the richness and size of the
U.S. market, the quality of the U.S. labor force, the inflation rate as it affects construction
costs, the avoidance of implicit and explicit trade barriers, the political stability of the
United States, the state of the U.S. dollar and the U.S. stock market, and other reasons
of lesser significance.

The growth in portfolio investment in the United States by foreign entities is no
less impressive. Of the $407 billion of T-notes and T-bonds outstanding at the end of
December 1980, $57.5 billion or 14.1 percent was held by foreign countries. During
the same month, the value of net purchases (purchases minus sales) of U.S. stocks
and bonds by foreign entities amounted to $562 million and $121 million respectively.
The net purchases of stocks and bonds for all of 1980 were $5,421 million and $5,461
million respectively. American investors, however, have been net sellers of foreign securities. Net sales of stocks and bonds were $5,460 million, $3,450 million, $4,729 million,
and $3,152 million for the years 1977, 1978, 1979, and 1980 respectively. Total U.S.
pension fund holdings of foreign securities at the end of 1980 was $3.25 billion, as
reported by Intersec Research Corporation. The estimate by Intersec for 1981 is $5.5
billion.

The fundamental motivations for these large capital flows across national borders,
as we will elaborate below, are the desire to diversify risk as well as the desire to
capitalize on a healthier economy in many western countries (Fig. 17.1) throughout
most of the 1970s, and on the correspondingly healthy stock markets[3] overseas (Fig.
17.2). The latest economic indicators of the six major countries and the returns in
foreign stock markets adjusted for changes in foreign exchange rates relative to returns
realized in the United States (Figs. 17.3 and 17.4) indicate, ceteris paribus, that the
capital flows at least over the short run will be in the direction of the United States.
The United States appears to hold the edge in rates of return (1980–1982) and political
and economic stability. Other incentives for international diversification stem from increased information flows on foreign money and capital markets (which reduce the
aversion of American investors to foreign securities), expanding opportunities overseas
(the market value of non-American securities is approximately equal to the $1 trillion
of U.S. stocks), and the increased international visibility and powers of non-American
multinational corporations.

17.2 MOTIVES FOR INTERNATIONAL INVESTMENTS

The primary reasons for international portfolio investments are risk diversification and/
or improved rates of return.

The issue of risk diversification on a domestic level was discussed in Chapters 5
and 6. To see how risk diversification can occur on an international scale,

let $\sigma_{P_1}^2$ = variance of a portfolio rate of return

σ_d^2 = variance of a portfolio made up of strictly domestic securities

[2] **Sarkis J. Khoury,** *Transnational Mergers and Acquisitions in the United States.* Lexington
Books, Lexington, Mass., 1980.

[3] An investment in the Hong Kong stock market between December 1969 and July 1980
would have yielded 645 percent, compared with 16 percent for U.S. securities in the same period.
The Hong Kong market is considerably more risky than its U.S. counterpart, however.

FIGURE 17.1   International comparisons of industrial production.

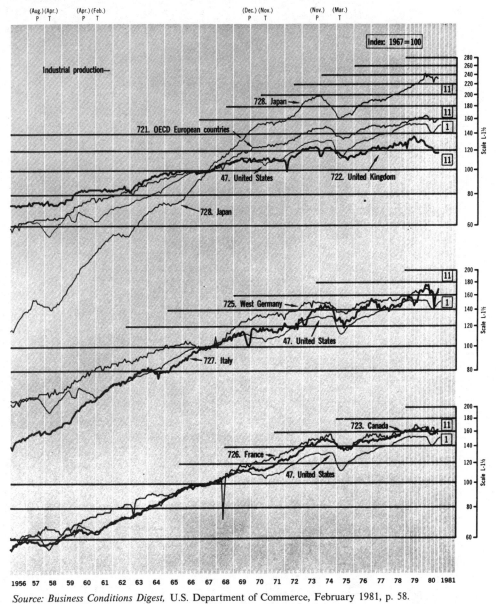

Source: *Business Conditions Digest,* U.S. Department of Commerce, February 1981, p. 58.

Therefore, in the absence of international diversification,

$$\sigma_{P_1}^2 = \sigma_d^2$$

If foreign securities are included in the portfolio, the variance of the new portfolio is calculated as follows:

$$\sigma_{P_2}^2 = W_d^2 \sigma_d^2 + W_f^2 \sigma_f^2 + 2 W_d W_f \sigma_{f,d} \qquad (17.1)$$

FIGURE 17.2 International comparisons of stock prices.

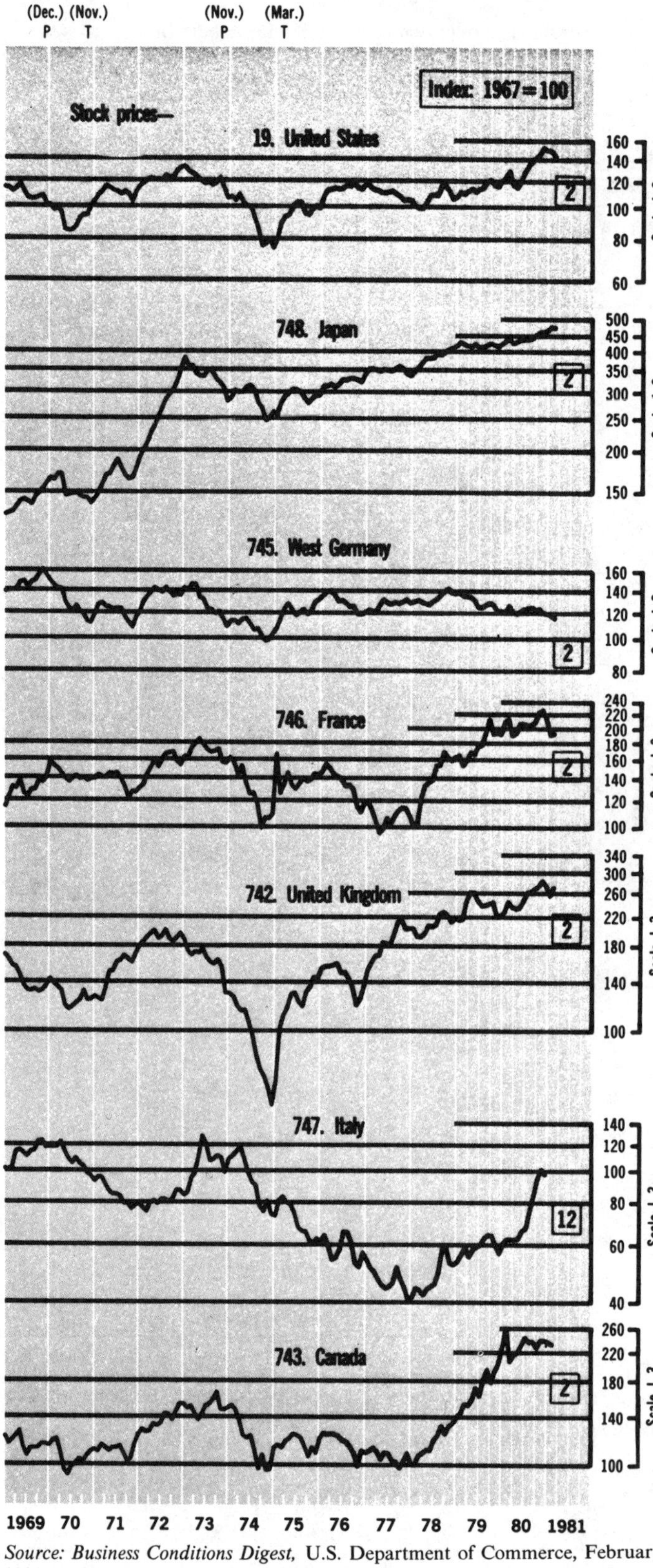

Source: *Business Conditions Digest*, U.S. Department of Commerce, February 1981, p. 59.

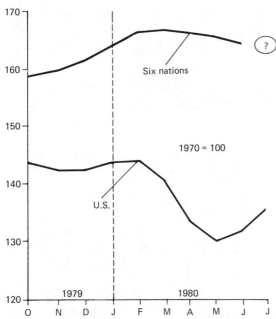

Source: Center for International Business Cycle Research and U.S. Department of Commerce.

FIGURE 17.4 Performance of selected world stockmarkets in the first quarter of 1981 (percent change for capital appreciation only).

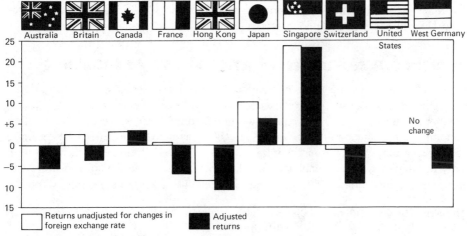

Reprinted by permission of Tribune Company Syndicate, Inc.

where W_d, W_f = proportion of total investable funds committed to domestic and foreign securities respectively; $W_d + W_f = 1$

σ_d^2, σ_f^2 = variances of rates of return on domestic and foreign securities in portfolio

$\sigma_{f,d}$ = covariance between foreign and domestic rates of return

$\rho_{f,d} = \sigma_{f,d}/\sigma_d\sigma_f$ = correlation between foreign and domestic rates of return

Thus, international diversification should prove valuable if $\rho_{f,d} < 1$; if $\rho_{f,d}$ equaled 1, the investor would be well advised to invest in that country with the lower variance.

International diversification can be achieved through various avenues. As corporations adopt geocentric (global) investment and marketing strategies, they diversify their geographic source of income. Investors who own shares in these multinational companies are effectively diversifying their portfolios internationally. The alternative to this indirect form of diversification is to purchase the securities of separate firms operating in various countries. If the international capital markets are efficient, the two methods should yield the same results.

The original work on international portfolio diversification was done by H. Grubel,[4] who showed that international diversification is advantageous to U.S. investors. H. Levy and M. Sarnat[5] extended the Markowitz-Tobin model to an international setting and showed that the advantages of international diversification were considerable during the 1951–1967 period.

The correlation of major foreign markets with the U.S. market is shown in Table 17.1. Clearly, the lower the correlation coefficient, the greater the potential for diversification. From Table 17.1, we can see that the largest potential for diversification for U.S. investors lies in investing in the United Kingdom during the period July 1975–June 1977. For the period Jan. 1, 1978–Dec. 29, 1980, the author has calculated the correlations (using monthly data) between the S&P 500 and the stock indexes of the same countries. The results are shown in Table 17.2.

Table 17.2 shows West Germany to have been the preferred country for risk reduction of securities portfolios held by U.S. investors. These results differ from those of Lessard because the time period is different and the market indexes used were unweighted.

In summary, therefore, international diversification, if possible, appears to be advantageous to U.S. investors (more evidence is given later in this chapter).

17.3 ISSUES/RISKS IN INTERNATIONAL DIVERSIFICATION

This section focuses on the problems encountered and trends observed in the international diversification of portfolios. Country-specific issues will be discussed later.

The increasing interdependence among world economies is increasing the correlation in economic performance among countries. Highly correlated economies may generate similar expectations, which indirectly link stock prices between countries. The integration of many economies is further enhanced by the emergence of new financial centers and the increased sophistication of existing ones. The extensive borrowing done by foreign

---

[4] **Herbert G. Grubel,** "Internationally Diversified Portfolios; Welfare Gains and Capital Flows." *American Economic Review,* December 1968, pp. 1299–1314.

[5] **Haim Levy** and **Marshall Sarnat,** "International Diversification of Investment Portfolios." *American Economic Review,* September 1970, pp. 668–675.

TABLE 17.1
Correlation of Major Foreign Markets with the U.S. Market[a] (Selected Periods[b])

Country	1961–65	1964–68	1967–71	1970–74
Canada	.828	.830	.813	.836
France	.364	.016	.081	.349
Germany	.563	.120	.343	.349
Japan	.181	.070	.224	.301
Netherlands	.695	.602	.570	.463
Switzerland	.559	.346	.532	.501
United Kingdom	.428	.187	.278	.483

Country	1973–77[c]	July 1971–June 1973	July 1973–June 1975	July 1975–June 1977
Canada	.727	—	—	—
France	.499	−.240	.683	.392
Germany	.431	.161	.487	.500
Japan	.396	.364	.293	.727
Netherlands	.609	.154	.671	.618
Switzerland	.629	.148	.689	.718
United Kingdom	.507	.312	.596	.256

Source: D. R. Lessard, "An Update on Gains from International Diversification." Unpublished, 1977, based on stock market data from *Capital International Perspective,* Capital International, S.A., Geneva, Switzerland.

[a] The S&P 500 is taken to represent the U.S. market.

[b] Based on monthly changes in value-weighted market indexes.

[c] Through June 1977, 54 observations.

TABLE 17.2
Correlation of Major Foreign Markets with the U.S. Market (Jan. 1, 1978–Dec. 29, 1980)

Canada	.914
France	.899
Germany	−.575
Japan	.843
Switzerland	.749
United Kingdom	.079

countries, the West European countries in particular, in the New York market serves to integrate their financial centers and consequently reduces the differential in interest rates across national borders. The interdependence among economies is further enhanced by the activities of multinational corporations, which give rise to nearly identical price behavior within limits imposed by impediments to capital flows.[6] Other factors contributing to increased levels of correlation are the following:

---

[6] See **R. Ripley,** "Systematic Elements in the Linkage of National Stock Market Indices." *Review of Economics and Statistics,* August 1973.

FIGURE 17.5   U.S. international transactions—goods and services movements.

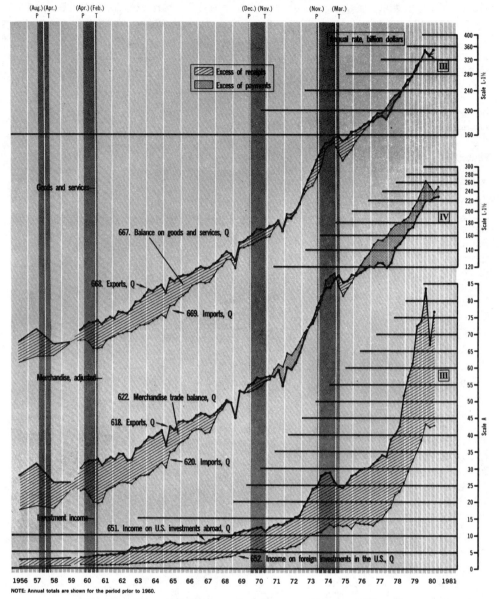

Source: Business Conditions Digest, U.S. Department of Commerce, February 1981, p. 57.

1. Foreign direct investment by U.S. firms.
2. Foreign direct investment by foreign firms in the United States.
3. Increased world trade resulting from the drive by many countries to expand their export sector, which has increased the interdependence among countries. The growth of U.S. trade is illustrated in Figure 17.5.

All of the factors reduce the payoffs from international diversification as they increase the correlation between stock market indexes across countries.

Factors unique to a country—political considerations, internal and unpredictable economic disruptions, and a host of others—can act to reduce the synchronization in economic performance across countries and have often done so. Correlations between stock market indexes may be increasing but are unlikely to reach +1. Therefore, the optimal efficient portfolio would still have to include international securities.

Other considerations in international investments besides increasing correlations are as follows:

1. *Foreign exchange risk.* Portfolio investments in foreign securities markets by U.S. residents require the conversion of U.S. dollars into the currency of the host country unless the foreign security is listed on the American stock exchanges and traded like a U.S. security (details are provided later in this chapter). The investor holding assets denominated in a foreign currency is exposed to foreign exchange risk, which can reduce the effective rate of return realized on the internationally diversified portfolio.

The volatility of foreign currencies in terms of the U.S. dollar is shown in Figure 17.6. This volatility makes default-free securities denominated in different currencies or securities in otherwise equivalent risk classes imperfect substitutes. Investors will, most economists argue, demand a risk premium for holding the asset denominated in a foreign currency.

The foreign exchange risk can easily be exaggerated, however. This risk can be reduced, if not eliminated, through the forward or the futures currency markets. Exchange rates moving in a direction opposite to that of domestic economic conditions reduce the riskiness of an internationally diversified portfolio compared to one made up strictly of domestic securities. Exchange-rate changes that are not completely correlated with each other (all currencies not moving in the same direction and by the same percent against the domestic currency) may well reduce the relative riskiness of internationally diversified portfolios. Finally, exchange-rate changes that are negatively correlated with returns on securities may well reduce the relative riskiness of internationally diversified portfolios.[7]

2. *Political risk.* This argues for international diversification to reduce political risk. The argument is hardly convincing, however, for a U.S. investor, who supposedly lives in the most politically stable country. On the other hand, the efficient functioning of financial markets in many countries will ensure that the American investor is adequately compensated for the increased risk assumed in venturing overseas.

3. *Limited size and depth of foreign markets.* Several studies point out that the thinness of a market accounts for the extra risk (variability in returns) in that market. Hawawini and Michel[8] suggest an inverse relationship between stability and significance of estimated risk measures and the size and structure of equity markets. They showed that in the Belgian case five additional factors also affected risk, and are all related to the thinness of the market. The factors are these:

a. *Behavior and size of investors.* Moderate portfolio adjustments and little institutional activity can significantly affect risk in a thin market.

---

[7] The evidence indicates, however, that the correlation between exchange rates and stock market returns is negligible. See **B. Jacquillat** and **B. Solnik,** "Multinationals are Poor Tools for Diversification." *Journal of Portfolio Management,* Winter 1978.

[8] **G. Hawawini** and **G. Michel,** "An Assessment of Risk in Thinner Markets: The Belgian Case. *Journal of Economics and Business,* Spring/Summer 1979, pp. 103–114.

b. *Degree of market isolation.* The freer the domestic market from external effects (outside the economy and caused by activities in other countries), the smaller the risk.

c. *Dividend policy.* The larger the share of dividends in total returns, the more stable the returns and the lower the risk.

d. *Obsolescence problem.* The longer certain companies are included in the calculation of a market index, the less drastic the impact on riskiness.

e. *Market inefficiency.* To the extent that foreign capital markets are inefficient,

FIGURE 17.6   Movements in exchange rates.[a]

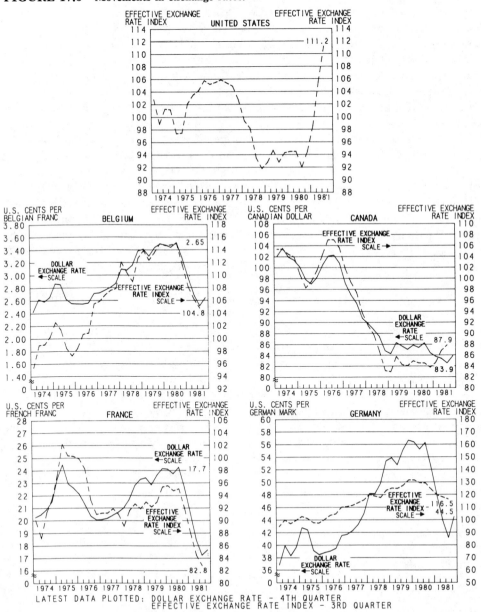

indigenous investors may be able to realize a rate of return superior to that realized by foreign investors. Indigenous investors may well be operating from a better information set.

4. *Degree of concentration in the financial markets.* The problem of limited size is aggravated by a large percentage of market capitalization consumed by a small number of firms. The extent of the concentration in various markets is shown in Table 17.3.

FIGURE 17.6 (continued)

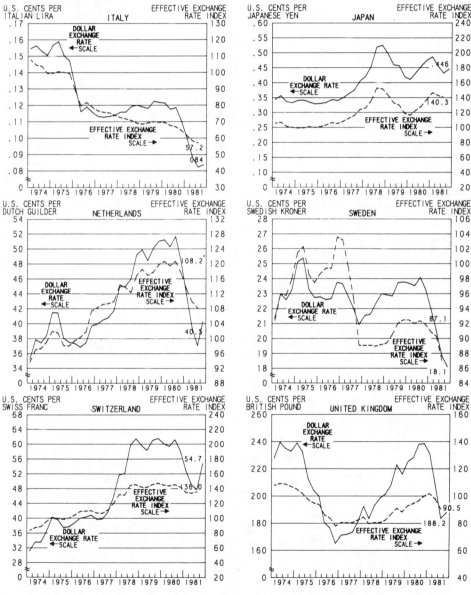

LATEST DATA PLOTTED: DOLLAR EXCHANGE RATE – 4TH QUARTER
EFFECTIVE EXCHANGE RATE INDEX – 3RD QUARTER

Source: International Economics Conditions. Federal Reserve Bank of St. Louis, Jan. 22, 1982.
[a] Latest data plotted: dollar exchange rate = 1st quarter; effective exchange rate index = 4th quarter.

TABLE 17.3
Stock Market Concentration Ratios (1972)

Exchange	Percentage of Total Equity Capitalization Accounted for by 10 Largest Stocks	Least Number of Stocks Accounting for Half Total Equity Capitalization
Amsterdam	77.4	3
Brussels	50.7	10
London	26.4	100
Milan	48.0	11
Paris	21.2	48
Germany (all exchanges)	37.8	17
Zurich	76.0	3
Japan	17.0	10
New York	23.9	60

Source: Europe and United States—D. C. Corner and Stafford, *Open End Investment Funds in the EEC and Switzerland.* Westview Press, Boulder, Colo., 1977. Japan—B. Jacquillat, "International Portfolio Investment: Opportunities and Pitfalls." Presentation to Stanford Investment Management Program, July 1975.

5. *High covariance in large markets.* A study by Hilliard points out that "the North American and European Exchanges have significant intra-continental commonalities."[9] This acts to reduce the benefits from international diversification.

6. *Taxes and restrictions on capital flows.* The taxes take the form of withholding taxes imposed by host countries on returns on securities. Some of these taxes are reduced or eliminated by treaty with the United States. For the countries most relevant to U.S. investors, the withholding taxes were as follows as of October 1980:

> Canada—15 percent to residents of the United States
> France—15 percent on dividends and 10 percent on negotiable instruments
> Germany—15 percent on dividends and no withholding tax on convertible or profit-sharing bonds
> Hong Kong—no withholding tax
> Japan—15 percent on dividends
> 10 percent on interest
> Switzerland—15 percent on dividends
> 5 percent on interest
> United Kingdom—no withholding tax

Although these taxes are deductible from U.S. tax liabilities, they have varying effects, depending on their tax bracket, on individual investors.

Some of the other obstacles to capital movements deal with restrictions placed by certain countries on types and amount of securities held and the lack of reliable and timely information.

These disadvantages do not appear to have eliminated the attractiveness of interna-

[9] **E. Jimmy Hilliard,** "The Relationship Between Equity Indices on World Exchange." *Journal of Finance,* vol. 34, no. 1 (March 1979), p. 109.

tional diversification. The risk reduction and the possible extra returns have validated the usefulness of international diversification. International securities should (and are) being held in the optimal portfolio.

We now proceed with a formal statement of the theory of international diversification.

17.4 THE THEORY OF INTERNATIONAL DIVERSIFICATION

Our discussion in this section will deal with the key issues in the area of international diversification. Our objective is to explain how the international equity markets function under differing states of the world.

Restating the capital asset pricing model developed in Chapter 6, we get:

$$E(R_i) = R_f + [E(R_M) - R_F] \frac{\sigma_{iM}}{\sigma_M^2}$$

$$E(R_i) = R_f + \frac{[E(R_M) - R_f]}{\sigma_M} \rho_{iM} \sigma_i \qquad (17.2)$$

where $E(R_i)$ = expected return on the ith security

R_f = risk-free rate

$E(R_M)$ = expected return on the market portfolio

σ_M = standard deviation of the return on the market portfolio

σ_i = standard deviation of the return on the ith security

ρ_{iM} = correlation coefficient of the rate of return of security i with the market rate of return

$\rho_{iM} \sigma_i$ = systematic or nondiversifiable risk

$[E(R_M) - R_f]/\sigma_M$ = price per unit of risk = slope of the capital market line = marginal rate of substitution of risk for return

In a portfolio context, therefore, the concern of the investor with the characteristics of individual securities is justified in terms of the effect that each security has on the distribution of the rate of return of a portfolio. The relevant risk of a single security is the nondiversifiable risk $\beta = \sigma_{iM}/\sigma_M^2$.

The interesting question in an international context, therefore, is what does international diversification do to the riskiness of the portfolio and to its rate of return?

Since the correlation coefficients between stock market indexes have been shown to be less than perfect, risk is bound to fall through international diversification. The low positive correlation among national markets presented earlier indicates that "only a fraction of national systematic risk elements is systematic in a world context"[10]—that is, that international diversification lowers systematic risk and hence the total risk of the portfolio, thus reducing $\rho_{iM} \sigma_i$ as the purely domestic market portfolio is broadened to include more low-correlation securities. In effect, international diversification, as Cohn

---

[10] **Donald R. Lessard,** "World, Country, and Industrial Relationships in Equity Returns: Implications for Risk Reduction Through International Diversification." *Financial Analyst's Journal,* January–February 1976, p. 2.

and Pringle[11] argue, changes the slope of the capital market line and lowers the value of the marginal rate of substitution between risk and return. The two effects will be reflected in a lower $E(R_i)$, as in Equation 17.2, and consequently in a higher market price of individual securities (assuming no barriers to international financial capital movements).

The essential question remains, however: does international diversification increase the welfare of the investor? The answer depends on whether the national securities markets are segmented; that is, security prices in each national market are not related to those in other countries, or are integrated; that is, security prices are not determined in a strictly national context. Also, the answer depends on the investment philosophy of the investor. We assume that his or her philosophy (strategy) is consistent with the mean-variance efficient portfolio hypothesis. Before discussing these two concepts, we examine the options open to the investor:

Markets	Options
1. Segmented	a. Invest strictly domestically—diversify intranationally b. Diversify internationally
2. Integrated	a. Invest strictly domestically—diversify intranationally b. Diversify internationally

Segmented Markets

The segmented markets theory argues that capital assets are priced in terms of their "domestic systematic risk."[12] The capital asset pricing model (CAPM) presented in Chapter 6 captures the pricing mechanism for a capital asset traded in a market isolated from the rest of the world, that is, the pricing mechanism in a strictly national context.

$$E(R_i) = R_F + [E(R_M) - R_F]\beta_i \tag{17.3}$$

where $E(R_M)$ represents the expected rate of return on a U.S. (national) market index, typically the S&P 500, which is made up of strictly domestic securities.

This model can be extended to account for the correlation between national securities markets in the determination of securities prices in a given national market.

$$E(R_i) = R_F + \beta'[E(R_M) - R_F] \tag{17.4}$$

where $\beta' =$ beta of the foreign market f in relation to the domestic market d
$$= (\rho_{f,d}\sigma_d\sigma_f)/\sigma_d^2 = (\rho_{f,d}\sigma_f)/\sigma_d$$

[11] **Richard A. Cohn** and **John J. Pringle**, "Imperfections in International Financial Markets: Implications for Risk Premia and the Cost of Capital to Firms." *Journal of Finance,* March 1973, pp. 59–66.

[12] **Donald Lessard**, "International Diversification." in Sumner and Levine, eds., *The Investment Manager Handbook.* Dow Jones-Irwin, Homewood, Ill., 1980, p. 368.

$E(R_M) =$ expected rate of return on the domestic market portfolio

$R_f =$ risk-free rate in the domestic market

The reader can see from Equation 17.4 that the lower the correlation between the two markets is and/or the lower σ_f is in relation to σ_d, the higher the payoffs from international diversification.

A fully segmented market in which securities are priced in terms of their national systematic risk should permit significant risk reduction through international diversification, for it "would turn previously undiversifiable risk into diversifiable risk in the context of world portfolio."[13] International diversification in this case is superior to intranational diversification.

We can conclude, therefore, that under the segmented market theory, an investor choosing option "a" would be assuming additional risk but would also be compensated for it, since securities are priced in terms of their domestic systematic risk.

However, that same investor could have been better off had he adopted a geocentric approach to investment. It is quite likely that in considering investments in other countries, the investor could have found an investment that would have produced a higher rate of return (than that available in the domestic market) for a given level of risk β or a lower risk (β) for a given level of return. Option "b" should be the preferred alternative, however, for the investor reduces the systematic risk of his portfolio through international diversification. A net welfare gain would accrue to the investor under this strategy if the rate of return on the international portfolio did not fall proportionately to the reduction in risk.

Integrated Markets

The integrated markets theory states that securities are priced in terms of their global systematic risk; that is,

$$E(R_i^J) = r + [E(R_w) - r]\beta_w^J \qquad (17.5)$$

where $E(R_i^J) =$ expected rate of return on security (portfolio) i in country J

$r =$ real rate of interest

$E(R_w) =$ expected rate of return on the world market portfolio

$\beta_w^J = (\rho_{i,w}^J \sigma_i \sigma_w)/\sigma_w^2$

$\rho_{i,w}^J =$ correlation coefficient between the rate of return on security (portfolio) i in country J and the world market portfolio

The riskiness of a security resulting from the covariance of its rate of return with that of a national stock market index is no longer the sole determinant of its price. The influence of the national market depends on its role in the world portfolio, which is not observable but is constructible. The method used by D. Lessard constructs the world portfolio as a weighted portfolio of the leading financial market indexes in the

---

[13] **Donald Lessard,** "The Structure of Returns and Gains from International Diversification: A Multivariate Approach," in **Edwin J. Elton** and **Martin J. Gruber,** eds., *International Capital Markets.* North-Holland Publishing Company, Amsterdam, 1975, p. 207.

world or of all financial market indexes in the world. The weights used must equal
the market value of all securities in a national index relative to the market value of
all securities in every national index included in the calculations. The weight of the
U.S. stock index relative to a world index is approximately 50 percent.

While this method is the best available, there remains considerable controversy over
which market index to use—whether stock markets in the world with varying levels
of efficiency can indeed be combined (treated as a homogeneous group) and what effects,
if any, the currency in which the national portfolio is denominated has on the results.
The latter issue will be addressed in the next section.

The implications of the integrated markets hypothesis depend, once again, on the
investment strategy. Option "a" would produce clearly inferior results. The investor
would bear unnecessary risk and would not receive compensation for it because the
market is pricing securities in terms of their global systematic risk and not with respect
to their higher domestic risk. Option "b" (international diversification) is clearly superior.
The effect of international diversification here would be a "pure diversification effect,"
that is, "a reduction in the contribution of the non-systematic risk of individual securities
to the total risk of the portfolio."[14]

The overall implication of the above for investment strategy is that investors must
behave as if national financial markets were integrated, that is, diversified internationally.
The net welfare gains from such a strategy can only be positive.[15]

Empirical Evidence

The empirical evidence on international diversification is steadily accumulating, with
much refinement remaining to be realized.

The early evidence dealt with the segmented market approach. The earliest work
was done by Grubel,[16] who found that international diversification did pay off if portfolios
were diversified across the 11 industrialized countries studied. The period covered by
the study extended from 1959 to 1966.

H. Grubel was later to collaborate with K. Fadner to further test the segmented
markets hypothesis. Grubel and Fadner[17] were able to demonstrate, once again, that
international diversification does pay off, but that the benefits from international diversification declined with longer holding periods.

Levy and Sarnat,[18] using a larger sample of countries (28), were also able to show
that internationally diversified portfolios were superior to domestic portfolios, although
markets are assumed to be segmented.

The testing of the integrated market hypothesis has received considerable attention

[14] **Lessard,** 1980.

[15] I owe this point to my colleague Professor Lee Tavis.

[16] **Herbert G. Grubel,** "Internationally Diversified Portfolios; Welfare Gains and Capital Flows."
American Economic Review, December 1968, pp. 1299–1314.

[17] **Herbert G. Grubel** and **Kenneth Fadner,** "The Interdependence of International Equity Markets." *Journal of Finance,* vol. 26, no. 1, March 1971, pp. 89–94.

[18] **Levy and Sarnat,** 1970.

[19] **Tamir Agmon,** "The Relations Among Equity Markets: A Study of Share Price Co-Movement
in the United States, United Kingdom, Germany, and Japan." *Journal of Finance,* September
1972, pp. 839–855.

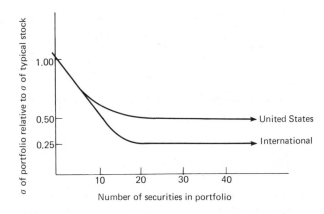

FIGURE 17.7 Impact of international diversification on portfolio risk.

from several scholars. Agmon,[19] using 145 stocks from four countries—the United States, United Kingdom, Japan, and Germany—tested whether stocks were priced as if the four countries made up a single multinational market. The results showed that country factors were *more* important than world factors, although the possibility of one multinational market could not be ruled out.

B. Solnik[20] provided, in addition to the evidence cited earlier, confirmation of portfolio risk reduction through diversification by country, by industry, or by both, as is shown in Figure 17.7. Internationally diversified portfolios containing more than thirty stocks had half the risk (measured in portfolios' standard deviation) of a well-diversified portfolio made up of strictly U.S. securities.

The empirical tests that address the two states of the world we have just discussed— one in which no barriers to capital flows exist and another in which capital markets are segmented—are neither numerous nor conclusive.

Using monthly security data and stock price indexes for Belgium, Canada, France, Germany, Italy, Japan, the Netherlands, Switzerland, the United Kingdom, and the United States for the period beginning with January 1956 and ending with December 1975, R. Stehle tested "whether the stocks traded on the New York Stock Exchange were priced nationally or internationally."[21]

The equation tested by Stehle was:

$$\tilde{r}_i = \alpha + b_i\,\tilde{\beta}_{iD} + b_2\,\tilde{\gamma}_i + \epsilon_i \tag{17.6}$$

where $\tilde{r}_{it}(\bar{r}) = (R_{it} - R_{ft})/R_{ft}$ = the realized (mean) deflated excess rate of return on the ith portfolio for month t

R_{ft} = risk-free rate

$\tilde{\beta}_{iD}$ = systematic risk when markets are segmented or when the rates of return on the domestic market portfolio are positively correlated with those on the international market portfolio

---

[20] **B. Solnik**, "Why Not Diversify Internationally Rather than Domestically." *Financial Analyst's Journal,* July–August 1974, pp. 48–54.

[21] **Richard Stehle**, "An Empirical Test of the Alternative Hypothesis of National and International Pricing of Risky Assets." *Journal of Finance,* May 1977, pp. 493–502.

$\tilde{\gamma}_i$ = systematic risk resulting from the correlation between the portfolio's rates of return and that segment of the international market portfolio which is not correlated with the domestic market portfolio

ϵ_i = error term

Using generalized least squares (ϵ_i's are heteroscedastic), Stehle obtained the following results:

$$\bar{r}_i = 0.00422 + 0.00117\,\beta_{iD} + 0.00280\,\gamma_i$$
$$\quad\;\;(1.73)\qquad\;\;(0.27)\qquad\quad(0.92)$$

The values in parentheses are t statistics. $\beta_{i,D}$ and γ_i measure rate-of-return variations that are nondiversifiable in an international capital market. The results for the purely domestic model are

$$\bar{r}_i = 0.00446 + 0.00089\,\beta_{i,D}$$
$$\quad\;\;(2.28)\qquad\;\;(0.22)$$

and the results for a reformulated international model are

$$\bar{r}_i = \alpha_i + b_1\beta_{i,D} + b_2\delta_i + w_i$$

where δ_i = risk that is diversifiable internationally but not domestically

$$\text{and } \bar{r}_i = \frac{0.00437 + 0.00096\,\beta_{iw} - 0.00017\delta_i}{(1.97)\qquad\;\;(0.23)\qquad\;\;(-0.05)}$$

The segmented markets theory, based on the regression results, cannot be rejected in favor of the international capital markets theory, and vice versa. The data support neither the segmented, nor the integrated model.

James H. Scott of Columbia University, in his discussion of Stehle's article, attributed the results to "too strong an assumption about beta."[22] The nonstationarity of beta may account for Stehle's conclusions.

D. Lessard[23] also studied the relative importance of world factors in the determination of equity returns. Again, national (country-specific) factors had significant impact on stock prices. Both national and international factors influenced securities prices, however, and the international effects manifested themselves through the national indexes.

More evidence on international diversification—which deals with whether or not the purchase of a stock in a multinational corporation is equivalent to international portfolio diversification—was presented by B. Jacquillat and B. Solnik.[24] Using data from April 1966 to June 1974 on 300 European and 100 American firms, Jacquillat and Solnik

[22] **James H. Scott,** discussion. *Journal of Finance,* May 1977, p. 516.

[23] **Donald P. Lessard,** "International Diversification," in Sumner and Levine, eds., *The Investment Manager Handbook.* Dow Jones-Irwin, Homewood, Ill., 1980.

[24] **Bertrand Jacquillat** and **Bruno H. Solnik,** "Multinationals are Poor Tools for Diversification." *Journal of Portfolio Management,* Winter 1978, pp. 8–12.

found that multinational firms are "poor substitutes for international portfolio diversification."[25]

The conclusions of Jacquillat and Solnik were strongly disputed by V. Errunza and L. Senbet (E&S).[26] The authors (E&S) argue that multinational firms, in the presence of market imperfections in the product and factor markets, possess a unique advantage over uninational firms because of their ability to capitalize on these imperfections and provide in the process an effective mode for indirect portfolio diversification. Using a valuation model of the Miller and Modigliani (M&M) type, E&S argued that:

> *If the U.S. market is well functioning, investors must accept a smaller equilibrium expected return on multinational stocks than on otherwise equivalent but purely domestic stocks. In other words, they pay a price premium. . . . An international firm is not a costless financial intermediary. Moreover, since the diversification services provided by multinationals are already "priced out," attempts to verify these services through traditional performance evaluation techniques as well as through risk-return generating processes are unwarranted.* [27]

Using data covering January 1959–December 1977 (a period made up of subperiods with varying degrees of market imperfection) E&S were able to show that international involvement was positively related to excess value (excess over the value of a purely uninational firm).

Effects of Exchange Rates

H. Grubel[28] and H. Levy and M. Sarnat,[29] argued that the introduction of exchange risk results in different optimum market portfolios for different countries (different currencies) once foreign exchange risk is incorporated. H. Grubel and K. Fadner[30] found, however, using weekly data for the period Jan. 1, 1965 to June 30, 1967, that accounting for foreign exchange risk did not have a significant impact on the variance of returns.

One of the latest studies using the mean-variance approach was undertaken by Nahum Biger.[31] Using returns on efficient portfolios from 13 industrialized countries from 1966 to 1976, Biger was able to show that risky assets were priced similarly across 6 selected nations, which implied that international capital markets are efficient. Each country's efficient portfolio was shown to contain both Japanese and Austrian stocks. The composition of efficient international portfolios from the perspective of French, West German, Danish, Canadian, British, and Japanese investors was shown to be superior (lower

[25] Ibid., p. 9.

[26] **Vihang R. Errunza** and **Lemma W. Senbet,** "The Effects of International Operations on the Market Value of the Firm: Theory and Evidence." *The Journal of Finance,* vol. 36, no. 2 (May 1981), pp. 401–417.

[27] Ibid., p. 408.

[28] **Grubel,** December 1968.

[29] **H. Levy** and **M. Sarnat,** "International Diversification of Investment Portfolios." *American Economic Review,* September 1970, pp. 668–675.

[30] **Herbert G. Grubel** and **Kenneth Fadner,** 1971.

[31] **Nahum Biger,** "Exchange Risk Implications of International Portfolio Diversification." *Journal of International Business Studies,* Fall 1979, pp. 64–74.

risk for a given return) than that of strictly national portfolios, and the fluctuations of foreign exchange rates did not seem "to matter excessively."

Biger's results contradict those of Grubel and of Levy and Sarnat (1970, 1975).[32] Levy and Sarnat showed that in a world of American and Israeli securities, the latter would not be part of the efficient set for U.S. investors. Both of the studies, however, confine their analysis to the Markowitz model, thus ignoring the issues dealing with the presence and the nature of a risk-free asset. In so doing, both studies fail to test the validity of the international CAPM.

Several recent studies have attempted to deal with exchange risk in a capital asset pricing context. Before discussing the major ones, we refer the reader to Equation 17.3. The model represented in this equation is a capital market equilibrium model where only one good, financial assets, is consumed. The model is based on rather stringent assumptions: homogeneous expectations of investors, commodity price stability, and a utility function completely defined by its first two moments. This model is applicable to an international setting where only one currency exists; it applies to a multicurrency world, as F. Grauer, R. Litzenberger, and R. Stehle (GLS) argue,[33] if the single good is freely traded and if a riskless asset (in real terms) exists. GLS argue that if investors' behavior is correctly perceived, the conclusions of Grubel and of Levy and Sarnat would not be accurate. Investors, GLS argue, evaluate investment opportunities in real terms (see Chap. 16) and are therefore uninfluenced in their consumption and asset choices by changes in nominal rates of return because such changes reflect changes in inflationary expectations (exchange risk) if markets are efficient (perfect purchasing power parity holds). GLS base their argument on the assumptions that economic agents have homogeneous tastes and expectations (a necessary assumption if expost data are used to test the international CAPM), that investors have a power utility function dependent on the consumption of many goods, and that international trade is free of barriers. The price of real goods and services is, therefore, equal throughout the world and any changes in price levels are caused purely by changes in monetary policy. In this environment, foreign exchange risk has no unique effect on value and an optimal world market portfolio would exist, confirming the validity of the Sharpe-Lintner model in an international context; that is, the separation theorem (see Chap. 6) holds internationally. To arrive at their conclusion, GLS assumed away international market segmentation and assumed the existence of a real risk-free asset.

B. Solnik[34] noted the assumptions made by GLS and the fact that they render the residence of the investor and the difference in currencies irrelevant in the derivation of an optimal international investment strategy. This is so because investors in a GLS world have identical tastes (they consume the same basket of goods) and differ only "in their propensity to lend or borrow."

Solnik allowed for significant heterogeneity in consumer taste across nations and

---

[32] **H. Levy** and **M. Sarnat,** "Devaluation, Risk and the Portfolio Analysis of International Investments," in Elton and Gruber, eds., *International Capital Markets.* North-Holland Publishing Company, Amsterdam, 1975.

[33] **F. L. A. Grauer, R. H. Litzenberger,** and **R. E. Stehle,** "Sharing Rules and Equilibrium in an International Capital Market Under Uncertainty." *Journal of Financial Economics,* June 1976, pp. 233–256.

[34] **Bruno H. Solnik,** "Testing International Asset Pricing: Some Pessimistic Views." *Journal of Finance,* vol. 32, no. 2 (May 1977), pp. 503–512.

consequently for the division of foreign exchange risk into two components: monetary and real. The real exchange risk is that risk stemming from the differential in taste patterns. Solnik further assumed that exchange risk and stock market risk are independent and that the international capital markets are free and perfect (the latter assumption is also made by GLS).

Solnik's world complicates considerably the mean–variance portfolio analysis. In the presence of a real risk-free asset, the market portfolio no longer consists of stocks only but of stocks and nominal risk-free T-bills.

Therefore, the models for testing the international CAPM in a world of uncertainty caused by exchange-rate changes should, according to Solnik, be as follows:

1. The GLS model, where exchange risk is nominal (purely monetary) and a riskless asset in real terms exists. The separation theorem in this world holds, and the optimum portfolio would consist of stocks only.

2. Solnik's model, where differences in consumption patterns exist, with the optimal risky portfolios consisting of stocks and nominal bills.

3. An ex post construct of a market portfolio made up of stocks only and a comparison of these stocks with those making up the portfolio in item 2, above.

While these hypotheses are interesting theoretically, Solnik himself is very skeptical of their testability. Solnik writes that "A test to discriminate between these three alternatives will not be easy to construct."[35]

Bernard Dumas,[36] in his comments on Solnik's study, argues that the empirical difficulties were caused by Solnik's effort to construct a world that is not. Specifically, the evidence suggests that consumer tastes are rather homogeneous[37] and that in the long run the purchasing power parity hypothesis (PPP) holds.[38] Short-run deviations from the PPP should be ignored when a theory of asset pricing is being constructed and tested.

For the above and other reasons, international asset pricing theories remain incomplete. Much additional research is needed. It can be said, however, that the reservations about an international CAPM are essentially similar to those of a purely domestic CAPM as expressed by R. Roll (see Chap. 6).

We now discuss investing in some foreign countries.

17.5 INVESTING IN THE LEADING COUNTRIES OF THE WORLD

The discussion here deals with countries on which American investors have traditionally focused: Canada, West Germany, Japan, and the United Kingdom. We develop a brief economic profile for each of these countries (retrospective and prospective) and outline the special characteristics of its capital markets. Sociopolitical issues are important but are not within the scope of this book.

---

[35] Ibid., p. 511.

[36] **Bernard Dumas,** Comments. *Journal of Finance,* May 1977, pp. 512–515.

[37] **I. B. Kravis** and others, *A System of International Comparisons of Gross Product and Purchasing Power.* Johns Hopkins University Press, Baltimore, 1975.

[38] **J. S. Hodgson** and **P. Phelps,** "The Distributed Impact of Price-Level Variation on Floating Exchange Rates." *Review of Economics and Statistics,* vol. J7 (February 1975), pp. 58–64.

We first present some comparative economic and market data to provide perspective on the relative position of the countries under examination. Figure 17.8 offers an index of the country's relative competitive position in terms of unit labor costs in manufacturing, average value of manufactured exports, and consumer prices. The trade position of the United States relative to the rest of the member countries of the Organization for Economic Cooperation and Development (OECD) has weakened steadily. This is reflected in the steady deficits in the U.S. balance-of-trade statistics. The most dramatic rise in the relative competitive position was registered by Japan, for which the trend is still upward.

On the inflation front, the U.S. economy experienced high levels of inflation, but only Japan and West Germany have been able to control prices to a greater degree than the United States (Fig. 17.9).

In terms of total economic performance, the U.S. economy underperformed those of Germany and Japan. Economic activity measured by the GNP and price stability measured by consumer prices were superior for Germany and Japan when compared with the United States.[39]

The relative performance of stock markets during the period Dec. 5, 1979, and Dec. 5, 1980, is shown in Table 17.4. The U.S. investor would have realized the highest rate of return had he invested in Hong Kong, followed by South Africa, Australia, Switzerland, and Canada, in that order.

The correlation between economic performance and stock market performance is illustrated in Figure 17.10. We shall, therefore, concentrate on the key economic variables in our analysis of the key foreign countries.

Canada

The Canadian economy is a mixed capitalistic economy the major part of which is privately controlled. Certain industries whose output is considered vital or which are characterized by little competition are either government-owned or are subject to substantial government regulation.

Canada imposes withholding taxes on returns realized by U.S. investors in Canada. The taxes are 15 percent on dividends, 15 percent on interest income, and 15 percent on royalties payments (associated with direct investment).

The vital statistics on the Canadian economy are provided in Figure 17.11. The real growth in GNP has been negative during the second and third quarters of 1980, reflecting perhaps the slowdown in the U.S. economy, on which Canada is very dependent. The lagging economic activity is reflected in low share prices (Fig. 17.11). Inflation in Canada—measured either by the GNP implicit price level, the producer price index, or the consumer price index—has been in the 10–15 percent range for 1979 and 1980 (10.7 percent in 1980).

The future of the Canadian economy, a major factor in the decision-making process for an investment in Canada, appears to be quite promising. The leading economic indicators began rising toward the middle of 1980, auguring a more optimistic level of economic activity. The strong drive toward nationalization and the preferential treatment of Canadian firms could prove harmful, however.

Canada has three major stock exchanges: the Toronto Stock Exchange, the Montreal

---

[39] See *Business Conditions Digest,* U.S. Department of Commerce, March 1981.

FIGURE 17.8 Measures of relative competitive position (indexes in common currency 1975 = 100).

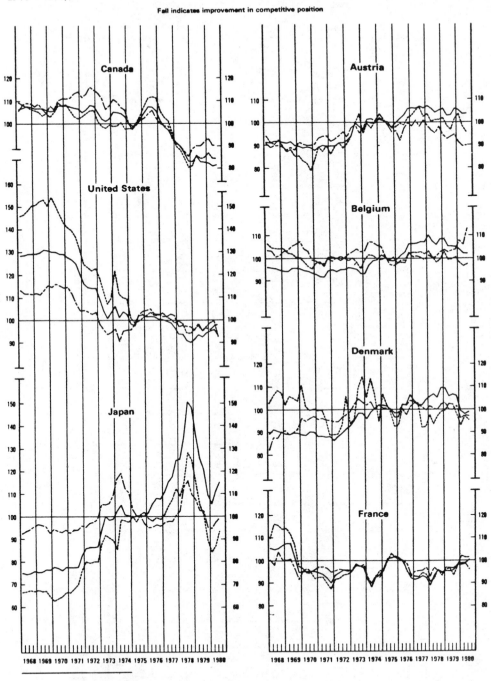

Fall indicates improvement in competitive position

Canada

United States

Japan

Austria

Belgium

Denmark

France

1968 1969 1970 1971 1972 1973 1974 1975 1976 1977 1978 1979 1980

1968 1969 1970 1971 1972 1973 1974 1975 1976 1977 1978 1979 1980

Relative indicators:
Unit labor costs in manufacturing ――――
Average value of manufactured exports ――-――
Consumer prices ―――――

Source: Main Economic Indicators, OECD, February 1981, p. 12.

FIGURE 17.9 International comparisons of consumer prices.

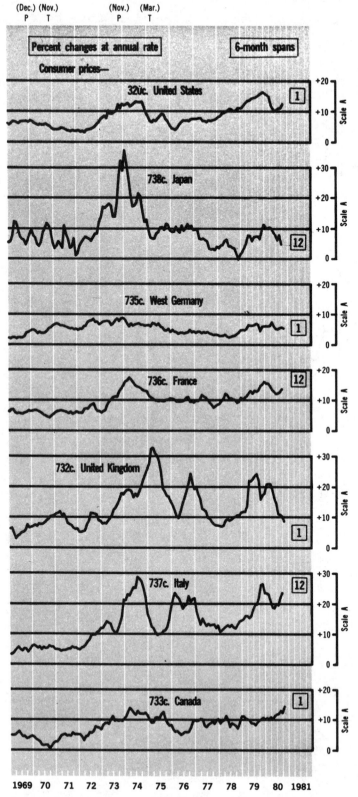

Current data for these series are shown on pages 95 and 96.

Source: Business Conditions Digest, U.S. Department of Commerce, February 1981, p. 59.

TABLE 17.4
International Comparison of Stock Market Performance Over the Past 12 Months Adjusted for Exchange Rate Fluctuations

Indices

DATE	Sydney All Ord.	Toronto Industrial	Paris Bourse	Commerzbank	Amsterdam Industrial	Hang Seng Bank	Tokyo New S.E.	R.D.M. Industrial	Swiss Bank Corp.	F.T.A. All Share	S. & P. Composite
5th December 1979	691.38	1728.70	96.50	728.00	67.10	772.12	451.83	432.10	307.60	230.39	107.25
5th December 1980	1000.95	2325.80	105.70	721.10	61.10	1382.51	492.25	613.30	298.10	295.44	134.03

Area of Investment

Country of Investor	Australia	Canada	France	West Germany	Holland	Hong Kong	Japan	South Africa†	Switzerland	U.K.	U.S.A.
Australia	+45	+23	− 7	−17	−22	+63	+19	+57	−18	+29	+17
Canada	+58	+35	+ 2	−10	−15	+78	+30	+72	−10	+41	+28
France	+71	+45	+10	− 3	− 8	+92	+40	+86	− 3	+52	+38
West Germany	+74	+48	+11	− 1	− 7	+95	+42	+89	− 1	+55	+41
Holland	+70	+44	+ 9	− 3	− 9	+91	+39	+85	− 3	+51	+37
Hong Kong	+59	+36	+ 2	− 9	−15	+79	+31	+73	− 9	+42	+29
Japan	+33	+13	−15	−24	−29	+50	+ 9	+45	−24	+19	+ 8
South Africa*	−	−	−	−	−	−	−	+42	−	−	−
Switzerland	+70	+45	+ 9	− 3	− 9	+91	+40	+85	− 3	+52	+38
United Kingdom	+44	+22	− 8	−18	−23	+62	+18	+56	−18	+28	+16
U.S.A.	+55	+31	− 1	−12	−17	+74	+27	+68	−12	+38	+25

Source: Cazenove, Inc., N.Y., Jan. 1981.

□ Perfromance of investment in investor's own market.

* South African residents are not permitted to invest overseas.

† Adjustment for performance based on the Financial Rand Exchange Rate.

Bold type indicates markets where performance has been better than investor's home market.

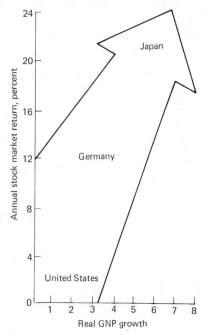

Annual stock market return, percent

Japan

Germany

United States

Real GNP growth

FIGURE 17.10 Relationship between stock prices and real economic growth (1966–1977 U.S. dollars).

Source: First National Bank of Chicago.

Stock Exchange, and the Vancouver Stock Exchange. In terms of number of shares listed and the value of these shares, the Toronto Stock Exchange is most important, followed by Montreal's and Vancouver's. About 1,280 shares are listed on the Toronto Stock Exchange. Some of the more prominent Canadian stocks with substantial participation by American investors are listed in Table 17.5. The attraction of Canadian securities to U.S. investors is concentrated in resource related enterprises, particularly energy. Canada is blessed by vast, mostly unexplored natural resources, for which worldwide demand is increasing.

On the debt securities side, Canada offers four types of instruments: federal government bonds, provincial government and agency bonds, municipal bonds, and corporate bonds. Canadian government entities do not issue tax-exempt securities.

West Germany

The boom, combined with the relatively stable prices that have characterized the economy of West Germany, seems to be coming to an end in the early 1980s. The official government forecast calls for slow growth in gross domestic product for 1982 and low inflation. Monetary policy has been tight in order to keep interest rates high and to reduce inflationary pressures, with the hope of shoring up the declining value of the DM in the foreign exchange markets.

The performance of the German economy over the last ten years is summarized in Figure 17.12. The real growth rate in GNP has been vigorous since 1976. It slowed down considerably in 1980 and continues at a low level. Leading economic indicators do not indicate a recovery in the immediate future. Prices since 1975, however measured, showed a remarkable stability for a country that imports most of its oil. The inflation rate for 1980, measured by consumer prices, was 5.2 percent. The economic weakness is reflected in share prices (Fig. 17.12). Returns on equity investment in Germany have been negative since the second quarter of 1979. Of particular concern to German policy-makers is the slowdown in the export sector, on which much of German prosperity

FIGURE 17.11   **Vital statistics on Canada's economy.**

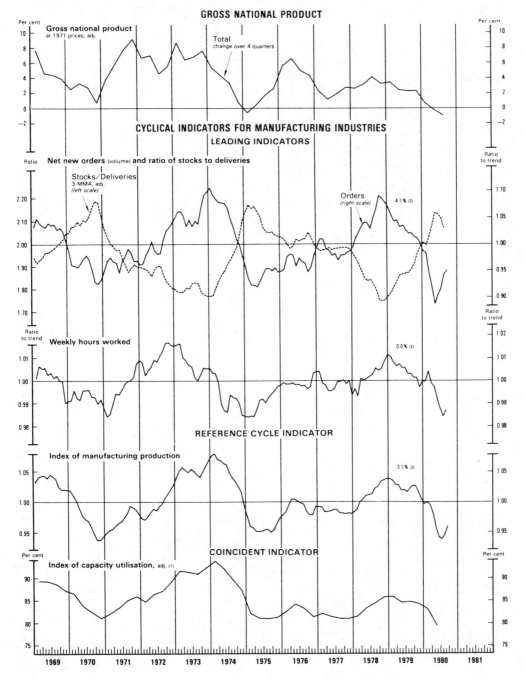

FIGURE 17.11 (continued)

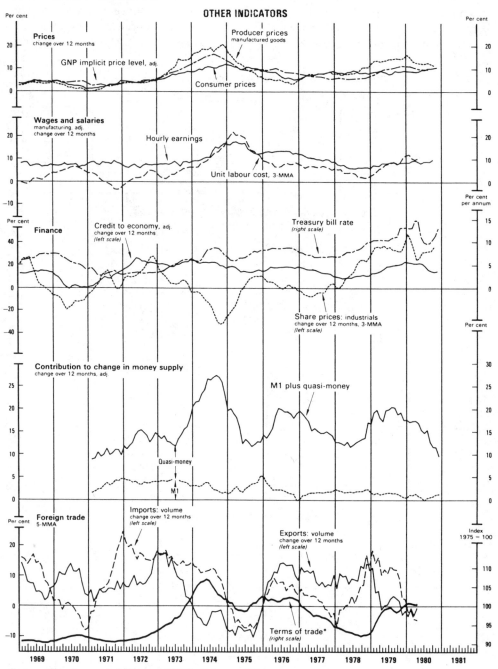

Source: Main Economic Indicators. OECD, February 1981.
(1) Ratio of export prices to import prices.
(2) Annual trend growth rate over last five years.

TABLE 17.5
Canadian Securities of Greatest Interest to U.S. Investors

Can. Dollars	Feb 18	Feb 11	Yr ago
Albitibi	26.63	24.88	23.88
Alcan	38.63	39.13	68.50
Bk Montreal	31.25	32.13	25.50
Bnk Nova Scotia	32.25	33.25	26.25
Bow Valley	18.50	19.63	18.67
BP Canada	42.75	44.50	46.75
Brascan	32.25	34.25	27.13
Camflo	35.88	37.13	20.38
Can NW Land	34.25	37.50	21.50
Can Pacific	42.38	44.38	47.25
Can Pac Ent	23.50	23.88	23.38
Cnd Tire	33.00	32.50	27.50
Chieftain	22.00	22.38	26.83
CIBC	30.13	29.50	25.00
Cominco	68.50	69.00	72.00
Cons Bath	23.75	24.75	18.38
Denison	51.88	52.75	47.38
Dome Mines	94.00	98.00	80.00
Dome Pet	79.00	80.00	81.25
Dom Bridge	21.00	20.25	8.07
Dom Stores	22.75	21.50	20.00
Domtar	28.50	28.75	28.13
Falcon Nickel	90.00	95.00	131.00
Genstar	36.25	36.75	31.13
Gulf Can	25.63	25.88	32.90
Hollinger	48.50	48.00	45.50
Hudson Bay Mining	30.13	31.00	34.38
Hud Oil & Gas	24.75	25.75	34.38
Imperial Oil	33.13	33.50	50.50
Inco	23.13	23.50	34.63
Indal	15.00	14.75	13.25
Kaiser Res	59.00	59.63	37.63
Macmil Bloedel	37.38	37.50	30.88
Massey-Ferg	5.00	5.12	11.75
McIntyre Mines	60.00	60.75	90.50
Moore	40.25	40.25	36.25
Noranda	27.25	29.00	27.88
N Telecom	33.50	33.50	45.25
Pancan Pet	88.50	88.13	78.00
Placer Dev	22.88	24.00	22.50
Power Corp	21.63	21.75	17.75
Ranger Oil	18.00	17.88	15.75
Reed Stenhs	11.75	12.00	8.75
Rio Algom	32.50	32.25	37.00
Royal Bank	59.50	60.00	44.75
Seagram	65.25	65.25	55.00
Shell Can	25.50	25.00	36.25
Stelco	34.13	35.00	30.63

TABLE 17.5
Canadian Securities of Greatest Interest to U.S. Investors
(*Continued*)

Can. Dollars	Feb 18	Feb 11	Yr ago
Thomson News A	20.88	20.75	15.13
Toronto Dom Bk	33.25	34.50	26.75
Trans Can Pipe	24.25	25.13	26.88
Walker Hiram	28.00	28.13	39.38
Westcst Trans	15.25	15.13	15.25
Weston Geo	33.25	33.25	27.75

Source: World Business Weekly, March 2, 1981.

depends. Germany is the third largest industrial nation in the Western world but is second only to the United States in exports. The federal government is pursuing a policy of technological intensification to expand export markets.

Germany has eight stock exchanges: Frankfurt, Dusseldorf, Hamburg, Munich, Berlin, Hanover, Bremen, and Stuttgart. The Frankfurt and the Dusseldorf exchanges are the largest. About 500 shares are listed on the exchanges. The stock markets are thin. A sample of German shares of greatest interest to the U.S. investors is shown in Table 17.6.

The debt market in Germany has been of great interest to American investors because of the strength of the German mark. Debt instruments with maturities exceeding four years are accessible, without restriction, to any foreign investor. Those with maturities below four years require a special permit. Germany imposes a 15 percent withholding tax on dividends but none on interest payments.

The bulk of financial activities in Germany is conducted by banks, who represent the dominant source of funds for firms.

Japan

The Japanese "economic miracle" has not ceased to fascinate American investors. The evidence presented in Figure 17.13 attests to the progress Japan has been able to realize. Real gross national product increased at a remarkable rate in the early 1970s and resumed a healthy growth pattern after the 1974–1975 recession, once the Japanese economy adjusted to the international oil crisis. The 1980 rate of inflation measured by consumer prices was 8.9 percent.

Share prices reflect to some degree the growth patterns in the Japanese economy. The leading indicators, however, point downward, signaling a weakening economy. The Economic Planning Agency of Japan is forecasting a real growth of 4.8 percent for the 1981 fiscal year, however. Worried about the increasing foreign interest in Japanese firms, the Japanese government has set limits on the level of foreign shareholdings, as specified in Table 17.7.

Most of the foreign interest in Japanese firms centers around technology, electronics, precision-optical companies, and energy-related issues. Of increasing interest to foreign investors are the small-technology-related issues in Japan, such as Canon, Olympus, and Minolta.

The Japanese government imposes a 10 percent withholding tax on dividend income earned by foreign investors and 10 percent on interest income.

The most important stock exchange in Japan is the Tokyo Stock Exchange (there are seven others), with approximately 1,500 listed securities. Individual investors account for 75 percent of the activity on the exchange. A sample of Japanese securities of interest to U.S. investors appears in Table 17.8.

FIGURE 17.12 **Vital statistics on Germany's economy.**

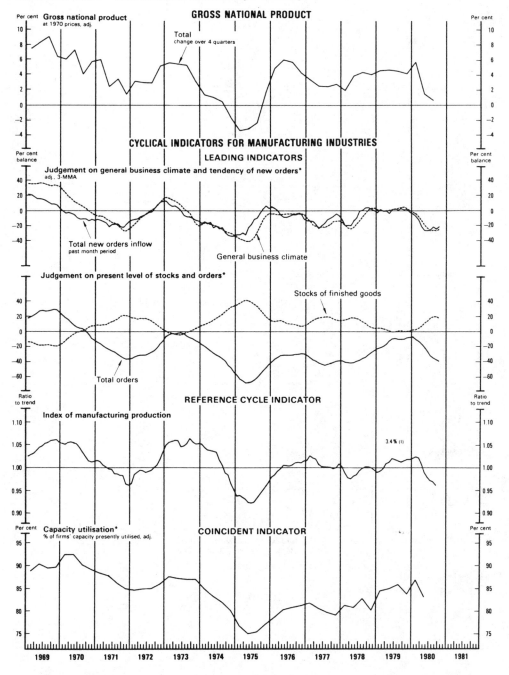

FIGURE 17.12 (continued)

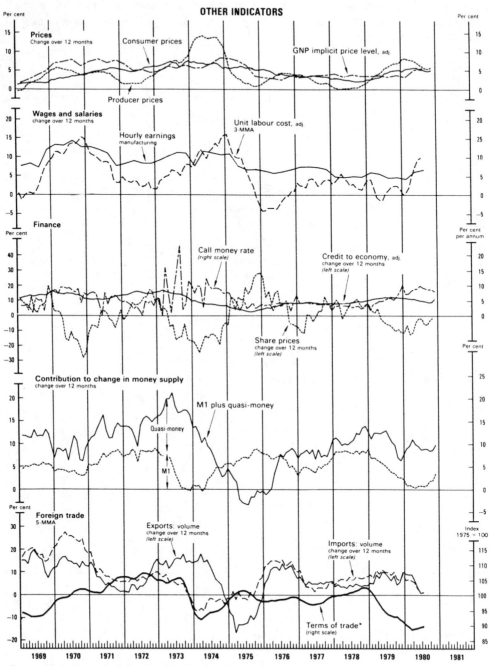

OTHER INDICATORS

Source: Main Economic Indicators. OECD, February 1981.
(1) Ratio of export prices to import prices.
(2) Annual trend growth rate over last five years.

TABLE 17.6
German Securities of Greatest Interest to U.S. Investors

German Marks	West Germany Feb 18	West Germany Feb 11	1980 Yr ago
AEG	59.0	64.0	38.9
Allianz Vers	454.0	456.0	383.0
BASF	120.3	119.5	147.2
Bayer	113.0	110.5	126.5
Bayer Hypo Bk	190.0	193.0	246.0
Bayer Ver Bk	284.0	286.0	275.5
BHF	186.0	187.0	194.0
BMW	153.5	147.0	169.0
Brown Boveri	245.0	252.0	304.0
Commerzbank	132.3	134.0	178.5
Conti Gummi	56.0	54.3	52.9
Daimler-Benz	267.2	267.5	266.6
Degussa	237.0	235.0	243.0
Demag	131.0	130.5	135.0
D'sche Babcock	173.0	178.2	274.9
Deutsche Bk	280.0	279.0	262.5
Dresdner Bk	156.0	158.0	189.6
Dyckerhoff	120.0	123.5	139.5
GHH	181.0	188.0	216.5
Hapag-Lloyd	60.5	63.0	72.0
Hoechst	116.4	114.7	123.3
Hoesch	24.0	23.6	36.0
Holzman (p)	373.5	370.0	400.0
Horten	136.5	137.0	134.5
Kali & Salz	221.5	222.5	167.0
Karstadt	183.0	189.5	238.0
Kaufhof	158.5	157.5	190.8
KHD	173.3	174.5	227.0
Kloeckner-Wk	53.0	51.0	65.5
Krupp	54.0	55.0	67.5
Linde	300.5	300.2	325.0
Lufthansa	62.8	63.0	74.5
MAN	165.0	168.5	199.0
Mannesmann	124.0	125.0	131.5
Mercedes Hlg.	231.0	232.0	216.5
Metallges	320.0	322.0	279.0
Munchner Ruck	680.0	670.0	605.0
Preussag	133.0	135.0	208.5
Schering	236.0	227.0	200.0
Siemens	247.5	250.8	275.0
Thyssen-Hutte	69.2	68.1	86.8
Varta	167.5	165.5	157.0
Veba	124.8	123.8	155.7
Vereins & West Bk	281.0	280.0	275.0
Volkswagen	146.0	140.0	185.3

Source: World Business Weekly, March 2, 1981.

The debt securities market in Japan consists mainly of government bonds, bank debentures, Nippon Telephone and Telegraph bonds, and corporate bonds (not abundant). Foreign participation is not extensive, however. The bond market and bank loans are the dominant source of funds for business entities.

FIGURE 17.13   Vital statistics on Japan's economy.

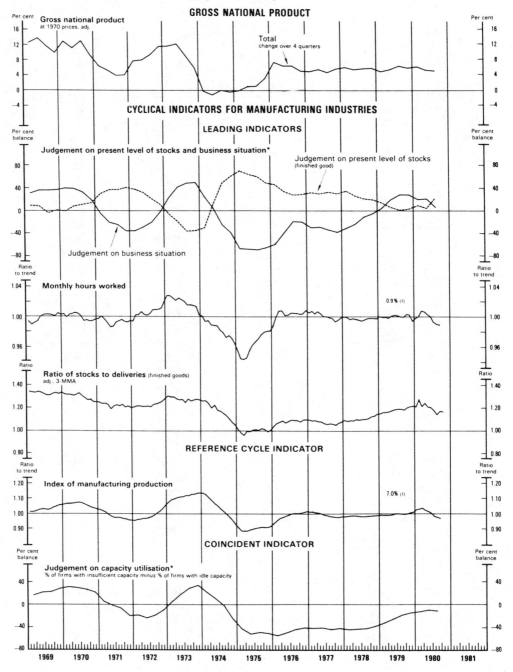

FIGURE 17.13 (continued)

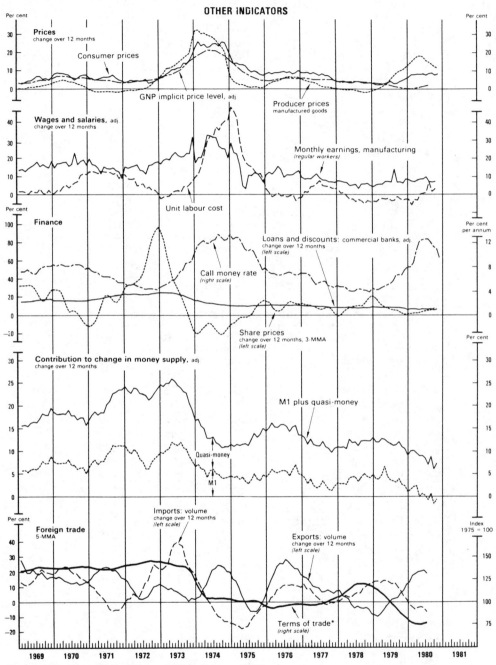

Source: Main Economic Indicators, OECD, February 1981.
(1) Ratio of export prices to import prices.
(2) Annual trend growth rate over last five years.

TABLE 17.7
Limits on Foreign Shareholdings in Japan

	Current Holding, Percent	Maximum Limit, Percent
Arabian Oil	20.0	25.0
Showa Oil	50.0	50.0
Mitsubishi Oil	50.0	50.0
Toa Nenryo Kogyo	50.0	50.0
Kao Oil	50.0	50.0
General Oil	49.0	49.0
Fuji Electric	23.4	25.0
Katakura Ind.	24.6	25.0
Sankyo	23.8	25.0
Tokyo Keiki	31.5	25.0
Hitachi	23.5	30.0

Source: Cazenove & Co., London, December 1980/January 1981.

TABLE 17.8
Japanese Securities of Interest to U.S. Investors

Yen	Feb 18	Feb 10	Yr ago
Ajinomoto	839	843	560
Asahi Chem	210	213	170
Asahi Glass	471	480	355
Banyu	558	568	578
Bk of Tokyo	205	205	218
Bridgestone	463	465	540
Calpis Food	549	548	536
Canon	796	823	650
Chugai Seiyaku	636	652	526
Daiei	705	710	970
Dai-Ichi Bk	454	454	390
Dai Nippon Pntg	581	586	535
Daiwa House	314	309	318
Daiwa Sec	269	270	268
Ebara	381	385	387
Eisai	1,070	1,050	1,010
Fuji Bk	451	451	411
Fuji Photo	1,040	955	517
Fujisawa Pharm	923	960	859
Fujitsu	486	530	471
Heiwa Real Est	557	564	628
Hitachi	312	321	259
Hitachi Koki	585	593	605
Honda	538	550	610
House Food	986	1,000	735
Indust Bk Japan	365	365	283
Isuzu Motors	215	227	242

TABLE 17.8
Japanese Securities of Interest to U.S. Investors
(*Continued*)

Yen	Feb 18	Feb 10	Yr ago
C Itoh	396	408	456
JAL	2,450	2,470	2,580
Kajima	290	290	281
Kansai Elec	915	934	895
Kao Soap	485	503	396
Kashiyima	673	676	520
Kirin Brew	445	448	405
Kokuyo	1,050	1,020	n.a.
Komatsu	345	353	346
Kubota	354	357	361
Kumagaigumi	404	392	361
Makita Elec	916	980	1,140
Marubeni	645	367	371
Marui	875	850	719
Matsushita Elec Ind	818	828	716
Matsushita Elec Wks	540	542	546
Mitsubishi Bk	460	462	415
Mitsubishi Chem	247	255	225
Mitsubishi Corp	645	669	719
Mitsubishi Est	400	400	417
Mitsubishi Hvy	188	190	195
Mitsui & Co	325	330	370
Mitsui Real Estate	504	518	544
Mitsukoshi	451	481	438
Mitsumi	445	445	503
Nikko Sec	339	341	364
Nippon Denso	900	910	1,210
Nippon Elec	544	561	407
Nippon Kogaku	569	575	474
Nippon Oil	1,450	1,460	1,900
Nippon Shinpan	778	813	613
Nippon Steel	143	143	137
Nippon Suisan	210	217	220
Nippon Yusen	297	288	331
Nissan Motor	704	705	725
Nomura Sec	374	380	417
Olympus Opt	1,250	1,320	750
Orient Leas	1,010	n.a.	900
Pioneer	2,780	2,850	1,980
Ricoh	619	645	595
Sanyo	382	386	405
Sekisui Prefab	620	621	703
Sharp	648	659	601
Shiseido	937	920	980
Sony	3,120	3,070	1,690
Sumitomo Bk	455	454	412
Taisei Const	211	208	221
Takada Chem	819	770	511
TDK	3,640	3,650	1,890

TABLE 17.8
Japanese Securities of Interest to U.S. Investors
(*Continued*)

Yen	Feb 18	Feb 10	Yr ago
Teijin	152	161	155
Tokio Marine	609	634	620
Tokyo Elec	955	972	895
Tokyo Gas	112	113	120
Toray	267	271	240
Toshiba	533	218	553
TOTO	497	484	441
Toyo Kogyo	309	325	405
Toyota	740	751	829
Wacoal	782	789	749
Yamaha Motor	811	850	870
Yamazaki	628	627	505
Yasuda Fire	274	289	299
Yokogawa Bridge	620	640	675

Source: World Business Weekly, March 2, 1981.

United Kingdom

The British economy has been characterized of late by negative economic growth, high unemployment, and high inflation. The tight monetary and fiscal policies that have been pursued by Prime Minister Margaret Thatcher have partially succeeded in reducing inflationary pressure, but only through unprecedented levels of unemployment. The inflation rate for 1980 was still a high 15.9 percent, however. The sluggishness of the British economy is demonstrable in Figure 17.14. The leading indicators have begun to point upward, but no one is yet forecasting a boom for Britain. The British government has thus far been unable to get public spending under control or to implement fully any element of the economic recovery program enunciated by Prime Minister Thatcher. The oil discoveries in the North Sea, although of great help, have proven insufficient to remedy Britain's economic ills.

The British stock market is more active than its European counterparts and is organized in a fashion similar to that of the United States. Some three thousand shares are listed in London. Transactions costs and stamp duties are very high, which encourages investors to trade off the exchanges.

The debt securities market in Britain is far more extensive than that of any other European market, with a volume four times as high as that in the equity market. The current (1980–1982) high interest rates in the United States compared with those of Britain have diminished the attractiveness of British debt securities, however. Britain remains the most important financial center in the world, helping to integrate world financial markets through issues denominated in its own currency or in other currencies (the Eurobond market, for example). British merchant banks play a major role in the flow and management of funds. The minimum-size portfolio of interest to merchant bankers is $100,000. Their activities reach other countries, in which they also manage portfolios. The 100 largest U.K. industrial companies are listed in Table 17.9.

We now look at a sound way of acquiring foreign securities.

FIGURE 17.14 Vital statistics on the economy of the United Kingdom.

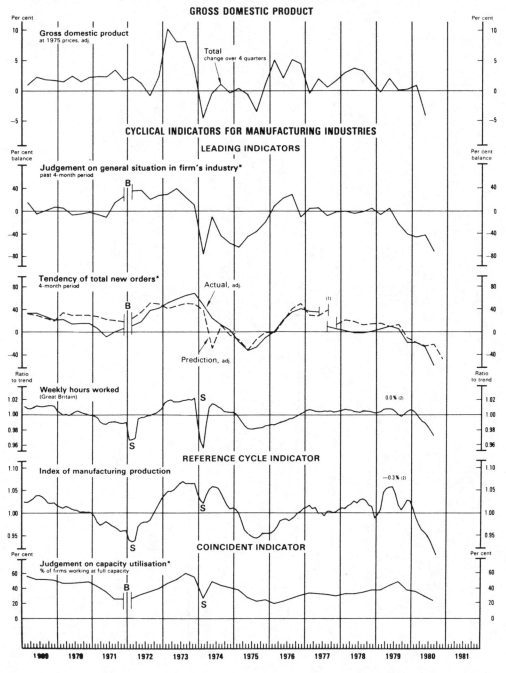

FIGURE 17.14 (continued)

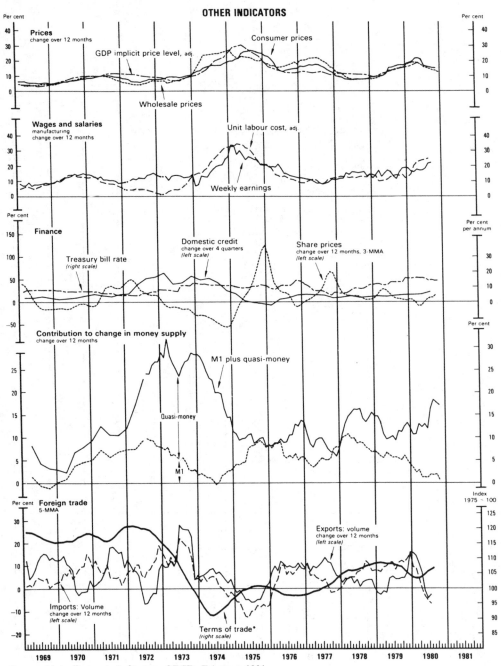

Source: Main Economic Indicators, OECD, February 1981.
* Ratio of export prices to import prices.
(1) From April 1977 in volume terms, in value terms previously.
(2) Annual trend growth rate over last five years.

TABLE 17.9
The 100 Largest UK Industrial Companies

Rank by Turnover	Company	Main Activity
1	British Petroleum Co.	Oil industry
2	'Shell' Transport & Trading	Oil industry
3	BAT Industries	Tobacco, retailing, paper & cosmetics
4	Imperial Chemical Industries	Chemicals, fibres, paints, etc.
5	Unilever Ltd.	Food products, detergents, etc.
6	Imperial Group	Tobacco, food, drink and packaging
7	BL	Motor vehicle manufacturers
8	Ford Motor Co.	Motor vehicle manufacturers
9	General Electric Co.	Electrical engineers
10	Shell UK	Oil industry
11	Esso Petroleum Co.	Oil industry
12	Allied Breweiries	Brewers, vintners, hoteliers, etc.
13	Rio Tinto-Zinc Corporation	Mining & industrial—metals & fuel
14	Grand Metropolitan	Hotel props., milk prds. brewers, etc.
15	Rothmans International	Tobacco manufacturers
16	Guest, Keen & Nettlefolds	Steel & eng. products, fastenings, etc.
17	George Weston Holdings	Food manufacturers & distributors
18	Courtaulds	Man-made fibres, textiles, chemicals
19	Inchcape & Co.	International merchants
20	Cavenham	Food, drink, tobacco, etc., products
21	Reed International	Paper, packaging, printing & publishing
22	Bowater Corporation	Paper manufacturers, intl. trading
23	Texaco	Oil industry
24	Gallaher	Tobacco, cigarette, cigar & snuff man.
25	Dunlop Holdings	Rubber goods & sports requisites, etc.
26	Marks & Spencer	General store proprietors
27	S. & W. Berisford	Sugar importers & mchts, etc.
28	C. T. Bowring & Co.	Insurance brokers, finance, eng., etc.
29	Ranks Hovis McDougall	Food manufacturers and distributors
30	Lonrho	Mining, agric., textiles, constr., etc.
31	BOC International	Manfrs. of gases & associated eqpmt.
32	P. & O. Steam Navigation Co.	Shipowners
33	Great Universal Stores	Stores & mail order
34	Tate & Lyle	Sugar refiners, etc.
35	Burmah Oil Co.	Oil industry
36	Tube Investments	General engineers
37	Sears Holdings	Footwear, stores, engineering, etc.
38	Czarnikow Group	Commodity brokers, etc.
39	Rank Xerox	Xerographic equipment, etc.
40	Thorn Electrical Industries	Electrical & electronic engineers
41	Boots Co.	Manfg., Wholesale & retail chemists
42	Thomas Tilling	Industrial holding co.
43	Bass	Brewers

TABLE 17.9
The 100 Largest UK Industrial Companies (*Continued*)

Rank by Turnover	Company	Main Activity
44	Cadbury Schweppes	Confectionery, soft drinks, food, etc.
45	Hawker Siddeley Group	Mech. & electrical eng. & metals
46	BICC	Cable makers, elec. engineers & contrs.
47	J. Sainsbury	Retail distribution of food
48	Unigate	Dairymen & food manufacturers, etc.
49	Lucas Industries	Vehicle & aircraft accessory manfrs.
50	Amalgamated Metal Corpn.	Metal & ores
51	Consolidated Gold Fields	Mining finance, industry, commerce
52	Tesco Stores (Holdings)	Multiple retailing
53	Tozer, Kemsley & Millbourn	Internl. finance & investment
54	Distillers Co.	Whiskey distillers
55	EMI	Music, electronics, leisure, TV, etc.
56	Beecham Group	Pharmaceuticals, toiletries, drinks, etc.
57	Trafalgar House	Contracting, civil eng., shipping, etc.
58	F. W. Woolworth & Co.	General retail merchants
59	Metal Box	Packaging containers & closures
60	Western United Inv. Co.	Foodstuffs & by-products
61	Vauxhall Motors	Motor vehicle manufacturers
62	Littlewoods Organization	Mail order trading & retail stores
63	Dalgety	International merchants
64	Babcock & Wilcox	Engineers & contractors
65	Brooke Bond Liebig	Tea, coffee, meat & other food prods.
66	Tarmac	Roadstone & civil eng.
67	Spillers	Millers, bakers, food manufacturers
68	Philips Electronic & Assoc.	Electric & electronic products
69	United Biscuits (Holdings)	Manfrs. of biscuits, cakes, crisps, etc.
70	Gill & Duffus Group	Commodity brokers, mchts. & processrs.
71	Rolls-Royce	Aero engines
72	Coats Patons	Thread, yarns, fashion & clothing
73	Mobil Oil Co.	Oil industry
74	George Wimpey	Bldg, civil, mech. & elec. eng. contrs.
75	Whitbread & Co.	Brewers
76	Arthur Guinness Son & Co.	Brewers
77	Ready Mixed Concrete	Building materials suppliers, etc.
78	British Electric Traction	Industrial holding co.
79	Trusthouse Forte	Hotels, catering and leisure group
80	Plessey Co.	Electric & electronic products
81	Reckitt & Colman	Food & h/hold products, pharms, etc.
82	Hanson Trust	Agriproducts, industrial services
83	Ultramar Co.	Petroleum exploration & development
84	Booker McConnell	International food, eng. & tdg co.
85	British Aircraft Corpn (Hds.)	Aircraft manufacturers

TABLE 17. 9
The 100 Largest UK Industrial Companies (*Continued*)

Rank by Turnover	Company	Main Activity
86	IBM United Kingdom Holdings	Information handling eqpt. mfrs.
87	Thomson British Holdings	Oil, travel, printing & publishing
88	Conoco	Petroleum products
89	House of Fraser	Department stores
90	Rowntree Mackintosh	Confectionery & grocery products
91	Harrisons & Crosfield	Eastern mchts., exporters & importers
92	Glaxo Holdings	Pharmaceutical preparations, etc.
93	Turner & Newall	Asbestos, plastics, insulation, etc.
94	Massey-Ferguson Holdings	Manfrs. of agricultural machinery
95	Associated Dairies	Dairymen, supermarkets, etc.
96	IMI	Metals, fabricated products, etc.
97	Nafta (GB)	Traders in petroleum products
98	Thomas Borthwick & Sons	International meat traders
99	ICL	Data processing systems
100	Standard Telephones & Cables	Telecommunications & electronics

Source: Cazenove & Co., New York, 1981.

17.6 AMERICAN DEPOSITORY RECEIPTS (ADRs)

Investing in a foreign stock may not require its direct purchase in the foreign country provided that an American depository receipt (ADR) exists for that stock.

ADRs are financial instruments issued by American banks (called depositories) against shares deposited with the bank's overseas branch or custodian. The underlying shares remain on deposit as long as the ADRs are outstanding.

ADRs were introduced in 1927 by Guaranty Trust Co. of New York (now Morgan Guaranty Trust Co.) as a mechanism for bridging the gap between foreign and American concepts of publicly traded securities. ADRs allow American investors to own, sell, and trade foreign securities without ever taking physical possession of them.

The price of ADRs represents not only the value of the underlying security but also the changes in the exchange rate. The American holder of ADRs can but usually does not determine the extent to which the change in the price of ADRs is due to changes in the market for securities and/or to changes in its intrinsic value or to changes in the exchange rate. The American investor pays dollars for ADRs and receives dividends in dollars. It is incorrect to conclude, however, that because the transaction and the returns are denominated in dollars the changes in the exchange rates do not matter.

Mechanics of ADRs

ADRs are ordinarily issued on a one-to-one basis: one ADR for every share held abroad. Foreign corporations with a large number of outstanding shares that sell for the equivalent of a few dollars are issued ADRs against more than one share: 10, 50, or 100. Some Japanese firms are prime examples. American investors can trade ADRs in exactly the same way as they do securities of American corporations. All ADRs are registered in the name of the owner. Upon receiving an order to sell an ADR, the bank, acting for the seller, notifies its foreign affiliate to supply an equivalent number of shares of the underlying security. A holder of ADRs may, on the other hand, elect to sell the underlying foreign shares overseas and give up the ADRs at home. An owner of ADRs may choose to take possession of the underlying stock abroad and surrender ADRs to the U.S. bank.

The functions of the bank are not limited to the issuance of the ADRs and to trades therein. Banks involved in this endeavor notify ADR holders of dividends and distribute those dividends in dollars (no guarantees as to the actual exchange rate) after deducting the applicable foreign taxes. The bank also furnishes information on stock rights, stockholders' meetings, new issues, tender offers, and other pertinent information to holders of ADRs. For these services the bank charges a fee.

ADRs are traded on the exchanges or over the counter. Listed ADRs (NYSE and AMEX) and their underlying shares must meet the requirements of the exchange and those of the SEC. Few ADRs are listed on the NYSE, many are listed on the AMEX, and most are traded over the counter. This makes the trading in ADRs cheaper and easier than trading in the underlying foreign shares.

The differences between the markets in which ADRs are traded and those in which the underlying shares are traded occasionally lead to differing prices. This creates an opportunity for arbitrage, which enhances the liquidity and the efficiency of the ADR market.

Advantages and Disadvantages of ADRs

The basic advantage of ADRs is in facilitating the ownership of foreign securities. Investors trading ADRs settle their transactions in exactly the same way as they do with securities issued by U.S. firms. The need to mail the foreign securities overseas (in case of a sale of a foreign-owned security) and to wait (a long time in many cases) for the receipt of funds is thus eliminated. The other advantages are as follows:

1. Escape from the payment of certain taxes imposed by foreign governments on securities holdings. Britain, for example, imposes a stamp tax on 1 percent of the value of a security.

2. Possibly increased information flow as the ADR-issuing bank may be more intent on providing information, considering the market norms and the expectations of American investors, than the corporations that have issued the underlying securities. This information (in English) is much more relevant and better focused than the investor could have generated on his or her own from an array of sources which may be written in a foreign language.

3. Escape from foreign regulations dealing with investment by Americans in indigenous markets.

4. Security. ADRs are issued by major U.S. banks, with Morgan Guaranty Trust Co. leading the way. ADRs are all registered (in the name of the owner) securities, whether the underlying security is a registered or a bearer security. Many foreign securities are bearer securities and therefore represent a great risk if lost or stolen. Moreover, the investor would not have to worry about currency convertibility and directly about exchange rates. Dividends are paid in the United States as soon as they are paid overseas, hence the elimination of the risk of having the check lost in the mail and of long delays, with the attended opportunity cost.

The disadvantages of owning ADRs, while few, may be significant nonetheless. Among them are the following:

1. Still insufficient information. The depository bank will not send information to ADR holders unless asked to do so in writing. Many investors are forgetful.

2. ADRs do not eliminate the requirement of paying withholding taxes to the host country. These taxes may be deductible from American tax liabilities, however.

3. ADRs may complicate the process of exercising a stock right. The SEC does not permit ADR owners to "exercise rights issued by foreign corporations unless the new stock issue is registered with the SEC. Such rights are automatically sold by the depository bank, and the proceeds are sent to the beneficial owner."[40]

Despite these disadvantages, ADRs remain the best way to participate in the world capital markets. A list of a few ADRs appears in Table 17.10.

We now turn to the Eurobond an increasingly popular instrument for participating in the international debt securities market.

17.7 THE EUROBOND MARKET

A Eurobond is an international bond denominated in a currency other than that of the country of the issuer.

Background

The development of the Eurobond market is mostly due to U.S. economic policies intended to stem the flow of capital outside the United States. In addition to Regulation Q, two programs are mainly responsible: The Interest Equalization Tax (IET), imposed in 1964 and abolished in 1974, and the Voluntary Foreign Credit Restraint (VFCR) program, which began in 1965 and ended in 1974. The IET was intended to discourage U.S. citizens from investing in foreign securities by increasing the tax on the returns from those securities. The VFCR, which was made mandatory in 1968, was intended to discourage U.S. bankers from lending overseas. This led U.S. banks to set up branches overseas to service their multinational clients and to the flourishing of the Eurodollar market.

After a rocky start, due mostly to the transfer systems for transactions in Eurobonds, The Association of International Bond Dealers (AIBD) was formed in 1968. AIBD brought about an efficient, uniform transfer system for Eurobonds.

The takeoff stage for Eurobonds began in 1968 and coincided with vigorous economic growth in the United States and Europe. After a short lull, the growth resumed at an explosive rate, reaching $23,879 million in 1980 (Table 17.11).

The center of activity in Eurobonds is Europe. The major operators in the Eurobond market are European banks and investment houses, followed by U.S. and Japanese banks, as shown in Table 17.12.

---

[40] *Dun and Bradstreet's Guide to Your Investments.* Thomas Y. Crowell, New York, 1978.

TABLE 17.10
Some Foreign Corporations Whose Shares Are Available Through American Depository Receipts (ADRs)[a]

Australia
Broken Hill Proprietary
G. J. Coles & Co.
M.I.M. Holdings
Santos
Union Carbide of Aust.
Woodside Burmah Oil
Western Holdings
Winkelhaak

France
Cie Financiere de Suez
Cie des Machines Bull
Michelin
Pechiney
Source Perrier
St. Gobain

Germany
AEG-Telfunken
BASF Bayer, AG
Commerzbank
Deutsche Bank
Dresdner Bank
Hoechst AG
Siemens AG
Volkswagenwerk

Japan
Canon, Inc.
Fuji Photo
Fujitsu
Hitachi, Ltd.
Japan Air Lines
Kansai Electric
Kirin Brewing
Mitsui & Co.
Nippon Electric
Nippon Optical
Pioneer Electronic
Sharp
Toshiba
Tokyo Marine & Fire
Tokyo Motors
Toyo Kogyo
Wacoal

Holland
Akzo, N.V.
Heineken's Bier.
KLM (N)
Philips Gloeil.
Royal Dutch (N)

Mexico
IEM, S.A.
Telefonas de Mexico
Tubos de Acero

South Africa
Anglo-American Corp.
Anglo-American Gold
Bkyvooruitzicht
Bracken
Buffelsfontein Doornfontein
Durban Deep
East Driefontein
East Rand Proprietary
Free State Geduld
Harmony
Hartebeestfontein
Kinross
Leslie
Libanon
Loraine
President Brand
President Steyn
Randfontein
St. Helena
Southvaal
Stilfontein
Vaal Reefs
Venterspost
Welkom
West Driefontein
Western Areas
Western Deep

United Kingdom
Assoc. British Foods
Beecham Group
Bowater Corp.
British-Amer. Tobacco (A)
Gestetner
Glaxo Holdings
Imperial Chemical (A)
Rank Organization
Rothman's International
Shell Transport (N)
Toreador Royalty
Unilever (N)
Woolworth (A)

Other
Amer. Israeli Paper (A)
Bank Leumi
Ericcson Telephone
Fiat Motors
IDBankholding
Montecatini Electric
Olivetti
Pirelli
Union Minere
Zambia Copper

Source: Carl Marks & Co., New York.
[a] Securities traded OTC Except (N) NYSE; (A) Amex.

TABLE 17.11
New International Bond Offerings (Millions of Dollars)

Year	Eurobonds	Foreign Bonds[a]	Total
1963	164	389	553
1964	719	264	983
1965	1,041	376	1,417
1966	1,142	378	1,520
1967	2,002	403	2,405
1968	3,573	1,135	4,708
1969	3,156	827	3,983
1970	2,966	378	3,344
1971	3,642	1,538	5,180
1972	6,335	2,060	8,395
1973	4,193	2,626	6,819
1974	2,134	1,432	3,566
1975	8,567	4,884	13,451
1976	14,328	7,586	21,914
1977	17,771	8,777	26,548
1978	14,125	14,359	28,484
1979	18,726	17,749	36,475
1980	23,879	14,521	38,400
Total	**128,463**	**79,682**	**208,145**

Source: Morgan Guaranty Trust Co., New York.

[a] Excludes foreign issues in the U.S. Foreign bonds are bonds issued by a foreign borrower in the domestic capital.

The distribution of international new issues by currency denomination during the 1975–1979 periods is shown in Table 17.13. The U.S. dollar plays a leading role. In fact, in 1980, Eurobonds denominated in U.S. dollars accounted for 67.74 percent of all new Eurobonds in 1980, followed by the German mark (18.75 percent).

Characteristics of the Eurobond Market

The characteristics of the Eurobond market are constantly changing as new currencies are introduced, new companies or industries enter the market, and new types of Eurobonds are introduced. What could generally be said is that the Eurobond market has the following characteristics:

1. *Low default risk.* Eurobond issues are invariably high-quality issues. Eurobond issuers are high-quality corporations or governments or government agencies with good credit ratings.

2. The average maturity of the Eurobond exceeds seven years.

3. Some foreign exchange risk is present. However, an American investor wishing to diversify a portfolio internationally can purchase a dollar-denominated Eurobond and avoid exchange risk altogether.

4. Some Eurobond issues are very thin and have little if any secondary market. Some experts estimate that upward of 40 percent of all Eurobond issues do not have a

TABLE 17.12
The 20 Leading Eurobond Managers of 1980 [a]

	Number of Issues	Amount (Millions of Dollars)
Credit Suisse First Boston	38	1,859.7
Deutsche Bank	29	1,713.0
Morgan Stanley	18	1,312.4
S G Warburg	20	843.9
Goldman Sachs	9	685.0
Paribas	9	678.6
Dresdner Bank	14	663.3
Societe Generale	10	621.3
WestLB	10	435.9
Orion Bank	9	417.5
Daiwa	14	366.8
Citicorp	8	364.4
Banque Nationale de Paris	10	351.4
Hambros Bank	9	330.9
Credit Commercial de France	7	329.5
Salomon Brothers	8	328.1
Union Bank of Switzerland	6	321.5
Commerzbank	8	315.8
Wood Gundy	7	310.5
Swiss Bank Corp	7	298.3

Source: Euromoney, February 1981.
[a] Includes all notes and bonds, but excludes New York issues.

genuine secondary market. This obviously decreases the liquidity of Eurobonds and increases transactions costs.

5. Eurobonds are denominated in an increasing number of currencies and group of currencies or special drawing rights (SDRs). The tracking of this market is becoming increasingly complex if not impossible. An individual investor is likely to be overwhelmed.

6. Eurobonds have historically produced a higher yield than U.S. bonds, even after adjusting for foreign exchange rate changes.

7. Eurobonds are invariably bearer bonds (not registered in the name of the holder), making it difficult for authorities to trace ownership and collect taxes. This, however, increases the risk of theft and decreases the probability of recovering a stolen Eurobond.

8. Interest on Eurobonds is usually paid on an annual basis.

9. Interest on Eurobonds is not subject to withholding taxes.

10. While the diversity of Eurobonds is confusing to some, it is an opportunity for others, the professionals in particular. We shall discuss the prominent types of Eurobonds in the next section.

11. Most Eurobonds provide for a sinking fund or a purchase fund. The sinking fund provision requires the issuer to retire a certain number of bonds after a specified time period. The purchase fund provision requires that the retirement of a certain number of bonds begin with the first year after issuance, but only if the bond is trading below the issue price. The retirement of bonds relies on the lottery system.

TABLE 17.13
International New Issue Offerings, 1975–79

	1975		1976		1977		1978		1979		Percent Change in Principal Amount 1978–79
	Principal Amount (Millions)	Number of Issues	Principal Amount (Millions)	Number of Issues	Principal Amount (Millions)	Number of Issues	Principal Amount (Millions)	Number of Issues	Principal Amount (Millions)	Number of Issues	
Dollars	$2,823	86	$7,538	166	$9,928	193	$5,512	107	$9,198	149	+67
Deutschemarks	Dm4,325	47	DM5,360	53	DM9,535	78	DM11,035	94	DM5,080	45	−54
Guilders	G1,460	23	G1,095	18	G670	9	G845	11	G549	8	−35
French francs	Ffr1,100	10	Ffr125	1	—	—	Ffr450	3	Ffr1,564	12	+248
Luxembourg francs	Lfr4,300	8	Lfr1,650	3	Lfr2,050	4	Lfr4000	1	—	—	−100
Belgian francs	Bfr2,000	1	—	—	—	—	—	—	—	—	—
Canadian dollars	C$575	23	C$1,370	47	C$575	20	—	—	C$479	12	—
Hong Kong dollars	—	—	—	—	HK$650	3	1—	—	7—	—	—
Australian dollars	—	—	A$15	1	A$10	1	A$27	2	A$15	1	−44
Austrian schillings	—	—	—	—	—	—	Sch400	1	Sch900	2	+125
Kuwaiti dinars	KD41	6	KD63	10	KD31	7	KD125	16	KD106	13	−15
Bahraini dinars	—	—	—	—	BD27	2	BD8	1	—	—	−100
Sterling	—	—	—	—	$120	6	$115	8	$120	4	+4
Swedish kronor	Skr30	1	—	—	—	—	—	—	—	—	—
Norwegian kroner	Nkr220	1	—	—	—	—	—	—	Nkr80	1	—
Yen	—	—	—	—	Y30,000	2	Y15,000	1	Y25,000	2	+67
Saudi riyals	—	—	—	—	SR35	1	—	—	—	—	—
European units of account	EUA292	14	EUA82	5	EUA25	1	EUA114	6	EUA161	6	+41
European composite units	Euro140	3	—	—	—	—	—	—	—	—	—
European Currency Units	ECU30	1	—	—	—	—	—	—	—	—	—
Special drawing rights	—	—	—	—	—	—	SDR25	2	SDR70	2	+180
Totals	$6,296 (dollar equivalent)	224	$11,937 (dollar equivalent)	304	$15,648 (dollar equivalent)	327	$12,709 (dollar equivalent)	252	$14,315 (dollar equivalent)	257	+13

Source: Euromoney, February 1980.

Types of Eurobonds

Eurobonds are more diverse than any other debt instrument. The innovative genius of investment bankers has produced an avalanche of Eurobonds, with peculiar provisions and special appeal to certain investors. At the same time, the perplexity of the Eurobond market has been compounded, making it very difficult for the individual investor to cope.

The following are among the more prominent and innovative Eurobonds:

1. *Straight debt Eurobond.* These Eurobonds are denominated in a single currency (the dollar, for example) and do not have an equity feature. These bonds could have a fixed rate or a floating coupon rate. Some floating-rate bonds are convertible into a fixed-rate bond and some include a put option (an option to sell the bond at a specific price during a period of time). This option reduces the risk of the bond resulting from fluctuations in the interest-rate levels.

2. *Multiple currency Eurobond.* This bond allows the investor to receive payment of interest and principal in any predetermined currency as well as in the currency of the loan in accordance with a predetermined exchange rate.

3. *European Unit of Account Eurobond.* The European Unit of Account (EUA) consisted originally of the 17 currencies in the European Payments Union (EPU). After the dissolution of the EPU in 1958, a new EUA emerged in 1973. The currencies it comprises are those of the members of the European Economic Community (EEC). The EUA is valued at 0.88867 grams of fine gold. A U.S. investor runs the risk of exchange loss if the dollar appreciates in value against the EUA.

4. *European monetary unit Eurobond.* This is a multicurrency bond denominated in the currencies of the six original EEC member countries. The investor is protected against exchange risk for the issuer guarantees the bond against exchange-rate fluctuations.

5. *Special drawing rights Eurobonds.* The growth of Eurobonds denominated in special drawing rights (SDRs) began only in the mid-1970s. SDRs are a form of currency created by the International Monetary Fund (IMF) to increase world liquidity. Countries that are members of the IMF accept payments in SDRs from each other in the settlement of international transactions. Those payments take the form of bookkeeping entries. SDRs are currently valued in terms of a group of currencies weighted by their relative position in world trade. These currencies are the U.S. dollar, the German mark, the Japanese yen, the French franc, and the British pound. The simplification of the definition of an SDR (in terms of 5 currencies instead of the old 16) should lead to an increase in SDR-denominated Eurobonds.

6. *Convertible Eurobonds.* These bonds are convertible into equity issues and carry all the advantages and disadvantages of convertible bonds. Convertible bonds may be partially or fully convertible.

7. *Deferred-purchase Eurobond.* This bond allows the investor to pay only 25 percent of the bond value at the time of purchase and the balance after a few months. The investor would earn interest on all the bonds purchased and could earn additional interest by investing 75 percent of the commitment in money market instruments until full payment is due.

Conclusion

Investors interested in the Eurobond market must be very careful. They must do their homework thoroughly or rely on a professional money manager to manage their funds separately or as part of a pool of funds; otherwise they must rely on internationally diversified mutual funds that are partially or exclusively invested in the Eurobond market.

17.8 INTERNATIONAL INVESTMENT FUNDS

The complexities of dealing in foreign-issued securities can be deferred, for a fee, to professional money managers. Several mutual funds with distinctly international flavors have emerged to meet the need for international portfolio diversification. They represent the simplest way to internationalize the portfolio. The funds accept dollars and distribute returns on their investment in dollars. The investor is indirectly exposed to exchange risk, however, because the funds assets (in whole or in part) are denominated in foreign currencies. Every investor can choose that fund which best meets the desired level and type (by geographic area) of international diversification. An American investor with particular interest in Japanese firms may purchase shares in the Japan Fund, which is traded on the New York Stock Exchange and on the Pacific Stock Exchange, or in the Nomura Capital Fund of Japan.

International mutual funds generally have the following advantages:

1. International risk diversification.
2. Professional management, particularly of foreign exchange risk.
3. *Liquidity.* Open-end funds (the most prevalent) allow the investor to redeem shares at net asset value.
4. *Flexibility.* Accumulated funds may be withdrawn in one lump sum or over a period of time suitable for example, for retirees, or they may be transferred from one type of fund to another, as from a common stock fund to an income-oriented fund. An investor is also able to make regular purchases in the fund—as, for example, part of a saving program. The minimum investment is dependent on the policy of the particular fund. Scudder International Fund, Inc., for example, requires a minimum investment of $1,000; Transatlantic Fund, Inc., on the other hand, requires a minimum initial investment of $25,000 and a minimum subsequent investment of $5,000.

The following factors must be kept in mind when an investor purchases an internationally diversified fund:

1. No returns are guaranteed; under professional management, foreign exchange risk is not always eliminated. Some funds enter into currency futures contracts to reduce foreign exchange risk.
2. Foreign securities markets are typically less liquid than their American counterparts, which increases the price volatility of the fund's shares.
3. Income from foreign securities may be reduced by withholding taxes. Fund shareholders may, in most cases, deduct or claim credits for taxes paid by the fund to foreign countries.
4. Most internationally diversified funds are no-load (no commission at time of purchase) funds. Their income is reduced, however, by management fees that are approxi-

mately equal to $\frac{1}{24}$ of 1 percent a month on the average daily net assets value of the fund during the preceding month.

5. Portfolio investments in foreign countries are subject to a variety of other risks: risk of expropriation, risk of exchange controls, political risk resulting from political instability which can translate into economic instability, and a host of other risks that can reduce if not eliminate the benefits of international diversification from a risk/return point of view.

6. A particular fund may well shift its investments in such a way as to have the majority of the fund's assets committed to one country or one specific region and/or to one industry or a group of industries of which the investor does not approve. Share owners must be on the guard for such changes. Notification to shareholders is *not* required every time the fund's management changes the profile of the portfolio provided that the investment objective is being met.

The available empirical evidence on the performance of internationally diversified mutual funds should be encouraging to investors. J. McDonald[41] studied the performance of eight French mutual funds and found that between 1964 and 1969 their performance was superior in relation to the market. Farber[42] found similar evidence with regard to internationally diversified European funds.

In conclusion, it can be said that internationally oriented funds are a worthwhile vehicle for investors to consider provided that they make a careful analysis before committing funds. The international investment service provided by companies like Business International Corporation should help the investors keep their hands on the economic pulse of the world.

Some corporations and some pension funds, unable or unwilling to manage an internationally diversified portfolio, have invested their funds in internationally diversified funds. Castle P. Cooke, for example, invested $2 million of its $90 million pension fund in the New Perspective Fund. The United Presbyterian Church,[43] with a retirement fund of $600 million, has decided to place some of its money (about $31 million) in a Templeton mutual fund in order to achieve international diversification. Other corporations go it alone (in-house management of pension funds), and still others use the services of major banks, investment bankers, or money management companies. The evidence is mixed as to which is the best alternative.

CONCLUSIONS

International portfolio diversification is necessary and desirable. Portfolios made up exclusively of domestic securities lie below the efficiency frontier of internationally diversified portfolios; that is, they yield a lower rate of return for a given level of risk or carry a higher risk for a given level of return.

---

[41] **John G. McDonald,** "French Mutual Fund Performance: Evaluation of Internationally Diversified Portfolios." *Journal of Finance,* vol. 28, no. 5 (December 1973).

[42] **Andre Farber,** "Systematic Exchange Risk in the International Capital Asset Pricing Model." Proceedings of the European Finance Association, North-Holland Publishing Company, Amsterdam, 1975.

[43] See *Institutional Investor,* March 1981, pp. 73–83.

Investors intent on international diversification can buy foreign stocks for their portfolios either directly or through ADRs, can manage their own portfolios, or can buy into a managed fund; they can also buy (directly or through a fund) foreign bonds or Eurobonds. Regardless of the chosen vehicle, careful analysis must be made prior to any commitment of funds.

QUESTIONS

1. Markowitz's portfolio theory arrives at a certain efficiency frontier. How is international diversification likely to change it?

2. Distinguish between direct and portfolio investment.

3. What is the essential criterion for successful international diversification of a portfolio of securities?

4. Provide reasons for the increasing interdependence of world economies. Do you view this as a favorable development?

5. Delineate the various risks inherent in foreign portfolio investment.

6. "The investor with a global investment strategy should operate under the assumption that markets are fully integrated." Comment.

7. How do the segmented and integrated theories differ in pricing an asset? What does each allow in terms of international diversification?

8. Look at Figure 17.5. What does this reveal to a small investor who is considering international diversification?

9. How might the purchase of a stock in a multinational corporation diversify a portfolio internationally? What does the empirical evidence suggest?

10. The economies of nations such as South Korea, Singapore, and Hong Kong currently enjoy impressive growth. What should an individual consider before investing funds in any of these nations?

11. How do exchange rates clutter the international diversification picture? Should this be a problem if foreign exchange markets are efficient? Could currencies themselves be used to diversify a portfolio?

12. What factors must an investor consider before investing in a foreign country?

13. How do ADRs enhance ownership of foreign securities? What factors can cause the value of an ADR to change?

14. "An ADR is a dollar-denominated instrument, thus does not represent international diversification." Comment.

15. American investors have, until recently, shied away from foreign equity investments. Why?

16. "The increased interdependence of world economies should help improve the performance of internationally diversified portfolios." Do you agree? Explain.

17. What factors led to the birth of the Eurobond market? To its development?

18. Distinguish between Eurobonds and corporate bonds. Who can issue Eurobonds?

19. In the Netherlands, three companies consume half the total equity capital (Table 17.4). How does this affect the Dutch capital market's efficiency? The Amsterdam index?

20. The construction of a world stock index is a difficult undertaking. Why? Propose an alternative. Suggest reasons for the necessity to arrive at a very accurate market index.

CHAPTER
18 | Financial Planning

18.1 INTRODUCTION

A world characterized by perfect certainty requires little if any planning. It is the uncertainty about the future that makes financial planning a requirement for all those who seek a secure future, a certain standard of living, and a certain level of wealth (human and physical) for themselves and their loved ones.

There is no magic formula for financial planning that applies to all individuals under all circumstances in all countries. Each individual situation requires its own plan, which only coincidentally may resemble another. We shall, therefore, concentrate on the identification of those issues and vehicles that must be considered in a financial plan. We shall conclude the chapter by taking a hypothetical case and by developing a reasonably comprehensive plan suitable for it.

Considering the critical role taxes play in any financial plan, we begin this chapter with a review of the basic and relevant elements of the tax laws as they apply to individual taxpayers. We incorporate in our discussion the Economic Recovery Tax Act of 1981, the most extensive revision of the Internal Revenue Code since 1954.

18.2 FEDERAL INCOME TAX

The federal personal income tax is a progressive tax payable to the U.S. Treasury on an annual basis.

The tax laws exclude certain incomes from taxation. Income in the form of social security payments, income from accident insurance, unemployment insurance benefits (generally),[1] and interest income earned on municipal bonds are a few examples of exclusions from income. Every taxpayer is entitled to these exclusions. In addition, a taxpayer is entitled to an exemption of $1,000 for each personal and dependency exemp-

---

[1] Three types of private unemployment insurance are distinguished. If insurance premiums are paid by the employer, the income is taxable to the employee. If paid by the employee, the income is nontaxable. If unemployment compensation income due to layoff, for example, exceeds $20,000, it is taxable.

tion claimed on his or her tax return. A taxpayer with five personal and dependency exemptions would have $5,000 of tax-exempt income (for example, a married taxpayer who has three children and files a joint return).

The tax laws also permit individuals to reduce their taxable income by taking certain deductions. A taxpayer may choose to take the standard deduction (referred to as the zero-bracket amount) or to itemize deductions. The standard deduction is $3,400 for married taxpayers filing joint returns and for surviving spouses; $2,300 for single taxpayers and for heads of households; $1,700 for married taxpayers filing separately; and $0 in every other case.

Itemized deductions apply only if they are incurred by the taxpayer and are subject to many qualifications and limitations. Among the deductible expenses are interest expenses, state and local taxes, casualty losses (in excess of $100), medical expenses (in excess of 3 percent of adjusted gross income), and charitable contributions.

The maximum tax rate on "earned taxable income" such as wages, salaries, professional fees, and compensation for personal services is 50 percent. Beginning in 1982, all income is taxed at a maximum rate of 50 percent. Effective after 1984, individual income tax brackets will be indexed to inflation, reducing the effective tax rate. The maximum tax rate on other income such as dividends, interest income, and capital gains (gains on the sale of a capital asset) is also 50 percent (60 percent of net long-term capital gains are deductible from taxable income, however).

Of great importance to investors are the capital gains taxes, which we discuss next.

18.3 CAPITAL GAINS TAXES

Taxation of gains realized from the sale of a capital asset is different from the taxation of other types of income. The law allows 60 percent of long-term capital gain to be deducted from income for tax purposes.

A capital asset is defined in the Internal Revenue Code as any asset except the following:

1. *Stock in trade or other inventory property.*
2. *Property held primarily for sale to customers in the ordinary course of business.*
3. *Depreciable or real property used in a trade or business.*
4. *The normal notes or accounts receivable derived by a business from the sale of goods or services.*
5. *A copyright; a literary, musical or artistic composition; or a letter or memorandum or similar property in the hands of the author, composer, or someone whose tax basis is determined by reference to the author.*
6. *Governmental non-interest-bearing discount obligations maturing in one year or less.* [2]

An example of a capital asset is a common stock, a preferred stock, a bond, a futures contract, or a residential property.

The determination of a capital gain or loss requires, as a first step, the determination of the cost basis of the asset. The cost basis for a purchased property, for example, is the original cost plus the cost of additions and improvements minus depreciation expense.

---

[2] Internal Revenue Code, Sec. 1221.

Regular maintenance costs are not included in the cost basis. The cost basis of a purchased common stock is the purchase price plus any transactions costs incurred at the time of purchase.

If the property were received as a gift, the basis is the "carry-over basis," that is, the basis of the donor becomes the basis of the donee. There are minor exceptions to this rule, as we shall later discuss.

An inherited property would have as a basis the value assigned the property for estate tax purposes, which is usually equal to the fair market value of the property at the time of death.

Having determined the cost basis of the capital asset and knowing the net sales price, we arrive at the difference, which would constitute the capital gain or loss. If the property were held for more than a year, the gains (losses) would be long-term gains (losses); if the holding period were one year or less, the gains (losses) would be short-term gains (losses). The holding period for futures contracts is only six months. Gains on a futures contract held for a period exceeding six months are long-term gains. This distinction between long- and short-term gains (losses) is of considerable importance in the determination of the tax liability.

Determination of Net Tax Effects

At the end of a tax year, an investor may have long-term gains, long-term losses, short-term gains, and short-term losses. Those gains and losses are combined as follows:

1. Short-term losses SL are used to offset short-term gains SG. If SL > SG, the excess will be used to offset net long-term gains NLG. If LG = 0, the following tax consequences obtain:

    a. SL > SG: Up to $3,000 of the excess can be used to reduce taxable income for the year. If the net short-term loss exceeds $3,000, the excess would be carried forward and applied against future short-term gains, net long-term gains, and ordinary income (limit of $3,000 per year), depending on the presence of those gains and on their size.

    b. SL < SG: The excess will be taxed as ordinary income with maximum tax rate of 50 percent. If LG > 0, then 40 percent of it is taxed as regular income.

2. Long-term losses LL offset long-term gains LG. If LL > LG, the net long-term loss NLL would be used to offset net short-term gains NSG, if any.

    a. NLL > NSG: The excess would be deducted from ordinary income on a 2-to-1 basis. That is, every $2 net long-term loss will offset $1 of ordinary income up to the maximum $3,000. It takes, therefore, $6,000 of NLL − NSG to obtain the maximum tax deduction from ordinary income ($3,000). The difference of $6,000 − $3,000 is lost forever; that is, it cannot be carried forward.

    b. NLL < NSG: The difference is taxed as ordinary income.

If LG > LL and net long-term capital gains LG − LL exceed net short-term capital losses SL − SG, the excess (LG − LL) − (SL − SG) is taxed at the preferred rate. That is, only 40 percent of the excess is taxable. Considering that the maximum tax is 50 percent, the maximum tax on net long-term capital gains is therefore equal to 20 percent (0.40 × 0.50).

If a situation arises where the investor has both short-term losses and long-term losses, he or she would use the short-term losses first to offset ordinary income up to the maximum allowable ($3,000). This is obviously more advantageous than using the long-term losses, because the 2-for-1 provision is avoided.

Net long-term losses are carried forward and are used to offset long-term gains, net short-term gains, and ordinary income (up to $3,000) in that order provided they are not exhausted after each step and that the gains exist.

Individuals who realize a loss from an investment in the stock of a small corporation may deduct up to $50,000 ($100,000 on a joint return) as an ordinary loss rather than a capital loss on stock issued after Nov. 6, 1978. An ordinary loss is deductible from ordinary income up to the limit allowed or the size of the income, whichever is less. If the loss exceeds current ordinary income, the excess is carried forward.

Other Capital Assets and Taxes

The tax implications of transactions in options contracts have been discussed in detail in Chapter 13. The reader is urged to review the sections in that chapter.

Capital gains resulting from the sale of a home are taxable at the preferred rate (60 percent of the gain excluded from taxation) if the holding period exceeds one year.

Homeowners over 54 years of age receive a once-in-a-lifetime exclusion from capital gains taxes on up to $125,000 of gain realized on the sale of a principal residence (effective after July 20, 1981). To qualify, the homeowner must have owned and occupied the property for three of the five years prior to the sale. The $125,000 exclusion is figured on a per household basis. Joint ownership by husband and wife does not qualify the owners for a $250,000 exclusion.

Homeowners who do not qualify for this exclusion may still avoid the payment of capital gains taxes under the two year roll-over provision. Under this provision, gains on the sale of a principal residence are not subject to taxation at the time of sale if, within two years, the homeowner reinvests all the proceeds in another residence of equal or greater value. In this case, capital gains are deferred, not forgiven.

The tax law also permits the seller of a home to spread the capital gains tax burden through the installment sale method. This method involves the sale of a house with the sale price paid over a period of time instead of in a lump sum at the time of sale. Effectively, the owner is financing the sale of his or her property. In this case, capital gains, if any, would be recognized on that portion of the total value of the property paid during the current tax year, and similarly for succeeding years. For example, if the sale price of a property is $50,000 with a 50 percent down payment and the remaining 50 percent payable two years later, half of the capital gains are deferred for two years.

18.4 INTEREST, DIVIDENDS, STOCK DIVIDENDS, STOCK SPLITS, STOCK RIGHTS, STOCK OPTIONS, AND TAXES

Interest

Interest income from obligations of business entities and the federal government are subject to federal income taxes. Interest on municipal bonds is not subject to federal income taxes (more about this later in this chapter). The Economic Recovery Tax Act of 1981 permits individuals to exclude up to $1,000 of interest income ($2,000 for individuals filing joint returns) on "All-Savers Certificates." These are one-year debt instruments issued by a qualified financial institution after Sept. 30, 1981, and before Jan. 1, 1983.

The maximum interest on these instruments could equal 70 percent of the yield on 52-week T-bills. Beginning on Jan. 1, 1985, an individual taxpayer who itemizes deductions can exclude up to $3,000 ($6,000 in case of a joint return) of interest income or net interest income from taxable income.

Interest expenses are deductible from taxable income if the taxpayer itemizes deductions. This deduction is disallowed if the funds were borrowed for the purpose of investing in tax-exempt interest income.

Dividends

Cash dividends paid by domestic corporations on common or preferred stock are subject to taxes except for the first $100 ($200 for a married couple filing a joint return) received annually.

If the corporation pays dividends in the form of a common stock, the dividend is not taxable unless the shareholder chooses cash instead of stock. The Economic Recovery Tax Act of 1981 allows for special treatment of dividends paid by a "qualified public utility." Here, a shareholder receiving a stock dividend after Dec. 31, 1981, and before Jan. 1, 1986, can exclude from income up to $750 ($1,500 for joint returns) of the value of the stock dividend received. The stock dividend increases the number of shares outstanding, leaving the proportionate ownership of the shareholder in the firm constant. The total value of the common shareholdings also remains constant, but the value per share drops. Since there is no change in wealth, a tax liability is not incurred. The effect of the stock dividend is simply to reduce the cost basis per share owned. Additionally, the holding period of a stock received in a stock dividend distribution is equal to that of the stock on which the dividend was distributed. If the newly received stock is sold immediately, long-term capital gains would be generated provided that the underlying stock had a long-term holding period.

The tax considerations in a stock split are the same as those of a stock dividend. A stock split increases the number of shares outstanding without increasing their total value.

Stock Rights

Occasionally corporations offer their shareholders the right to buy additional shares at a reduced price. The acquisition of the extra shares requires the exercise of the stock rights. The stock right has a limited life, is transferable, and has a market value. If the stock right is sold, the proceeds are subject to capital gains taxes: long-term if the holding period of the underlying stock exceeds one year at the time the stock right is being sold and short-term otherwise. If the stock rights are exercised, the holding period of the newly acquired shares begins at the time of their acquisition. The holding period of the underlying shares is, in this case, irrelevant.

The effect of stock rights on the cost basis of the stock depends on the value of the right relative to that of the stock. If the value of a right is 15 percent or more of that of the stock, the cost basis of the stock must be allocated between the stock and the right. If the value of the right is less than 15 percent of the value of the stock, the owner has the option of leaving the cost basis of the stock unaltered—that is, to assign the stock right a cost basis of zero or to allocate the cost basis of the stock between the stock and the right.

Example

XYZ Corporation, with its stock selling at $50, issues stock rights entitling existing stockholders to purchase new shares at $40 plus four rights. The value of one right R is equal to:

$$R = \frac{50 - 40}{4 + 1} = \frac{10}{5} = \$2$$

The value of the right is, therefore, equal to 4 percent of the value of the stock. The stockholder can now choose between the two alternatives. If the choice to allocate is made, the cost basis of the stock will be divided as follows:

	Market Value	*Basis*
Stock	50	$\frac{50}{52} \times 100 = 96.15\%$
Right	2	$\frac{2}{52} \times 100 = 3.85\%$
Total value	**52**	

Assuming that the cost basis of the stock is $35, its new cost basis becomes 35 × 96.15% = $33.65; that of the right is $1.35.

Employee Stock Options

Employee stock options are given to corporate employees as a fringe benefit. These options can be exercised at advantageous prices compared with prevailing stock prices. Under the current tax law, the difference between the market value of the stock and the exercise price of the option is taxable.

The Economic Recovery Tax Act of 1981 creates a new stock option known as an *incentive stock option*. This type option, if it qualifies, eliminates the tax liability provided that:

1. The stock is not sold or transferred within two years after the option was granted and one year after the option was exercised
2. The option recipient is an employee of the option granting corporation from the time of the grant until three months before the exercise date of the option (12 months if disabled)

The sale of the stock received from the exercise of the option qualifies for the preferential long-term treatment if the above conditions are met.

If the employee stock option is a nonqualified option, that is, it does not qualify as an incentive stock option, the appreciation over the original option price is taxed as ordinary income when the option is exercised. Further appreciation in the price of the stock will be taxed at the preferred capital gains rate if the stock is held for at least one year from the exercise date.

18.5 SHORT SALES

Short selling involves the following activities:

1. Borrow the stock you intend to sell from a broker (expect to pay a fee for the privilege).
2. Sell the stock in the market and deliver the borrowed shares.
3. When the price of the stock later falls to the desired level, buy the same number of shares you have sold and return them to the broker.
4. The difference between the sale price and the purchase price represents the profit.

If the price of the security in which the short position was established rises instead, a loss would be incurred. Thus a short position is a vehicle for capitalizing on a decline in the price of a security.

From the point of view of the Internal Revenue Service, the short position is not a position at all. The investor has not held the stock and his or her holding period is equal to zero. Any gains or losses on a short position are, therefore, short-term gains or losses.

18.6 WASH SALES

Investors with realized capital gains and book losses in securities currently held may decide to sell the securities with the book loss merely to offset the realized capital gains, only to repurchase those same securities at a later period. If a repurchase of the same or of "substantially identical" securities (securities issued by the same company which are convertible to the securities sold, such as convertible bonds and convertible preferred stocks) takes place 30 days before or after the sale, the sale is a "wash sale" and the tax loss is disallowed.

In a wash sale, the IRS deems the transaction to have no economic content and is done solely for the purpose of avoiding the payment of taxes.

The investor should, in this case, wait for more than 30 days or buy securities of other companies with the same characteristics and in the same industry in order to be allowed the tax deduction.

The wash-sale rule provides the taxpayer with a unique tax-planning opportunity. Stock can be sold at a loss on Dec. 20 (by a calendar-year individual) and the loss can be eliminated (*if it is not needed in the recently completed calendar year*) by reacquiring the same company's stock on or before Jan. 19 of the following year. On the other hand, the loss will be realized (if needed) by not reacquiring the stock of the same company.

The wash-sale rule, it must be noted, does not apply to securities with a book gain. An investor with realized capital losses can sell securities with book capital gains to offset the losses. The repurchase of the securities would not disallow the deduction no matter when it takes place. The gains, when realized, would also reduce if not eliminate the concern with the $3,000 deduction from ordinary income and/or the 2-to-1 deduction for net long-term capital losses.

18.7 METHODS FOR REDUCING THE TAX BURDEN

The methods for reducing the tax burden (sheltering income from taxes) covered in this section represent those whose effectiveness has been proven.

Investors must keep in mind that tax shelters are not only for the rich and that each form of tax shelter must be judged in terms of its investment merits in addition to its potential as a tax sheltering device.

A very common tax shelter involves fringe benefits provided by employers in the form of life insurance premiums, health insurance premiums, dental benefits, free legal counsel benefits, profit sharing plans, etc. Employees of firms should carefully consider the costs/benefits of receiving additional compensation in the form of higher salaries or in the form of higher fringe benefits.

Buying stocks that pay little or no dividends or that have a history of paying nontaxable stock dividends is a way of reducing the tax burden by transforming current income into capital gains.

Other sheltering techniques include the following:

1. Buy municipal bonds. Interest income on municipal bonds does not have to be reported for federal tax purposes.

2. Buy real estate. Real estate shelters income through the tax deductibility of interest payments and the tax payments (such as property taxes) and through depreciation allowance on the non-land portion used for business purposes.

3. Buy raw land. The appreciation on raw land is taxed at the capital gains rate after it has been held for more than one year. Investors should consider the fact that land is not very liquid and does not generate periodic cash flows.

4. Make maximum contributions to retirement plans for which you are eligible. We shall discuss this below. In addition, an individual may buy annuities from insurance companies. Payments to the insurance companies are made during the individual's working years. Upon retirement, the insurance company begins regular payments to the annuitant for life or some other period. The contributions made during the working years may not be taxable nor is the income accumulated thereon.

5. Take, whenever possible, long-term capital losses against short-term capital gains. Long-term capital losses must offset long-term gains, but the excess can be used to reduce short-term gains, which are subject to regular income taxes.

6. Use options. Options can be an effective tool for reducing the tax burden, as was detailed in Chapter 13.

7. Sell short against the box. This involves the sale of a borrowed stock while the investor holds a long position in the same security. In this case, the investor has decided to sell the stock but wishes not to pay the taxes this year and to postpone the payment of taxes to the next year. The short sale results in the investor collecting the full market value of the stock. Since a short position is not a position as far as the IRS is concerned, the investor maintains the long position in the stock and thus owes no taxes. During the next tax year, the short position is covered by the investor, who delivers the stocks he or she holds. If the short position has a loss in it, it will exactly offset the gains in the long position; if the short position produces gains, they would offset the losses in the long position. What the investor has effectively achieved is to lock in the sale price for the stock at the time he or she decided to sell and postpone the payment of taxes.

8. Charitable and political contributions also reduce the tax burden.

9. Buy certificates of deposits (CDs), on which the interest is not credited to your account until the maturity date. This allows you to postpone the payment of taxes from one tax year to the next. Also buy All Savers Certificates, which, under the Economic Recovery Tax Act of 1981, allow the investor $1,000 ($2,000 on joint returns) in tax-free interest income. The certificates must be purchased before Dec. 31, 1982.

10. Buy into real estate, gas and oil, and other tax shelters. This will be discussed below.

11. Use the provisions of the gift and estate tax laws to your advantage and as part of a comprehensive tax planning program. Details on this are provided below.

12. Use trusts to reduce the tax burden and to maximize control over your wealth even after your death. A summary on trusts will be provided later.

We begin our detailed discussion of major tax shelter programs with retirement plans.

Retirement Plans

The prevalent retirement plans can be classified into three categories: private group pension plans, Keogh plans, and Individual Retirement Accounts (IRAs).

Private Group Pension Plans

Private pension plans are set up by employers to benefit their employees after retirement. These plans can be distinguished by (1) defined contribution vs. defined benefit; (2) insured vs. uninsured; and (3) contributory vs. noncontributory plans.

A defined contribution, as its name implies, requires that a certain sum be contributed periodically for each employee covered by the pension plan; upon the employee's retirement, the accumulated sum would be used to buy an annuity for him or her.

The defined benefit program works in the opposite direction. The desired level of retirement benefits is set and the required contributions are made.

An insured plan is one which is partially or totally insured by an insurance company. It is a pension plan funded by a life insurance company.

An uninsured pension fund is usually a trust fund. Contributions are made to a trust managed by a bank or a trust company.

A contributory plan is one in which the employee pays a portion of the pension plan.

These vesting schedules are minimal standards that an employer can choose to *improve* upon, and they apply only to the portion contributed by the employer. Employee contributions are fully and immediately vested.

Vesting, once it is realized, becomes a permanent right even if employment is terminated.

The benefits from a pension plan generally depend on the length of service, the level of compensation, or both. The maximum annual benefit is the smaller of $124,500[3] or 100 percent of the average compensation for the three highest-paid years. The 100 percent rule is waived for lower-income employees. These maximum benefits are normally achieved after 30 to 35 years of work with the same firm.

---

[3] This ceiling changes from one year to the next for it is indexed to inflation. The $124,500 was the ceiling at the end of 1981.

Taxability.   Pension income is ordinarily fully taxable. However, there are conditions under which a portion of the pension income is not taxable.

Condition 1.   Pension income from a noncontributory plan is fully taxable. If the employee did contribute to the plan but got back his or her entire contribution prior to 1979, the pension income is again fully taxable.

Condition 2.   Pension income may not be taxable until a later year if both employee and employer have contributed to the plan and if the employee expects to receive the full amount contributed to the plan in three years or less. This is called the three-year rule.

Condition 3.   This condition is referred to as the *general rule*. It involves the calculation of the total investment in the contract by the employee, including contributions made by the employer that were included in the employee's reported income.

The second step involves the determination of the total amount the employee expects to receive under the contract. The ratio of the investment to this expected return represents the exclusion percentage—that is, that portion of the pension income not subject to taxation.

The issues in group pension plans are much more complex than implied in the aforementioned discussion. This is only an outline, and the reader is encouraged to study some of the many sources dealing exclusively with this subject. Our discussion shifts now to the individual retirement plans.

Keogh Plan

The Keogh plan is a tax-deferred retirement plan named after Eugene J. Keogh, the sponsor of the legislation, officially titled the Self-employed Individuals Tax Retirement Act of 1962, sometimes referred to as HR-10. Prior to the enactment of the Keogh Act, self-employed individuals could reap the benefits of a qualified retirement plan only by incorporating and employing themselves. Individual proprietorships and partnerships were discriminated against.

Basic Features of the Keogh Act.   The Keogh Act covers full- and part-time self-employed persons under the age of 70½, from the plumber to the physician. Full-time employees of a Keogh employer who have worked for the company for three years or since its inception, whichever is sooner, must also be covered by the plan. An employer may, however, choose to extend the coverage before the required three years but cannot set the minimum or maximum age for qualification or anything but a uniform period of employment for every employee.

A full-time employee is defined as one who works at least 1,000 hours per year. A spouse is covered under the plan if he or she qualifies as a bona fide employee.

In the case of a partnership, each partner may participate in a Keogh plan set up by the partnership, but an individual partner may not set up a plan solely for his or her own benefit. Partners with less than 10 percent interest in the partnership are treated as employees and must be included in the plan.

The maximum contribution by each Keogh plan participant is 15 percent of earned income or $15,000 whichever is less. This contribution is deductible from taxable income and thus reduces the tax liability for the period during which the contribution was made. The same percentage must be contributed for all participants in the plan. Contributions can be made in one annual lump sum or on a periodic basis throughout the year. Contributions do not have to be made every year. A participant may stop making contributions and then start without any penalty. The contributions must be handled by a qualified trustee, including banks, insurance companies, and savings and loan associations; they may be invested in savings certificates, annuity contracts, mutual funds shares, securities (stocks and bonds), and even real estate.

Once the contributions are made, all earnings (interest, dividends) and capital gains derived therefrom will not be taxed when earned. Taxes are deferred until retirement, when the retiree is usually in a lower tax bracket.

Participants in a Keogh plan are fully and immediately vested; that is, they have full and immediate right to receive future benefits. The participant is guaranteed retirement benefits in the event of termination of employment, death, retirement, or disability.

The distribution of benefits to a participant may not begin before age of 59½ (except in the case of disability) and no later than age 70½. Early withdrawals subject the participant to a penalty tax and bar him or her from making further contributions for the next five years. The Economic Recovery Act of 1981[4] allows premature distribution if made because of the plan's termination. Accumulated contributions *cannot* be used as collateral for a loan, nor can they be attached by creditors.

There are several options for withdrawing funds upon qualification. A lump-sum withdrawal is possible, although it is costly, since it means that the entire tax burden will be borne at once. A reprieve is available, however. The law allows the participant choosing a lump-sum distribution to apply capital gains treatment to those withdrawals representing pre-1974 contributions and a special ten-year averaging formula to the rest. Other withdrawal options consist of periodic withdrawals, of conversion of the Keogh funds into retirement bonds or insurance annuities, and other, more imaginative methods.

Individual Retirement Accounts

IRAs represent a retirement savings program similar to Keogh. It came into existence in 1975 after the passage of the Employee Retirement Income Security Act (ERISA) in 1974. The requirements of ERISA were quite stringent, forcing many small firms to drop existing retirement plans and seek new alternatives. IRAs may be set up by individuals or by a firm on behalf of its employees. Contributions by the firm can go up to $7,500 or 15 percent of the worker's income, whichever is less. The maximum contributions by individuals to IRAs are less generous. The maximum contribution is $2,000 regardless of the level of income (the contribution cannot exceed 100 percent of compensation, however); that is, there is no percentage limitation. The employer maintains the privilege of making additional contributions.

To qualify for an IRA, the individual must earn some income (excluding dividend and interest) during the year in which the contribution is made. The IRA can be set up even if the employee is an active participant in a qualified employer or government

---

[4] The Economic Recovery Tax Act of 1981 increases the dollar amount upon which contributions are based from $100,000 to $200,000, and requires a minimum of 7.5 percent contribution by employer if contributions are based on compensation in excess of $100,000.

plan. Contributions to the IRA plan can be made directly by the employee or indirectly through the employer if the latter so permits.

IRA is also a viable alternative for self-employed people who want to escape the expensive requirements of a Keogh plan, such as the coverage of employees.

The maximum contribution, as mentioned earlier, is $2,000. An employer choosing to set up IRAs for employees must cover every employee age twenty-five and over who has worked for the firm for any part of the previous five years. The employer's contribution must be included in the employee's income, however. While contributions have a maximum, they have no minimum and do not have to be made every year. Contributions in excess of the maximum allowed are subject to a 6 percent penalty tax imposed annually until the excess is withdrawn or contributions in subsequent periods are reduced by a sum equivalent to the excess.

As in Keogh plans, the contributions must be handled by a qualified trustee, are not subject to income tax (nor are incomes derived therefrom) until retirement, and cannot be withdrawn before the age of 59½; withdrawal must start by age 70½. Participants are fully and immediately vested and can choose the appropriate vehicle in which to place their periodic contributions. None of the contributions, however, may be used to buy a life insurance policy. Only in the case of death or disability can funds be borrowed or withdrawn from an IRA plan.

Special Types of IRA's.   Two other types of IRA plans can be set up in addition to the regular IRA. We will discuss the spousal IRA and the rollover IRA.

Spousal IRA.   An individual with a regular IRA may set up an IRA for his or her spouse provided that the spouse is not employed. The maximum contribution to both accounts is $2,250. The additional contribution (above that permitted under an individual IRA) must be contributed to the IRA of the nonworking spouse.

Rollover IRA.   A rollover consists of a transfer of accumulated funds from one type of retirement plan to another. Two rollovers are possible: (1) from a company pension plan to an IRA upon termination of employment, retirement, or cancellation of retirement plan by company and (2) from one IRA to another. Both rollovers are tax-free provided the full amount received (minus any voluntary contribution made) is invested within 60 days and lump-sum payment of the full amount owed the employee is made. In the event that a portion of the lump sum received is rolled over, the balance is taxed as income in the year received.

A surviving spouse may also select a rollover upon receipt of a lump-sum distribution upon the death of a husband (wife) who participated in a qualified pension plan or a profit-sharing plan.

Real Estate, Oil, and Gas Tax Shelters

The desire of the wealthy to avoid sharing their wealth with the U.S. Treasury Department has produced an avalanche of tax-shelter offerings by many investment houses with varied degrees of sophistication and different underlying assets. We shall only attempt to shed light on the basic characteristics of real estate, oil, and gas tax shelters and leave it up to the interested investor to search further, with the help of a broker, lawyer, and/or accountant.

Real Estate Tax Shelters

A real estate tax shelter, like any other tax shelter, produces accounting and tax losses while cash flows may be positive. The tax shelter results, as we shall demonstrate, from the interest payments, the depreciation expense, and the conversion of ordinary income into capital gains.

Organizing a Real Estate Tax Shelter. Two often used ways[5] of organizing real estate tax shelters are the limited partnership and the Subchapter S Corporation.

A limited partnership has two main actors: the general partner and the limited partner. The general partner organizes the partnership, manages the property, and assumes responsibility for the partnerships debts and other obligations. For this the general partner charges a commission equal to approximately 20 percent of the total investment for which the limited partnership was formed. The limited partner merely puts up the capital by buying units (usually equal to $5,000 or $10,000) in the limited partnership. His or her liability is limited to the amount of cash invested.

In real estate tax shelters, the at-risk provision does not apply. That is, a limited partner in a real estate tax shelter may deduct losses incurred by the partnership in excess of the aggregate amount with respect to which the partner is at risk (his or her equity investment) during the tax year. A limited partner can, therefore, invest, say, $5,000, sign a nonrecourse note for $50,000, and be able to take a tax loss on the $55,000 although nothing is pledged against the $50,000 note.[6]

If the accelerated deductions the first year come to $15,000, for example, the investor in the 50 percent tax bracket would save $7,500 ($15,000 × 0.50) on the tax. This sum is 150 percent of the original investment. This means that after the first year of the investment's life, the investor has no money (equity) at-risk but can still take deductions against future income for tax purposes, although his or her obligation to the partnership is limited to the initial investment. The at-risk provision accounts for the great demand for real estate tax shelters as compared with other tax shelters, all of which are subject to the at-risk provision.

A limited partnership has a limited life span. The date the partnership is scheduled to end is specified at the time of its formation. On that day, the property is sold, the partnership ends, and the proceeds are distributed to the partners in accordance with each individual's proportionate share in the partnership.

The Subchapter S Corporation allows for a flow-through accounting, that is, profits and losses realized by the corporation are claimed by the owners of the corporation on their tax returns. The Subchapter S Corporation is thus, in general, not taxed as a separate legal entity.

To qualify for a Subchapter S Corporation, the following conditions must be met:

1. The number of original stockholders cannot exceed 25.
2. Stockholders must be individuals, estates, and certain types of trusts.
3. Subchapter S Corporations can issue only one class of stock.

---

[5] There are seven ways of owning real estate: individual ownership, concurrent ownership (e.g., joint tenancy), general partnership, limited partnership, regular corporation, Subchapter S Corporation, and trust.

[6] A nonrecourse loan increases the cost basis of the investment and is collectible out of the value of the properties.

4. The maximum percentage of gross income coming from passive investment (such as dividends) cannot exceed 20 percent. Foreign income is limited to 80 percent.
5. Allocation of profits or losses can be made only in accordance with stock ownership.

The preferred organizational form of real estate tax shelter has, however, been the limited partnership. The reason is that a limited partnership allows for flow-through accounting. The losses of the partnership become the losses of the partners and hence are tax-deductible. Also, a limited partnership is preferred to a corporation of the Subchapter S type because the latter has a maximum number of stockholders (currently 25), while the number of limited partners has no ceiling; also, the excess of losses over the partner's basis in the partnership interest can be tax-deductible under a limited partnership arrangement if the limited partner commits additional capital equal to the excess, while this excess is lost permanently under a Subchapter S arrangement despite the fact that a Subchapter S corporation allows for flow-through accounting.

The Workings of a Real Estate Tax Shelter.   The manner in which real estate investment provides a tax shelter can be summarized by these basic steps:

Rental income	XXXX
− Operating expenses	XXXX
Net operating income	XXX
− Mortgage payments (principal + interest)	XXX
Cash flow	XXX
+ Principal (principal payments are not tax deductible)	XXX
Adjusted cash flows	XXX
− Depreciation allowance (usually at an accelerated rate)	XXX
Taxable income	**XXX**

The tax shelter provided by a real estate investment is equal to net operating income minus taxable income. The key ingredients of the tax shelter are, therefore, the interest expenses and the depreciation expenses.

It is likely that in the early years of a real estate investment the taxable income will be negative because of the high depreciation expenses due to accelerated depreciation. This may be so while net cash flow is positive. This negative taxable income is deductible from the taxpayer's ordinary income up to the size of the latter.

If the investment in the real estate venture were financed by debt, the maximum interest payments deductible from ordinary income would be limited to $10,000 plus net investment income. Amounts that are disallowed in a given year may be carried forward indefinitely and applied against future incomes.

A real estate tax shelter also provides for the transformation of ordinary income into capital gains. An investor who committed $20,000 to a real estate tax shelter and was able to take depreciation deductions equal to $14,000 (which reduce ordinary income by the same amount and hence reduce ordinary income taxes) has an adjusted cost basis of $20,000 − $14,000 = $6,000. If the interest in the property is sold for $20,000, the $14,000 profits (20,000 − 6,000) will be taxed as a capital gain if straight-line depreciation is used. If accelerated depreciation were used, on the other hand, complete recapture of all prior depreciation deductions is required and the balance, if any and if positive, is taxed as capital gains. This is true if the underlying property is a nonresidential real property.

If the underlying property is a residential property, the $14,000 will be taxed as ordinary income unless the property was held for 200 months or more.[7] Had the property been sold for $25,000, the gain would be $19,000. The first $14,000 will be considered as a depreciation recapture and thus is taxable as ordinary income, but the remaining $5,000 [$25,000 (sale price) minus $20,000 (purchase price)] would be taxed as capital gain even if the property is a residential property and is held for less than 200 months.

While the advantages of real estate tax shelters are numerous, interested investors must also incorporate the disadvantages in evaluating their prospects. General economic conditions—local economic conditions in particular—exert a significant influence on real estate values and hence on the prospects of the tax shelter; renters may move out or may default on their rent liabilities; management of the tax shelter may be incompetent, unscrupulous, or both; and the real estate tax shelter has a built-in weakness resulting from lower depreciation and interest deductions as the life of the investment increases. A real estate tax shelter is a vanishing tax shelter. This may account for the short holding periods of real estate tax shelter units as investors seek larger and larger shelters.

Oil and Gas Tax Shelters

Oil and gas tax shelters operate on the same principle as real estate tax shelters. They are normally organized as limited partnerships and produce a tax shelter to the limited partner from the following major deductions from income:

1. Intangible drilling expenses of oil or gas wells, up to 80 percent of the value of the investment, are deductible from ordinary income. The 1976 Tax Reform Act requires, however, that this deduction be recaptured upon the sale of the property and taxed as ordinary income. The recapture is equal to the actual deduction minus that amount equal to the amortization of capitalized intangible drilling costs over the useful life of the well.

2. The oil depletion allowance excludes 22 percent of gross income from the well from taxation. This exclusion cannot exceed 50 percent of the investor's taxable income, however.

3. Depreciation on the tangible equipment used in exploration and promotion reduces taxable income.

Oil and gas tax shelters also allow the investor to transform ordinary income into capital gains and hence to reduce the tax liability. This is achieved through the sale of the interest in the well after a one-year holding period.

Oil and gas investments fall into three main categories: producing property when producing wells already exist, development drilling near producing wells, and exploratory

---

[7] The rule since 1975 is that ordinary gain is recognized to the extent that accelerated depreciation exceeds the straight-line depreciation.

drilling in previously unproductive areas. These categories have differing risks and tax shelter characteristics and thus are suitable only for certain portfolios.

All oil and gas tax shelters carry considerable risk, which is due to the following factors:

1. A limited success rate in the discovery of oil or gas. Only one in ten drills finds oil. Even if a discovery is made, only about 15 percent of the wells prove commercially viable.

2. Oil and gas deals tend to attract more than their fair share of unscrupulous operators, and the prospect of a "major oil discovery" makes many investors particularly vulnerable. Experts recommend that the general partner be closely scrutinized as to experience and potential conflict of interest.

3. Oil and gas production is subject to strict environmental regulations and to stiff competition for labor and materials.

4. The size of the tax shelter is not very large considering the average size of the intangible drilling costs and the depletion allowance. In any case, the size of the tax shelter is limited to the amount of money at risk.

5. Units in oil and gas shelters are not very liquid. Their transferability requires the consent of the general partner.

The advantages and disadvantages of tax shelters must be carefully weighed. Tax shelters should be considered on the merits of the underlying investment and not solely on the basis of the tax benefits they are likely to produce. An investor in the 50 percent tax bracket who loses $100 in a tax shelter program can surely deduct it from ordinary income and save $50 in current taxes. The risk-averse investor, however, laments the other $50, which represents a reduction in wealth.

Gift Taxes

A gift tax is a tax imposed on property transfers of all kinds: tangible or intangible, business or nonbusiness, present or future interest in property or income therefrom, etc.

The issues in property transfers are occasionally complex and do not always have standard answers. They are as follows:

1. The determination of what constitutes a gift. For a transfer of property to constitute a gift, no control over the property can be exercised by the donor and the transfer must be final. A sale of property at substantially below market value can constitute a gift and thus is subject to a gift tax.

2. The determination of the market value of the property being transferred. If future income from a property is being transferred, the present value of the income stream will be subject to gift tax.

3. The determination of the taxable portion of the value of the transferred property.

The Economic Recovery Tax Act of 1981 allows the following exclusions from the gift tax:

1. An individual may give up to $10,000 per year per person, without limit, without incurring a gift tax.

TABLE 18.1
Unified Tax Credit Provided by Economic Recovery Tax Act of 1981

Transfers Made and Decedents Dying in	Unified Credit	Amount of Transfers Not Taxed	Lowest Tax Bracket Rate
1982	$ 62,800	$225,000	32%
1983	79,300	275,000	34
1984	96,300	325,000	34
1985	121,800	400,000	34
1986	155,800	500,000	37
1987 and later	192,800	600,000	37

2. Effective Jan. 1, 1982, whatever one spouse gives or leaves to the other will not be subject to gift tax.

3. An individual may give up to $20,000 a year if income splitting is chosen, that is, if his or her spouse concurs with the decision to transfer $20,000 in property. The $10,000 goes to each spouse if different individuals receive the gift, although one spouse owns all the property being transferred.

4. A husband and wife are entitled to a combined maximum deduction of $20,000 per year per donee even if only one spouse owned the property being transferred.

5. If a gift in excess of $10,000 ($20,000, depending on the circumstances) is made, the excess is taxable. No tax may be paid, however, because of the unified credit of $47,000. The tax on the excess gift is applied against the credit until the credit is exhausted.

The Economic Recovery Tax Act of 1981 increases the unified tax credit as shown in Table 18.1.

The taxable portion of every gift, however, must be included in the estate and the applicable tax paid. The estate tax and the gift tax have been unified under the Tax Reform Act of 1976.

The taxability of the excess gift as part of the estate should not discourage making the gift now for the following reasons:

1. The recipient is likely to be in a lower tax bracket than the donor.
2. Any postgift appreciation in the value of the property is not subject to transfer tax.
3. If the gift is later included in the estate, it is valued as of the time of the gift and not at its current market value.

These advantages must be tempered, however, by considerations involving the time value of money. If a gift tax is owed now, it must be paid now. If less property is transferred, the tax will be postponed and paid later in the form of an estate tax.

Gifts to charitable, religious, literary, educational, and scientific organizations must be reported if they exceed $10,000. If the donor retains the use of the property while still alive (the use of a house donated to a university, for example), the donation is still exempt (except for the value of the retained life estate) provided that the will contains a provision guaranteeing the transfer of said property upon death.

A husband or wife may give his or her spouse any amount in gifts without incurring

TABLE 18.2
Tax Rates Applicable to Gifts and Estates

A Exceeding	B But not Exceeding	Tax on Amount in Column A	Tax Rate on Amount in Excess of Column A, Percent
$ 0	$ 10,000	—	18%
10,000	20,000	$ 1,800	20
20,000	40,000	3,800	22
40,000	60,000	8,200	24
60,000	80,000	13,000	26
80,000	100,000	18,200	28
100,000	150,000	23,800	30
150,000	250,000	38,800	32
250,000	500,000	70,800	34
500,000	750,000	155,800	37
750,000	1,100,000	248,300	39
1,100,000	1,250,000	345,800	41
1,250,000	1,500,000	448,300	43
1,500,000	2,000,000	555,800	45
2,000,000	2,500,000	780,800	49
2,500,000	3,000,000	1,025,800	53
3,000,000	3,500,000	1,290,800	57
3,500,000	4,000,000	1,575,800	61
4,000,000	4,500,000	1,880,000	65
4,500,000	5,000,000	2,205,800	69
5,000,000	—	2,550,800	70

Column headings: Amounts Subject to Tax (A, B)

gift or estate tax. The elimination of all the quantitative restrictions on transfer of property between spouses was affected by the Economic Recovery Tax Act of 1981.

The tax rates applicable to gifts and to estates are shown in Table 18.2.

The Economic Recovery Tax Act reduces the unified tax rate from a maximum of 70 percent to 50 percent over a four-year period, as shown in Table 18.3.

It is highly recommended that a systematic gift program using joint gifts, if possible, be established as part of an overall financial plan. The personal needs and preferences of the donor and the maturity and competence of the donee must be kept in mind, however.

TABLE 18.3
Unified Tax Rate According to Economic Recovery Tax Act of 1981

Transfers Made and Decedents Dying in	Top-Bracket Rate	Top-Bracket Amount in Excess of
1982	65%	$4,000,000
1983	60	3,500,000
1984	55	3,000,000
1985 and later	50	2,500,000

Estate Tax

The estate tax is a tax on the right to transfer property upon death.

The cost basis of the property transferred at death is its fair market value on the day of the decedent's death.

An estate includes the following items:

1. Everything owned by the decedent.
2. All taxable gifts made by the decedent during his or her lifetime.
3. All gifts over which the decedent had control.

These items represent the gross value of the estate. From this value the following are deductible:

1. Funeral expenses.
2. Debt at the time of death.
3. Expenses for the administration of the estate.
4. Legal expenses.
5. Certain losses.
6. Charitable contributions.
7. Marital deductions. By the end of 1981, half of the adjusted gross estate (which includes items 1 through 5 above or $250,000, whichever is larger) was deductible from the taxable estate. The Economic Recovery Tax Act of 1981 changes this provision. Effective in 1982, an unlimited marital deduction is allowed for estate and gift tax purposes.

The gross estate minus the deductions equals the taxable estate. The applicable tax rates are shown in Table 18.1. Against the tax liability, certain credits can be taken: (1) a unified credit of $47,000, (see Table 18.1 for future unified credits) and (2) credits for state death taxes and federal gift taxes previously paid.

The issue of what is included in the gross estate can be complex at times. The complication results, among other things, from having to determine what is jointly or individually owned; the nature of the life insurance policy; and the nature of the pension plan, stock plan, or profit-sharing plan the decedent had participated in. Annuities from a qualified retirement plan are excluded except to the extent of the decedent's past contributions to the plan. Proceeds from a life insurance policy are *not* included in the estate if the wife is made the owner as well as the beneficiary of the estate more than three years prior to death.

It is apparent by now that competent legal advice should be sought to handle estate matters.

We now offer an example of estate tax calculations.

Example

When John Alive passed away (June 1, 1981), he left a will specifying that all property should pass to his wife except $20,000 for his alma mater. John had given $200,000 in taxable gifts prior to June 1, 1978, but after December 31, 1976. The gift tax paid on these was $40,000. The estate tax is calculated as follows:

Gross Estate

Cars (3)	$ 17,000
Residences	190,000
Stocks and bonds	200,000
Life insurance	350,000
Checking and savings accounts	12,000
Gross estate	$769,000

Taxable Gifts

Donated after 12/31/76	$200,000	
Taxable estate		**$969,000**

Deductions

Total debt (mortgage, credit cards, etc.)	$ 62,000	
Funeral expenses	4,500	
Executor and legal fees	10,000	
Total	$ 76,500	
Marital deduction		
(($969,000 − $76,500) (0.50))[8]	$446,250	
Contributions to alma mater	20,000	
Total deductions		$542,750
Amount subject to tax		**$426,250**

Estate Tax (Table 18.1)

Estate tax before credits		
70,800 + (445,850 − 250,000) (0.34)		$130,725
less Unified credit	$ 47,000	
Gift taxes on post-1976 gifts	40,000	
Inheritance tax (depends	20,000	
on the stock—we use an		
estimated figure)		
Total credits		$107,000
Net estate tax owed		**$ 23,725**

18.8 FINANCIAL PLANNING

The topics discussed in the previous sections have a strong influence on the financial welfare (if not also the physical welfare) of the individual (and his or her family) during the working years and beyond. We shall attempt to integrate the concepts introduced earlier into a unified comprehensive financial plan which takes into consideration the needs of the individual and family before and after retirement.

Our focus will be on a forty-year-old physician who is married and has two children: a boy of six and a girl of four. Our financial plan begins on Jan. 1, 1980. The doctor's current earnings are $85,000, with half derived from private practice and the other

---

[8] In 1982 and beyond, if a spouse dies leaving a will transferring all the property to the surviving spouse, the $969,000 estate will not be taxable. If the will specifies that 50 percent, for example, of the estate should pass to the wife, the calculations above would apply.

half from a local hospital, and his income is expected to grow at a compounded rate of 8 percent. He expects to send his two children to college when they complete high school at the age of eighteen, expects to retire at age sixty, and hopes to leave a minimum estate of $2 million to his family. The medical history of the doctor's family allows him to think in terms of an 80-year life span for himself. Upon retirement, he wishes to have an income of $50,000 a year for the rest of his life, or about 20 years. The doctor's current assets consist of the following:

1. A suburban home valued at $185,000. The mortgage on the property will be completely paid off in 20 years. The monthly mortgage payment is equal to $1,000.
2. A savings account of $12,000.
3. A portfolio of securities valued (current market prices) at $15,000.
4. A life insurance policy for $200,000.
5. Jewelry and other precious items valued at $30,000.

Our objective is to develop a financial plan for the doctor consistent with his objectives and with his risk profile.

We begin with a review of each of the securities held in the portfolio and make the appropriate sell/buy decisions, if any. The resulting portfolio must be consistent with the doctor's risk characteristics and must be efficient in a Markowitz sense.

The next step is the life insurance policy. The current policy is clearly inadequate. In the event of the doctor's death, his family will have about two years of income to live on. It is, therefore, recommended that the insurance coverage be increased to five times (the minimum standard multiple) current income or to about $400,000.

Planning for College

One year of college education is expected to cost $20,000 in the year 1992. It is expected that tuition costs will rise at an annual compound rate of 10 percent. The doctor expects that half the college costs will be paid by the children themselves through summer employment and various scholarship programs.

The net college costs and their present value in 1992 are shown in Table 18.4. The doctor's objective, therefore, is to systematically accumulate sufficient funds in order to meet the $68,404 expenditures. Assuming that the doctor is in the 50 percent tax bracket and that the average return on investments is currently 12 percent and is expected to continue into the foreseeable future, the following options present themselves:

Option 1
The $68,404 could be thought of as the future value FV of an annuity of A. Therefore

$$FV = A \sum_{t=1}^{n} (1 + K)^t \tag{18.1}$$

where $\sum_{t=1}^{n} (1 + K)^t$ = compound value interest factor (CVIF)

K = interest-rate factor = before-tax rate of return = 12 percent

n = time horizon = 12 years

Let K_T = after-tax rate of return

TABLE 18.4
Expected College Costs

Date	Cost/ Person	Children's Expected Income and Scholarship	Net Educational Costs	Total Educational Expenses by the Doctor	PVDF[a]	Present Value of Educational Expenses in 1992
Jan. 1992	$20,000	$10,000	$10,000	$10,000	1.000	$10,000
1993	21,000	10,500	10,500	10,500	.893	9,377
1994	22,050	11,025	11,025	22,050 }[b]	.797	17,574
1995	23,153	11,577	11,577	23,153 }	.712	16,485
1996	24,310	12,155	12,155	12,155	.636	7,731
1997	25,525	12,763	12,763	12,763	.567	7,237
Total educational funds needed						**$68,404**

[a] PVDF = present value discount factor.
[b] Overlap period when both children are in school.

Therefore $K_T = K(1 - T)$

$$K_T = 12(1 - 0.5) = 6\%$$

where T = personal tax rate

= 50% (here)

From Equation 18.1, we find that

$$A = \frac{FV}{\sum_{t=1}^{n} (1 + K)^t} \text{ or } A = \frac{FV}{\sum_{t=1}^{n} (1 + K_T)^t} \tag{18.2}$$

The $A represent the annual saving (contribution) which, if invested at an after-tax rate of 6 percent, will produce a sum equal to $68,404.

$$A = \frac{68,404}{CVIF_{12,6\%}} = \frac{68,404}{16.870} = \$4,054.77$$

where $12,6\% = 12$ years at 6 percent interest

The doctor must, therefore, invest $4,054.77 each year for 12 years in order to meet the educational expenses of his children assuming that the realized after-tax rate of return is equal to the expected.

Option 2

The gift tax law, discussed earlier, allows $10,000 of gift to each person (no limit on the number of persons) per year without incurring gift tax. If the doctor makes a gift of $6,000 annually to his children, it would effectively shift the tax burden (on the income earned) from the father to the donees, with the father having fiduciary responsibility over the donated funds if desired. The $20,000 in maximum nontaxable gifts currently permitted would, if used, seriously disrupt the doctor's budget and living standards; thus our choice to use the old limit ($3,000 per donee, or $6,000 per donee if a joint gift is made) to allow some room for maneuver at least for the immediate future. The doctor could later decide to be more generous with his children and possibly use the limit allowed by law. Assuming that the applicable tax rate to the children is 20 percent, the effective after-tax rate of return would equal

$$K_T = 12(1 - 0.2) = 9.6 \text{ percent}$$

At this rate, the annual savings requirement for the education of the children would equal

$$A = \frac{68,404}{\text{CVIF}_{12,9.6\%}} = \frac{68,404}{20.890} = \$3,274.49$$

The remainder (\$6,000 − \$3,274.49 = \$2,725.51) could be used by the children to accumulate their own personal wealth and eventually to reduce the work burden necessary to meet the full education expenditures. The reinvestment of the \$2,725.51 will bring additional tax saving as the income is reported by the children instead of the father.

Option 3: Clifford Trust

A Clifford Trust is an irrevocable trust set up for a limited objective and having a limited life exceeding ten years. This form of trust allows parents to borrow the present value of the education costs of their children, secured by existing assets, and to contribute funds to the trust that, they hope, will accumulate at the desired rate to meet the anticipated expenses. The trust requires, however, that the income from the trust be distributed *currently* to the children if they so demand. Also, upon its termination (after ten years), the original contribution to the trust must be returned to the parents. The college expenses are then met by withdrawals of sufficient funds as needed. The trust ends when the beneficiaries reach college age or upon the beneficiaries' death or when the trust's life expires, whichever occurs first. Income from the trust is taxable to the trust if not distributed to the beneficiaries (\$600 deduction is allowed) and to the beneficiaries if distributed.

The size of the borrowed funds could be either of the following:

1. The present value of the required \$68,404. The accumulated value of this principal should meet the educational expenditures beginning in 1992, although the principal will have reverted back to the parents.

$$\text{PV} = 68,404 \left[\frac{1}{(1 + 0.096)^{12}} \right] = 68,404 \times 0.334 = \$22,847$$

2. Borrow \$68,404 and place in trust so that this full amount will revert back to the parents upon the expiration of the trust.

3. Borrow the necessary funds such that the accumulated compounded earnings will equal \$68,404 in 12 years.

The determination of the amount to be borrowed is done as follows:

Let X = amount borrowed

$$X(1 + K_T)^t = X + 68,404$$

where $K_T = 9.5\%$, the interest rate
          $t = 12$, the life of the trust

$$X(1 + K_T)^t - X = 68,404$$
$$X[(1 + K_T)^t - 1] = 68,404$$

$$X = 68,404 \left[\frac{1}{(1 + K_T)^t - 1} \right]$$

Dividing by $(1 + K_T)^t$,

$$X = 68,404 \left\{ \frac{1/(1 + K_T)^t}{[(1 + K_T)^t/(1 + K_T)^t] - [1/(1 + K_T)^t]} \right\}$$

$$X = 68,404 \left\{ \frac{[1/(1 + K_T)^t}{1 - [1/(1 + K_T)^t]} \right\}$$

$$X = 68,404 \left[\frac{\text{PVDF}_{12,9.6\%}}{1 - \text{PVDF}_{12,9.6\%}} \right]$$

$$X = 68,404 \left[\frac{0.334}{1 - 0.334} \right]$$

$$= \$34,305$$

The choice between the three alternatives depends on the relative cost of each and its affordability in terms of the doctor's income. The second alternative, borrowing $68,404, requires the largest annual payments of interest and principal; $983/month $\times$ 12 = $11,796 at a borrowing rate of 14 percent. Since interest payments are tax-deductible, the interest portion of the $11,796, or $8,400, would constitute a tax shelter. In addition, the income from $68,404 would be taxed at the assumed 20 percent instead of the 50 percent rate. The advantages consist, therefore, of the tax shelter derived from interest expenses and from shifting the interest income from the doctor to the trust. The problem with this alternative, however, is its affordability. The $11,796 represents 11,796/85,000 = 13.87% of the doctor's current income. Allowing for the tax deductibility of interest, the cost as percent of income would be [(11,796 − 8,400) + 8,400(0.50)]/85,000 = 8.93%. This percent is still excessive considering the doctor's other commitments. The choice, therefore, is the third alternative, which calls for borrowing $34,305 at 14 percent, and an annual payment of 493/month $\times$ 12 = $5,916.

Choosing Among the Options

The first option calls for an annual contribution of $4,055 with no subsequent reduction in estate taxes due to the interim reduction in the value of the estate through gifts.

The second option clearly dominates the first. It calls for lower (required) contributions and provides for potential savings on estate taxes. The only concern is with the issue of control over the resources as funds are donated by the doctor to his children.

The third option which calls for borrowing and contributing $34,305 to a Clifford trust requires, assuming *annual* (for ease of exposition) payments of principal and interest

TABLE 18.5
Amortization of $34,305 Loan Contributed to a Clifford Trust

	(1)	(2)	(3)	(4)	(5)	(6)	(7)
Year	Annual Payment	Principal	Interest	After-Tax Interest Costs (3) × (1 − 0.5)	Net Contribution (2) + (4)	PVDF	PV or Net Contribution (5) × (6)
1	6,061	1,258	4,803	2401.5	3659.5	.912	3,337.46
2	6,061	1,434	4,627	2313.5	3747.5	.832	3,117.92
3	6,061	1,635	4,426	2213.0	3848.	.759	2,920.63
4	6,061	1,864	4,197	2098.5	3962.5	.693	2,746.01
5	6,061	2,125	3,936	1968.	4093.0	.633	2,590.87
6	6,061	2,422	3,639	1819.5	4241.5	.577	2,447.34
7	6,061	2,762	3,299	1649.5	4411.5	.527	2,324.86
8	6,061	3,148	2,913	1456.5	4604.5	.481	2,214.76
9	6,061	3,588	2,473	1236.5	4824.5	.438	2,113.13
10	6,061	4,091	1,970	985.	5076.0	.400	2,030.40
11	6,061	4,763	1,398	699.	5462.0	.365	1,993.63
12	6,061	5,316	745	372.5	5688.5	.333	1,894.27
			Present value of total contributions				**$29,731.28**

at 14 percent, an annual payment (interest and principal) of $6,061 (a higher value than the $5,916 resulting from monthly payments). The distribution of the payments between interest and principal is shown in Table 18.5. The present value of all the contributions is equal to $29,731.28. This must be reduced by the present value of the sum, $34,305, that the doctor will receive in 12 years. That value is equal to

$$PV = 34,305(0.333) = \$11,423.56$$

The net contribution under option 3 is then equal to: 29,731.28 − 11,423.56 = $18,307.72.

The present value of the $3,274.49 annual contribution under option 2, using a 9.6 percent discount rate, is equal to 3,274.49(6.953) = 22,767.529. This sum must be subtracted from the savings on estate taxes.

According to the values calculated above, the doctor should choose option 3. Option 2, however, may still be the choice, depending on the personal biases of the doctor. We shall use the option 2 figures in the calculations to come on the basis that personal considerations could be more important than raw figures.

Planning for Retirement

Having decided that the desired level of retirement income is $50,000 per year, the doctor is concerned with the optimum way of achieving it. One source of retirement income is currently available to the doctor: social security. The doctor can also count on his savings. We shall also recommend another source of retirement income—a Keogh plan to be set up now for the income generated from private practice and from the hospital.[9]

The present value of the required retirement income at age sixty, given that the doctor's life expectancy is 80 years, is equal to

$$PV = 50,000 \sum_{t=1}^{n} \frac{1}{(1 + K)^t}$$

For $K = 12\%$, $PV = 50,000(7.469) = \$373,450$

The financial plan should be so structured so as to produce \$373,450 in 20 years. We start our analysis with the social security benefits.

Social Security

The status of social security benefits is currently under examination by the Reagan administration. We shall, therefore, deal with social security benefits as currently calculated, leaving potential changes for speculators.

To qualify for full social security benefits, a worker must be in the program for a specified period of time. The maximum time required for anyone is ten years, or 40 quarters of coverage. Assuming an average working life of 40 years, the worker must be under the social security program for about one-fourth of the time from age twenty-one (or 1950, whichever is later). In 1981, a quarter of coverage is earned for each \$310 of wages paid, with a maximum of four earned quarters per year.

The benefits from the Social Security System, assuming the individual qualifies, are a function of the worker's earnings and of the continuity of work under the Social Security System. The formula for calculating the benefits is weighted more heavily in favor of workers with low average earnings. These workers get a larger percentage of their earnings in social security benefits. Social security benefits can only begin at age sixty-two. If the worker wishes to retire at age sixty-two—that is, prior to the "normal" retirement age of sixty-five—he or she is penalized by a benefit reduction of 0.2536 of 1 percent for every month of retirement prior to age sixty-five.

The maximum monthly income from social security, given that the individual has earned at least \$29,700 per year during the qualifying years is currently \$650. The

---

[9] The assumptions here are as follows:
  1. The doctor is not a common-law employee of the hospital but a contract employee. That is, he provides services to the hospital and his incorporated practice bills the hospital for the costs of the services provided. This, therefore, does not allow the doctor to participate in any group retirement plan in the hospital. Had the doctor been a regular (full- or part-time) employee, he would have qualified for the group pension plan, have been able to contribute 4 percent (a taxable contribution) of his income at the hospital toward his retirement, and have been able to set up a tax shelter annuity program which would have allowed for the following:
     a. An annual tax-deductible contribution of up to *20 percent* of the income derived from the hospital
     b. the right to change the size of the contribution once a year in accordance with the doctor's financial needs
     c. the right to withdraw the funds without penalty at any time
  2. The Keogh is the most suitable retirement plan for the doctor. The 15 percent maximum contribution applies to earned income from the hospital and from private practice.

doctor, we assume, qualifies for this maximum. If the annual inflation rate is 10 percent for the next 22 years, and accounting for the penalty for early retirement, the doctor should expect to receive:

$$PV = (12)[650 - (650)(0.002536 \times 36 \text{ months})] \sum_{t=1}^{n} \frac{(1+f)^t}{(1+K)^t}$$

where f = inflation adjustment factor resulting from the indexing of the social security payments = an assumed 10%

K = discount factor = 12%

t = 18 years (the difference between 80 years and the earliest allowable retirement of 62)

The formula assumes also that the social security payments are received once a year. This is so in order to facilitate the analysis. Hence, the multiplication by 12. Therefore

$$PV = (12)(590.65)\left(\sum_{t=1}^{n} \frac{(1+0.10)^t}{(1+0.12)^t}\right)$$

$$= 7,087.80 \frac{\text{CVIF}_a}{\text{PVDF}_a} = 7,087.80 \left(\frac{45.599}{7.250}\right)$$

$$= \$44,580$$

This is the present value at age sixty-two. At age sixty, the desired retirement age, the sum shrinks further.

$$PV \text{ (year 2,000)} = \frac{\$44,580}{(1+0.12)^2} = \$44,580(0.797) = \$35,530$$

At this point the doctor is still far short of the $373,450 he needs to ensure the desired retirement income.

Income from Keogh

The maximum contribution to a Keogh plan cannot exceed 15 percent of earned income or $15,000, whichever is lower. Considering the doctor's current income, commitments, and desired standard of living, the 15 percent, $15,000 maximum deduction is out of the question for the first five years at least; thus our decision to follow the old rule allowing a maximum of $7,500. The contributions are shown in Table 18.6, in the third column. At the age of sixty, the accumulated sum (FV) is equal (assuming a 12 percent rate of return) to

$$FV = 7,500 \text{ (CVIF}_{a, 20 \text{ yr.}}) = 7,500(72.052) = \$540,390$$

This sum alone far exceeds the financial requirements for retirement. It requires, however, a saving rate of 21.24 percent (Table 18.6) in the first year of the implementation of a Keogh plan. The doctor may choose to spend more than the current plan allows. The choice, therefore, is between

TABLE 18.6
Requisite Retirement Data

		(1)	(2)	(3)	(4)	(5)
Age	Year	Income, Private[a]	Income, Hospital	Keogh[b]	Deductions and Exemptions (5% Growth Rate)	Contribution for College Education
40	80					
1	1	42,500	42,500	(7,500)	(12,500)	(3,275)
2	2	45,900	45,900	(7,500)	(13,125)	(3,275)
3	3	49,572	49,572	(7,500)	(13,781)	(3,275)
4	4	53,538	53,538	(7,500)	(14,470)	(3,275)
45	85	57,821	57,821	(7,500)	(15,194)	(3,275)
6	6	62,447	62,447	(7,500)	(15,953)	(3,275)
7	7	67,442	67,442	(7,500)	(16,751)	(3,275)
8	8	72,838	72,838	(7,500)	(17,589)	(3,275)
9	9	78,665	78,665	(7,500)	(18,468)	(3,275)
50	90	84,958	84,958	(7,500)	(19,391)	(3,275)
1	1	91,755	91,755	(7,500)	(20,361)	(3,275)
2	2	99,095	99,095	(7,500)	(21,379)	(3,275)
3	3	107,022	107,022	(7,500)	(22,448)	(3,275)
4	4	115,584	115,584	(7,500)	(23,571)	(3,275)
55	95	124,831	124,831	(7,500)	(24,479)	(3,275)
6	6	134,817	134,817	(7,500)	(25,987)	(3,275)
7	7	145,603	145,603	(7,500)	(27,286)	(3,275)
8	8	157,251	157,251	(7,500)	(28,650)	(3,275)
9	9	169,831	169,831	(7,500)	(30,083)	(3,275)
60	00	183,418	183,418	(7,500)	(31,587)	(3,275)

[a] Based on standard percentages from 1980 tax returns.

[b] This contribution is in addition to that made by the hospital in the group pension plan. The reported amount is 15 percent of income or $7,500, whichever is lower.

1. Reducing annual contributions in order to increase current spendable income. This is necessary for the first 5 years at most.
2. Letting the contributions stand and using the excess to increase the value of the estate.

We shall, henceforth, assume that the doctor is willing to make short-run sacrifices. Our reason is that life expectancy is just an expectation. An early and substantial saving program is thus desirable. The doctor, should he achieve his life expectancy, will have all the excess income he needs to satisfy his pent up demand.

The total retirement income including social security benefits is equal to

$540,390 + $35,530 = $575,920

The excess over the requisite retirement income is equal to

$575,920 − $373,450 = $202,470

(6)	(7)	(8)	(9)	(10)	(11)	(12)
Total Deductions from Income (3) + (4)	Taxable Income [(1) + (2)] − (6)	Income After Tax (7)(1 − 0.5)	Total Regular Saving (3) + (5)	Tax Saving from Keogh (3)(0.50)	Actual Saving Required (9) − (10)	Actual Saving as Percent of Income (11)/7
(18,875)	66,125	33,062.5	10,775	3,750	7,025	21.24%
(20,010)	71,790	35,895.	10,775	3,750	7,025	19.57
(21,217)	77,927	38,963.5	10,775	3,750	7,025	18.03
(21,970)	85,106	42,553.	10,775	3,750	7,025	16.51
(22,694)	92,998	46,474.	10,775	3,750	7,025	15.11
(23,453)	101,441	50,720.5	10,775	3,750	7,025	13.85
(24,251)	110,663	55,331.5	10,775	3,750	7,025	12.70
(25,089)	120,587	60,293.5	10,775	3,750	7,025	11.65
(25,968)	131,362	65,681.	10,775	3,750	7,025	10.70
(27,431)	142,458	71,229.	10,775	3,750	7,025	9.86
(27,861)	155,644	77,824.5	10,775	3,750	7,025	9.03
(28,879)	169,311	84,655.5	10,775	3,750	7,025	8.30
(29,948)	184,096	92,048.	10,775	3,750	7,025	7.63
(31,071)	200,097	100,048.5	10,775	3,750	7,025	7.02
(31,979)	217,683	108,841.5	10,775	3,750	7,025	6.45
(33,487)	236,146	118,073.5	10,775	3,750	7,025	5.95
(34,786)	256,420	128,210.	10,775	3,750	7,025	5.48
(36,150)	278,352	139,176.	10,775	3,750	7,025	5.05
(37,583)	302,099	151,049.5	10,775	3,750	7,025	4.65
(39,089)	327,749	163,874.5	10,775	3,750	7,025	4.29

The accumulation of this sum at an after-tax rate of only 4 percent (distributions from a Keogh plan are taxable) will produce

$$\$202,470 \times 2.191(CVIF) = \$443,612$$

This sum will be on hand at the end of the doctor's expected life in the year 2020.

Estate Planning

The doctor's objective is to leave a $2 million estate to his children. The excess over the required retirement income promises $202,470. The value of the house in 40 years, with an average appreciation of 5 percent a year, would contribute an additional sum of

$$\$185,000 \, (CVIF) = \$185,000 \, (7.04) = \$1,302,400$$

The required accumulation of savings to meet the targeted value of the estate is, therefore, equal to

$$\$2,000,000 - (1,302,400 + 443,612) = \$253,988$$

This sum will be covered by the insurance policy proceeds upon death: $400,000.

The doctor, faced with such prospects, should feel quite secure. Much can happen to change the circumstances or prove our assumptions incorrect and, in fact, reduce the doctor's optimism. Thus, the inclination is to continue saving above the "required" sum.

The investment of the savings should be consistent with the doctor's risk profile. The portfolio should include the following:

1. A sufficiently large number of domestic (U.S.) securities (about 15) to eliminate unsystematic risk. These securities should include stocks and bonds and some options
2. At least 10 percent of foreign-issue securities to achieve international risk diversification
3. At least 5 percent in gold and in precious stones
4. Some art work or antiques depending on the doctor's taste

All the risks and benefits associated with these investment vehicles must be kept in mind, as was explained in detail in the preceding chapters.

Other Major Considerations in Estate Planning

Planning an estate requires much more than the systematic accumulation of funds. In particular, it requires an efficient method for the transfer of funds at the time of death. This is accomplished through wills and/or trusts.

Wills

A will is a document, prepared in accordance with the laws of a state, by which a person disposes of his or her property after death. A will is not effective prior to the death of its writer, who is referred to in the legal vernacular as the testator (if male) or testatrix (if female). A will can be changed or canceled at any time by its writer.

For a will to have legal standing, it must be in writing. It requires, in addition, that the testator be of legal age and of sound mind, that the testator wrote it of his own free will and not under duress, and that the will has been signed and "witnessed."[10]

Preparing a will requires (1) nominating an executor, (2) defining the power of the executor, and (3) stating who gets the property after debts, funeral expenses, taxes, and costs of administration are paid. The term of an executor is one to three years. One or more executors of the will should be named in the event something befalls the preferred one. An executor goes to court to probate (prove) the existence and the validity of the will; distributes the designated property to the intended party or parties after funeral expenses, debts, estate taxes, and other expenses and taxes are paid; gets a court order to sell property not designated to go to named persons and distributes the proceeds in accordance with the will and the law; and has the power to buy and sell real estate. An executor can also be the trustee if the will so specifies. It is common for testators

---

[10] Unwitnessed wills have been admitted to probate (proving) in many states. Not all states admit them, and those that do set a minimum limit on the value of the property that can be passed.

to designate their banks, or their bank with their spouse, as partner of the executor and/or trustee of the estate.

The compelling reason for a will is that unless it exists,[11] the estate will be disposed of in accordance with state laws, which may not coincide with the wishes of the deceased. In some cases, in fact, the whole estate may pass to the state. A carefully prepared will can avoid these pitfalls and can, in addition, substantially reduce if not eliminate current and/or future estate taxes.

Certain individuals delude themselves in the belief that small estates and/or jointly held property (joint ownership between husband and wife) do not necessitate a will. Jointly held property may be included, in certain cases, in its entirety in the estate of the deceased and once again in the estate of the surviving spouse. Joint ownership may also reduce the flexibility in setting up certain trusts (which we discuss below) and may not allow for the fulfillment of the objectives of either spouse if they both die at the same time (an automobile accident, for example).

A simple will is sufficient for most people, particularly if the estate is to be left outright to someone. If only the benefits from the estate are to accrue for life to one person or a group of persons, if the size of the estate warrants careful tax considerations, or if the property is to be divided in a certain fashion after the death of the first beneficiary or beneficiaries, the creation of a trust must be considered.

Trusts

A trust is an instrument used for transferring property owned by the creator of the trust to a fiduciary called a trustee for the benefit of a third party, the beneficiary.

The creation of a trust requires that it be done in writing, that the creator have the legal capacity to transfer property and in fact intends to, and that both the trustee and the beneficiary be "capable" in the eyes of the law.

A trust can be set up during the life of the creator, in which case it is referred to as an inter vivo trust, or it can be established through a will, when it is called a testamentary trust.

Inter Vivo Trusts. Inter vivo trusts, also known as living trusts, are created during the grantor's lifetime. The grantor may specify himself or herself or a third party as beneficiary. They are of two types: irrevocable and revocable trusts.

Irrevocable Trusts. The creator of the irrevocable trust relinquishes any and all control over the property being transferred without any possibility of changing his or her mind or invading the corpus (the property) held in trust.

Revocable Trusts. As its name implies, a revocable trust allows the grantor to change his or her mind and to retain control over the funds. This type of trust can, under certain circumstances, produce a tax saving by shifting the benefits of the donated property from the grantor to the trust or to the beneficiary's lower tax bracket.

Testamentary Trust. A testamentary trust is created through a will. It is done usually to protect the interest of the beneficiary who may not be equipped to handle the complex estate being transferred, to protect the estate from the irresponsible tendencies of the beneficiary, and/or to minimize the payment of taxes.

---

[11] A person who dies without a will is said to have died intestate.

Trust and Financial Planning. Our focus, once again, is on the doctor whom we have used as an example earlier in this chapter. As a first step, a will is drawn consistent with the objectives of the doctor and the interests of his wife and two children.

If the assets of the estate are all in the doctor's name, they will be included in the probate settling of his estate. It is desirable to have assets avoid probate for a number of reasons. First, the cost of probate is determined by the size of the estate. If any asset can avoid probate, this cost will be reduced proportionately. Second, assets that are in probate cannot be touched until the estate has been settled. This can often lead to problems in that the surviving spouse and children may not be able to get at funds that they need during the time that it takes to settle the estate. Last, the probate estate is a matter of public record that can be viewed by anyone. The owner often wants to keep his or her financial dealings secret to the greatest degree possible.

Probate can be avoided in two ways. The first is through the use of a trust, which will be discussed in more detail below, and the other is by joint tenancy. Joint tenancy entails putting property in the names of both the husband and the wife. When one spouse dies, the property immediately and entirely vests in the survivor, and such property is not subject to probate. Due to estate tax consequences, this method should be used only to the extent necessary, with the concerns expressed earlier in mind. The assets that the doctor should put in joint ownership are the principal family residence, the car, and a sufficient dollar amount of the checking and savings accounts to cover short-term living expenses adequately.

The use of a trust for the remainder of the assets will not only avoid probate costs but can also help reduce income and estate taxes. The trust method has other advantages in that it can be used to assure the financial well-being of the remaining family and provide funds to secure the college education of the children. At the same time, it can be used to relieve the spouse and children of the burden of managing the assets, which they more than likely would not have the experience or expertise to do. Trusts can also be drafted, through provisions called spendthrift clauses, that prevent the beneficiaries of a trust from squandering the funds before an objective such as college education can be achieved. The trust can still be structured so that, in the event of an unexpected emergency, the principal (or corpus) of the trust can be invaded to cover the needed costs (sprinkling costs).

CONCLUSIONS

Financial planning requires considerable knowledge of the tax laws and investment theory and strategy as well as considerable foresight. Much of the family's future security may depend on the quality of current plans. Thus, financial planning should be done with utmost seriousness and diligence.

QUESTIONS

1. Various taxes complicate financial matters. Would financial planning be necessary in a world without taxes?

2. How do the actions of the IRS reduce the net borrowing costs of the treasury? How does this affect the real after-tax return to investors in T-bills?

3. How can shorting against the box defer a tax liability?

4. Why is the timing of a transaction in a capital asset so important?

5. Describe how a real estate tax shelter works.

6. "Life insurance leads to the creation of an immediate estate." Comment. Why is life insurance a critical part of any financial plan?

7. Discuss incentive stock options. How should an employee evaluate this and other fringe benefits vs. higher pay?

8. Outline the various types of retirement plans. What is their chief benefit? What must an individual consider before selecting a plan?

9. Assumptions made in the chapter example of the physician are, at best, estimates. What does this suggest for a retirement strategy in terms of uncertainty? What does it reveal about the nature of financial planning?

10. What are the major considerations in financial planning?

11. How do trusts facilitate wealth transfer?

12. Explain the importance of a will. Who should have one?

PROBLEMS

1. Mr. I. T. Money owns 100 shares of SAO common stock. He receives a 10 percent stock dividend. If he paid $4,000 for the 100 shares, what is the new tax basis of the shares? If he sold the stock for $38 per share, what would be his gain?

2. Mrs. Money owns 200 shares of MES stock, which she bought for $21 per share. MES now trades at $22. If the company issues one right for each share and it takes five rights to purchase a new share for $10, find the value of one right and the tax basis for the right and stock.

3. A lady who is in the 38 percent tax bracket reports the following results on security transactions for the year 1981:

Long-term capital gains	$1,500
Long-term capital losses	$ 900
Short-term capital gains	$ 100
Short-term capital losses	$ 400

Determine her tax liability on the transactions.

4. Mr. W. G. McKenna lists the following results from transactions during the year:

Long-term capital gains	$ 200
Long-term capital losses	$ 600
Short-term capital gains	$ 350
Short-term capital losses	$1,600

If his wages were $25,000, find his new taxable income.

5. An investor reports net short-term capital losses of $3,800 and net long-term capital losses of $4,300. What is the maximum deduction against income to which he is entitled? What happens to the balance of the losses beyond the allowable deduction? Repeat the problem if the net short-term capital losses had been $1,800.

6. Mr. Noah Lott bought 100 shares of Uxxen stock 11 months ago for $40 per share. The stock now trades at $58, and Mr. Lott feels that Uxxen will advance no further. Outline a strategy for him to lock in his profit yet retain ownership of the share for another month, making his gain long-term.

7. Mr. Lew Zuhr bought 100 shares of Daring Corp. stock at $35. It now trades at $18; he has held the stock for ten months. If he feels the stock will not recover in the near future, what would you recommend in terms of a tax strategy: sell now or later? What are the possible drawbacks to your recommendation?

8. A young golf pro, Longen Strait, has realized a $17,000 long-term capital gain on a shrewd purchase and sale of antiques. He also owns 100 shares of Sleazy Co. stock selling at $23, which is $30 below the price at which he bought the stock three months ago. On Dec. 10, he wants to determine whether to sell the stock now or wait until next year. He feels that the stock will remain static for the next six months. Which strategy will lower his tax burden if no other transactions have occurred or are anticipated in the near future? What is the taxable income under each strategy? What other considerations may come to bear on the decision?

APPENDIX

Mathematical Tables

TABLE 1. Compound Sum of $1 (CIF)

Period	1%	2%	3%	4%	5%	6%	7%
1	1.010	1.020	1.030	1.040	1.050	1.060	1.070
2	1.020	1.040	1.061	1.082	1.102	1.124	1.145
3	1.030	1.061	1.093	1.125	1.158	1.191	1.225
4	1.041	1.082	1.126	1.170	1.216	1.262	1.311
5	1.051	1.104	1.159	1.217	1.276	1.338	1.403
6	1.062	1.126	1.194	1.265	1.340	1.419	1.501
7	1.072	1.149	1.230	1.316	1.407	1.504	1.606
8	1.083	1.172	1.267	1.369	1.477	1.594	1.718
9	1.094	1.195	1.305	1.423	1.551	1.689	1.838
10	1.105	1.219	1.344	1.480	1.629	1.791	1.967
11	1.116	1.243	1.384	1.539	1.710	1.898	2.105
12	1.127	1.268	1.426	1.601	1.796	2.012	2.252
13	1.138	1.294	1.469	1.665	1.886	2.133	2.410
14	1.149	1.319	1.513	1.732	1.980	2.261	2.579
15	1.161	1.346	1.558	1.801	2.079	2.397	2.759
16	1.173	1.373	1.605	1.873	2.183	2.540	2.952
17	1.184	1.400	1.653	1.948	2.292	2.693	3.159
18	1.196	1.428	1.702	2.026	2.407	2.854	3.380
19	1.208	1.457	1.754	2.107	2.527	3.026	3.617
20	1.220	1.486	1.806	2.191	2.653	3.207	3.870
25	1.282	1.641	2.094	2.666	3.386	4.292	5.427
30	1.348	1.811	2.427	3.243	4.322	5.743	7.612

Period	8%	9%	10%	12%	14%	15%	16%
1	1.080	1.090	1.100	1.120	1.140	1.150	1.160
2	1.166	1.186	1.210	1.254	1.300	1.322	1.346
3	1.260	1.295	1.331	1.405	1.482	1.521	1.561
4	1.360	1.412	1.464	1.574	1.689	1.749	1.811
5	1.469	1.539	1.611	1.762	1.925	2.011	2.100
6	1.587	1.677	1.772	1.974	2.195	2.313	2.436
7	1.714	1.828	1.949	2.211	2.502	2.660	2.826
8	1.851	1.993	2.144	2.476	2.853	3.059	3.278
9	1.999	2.172	2.358	2.773	3.252	3.518	3.803
10	2.159	2.367	2.594	3.106	3.707	4.046	4.411
11	2.332	2 580	2.853	3.479	4.226	4.652	5.117
12	2.518	2.813	3.138	3.896	4.818	5.350	5.926
13	2.720	3.066	3.452	4.363	5.492	6.153	6.886
14	2.937	3.342	3.797	4.887	6.261	7.076	7.988
15	3.172	3.642	4.177	5.474	7.138	8.137	9.266

CIF = Compound interest factor.

(continued)

TABLE 1. Compound Sum of $1 (CIF) (*continued*)

Period	8%	9%	10%	12%	14%	15%	16%
16	3.426	3.970	4.595	6.130	8.137	9.358	10.748
17	3.700	4.328	5.054	6.866	9.276	10.761	12.468
18	3.996	4.717	5.560	7.690	10.575	12.375	14.463
19	4.316	5.142	6.116	8.613	12.056	14.232	16.777
20	4.661	5.604	6.728	9.646	13.743	16.367	19.461
25	6.848	8.623	10.835	17.000	26.462	32.919	40.874
30	10.063	13.268	17.449	29.960	50.950	66.212	85.850

Period	18%	20%	24%	28%	32%	36%
1	1.180	1.200	1.240	1.280	1.320	1.360
2	1.392	1.440	1.538	1.638	1.742	1.850
3	1.643	1.728	1.907	2.067	2.300	2.515
4	1.939	2.074	2.364	2.684	3.036	3.421
5	2.288	2.488	2.932	3.436	4.007	4.653
6	2.700	2.986	3.635	4.398	5.290	6.328
7	3.185	3.583	4.508	5.629	6.983	8.605
8	3.759	4.300	5.590	7.206	9.217	11.703
9	4.435	5.160	6.931	9.223	12.166	15.917
10	5.234	6.192	8.594	11.806	16.060	21.647
11	6.176	7.430	10.657	15.112	21.199	29.439
12	7.288	8.916	13.215	19.343	27.983	40.037
13	8.599	10.699	16.386	24.759	36.937	54.451
14	10.147	12.839	20.319	31.961	48.757	74.053
15	11.974	15.407	25.196	40.565	64.359	100.712
16	14.129	18.488	31.243	51.923	84.954	136.970
17	16.672	22.186	38.741	66.461	112.140	186.280
18	19.673	26.623	48.039	85.071	148.020	253.340
19	23.214	31.948	59.568	108.890	195.390	344.540
20	27.393	38.338	73.864	139.380	257.920	468.570
25	62.669	95.396	216.542	478.900	1033.600	2180.100
30	143.371	237.376	634.820	1645.500	4142.100	10143.000

Period	40%	50%	60%	70%	80%	90%
1	1.400	1.500	1.600	1.700	1.800	1.900
2	1.960	2.250	2.560	2.890	3.240	3.610
3	2.744	3.375	4.096	4.913	5.832	6.859
4	3.842	5.062	6.544	8.352	10.498	13.032
5	5.378	7.594	10.486	14.199	18.896	24.761
6	7.530	11.391	16.777	24.138	34.012	47.046
7	10.541	17.086	26.844	41.034	61.222	89.387
8	14.758	25.629	42.950	69.758	110.200	169.836
9	20.661	38.443	68.720	118.588	198.359	322.688
10	28.925	57.665	109.951	210.599	357.047	613.107

(continued)

Period	40%	50%	60%	70%	80%	90%
11	40.496	86.498	175.922	342.719	642.684	1164.902
12	56.694	129.746	281.475	582.622	1156.831	2213.314
13	79.372	194.619	450.360	990.457	2082.295	4205.297
14	111.120	291.929	720.576	1683.777	3748.131	7990.065
15	155.568	437.894	1152.921	2862.421	6746.636	15181.122
16	217.795	656.840	1844.700	4866.100	12144.000	28844.000
17	304.914	985.260	2951.500	8272.400	21859.000	54804.000
18	426.879	1477.900	4722.400	14063.000	39346.000	104130.000
19	597.630	2216.800	7555.800	23907.000	70824.000	197840.000
20	836.683	3325.300	12089.000	40642.000	127480.000	375900.000
25	4499.880	25251.000	126760.000	577060.000	2408900.000	9307600.000
30	24201.432	191750.000	1329200.000	8193500.000	45517000.000	230470000.000

TABLE 2. Present Value of $1 (PVDF)

Period	1%	2%	3%	4%	5%	6%	7%	8%	9%	10%	12%	14%	15%
1	.990	.980	.971	.962	.952	.943	.935	.926	.917	.909	.893	.877	.870
2	.980	.961	.943	.925	.907	.890	.873	.857	.842	.826	.797	.769	.756
3	.971	.942	.915	.889	.864	.840	.816	.794	.772	.751	.712	.675	.658
4	.961	.924	.889	.855	.823	.792	.763	.735	.708	.683	.636	.592	.572
5	.951	.906	.863	.822	.784	.747	.713	.681	.650	.621	.567	.519	.497
6	.942	.888	.838	.790	.746	.705	.666	.630	.596	.564	.507	.456	.432
7	.933	.871	.813	.760	.711	.665	.623	.583	.547	.513	.452	.400	.376
8	.923	.853	.789	.731	.677	.627	.582	.540	.502	.467	.404	.351	.327
9	.914	.837	.766	.703	.645	.592	.544	.500	.460	.424	.361	.308	.284
10	.905	.820	.744	.676	.614	.558	.508	.463	.422	.386	.322	.270	.247
11	.896	.804	.722	.650	.585	.527	.475	.429	.388	.350	.287	.237	.215
12	.887	.788	.701	.625	.557	.497	.444	.397	.356	.319	.257	.208	.187
13	.879	.773	.681	.601	.530	.469	.415	.368	.326	.290	.229	.182	.163
14	.870	.758	.661	.577	.505	.442	.388	.340	.299	.263	.205	.160	.141
15	.861	.743	.642	.555	.481	.417	.362	.315	.275	.239	.183	.140	.123
16	.853	.728	.623	.534	.458	.394	.339	.292	.252	.218	.163	.123	.107
17	.844	.714	.605	.513	.436	.371	.317	.270	.231	.198	.146	.108	.093
18	.836	.700	.587	.494	.416	.350	.296	.250	.212	.180	.130	.095	.081
19	.828	.686	.570	.475	.396	.331	.276	.232	.194	.164	.116	.083	.070
20	.820	.673	.554	.456	.377	.312	.258	.215	.178	.149	.104	.073	.061
25	.780	.610	.478	.375	.295	.233	.184	.146	.116	.092	.059	.038	.030
30	.742	.552	.412	.308	.231	.174	.131	.099	.075	.057	.033	.020	.015

Period	16%	18%	20%	24%	28%	32%	36%	40%	50%	60%	70%	80%	90%
1	.862	.847	.833	.806	.781	.758	.735	.714	.667	.625	.588	.556	.526
2	.743	.718	.694	.650	.610	.574	.541	.510	.444	.391	.346	.309	.277
3	.641	.609	.579	.524	.477	.435	.398	.364	.296	.244	.204	.171	.146
4	.552	.516	.482	.423	.373	.329	.292	.260	.198	.153	.120	.095	.077
5	.476	.437	.402	.341	.291	.250	.215	.186	.132	.095	.070	.053	.040
6	.410	.370	.335	.275	.227	.189	.158	.133	.088	.060	.041	.029	.021
7	.354	.314	.279	.222	.178	.143	.116	.095	.059	.037	.024	.016	.011
8	.305	.266	.233	.179	.139	.108	.085	.068	.039	.023	.014	.009	.006
9	.263	.226	.194	.144	.108	.082	.063	.048	.026	.015	.008	.005	.003
10	.227	.191	.162	.116	.085	.062	.046	.035	.017	.009	.005	.003	.002
11	.195	.162	.135	.094	.066	.047	.034	.025	.012	.006	.003	.002	.001
12	.168	.137	.112	.076	.052	.036	.025	.018	.008	.004	.002	.001	.001
13	.145	.116	.093	.061	.040	.027	.018	.013	.005	.002	.001	.001	.000
14	.125	.099	.078	.049	.032	.021	.014	.009	.003	.001	.001	.000	.000
15	.108	.084	.065	.040	.025	.016	.010	.006	.002	.001	.000	.000	.000
16	.093	.071	.054	.032	.019	.012	.007	.005	.002	.001	.000	.000	
17	.080	.060	.045	.026	.015	.009	.005	.003	.001	.000	.000		
18	.089	.051	.038	.021	.012	.007	.004	.002	.001	.000	.000		
19	.060	.043	.031	.017	.009	.005	.003	.002	.000	.000			
20	.051	.037	.026	.014	.007	.004	.002	.001	.000	.000			
25	.024	.016	.010	.005	.002	.001	.000	.000					
30	.012	.007	.004	.002	.001	.000	.000						

PVDF = Present value discount factor.

TABLE 3. Sum of an Annuity of $1 for *N* Periods (CIF)

Period	1%	2%	3%	4%	5%	6%
1	1.000	1.000	1.000	1.000	1.000	1.000
2	2.010	2.020	2.030	2.040	2.050	2.060
3	3.030	3.060	3.091	3.122	3.152	3.184
4	4.060	4.122	4.184	4.246	4.310	4.375
5	5.101	5.204	5.309	5.416	5.526	5.637
6	6.152	6.308	6.468	6.633	6.802	6.975
7	7.214	7.434	7.662	7.898	8.142	8.394
8	8.286	8.583	8.892	9.214	9.549	9.897
9	9.369	9.755	10.159	10.583	11.027	11.491
10	10.462	10.950	11.464	12.006	12.578	13.181
11	11.567	12.169	12.808	13.486	14.207	14.972
12	12.683	13.412	14.192	15.026	15.917	16.870
13	13.809	14.680	15.618	16.627	17.713	18.882
14	14.947	15.974	17.086	18.292	19.599	21.051
15	16.097	17.293	18.599	20.024	21.579	23.276
16	17.258	18.639	20.157	21.825	23.657	25.673
17	18.430	20.012	21.762	23.698	25.840	28.213
18	19.615	21.412	23.414	25.645	28.132	30.906
19	20.811	22.841	25.117	27.671	30.539	33.760
20	22.019	24.297	26.870	29.778	33.066	36.786
25	28.243	32.030	36.459	41.646	47.727	54.865
30	34.785	40.568	47.575	56.805	66.439	79.058

Period	7%	8%	9%	10%	12%	14%
1	1.000	1.000	1.000	1.000	1.000	1.000
2	2.070	2.080	2.090	2.100	2.120	2.140
3	3.215	3.246	3.278	3.310	3.374	3.440
4	4.440	4.506	4.573	4.641	4.770	4.921
5	5.751	5.867	5.985	6.105	6.353	6.610
6	7.153	7.336	7.523	7.716	8.115	8.536
7	8.654	8.923	9.200	9.487	10.089	10.730
8	10.260	10.637	11.028	11.436	12.300	13.233
9	11.978	12.488	13.021	13.579	14.776	16.085
10	13.816	14.487	15.193	15.937	17.549	19.337
11	15.784	16.645	17.560	18.531	20.655	23.044
12	17.888	18.977	20.141	21.384	24.133	27.271
13	20.141	21.495	22.953	24.523	28.029	32.089
14	22.550	24.215	26.019	27.975	32.393	37.581
15	25.129	27.152	29.361	31.772	37.280	43.842
16	27.888	30.324	33.003	35.950	42.753	50.980
17	30.840	33.750	36.974	40.545	48.884	59.118
18	33.999	37.450	41.301	45.599	55.750	68.394
19	37.379	41.446	46.018	51.159	63.440	78.969
20	40.995	45.762	51.160	57.275	72.052	91.025
25	63.249	73.106	84.701	98.347	133.334	181.871
30	94.461	113.283	136.308	164.494	241.333	356.787

CIF = Compound interest factor.   *(continued)*

TABLE 3. Sum of an Annuity of $1 for *N* Periods (CIF) (*continued*)

Period	16%	18%	20%	24%	28%	32%
1	1.000	1.000	1.000	1.000	1.000	1.000
2	2.160	2.180	2.200	2.240	2.280	2.320
3	3.506	3.572	3.640	3.778	3.918	4.062
4	5.066	5.215	5.368	5.684	6.016	6.362
5	6.877	7.154	7.442	8.048	8.700	9.398
6	8.977	9.442	9.930	10.980	12.136	13.406
7	11.414	12.142	12.916	14.615	16.534	18.696
8	14.240	15.327	16.499	19.123	22.163	25.678
9	17.518	19.086	20.799	24.712	29.369	34.895
10	21.321	23.521	25.959	31.643	38.592	47.062
11	25.733	28.755	32.150	40.238	50.399	63.122
12	30.850	34.931	39.580	50.985	65.510	84.320
13	36.786	42.219	48.497	64.110	84.853	112.303
14	43.672	50.818	59.196	80.496	109.612	149.240
15	51.660	60.965	72.035	100.815	141.303	197.997
16	60.925	72.939	87.442	126.011	181.870	262.36
17	71.673	87.068	105.931	157.253	233.790	347.31
18	84.141	103.740	128.117	195.994	300.250	459.45
19	98.603	123.414	154.740	244.033	385.320	607.47
20	115.380	146.628	186.688	303.601	494.210	802.86
25	249.214	342.603	471.981	898.092	1706.800	3226.80
30	530.312	790.948	1181.882	2640.916	5873.200	12941.00

Period	36%	40%	50%	60%	70%	80%
1	1.000	1.000	1.000	1.000	1.000	1.000
2	2.360	2.400	2.500	2.600	2.700	2.800
3	4.210	4.360	4.750	5.160	5.590	6.040
4	6.725	7.104	8.125	9.256	10.503	11.872
5	10.146	10.846	13.188	15.810	18.855	22.370
6	14.799	16.324	20.781	26.295	33.054	41.265
7	21.126	23.853	32.172	43.073	57.191	75.278
8	29.732	34.395	49.258	69.916	98.225	136.500
9	41.435	49.153	74.887	112.866	167.983	246.699
10	57.352	69.814	113.330	181.585	286.570	445.058
11	78.998	98.739	170.995	291.536	488.170	802.105
12	108.437	139.235	257.493	467.458	830.888	1444.788
13	148.475	195.929	387.239	748.933	1413.510	2601.619
14	202.926	275.300	581.859	1199.293	2403.968	4683.914
15	276.979	386.420	873.788	1919.869	4087.745	8432.045
16	377.690	541.990	1311.700	3072.800	6950.200	15179.000
17	514.660	759.780	1968.500	4917.500	11816.000	27323.000
18	700.940	1064.700	2953.800	7868.900	20089.000	49182.000
19	954.280	1491.600	4431.700	12591.000	34152.000	88528.000
20	1298.800	2089.200	6648.500	20147.000	58059.000	159350.000
25	6053.000	11247.000	50500.000	211270.000	824370.000	30111000.000
30	28172.000	60501.000	383500.000	2215400.000	11705000.000	56896000.000

TABLE 4. Present Value of an Annuity of $1 (PVDF)

Period	1%	2%	3%	4%	5%	6%	7%	8%	9%	10%
1	0.990	0.980	0.971	0.962	0.952	0.943	0.935	0.926	0.917	0.909
2	1.970	1.942	1.913	1.886	1.859	1.833	1.808	1.783	1.759	1.736
3	2.941	2.884	2.829	2.775	2.723	2.673	2.624	2.577	2.531	2.487
4	3.902	3.808	3.717	3.630	3.546	3.465	3.387	3.312	3.240	3.170
5	4.853	4.713	4.580	4.452	4.329	4.212	4.100	3.993	3.890	3.791
6	5.795	5.601	5.417	5.242	5.076	4.917	4.766	4.623	4.486	4.355
7	6.728	6.472	6.230	6.002	5.786	5.582	5.389	5.206	5.033	4.868
8	7.652	7.325	7.020	6.733	6.463	6.210	5.971	5.747	5.535	5.335
9	8.566	8.162	7.786	7.435	7.108	6.802	6.515	6.247	5.995	5.759
10	9.471	8.983	8.530	8.111	7.722	7.360	7.024	6.710	6.418	6.145
11	10.368	9.787	9.253	8.760	8.306	7.887	7.499	7.139	6.805	6.495
12	11.255	10.575	9.954	9.385	8.863	8.384	7.943	7.536	7.161	6.814
13	12.134	11.348	10.635	9.986	9.394	8.853	8.358	7.904	7.487	7.103
14	13.004	12.106	11.296	10.563	9.899	9.295	8.745	8.244	7.786	7.367
15	13.865	12.849	11.938	11.118	10.380	9.712	9.108	8.559	8.060	7.606
16	14.718	13.578	12.561	11.652	10.838	10.106	9.447	8.851	8.312	7.824
17	15.562	14.292	13.166	12.166	11.274	10.477	9.763	9.122	8.544	8.022
18	16.398	14.992	13.754	12.659	11.690	10.828	10.059	9.372	8.756	8.201
19	17.226	15.678	14.324	13.134	12.085	11.158	10.336	9.604	8.950	8.365
20	18.046	16.351	14.877	13.590	12.462	11.470	10.594	9.818	9.128	8.514
25	22.023	19.523	17.413	15.622	14.094	12.783	11.654	10.675	9.823	9.077
30	25.808	22.397	19.600	17.292	15.373	13.765	12.409	11.258	10.274	9.427

Period	12%	14%	16%	18%	20%	24%	28%	32%	36%
1	0.893	0.877	0.862	0.847	0.833	0.806	0.781	0.758	0.735
2	1.690	1.647	1.605	1.566	1.528	1.457	1.392	1.332	1.276
3	2.402	2.322	2.246	2.174	2.106	1.981	1.868	1.766	1.674
4	3.037	2.914	2.798	2.690	2.589	2.404	2.241	2.096	1.966
5	3.605	3.433	3.274	3.127	2.991	2.745	2.532	2.345	2.181
6	4.111	3.889	3.685	3.498	3.326	3.020	2.759	2.534	2.339
7	4.564	4.288	4.039	3.812	3.605	3.242	2.937	2.678	2.455
8	4.968	4.639	4.344	4.078	3.837	3.421	3.076	2.786	2.540
9	5.328	4.946	4.607	4.303	4.031	3.566	3.184	2.868	2.603
10	5.650	5.216	4.883	4.494	4.193	3.682	3.269	2.930	2.650
11	5.938	5.453	5.029	4.656	4.327	3.776	3.335	2.978	2.683
12	6.194	5.660	5.197	4.793	4.439	3.851	3.387	3.013	2.708
13	6.424	5.842	5.342	4.910	4.533	3.912	3.427	3.040	2.727
14	6.628	6.002	5.468	5.008	4.611	3.962	3.459	3.061	2.740
15	6.811	6.142	5.575	5.092	4.675	4.001	3.483	3.076	2.750
16	6.974	6.265	5.669	5.162	4.730	4.033	3.503	3.088	2.758
17	7.120	5.373	5.749	4.222	4.775	4.059	3.518	3.097	2.763
18	7.250	6.467	5.818	5.273	4.812	4.080	3.529	3.104	2.767
19	7.366	6.550	5.877	5.316	4.844	4.097	3.539	3.109	2.770
20	7.469	6.623	5.929	5.353	4.870	4.110	3.546	3.113	2.772
25	7.843	6.873	6.097	5.467	4.948	4.147	3.564	3.122	2.776
30	8.005	7.003	6.177	5.517	4.979	4.160	3.569	3.124	2.778

PVDF = Present value discount factor of an annuity.

Index